Group Counseling

Group Counseling
A Developmental Approach

Fourth Edition

George M. Gazda
University of Georgia

Allyn and Bacon
Boston   London   Sydney   Toronto

Series Editor: Ray Short
Cover Administrator: Linda K. Dickinson
Text Designer: Suzanne Harbison
Editorial-Production Service: Kathy Smith

Library of Congress Cataloging-in-Publication Data

Gazda, George Michael, 1931–
    Group counseling.

    Includes bibliographies and index.
    1. Group counseling   I. Title.
BF637.C6G36   1989   158'.3   88-33340
ISBN 0-205-11985-9

Printed in the United States of America

10   9   8   7   6   5   4

*Dedicated
to
the late Dr. Fred C. Proff,
Teacher and Friend*

Brief Contents

Contents

APPENDIXES

Preface

The purpose of this book is to provide students, practitioners, and practicum supervisors of group counseling a comprehensive guide for counseling with all age levels and with selected specialty groups. My experience has convinced me that we must have a theory and a method of group counseling that is relevant to the identifiable age groups with which we work: the young child, the preadolescent, the adolescent, and the adult.

The needs of children, preadolescents, adolescents, and adults can be related to their developmental stages of growth and the coping behaviors (knowledge and skills) appropriate to their developmental levels. How they ultimately function can be related directly to the degree that they acquire the appropriate understanding and skills of each developmental stage. The knowledge and skills of each age group have been categorized into four generic life-skill areas: Interpersonal Communication/Human Relations, Physical Fitness/Health Maintenance, Identity Development/Purpose in Life, and Problem-Solving/Decision-Making. The knowledge and skill areas are listed in Appendix A for use in identifying preventive and remedial interventions.

Group counseling is described as a preventive, growth-engendering, and remedial process. It is preventive if it is implemented at the first sign of inappropriate coping behaviors for given developmental tasks; it is growth engendering for those who are not debilitated and who serve as healthy models in groups; and it is remedial to the extent that it is applied before persons have become debilitated to the extent that they have extreme difficulty functioning in society.

The developmental model provides a comprehensive approach for the application of group counseling, guidance, and skills training. A rationale and methods for working with the *child* from age five through nine, the *preadolescent* from age nine through thirteen, and the *adolescent* and *adult* from age thirteen through old age have been developed in chapters 4, 5, and 6, respectively. Each of these chapters is supported with tables in Appendix A that summarize the knowledge and skills appropriate for specific age groups. The focus of each of these chapters is on group counseling with its rationale and methodology. In each chapter, also, I have used examples or protocols of group sessions to illustrate the elements that are interacting to produce change.

Essential to the success of the group counseling interventions are appropriate selection procedures and group composition, group size, media utilized, group setting, frequency and length of sessions, and duration of treatment. Each of these areas is treated extensively in chapters 4, 5, and 6 and in chapters 7–10 and 14–20. Chapter 2 is related to chapters 4, 5, and 6 insofar as it provides an overview of the theoretical rationale and methodology. The conditions essential for group counselors to facilitate growth in counselees are developed around the core conditions of a helping relationship, à la Carkhuff. The dynamics operative in a group, which must be understood and controlled, are detailed in Chapter 3 under the topics of leadership, structure, goal setting, cohesiveness, roles, and strategies for dealing with problem members and stages of group development.

Chapter 1 completes the gestalt in Part One. It traces the history and development of group counseling and guidance, supplemented with a historical time line, and shows the interrelationship among the contributing disciplines. In addition, definitions are given for group counseling, group psychotherapy, life-skills training, and related group procedures.

Part Two includes chapters on the application of group counseling to special populations. Chapter 7 has been included because of the rapidly increasing use of family group counseling in community agencies, as well as educational institutions. A family group counseling model consistent with the developmental model of this text fills an area of great interest and need.

Chapter 8 presents a developmental model applied to group counseling with the aged, an area of rapid growth.

Chapter 9 treats another specialty issue of great concern—the treatment of substance abuse/chemical dependency. This chapter illustrates the application of life-skills training to the prevention and remediation of substance abusers and the application of traditional interview group counseling to the remediation of substance abusers.

Chapter 10 is an entirely new chapter devoted to self-help groups. Self-help groups are among the most rapidly increasing group procedures. Although they most often function without professional leadership, it is important for professional group counselors and therapists to be acquainted with them and perhaps to provide consultation to them.

Part Three consists of three chapters. Chapter 11 presents a comprehensive treatment of nonverbal communication. It provides the parameters to assist group counselors in improving their own nonverbal communication, as well as improving their understanding of their group counselees.

Chapter 12 is a revision of a similar chapter in the third edition. The revision consists of updating ethical practices and legal issues that have been recently applied to group counseling and therapy.

Chapter 13 represents an updating of the review of group counseling research (from 1938 to 1970) reported in the first edition, from 1938 to 1976 reported in the second edition, and from 1938 to 1982 reported in the third edition. The number of studies evaluated is approximately 680 from 1938 to 1987.

Part Four represents an entirely new section. It summarizes seven basic group counseling/therapy theories and provides in the outline of each chapter a method for comparing each theory. This section was added to enable instructors to focus on group counseling/therapy positions in addition to the Developmental Group Counseling position emphasized in Parts One and Two. It is placed as a separate section at the end of the text since it is somewhat independent of the remainder of the text.

In closing the preface to the first edition of this book, I indicated that I had delayed writing the first edition until I felt my model was relatively complete. The second edition attempted to fill gaps in the Developmental Group Counseling model. The third edition represented a rather radical change by the addition of the theoretical model of life-skills training—a significant preventive and remedial strategy. This edition places the traditional interview group counseling model in the position of preparing group members for referral to life-skills training groups if their problems are not subject to change through the interview/discussion approach.

I offer this edition for application and evaluation. Once again I thank those of you who have used the first three editions of this book for both your plaudits and constructive criticism.

Acknowledgments

Innumerable persons and experiences—too many to recall and recognize adequately—have influenced me in what I have tried to present in this book. To my teachers who shared their knowledge with me and stimulated me, to my students who challenged and supported me, to the many professionals who shared their knowledge and experience with me through their writing, and to my wife, my son, my parents, and my brothers, who provided me the warmth of human nourishment, I express my appreciation.

While recognizing in a general way the many individuals who assisted me in preparing the three earlier editions of this text, I wish to give special recognition to those who made direct contributions by authoring or coauthoring chapters: Dr. Jerry Mobley for authoring Chapter 7, Dr. Frances Hendrix and Charlalee Sedgwick for coauthoring Chapter 8, Dr. Michael Kavkewitz for authoring Chapter 9, Inese Wheeler for authoring Chapter 10, Dr. Richard Walters for authoring Chapter 11, Dr. R. Ernest Taylor for authoring Chapter 12, and Charlalee Sedgwick for authoring Chapter 20. In addition, Dr. Joe Hill assisted in reviewing and classifying the research from 1982 to 1987 in Chapter 13 and Charlalee Sedgwick also assisted in the research literature review for this chapter. Inese Wheeler updated the resource material in Chapters 4, 5, and 6 and assisted in the overall literature review for Part One. Mildred Powell developed the case example in Chapter 2, and Dr. David K. Brooks, Jr., assisted in the development of Appendix A.

I would like to thank Allyn and Bacon's reviewers: Jack A. Duncan of Virginia Commonwealth University, Mark E. Meadows of Auburn University, and T. F. Renick of St. Lawrence University.

Cynthia Pool, Charlalee Sedgwick, and Barbara Gazda assisted me with the typing, reproduction, and assembling of the manuscript. Kathy Smith did the copyediting and gave generously of her time and expertise. My wife Barbara and son David, by their very existence, provided me with the inspiration to develop all four editions of this book and the inspiration for many other endeavors. To all of these helpers I express my sincere gratitude.

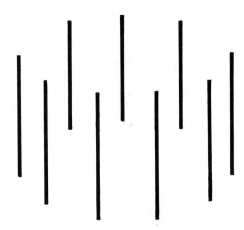

PART ONE

Part One contains the six chapters that represent the core of Developmental Group Counseling. Chapter 1 traces the history and development of group counseling, Chapter 3 focuses on group dynamics in group counseling, and Chapters 2, 4, 5, and 6 discuss the theoretical rationale for Developmental Group Counseling.

CHAPTER 1

Group Counseling and Group Guidance
Origins, Definitions, and Significant Contributors

ORIGINS

Group Guidance

Group guidance is probably as old as the guidance movement itself. The guidance movement began essentially as *vocational guidance* when Frank Parsons founded the Vocations Bureau of Boston in 1908 (Brewer, 1942). Just when, where, and by whom the word *group* was added to the word *guidance* is not known; however, according to Brewer (1942), Charles L. Jacobs of San Jose, California, was one of the first to suggest a wider use of the term *guidance* when, in the October 1915 issue of *Manual Training and Vocational Education*, he stated that his work included three departments— educational guidance, vocational guidance, and avocational guidance.

Vocational Guidance
According to Glanz and Hayes, "As early as 1907, Jesse B. Davis, principal of the Cedar Rapids High School in Iowa, devoted weekly periods in English classes to 'Vocational and Moral Guidance,' and George Boyden in 1912 introduced a course in vocations at the Beauport, Connecticut, high school. So 'group guidance' was 'born' " (1967, p. 3). Glanz and Hayes caution that these first group guidance courses were instructional groups and the techniques used were instructional and devoid, for the most part, of systematic use of group dynamics principles and techniques.

Classes in Occupational Information

As early as 1908, William A. Wheatley was instrumental in introducing a course in occupational information for freshman boys at the Westport, Connecticut, high school. Similar courses were offered in Boston and New York City soon after Wheatley's course (Brewer, 1942). The movement continued to grow until, according to Glanz and Hayes, "The 1930's became the era of the group guidance class, where units on character, vocation, and citizenship were prominent. Hardly a city junior high or high school was without such a program, and the guidance literature of the era was saturated with texts on 'group guidance'" (1967, p. 3).

Home Room

In 1934 McKown authored a text, *Home Room Guidance*. The content of the text and the fact that McKown proposed the director of guidance as the director of homeroom guidance suggest its close association to group guidance and counseling. In fact, some schools referred to the homeroom as "the 'guidance hour' or 'guidance room'" (McKown, 1934, p. 53). Strang (1935) cited the contribution of the homeroom teacher as being fourfold: "to establish friendly relationships, to discover the abilities and needs, and to develop right attitudes toward school, home, and community" (p. 116). Here again the group guidance and counseling flavor was evident in the work of the homeroom teacher.

Extracurricular Activities

Foster authored a book, *Extra-Curricular Activities in High School*, in 1925 in which he recognized guidance as an extracurricular activity. In the same text Foster also urged the counselor to "hold many group conferences with the students on the subject of future educational or vocational plans" (p. 182). Pittsburgh schools were cited by Foster as including instructional guidance taking "the form of tenth grade group conferences which were held for the purpose of discussing Pittsburgh's industrial life and the opportunities it affords the young people" (p. 183).

Group Dynamics

The group dynamics movement, under the leadership of Kurt Lewin, began to influence education in the 1930s and early 1940s. At this time the group or vocational guidance movement was affected by the application of group dynamics principles to the group guidance classes. At this point also, group guidance was heavily vocational, and students were "taught" how to make career or vocational decisions. Those teachers and the few school counselors available in the 1930s and 1940s who were responsible for group guidance tried to instruct the group guidance classes as they would any other academic class. Some students were even given grades in group guidance. Where these procedures were employed, group guidance failed. However, where teachers and school counselors were influenced by the group dynamics movement and applied the principles and techniques to group guidance classes, the classes were more successful. Unfortunately for group guidance, too few teachers and counselors were acquainted with group dynamics, and consequently the 1950s saw a decline in the enthusiasm of school administrators toward group guidance.

Structured Groups

In the 1970s a variation on traditional group guidance appeared. This new movement was influenced by the behavioral counseling and the skills training movements. These movements returned to the educational emphasis of group guidance, but were different insofar as the skills emphasized were more focused and intensive. For example, individuals were taught or trained to become assertive, better in their communication skills, and better problem solvers. Other focused approaches stressed consciousness raising on such issues as race, gender, and age. I have developed a rationale and a system for developmental life-skills training. An overview of this rationale and system will be presented in Chapter 2.

Conclusions.   Group guidance is almost synonymous with "guidance" in general. Guidance got its start with Parsons' Vocations Bureau of Boston in 1908, although one can point to isolated guidance practices that antedate 1908. When *group* was added to *guidance* is not precisely known, but it is likely that it occurred on several fronts at the same time—probably before 1915. Glanz and Hayes (1967) suggest that it was during the period 1907–1912.

Vocational guidance, homeroom guidance, classes in occupational information, certain extracurricular activities, the group dynamics movement, and structured groups all influenced group guidance. In turn, the group guidance movement, along with several other related movements, contributed significantly to the evolution and emergence of group counseling that has eclipsed group guidance. Traditional group guidance is a thing of the past, except for occasional use in some elementary schools. For example, the American Personnel and Guidance Association Senate voted at its annual convention in 1983 to change its name to American Association for Counseling and Development.

Group Counseling

The origin of the term *group counseling* is also somewhat obscure. Its historical antecedent was most likely group guidance or case conference. Thus, much like its counterpart, group psychotherapy, group counseling in its inception was very likely a class method similar to what is referred to today as group guidance. One of the earliest appearances of the term *group counseling* in print in the United States seems to have been in 1931. Dr. Richard D. Allen used *group counseling* in the following context:

> Group thinking and the case-conference method usually take the place of the recitation. . . . Problems of educational and vocational guidance require teachers who are specially selected and trained for the work, who understand problems of individual differences and are continually studying them. These teachers require continuous contacts with the same pupils for several years, a knowledge of occupations and occupational problems, and special training in methods of individual and group counseling.
>
> All of these considerations draw attention to the class counselor as the logical teacher of the new unit. There is much similarity between the techniques of individual guidance and group guidance. When the counselor finds by individual interviews that certain problems are common to most of the pupils, such problems become units in the group guidance courses. The class discussions of these problems should reduce the length and number of individual interviews with a saving of considerable time and expense. In fact, the separation of group counseling from individual counseling would seem very short-sighted.
>
> If the above principle prevails, the next serious problem concerns its practical application in the time schedule of the school. Ideally, such a course should be *extensive* rather than *intensive* in its nature, in order to accomplish its objectives effectively. Its purpose is to arouse interests in current educational, vocational and social problems, to develop social attitudes, and to build up a back-ground of occupational information. Such objectives require considerable time extended over several years. (p. 190)

This quotation demonstrates that what Allen described as group counseling in 1931 is today generally referred to as group guidance. Also, it should be noted that Allen used the terms *case-conference, group guidance,* and *group counseling* interchangeably.

Although Allen's use of *group counseling* appeared in print in 1931, it is quite possible that he had used the expression before 1931. For example, Brewer (1937), writing the introduction to Allen's *Organization and Supervision of Guidance in Public Education,* published in 1937, wrote, "For more than a decade his colleagues in the Harvard Summer School have urged Dr. Allen to put his ideas into permanent form" (p. xxi).

Jones, as early as 1934 in his second edition of *Principles of Guidance,* stated "It [group guidance] is a term that has come into use chiefly through the excellent work of Richard D. Allen in Providence, R.I. It includes all those forms of guidance activities that are undertaken in groups or in classes" (p. 284). Jones also refers to the "Boston Plan for Group Counseling in Intermediate Schools" and cites the source as two circulars[1] developed by the Committee on Guidance of the Boston Public Schools (p. 291). Although group counseling is used in the title of the Boston publication, the description of the nature of the process Jones described places it squarely in the realm of group guidance and not group counseling as it is defined today.

In his fifth edition of *Principles of Guidance*, published in 1963, Jones had this to say about Allen's case conference procedures: "A technique that combined the techniques of counseling in groups and group counseling was used by Allen and practiced in the public schools of Providence, Rhode Island, more than twenty-five years ago" (pp. 218–219). Jones believed that the purpose of the case conference was to provide the counselor with a means for students to discuss their personal and social relationships. The general approach was to use common problems of group members as the basis for discussion. A case was presented to the group to illustrate the problem, and each student was expected to compare his or her own experiences with those revealed through the case. The leader encouraged the group to seek the "more permanent values" exposed rather than the more "immediate temporary" ones and also encouraged the participants to consider the effect of their proposed action upon others. Conclusions were summarized to formulate generalizations for other situations. Jones stated that Allen believed his method worked best when "each case represented a common, usual, or typical situation that concerned most of the group. The case should involve persons and personal or social relations" (Jones, 1963, p. 219).

According to Jones, Allen characterized the case conference leaders as individuals who never expressed approval or disapproval of any opinion or attitude and never stated opinions of their own. In addition, the leaders were impartial and open minded and encouraged the expression of all points of view. They would occasionally restate and summarize the group thinking and organize the group so that it was large enough to guarantee a diversity of opinions, but not so large as to prevent each member from having the opportunity to enter into discussion.

The goals and procedures of Allen's case conference approach are similar to those of contemporary group counselors. However, most contemporary group counselors do not structure their groups around specific cases.

Although Allen may have been the first person to introduce the term *group counseling*, he is not recognized by contemporary group counselors as

1. Boston Public Schools, Guidance—educational and vocational, a tentative plan for group counseling, Board of Superintendents' Circular No. 2, 1928–1929, and Board of Superintendents' Circular No. 17, 1928–1929. First Supplement to Board of Superintendents' Circular No. 2. Boston: Printing Department, 1929.

having significantly influenced the group guidance or counseling movement. It was not until about ten years after World War II that group counseling received much of an impetus. During that era, group guidance, group dynamics, and group therapy began their rapid rise in popularity, and group counseling seemed to be an outgrowth of these disciplines.

There were few, if any, textbooks devoted primarily to group counseling as such before Driver's (1958) *Counseling and Learning through Small Group Discussion*. The group guidance specialists such as Bennett, Warters, Ohlsen, and Froehlich had written chapters on group counseling that were part of their texts in group guidance and general guidance in the mid-1950s and early 1960s. In 1961 Lifton's *Working with Groups* was the most comprehensive effort to apply client-centered counseling to group work, and at the same time Mahler and Caldwell (1961) produced a booklet, *Group Counseling in Secondary Schools*.

Historically, as group guidance seemed to lose its impetus in the late 1950s and early 1960s, group counseling took its place, especially within educational institutions, as a potential source for bringing about behavioral change. Whereas in the 1950s there were no popular complete texts on group counseling, the late 1960s saw the emergence of at least six texts. In the first half of the 1970s, at least a dozen new group counseling texts were added to the field. With the current keen interest in group counseling, a considerable expansion of practice, research, and writing can be predicted. Nevertheless, instead of group guidance influencing group counseling as it once did, the direction has been reversed, and the group counseling movement seems to be effecting a rebirth of interest and activity in group guidance, especially at the elementary school level, and through structured groups at all age levels.

DEFINITIONS: GROUP GUIDANCE, GROUP COUNSELING, AND GROUP PSYCHOTHERAPY

Group Guidance

Group guidance was organized to prevent the development of problems (see Figure 1–1). The content included educational-vocational-personal-social information not otherwise systematically taught in academic courses. The typical setting was the classroom. Typical class size ranged from approximately twenty to thirty-five. Providing accurate information for use in improved understanding of self and others was the direct emphasis in group guidance; attitude change frequently was an indirect outcome or goal. The leadership was provided by a classroom teacher or a counselor who utilized a variety of instructional media and group dynamics concepts in motivating students and in obtaining group interaction. Instructional

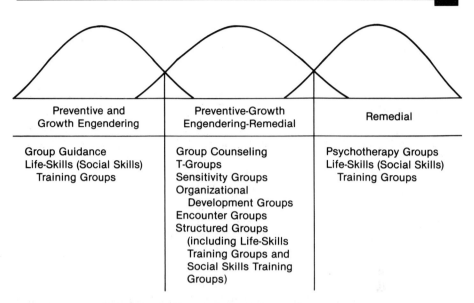

Preventive and Growth Engendering	Preventive-Growth Engendering-Remedial	Remedial
Group Guidance Life-Skills (Social Skills) Training Groups	Group Counseling T-Groups Sensitivity Groups Organizational Development Groups Encounter Groups Structured Groups (including Life-Skills Training Groups and Social Skills Training Groups)	Psychotherapy Groups Life-Skills (Social Skills) Training Groups

Figure 1–1   Relationships among group processes

media included unfinished stories, puppet plays, movies, films, filmstrips, guest speakers, audio and videotaped interviews, and student reports. Group dynamics concepts referred to the process employed in group guidance, such as sociodramas, buzz groups, panels, and other related techniques.

In addition to the classroom-size unit in which group guidance was provided by either the teacher or counselor, group guidance was also implemented in junior and senior high schools through units taught in courses such as social studies, language arts, and home economics. A third means of implementing group guidance was through credit courses such as psychology, senior problems, and occupations.

With the "back to basics" emphasis in the 1980s, one can expect fewer credit courses in areas related to group guidance. Universities can be expected to continue to present guidance-type (skills training) content through their health and counseling centers and student union functions. Other adults will be able to obtain a type of group guidance through the mass media and adult education courses, but the emphasis will be on life-skills/social skills training.

At the early elementary and middle school levels, group guidance still exists and is a part of the interest in affective education that includes units taught through the use of the magic circle, kits such as DUSO, "class meetings," "developmental guidance units," and similar approaches. My own recommendations would provide an impetus for increasing direct teaching of nonacademic content and skills (life skills) in elementary, secondary, higher education, and community mental health agencies. Life-skills training, therefore, replaces group guidance for elementary age children, as well as the whole age spectrum.

Group Counseling

Whereas the goal of traditional group guidance was to provide students with accurate information that would help them make more appropriate plans and life decisions (and in this sense it is prevention-oriented), group counseling is growth engendering and prevention and remediation oriented (see Figure 1–1). Group counseling is prevention-oriented in the sense that the counselees or clients are capable of functioning in society, but may be experiencing some "rough spots" in their lives. If counseling is successful, the rough spots may be successfully smoothed, with no serious personality defects incurred.

Group counseling is growth engendering insofar as it provides the participants with incentive and motivation to make changes that are in their best interest (that is, the participants are motivated to take actions that maximize their potential through self-actualizing behaviors).

Group counseling is remedial for those individuals who have entered into a spiral of self-defeating behavior, but who are nevertheless capable of reversing the spiral without counseling intervention. However, with counseling intervention, the counselee is likely to recover, and recover more quickly and with fewer emotional scars.

Group counseling is defined as follows:

> Group counseling is a dynamic interpersonal process focusing on conscious thought and behavior and involving the therapy functions of permissiveness, orientation to reality, catharsis, and mutual trust, caring, understanding, acceptance, and support. The therapy functions are created and nurtured in a small group through the sharing of personal concerns with one's peers and the counselor(s). The group counselees are basically normal individuals with various concerns which are not debilitating to the extent requiring extensive personality change. The group counselees may utilize the group interaction to increase understanding and acceptance of values and goals and to learn and/or unlearn certain attitudes and behaviors. (Gazda, Duncan, & Meadows, 1967, p. 305)

Although the content of group counseling is very similar to group guidance—including educational, vocational, personal, and social concerns—a number of other factors are quite different. First, *group guidance* was recommended for everyone on a regularly scheduled basis; *group counseling* is generally recommended only for those experiencing continuing or temporary problems that information alone will not resolve.

However, in order to remove the stigma sometimes attached to counseling, I recommend that group counseling also be made available to everyone. Another reason to include everyone in group counseling, or preferrably life-skills/social skills training, is the need to form heterogeneous groups and in this manner provide healthy models in every counseling group.

Second, traditional group guidance made an *indirect* attempt to change attitudes and behaviors through accurate information or an emphasis on cognitive or intellective functioning; group counseling and skills training make a *direct* attempt to modify attitudes and behaviors by emphasizing total involvement. Finally, traditional group guidance was applicable to groups of fifteen to thirty, whereas group counseling is dependent on the development of strong group cohesiveness and the sharing of personal concerns, which are most applicable to small, intimate groups of three or four (children) or eight to twelve (adolescents and adults).

Group Psychotherapy

The term *group psychotherapy*, the third part of the guidance, counseling, therapy continuum, was coined by J. L. Moreno in 1936 (Corsini, 1957). Moreno's definition is a general one: "Group psychotherapy means simply to treat people in groups" (1962, p. 263). It is generally accepted that there is a difference between group counseling and group psychotherapy, although there is also overlap between them. Brammer and Shostrom have characterized these differences by the following series of adjectives in which counseling is described as

> educational, supportive, situational, problem-solving, conscious awareness, emphasis on "normals," and short-term. Psychotherapy is characterized by supportive (in a more particular sense), reconstructive, depth analysis, analytical, focus on the unconscious, emphasis on "neurotics" or other severe emotional problems, and long-term. (1960, p. 6)

Although these differentiations were applied to individual counseling and psychotherapy, they are equally applicable to group counseling and group psychotherapy.

SENSITIVITY, T-GROUPS, AND ENCOUNTER GROUPS

Eddy and Lubin (1971) defined sensitivity (group) training, T-groups, and encounter groups as follows.

Sensitivity Groups

Sensitivity [group] training: Sensitivity training is one of the first and most generic terms in the field. It originally referred to the small group training conducted by the National Training Laboratories. Currently, it is used by some to subsume all small group training approaches. However, most practitioners do not find it a useful term because it is frequently used so broadly (to include group therapy, for example) that it has lost its power to define. (p. 627)

Eddy and Lubin recommend the use of the term *laboratory training* over sensitivity training because

it is used to refer to an educational method that emphasizes experience-based learning activities. Participants are involved in a variety of experiences, usually including small group interaction, and their behavior provides data for learning. Thus laboratory training involves learning by doing. The subject matter of such programs deals with some aspect of human interaction, and the goal is to be more aware of and responsive to what is going on. A specific laboratory training program may run from a few hours to two or more weeks and may contain a combination of elements designed to provide experiential learning. (p. 627)

T-Groups

A basic element of most laboratories is the *T-group* (T for training). In the standard NTL-type of T-group, participants find themselves in a relatively unstructured environment in which their responsibility is to build out of their interaction a group that can help them meet their needs for support, feedback, learning, etc. The behaviors exhibited by members as they play out their roles provide the material for analysis and learning. Thus, T-group members have the opportunity of learning ways in which their behavior is seen by others in the group, the kinds of roles, ways of being more sensitive to the feelings and behaviors of other group members, methods for understanding group behavior dynamics, etc. Time is usually provided for trainees to integrate what they have learned and plan to apply their new knowledge after the laboratory ends. (p. 627)

Encounter Groups

Encounter groups, as we define the term, refers to intensive small group experiences in which the emphasis is upon personal growth through expanding awareness, exploration of intrapsychic as well as interpersonal issues, and release of dysfunctional inhibitions. There is relatively little focus on the group as a learning instrument; the trainer takes a more active and directive role; and physical interaction is utilized. Other modes of expression and sensory exploration such as dance, art, massage, and nudity are currently being tried as a part of the encounter experience. (pp. 627–628)

ORGANIZATIONAL DEVELOPMENT

Organizational Development (OD) has its origin in laboratory training group procedures and would likely be placed in the same area of the continuum as the T-group (see Figure 1–1). Golembiewski (1972) has characterized OD as follows:

OD basically reflects a variety of group-oriented strategies for conscious and deliberate change in social systems. In essence, changes in group level phenomena such as social norms and values are seen as the primary motivators of organizational change, via their influence on the behaviors of individuals. (p. 13)

In other words, OD specialists diagnose communication and interaction problems within and between work units in educational, governmental, and industrial settings. Having diagnosed problem areas, the OD specialist recommends modifications intended to lead to improved work conditions and productivity.

STRUCTURED GROUPS

Structured groups include numerous variations, the most common of which are the *social skills training groups*. A sample of the varieties include Human Resources Development (Carkhuff, 1969; Egan & Cowan, 1979), Structured Learning Therapy (Goldstein, et al. 1976), Deliberate Psychological Education (Mosher & Sprinthall, 1971), Focusing (Gendlin, 1981), Relationship Enhancement (Guerney, 1977), Multimodal Behavior Therapy (Lazarus, 1976), Life Skills Education (Adkins, 1984), Life Skills (Smith, 1982), Life-Skills Training (Gazda, et al. 1987), and Social Skills Training (Hersen & Bellack, 1976; Patterson, 1967; Wolpe & Lazarus, 1976; Zigler & Phillips, 1960).

Drum and Knott (1977) define the structured group as follows:

A structured group is a delimited learning situation with a predetermined goal, and a plan designed to enable each group member to reach this identified goal with minimum frustration and maximum ability to transfer the new learning to a wide range of life events. (p. 14)

The use of structure in counseling groups, according to Drum and Knott, allows the group facilitator: (1) to focus precisely on a specific goal and include relevant goal-oriented activities while eliminating goal-detracting influences; (2) to converge resources and exercises in order to amplify learning; and (3) to assess the degree of goal accomplishment for each participant. (p. 14)

Social Skills Training

Social skills training has become the generic term in the 1980s for all skills training groups; however, there has been difficulty in producing an acceptable definition of the term. Phillips (1985) integrated the numerous definitions and drew the following conclusion:

> It may be, today that the plethora of social skills written about are mainly the almost endless lists of strategies that complex social interaction requires, and social skills is the ability to shift and pivot according to a variety of demands, thus making skill a matter of versatility rather than a hard and fast contribution to a repertoire (it is that social skill is more a matter of managing a 'behavioral' economy than drawing on a repertoire in the musical analogy sense). (p. 5)

The specific methods that constitute *social skills training* reflect psychology's modern social learning theory and education's contemporary pedagogical principles and procedures (Goldstein, 1981). These definitional characteristics of social skills training are identical to or very similar to a variety of other psychological/educational intervention programs such as Life-Skills Training (Gazda, Childers, & Brooks, 1987), Structured Learning (Goldstein, Sprafkin, & Gershaw, 1976), Parent–Child Communication Skill (Terkelson, 1976) , Alive and Aware (Miller, Nunnally, & Wackman, 1975), Dating and Social Skills (Curran, 1977), Interpersonal Career Skills (Johnson, 1978), Facilitative Interpersonal Functioning (Carkhuff & Berenson, 1967), Basic Social Communication Skills (Hansen, 1972), Effective Communication (Rhodes, Rasmussen & Heaps, 1971), and Problem Solving Communication Training (Robin, 1979).

The most common social skills training paradigm is based on the *skill deficit model*, which is constructed on the premise that the individual who evidences poor social skills lacks certain specific responses from his or her repertoire and/or is using inappropriate ones. The intervention for skills deficits is to teach appropriate skills. In social skills training programs based on the conditioned-anxiety model, which assumes that the individual has the requisite skills in his or her repertoire, but is inhibited from responding in a socially appropriate fashion because of conditioned anxiety responses, the teaching of anxiety reduction techniques constitutes the primary component of the training.

Social skills training has been conducted on both an individual basis and in groups, and in various combinations. Gazda, et al. (1987), Bellack and Morrison (1982), Goldsmith and McFall (1975), Hersen and Bellack (1977), and Monti, Corriveau, and Curran (1982) are all advocates of the group approach.

Various programs have been applied or recommended for a wide variety of dysfunctions such as schizophrenia (Bellack, Hersen, & Turner, 1976), social isolation in children (Whitehill, Hersen, & Bellack, 1980), depression (Bellack, Hersen, & Himmelhock, 1980), hyperaggressivity (Frederikson, Jenkins, Foy, & Eisler, 1976), sexual deviation (Barlow, Abel, & Blanchard, 1977), marital conflict (Birchler, 1979), drug addiction (Van Hasselt, Hersen, & Milliones, 1978), juvenile delinquency (Ollendick & Hersen, 1979), wife abuse (Rosenbaum & O'Leary, 1981), hysterical neurosis (Bellack & Hersen, 1978), heterosocial failures and shyness (Galassi & Galassi, 1979), assertive deficits in women (Lineham & Egen, 1979), and hospitalized psychiatric patients (Powell, Illovsky, O'Leary, & Gazda, 1988). (For a detailed exposition of the Life-Skills Training model, see *Foundations of Counseling and Human Services*, Gazda, Childers, & Brooks, 1987.)

SUMMARY OF GROUP PROCEDURES ⎯⎯⎯⎯⎯⎯ ▬

Gazda, Duncan, and Sisson (1971) surveyed 1,000 members of the American Personnel and Guidance Association's (now American Association of Counseling and Development) Interest Group on Group Procedures in order to differentiate among various group processes. (The majority of the 164 respondents held the doctorate degree and were members of the American Personnel and Guidance Association, the American Psychological Association, or both.)

The respondents were asked to indicate distinctions they would make among group guidance, group counseling, group psychotherapy, T-groups, sensitivity groups, and encounter groups on each of the following: (1) purposes of each, (2) clientele best served, and (3) "essential" professional preparation requirements. Group guidance was viewed as essentially different from the other group procedures on all three criteria. The differences were consistent with my earlier definition (instructional/informational in purpose, most applicable to normal individuals, and implemented by classroom teachers or master-degree or master-degree-level counselors).

Group psychotherapy was also considered essentially different from all the other group processes and in the direction of my definition (that is, the purpose was considered remedial, the clientele were relatively seriously emotionally disturbed, and the training for the leaders was intensive psychological and/or medical at the doctoral level).

The respondents did not distinguish clear differences among the following groups: counseling, T-, sensitivity, and encounter. (Organizational development, structured groups, and life-skills/social skills training groups were not included in the questionnaire.) In other words, they perceived these groups as essentially similar on the three criteria. Their descriptions of purpose, clientele best served, and preparation of the leaders for these group processes were very similar and consistent with my definition of, purpose of, and clientele best served through group counseling. Eddy's definitions of sensitivity, T-, and encounter groups suggest a continuum, with sensitivity groups and T-groups being very similar and encounter groups more like counseling and psychotherapy groups.

Although the lines between group processes, especially group counseling, encounter groups, and therapy groups are becoming more and more blurred because of each of the various group disciplines borrowing from the others, there is still a need, in my opinion, to make the distinctions that I have made in the preceding definitions and in Figure 1–1, which shows the relationships among group guidance, group counseling, T-groups, sensitivity groups, organizational development groups, encounter groups, structured groups, life-skills/social skills training groups, and psychotherapy groups.

DISCIPLINES CONTRIBUTING TO GROUP COUNSELING

The previous reference to R. D. Allen's use of the term *group counseling* suggests that Allen may have coined the expression; however, I do not contend that I have discovered the missing link. More likely than not, other individuals were also using the term in Allen's era.

Other related movements that have contributed to the group counseling movement must also be considered when attempting to trace its historical development. The most significant of these contributing movements were group guidance (previously described), group psychotherapy, child guidance, social casework, group work, group dynamics, self-help, and human potential.

Group Psychotherapy

Corsini (1957) has referred to *group psychotherapy* as "a conglomerate of methods and theories having diverse multiple origins in the past, resulting inevitably from social demands, and developed in various forms by many persons" (p 9). On the other hand, J. L. Moreno (1966) has contended that group psychotherapy had its roots in medicine, sociology, and religion. However, if we accept July 1, 1905 (Hadden, 1955), the date that J. H. Pratt introduced his "class method," as the beginning of group psychotherapy, rather than some ancient ritual such as Mesmer's group treatment through suggestion, the history of group psychotherapy covers approximately eighty-five years.

The term *group therapy* was introduced by J. L. Moreno in 1931 (Z. Moreno, 1966), and *group psychotherapy* was introduced, also by J. L. Moreno, in 1932 (Corsini, 1957). For the most part, group therapy and group psychotherapy are used synonymously in current discourse. Specifically, group therapy has become the shortened or colloquial version of group psychotherapy.

Even though the term *group psychotherapy* was not coined until 1932 by J. L. Moreno, an emigrant to America, there is considerable evidence that group psychotherapy is an American invention and that various forms were being practiced in the United States, mostly by psychiatrists and ministers, long before Moreno coined the term. *Group therapy* was coined by Moreno about the same time as the expression *group counseling* was used in the literature by R. D. Allen; however, there is every reason to believe that Allen's use of *group counseling* was more closely related to group *instruction* than was the meaning that Moreno intended when he coined *group therapy* and *group psychotherapy*.

Numerous systems of group psychotherapy were described in the professional literature well in advance of the appearance of group counseling professional literature. It is recognized, therefore, that group psychotherapy, as practiced and as described in the literature, provided much of the theoretical rationale for the emergence of group counseling. Just how much credit the group psychotherapy movement should receive for the emergence and development of group counseling is uncertain, but I believe it to be considerable, probably the most significant of the several disciplines or movements contributing to its emergence and growth.

Child Guidance

The possibility exists that group counseling originated in Europe. Dreikurs and Corsini (1954) contend that between 1900 and 1930 major steps were being made in Europe toward a systematic use of the group method called "collective counceling" [sic]. They believe that Alfred Adler, in his child guidance clinic in Vienna, was probably the first psychiatrist to use *collective counseling* formally and systematically.

Ansbacher and Ansbacher (1956) translated many of Adler's works, and in their commentary on his writing, they stated, "Although Adler himself never practiced group therapy, he suggested its use for the treatment of criminals" (p. 347). It is not because of his suggestion for using group therapy with criminals that Adler is considered by some to be the father of the movement, but rather because of his application of group techniques in his child guidance clinics. According to the Ansbachers, Adler was conducting group procedures—perhaps collective counseling—as early as 1922.

The rationale and methods employed by Adler and his followers are described by Ansbacher and Ansbacher (1956). However, the Ansbachers, because they were unable to find "more than a mere mention" of Adler's rationale and methods in his own writings, were forced to turn to secondary sources (the writing of Seidler and Zilat, and Rayner and Holub). Seider and Zilat described the "public" character of Adlerian child guidance clinics in which the child was interviewed in the presence of an adult audience. Doris Rayner defends this form of treatment by stating that the children benefit because they come to view their difficulties as a "community problem," and their audience (parents) receive an education in parent-child behavior.

In 1942 Brewer described the child guidance movement "as yet largely dissociated from the work of the schools" (p. 263). Nevertheless, because of its many similarities, the child guidance movement *may* have influenced, directly or indirectly, and/or have been somewhat akin to the group counseling movement.

Social Casework

In reviewing the history of the Marriage Council of Philadelphia, Gaskill and Mudd (1950) stated that group counseling and family life education had been part of the "Marriage Council's service from the agency's inception in 1932" (p. 194). Whether the term *group counseling* itself was actually used by the council as early as 1932 and whether the treatment was similar to current group counseling is not indicated. However, Gaskill and Mudd (1950) gave the following definition of group counseling, which they attributed to Hazel Froscher, Margery Klein, and Helen Phillips:

> a dynamic relationship between a counselor and the members of a group, involving presentation and discussion of subjects about which the counselor has special knowledge, which is of general or specific concern to the group, and around which emotions may be brought out and attitudes developed or changed. The relationship between the group members themselves and the counselor's use of this is essentially important in the total process. (1950, p. 195)

The definition implies that the counselor gives a presentation and encourages discussion of it. Gaskill and Mudd (1950), in their description of the group counseling session, indicated that the group ranged between thirty-five and fifty persons in size, and they further described the group session as a *course* including speakers other than the group counselor. This approach to group counseling seems more closely related to group guidance or a family living class rather than the typical small, eight- to ten-member counseling groups where leader-imposed content is absent or minimal.

Group Work

Sullivan (1952) described a *group* in the following manner:

The group must be a small stable one which feels itself as an entity and which the individual can feel close identification. Membership . . . is voluntary. There is a group leader, who is consciously making constructive use of the process of personality interaction among the members. The leader utilizes the desire of a normal person to be accepted by his fellows. He establishes the dignity of the individual and teaches acceptance of differences in race, creed, and nationality. Group work stresses programs evolved by the group itself, in consultation with the leader who guides toward socially desirable ends. Creative activities are encouraged to provide legitimate channels of self-expressions and to relieve emotional stress. Competition for its own sake is minimized and group members learn from situations where cooperation brings rich satisfaction. The trained leader arranges for leadership practice by group members; individual responsibility and group responsibility grow as the group takes on new functions. The atmosphere is friendly, informal, and democratic. (p. 189)

Since this description of group work contains many of the ingredients present in definitions of group counseling, the possible influence on group counseling of the group work specialists becomes readily apparent.

Group Dynamics

Bonner (1959) has outlined the development of the group dynamics movement as beginning in the late 1800s, notably in Europe, and including contributions from sociology, psychology, philosophy, and education—but primarily contributions came from sociology and psychology. Bonner was cautious not to credit a single individual or a single discipline for the origin of group dynamics; however, Kurt Lewin and J. L. Moreno are cited for making significant, yet differing contributions to the discipline during its contemporary phase of development—the 1930s to the present.

Although the National Training Laboratory (NTL) was established in Bethel, Maine, in 1946, "it was not until the middle to late 1950s before the tools and techniques of group dynamics really found their way into education and more specifically, into guidance" (Glanz & Hayes, 1967, p. 4). In 1964, Durkin, after a careful survey of group dynamicists and group therapists, wrote,

In spite of the general impression to the contrary, there was almost no therapy actually being conducted on solely group dynamic principles by group dynamicists. From private correspondence with some of the leading social scientists, I learned that they did not acknowledge group dynamics therapy as an identifiable approach and that they were meticulous in distinguishing between their work and group therapy. (p. 4)

The statement by Glanz and Hayes suggests that group dynamics principles and concepts only very recently have begun to affect the field of group *guidance*. And Durkin stressed the point that although group dynamics had begun to affect the field of group therapy as late as 1964, there was still no complete theory of group dynamics being applied to group therapy.

In 1966, I began to assemble a book, *Innovations to Group Psychotherapy* (1968), and was able to secure a contribution from some group dynamicists, Jack and Lorraine Gibb, of a theory of group dynamics applied to group therapy. They referred to their theory as Emergence Therapy: The TORI Process in an Emergent Group. This theory really represents a leaderless approach to group therapy as well as to small and large groups in general.

The application of group dynamics principles to group *counseling* has a very recent history. The formulations can be found in the writings of Bonney (1969), Fullmer (1971), Mahler (1969), Ohlsen (1966), and in this text.

Self-Help Movement

In the last twenty years we have witnessed a striking increase in the formation and utilization of self-help groups in our society. This self-help movement represents the rediscovery of the oldest and most pervasive system of caring for human ills (Katz, 1981). Kropotkin (1914/1972) argued that mutual aid is the very essence of civilization. The present day self-help group embodies the most recent expression of the human tendency to join together for mutual benefit.

The power and potential of the self-help group has only recently been rediscovered by scholars and health-care professionals. Social scientists showed little interest in self-help/mutual aid until the early 1970s. Only one empirical investigation appeared in the literature before 1957. By the 1970s a number of disciplines were paying considerable attention to the self-help phenomenon. Currently self-help is enjoying an upsurge of interest and activity, reflecting the growing realization of its unique potential (Katz, 1981).

The unique contribution of the self-help movement is its emphasis on the mutuality of the helping process. Peers give and receive help. Giving help is as important to recovery as being helped. Riessman (1965) has called the phenomenon the "helper-therapy principle." Rather than passively relying on a higher-status professional to conduct treatment, group members assume responsibility for helping themselves and each other. Rappaport (1985) describes the benefits of this type of therapy as "empowerment."

Human Potential Movement

The Human Potential Movement is a recent (middle and early 1960s) movement. It has multiple and diverse origins, but is probably most closely related to the efforts of humanistic psychologists (for example, Herbert Otto, Carl Rogers, Abraham Maslow, Jack Gibb, and William Schutz). In its more practical emphasis, features of the movement are being adapted to classroom instruction and in that sense are group guidance-oriented. In the highly experimental and perhaps even ethically questionable forms of group application, it is affecting group counseling by introducing more body contact and more structured game playing.

Conclusions.   The tracing of the development of group counseling suggests that it is a hybrid. Perhaps that is why it has always been difficult to arrive at a definition that is satisfactory to group counseling theorists and practitioners. Those who were most influenced by group guidance also reflect a vocational guidance orientation and prefer a leader-centered and topic-centered approach with an emphasis on educational and vocational counseling. They also prefer a definition that reflects these elements.

Those group counseling theorists and practitioners, on the other hand, who have been significantly influenced by the discipline of group psychotherapy, tend to emphasize the rehabilitative or adjustive (personal–social) qualities of the process. In addition, they tend to use less structure as leaders and to focus on the uniqueness of the individual problems brought to the group, rather than "group" problems.

Some group counseling theorists and practitioners have come from a background of study and/or practice in the group dynamics movement. For these practitioners, the group themes or goals are developed, emphasized, and dealt with. The process the group follows and the nature of leadership are of considerable interest to this type of practitioner. Often they practice leaderless, that is, defaulted leadership and also literally leaderless groups or instrumented group procedures.

Group counselors influenced by the self-help movement encourage and support peer leadership. They believe that nonprofessional group leaders are a potential resource that will allow for the expansion of psychotherapeutic services. They envision their role as trainers of and consultants to the peer leaders.

The group counselors who have evolved from the group work and social casework disciplines frequently bring to their groups a group dynamics emphasis with a psychoanalytic orientation. The psychoanalytic orientation reflects their social work training.

Child guidance-oriented group counselors reflect an Adlerian theoretical influence. As such, they tend to concentrate on family counseling, working especially with elementary school children, their parents, and their teachers. They also tend to be leader-centered and, as such, oriented toward advisement.

The Human Potential Movement may prove to have profound effect on the group counseling movement. The heavy emphasis on body contact and nonverbal "games" introduces experimental processes that have high potential for helping or harming. They have not been experimentally validated, and the theoretical underpinnings are all but absent at the moment. Nevertheless, there are those practitioners of this very broad and inclusive movement who emphasize positive verbal reinforcement techniques and deemphasize responding to or recognizing negative behavior. This subgroup of the Human Potential Movement seems to be the most theoretically sound subgroup and may offer means for improving group counseling techniques, as well as extending the practices to other settings, such as the classroom. The emphasis on body contact in small group work, including group counseling, seems to offer the greatest threat to the professional respectability of group counseling.

SIGNIFICANT CONTRIBUTORS

To attempt to appraise and record some of the most significant contributors to the specialty of *group counseling* while living in the era of the beginning of the movement is to court professional suicide. Nevertheless, an attempt will be made to sketch briefly my perception of those who have been and, in most instances, are still making significant contributions to the group counseling movement. My conclusion that the leaders of the group counseling movement are citizens of the United States seems supported by Brewer (1942). If this conclusion is erroneous, it might at least stimulate others to investigate and challenge it.

The credit for coining the term *group counseling* may be attributed to Richard D. Allen, although there is no absolute proof of this. Others who were among the first to publish and teach in the field of group counseling were Margaret Bennett, Ruth Strang, and Jane Warters. Evelyn Gaskill and Emily Mudd should be cited for their early use of group counseling in social casework and Hanna Grunwald for the current application of group counseling in casework agencies.

Clifford Froehlich and Helen Driver have influenced the group counseling movement with their introduction of multiple counseling, and E. Wayne Wright, upon the death of Froehlich, continued the multiple counseling emphasis. However, *multiple counseling* is now only rarely accepted as the preferred term for group counseling (Gazda, Duncan, & Meadows, 1967).

Merle Ohlsen, Fred Proff, and several of their colleagues and students at the University of Illinois, the author among them, are known for their early attempt to research group counseling. Ohlsen has also contributed two significant texts to the field. Clarence Mahler and Edson Caldwell coauthored one of the first texts on group counseling in the schools, and Mahler has since produced his own very useful text. C. Gratton Kemp also contributed an early useful text, *Foundations of Group Counseling*.

Among those representing the various schools of group counseling, Walter Lifton has been the most prominent proponent of the client-centered approach to group counseling. Rudolf Dreikurs, Manford Sonstegard, Oscar Christensen, Donald Dinkmeyer, James Muro, James Bitter, and G. Edward Stormer are among the most significant Adlerian-oriented contributors to the field of group counseling. John Krumboltz, Barbara Varenhorst, and Carl E. Thoresen have made their contributions with a behavior-oriented application of group counseling.

Dan Fullmer and Harold Bernard have introduced to the field *family group-consultation*, whereas Joseph Knowles has been instrumental in the successful application of the group approach to *pastoral counseling*.

Robert Carkhuff (1971) has influenced the direction that group counseling and counseling in general is taking because of his research and writings regarding the "core dimensions" of a helping relationship and his overall model—Systematic Human Resources Development (HRD).

More recent contributions to group counseling have been through eclectic positions presented by the following individuals: Sheldon D. Glass, *The Practical Handbook of Group Counseling* (1969); Wayne Dyer and John Vriend, *Group Counseling for Personal Mastery* (1980); Jack Duncan and James Gumaer, *Developmental Groups for Children* (1980); James Hansen, Richard Warner, and E. J. Smith, *Group Counseling: Theory and Process* (1980); Robert Conyne, *The Group Workers' Handbook: Varieties of Group Experience*, (1985); Gerald Corey, *Theory and Practice of Group Counseling* (1985), and with Marianne Corey, several other related group books; and Edward E. Jacobs, Riley L. Harvill, and Robert L. Messon, *Group Counseling: Strategies and Skills* (1988).

There are many others who have contributed significantly to the development of group counseling through their training procedures, research, and writing.

Lechowicz (1973) identified over 229 "experts" in group counseling. His criteria for defining an expert included:

1. The author must have published in the area of group counseling, group guidance, group psychotherapy, or multiple counseling.
2. At least two different publications of each author had been cited by other authors.
3. The cited publications were dated between 1950 and 1972. (p. 41)

In 1966, Dwight Arnold assumed a leadership role in developing an "interest group" among the American Personnel and Guidance Association members for the purpose of defining the field, sharing information on training programs, and establishing communication among practitioners to provide some form of organization to the loose-knit group counseling movement. I assumed Dr. Arnold's coordinator role in 1968 and developed

Group Psychotherapy

J.H. Pratt ("class method") (1905) Boston, Mass.

Group Guidance

G. Boyden (1912)
Beaufort, Connecticut

A. Adler
(1921)
Vienna

Group Counseling

R.D. Allen (1931)
Providence, R.I.

First Annual Meeting
of ASGPP at the
Sociometric Institute,
New York City, 1943.

J.L. Moreno (1910) Vienna

A. Adler (1921) Vienna
L.C. Marsh and E.W. Lazell (1921) U.S.A.
T. Burrow (1925) U.S.A.
L. Wender (1929) U.S.A.
P. Schilder (1930s) U.S.A.
S.R. Slavson (1930s) U.S.A.

J.L. Moreno coined term "group therapy" (1931)
J.L. Moreno coined term "group psychotherapy" (1932)
J.L. Moreno founded the American Society of Group
Psychotherapy and Psychodrama (ASGPP—1941-1942)
S.R. Slavson founded the American Group Psychotherapy
Association (AGPA) (1942)
First Annual Conference of AGPA held at Russell Sage
Foundation, January 14 and 15, 1944.

*Sociatry (Group Psychotherapy
and Psychodrama)* founded by
J.L. Moreno, 1947

*International Journal of Group
Psychotherapy* founded by
S.R. Slavson (1949-1951)

T-Groups

K. Lewin, L. Bradford, R. Lippitt,
and K. Benne (Connecticut
Laboratory, 1946)

L. Bradford, R. Lippitt, and
K. Benne (Gould Academy,
Bethel Maine "Basic Skill
Training Groups," 1947)

"T-group" name change from
BST Group, 1949

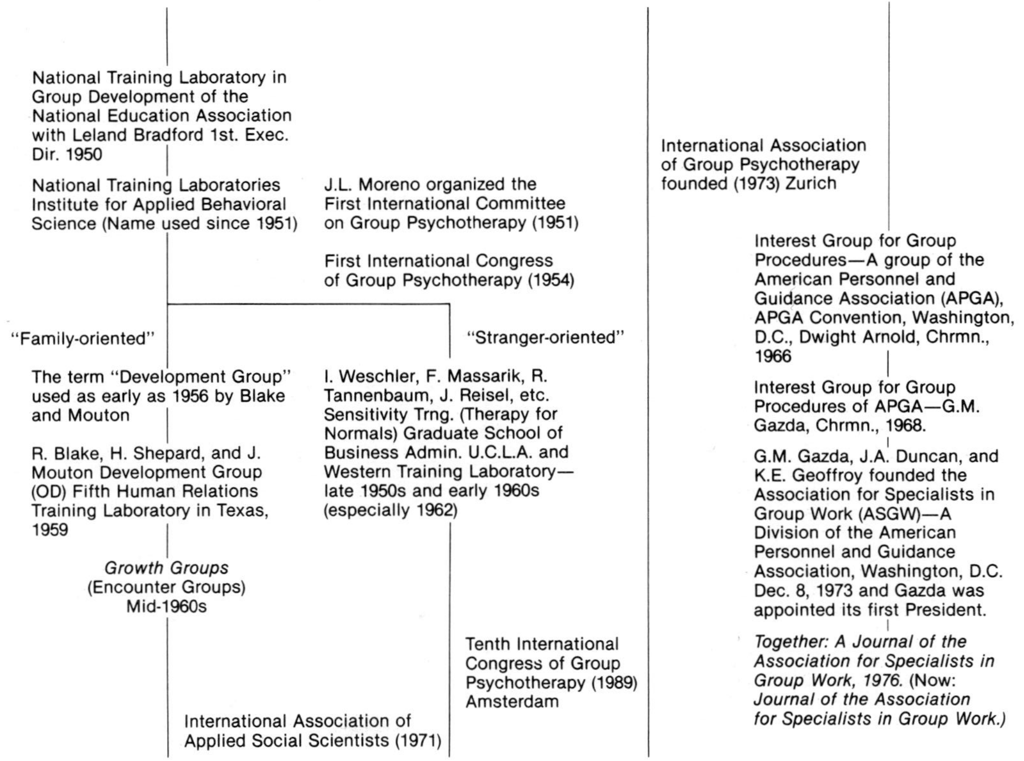

Figure 1–2 Group procedures historical time line

Source: G. M. Gazda, Group psychotherapy and group counseling: Definition and heritage. In G. M. Gazda (Ed.), *Basic approaches to group psychotherapy and group counseling.* 3d Ed. Courtesy Charles C. Thomas, Publisher, Springfield, Illinois.

National Training Laboratory in Group Development of the National Education Association with Leland Bradford 1st. Exec. Dir. 1950

National Training Laboratories Institute for Applied Behavioral Science (Name used since 1951)

"Family-oriented"

The term "Development Group" used as early as 1956 by Blake and Mouton

R. Blake, H. Shepard, and J. Mouton Development Group (OD) Fifth Human Relations Training Laboratory in Texas, 1959

Growth Groups (Encounter Groups) Mid-1960s

International Association of Applied Social Scientists (1971)

J.L. Moreno organized the First International Committee on Group Psychotherapy (1951)

First International Congress of Group Psychotherapy (1954)

"Stranger-oriented"

I. Weschler, F. Massarik, R. Tannenbaum, J. Reisel, etc. Sensitivity Trng. (Therapy for Normals) Graduate School of Business Admin. U.C.L.A. and Western Training Laboratory— late 1950s and early 1960s (especially 1962)

Tenth International Congress of Group Psychotherapy (1989) Amsterdam

International Association of Group Psychotherapy founded (1973) Zurich

Interest Group for Group Procedures—A group of the American Personnel and Guidance Association (APGA), APGA Convention, Washington, D.C., Dwight Arnold, Chrmn., 1966

Interest Group for Group Procedures of APGA—G.M. Gazda, Chrmn., 1968.

G.M. Gazda, J.A. Duncan, and K.E. Geoffroy founded the Association for Specialists in Group Work (ASGW)—A Division of the American Personnel and Guidance Association, Washington, D.C. Dec. 8, 1973 and Gazda was appointed its first President.

Together: A Journal of the Association for Specialists in Group Work, 1976. (Now: *Journal of the Association for Specialists in Group Work.*)

this interest group from approximately 100 to over 1,500. On December 8, 1973, I succeeded, with the help of Jack Duncan and Kevin Geoffroy, in establishing the Association for Specialists in Group Work (ASGW) as the eleventh division of the American Personnel and Guidance Association (the parent organization of now over 55,000 members now renamed the American Association of Counseling and Development). I also served as the new division's first president. With the establishment of this new division for group work, of which group counseling is the core, the continued growth and impact of group counseling seems likely. The current membership of ASGW exceeds 4,500.

Although this chapter has focused primarily on the historical development of group guidance and group counseling, many other related group procedures were developing and influencing these two group specialties. In the 1960s especially, clear differentiations among the many group procedures and disciplines became difficult. Figure 1–2 is included to illustrate the concurrent development of several group disciplines, to illustrate the possible mutual influence of the discipline procedures on each other, and to serve as a brief summary of several significant group developments.

SUMMARY

This chapter traces the history of the development of group counseling and guidance. Attempts were made to identify the persons responsible for coining the terms and the related disciplines contributing to their growth and development.

The related disciplines found to have contributed to the evolution and development of group counseling include group guidance, group psychotherapy, child guidance, social casework, group work, group dynamics, and the Human Potential Movement. These disciplines and the manner in which they have most likely influenced group counseling are systematically described. The disciplines contributing to group guidance are also cited.

Group counseling and group guidance are defined as well as contrasted with other related group procedures. In addition, a paradigm for group guidance, group counseling, group psychotherapy, and other group procedures is outlined.

This chapter closes with an enumeration of some of the more prominent contributors to group counseling and group guidance. Included is a brief description of the nature of their contribution followed by a historical time line.

REFERENCES

Adkins, W. R. (1984). Life skills education: A video-based counseling/learning system. In D. Larsen (Ed.), *Teaching psychological skills: A model for giving psychology away* (pp. 44–68). Monterey, CA: Brooks/Cole.

Allen, R. D. (1931). A group guidance curriculum in the senior high school. *Education, 52,* 189–194.

Ansbacher, H. A., & Ansbacher, R. R. (Eds.). (1956). *The individual psychology of Alfred Adler.* New York: Basic Books.

Barlow, D. H., Abel, G. G., & Blanchard, E. B. (1977). Gender identity change in a transsexual: An exorcism. *Archives of Sexual Behavior, 6,* 387–395.

Bellack, A. S., & Hersen, M. (1978). Chronic psychiatric patients: Social skills training. In M. Hersen & A. S. Bellack (Eds.), *Behavior therapy in the psychiatric setting* (pp. 169–195). Baltimore: Williams & Wilkins.

Bellack, A. S., Hersen, M., & Himmelhock, J. M. (1980). Social skills training for depression: A treatment manual. *JSAS Catalog of Selected Documents in Psychology, 10,* 92, (Ms. No. 2156).

Bellack, A. S., Hersen M., & Turner, S. M. (1976). Generalization effects of social skills training in chronic schizophrenics: An experimental analysis. *Behavior Research and Therapy, 14,* 391–398.

Bellack, A. S., & Morrison, R. L. (1982). Interpersonal dysfunction. In A. S. Bellack, M. Hersen, & A. E. Kazdin (Eds.), *International handbook of behavioral modification and therapy* (pp. 277–310). New York: Plenum Press.

Birchler, G. R. (1979). Communication skills in married couples. In A. S. Bellack & M. Hersen (Eds.), *Research and practice in social skills training* (pp. 273–315). New York: Plenum Press.

Bonner, H. (1959). *Group dynamics.* New York: Ronald Press.

Bonney, W. C. (1969). Group counseling and developmental processes. In G. M. Gazda (Ed.), *Theories and methods of group counseling in the schools.* (pp. 157–180). Springfield, IL: Charles C. Thomas.

Brammer, L. M., & Shostrom, E. L. (1960). *Therapeutic psychology.* Englewood Cliffs, NJ: Prentice-Hall.

Brewer, J. M. (1937). Introduction to R. D. Allen (Ed.), *Organization and supervision of guidance in public education.* New York: Inor.

Brewer, J. M. (1942). *History of vocational guidance.* New York: Harper.

Carkhuff, R. R. (1969a). *Helping and human relations: A primer for lay and professional helpers: Vol. 1. Selection and training.* New York: Holt, Rinehart and Winston.

Carkhuff, R. R. (1969b). *The development of human resources: A primer for lay and professional helpers: Vol. 2. Practice and research.* New York: Holt, Rinehart and Winston.

Carkhuff, R. R. (1971). *The development of human resources: Education, psychology and social change.* New York: Holt, Rinehart and Winston.

Carkhuff, R. R., & Berenson, B. G. (1967). *Beyond counseling and therapy.* New York: Holt, Rinehart & Winston.

Conyne, R. K. (Ed.). (1985). *The group workers' handbook: Varieties of group experience.* Springfield, IL: Charles C. Thomas.

Corey, G. (1981). *Theory and practice of group counseling.* Monterey, CA: Brooks/Cole.

Corsini, R. J. (1957). *Method of group psychotherapy.* Chicago: William James Press.

Curran, J. P. (1977). Skills training as an approach to the treatment of heterosexual social anxiety: A review. *Psychological Bulletin, 84,* 140–157.

Dreikurs, R., & Corsini, R. J. (1954). Twenty years of group psychotherapy, *American Journal of Psychiatry, 110,* 567–575.

Driver, J. I. (1958). *Counseling and learninq through small-group discussion.* Madison, WI: Monona Publications.

Drum, D. J., & Knott, J. E. (1977). *Structured groups for facilitating development: Acquiring life skills, resolving life themes, and making life transitions.* New York: Human Sciences Press.

Duncan, J. A., & Gumaer, J. (1980). *Developmental groups for children.* Springfield, IL: Charles C. Thomas.

Durkin, H. E. (1964). *The group in depth.* New York: International Universities Press.

Dyer, W. W., & Vriend, J. (1980). *Group counseling for personal mastery.* New York: Sovereign Books.

Eddy, W. B., & Lubin, B. (1971) Laboratory training and encounter groups. *Personnel and Guidance Journal, 49,* 625–635.

Egan, G., & Cowan, M. A. (1979). *People in systems.* Monterey, CA: Brooks/Cole.

Foster, C. R. (1925). *Extra-curricular activities in high school.* Richmond, Va.: Johnson.

Frederickson, L. W., Jenkins, J. O., Foy, D. W., & Eisler, R. M. (1976). Social skills training in the modification of abusive verbal outbursts in adults. *Journal of Applied Behavior Analysis, 9,* 117–125.

Fullmer, D. W. (1971). *Counseling: Group theory and system.* Scranton, PA: International Textbook.

Galassi, J. P., & Galassi, M. D. (1979). Modification of heterosexual skills deficits. In A. S. Bellack, & M. Hersen (Eds.), *Research and practice in social skills training.* (pp. 131–187) New York: Plenum Press.

Gaskill, E. R., & Mudd, E. H. (1950). A decade of group counseling. *Social Casework, 31,* 194–201.

Gazda, G. M. (Ed.). (1968). *Innovations to group psychotherapy.* Springfield, IL: Charles C. Thomas.

Gazda, G. M., Childers, W. C., & Brooks, D. K., Jr. (1987). *Foundations of counseling and human services.* New York: McGraw-Hill.

Gazda, G. M., Duncan, J. A., & Meadows, M. E. (1967). Group counseling and group procedures—Report of a survey. *Counselor Education and Supervision, 6,* 305–310.

Gazda, G. M., Duncan, J. A., & Sisson, P. J. (1971) Professional issues in group work. *Personnel and Guidance Journal, 49,* 638–643.

Gendlin, E. T. (1981). *Focusing.* New York: Bantam Books.

Glanz, E. C., & Hayes, R. W. (1967). *Groups in guidance* (2nd ed.). Boston: Allyn and Bacon.

Glass, S. D. (1969). *The practical handbook of group counseling.* Baltimore: BCS Publishing Co.

Goldsmith, J. B., & McFall, R. M. (1975). Development and evaluation of an interpersonal skills-training program for psychiatric patients. *Journal of Abnormal Psychology, 84*(1), 51–58.

Goldstein, A. P. (1981). *Psychological skills training:* The structured learning technique. New York: Pergamon Press.

Goldstein, A. P., Sprafkin, R. P., & Gershaw, N. J. (1976). *Skill training for community living: Applying structured learning therapy.* New York: Pergamon Press.

Golembiewski, R. T. (1972). *Renewing organizations. The laboratory approach to change.* Itasca, IL: F. E. Peacock.

Guerney, B. G., Jr. (1977). *Relationship enhancement.* San Francisco: Jossey–Bass.

Hadden, S. B. (1955). Historic background of group psychotherapy. *International Journal of Group Psychotherapy, 5,* 162–168.

Hansen, J. C., Warner, R. W., & Smith, E. J. (1980). *Group Counseling. Theory and process* (2nd ed.). Chicago: Rand McNally.

Hansen, R. W. (1972). *Training program in basic communication skills.* Unpublished manuscript. Palo Alto, CA: Veterans Administration Hospital.

Hersen, M., & Bellack, A. S. (1976). Social skills training for chronic psychiatric patients: Rationale, research findings and future directions. *Comprehensive Psychiatry, 17,* 559–580.

Hersen, M., & Bellack, A. S. (1977). Assessment of social skills. In A. R. Ciminero, K. S. Calhoun, & H. E. Adams (Eds.), *Handbook for behavioral assessment.* (pp. 509–554). New York: Wiley.

Jacobs, E. E., Harvill, R. H., & Messon, R. L. (1988). *Group counseling: Strategies and skills.* Pacific Grove,CA: Brooks/Cole.

Johnson, D. W. (1978). *Human relations and your career. A guide to interpersonal skills.* Englewood Cliffs, NJ: Prentice-Hall.

Jones, A. J. (1934). *Principles of guidance* (2nd ed.). New York: McGraw-Hill.

Jones, A. J. (1963). *Principles of guidance* (5th ed.). New York: McGraw-Hill.

Katz, A. H. (1981). Self-help and mutual aid: An emerging social movement. *Annual Review of Sociology, 7,* 129–155.

Kemp, S. D. (1970). *Foundations of group counseling.* New York: McGraw-Hill.

Kropotkin, P. (1972). *Mutual aid: A factor in evolution.* New York: New York University Press. (Original work published 1914.)

Lazarus, A. A. (1976). *Multi-modal behavior therapy.* New York: Springer Publishing.

Lechowicz, J. S. (1973). Group counseling instruction: A model based on behavioral objectives developed via the delphi technique. Ph.D dissertation, University of Georgia.

Lifton, W. M. (1961). *Working with groups.* New York: Wiley.

Linehan, M. M., & Egan, K. J. (1979). Assertion training for women. In A. S. Bellack, & M. Hersen (Eds.), *Research and practice in social skills training.* (pp. 237–271). New York: Plenum Press.

MacLennen, B. W., & Felsenfeld, N. (1968). *Group counseling and psychotherapy with adolescents.* New York: Columbia University Press.

Mahler, C. A. (1969). *Group counseling in the schools.* Boston: Houghton Mifflin.

Mahler, C. A., & Caldwell, E. (1961). *Group counseling in secondary schools.* Chicago: Science Research Associates.

McKown, H. A. (1934). *Home room guidance.* New York: McGraw-Hill.

Miller, S., Nunnally, E. W., & Wackman, D. B. (1975) *Alive and aware: Improving communication in relationships.* Minneapolis: Interpersonal Communications Program.

Monti, P. M., Corriveau, D. P., & Curran, J. P. (1982). Social skills training for psychiatric patients: Treatment and outcome. In J. P. Curran, & P. M. Monti (Eds.), *Social skills training.* New York: Guilford.

Moreno, J. L. (1962). Common ground for all group psychotherapists. What is a group psychotherapist? *Group Psychotherapy, 15,* 263–264.

Moreno, J. L. (Ed.) (1966). *The international handbook of group psychotherapy.* New York: Philosophical Library.

Moreno, Z. T. (1966). Evolution and dynamics of the group psychotherapy movement. In J. L. Moreno (Ed.), *The international handbook of group psychotherapy.* New York: Philosophical Library.

Mosher, R. L., & Sprinthall, N. A. (1971). Psychological education: A means to promote personal development during adolescence. *The Counseling Psychologist, 2*(2), 3–82.

Ohlsen, M. M. (1966). Adapting principles of group dynamics for group counseling. *School Counselor, 33,* 159–161.

Ollendick, T. H., & Hersen, M. (1979). Social skills training for juvenile delinquents. *Behavior Research Therapies, 17,* 547–554.

Phillips, E. L. (1985). Social skills: History and prospect. In L. L'Abate, M. A. Milan, (Eds.), *Handbook of social skills training and research* (pp. 101–135). New York: Wiley & Sons.

Powell. M., Illovsky, M., O'Leary, W., & Gazda, G. (1988). Life-skills training with hospitalized psychiatric patients. *International Journal of Group Psychotherapy, 38*(1), 109–117.

Rappaport, J. (1985). The power of empowerment language. *Social Policy, 16,* 15–21.

Rhodes, N., Rasmussen, D., & Heaps, R. A. (1971). *Let's communicate: A program designed for effective communication.* Presented at American Personnel and Guidance Association.

Riessman, F. (1965). The helper therapy principle. *Social Work, 10,* 27–32.

Robin, A. L. (1979). Problem-solving communication training: A behavioral approach to the treatment of parent-adolescent conflict. *American Journal of Family Therapy, 7*(2), 69–82.

Rosenbaum, A., & O'Leary, K. D. (1981). Marital violence: Characteristics of abusive couples. *Journal of Consulting and Clinical Psychology, 49,* 63–71.

Smith, P. (1982). *The development of a taxonomy of the life skills required to become a balanced self-determined person.* Ottowa, Canada: Employment and Immigration, Canada.

Strang, R. (1935). *The role of the teacher in personnel work.* New York: Bureau of Publications, Teachers College, Columbia University.

Sullivan. D. F. (Ed.). (1952). *Readings in group work.* New York: Association Press.

Terkelson. C. (1976). Parent-child communication skill program. *Elementary School Guidance and Counseling, 11,* 89–99.

Van Hasselt, V. B., Hersen, M., & Milliones, J. (1978). Social skills training for alcoholics and drug addicts: A review. *Addictive Behaviors, 3,* 221–233.

Whitehill, M. T., Hersen, M., & Bellack. A. S. (1980). Conversation skills training for socially isolated children. *Behavior Research and Therapy, 18,* 217–225.

SUGGESTED READINGS

Allen, R. D. (1931). A group guidance curriculum in the senior high school. *Education, 51,* 189–194.

Bonner, H. (1959). *Group dynamics.* New York: Ronald Press.

Corsini, R. J. (1957). *Methods of group psychotherapy.* Chicago: William James Press.

Dreikurs, R., & Corsini, R. J. (1954). Twenty years of group psychotherapy. *American Journal of Psychiatry, 110,* 567–575.

Drum, D. J., & Knott, J. E. (1977). *Structured groups for facilitative development*. New York: Human Sciences Press.

Durkin, H. (1964). *The group in depth*. New York: International Universities Press.

Fullmer, D. W. (1971). *Counseling: Group theory and system*. Scranton, PA: International Textbook.

Hadden, S. B. (1955). Historic background of group psychotherapy. *International Journal of Group Psychotherapy, 5,* 162-168.

Moreno, J. L. (Ed.) (1966). *The international handbook of group psychotherapy*. New York: Philosophical Library.

Rosenbaum, M. (1976). Group psychotherapy. In M. Rosenbaum and A. Snadowsky (Eds.), *The intensive group experiences*, (pp. 1–49). New York: Free Press.

Zimpfer, D. G. (1976). Groups: Foundations, philosophy, purposes, definitions. In D. G. Zimpfer (Ed.), *Group work in the helping professions: A bibliography*, (pp. 1–3). Washington, D.C.: Association for Specialists in Group Work, American Personnel and Guidance Association.

C H A P T E R 2

Theoretical Rationale for Developmental Group Counseling

This chapter will develop the rationale for Developmental Group Counseling as it applies to all age groups and it will include goals ranging from prevention to remediation. Two different models of group intervention, the interview model and the life-skills model, are examined in terms of their theoretical assumptions and applications.

Interview group counseling consists primarily of counselor–counselee and counselee–counselee talk, the primary purpose of which is to explore one's strengths and deficits and to arrive at an understanding of the need for a commitment to change. In other words, the basic goals of interview group counseling are to develop insight into oneself and to initiate a plan of positive change. Assuming that the client's problems are not seriously debilitating, insight-oriented interview counseling may be sufficient to help the counselee resolve his or her problems.

In situations in which the counselee's problems reflect deficits in life-coping skills, the life-skills model is the recommended approach. This model focuses on structured skills training for both preventive and remedial purposes.

Life-skills training is recommended for primary prevention, where it is presented to persons still in the process of development. This educational emphasis may be operationalized through a curriculum of life-skills training, especially in the school setting. A comprehensive life-skills training model represents my preferred substitute to the traditional group guidance models that have been applied to groups of children and adolescents and that have been extended to groups of adults.

The two models are not mutually exclusive. In fact, they may be used effectively in combination. The interview model can serve to ready the client. Once deficits are identified, the life-skills model can be used for structured skills training. The integration of the two approaches to group intervention provides a comprehensive framework which fits the needs of all age groups and satisfies the goals of prevention and remediation.

DEVELOPMENTAL APPROACH TO GROUP COUNSELING

Heretofore no systematic attempt has been made to provide an approach to group *counseling* applicable to all age levels. Previous attempts have singled out methods of group counseling with children, with adolescents, or with adults. Slavson (1945), however, long ago recognized the need for differential treatment for different age groups in *group therapy*. "Group therapy," he said, "is practiced on different levels, and in discussing its functions in therapy, it is necessary that these levels be kept in mind" (p. 201).

My experience also has demonstrated the need for a position that allows for and accommodates a different emphasis with different age groups in interview group counseling and life-skills training. The developmental approach to interview group counseling and life-skills training therefore uses the developmental task concept (Havighurst, 1948, 1952, 1953) with subsequent coping behaviors to serve as broad guidelines for the group counselor and life-skills leader. Havighurst defines *developmental task* as follows:

> A developmental task is a task which arises at or about a certain period in the life of the individual, successful achievement of which leads to his happiness and to success with later tasks, while failure leads to unhappiness in the individual, disapproval by society, and difficulty with later tasks. (1952, p. 2)

Havighurst (1952) also cites two reasons why the concept of developmental task is useful to educators. His reasons seem equally applicable to counselors and life-skills trainers: "First, it helps in discovering and stating the purpose of education [group counseling and life-skills training] in the schools. . . . The second use of the concept is in the timing of educational [group counseling and life-skills training] efforts" (p. 5). He describes timing to mean *teachable moment* (1952, p. 5). Readiness for life-skills training is determined by the developmental level of individuals and their corresponding need systems, whereas readiness for group counseling is determined by the dissonance between the developmental task and its subsequent coping behavior.

Zaccaria (1965) gives a more comprehensive interpretation of developmental tasks than does Havighurst. His interpretation includes Havighurst's (1952) "bio-socio-psychological" emphasis, the "vocational development" emphasis of Super et al. (1957, 1963), and Erikson's (1950, 1959, 1963) "psychosocial crises."

In addition to accepted classification of human development along psychosocial and vocational domains, we have well-defined developmental stages in the physical-sexual area (Gesell, Ilg, & Ames, 1956; Gesell, Ilg, Ames, & Bullis, 1946), the cognitive area, à la Piaget (Flavell, 1963; Wadsworth, 1971: Zigler & Child, 1973), the moral area, according to Kohlberg (Duska & Whelan, 1975; Kohlberg, 1973; Kohlberg & Turiel, 1971), the ego developmental stages of Loevinger (1976), and the affective stages of Dupont (1978, 1979). When individuals are viewed along these seven areas of human development, one can obtain a rather complete picture of them. If we use these developmental parameters to gauge normal progress in one's total development, we shall be in a unique position to provide timely assistance in the area(s) (tasks) where mastery is lagging.

Cognitive, moral, ego, and affective developmental *stage* theorists differ from the physical-sexual, psychosocial, and vocational *age* developmental theorists insofar as they do not generally relate stage development

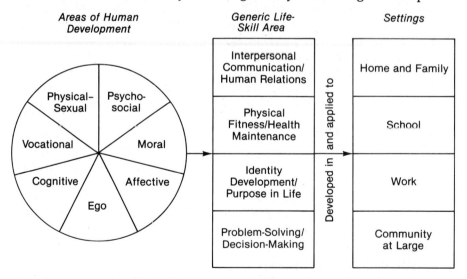

Figure 2–1   A model for the development and application of generic life-skills.

Source: From *Foundations of counseling and human services* by George M. Gazda. Copyright © 1987 by McGraw-Hill Publishing Company. Reproduced by permission.

in these areas to age development. Therefore, using the developmental models places certain interpretive restrictions on the counselor since he or she cannot evaluate stage development based on age development. Nevertheless, certain general classifications can be made. Research by Brooks (1984) showed that the developmental tasks could be classified according to the developmental age group: childhood, adolescence, and adulthood. Furthermore, Figure 2–1 illustrates that the seven areas of human development could be collapsed into four generic life-skill areas: Interpersonal Communication/Human Relations, Physical Fitness/Health Maintenance, Identity Development/Purpose in Life, and Problem Solving/Decision Making. In turn, these generic life-skills are utilized and developed in four settings: home and family, school, work, and the community at large.

Appendix A will assist counselors and life-skills trainers in understanding approximately what knowledge and skills a person should usually possess for each of the three age levels for the four generic life-skill areas. Counselors and trainers can use the descriptors in Appendix A to help them assess what knowledge and skills are relevant for a person's given age. They can intervene with appropriate preventive or remedial counseling and/or training strategies.

Our society and much of the rest of Western culture is organized on the basis of expected progressive development in the biological, intellectual, vocational, sociological, and psychological realms of its citizens, and, as such, the concept of developmental task has general applicability. For example, our schools are organized on a preschool and kindergarten, early elementary school, middle school, and high school basis; state laws govern marriageable ages of its citizens; federal laws govern legal retirement age; and so forth (Muuss, 1962).

Although there are variations in individual biological, social, intellectual, vocational, and psychological development, there are classifiable periods between and within age groups. Several individuals (Blocher, 1974; Brammer & Shostrom, 1960; Erikson, 1950; Havighurst, 1952; Super et al., 1957, 1963) have developed various classification schemes for the developmental phases. For group counseling purposes, the phases can be divided into (1) early childhood or preschool and early school, ages 5–9; (2) preadolescent, ages 9–13; (3) adolescent, ages 13–20; and (4) adult. That there is sometimes considerable overlap between age groups is well documented. There is also a special discrepancy between the sexes at the end of the latency period and the beginning of pubescence—beginning from ages 8 to 13 for girls and 10 to 15 for boys.

Group counselors therefore must be alert to individual differences and organize their groups to accommodate them. Since "little is known as to what the values of a group to a child of 3 or 4 may be" (Slavson, 1945, p. 203), the emphasis of my approach begins with the kindergarten child of age 5.

INTERVIEW MODEL

The interview approach to group counseling is based on the assumption of blockage/barriers to growth. Figure 2–2 represents Lazarus's (1982) illustration of the blockage model. According to Lazarus, in this model the removal of the barrier through empathic reflection, self-understanding, and similar factors (such as the generation of insight and removal of inhibitions or repression) will restore the person to the original pathways of adaptive functioning. In other words, the counselor facilitates the counselee in gaining insight and releasing his or her potential to resolve problems. Therefore, when problems stem from inhibitions, depressions, conflicts, and other barriers, the interview group counseling model is the preferred intervention.

Theoretical Foundations

The position taken in this approach is that humans are endowed with *free will* and therefore have the capacity to make choices, for "good or evil." Certain brain-damaged, severely retarded, or acutely disturbed persons may be exempted from this hypothesis to varying degrees. Even "normals," because of their condition of birth, may have varying degrees or spheres within which they can exercise free will. However, a further assumption is made that humans have a conscience that cannot be reduced to the consequences of learning father images, or anything else. This conscience lies in what may be called tensions of the human spirit (Fabry,

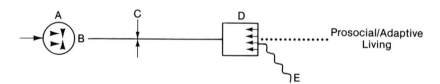

Figure 2–2   Blockage model

   A. The individual at birth is a product of a genetic endowment and the impact of intrauterine and subsequent environmental influences.
   B. The life trajectory proceeds toward "prosocial/adaptive living" or nonneurotic functioning.
   C. Events create conflicts and/or are perceived as traumatic.
   D. A barrier or blockage arises.
   E. The individual departs from the "normal" pathway and is now dysfunctional and/or emotionally disturbed.

Reproduced from A. A. Lazarus, Multimodal group therapy. In G. M. Gazda (Ed.) *Basic approaches to group psychotherapy and group counseling,* 3rd ed. Springfield, IL: Charles C. Thomas, Publisher.

1980). Frankl (cited in Fabry, 1980) puts it this way: "to be human means to be caught in the tensions between what we are and what we are meant to be, to be aware that we do not need to remain the way we are but can always change" (pp. 84–85).

In his book *Life after Life*, Moody (1975) contends that persons clinically dead experienced a powerful need to respond to an out-of-body experience that urged them to strive "to know and to love." Assuming that this "healthy" human tension exists, humans would appear to possess an innate need to know and to understand. This need, therefore, provides a basis for many of the *educational* and *insight*-generating assumptions underlying the interview and life-skills training models described here.

Structuring the Interview Group

The structure of the interview group varies greatly depending on the theoretical orientation used by the leader and the age of the participants. Consequently, issues related to structure, such as group selection, setting, and size, will be covered both in the chapters dealing with the developmental approach to group counseling (Chapters 4, 5, and 6) and the chapters dealing with theoretical approaches to group counseling (Chapters 14–20).

All interview groups, however, depend on the members' willingness to commit themselves to the group. This commitment involves both a willingness by an individual to explore his or her own issues in the group and a willingness to support others in their exploration. Ground rules that facilitate this process, therefore, can be applied to all interview groups, regardless of age level or theoretical framework. The following ground rules are geared toward use with adolescent and adult groups. They can be modified or abbreviated for children's groups.

Ground Rules

Following the counselor's hopeful and positive introduction in the screening interview, the counselor reviews for the candidate the following ground rules that the candidate will be expected to follow as a member of the group.

1. Set a goal or goals for yourself before you enter the group, or at the very latest, as early as you can isolate and define your direction of change. Revise these goals as clarification and/or experience dictates.
2. Discuss as honestly and concretely as you can the nature of your trouble, including the successful and unsuccessful coping behaviors you have employed.

3. When you are not discussing your own difficulties, listen *intently* to the other group members and try to help them say what they are trying to say and to communicate your understanding, caring, and empathy for them.

4. Maintain the confidentiality of all that is discussed in the group. (There are no exceptions to this rule other than those that pertain to you only.)

5. Be on time and attend regularly until termination of the group (if a closed group) and until you have met your goals (if the group is open-ended).

6. Give the counselor the privilege of removing you from the group if the counselor deems it necessary for your health and for the overall benefit of the group.

7. Concur that all decisions affecting the group as a whole will be made by consensus only.

8. Inform the group counselor in private, before the group is constituted, of individuals who would for various reasons constitute a serious impediment to your group participation. (I feel that the "cards should be stacked in the counselee's favor" as much as possible; therefore those individuals who could inhibit the counselee should be excluded from the group if at all possible.)

9. You may request individual counseling interviews, but what is discussed in these interviews should be shared with the group at the appropriate time and at the discretion of the counselor and yourself.

10. When fees are involved, concurrence on amounts and payment schedules is made with counselor before counseling begins.

Values and Uniqueness of Interview Group Counseling

There are certain unique features and values of interview group counseling and psychotherapy in general that should be recognized. These values and features are cited below with full awareness that they are not limited to Developmental Group Counseling and that all have not been experimentally validated.

Respondents to a national survey (Gazda, Duncan, & Meadows, 1967) cited the following advantages—values and uniqueness:

1. Approximates a real life situation, or small community of peers, through which each member can test reality, practice identification, obtain feedback and support, and share ideas, feelings, and concerns, leading to personal growth and improved interpersonal relations.

2. Provides for more economical and better use of counselor's time.
3. Facilitates an effective use of peer group pressure.
4. Makes certain individuals (for example, the defensive, shy, dependent, and school behavior problem) more amenable to individual counseling.
5. Enables counselees to serve as co-counselors.
6. Provides a method for counselor training.
7. Implements subsequent individual counseling.

The limitations and disadvantages of Developmental Group Counseling are not believed to be any different from those of any other form of group counseling or psychotherapy. For example, when authors were asked to list the limitations and disadvantages of group counseling as a part of a survey questionnaire (Gazda, Duncan, & Meadows, 1967), their responses, in order of frequency, included the following:

inappropriate treatment for certain problem types, e.g., sociopathic or psychopathic children, and the severely disturbed; difficult to control confidentiality, depth of involvement, collusion of unhealthy effects, and anxiety level; requires a more skillful counselor, including a greater sensitivity and expertness in group dynamics; is difficult to select appropriate combinations of group members; permits certain participants, e.g., the shy and withdrawn, to refrain from participation; does not provide for adequate individual attention for some counselees; can be difficult, especially in the school setting, to arrange a convenient time for a group meeting; does not represent an economical use of counselor's time; may lead to acceptance of the group milieu which may become artificial; and it is difficult to train adequate practitioners. (p. 307)

Still other limitations of interview group counseling and therapy are cited. Beck (1958) calls attention to the unsuitability of group therapy for those lacking communication skills, the lessened control of the group therapist, the unpredictability of group process, intragroup jealousies, and lack of opportunity for depth treatment at critical moments. Prados (1953) cites as a weakness the tendency of members to act out unconscious infantile impulses, and Spotnitz (1961) cites the tendency of some participants, because of group comfort and a decrease in the urgency to tackle their problems, to drop out of therapy prematurely.

Data on group dropouts provide information on the limitations of group counseling. Early termination could be considered a failure, and consequently a limitation, of the group process. Yalom (1966), in a study of group dropouts, found the following reasons for early termination: (1) external factors, (2) group deviancy, (3) problems of intimacy, (4) fear of emotional contagion, (5) inability to share the doctor, (6) complications of concurrent individual and group therapy, (7) early provocateurs, (8) inadequate orientation to therapy, and (9) complications arising from subgrouping.

Yalom (1985) surveyed recent premature termination studies and concludes that dropouts have the following characteristics: high denial; high somatization; lower motivation; lower psychological mindedness; more severe, psychotic pathology; less likeable (to the therapist); and lower socioeconomic class, social effectiveness, and I.Q.

Therapists who practice psychoanalytic psychotherapy on an individual basis frequently contend that the use of a group interferes with or makes impossible the development of a transference relationship and hence is not effective therapy. Some psychoanalytically oriented group therapists feel that the transference relationship between counselees and therapist is sometimes interfered with by the presence of other counselees.

In summary, it seems possible that the same elements that make for a potent therapeutic climate and force are those that also add greater risks to the treatment (for example, the presence of several counselees in a group decreases the counselor's control and thus subjects the counselees to greater risks of the group's ostracism, pressure, rivalry, breaking of confidence, and the like, with the possible resultant harmful effects). Still other limitations or weaknesses of group counseling lie in the difficulty of bringing together regularly a number of counselees at the same time and the reduced ability of the counselor to focus on nonverbal behavior.

LIFE-SKILLS MODEL ⸻

The life-skills training aspect of Developmental Group Counseling is based on the theory that many people develop emotional problems and/or fail in personal adjustment because they failed to learn the necessary coping skills, either because of poor role models or impoverished learning environment in general, or both. Lazarus (1982) depicts the *deficits* theoretical explanation of personal maladjustment in Figure 2–3. Curran (1979), in discussing the hypothesis for explaining poor social performance and hence the rationale for social skills training, indicates that the most documented and researched hypothesis is the skills-deficit model. Curran gives a variation of the skills-deficit hypothesis, indicating that while an individual at some point in time may have possessed the requisite skills, his or her behavior is no longer readily available to him or her because of some decaying process.

The treatment for the skills-deficit model proceeds by training the individual on each deficient response element (one at a time in order of increasing difficulty) in a series of problem situations. The training usually consists of five techniques: (1) instruction, (2) role play, (3) feedback and social reinforcement, (4) modeling, and (5) practice. Curran (1979) refers to these techniques as a response acquisition approach to treatment.

Bellack and Morrison (1982) describe the conditioned-anxiety hypothesis or model to explain poor social performance. The assumption in this model is that the individual has the requisite skills in his or her repertoire, but is inhibited from responding in a socially appropriate way because of conditioned anxiety. Anxiety-reduction techniques, therefore, constitute the primary component of training.

Both Lazarus and I concluded that dysfunctional individuals may develop this condition through either the blockages or deficits route, or both. Therefore, treatment must be appropriate to the cause(s) of the dysfunction. Frequently the causes are multiple and call for a strategy of multiple interventions. I have already described the four generic areas of life-skills that I use to diagnose and develop intervention strategies (see Figure 2–2). Lazarus (1982) has chosen to compartmentalize the person according to seven areas of personality functioning: behavior, affective responses, sensations, images, cognitions, interpersonal relationships, and biological functioning. Goldstein, Sprafkin, and Gershaw (1976), on the other hand, developed a list of some fifty-nine life-skills areas, including social, personal, and interpersonal functioning, in their model of structured learning therapy.

Recently Smith (1982) described a taxonomy of 222 life skills "required to become a balanced self-determined person." This taxonomy includes "elementary," "complex," and "very complex" skills from the five content areas of self, family, job, leisure, and community.

In 1918 the Commission on the Reorganization of Secondary Education (Shane, 1979) developed the cardinal principles of secondary education: (1) health, (2) command of fundamental processes, (3) worthy home member-

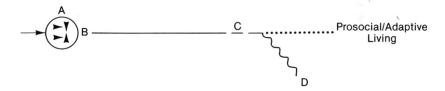

Figure 2–3   Deficits model

A. The person at birth is a product of a genetic endowment and the impact of intrauterine and subsequent environmental influences.

B. The life trajectory proceeds toward "prosocial/adaptive living."

C. Gaps or deficits in the person's learning history create discontinuities in the "normal" pathway.

D. These response deficits lead the person away from adaptive functioning into self-defeating action.

Reproduced from A. A. Lazarus, Multimodal group therapy. In G. M. Gazda (Ed.) *Basic approaches to group psychotherapy and group counseling.* 3rd ed. Springfield, IL: Charles C. Thomas, Publisher.

ship, (4) a vocation, (5) good citizenship, (6) worthy use of leisure time, and (7) career and occupational development skills. These seven principles, for the most part, have been the forerunners of some currently identified life skills.

In 1969 the yearbook of the Association for Supervision and Curriculum Development of the National Education Association was titled *Life Skills in School and Society*. Although the book was published a number of years ago, the problems that the writers cited then are still with us today, and perhaps we have even regressed somewhat with our current emphasis on "back to basics." In the prologue, Rubin cited some of the major shortcomings of the educational system:

> Other criticism of relevance to the matter of skill development points to the school's lack of concern for personal development and the betterment of society. We frequently have been charged with compartmentalizing knowledge in the curriculum so that the learner rarely can relate the ideas of science and the ideas of art, not only to each other, but to the social scene atlarge. The intellectual skills we use, it is said, are too narrow and too disjointed. Skills and knowledge are treated in the abstract so that they do not become a part of the child's personal mechanism for dealing with his world.
> ... The fact that our notions about the disciplines and traditional subject matter are man-made is overlooked, and the schools behave as if people can approach life through biology, phonics, or a unit in community orientation. Schooling, some critics maintain, is closed to all save preparation for entrance into college for the able and temporary custody for those who are less able. (Rubin, 1969, p. 5)[1]

With respect to the need for the inclusion of life-skills training in the curriculum of the schools, Rubin had this to say:

> The ability to manage one's emotions, to take advantage of one's creative potential, to cope with difficult problems, to spend one's leisure wisely, to think rationally, to know one's self and other skills referred to in several chapters of this volume cannot be pasted onto the present curriculum. If they have merit, they must be established in a reasonably fertile environment and nurtured with at least minimal care. Many of the recommendations, moreover, are antithetical to our prevailing assumptions and our standard operating procedures. Where this is the case, either the system must be altered to accommodate the ideas, or the ideas must be ignored in deference to the system. We cannot have both. (Rubin, 1969, p. 9)[2]

---

1. From L. J. Rubin (Ed.) *Life skills in school and society: 1969 yearbook*. Reprinted with permission of the Association for Supervision and Curriculum Development, National Education Association. Copyright © 1969 by the Association for Supervision and Curriculum Development. All rights reserved.
2. See note 1 above.

David Brooks (1984) and I have used the pool of life-skills descriptors from the seven areas of human development shown in Figure 2–1 to develop a series of questionnaires that were sent to developmental psychologists with expertise in child development, adolescent development, and adult development. We used the Delphi research model to determine life-skill components for each of the three age groupings of childhood, adolescence, and adulthood and to identify and name the generic life-skill areas. Some 500 life-skill descriptors were obtained from the developmental theories in Figure 2–1. These descriptors were reduced to approximately 350 when duplicate descriptors were eliminated. Based on the consensus of the experts, the life-skill descriptors were rated for their value to each of the three age groupings: childhood, adolescence, and adulthood.

Each expert rater was also asked to classify the life-skill descriptors on the third and final round of ratings. The purpose of classifying descriptors was to place related items into common or generic categories. The following categories emerged: interpersonal communication/human relations skills, problem-solving/decision-making skills, fitness/ health maintenance skills, and identity development/purpose-in-life skills. Four *settings* were also identified in which the generic skills were practiced. They were family, community, work, and school.

An educational or training model by definition makes certain assumptions about the nature of personal dysfunctioning. Although more specific assumptions will be enumerated later, the underlying assumption is that individuals become mentally or emotionally disturbed because they lack certain life skills or levels of these skills needed to cope with the day-to-day requirements of living. Furthermore, these deficits occur because the person failed to learn the skill or, more frequently, has not mastered it at an effective level. Another possibility exists that through some trauma or anxiety the person is unable to apply life skills that he or she has mastered.

Using the life-skills descriptors that were validated by developmental psychologists as teaching/training objectives, a comprehensive training program eventually will be developed for each of the three age groups. Some partial programs have already been developed (Gazda, Childers, & Brooks, 1987).

Since many life skills are developmentally acquired and since they are learned progressively or hierarchically, the mastery model of Bloom (1976) provides a very appropriate educational paradigm. Instructional models are varied to appeal to all of the chief modes through which people learn: auditory, visual, kinesthetic, and olfactory (Bandler & Grinder, 1975; Grinder & Bandler, 1976). Considerable use is also made of modeling, role playing and simulation, and homework. Practice is a key ingredient of the instructional approach. It is hypothesized that behavioral responses are more likely to be transferred to real life situations if they are first well integrated into the person's repertoire of responses.

LIFE-SKILLS TRAINING

Basic Assumptions of Life-Skills Training Applied in Prevention

The preventive application of the life-skills training model is based on the following assumptions:

1. Effective personal functioning is dependent on achievement of a certain basic level of mastery of the seven areas of human development.
2. Individuals who function effectively progress through certain identifiable stages.
3. Coping skills are optimally learned during certain age ranges.
4. Although the capacity for learning is inherited, the degree to which one's potential is achieved is closely related to one's environment or life experiences.
5. Life skills are most effectively and efficiently taught in the small group and when the learners are developmentally at the peak of readiness.
6. Life skills will be learned and transferred to out-of-group situations when the entire life-skills curriculum is taught simultaneously at the age/stage level appropriate to the learner's readiness. In other words, in a fashion similar to the teaching of reading, writing, and arithmetic at all age/grade levels, the four generic life skills should be so organized that they would be taught daily at all age/grade levels for children and youth and at least weekly for adults.

Basic Assumptions of Life-Skills Training Applied in Remediation

The assumptions that apply to the preventive use of life-skills training also apply to its application to remediation, plus the following four additional assumptions:

1. The basic cause of neuroses and functional psychoses is the failure to learn life skills.
2. Counselees/patients assisted by counselors/therapists can determine their life-skills strengths and deficits.
3. Individuals suffering from neuroses or functional psychoses typically have several life-skills deficits.
4. The most effective and efficient remedy for neuroses and functional psychoses is the direct concurrent teaching/training of counselees/patients in their generic life-skills deficits.

Because space does not permit separate treatment of group selection, size, composition, and other factors for both the interview modality and the life-skills modality by age group, these topics will be included here. The topics will be given general treatment as they relate only to the life-skills modality. Following the treatment of these topics, a case report is provided to illustrate a remedial application of the life-skills training modality.

Structuring Life-Skills Groups

Selection of Group Members

When the life-skills curriculum is applied in the school setting for the purpose of *prevention*, no screening is necessary. All students/trainees within a given group can be expected to learn something from the classes.

The selection process typically involves the group leader and the potential counselee or trainee. The traditional interview group counseling medium provides an excellent experimental medium through which potential group members can be selected. During the first three or four sessions of an open-ended traditional interview counseling group, the potential trainee has the opportunity to present his or her strengths and deficits. These are translated to life skills, and together with the group leader, the client decides with which of the usually several areas of life-skill deficits he or she wishes to seek help. Essentially this list constitutes a prioritizing by the client, and if the group leader concurs, the client is referred to one or more life-skills training groups.

Individual interviews with potential trainees represent another medium to identify life-skill deficits in counselees. These are usually the result of self-referrals or professional referrals. Additional criteria for selection can be obtained from interviews with teachers, relatives, on-site observation of behavior, and assessments through the use of psychological tests. Life-Skills Assessment Scales are currently under development by the author for the age groups: childhood, adolescence, and adulthood.

Because trainees are selected for a life-skills group on the basis of a given life-skill deficit, the groups are homogeneous on that index. Differences in age ranges can be tolerated as long as children are with other children, youth with other youth, and adults with other adults. Because the emphasis is on education rather than treatment, there is no age range where the sexes should not be combined.

Only when a potential trainee is so disruptive or incoherent that he or she cannot learn the life skill being taught would he or she be excluded from the group. Generally, then, actively psychotic persons, individuals who are severely depressed, and those who cannot control themselves would be excluded.

Group Composition

Unlike many traditional counseling groups, life-skills training groups are selected for homogeneity of life-skills deficits; therefore they are homogeneous with regard to problem, but not necessarily with respect to sex, age, or other factors. Since life-skills training is primarily an educational intervention, homogeneous grouping with respect to a life-skill deficit can become an asset rather than a liability insofar as it is easier to teach persons with similar interests and readiness.

Mixed-sex groups are generally preferred because they allow for optimal feedback to participants. There may be a rare exception to mixed-sex groups, such as for youth groups when the content is sexual in nature, as in a physical fitness/health maintenance life-skills group.

Only those persons who are disruptive or incoherent would be excluded from life-skills training groups. Preferred groupings, especially for closed groups, would be members who suffered approximately the same *degree* of skill deficit. These individuals would be expected to progress in learning the life skill at about the same rate, and the group would not be slowed by lagging members. In open-ended groups, larger discrepancies in life-skills deficits would be permitted because the more advanced members could assist the less advanced members in increasing their life skill.

Group Size

Group size is related to a number of other factors such as age of persons, degree of life-skill deficit, number of training sessions, length of training sessions, and duration of training sessions. Generally the smaller the group size, the more intense the involvement per group member. Therefore, if there is little time for training, groups should be limited to about six. (Since training frequently involves pairing of individuals for practice, an even number is recommended.) If time is not a problem, groups could range upward to twelve or fourteen—even larger when the skill deficits are slight, good audiovisual instructional material is available, and peer facilitators are utilized.

A rule of thumb to follow is that when disturbance is high and self-control is low (either because of degree of disturbance or age level of the group members), groups should be small—six or eight members. When these conditions are reversed, groups can be larger—twelve to fourteen, or even classroom size when peer facilitators are utilized.

Group Setting(s)

As with any other setting where teaching and learning is the primary goal, the room or space should be physically comfortable and accommodating. In addition, it should be free from loud or continuous noises and distractions. Small, carpeted rooms where chairs can be moved easily into groups of twos and threes, or more, are preferred. These rooms should include audiovisual equipment, especially videotape cameras and recorders, audio-tape recorders, slide projectors, chalkboards or the equivalent, and the like. An audiovisual room nearby may serve equally well.

The setting for life-skills training may vary considerably more than a typical classroom or therapy room. For example, training in physical fitness/health maintenance may include a gym or the outdoors as well as the typical classroom. Since life-skills training attempts to include at least one-half of the training through simulation or vicarious experiencing and practice, the use of closed circuit television is almost a necessity in order to provide audio and visual feedback to each group member.

Frequency, Length, and Duration of Group Sessions

Unlike traditional group counseling, life-skills training of the type described here is so recent that tested frequencies for group sessions, lengths per session, and duration of training are unavailable. A curriculum for life-skills training in schools is being developed. This plan involves daily or minimally weekly instruction in the generic or basic life-skills. Students will be introduced to concepts and skills that are within their developmental readiness levels and proceed up the developmental hierarchy through at least twelve grades. Similar units of instruction and practice will need to be developed for adults. Currently, only general goals and limited materials and syllabi are available for adults, and these, for the most part, represent the efforts of the interdisciplinary staff at the Veterans Administration Medical Center, Augusta, Georgia. Appendix A includes the life-skill descriptions that can be used as goals for the development of training units at all age levels.

Once again, one needs to resort to rule of thumb or general guidelines when dealing with frequency, length, and duration of group sessions. The trainee's available time for training will influence the nature of the teaching/training program. Some skills are learned best through massed practice, while others are learned best through spaced or intermittent practice. Research will be needed to determine the optimum training session length, frequency, and duration. However, since each group will vary in its skill deficit and learning rates, no immediate clear and definitive guidelines can be given. When using television feedback, however, one should plan sufficient time for the original taping and the playback and analysis. Because taping and playback is quite time-consuming, it must be scheduled carefully to conserve training time.

Media Employed

Types of media employed are practically unlimited because of the variety of life skills to be taught. The use of audiovisual media, especially closed circuit television, has been recommended. Video feedback is especially helpful in teaching interpersonal communication skills, assertiveness, group relationship skills, and self-evaluative skills.

Because life-skills training is an educational model, the learning of all of the life skills can be facilitated through the use of prescribed readings of books, pamphlets, and appropriate articles. Selected video, interactive video discs, and audio tapes and movies would facilitate the learning of most, if not all, life skills.

Since the goal in life-skills training is to provide as much practice and experiential involvement as possible in each life-skill area, simulations, role playing, and role-rehearsal-type activities are used extensively. In other words, life-skills training makes maximum use of the so-called action therapies.

Self-evaluation and monitoring (self-feedback) is an important goal for training in each life-skill area; therefore rating scales, (e.g., life-skills assessment scales under development by the author), physical monitoring devices, and the like are essential training media. In some instances certain standardized self- and external-report psychological assessment devices would be used. Of course, trainer and peer trainer feedback are frequently used media.

Trainer(s) Role(s)

Life-skills training consists of training/teaching in several generic life skills; therefore the role(s) of the trainer(s) will vary with the type of life skill being taught. In general, trainers will be expected to provide information through didactic methods such as minilectures, audiovisuals, and print material. In addition to providing accurate information through these methods, trainers will be required to demonstrate the "model" life skills being taught. The trainer must be able not only to tell about preferred behavior, but he or she should be able to illustrate it through a personal demonstration.

In addition to having a thorough understanding of the life skill for which the trainer is responsible, he or she must also be able to direct or provide the trainees with appropriate print material—in other words, be a resource person for trainees.

In order to teach a life skill most effectively, trainers will need to have a knowledge of preferred educational/training procedures for the life-skills areas for which they are responsible. Skills in field research to test training models would therefore be quite useful.

Since life-skills development constitutes rather personal and pervasive involvement of trainees, the trainers must develop a sense of trust and confidentiality among the trainees. Trainees should be alerted to content that is not to be shared outside the training group. On these occasions, the trainer fills a counselor/therapist role. The trainer is *always* expected to be a group facilitator and, in that role, functions as a group counselor/therapist.

Peer facilitators are recommended in grades 7 through 12 whenever possible. The training materials presented in Appendix B were developed to incorporate peer facilitators for these grades. They would also be appropriate for age groups above twelfth grade. In all cases peer facilitators should first be trained in interpersonal communication and group leadership skills.

Ground Rules for the Group

Ground rules can be considered preliminary elements of a normative system. These are the conditions that are more or less predetermined by the leader or the environment. It is not unusual for group leaders to set such specific guidelines as "Smoking is not allowed," "Fighting is not permitted," or "Confidentiality is expected to be upheld by group members." Only when ground rules become a part of the group's standard operating procedures, in other words—internalized by the members, do they become norms (Dagley, Gazda, & Pistole, 1986, pp. 141). Inasmuch as each training group has its own ground rules, no comprehensive coverage of all these rules would be possible in the space allotted. What can be accomplished here is to illustrate some ground rules that would be appropriate in general.

Even though the emphasis in each group is on education/training and not treatment in the traditional sense, much of the training is experimental. That is, new behaviors are "tried on" or practiced in the training group. Insofar as the practice involves personally relevant material, each training group should require confidentiality of all members. Since several members in remedial groups may be involved in one or more training groups in common, members will need to be cautioned not to carry over personally relevant disclosures of members from one group to another unless permission is obtained.

Other ground rules that would help to ensure a successful remedial training group experience would be regular and prompt attendance, consensus on all issues affecting the group, agreement on the minimum number of group sessions that any given individual will attend, acceptance by group members of the responsibility of the leader(s) to compose the groups so as to be most helpful to each group member, agreement on a mutually (trainee and leader) acceptable fee and payment schedule (if a fee is to be charged), and agreement among the members to be willing to participate in experiences that might be helpful to other group members even though the experience would be of minimal or no interest to a given trainee.

Research

Hundreds of studies have been completed on skills training. In the period from 1970 to 1981 alone, Marshall and Kurtz (1982) cited 140. Current research, however, does not confirm the unequivocal superiority of one skills training model over another (Marshall, Charping, & Bell, 1979).

Matarazzo (1978) reported, nevertheless, that skills training models seem to produce results superior to control group results.

A large body of literature exists that documents the effectiveness of social skills training as a therapeutic intervention for a variety of populations. These include children and adolescents (Fedoravicus, 1973; Grawbard, Rosenberg, & Miller, 1971; Seymour & Stokes, 1976), elderly populations (Berger & Rose, 1977; Gambrill, 1985), people with overly aggressive reactions (Foy, Eisler, & Pinkston, 1975), college students (McFall & Twentymen, 1973), and many other populations.

There have been two rather comprehensive research studies completed in which the *multiple impact life-skills training* model has been applied. These studies (May, Powell, Gazda, & Hauser, 1985; Powell, Illovsky, O'Leary, & Gazda, 1988) were conducted in the psychiatric division of the Veterans Administration Medical Center in Augusta, Georgia, where the author is a consultant and where the life-skills training model has been incorporated.

The first study (May et al., 1985) provided for concurrent training of the experimental group of patients in: interpersonal communications skills, purpose-in-life skills, and physical fitness/health maintenance skills. The life-skills training group received twelve hours of training in interpersonal communications skills over a two-week period. They were assessed by pre–post participation in a standard role-play situation where they were asked to respond to the role player in a "helpful" way. Raters evaluated their level of response on the Gazda, Walters, and Childers (1982) Global Scale. The trained group of patients responded at significantly higher levels ($p < .05$) than a traditional treatment control group.

Six hours of training were provided in the life-skill purpose-in-life. Pre–post testing on the Purpose-in-Life test (Crumbaugh & Maholick, 1964) showed that the life-skill-trained group obtained purpose-in-life scores significantly higher ($p < .025$) than the traditional treatment control group.

For the physical fitness/health maintenance life-skill training, the experimental treatment group received ten hours of exercise and education in physical fitness and health maintenance, including information on diet and nutrition. Change measures were blood pressure, heart rate, and forced vital capacity. The experimental treatment group and traditional treatment group did not differ significantly on these three factors. However, the experimental treatment group showed significant pre- to post-gains in forced vital capacity ($p < .05$). A trend toward a significant decrease for pre- to post- treatment was also found for heart rate ($p < .10$) and blood pressure ($p < .05$). The treatment control group, however, showed a significant pre–post increase in forced vital capacity ($p < .001$) and decrease in blood pressure ($p < .05$) and heart rate ($p < .05$).

A significant decrease in pathology as measured by staff ratings on the Nurses' Observation Scale for Inpatient Evaluation (NOISE-3) (Honigfeld &

Klett, 1965) showed significant pre–post decreases in psychopathology for both the experimental and traditional groups ($p < .01$), but no significant differences between groups. A two-year follow-up showed that rehospitalization and employment rates were highly similar for the life-skills treatment group and the treatment control group.

The other study (Powell et al., 1988) compared the effectiveness of two life-skills components in treatment of psychiatric patients. Patients in the experimental group received life-skills training in communication and vocational skills. Patients in the control group received treatment available at the time in a Veterans Administration psychiatric hospital.

Communication skills were assessed by the Global Scale (Gazda, et al. 1983). Vocational skills were assessed by the Vocational Development Rating Scale (O'Leary, Powell, & Gazda, n.d.) and the Career Maturity Inventory (Crites, 1965). The patients receiving direct skills training obtained significantly higher scores on all measures than the patients in the control group.

Results of a one-year follow-up study using a self-report questionnaire indicated that the experimental group had proportionally fewer rehospitalizations and less tendency to receive mental health treatment after discharge. Members of the experimental group were twice as likely to be employed. Their communications with others showed greater improvement, as did their relationships with others.

The results of the two studies showed that important life skills can be taught to patients in a psychiatric hospital in a relatively short period of time and that the multiple-impact life-skills training approach is more effective than the traditional treatment approach.

Ethical Considerations

Confidentiality cannot be guaranteed in any form of group treatment. In this respect, group treatment procedures are uniquely different from individual treatment modalities where the counselor can be expected to maintain confidentiality. Group treatment procedures also rely on group support. Again, this feature of group treatment can be more potent than the support from an individual counselor.

Good group leaders rely on positive modeling of certain group members to effect positive change in other group members. Multiple models are available in groups, unlike in individual counseling.

Groups can contain a microcosm of society, unlike an individual counselor; therefore generalizability of responding can be enhanced.

These are a few of the more basic differences or degrees of difference between group and individual treatment modalities in general. For life-skills training, the same differences exist and raise the same ethical problems; however, at least two of these are even more present. Group members in remedial groups will need to be cautioned about confidentiality even more so than in traditional counseling groups because of the carry-over of content from one life-skills group to another where the same individuals are participants. On the other hand, since life-skills training emphasizes an educational/training model, personally relevant disclosures will be lessened somewhat.

The other major unique ethical issue highlighted through life-skills training lies in the basic assumption that the person is suffering from lack of knowledge/skill in one or more (usually more than one) life-skills areas. This assumption presupposes that the group leader(s) are capable of teaching these life skills, or, more provocative, that they "know better than the trainee" how he or she should respond. This is no minor consideration, and it behooves the leader to become thoroughly competent in the life-skill area(s) that he or she teaches/trains. Assuming competence, the leader must still permit group members to reject the leader's life-skill model even if it means that the trainee/patient/client will deteriorate further.

Group Protocol (Case Report)

Since space does not permit protocols from the many different remedial life-skills training groups, a single case shall be reported. The name is fictitious to protect the identity of the patient/trainee.

Presenting History

This is the third admission for this forty-year-old veteran. His chief complaint is being unable to cope with everyday living responsibilities. This divorced veteran feels inadequate in caring for his six-year-old son. A major problem is that he socially isolates himself from others and abuses drugs and alcohol. Feeling that his parents do not understand him, he fails to discuss his problems and feelings with them. Mr. Fannin states that he cannot communicate in groups and requests individual therapy sessions. Preoccupied with concerns of insomnia, guilt feelings, flashbacks of Vietnam, depression, and feeling stressed out, this client lacks interest in the problems of others. He communicates Post-Traumatic-Stress as his major problem and is unable to identify specific problem areas that he wants to improve. This unemployed car salesman questions if he will ever be able to function productively. Mr. Fannin has a degree in business administration, but has difficulty concentrating and attending to day-to-day tasks. Having a past interest in sports, jogging, swimming and fishing, this client has become apathetic and inactive. This veteran has a low self-concept and a poor self-image, and lacks self-confidence, spiritual meaning, and purpose for his life.

During two prior hospitalizations, Mr. Fannin received implosive therapy, anger management, Post-Traumatic-Stress counseling, manual arts therapy, and attended the Problem-Solving/Decision-Making Group. Each of these hospitalizations averaged a month. Mr. Fannin lacked commitment for involvement in his treatment program and thus feels that he did not benefit from his past hospital stays. Currently he is requesting help and is willing to commit himself to a treatment program.

Patient's Life-Skills Deficits

Patients in this treatment program are assessed against the four generic life-skills and the sub-skills areas that are appropriate and available in this Veterans Administration Medical Center. The following life-skills deficits were identified by the therapists (see Table 2–1):

> *Interpersonal Communication* —Withdraws from others. Cold, rigid, and indifferent to feelings of others. Responds in a mechanical way and fails to communicate on an emotional level. Focuses conversation on self. Unable to self-disclose in groups. Unable to discuss problems and feelings with parents. Unable to communicate with son and lacks parenting skills. Divorced in 1983 and lacks interest in dating. Unable to make eye contact and lacks concreteness in making requests for help.
>
> *Assertiveness* —Unable to express anger without being verbally abusive.
>
> *Problem-Solving/Decision-Making* —Unable to identify problem areas. Complained of symptoms. Denies specific problem areas and focuses on diagnostic classification with signs and symptoms.
>
> *Physical Fitness/Health Maintenance* —Inactive. Fails to carry out physical activities because of lack of energy. Dull flat affect.
>
> *Relaxation Training* —Tense, anxious, and restless. Poor sleep-rest pattern. High stress level. Low tolerance for frustration.
>
> *Exploring Leisure Time* —Spends most of time alone on a farm.
>
> *Purpose-in-Life* —Poor self-image. Loss of religious interests. Lacks self-confidence. Depressed and feels guilty.
>
> *Vocational/Career Development* —Unemployed. Unable to take the pressure of job as a car salesman and feels stressed out. Insecure about changing vocations.
>
> *Other maladaptive coping behavior* —Unable to cope with everyday living responsibilities. Past history of drug and alcohol abuse.

Patient's Progress

This patient's rapid progress was attributed to several factors. The primary reason was that he had a readiness for commitment to a treatment program. The multiple impact of life-skills training groups was also very effective, however, in affecting his progress.

Table 2-1   Mr. Fannin's Treatment Program

	Operational Skills Training Groups										
Generic Life Skills	Interpersonal Communications	Assertiveness Training	Problem-Solving/ Decision-Making	Physical Fitness	Weight Management	Stress Awareness	Relaxation Training	Exploring Leisure Time	Purpose in Life	Vocational/ Career Development	Group Process
Interpersonal Communications/ Human Relations	X	X									
Problem-Solving/ Decision-Making			X								X
Physical Fitness/ Health Maintenance				X			X	X			
Identity Development/ Purpose in Life									X	X	

Table 2-2   Patient Progress Report

Client—Fleming Fannin			**Counselor**—Midge Powell, M.S.N., C.S.			
Dates	7/1	7/8	7/15	7/22	7/29	8/6
	1	2	3	4	5	6
Interpersonal Communications/ Human Relations	D	C	B	B	A	A
Problem-Solving/ Decision-Making	D	D	C	B	B	B
Physical Fitness/ Health Maintenance	D	C	B	A	A	A
Identity Development/ Purpose in Life	D	D	C	B	B	B

Legend: D gross deficit;   C deficit;   B average;   A good

The progress of patient Fannin (see Table 2–2) was as follows:

Interpersonal Communication —Able to communicate more effectively. Friendly, pleasant, congenial, and initiates interactions with others. Serves as a peer helper in interpersonal communications training. Discusses concrete problems relating to family. Actively participates in other groups. Demonstrates warmth to others.

Assertiveness —Discusses angry feelings with others. Discusses upset feelings with father.

Problem-Solving/Decision-Making — Demonstrates genuineness in outlining plan for improving communications with family. Works on parenting plan to show more warmth and understanding toward son. Outlines plan for physical and leisure time activities. Discusses plans to change career goals and cites steps to carry out plan. Outlines life-style changes.

Physical Fitness/Health Maintenance —Jogs and works out daily in corrective therapy. Alert and increased energy level. Feels better and increases physical activities to include aquatic therapy. Neat and attractively dressed.

Relaxation Training —Improving sleep-rest pattern. Decreasing tension and anxiety. Constructively managing day-to-day frustrations.

Exploring Leisure Time —Increases time improving concentration and relaxation.

Purpose-in-Life —Making plans to attend church. Reading religious books. Talking out guilt feelings with chaplain. Increases self-confidence.

Vocational/Career Development —Initiates plan to reinstate driver's license. Seeking vocational counseling to change career to two-year program in Sociology.

Other coping behavior —Improved general coping skills and handling responsibility for privileges and passes. Attending A.A. No drug abuse. Drank one time during hospital stay. Plans to attend Mental Hygiene outpatient services in hometown on discharge.

SUMMARY

This chapter develops the rationale and application for Developmental Group Counseling. The chapter is divided into two major parts. In the first part, the rationale for the application of the interview group counseling modality is developed. The interview modality is the major intervention developed in Chapters 4, 5, and 6 of this book.

The second part of this chapter is devoted to explicating the rationale for a new intervention of Developmental Group Counseling in the life-skills training modality. This new modality provides Developmental Group Counseling with a more complete intervention system. How this modality complements the interview modality is developed. The life-skills modality is illustrated with a case report.

REFERENCES

Bandler, R., & Grinder, J. (1975). *The structure of magic I.* Palo Alto, CA: Science and Behavior Books.

Beck, D. F. (1958). The dynamics of group psychotherapy as seen by a sociologist. Part I: The basic process. *Sociometry, 21,* 98–128.

Bellack, A. S., & Morrison, R. L. (1982). Interpersonal dysfunction. In A. S. Bellack, M. Hersen, & A. E. Kadzin (Eds.). *International handbook of behavioral modification and therapy* (pp. 717–747). New York: Plenum Press.

Berger, R. M., & Rose, S. D. (1977). Interpersonal skill training with institutional-ized elderly patients. *Journal of Gerontology, 32,* 346–353.

Blocher, D. H. (1974). *Developmental counseling.* (2nd ed.). New York: Roland Press.

Bloom, B. S. (1976). *Human characteristics and school learning.* New York: McGraw-Hill.

Brammer, L. M., & Shostrom, E. L. (1960). *Therapeutic psychology.* Englewood Cliffs, NJ: Prentice-Hall.

Brooks, D. K., Jr. (1984). A life-skills taxonomy: Defining the elements of effective functioning through the use of the Delphi technique. Ph.D. dissertation, University of Georgia.

Crites, J. O. (1965). Measurement of vocational maturity in adolescence: 1. Attitude test of the vocational development theory. *Psychological Monographs, 79,* 1–36.

Crumbaugh, J. C., & Maholick, L. T. (1964). An experimental study of existential-ism: The psychometric approach to Frankl's concept of noogenic neurosis. *Journal of Clinical Psychology, 20,* 200–207.

Curran, J. P. (1979). Social skills: Methodological issues and directions. In A. S. Bellack & M. Hersen (Eds.), *Research and practice in social skills training* (pp. 319–354). New York: Plenum Press.

Dagley, J. C., Gazda, G. M., & Pistole, M. C. (1986). Groups. In M. D. Lewis, R. L. Hayes, & J. A. Lewis (Eds.), *The counseling profession* (pp. 130–166). Itasca, IL: F. E. Peacock.

Dupont, H. (1978, February 3–4). Affective development: A Piagetian model. Paper presented at the UAP-USC Eighth Annual Interdisciplinary International Conference "Piagetian Theory and the Helping Professions," Los Angeles, CA.

Dupont, H. (1979). Affective development: Stage and sequence. In R. L. Mosher (Ed.), *Adolescents' development and education.* Berkeley, CA: McCutchon.

Duska, R., & Whelan, M. (1975). *Moral development: A guide to Piaget and Kohlberg.* New York: Paulist Press.

Erikson, E. H. (1950). *Childhood and society.* New York: Norton.

Erikson, E. H. (1959). Growth and crises of the healthy personality. *Psychological Issues, 1,* 50–100.

Erikson, E. H. (1963). *Childhood and society.* (2nd ed.). New York: Norton.

Fabry, J. A. (1980). *The pursuit of meaning.* New York: Harper & Row.

Fedoravicus, A. S. (1973). The patient as shaper of required parental behavior: A case study. *Journal of Behavior Therapy and Experimental Psychiatry, 4*, 395–396.

Flavell, J. H. (1963). *The developmental psychology of Jean Piaget*. Princeton: D. Van Nostrand.

Foy, D. W., Eisler, R. M., & Pinkston, S. (1975). Modeled assertion in case of explosive rage. *American Journal of Mental Deficiency, 89*, 9–15.

Gambrill, E. (1985). Social skills training with the elderly. In L. L'Abate & M. A. Milan (Eds.). *Handbook of social skills training and research* (pp. 326–360). New York: Wiley & Sons.

Gazda, G. M., Asbury, F., Balzer, F., Childers, W., & Walters, R. (1983). *Human relations development: A manual for educators*. (3rd ed.). Boston: Allyn & Bacon.

Gazda, G. M., Childers, W. C., & Brooks, D. K., Jr. (1987). *Foundations of counseling and human services*. New York: McGraw-Hill.

Gazda, G. M., Childers, W. C., Walters, R. R. (1982). *Interpersonal communication: A handbook for health professionals*. Rockville, MD: Aspen System Corporation.

Gazda, G. M., Duncan, J. A., & Meadows, M. E. (1967). Group counseling and group procedures—Report of a survey. *Counselor Education and Supervision, 6*, 305–310.

Gazda, G. M., Walters, R. P., & Childers, W. C. (1975). *Human relations development: A manual for health sciences*. Boston: Allyn and Bacon.

Gesell, A., Ilg, F. L., & Ames, L. B. (1956). *Youth: The years from ten to sixteen*. New York: Harper.

Gesell, A., Ilg, F. L., Ames, L. B., & Bullis, G. E. (1946). *The child from five to ten*. New York: Harper.

Goldstein, A. P., Sprafkin, R. P., & Gershaw, N. J. (1976). *Skill training for community living: Applying structural learning therapy*. New York: Pergamon Press.

Grawbard, P. S., Rosenberg, H., & Miller, M. B. (1971). Student application of behavior modification to teacher and environments or ecological approaches to social deviancy. In E. R. Ramp, & B. L. Hopkins (Eds.), *A new direction for education* (pp. 80–101). Lawrence, KS: Department of Human Development, University of Kansas.

Grinder, J., & Bandler, R. (1976). *The structure of magic II*. Palo Alto, CA: Science and Behavior Books.

Havighurst, R. J. (1948). *Developmental tasks and education*. Chicago: University of Chicago Press.

Havighurst, R. J. (1952). *Developmental tasks and education*. (2nd ed.). New York: Longmans, Green.

Havighurst, R. J. (1953). *Human development and education*. New York: David McKay.

Honigfeld, G. H., & Klett, C. J. (1965). The Nurses' Observation Scale for Inpatient Evaluation: A new scale for measuring improvement in chronic schizophrenia. *Journal of Clinical Psychology, 21*, 65–71.

Kohlberg, L. (1973). Continuities and discontinuities in childhood and adult moral development revisited. In P. B. Baltes, & K. W. Schaie (Eds.), *Life-span development psychology: Research and theory*. New York: Academic Press.

Kohlberg, L., & Turiel, P. (1971). Moral development and moral education. In G. Lesser (Ed.), *Psychology and educational practice*. New York: Scott, Foresman.

Lazarus, A. A. (1982). Multimodal group therapy. In G. M. Gazda (Ed.), *Basic approaches to group psychotherapy and group counseling*. (3rd ed.). (213–234). Springfield, IL.: Charles C. Thomas.

Loevinger, J. (1976). *Ego development*. San Francisco: Jossey-Bass.

Marshall, E. K., Charping, J. W., & Bell, W. J. (1979). Interpersonal skills training: A review of research. *Social Work Research and Abstracts, 15*(1), 10–17.

Marshall, E. K., & Kurtz, P. D. (Eds.) (1982). Interpersonal helping skills. San Francisco: Jossey-Bass.

Matarazzo, R. G. (1978). Research on the teaching and learning of psychotherapeutic skills. In S. L. Garfield and A. E. Bergin (Eds.), *Handbook of psychotherapy and behavior change*. (2nd ed.). New York: Wiley.

May, H. J., Powell, M., Gazda, G. M., & Hauser, G. (1985). Life skill training: Psychoeducational training as mental health treatment. *Journal of Clinical Psychology, 41*(3), 359–367.

McFall, R. M. & Twentyman, C. T. (1973). Four experiments on the relative contribution of rehearsal, modeling and coaching to assertion training. *Journal of Abnormal Psychology, 81*, 199–218.

Moody, R. (1975). *Life after life*. Atlanta: Mockingbird Books.

Muuss, R. E. (1962). *Theories of adolescence*. New York: Random House.

O'Leary, W., Powell, M. F., & Gazda, G. M. (unpublished), Vocational Development Rating Scale.

Powell, M., Illovsky, M., O'Leary, W. & Gazda, G. (1988). Life-skills training with hospitalized psychiatric patients. *International Journal of Group Psychotherapy 38*(1), 109–117.

Prados, M. (1953) Some technical aspects of group psychotherapy. *International Journal of Group Psychotherapy, 3*, 131–142.

Rubin, L. J. (Ed.) (1969). *Life skills in school and society: 1969 Yearbook*. Washington, D.C.: Association for Supervision and Curriculum Development, National Education Association.

Seymour, F. W., & Stokes, R. F. (1976). Self-recording in training girls to increase work and evoke staff praise in an institution for offenders. *Journal of Applied Behavior Analysis, 9*, 41–45.

Shane, H. G. (1979). Education in and for the future. In E. Ignas, & R. J. Corsini (Eds.). *Alternative educational systems*. Itasca, IL: F. E. Peacock.

Slavson, S. R. (1945). Differential methods of group therapy in relation to age levels. *Nervous Child, 4*, 196–210.

Smith, P. (1982). *The development of a taxonomy of life skills required to become a balanced self-determined person*. Ontario, Canada: Employment and Immigration Canada, Occupational and Career Analysis Development.

Spotnitz, H. (1961). *The couch and the circle*. New York: Alfred A. Knopf.

Super, D. E., Crites, J., Hummel, R., Mosher, H., Overstreet, C. B., & Warnath, C. B. (1957). *Vocational development: A framework for research*. Monograph No. 1. New York: Bureau of Publications, Teachers College, Columbia University.

Super, D. E., Starishevesky, R., Matlin, N., & Jordaan, J. P. (1963). *Career development: Self-concept theory*. New York: College Entrance Examination Board.

Wadsworth, B. J. (1971). *Piaget's theory of cognitive development*. New York: David McKay.

Yalom, I. D. (1966). A study of group therapy dropouts. *Archives of General Psychiatry, 14*, 393–414.

Yalom, I. D. (1985). *The theory and practice of group psychotherapy*. (3rd ed.). New York: Basic Books.

Zaccaria, J. S. (1965). Developmental tasks: Implications for the goals of guidance. *Personnel and Guidance Journal, 24,* 372–375.

Zigler, E. F., & Child, I. L. (Eds.) (1973). *Socialization and personality development.* Reading, Mass.: Addison-Wesley.

SUGGESTED READINGS

Blocher, D. H. (1966). *Developmental counseling.* New York: Ronald Press.

Brooks, D. K., Jr. (1984). A life-skills taxonomy: Defining the elements of effective functioning through the use of the Delphi technique. Ph.D. dissertation, University of Georgia.

Carkhuff, R. R. (1969a). *Helping and human relations. Vol. 1. Selection and training.* New York: Holt, Rinehart and Winston.

Carkhuff, R. R. (1969b). *Helping and human relations. Vol. 2. Practice and research.* New York: Holt, Rinehart and Winston.

Dupont, H. (1979). Affective development: Stage and sequence. In R. L. Mosher (Ed.), *Adolescents' development and education.* Berkeley, CA: McCutchon.

Erikson, E. H. (1963). *Childhood and society.* (2nd ed.). New York: Norton.

Flavell, J. H. (1963). *The developmental psychology of Jean Piaget.* Princeton: D. Van Nostrand Company.

Gazda, G. M., Childers, W. C., & Brooks, D. K. Jr. (1988). *Foundations of counseling and human services.* New York McGraw-Hill.

Gesell, A., Ilg, F. L., & Ames, L. B. (1956). *Youth: The years from ten to sixteen.* New York: Harper.

Gesell, A., Ilg, F. L., Ames, L. B., & Bullis, G. E. (1946). *The child from five to ten.* New York: Harper.

Goldstein, A. P., Sprafkin, R. P., & Gershaw, N. J. (1976). *Skill training for community living: Applying structural learning therapy.* New York: Pergamon Press.

Kohlberg, L. (1973). Continuities and discontinuities in childhood and adult moral development revisited. In P. B. Baltes, & K. W. Schaie (Eds.). *Life-span development psychology: Research and theory.* New York: Academic Press.

Kohlberg, L., & Turiel, P. (1971). Moral development and moral education. In G. Lesser (Ed.), *Psychology and educational practice.* New York: Scott, Foresman.

Loevinger, J. (1976). *Ego development.* San Francisco: Jossey-Bass.

Rubin, L. J. (Ed.) (1969). *Life-skills in school and society: 1969 Yearbook.* Washington, D.C.: Association for Supervision and Curriculum Development, National Education Association.

Smith, P. (1982). *The development of a taxonomy of life skills required to become a balanced self-determined person.* Ontario, Canada: Employment and Immigration Canada, Occupational and Career Analysis Development.

Super, D. E., Crites, J., Hummel, R., Mosher, H., Overstreet, C. B., & Warnath, C. B (1957). *Vocational development: A framework for research.* Monograph No. 1. New York: Bureau of Publications, Teachers College, Columbia University.

Super, D. E., Starishevesky, R., Matlin, N., & Jordaan, J. P. (1963). *Career development: Self-concept theory.* New York: College Entrance Examination Board.

Zaccaria, J. S. (1965). Developmental tasks: Implications for the goals of guidance. *Personnel and Guidance Journal, 24,* 372–375.

C H A P T E R   3

Group Dynamics Applications to Developmental Group Counseling

This chapter summarizes basic group dynamics theory and research that relate to group counseling in general and Developmental Group Counseling in particular. Inasmuch as research evidence with respect to the group dynamic elements of group counseling is not conclusive, an attempt is made to focus on those important features of group counseling where at least research trends are available. Most group dynamics research is not age specific; therefore the group counselor implementing the Developmental Group Counseling model will need to make his or her own translations of the findings to the specific age group with which he or she works.

GROUP DYNAMICS

The term *group dynamics* is used by professionals in more than one way. For some, "group dynamics is a field of inquiry dedicated to advancing knowledge about the nature of groups, the laws of their development, and their interrelations with individuals, other groups, and larger institutions" (Cartwright & Zander, 1968, p. 19). Others use *group work* in a similar manner, differing only in focus, with primary attention given to the study of the complex and interdependent forces of the small group for the express purpose of improving professional work in such areas as leadership and involvement. For instance, Knowles and Knowles (1959) refer to group dynamics as the complex forces that act on every group, whether known to members or not, and influence the behavior of the group. Although a group has certain static characteristics such as size, it also has dynamic aspects. "It is always moving, doing something, changing, becoming, interacting, and reacting" (Knowles & Knowles, 1959, p. 12). The interactive effect of these internal and external forces on the group's direction and movement constitute its dynamics (Dagley, Gazda, & Pistole, 1986, pp. 138–139).

Several concepts are important to understanding group dynamics. Among these are leadership variables, structure, goals, cohesiveness, norms, feedback, roles, and stages of development. These and related variables will be described in the remainder of this chapter.

Counselor's Ability to Help

Stockton and Morran (1982) surveyed the group leadership research and reported that there are inconclusive results: "There is very little research that provides clear evidence for a particular style of leadership as being most effective" (p. 48). Having issued this caution, let us review some of the more significant results from their survey.

Stockton and Morran concluded that leadership is multidimensional, thus making it difficult to control for unidimensional examination. Nevertheless, they also concluded that the Lieberman, Yalom, and Miles (1973) study of encounter groups comes closest to supporting a specific style of leadership. Their results are summarized as follows:

> The most effective encounter group leaders (a) were moderate in amount of emotional stimulation (emphasizing disclosure of feelings, challenging, confronting, etc.), (b) were high in caring (offering support, encouragement, protection, etc.), (c) had meaning-attribution utilization (providing concepts for how to understand, clarifying, interpreting, etc.), and (d) were moderate in expression of executive functions (setting rules, limits, norms, time management, etc.). (Stockton & Morran, 1982, pp. 70–71).

The Lieberman et al. study has been criticized for a variety of reasons, but a reanalysis of the data by Russell (1978) appeared to identify two major leader dimensions: "Effective leaders were found to foster both a warm, supportive relationship and a high degree of emotional stimulation" (Stockton & Morran, 1982, p. 70). Stockton and Morran also reported a study by Hurley and Pinches (1978) that found more effective group leaders to be more self-accepting, dominant, and self-assertive than relatively less effective leaders.

Lieberman, Yalom, and Miles (1973) also discovered that the group leader's style (not theoretical rationale) was the major cause of casualties. Leaders represented all of the major group counseling and therapy theoretical models and varied considerably with respect to effectiveness within a given model. The most destructive leaders were aggressive, authoritarian, and showed little "respect" (insofar as they frequently intruded on and challenged group members). They also used frequent confrontations; were impatient with members' progress; and pressed for immediate self-disclosure, emotional expression, and attitude change. In other words, it appears that the harmful leaders were low on the "respect" dimension and high on the "confrontation" dimension. (In an extensive and intensive analysis of the confrontation dimension, or the use of confrontation in counseling and therapy, Berenson and Mitchell (1974) concluded that confrontation is never necessary, but it can be used effectively by very *high functioning* helpers.)

The ineffective leaders were also described as high self-disclosers (evidently inappropriately so) and rather egocentric (high ego needs). My appraisal of their behavior suggests that they were unable to allow their group members to self-disclose and get emotionally involved at the rate that the members could deal with. They pushed the members too hard to change too fast (perhaps to meet their own ego needs to see change). Their timing was way off, especially regarding their use of confrontation and self-disclosure. They did not allow their group members to *pace* themselves, to be responsible for the progress of their own change.

Truax and Carkhuff (1967, p. 1) described effective counselors as integrated, nondefensive, and authentic or *genuine* in their therapeutic encounter. They also described them as providing a nonthreatening, safe, trusting, or secure atmosphere by their acceptance, unconditional positive regard, love, or *nonpossessive warmth* for the client. And finally, they are able to "be with," "grasp the meaning of," or *accurately and empathically* understand the client on a moment-by-moment basis. Bergin (1975) concluded that "therapists who are themselves psychologically healthier, and who have a capacity to form deep, trusting relationships with others get the best results" (p. 100).

Bergin (1975) reported that an analysis of about a dozen carefully designed and controlled studies on the effects of various types of therapy with nearly 1,000 cases showed that therapy helped 25 percent more than a control (untreated) group, but that it harmed an additional 5 percent. Sixty-five percent of the treated cases showed improvement versus 40 percent of the untreated controls; 25 percent of the treated group were unchanged versus 55 percent of the untreated group; and 10 percent of the treated group deteriorated versus only 5 percent of the untreated group.

Leader Orientation

The qualities of a group counselor who is likely to be helpful were outlined in the preceding section. At this point emphasis will be placed on relating the effects of the leader's interaction to what happens in a counseling group. Once more we need to turn to the group dynamics research for direction. Goldstein, Heller, and Sechrest (1966), following a review of research in both group psychotherapy and group dynamics, concluded that the research

> pointedly provides basic evidence of the prediction of more favorable patient response to a leader-centered versus a group-centered therapist orientation in the early stages of group psychotherapy. . . . However, in spite of its less favorable early effects, there is a considerable body of group dynamics research suggesting that the group-centered approach is very likely to result in patient behavior much more highly related to a favorable therapeutic outcome than would be the case if an essentially leader-centered approach persisted beyond the first 10 to 20 therapy sessions. (p. 377)

The findings reported by Goldstein, Heller, and Sechrest are based to a considerable extent on patient expectancies of group leadership. In this regard they found:

> In sum, these diverse studies focusing on leadership expectancies in psychotherapy and other settings appear to converge in the general conclusion that the more discrepant the expectancies, the less the attraction to the group, the less the satisfaction of group members, and the more the strain or negative affect between leader and led or therapist and patient. (p. 375)

Stockton and Morran (1982) cited the research by Lewis and Mider (1973) on short-term therapy groups in which they found that "work" and "member-centered" behavior, as measured by the Hill Interaction Matrix, significantly increased where "experiential" leaders focused on feelings in the here-and-now. Leaders who assumed a "cognitive" approach and encouraged a discussion of topics and goals did not increase similar positive member behavior.

In a study on leader style applied to therapy groups, Gruen (1977) concluded:

> (a) when the leader correctly anticipates group themes in a session, there is visible movement in the session, and patients supply more insight for each other; (b) when the leader exerts a moderate amount of control over group processes in a session, the movement of the group through resolution of problems is accelerated; and (c) when the leader's interpretations are far-reaching or make deep connections in a given session, movement is accelerated, interpretations from patients increase, and the group expresses a great spirit of cohesion. (Stockton & Morran, 1982, p. 71)

Coleadership

From Stockton and Morran's (1982) review of coleadership research, the following conclusions seem warranted:

1. Coleaders' caring and self-expressiveness is positively related to group cohesiveness in adolescent groups.
2. Both coleaders need to exhibit effective styles for cohesion to develop in adolescent groups (one coleader cannot compensate for a lack in the other).
3. Self-disclosing coleaders are generally viewed as more constructive in quality of interpersonal feedback and improved member functioning on a number of important process and outcome variables.
4. Consistency of the coleaders over time in style and type of intervention produced significantly higher levels of documented work and better improvement on social shyness, inhibition, and psychosomatic problem measures than coleaders with inconsistent styles and interventions.
5. Similarity of the coleaders—the degree that the coleaders led in the same or different directions of each other—produced results in favor of dissimilar coleaders insofar as they produced significantly higher levels of undocumented work and reported significantly better improvements on outcome scores of interpersonal functioning. (The researchers suggested that coleader differences were accepted by group members and possibly provided a wider, and thus more beneficial, variety of interactions and interventions.)

These research results suggest a number of important considerations when group counselors pair up to colead groups. First, the leaders must have the caring and self-expressive qualities documented earlier for group leaders, whether or not they colead. Second, *both* leaders must be effective or competent. One cannot make up for serious weaknesses in the other. Third, coleaders must be able to be sufficiently self-disclosing to model this behavior for group members. The timing, depth of self-disclosure, and composition of the group, of course, determine how it is received and used. In a very healthy adult group, members can accept deep self-disclosures; however, in groups where members are quite unstable or too young to interpret the self-disclosures, they are likely to interpret it to mean that the leader is unstable. Fourth, coleaders need to be consistent in their styles and types of interventions. Inconsistency leads to member confusion, frequently the result of competition for the leadership position by the coleaders. Fifth, leadership differences in such areas as sex and the group themes that they choose to follow may prove to be beneficial insofar as members are exposed to a wider and more beneficial variety of interactions and interventions.

When groups are coled, teachers gain considerably by meeting regularly to discuss and analyze their group leaderships. Supportive feedback, mutual trust and respect, and a liking for each other appear to be at least minimal requirements for coleaders to benefit mutually.

Conclusions. If one can conclude that patients seeking group psychotherapy or, similarly, counselees seeking group counseling will approach the experience expecting direction and assistance from the leader, a rule of thumb to follow would be for the group counselor to be more active in the early group sessions and to move gradually from a leader-centered approach to a group-centered approach as counseling proceeds. This practice should reduce initial counselee hostility, increase receptiveness, and provide the best overall plan for building a therapeutic climate.

This rule-of-thumb procedure is congruent with the model described by Carkhuff (1969a), the model that seems to have the greatest support or application to group counseling. Carkhuff, in describing guidelines for the communications of empathy (a prerequisite for developing a facilitative base), stated that especially at the beginning of helping, the helper would find that increasing verbal responsiveness would not only provide a model for an increasingly active helpee, but would also serve to increase the probability of accuracy in communication.

In the beginning of a counseling group, the counselor tries to build a base of mutual trust by responding empathetically, warmly, and with respect. As the counselees develop this base, they will provide cues that indicate they want to go deeper into their problems. The group counselor assists the counselees in exploring in greater depth; this in turn leads to greater understanding, commitment to change, and eventual positive action. This personal exploration is made possible by the counselor's application of the more action-oriented core conditions of genuineness, appropriate self-disclosure, concreteness, confrontation, and immediacy (Carkhuff, 1969a). Figure 3–1 shows the phases of the helping relationship. Appendix D contains the Global Scale that describes the levels of core conditions in Figure 3–1.

GROUP STRUCTURE ⎯⎯⎯⎯⎯⎯⎯⎯⎯⎯ ▬

Bednar and Battersby (1976) define *structure* as "a multidimensional concept potentially useful for deliberately influencing encounter, therapy, and growth group processes by focusing and controlling group attention and behavior" (p. 515). Roark and Roark (1979) contend that group structure is not a unidimensional construct ranging from complete ambiguity to complete structure because even in unstructured groups, *implicit* structure exists. Implicit structure, they point out, includes such issues as selection of members, goals modeled by the leader(s), physical setting, and the evolving norms of the group. They conclude, therefore, that it is impossible not to structure a group.

Leaders take part in the development of group structure, particularly in the early stages of a group. Structuring on the part of the leader is a

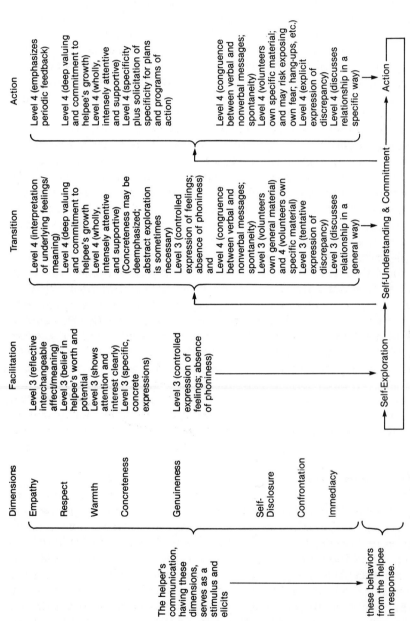

Figure 3–1 Phases of the helping relationship

Adapted from Gazda, G. M., Walters, R. P., and Childers, W. C. (1975). *Human relations development: A manual for health sciences.* Boston: Allyn and Bacon, Inc. Reproduced by permission.

directive technique used to define goals, to orient the group to expectations, and to communicate basic rules and procedures (Gazda, 1976; Muro & Dinkmeyer, 1977; Wilborn & Muro, 1979). Others used the term *structure* to refer to activities designed to facilitate skill development (Drum & Knott, 1977; Johnson & Johnson, 1975). Some group leaders consciously refrain from structuring a group and, by so doing, end up actually providing a very specific type of structure. Thus, what at first appears to be an unstructured situation is actually a deliberate move to structure expectations and procedures (Dagley, Gazda, & Pistole, 1986, p. 140).

Bednar, Melnick, and Kaul (1974) presented a model for initiating group work. In this model, client risk, personal responsibility, and group structure are the basic parameters that affect early group development. This model proposes that client exposure to the levels of personal risk and responsibility most conducive to optimal group and/or individual development can be regulated by the group structure. The model includes the basic assumption that structure tends to reduce group participants' personal responsibility for their behavior in early group sessions, thereby increasing the potential for high risk-taking behavior and the development of group cohesion in later sessions. Stockton and Morran (1982, p. 42) interpreted this general model for novice groups to include the following sequence (1) initial ambiguity, (2) increased structure through specific instructions, (3) increased risk taking, (4) increased cohesion, and (5) increased personal responsibility. The impact of structuring and client risk taking on early group (therapy/encounter) development is summarized in this way:

1. Specific *behavioral* instructions were associated with higher levels of group cohesion, more favorable attitudes toward group experiences, higher frequency of work-oriented interpersonal communications, and lower frequencies of conventional and socially appropriate communications than were instructions focusing on *goal clarity* and *persuasion* (Bednar & Battersby, 1976).
2. The highest frequency of therapeutically relevant behaviors occurred in the high-structure and high risk-taking disposition treatment conditions. Structure (message specificity) was particularly influential in increasing the target behaviors of low risk-taking persons (Lee & Bednar, 1978). This result is consistent with the theoretical model of Bednar, Melnick, and Kaul (1974) suggesting "that structure reduces personal responsibility, thereby increasing the freedom to engage in higher risk interpersonal behavior. . . . The high-structure condition dramatically increased the level of relevant, and presumably risky, communications of the low risk-taking subjects. In fact, the observed behavior of the low risk-taking subjects in the high-structure conditions was virtually identical to that of the high risk-taking subjects" (Lee & Bednar, 1978, p. 198).

3.   Unexpectedly, low risk takers receiving high structure tended to give poorer evaluations of the workshop and rated their group as less cohesive (Lee & Bednar, 1978). Lee and Bednar (1978) suggest that the high-structure and high risk-taking disposition treatment conditions produced the highest frequency of personal and inter-personal communications that were simultaneously the most meaningful, but subjectively distressing.

4.   High risk takers exposed to behavioral structuring reported the highest levels of group cohesion, positive attitudes, and frequency of target behaviors. The optimal structure for low risk takers was the cognitive-behavioral condition (Evensen & Bednar, 1978).

Based on their review of research on group structure, Stockton and Morran (1982) conclude:

> Findings show that the establishment of structure in the early meetings of the group tends to facilitate the development of cohesion and risk-taking by members in performing selected behaviors, such as self-disclosure and feed-back exchange. In addition, direct instruction also appears to facilitate this group development, particularly in its formative stages. The most salient find-ings from the research on structure suggest that the effects of structure on behavioral performance, perceived cohesion, and attitudes toward the group tend to vary as a function of members' personal characteristics, includ-ing their risk-taking. (p. 45)

Structuring research results also support the use of the following proce-dures:

1.   Be positive in building expectancy states. Group members should be told that they most likely will like and will be liked by other members of the group (Schachter et al., 1960) and the group was set up to consist of individuals who share similar opinions and values (Festinger, Schachter, & Back, 1950).

2.   Stress the hard work that will be involved in the group counseling process. This should increase the effort expended by counselees (Cohen, 1959; Yaryan & Festinger, 1961; Zimbardo, 1960).

3.   Stress the careful screening that went into selection of the group members. (This procedure should increase the attractiveness of the group to the counselees—see research reviewed by Goldstein, Heller, & Sechrest, 1966, pp. 344–348.)

4.   Define the norm of the group as different from the usual social norm, that is, that it is appropriate and beneficial to discuss one's personal concerns in the counseling group. Reinforcement of this new norm should make the transition to self-disclosure and revela-tion of one's problems more acceptable to group members (Bonney & Foley, 1963).

Pretraining

Bednar and Lawlis (1969) reported the following three objectives of pre-group training: (1) the clarification of expectations, (2) the presentation of guidelines of group therapy and group development, and (3) the provision of models of effective behavior. Stockton and Morran (1982) reviewed the group research on the application of the three objectives reported by Bednar and Lawlis. They reported that all of the studies that they reviewed met two of the three objectives. They also found that techniques could be divided into four categories: written instructions, interviews, recordings, and practice.

The use of written instructions or handouts was reported to have served as a means of assurance, provided a stimulus for group interaction and learning, eased members' entry into the group, and accelerated the treatment process. Cohesiveness was not increased through the use of written instructions.

When interviews were used, they ranged from twenty-five-minute lectures to role induction interviews. The lecture method was reported to have brought about more immediate and deeper levels of intermember communication. The role induction interview method led to behavior in which group members communicated more frequently and engaged in self-exploration efforts more frequently in a greater percentage of their communication than controls.

The use of audiotapes in vicarious therapy pretraining resulted in hastening therapeutic self-exploration, improving self-concept, changing in the direction of a theoretical ideal, and increasing social awareness. The modeling of interpersonal openness viewed on film with detailed descriptive instructions led to more self-disclosure and group interaction than for subjects who received only one of these treatments. Group members who received either pretraining instruction by film or role induction or both were higher in satisfaction with interpersonal group relations, progress in therapy, and perceived improvement than were controls.

Experiential pregroup training intended to teach general anxiety reduction skills and use of defenses led to significant increases on the extraversion scale of the Eysenck Personality Inventory (interpreted as leading to fewer inhibition and more approach behaviors).

Stockton and Morran (1982) concluded that their overview of research suggested "that successful pretraining includes both a cognitive and a behavioral component. Studies have consistently shown that groups receiving both instructions and modeling do better than those receiving only one treatment or neither" (p. 53).

My own experience with the pretraining type of structure suggests that the group will make greater progress if they are first taught basic helping skills of attending, perceiving, and responding (interpersonal communication skills). When group counseling members are taught how to attend, listen, and respond, they give fewer low-level or hurtful responses and more high-level responses to each other, and as a result there are fewer occasions when there are hurt feelings among the group and a need to delay group progress just to repair or "mend the fences" (damaged egos). For more efficiency in group counseling, pretraining in basic helping skills seems to be warranted.

Games

Other forms of group structuring include the use of structured activities or games. There are certain advantages and disadvantages in the use of games to facilitate group counseling. First let me suggest that games (gaming) can only be useful when the group leader has had considerable experience with the game and can predict its effects at a certain juncture in the group's development. The game can serve as a catalytic agent to increase cohesiveness, self-disclosure, and trust. My observations of the use of games, however, suggest that they are used in lieu of the counselor's interpersonal or helping skills; when they are used in this way, one game after another is introduced to activate the group. Frequently under these conditions the games become recreational at best because there is no coherent theoretical rationale or encompassing plan for their use.

Group counselors may also find games to be a problem when they lose control of the pacing mechanism of the group as a result of the use of a game. The game has the quality of a foreign substance placed into a chemical compound, the reaction of which is unknown to the group leader and often may be explosive, uncontrollable, and harmful to the participants.

Some games also lead to questionable ethical practices. For example, writing one's secrets on a piece of paper, placing them in a hat or receptacle, having them drawn out, read, and then guessing whose secret it is exposes many people before they are ready for this kind of exposure. Thus, they are frequently precipitated into premature self-disclosure.

The frequent employment of games also has the potential of reducing the counselor's sensitivity and responsibility to the group. Counselors take the risk of depending too much on the game activities and too little on their own skills.

In addition to the potential of games leading to counselor apathy and reduction of effort, there is the distinct possibility that the group members will also assume less responsibility for their own behavior because of the opportunity to hide behind the rules of the game. The game becomes the safe scapegoat.

More research on the effective use of games and similar structure is needed, but until it is forthcoming games should be used cautiously. See Duncan's (1976) discussion of this issue for a more complete treatment.

GOAL SETTING

Several studies, except for Bednar and Battersby (1976), have shown that clarity of group goals and means of achieving them increases the group's attraction for members, improves communication, generates greater group cohesiveness, and reduces intragroup hostility. Thoresen and Potter (1975) have pointed out that the group counselor "must conceptualize and relate to the group on two levels: as a collection of discrete persons and as an entity itself. The leader's task goals are aimed at the person within the group; interaction goals are focused on the group as a whole" (p. 455). My own choice, and the more commonly understood description of group goals, are *task* and *process*, but interaction is also quite appropriate. Task and process are also used to describe the purpose of the group, to differentiate, for example, a work group or committee (task group) from a T-group (process group).

The counselor focuses on the group as a whole primarily to maximize the group effect on the separate individuals within it. The power of the group in terms of its norms, cohesion, and trust is harnessed in the service of helping each individual accomplish his or her unique goal(s). Also in the service of accomplishing individual goals is the use of the group goal or metagoal, as developed by Thoresen and Potter (1975). The metagoal is really the description that best characterizes the reason the collection of individuals was organized. It might be as general or as specific (depending how perceived) as reducing anxiety, reducing feelings of loneliness, or increasing interpersonal skills.

Counselees' purposes for seeking help or goal setting should be verbalized in initial interviews before they enter a group; however, they are encouraged to repeat these in the first session of the group. Therefore, to increase the possibility of goal achievement through group counseling, the counselor should encourage the counselees to verbalize their goals as specifically and concretely as they can in the beginning and to increase their specificity as clarity occurs through the counseling experience by operationalizing them through the use of behavioral objectives.

Berne (1966) has referred to goal setting as the therapist-patient contract. He considers that a contract exists between therapists and the institutions that employ them and between the therapist and patient. Therefore the patient should know the therapist's institutional obligations that may impinge on the patient's goals. For example, if the counselor has an obligation to report the use of drugs by counselees, the counselee should know this to avoid being placed in jeopardy. Berne also cautions that the contract between therapist and patient may need to be amended from time to time as determinants underlying symptoms or responses are made more explicit. The same opportunity for goal modification should be applied to group counselees.

On occasion, subgroups develop within a counseling group and fre-quently begin to compete with each other to the point of creating severe friction within the total group. This situation usually calls for reconstituting the group or instituting a superordinate goal, such as the counselor's intro-ducing a legitimate threat to the total group that is sufficient to bring together the warring factions in a total group effort to counteract the out-side threat. The threat might be impending loss of a meeting place, the revocation of institutional time for group counseling, or some other admin-istrative threat to the group's existence.

Establishing and Maintaining Cohesiveness

Truax (1961) studied the effects of cohesiveness in therapy groups and observed that "cohesion, long a central concept in the analysis of small group behavior, is also of importance in the analysis of group psychother-apy: successful psychotherapy groups are cohesive. . . . These findings . . . point to a variable unique to the group setting and one which is susceptible to external manipulation" (p. 16). Lakin (1976) describes group cohesive-ness as "the collective expression of personal belongingness" (p. 59). He contends that cohesiveness is demonstrated by (1) binding members emo-tionally to the common task as well as to one another, (2) assuring greater stability of the group even in the face of frustrating circumstances, and (3) developing a shared frame of reference among group members that allows for more tolerance for diverse aims of group members. Obviously, then, a cohesive group is a stable and productive group that can be quite task or goal oriented.

Behaving in Conformity with Group Norms

The concept of norm setting in the context of group counseling refers to what is expected and/or allowable in the group. The norm may be either explicit or implicit, but in either case the group members know what they are permitted to do (with its subsequent rewards) and what they are forbid-den to do (with its subsequent punishments).

Included in the setting of group norms, of course, is the group coun-selor. Counselors are active in helping the group develop the norms and are themselves being influenced by the group with respect to the role or roles they will be expected to follow within the group. Counselors' actions are especially significant in determining group norms in the first few ses-sions. Their own modeling, such as responding empathically and showing warmth and respect to all members and supporting shy members, can go a long way toward setting the climate for the group. That is, when the group is most in need of leadership early in its Exploratory Stage, the counselor has perhaps the greatest opportunity to influence its direction. Bonney (1969) contends that the leader should assume an active though not highly directive part in the formation of the group's norms. Ideally the setting of norms should emanate from the group itself.... The eventual acceptance of a group norm should ... be left to the consensus of the group and not forced by the leader, particularly in the early stages of the group's development. (p. 167)

Provided the group members have had the opportunity to be involved in the development of the group norms, each should feel a commitment to them. The commitment will be stronger if the members accept the group as their own. The desire for social approval is also inherent in conforming to group norms. Therefore group leaders will have the benefit of social pressure supporting them if they are skillful in creating the appropriate therapeutic climate. Lakin and Carson (1966) point out that "the pressures to adhere to group norms and to facilitate the task and maintenance functions of the group generally operate to 'socialize' the individual within the particular group's culture" (p. 30).

Consensual Validation of Personal Perceptions and the Use of Feedback

According to Lakin and Carson (1966), many people experience difficulty in living because they suffer from nonvalidated views of themselves and their environment. Since views about the self and others are generally organized as attitudes, they are typically highly resistant to change. When, however, the group process includes feedback at a level and rate that is not so threatening to the group members that they have to reject it, the opportunity for validating one's perceptions about the self and others and changing one's attitudes is present.

Jacobs (1975) reported the results of eleven independent studies on feedback in small groups. About half the studies dealt with the sequencing of positive and negative feedback, and the other half were devoted to type and valence of feedback. The results of these studies hold great promise of direction for group leaders and members. The effects seem especially relevant to consensual validation of personal perceptions and thus are briefly summarized here.

Jacobs found that positive feedback is almost inevitably rated as more believable, desirable, and potent by recipients and donors. He also stated that believability of information seems likely to be a necessary, although perhaps not always sufficient, condition for attitudinal and behavioral change. Negative feedback (especially massed following self-disclosures by participants) operated to deflate groups. *No evidence was found that negative feedback was advantageous to the group or recipient.* Therefore, Jacobs was led to investigate methods for detoxifying negative feedback. Preliminary results of his research suggest three methods for detoxifying feedback: (1) present information referring to desirable improvement in a positive behavioral statement and in association with positive affect, (2) increase the credibility of the feedback by emphasizing in its delivery its origin in the deliverer and/or its repugnance to him or her, and (3) use positive to negative sequences (precede negative feedback with positive) that are generally more effective overall than the reverse order.

Stockton and Morran (1982) used personal growth groups to test the effects of feedback on group members. Generally, their findings concurred with those of Jacobs's findings; however, they found that positive feedback exchanges among members were better accepted in early sessions (the first two), whereas there was no difference in the acceptance of positive or negative acceptance after four and six weeks (supporting the idea that counselees will accept negative feedback after a base of trust has been built). Stockton and Morran also found negative feedback to be more desirable by high self-concept group members than by low self-concept group members. This finding would be expected, but the difficulty for the counselor is knowing "how high is high" when considering negative feedback.

Differentiation of Roles

The counseling group, depending on the heterogeneity of membership and purpose, allows many roles to be taken. Lifton (1972) has classified group roles as task, growth/vitalizing, and antigroup. His task roles include initiator, information seeker, opinion seeker, elaborator, opinion giver, energizer, information giver, coordinator, orienter, evaluator, energizer, procedural technician, and recorder. Growth/vitalizing roles include encourager, gatekeeper/expediter, harmonizer, compromiser, standard setter, group observer/commentator, and follower. Antigroup roles include aggressor, blocker, recognition seeker, self-confessor, playboy, dominator, help seeker, and special-interest pleader.

In order to cope effectively with problem members, or those assuming antigroup roles, the group counselor should first take a self-inventory. The group counselor should ask himself or herself the following kinds of questions:

1. How do I feel?
2. Why do I feel this way?
3. Is the group member:
   a. challenging me?
   b. distracting the group?
   c. seeking attention?
   d. resisting involvement?
4. What payoff is the group member receiving?
   a. Reward?

      b.   Punishment?
      c.   Attention?
      d.   Safety?
5.   Do other members of the group appear to feel the same as I do toward the "problem" member?
      a.   What verbal behavior confirms their feelings?
      b.   What nonverbal behavior confirms their feelings?
6.   Does the "problem" group member require an intervention? If so, from whom?
      a.   Me?
      b.   Another member?
      c.   Self?
      d.   Co-counselor?

Following the self-analysis, the group counselor may wish to classify the "problem" member according to one or more of the antigroup/ "problem" member types and use one or more of the following suggested coping strategies.

Problem Member	*Counselor Coping Strategies*
Aggressor	Avoid negative confrontation.
	Encourage the member to be specific about personal feelings.
	Place the member in a role-play situation that involves personal self-disclosure and look for clues to the aggressiveness.
	Ask for a private conference, share your feelings, and ask for cooperation; point out harmful effects on others; or as a last resort, ask member to leave the group.
Recognition seeker/ attention-getter	Avoid negative confrontation.
	Respond to member's feelings of insecurity, if present.
	Avoid eye contact.
	Do not respond to off-task comments/behavior.
	Ask for private conference and evaluate member's reasons for the behavior.
Monopolist	Avoid negative confrontation.
	Respond to feelings of insecurity, if present.

Problem Member	*Counselor Coping Strategies*
	Avoid eye contact during irrelevant conversation.
	Respond only to relevant statements.
	Assign a role of facilitator/helper in a role-play situation.
	Ask for private conference and refer to individual counseling if member cannot change group role.
Hostile/acting out	Avoid negative confrontation.
	Respond to possible negative transference phenomena.
	Keenly observe nonverbal behavior and respond appropriately.
	Remind member of ground rules and set limits firmly, but not angrily.
	Ask for private conference and try to resolve member's feelings toward the leader or significant others; refer member if problems cannot be resolved.
Advice giver	Avoid negative confrontation.
	Respond to feelings of insecurity.
	Observe the reaction to the advice on the member who receives it.
	Encourage self-disclosure on the part of the advice giver.
	Place in a role-play situation that limits advice giver's responses to helpee's feelings only.
	Avoid reinforcing advice giver's inappropriate advice.
Silent/withdrawn	Avoid negative confrontation; use positive confrontation.
	In general, respect silence.
	Respond to nonverbal behavior and try to "read" meaning of silence.
	Make direct requests to member to respond to statements and or behavior of other group members and offer his or her own opinions and feelings.

Notice that for each "problem" member type, the group counselor is admonished not to employ negative confrontation. To do so would not be consistent with the goals of the facilitative model. Unless the counselor has a strong facilitative base with the counselee, negative confrontation will produce further defensiveness, withdrawal, or other problems. Since the group member is viewed as a "problem," obviously the counselor does not have a strong base rapport, and it would be premature to use negative confrontation (confrontation of one's deficits). However, positive confrontation (confrontation of one's strengths) may be in order.

A basic ground rule would have it that each and every counselee be shown respect; therefore, if a counselee may need to be removed from the group, a private discussion of the issues is in order. This discussion may prove to motivate the counselee to greater communication and less disruptive behavior if he or she wishes to remain in the group.

In any event, the group counselor must avoid defensive and confrontive behavior, and instead must model facilitative behavior. There is nothing to be gained by using one's role as leader to put down a group member.

Because of the large variety of roles available in a counseling group, the participants can experiment with roles they wish to try out. However, there is a tendency for groups to stereotype participants into certain roles. Often these roles are not desirable, and the leader should be alert to help individuals break out of their stereotypic roles.

Therapeutic Factors[1]   Beginning with Corsini and Rosenberg's (1955) classification and enhanced by Yalom's (1975) taxonomy, professionals have been involved in delineating therapeutic factors that contribute to positive outcomes in group therapy. Yalom's (1975) comprehensive list includes eleven categories of curative factors: instillation of hope, universality, imparting of information, altruism, the corrective recapitulation of the primary family group, development of socializing techniques, imitative behavior, interpersonal learning, group cohesiveness, catharsis, and existential factors (pp. 3–4; see Yalom, 1975, 1985 for more detail). The reader should be aware of these therapeutic factors as an explanation of how therapeutic change occurs. Supposedly, through the therapist's facilitation of the complex interdependent action of these factors, clients improve their functioning. Yalom (1985), in discussing therapeutic factors states:

> Their interplay and differential importance can vary widely from group to group. Furthermore, patients in the same group may be benefited by widely differing clusters of therapeutic factors. (p. 4)

---

[1] From J. Dagley, G. M. Gazda, & M. C. Pistole, Groups. In M. D. Lewis, R. Hayes, & J. A. Lewis (Eds.), *The counseling profession* (pp. 130–166). Itasca, IL: Copyright © 1986 by F. E. Peacock, Publisher. Reproduced by permission.

The purpose of clinical and research interest in these factors is to develop a set of systematic guidelines that will enable the therapist to be more expert in facilitating productive change. After reviewing the theoretical, empirical, and clinical research on therapeutic factors (from 1955 to 1979), Bloch, Crouch, and Reibstein (1981) agreed with Yalom's (1975) statement: "There is little truly definitive research demonstrating the efficacy of any of the curative factors and even less research bearing on the question of the comparative value or the interrelation of these factors" (pp. 70–71). In 1985 Yalom made the following statement about curative factors:

> I do not present these factors as definitive; rather, I offer them as provisional guidelines which may be tested and perhaps expanded by other clinical researchers. For my part, I am satisfied that they derive from the best available evidence and constitute the basis of an effective approach to therapy (p. 6).

Although it would be useful to have strong research evidence supporting and specifying the operation of these factors in group therapy, they currently have, at least, heuristic usefulness. Not only do they provide a way to talk about mechanisms of change, but also they can be used singly or in clusters to specify the treatment modality used in group therapy research. For instance, the group leader may focus on universality as the treatment technique (see, for example, Oppenheimer, 1984). Specifying a therapeutic factor as the focus of treatment enables researchers to communicate meaningfully about a somewhat standardized treatment technique. The differences between groups can then be more surely considered a result of the variable under study than the result of a variable that is extraneous to the research project, such as treatment.

A number of group therapists and group counselors (Bach, 1954; Bonney, 1969; Gendlin & Beebe, 1968; Mahler, 1969) have identified stages or phases through which counseling and therapy groups purportedly pass, ranging from three phases (Gendlin & Beebe, 1968) to seven (Bach, 1954). The stages through which counseling groups progress are most clearly visible in closed groups, that is, groups that retain the same membership throughout the duration of the group's existence. In open groups, or groups that add new members as old members terminate and especially when the influx of new members is frequent, the stage development is affected and, as Gendlin and Beebe (1968) have noted, the old members reach a Tired Phase because of the constant necessity of the old members assisting the new members through the Breaking Through Phase—the phase during which the member experiences an explosive freeing and growth process. With open groups, then, it is incumbent on the counselor to know the potential effect of too rapid a turnover in an ongoing group. It is necessary to protect the Sustaining Phase (Gendlin & Beebe, 1968), or Work Phase of the core members of a group and to prevent them from reaching the Tired Phase.

Hill (1961, 1963, 1965) has developed an Interaction Matrix based on a hypothesis that therapy groups proceed along two dimensions of *content* and *work* and through approximately sixteen to twenty cells or levels of interaction. The Hill model has many of the same elements included in the model developed by Carkhuff (1969a). The Carkhuff model emphasizes the need to build a facilitative base through high-level expressions of empathy, respect, and warmth in the early phases of developing sound relationships. Building a facilitative base is prerequisite to the implementation of the action-oriented dimensions at later stages in helping relationships. The action-oriented dimensions are geared to changing behavior. The facilitative action-oriented dimensions include genuineness, specificity or concreteness of expression, and appropriate self-disclosure by the leader, whereas the action-oriented dimensions include the leader behavior just cited plus *appropriate* confrontation and immediacy or "telling it like it is" between leader and helpees in the here-and-now.

The amount, the kind, and the timing of counselor intervention in groups is therefore related to the stage or phase of a group's development. It cannot be independent of the stage, however, since the group is influenced by counselor behavior and vice-versa. It has been my experience that counseling groups go through four rather definite stages: (1) Exploratory Stage, (2) Transition Stage, (3) Action Stage, and (4) Termination Stage. These four stages are named similarly by others. For example, Bonney (1969) refers to the Exploratory Stage as the Establishment Stage, and Mahler (1969) calls it the Involvement Stage. Both Bonney and Mahler have a second or Transition Stage. The Action Stage can be equated with Mahler's Working Stage. The fourth or Termination Stage is equivalent to Mahler's Ending Stage. (See Table 3–1.)

Exploratory Stage

During this stage the group members introduce themselves and each member describes the goals he or she hopes to achieve. They also agree on some basic ground rules. Following the initial session, the counselees usually engage in social and superficial discussions about themselves, each parrying with the other to present himself or herself in an acceptable fashion. This is the kind of activity in which members assign to each other what Hollander (1964) has called "idiosyncratic credits." Bonney (1969) has referred to this as the "process by which the group, consciously and unconsciously, assigns power and influence, in varying degrees to each member of the group" (p. 166). It is also a means of establishing various roles that each person will first assume in the group. Hidden agendas also begin to emerge and the group begins to establish norms that will eventually become the unofficial controlling ground rules.

It is especially important that group counselors be actively helpful during the Exploratory Stage. They show their helpfulness by clarifying

Table 3–1 Stages in the group counseling relationship

Counselor Offered Conditions For Therapeutic Change (Part A)ᵃ	Phase I (Downward or Inward Phase of Self-Exploration)		Phase II (Upward or Outward Phase of Emergent Directionality and Action)
	Initial Stage of Individual Dimensions	Intermediary Stages of Individual Dimensions	Final Stage of Individual Dimensions
Empathy	Level 3 (interchangeability)	Levels 4 and 5 (additive responses)	Levels 4 and 5 (emphasizing periodic feedback only)
Respect	Level 3 (unconditionality)	Level 4 (positive regard)	Levels 4 and 5 (regard and conditionality)
Concreteness	Levels 3 and above (specificity of exploration)	De-emphasized (abstract exploration)	Levels 4 and 5 (specificity of direction)
Genuineness	Level 3 (absence of ingenuineness)	Levels 4 and 5 (self-disclosure and spontaneity)	Levels 4 and 5 (spontaneity)
Confrontation		Level 3 (general and open)	Levels 4 and 5 (directionful)
Immediacy		Level 3 (general and open)	Levels 4 and 5 (directionful)
GROUP (COUNSELEE) STAGES IN THERAPEUTIC CHANGE (PART B)	Stage 1 Exploratory	Stage 2 Transition Stage 3 Action	Stage 4 Termination

ᵃSource: From *Helping and human relations: A primer for lay and professional helpers,* vol. 2 by Robert R. Carkhuff. Copyright © 1969 by Holt, Rinehart and Winston, reproduced by permission of Holt, Rinehart and Winston.

both the goals for the group and the group means for achieving them, by telling the group something about themselves and, most important, by modeling the facilitative dimensions of empathy, respect, warmth, and genuineness. In the Carkhuff (1969a) sense, the counselors consistently give responses to each counselee that are *interchangeable* with those of the counselee—interchangeable especially with respect to the affect expressed by the counselee and also to the content or message expressed. It is during this initial or Exploratory Stage that a facilitative base of mutual trust and caring is built. Without this, the group fails to reach the next stage in its development.

Transition Stage

The Transition Stage occurs at a point when one or more counselees begin to self-disclose at a level significantly deeper than the "historical" type of disclosures heretofore given in the group. At this point the group members experience a feeling of threat since the typical social group does not usually function in this manner. The members may attempt to block the self-disclosures with overly supportive responses or by attempts to change the subject—more precisely to revert to the superficial conversation of a historical nature found in the Exploratory Stage.

To move the group as a whole through the Transition Stage to the Action Stage, or work stage, requires high levels of discrimination or sensitivity and accuracy in *timing* of counselor responses. Counselors must be able to encourage volunteers to self-disclose at a level that gives them a feeling of involvement, and simultaneously they must be able to hold the anxiety level of the more threatened group members to a level that will not force their defense systems to overact. Following the Carkhuff model for moving from counselee exploration to understanding to action, counselors must be able to give responses that are at least minimally action oriented (they must begin to add the facilitative action-oriented dimensions of genuineness, concreteness, and appropriate self-disclosure to those of empathy, warmth, and respect). The counselors themselves should be willing to self-disclose, when appropriate, at a depth equal to that of the most advanced counselee. In that way they model for the counselees who are beginning to involve themselves in the action-oriented dimensions of problem resolution, that is, goal-related work.

Action Stage

The Action Stage is synonymous with the work or productive stage of a counseling group. Also, it involves the implementation of the action-oriented dimensions, *à la* Carkhuff's model, of confrontation and immediacy plus the facilitative action dimensions of genuineness, concreteness, and appropriate self-disclosures.

The group counselor must orient the counselees toward a belief that their condition will not change until they take definite steps (action) to modify it. Insofar as the counselees' goals can be achieved by modifying their behavior in the group itself, they should be encouraged to do so and rewarded when they do. In this regard talking about how they are planning to change is no longer defensible; they must demonstrate it in the here-and-now of the group experience. Counselors use appropriate confrontations and share with the counselee their here-and-now feelings about the counselee's ingroup behavior. They also encourage other group members to do similarly.

In the final analysis, counselee action is goal related and dependent on behavioral modifications to be employed outside of the group setting. It is encouraged in the form of *homework* to be done and then reported back to the group at the next session. Attempts that fail to achieve the desired goal can be appraised and modified, even role played in the group, until counselee satisfaction is achieved.

If group counselors involve all group members in the Action Stage of group counseling, they will seldom need to confront group members themselves. Rather the group members will confront each other, and the group counselors will become gatekeepers of group safety. They will be the most expert timing devices in the group—the ones who can best predict when a given counselee is ready to be confronted with decision making and/or action. In this view they not only confront, but also solicit confrontation by the counselees through their openness.

Termination Stage

The Termination Stage begins with a tapering off of counselee self-disclosures, especially in new areas of concern. In a closed group with a preset termination date, the tapering off usually begins naturally two or three sessions before this date and frequently includes halfhearted attempts by the counselees to continue the sessions beyond the present deadline. Not unusual during the last three or four sessions is the initiation of a "going around" procedure wherein each member solicits frank feedback from every other member. Also common during the Termination Stage is a general and spontaneous need of counselees to tell how much the group members and the group experience have meant to them. They are reluctant to see the group experience terminate, and sometimes they make plans for a group reunion at some specific date in the future.

The group counselor's responsibility at termination is to reinforce the growth made by group members and to make sure that all group counselees have had the opportunity to work out their differences with the counselor and other group members before leave-taking. If any member of the group, for whatever reason, continues to require counseling, the counselor must assume this responsibility or assist the member in a mutually satisfactory referral.

SUMMARY

This chapter contains a summary of the group dynamics theory and research that pertain to group counseling. It begins with leadership research and outlines those leadership characteristics that have proved to be effective in small group work. Also, leadership characteristics that are not effective are cited. Coleadership research findings are also reported.

Group structure is discussed in detail. According to Stockton and Morran (1982), the most salient findings from the research on structure suggest that the effects of structure on behavioral performance, perceived cohesion, and attitudes toward the group tend to vary as a function of members' personal characteristics, including their risk taking.

Research on *pretraining* procedures shows that groups receiving both instruction and modeling do better than those receiving only one treatment and those receiving neither treatment. The value of goal setting for group members is also outlined.

The *core processes* of a group are summarized. These are: leadership, structure, goals, cohesiveness, norms, feedback, and roles. Suggested counselor coping actions are included for antigroup roles or "problem" members under the role-differentiation topic.

Finally, the chapter concludes with a description of the author's four stages of group development: exploratory, transition, action, and termination.

REFERENCES

Bach, G. R. (1954). *Intensive group psychotherapy*. New York: Ronald Press.

Bednar, R. L., & Battersby, C. P. (1976). The effects of specific cognitive structure on early group development. *Journal of Applied Behavioral Sciences, 12*, 513–522.

Bednar, R. L., & Lawlis, G. F. (1969). Empirical research in group psychotherapy. In A. E. Bergin & S. L. Garfield (Eds.), *Handbook of psychotherapy and behavior change: An empirical analysis*. New York: Wiley.

Bednar, R. L., Melnick, J., & Kaul, T. (1974). Risk responsibility and structure: a conceptual framework for initiating group counseling and psychotherapy. *Journal of Counseling Psychology, 21*, 31–37.

Berensen, B. G., & Mitchell, K. M. (1974). *Confrontation: For better or worse*. Amherst, MA: Human Resource Development Press.

Bergin, A. E. (1975). Psychotherapy can be dangerous. *Psychology Today, 9*, 96, 98, 100, 104.

Berne, E. (1966). *Principles of group treatment.* New York: Oxford University Press.

Bloch, S., Crouch, E., & Reibstein, J. (1981). Therapeutic factors in group psychotherapy. *Archives of General Psychiatry, 38,* 519–526.

Bonney, W. C. (1969). Group counseling and developmental processes. In G. M. Gazda (Ed.), *Theories and methods of group counseling in the schools.* Springfield, IL: Charles C. Thomas.

Bonney, W. C., & Foley, W. J. (1963). The transition stage in group counseling in terms of congruity theory. *Journal of Counseling Psychology, 10,* 136–138.

Carkhuff, R. R. (1969a). *Helping and human relations.* Vol. 1. *Selection and training.* New York: Holt, Rinehart and Winston.

Carkhuff, R. R. (1969b). *Helping and human relations.* Vol. 2. *Practice and research.* New York: Holt, Rinehart and Winston.

Cartwright, D., & Zander, A. (1968). *Group dynamics: Research and theory* (3rd ed.). New York: Harper & Row.

Cohen, A. R. (1959). Communication discrepancy and attitude change: A dissonance theory approach. *Journal of Personality, 27,* 386–396.

Corsini, R., & Rosenberg, B. (1955). Mechanisms of group psychotherapy: Processes and dynamics. *Journal of Abnormal Social Psychology, 51,* 406–411.

Dagley, J., Gazda, G. M., & Pistole, M. C. (1986). In M. O. Lewis, R. Hayes, & J. A. Lewis (Eds.). *The counseling profession* (pp. 130–166). Itasca, IL: F. E. Peacock.

Drum, D. J., & Knott, J. E. (1977). *Structured groups for facilitating development: Acquiring life skills, resolving life themes, and making life transitions.* New York: Human Sciences.

Duncan, J. A. (1976). Games people play in groups. *Together: ASGW, 1,* 54–62.

Evensen, E. P., & Bednar, R. L. (1978). Effects of specific cognitive and behavioral structure on early group behavior and atmosphere. *Journal of Counseling Psychology, 25,* 66–75.

Festinger, L., Schachter, S., & Back, K. (1950). *Social pressures in informal groups.* New York: Harper.

Gazda, G. M. (Ed.). (1976). *Theories and methods of group counseling in the schools* (2nd ed.). Springfield, IL: Charles C. Thomas.

Gendlin, E. T., & Beebe, J. (1968). Experiential groups: Instructions for groups. In G. M. Gazda (Ed.), *Innovations of group psychotherapy.* Springfield, IL: Charles C. Thomas.

Goldstein, P., Heller, K., & Sechrest, L. B. (1966). *Psychotherapy and the psychology of behavior change.* New York: Wiley.

Gruen, W. (1977). Effects of executive and cognitive control of therapist or work climate in group therapy. *International Journal of Group Psychotherapy, 27,* 139–152.

Hill, W. F. (1961). *Hill interaction matrix: Scoring manual.* Pocatello, ID: Author.

Hill, W. F. (1963). *Hill interaction matrix (HIM) scoring manual.* Salt Lake City, UT: Dye, Smith, & Co.

Hill, W. F. (1965). *Hill interaction matrix (HIM)* (rev. ed.), Los Angeles: University of Southern California Youth Studies Center.

Hollander, E. P. (1964). *Leaders, groups and influence.* New York: Oxford University Press.

Hurley, J. P., & Pinches, S. K. (1978). Interpersonal behavior and effectiveness of T-group leaders. *Small Group Behavior, 9,* 529–539.

Jacobs, A. L. (1975, April). Research on methods of social intervention: The study of the exchange of personal information in brief personal growth groups. Paper presented at the University of Indiana's Invitational Conference on Experimental Small Group Research: Perspectives on Current Issues and Future Directions, Bloomington.

Johnson, D. W., & Johnson, F. P. (1975). *Joining together: Group theory and group skills*. Englewood Cliffs, NJ: Prentice-Hall.

Jourard, S. (1964). *The transparent self*. Princeton: D. Van Nostrand Company.

Knowles, M., & Knowles, H. (1959). *Introduction to group dynamics*. New York: Association Press.

Lakin, M. (1976). The human relations training laboratory: A special case of the experiential group. In M. Rosenbaum & A. Snadowsky (Eds.), *The intensive group experience* (p. 50–86) New York: The Free Press.

Lakin, M., & Carson, R. C. (1966). A therapeutic vehicle in search of a theory of therapy. *Journal of Applied Behavioral Science, 2,* 27–40.

Lee, F., & Bednar, R. L. (1978). Effects of group structure and risk-taking, disposition on group behavior, attitudes, and atmosphere. *Journal of Counseling Psychology, 24,* 191–199.

Lewis, J., & Mider, P. A. (1973). Effects of leadership style on content and work styles of short-term therapy groups. *Journal of Counseling Psychology, 20,* 137–141.

Lieberman, M. A., Yalom, I. D., & Miles, M. B. (1973). Encounter: The leader makes the difference. *Psychology Today, 6,* 69ff.

Lifton, W. (1972). *Groups: Facilitating individual growth and societal change*. New York: Wiley.

Mahler, C. A. (1969). *Group counseling in the schools*. Boston: Houghton Mifflin.

Muro, J. J., & Dinkmeyer, D. (1977). *Counseling children in the elementary and middle schools*. Dubuque, IA: Wm. C. Brown.

Oppenheimer, B. (1984). Short-term small group intervention for college freshmen. *Journal of Counseling Psychology, 31,* 45–53.

Roark, A. E., & Roark, A. B. (1979). Group structure: Components and effects. *Journal for Specialists in Group Work, 4,* 186-191.

Russell, E. W. (1978). The facts about encounter groups: First facts. *Journal of Clinical Psychology, 34,* 130–137.

Schachter, S., Ellertson, N., McBride, D., & Gregory, D. (1960). An experimental study of cohesiveness and productivity. In D. Cartwright and A. Zander (Eds.), *Group dynamics*. Evanston, IL: Row, Peterson.

Shane, H. G. (1977). *Curriculum change toward the 21st century*. Washington, D. C.: National Education Association.

Stockton, R., & Morran, D. K. (1982). Review and perspective of critical dimensions in therapeutic small group research. In G. M. Gazda (Ed.), *Basic approaches to group psychotherapy and group counseling* (3rd ed.). Springfield, IL: Charles C. Thomas.

Thoresen, C. E., & Potter, B. (1975). Behavioral group counseling. In G. M. Gazda (Ed.), *Basic approaches to group psychotherapy and group counseling* (2nd ed.). Springfield, IL: Charles C. Thomas.

Truax, C. B. (1961). The process of group psychotherapy. *Psychological Monograph, 75* (Whole No. 511).

Truax, C. B., & Carkhuff, R. R. (1967). *Toward effective counseling and psychotherapy: Training and practice.* Chicago: Aldine.

Wilborn, B. L., & Muro, J. J. (1979). The impact of structuring technique on group functions. *The Journal for Specialists in Group Work, 4,* 193–200.

Yalom, I. D. (1975). *The theory and practice of group psychotherapy* (2nd ed.). New York: Basic Books.

Yalom, I. D. (1985). *The theory and practice of group psychotherapy* (3rd ed.) New York: Basic Books.

Yaryan, R., & Festinger, L. (1961). Preparatory action and belief in the probable occurrence of future events. *Journal of Abnormal and Social Psychology, 63,* 603–606.

Zimbardo, P. G. (1960). Involvement and communication discrepancy as determinants of opinion. *Journal of Abnormal and Social Psychology, 60,* 86–94.

SUGGESTED READINGS

Bednar, R. L., & Kaul, T. J. (1978). Experiential group research: Current perspectives. In S. L. Garfield & A. E. Bergin (Eds.), *Handbook of psychotherapy and behavior change: An empirical analysis.* (2nd ed.). New York: Wiley.

Carkhuff, R. R. (1969). *Helping and human relations.* Vol. 1. *Selection and training.* New York: Holt, Rinehart and Winston.

Carkhuff, R. R. (1969). *Helping and human relations.* Vol. 2. *Practice and research.* New York: Holt, Rinehart and Winston.

Cartwright, D., & Zander, A. (Eds.) (1968). *Group dynamics: Research and theory* (3rd ed.). New York: Harper and Row.

Goldstein, A. P., Heller, K., & Sechrest, L. B. (1966). *Psychotherapy and the psychology of behavior change.* New York: Wiley.

Kipper, D. A. (1986). *Psychotherapy through clinical role playing.* New York: Brunner/ Mazel.

Kottler, J. A. (1983). *Pragmatic group leadership.* Monterey, CA: Brooks/Cole.

Marcovitz, R. J., & Smith, J. E. (1983). Patients' perceptions of curative factors in short-term group psychotherapy. *International Journal of Group Psychotherapy, 33*(1), 21–39.

McGrath, J. E., & Kraviz, D. A. (1982). Group research. In *Annual Review of Psychology, 33,* 195–230. Annual Reviews, Inc.

Ohlsen, M. M., Horne, A. M., & Lawe, C. F. (1988). *Group counseling* (3rd ed.). New York: Holt, Rinehart and Winston.

Shaw, M. E. (1981). *Group dynamics: The psychology of small group behavior* (3rd ed.). New York: McGraw-Hill.

Trotzer, J. P. (1979). Developmental tasks in group counseling: The basis for structure. *Journal for Specialists in Group Work, 4,* 177–185.

Zimpfer, D., & Waltman, D. (1982). Correlates of effectiveness in group counseling. *Small Group Behavior, 13*(3), 275–290.

CHAPTER 4

Group Counseling via the Playgroup for the Preschool and Early School Child

For the purposes of group treatment, preschool and early school includes the ages from approximately 5 through 9. "Little is known as to what the values of a group to a child of 3 or 4 may be," according to Slavson (1945, p. 203); therefore, until more information becomes available on how to treat the child of 3 or 4 in groups, one may risk extrapolating downward from age 5 and use basically the same rationale and group procedures for the period described in this chapter—at least for the more mature 3- and 4-year-olds.

The descriptors of knowledge and skills appropriate to the preschool and early school child (the four generic life-skill areas of Interpersonal Communication/Human Relations, Problem-Solving/Decision-Making, Physical Fitness/Health Maintenance, and Identity Development/Purpose in Life) may be found in Appendix A. The purpose of reproducing the life-skills descriptors is to give a guide for evaluating a child's total developmental progress so that the reader can introduce group counseling or Life-Skills Training, or both. Appendix C provides the reader with additional help in isolating developmental tasks appropriate for levels below age 5 through age 15. Acceptable behavioral characteristics are listed, as well as those showing minimal and extreme psychopathology for the child and parent(s).

GROUP COUNSELING

Play Techniques

The primary mode of group counseling for the age group 5 through 9 involves play and action. Slavson (1945, 1948) has advocated play group therapy for young children under 12 years of age, and I concur with him. However, I prefer to refer to it as *group play techniques* or *play group counseling* when it is applied to basically normal children who are not hospitalized. Although the basic rationale for emphasizing play and action techniques for this age group is the same whether it be play therapy or play techniques or play group counseling, the degree of disturbance of the child, the training of the therapist (counselor), and the setting are different. I discourage school personnel from working with seriously disturbed children and from doing "therapy" in the school setting unless they are sufficiently trained at the doctoral level in school counseling, school psychology, or clinical psychology. Nevertheless, when one considers the various processes of therapy that are currently practiced, save for psychopharmacological, electroshock, and surgical therapies, there is probably very little reason to insist that a therapist be required to receive training in medicine, or for that matter, at the doctoral level in other disciplines, although doctoral-level training should provide the therapist or counselor with greater sophistication of techniques and, it is hoped, with higher-level ethical practices. In other words, there is no reason why most group play therapy techniques cannot be modified for use by counselors in the school and community mental health settings, providing the group members are not seriously disturbed and the counselor is trained in group counseling and play techniques and has the appropriate playroom facilities and play media available.

Lebo (1955) has credited Rosseau as the first to recommend that children be educated through play, although Klein (1955) has taken credit for the development in 1919 of psychoanalytic play techniques. Readers should refer to the Suggested Readings at the end of this chapter for a representative sampling of the play therapy literature.

Harms (1948) has referred to play as the "language of childhood" (p. 237), and Frank (1955) has stated that "in play we . . . observe various themes or schemes in which this [child's] immediate concerns are focused and more or less symbolically played out" (p. 585). Frank also has referred to play as "learning to learn: . . . cope with life tasks" (p. 583). It is generally agreed that all psychotherapy constitutes some form of learning. Axline (1955) succinctly conveys my feeling on this issue in the following assertion regarding learning and psychotherapy: "It [psychotherapy] seems to be a cumulative, compound, integrative, effective experience that can be used to illustrate many learning theories. At the same time, it raises many questions as to the adequacy of any existing theory to explain conclusively the learning experience that occurs during psychotherapy" (p. 622).

She explains the value of play therapy as follows: "Play therapy is based upon the fact that play is the child's natural medium of self-expression. It is an opportunity which is given to the child to 'play out' his feelings and problems just as in certain types of adult therapy, an individual 'talks out' his difficulties" (Axline, 1969, p. 9).

In regard to therapeutic play, Conn (1951) has stated, "Every therapeutic play method is a form of learning process during which the child learns to accept and to utilize constructively that degree of personal responsibility and self-discipline necessary for effective self-expression and social living" (p. 753).

Lowrey (1955) has argued that "we should be more accurate if we spoke of 'activity' (or activities) instead of 'play' with reference to therapy. For it is the activity with its release of fantasy, imagery, fears, hostility, and other feeling and thoughts which give us quick insights into the problems besetting our child patients" (p. 574).

Until now, we have been speaking of play therapy without regard to its use in groups. What are the unique features or values that play in a group setting offers? Slavson (1945) has claimed that the function of the group in the treatment of young children lies in three areas: "(1) play and activity; (2) association with other children of the same age; [and] (3) the role of the worker" (p. 208). The play and activity, according to Ginott (1961), should facilitate contact with the child, catharsis, insight, reality testing, and sublimation.

Slavson (1945) also has stated that in all instances the value of a group to children

> lies in the fact it supplies a field in which the child may relate himself to others, thus helping him to break through isolation, withdrawal, and aggressive rejection of people . . . to go out . . . into the human environment, thus leading from egocentricity and narcissism to object relationships . . . to test himself against others and discover the boundaries of his ego . . . [and] offers the possibility of developing patterns of relationship with human beings of the same intellectual, emotional, and social development, in which the feeling of sameness and therefore of comfort and security is greatest. (p. 209)

The role of the group leader or "worker," according to Slavson (1945), varies with the age of the children; leaders are more active with the young child who is dependent on them for support, and of necessity, for young children, much of the authority must come from the therapist. The leader's role changes both with the ages of the children and their changing personalities. "While he functions at first as a source of security and support, his role changes to one of guidance and authority" (p. 209).

Some specific values attached to play therapy are suggested by Solomon (1955). It is his belief that through

> the use of play, the child is able to express his own regressive tendencies, thereby lessening the need to act out such forms of behavior in his real life situation . . . and the release of aggression or hostility with its appropriate emotion, that of anger, and the lessening of fears through the amelioration of the catastrophic results from the expression of the primitive impulses of gains which accrue from the judicious use of play therapy. (p. 594)

He has summarized the therapeutic values of play therapy as follows: "(1) release of hostility toward parents, siblings, etc.; (2) alleviation of guilt feelings; (3) opportunity to express freely all love fantasies; (4) incorporation of therapeutic suggestions in direction of growth; and (5) desensitization by means of repetition (Solomon, 1940, p. 763).

Amster (1943) succinctly conveyed part of my purpose for advocating the use of play and action techniques when she stated:

> Essentially play is an activity a child comprehends and in which he is comfortable, an integral part of his world, his method of communication, his medium of exchange, and his means of testing, partly incorporating and mastering external realities.
>
> ... Provision of play materials means the provision of a natural means of communication, through which the child's problems may be expressed more readily and the treatment more likely to succeed.
>
> In treatment of children, play is always a medium of exchange and it is comparable to words, the adult's medium of exchange. It is not a therapy in itself any more than words can be. All therapies require a therapeutic relationship and a medium of exchange. The purpose of the play activity determines its role and importance in treatment. Therefore, play as a medium differs from play as a technique even as words differ from any purposive use of them. Play is a technique when it is used in treatment for definite diagnostic and therapeutic purposes. (p. 62)

Amster (1943, pp. 62–67) has listed and defined six uses of play:

1. *Play can be used for diagnostic understanding of the child.* ... We can observe the child's capacity to relate himself to others, his distractibility, his rigidity, his areas of preoccupation, his areas of inhibition, the direction of his aggression, his perception of people, his wishes, and his perception of himself. In the play, his behavior, ideas, feelings, and expressions help our understanding of his problem and how he sees it. (p. 63)
2. *Play can be used to establish a working relationship.* This use of play is helpful with the young child who lacks the adult's facility for verbal self-expression and with the older child who shows resistance or inability to articulate. (p. 64)
3. *Play can be used to break through a child's way of playing in his daily life and his defenses against anxiety.* This use is helpful as an additional way of treating distortions in a child's way of playing. (p. 65)
4. *Play can be used to help a child verbalize certain conscious material and associated feelings.* This use is helpful when a child blocks in discussing certain material and an impasse in treatment is created. (p. 65)
5. *Play can be used to help a child act out unconscious material and to relieve the accompanying tension.* This cathartic use of play deals with symbolic material which has dangerous significance to the child. The therapist must be aware of how much release in play the particular child

can tolerate without panic and must be aware of the kind of participation and interpretation in which to engage. (p. 67)

6. *Play can be used to develop a child's play interests which he can carry over into his daily life and which will strengthen him for his future life.* This use of play has particular importance because of the correlation between the play and the work capacities of an individual. (p. 67)[1]

On the other side of the ledger, Bender (1955) wrote:

If the play technique used is important to the adult and gives him a tool with which he can understand the child and relate to him with confidence and warmth, the play setup will undoubtedly contribute to the relationship. Beyond this I doubt if there is any specific therapeutic value to the play procedures. (p. 785)

Nelson (1972) cautions that play activities may distract the child who is ready to deal directly with a problem and thus interfere with communication.

Theoretical Rationale of Play and Action Methods for Group Counseling with a Child from 5 to 9: Modeling

A small group represents a slice of society. Its composition determines how closely it will represent the society of a given member. Group counseling provides an opportunity for social learning or behavior change that is maximized by the presence (modeling) of other individuals. Whether the group setting is the preferred mode for assisting a given individual's behavior and feelings of self-worth depends on many factors discussed later in this chapter. The topic of import at this point is how to maximize opportunities for behavioral change for the young child from the ages of 5 to 9.

Play and action-oriented techniques such as sociodrama, child drama, and psychodrama are natural media or modes through which young children communicate and express themselves; therefore following the emphasis on developmental group procedures, the group counselor is encouraged to take advantage of these media. In addition to maximizing the relationship-engendering procedures through the use of play and action methods, group counselors must also use relevant learning principles if their counseling armamentarium is to be complete. In the following paragraphs a model will be developed that will assist practicing group counselors in their understanding and treatment of young children in groups.

1 From Amster, F. Differential uses of play in treatment of young children. (1943). *American Journal of Orthopsychiatry, 13*, 62–68. Copyright © 1943 the American Orthopsychiatric Association, Inc. Reproduced by permission.

Young children have not developed their verbal facility to a high level, and thus verbally loaded (interview-type) group treatment is of limited value. Young children in particular are dependent on the imitation (modeling) of others for much of their learning both because of their relatively low verbal facility and also because of their relatively undeveloped behavioral response repertoire. However, as children develop verbal and behavioral repertoires, combinations of modeling and operant conditioning models may be used in modifying their behavior.

Modeling, sometimes referred to as no-trial learning or observational learning (Bandura, 1965), can be a very efficient method for changing the behavior of the young child. A model can exhibit a preferred way of behaving, relating, or problem solving. This real-life model can be a peer or the adult group counselor or both. It is apparent that the peer and adult models must be capable of providing exemplary behavior; peers must be chosen with care to ensure mutual helpfulness. The group counselor, too, must be able to model appropriately. (This subject is dealt with in Chapter 3. Peer selection will be discussed under Selection in this chapter.)

Rose (1973) describes the modeling procedure as "a set of therapist activities designed to increase the observer's probability of matching behavior. Modeling procedures include introducing potential models, pointing out behavior to be imitated, modifying situational conditions to facilitate imitation, teaching observational and imitational skills, reinforcement, and roleplaying" (p. 107). Rose contends that modeling procedures lend themselves especially to group treatment because the group contains an abundance of potential models, new models can be introduced without seriously disrupting the existing social patterns, multiperson role playing can be used, and group pressures can be stimulated to encourage imitation.

In addition to modeling opportunities made available through group peers and the counselor, symbolic models can be presented in the playroom in the form of dolls and puppets and verbally through counselor-read stories, counselor-led puppet plays, and psychodrama. Structured play settings will give the counselor the greatest control over modeling since the counselor will be able to recreate the setting, characters, and other factors responsible for precipitating and maintaining the child's problem behavior. (Structured play and modeling may be the equivalent of simulation or gaming techniques applied to older groups.) Since the structured problem situation may be anxiety producing for the young child, it should be introduced only after the group counselor has developed a strong base of mutual trust and understanding in the free play situation used in the early stages of treatment. The free play situation can also provide the group counselor an opportunity to validate a diagnosis of the child's problem based on interview and case history data.

Research studies such as those of Chittenden (1942); Bandura, Ross, and Ross (1963); Beach (1967); and Hansen, Niland, and Zani (1969) demonstrated that symbolic or vicarious modeling can produce change similar to real-life models. In vicarious modeling the counselor or someone in a story, movie, or puppet play rewards certain characters for prosocial behaviors and punishes the characters in pantomime, verbally, or both ways for asocial and antisocial behavior. Through the use of vicarious modeling, the group counselor can structure the kind and amount of modeling opportunities that seem necessary to modify the child's behavior.

Psychodrama or role playing can also be used to involve all the members in the counseling or play group in minimally structured areas of problem behavior. In the psychodrama the group counselor is the director, one of the children is the protagonist or the person with an avowed problem, and the other children become the auxiliary egos. A vicarious psychodrama can be created from puppet characters with the counselor assuming all roles and structuring the problem and its resolution as he or she chooses.

Modeling as described here is first of all a method for producing *new* learning. Bandura (1965) explains this occurrence by postulating the existence of *component responses* in the person's behavioral repertoire of prior learnings that are reproduced in unique combinations by new stimuli. Second, he postulates that

> Exposure to models may also strengthen or weaken inhibitory responses in the observer. . . . Reinforcers administered to a model undoubtedly serve a discriminative function signifying the probable reinforcement contingencies associated with the modeled classes or responses. In addition, rewarding consequences may result in vicarious extinction of inhibitory responses. Conversely, observed aversive outcomes tend to establish conditioned emotional responses . . . that help to support avoidant and inhibitory repertoires. (p. 321)

A third effect of modeling, according to Bandura (1965), is that

> the behavior of models may elicit previously learned responses that match precisely or bear some resemblance to those exhibited by the model. This *response facilitation effect* can be distinguished from disinhibition when the behavior in question is not likely to have incurred punishment and, therefore, any increase in responsivity is not attributable to the reduction of inhibitory responses. (p. 321)

It is not my intention to portray modeling (real-life or vicarious) as the only method or learning principle applicable to the young child treated in a play group setting. Modeling and various conditioning procedures should be viewed as complementary methods for modifying or shaping behavior. Illustrations of the combined use of modeling and social reinforcement procedures to increase the assertiveness of relatively inhibited children are provided in early studies by Jack (1934) and Page (1936). Also, the acquisition of psychomotor skills governed largely by proprioceptive stimuli that are not observable or easily described verbally requires more than modeling. Varying amounts of overt practice in addition to modeling are usually necessary in the acquisition of psychomotor skills (Bandura, 1965).

Since "self-administered primary and conditioned rewards may frequently overweigh the influence of external stimuli in governing social behavior" (Bandura, 1965, pp. 331–332), children's self-concept or feelings of worth may very well be a significant determinant of the ease and/or degree to which they can learn from a good model. Thus the necessity of "relationship therapy" or, as Carkhuff (1969a,b) would describe it, building a strong facilitative base through the use of empathy, respect, and warmth, cannot be ignored in treatment. Otherwise, the more action-oriented principles such as modeling and conditioning will prove to be of limited applicability. Arnold Lazarus (1968), a well-respected behavioral therapist, has stated that "there is nothing in modern learning theory to justify withholding the combined advantages of interpretation and desensitization, or any other method or technique which seems to have beneficial effects" (p. 155).

Prerequisites for Effective Modeling

In order to assure that modeling is effective, certain conditions need to be satisfied. Rose (1982, Chapter 15) has succinctly summarized these prerequisite conditions. Some of the attributes that may effectively increase the probability of the model include demonstrated competence in areas highly regarded by the observer; possession of general renown as perceived by the observer; possession of some of the observer's population attributes (such as race, sex, age, and experience); possession of skill status that the observer could realistically expect to achieve; and possession of power as perceived by the observer.

Bandura (cited in Rose, 1973) has shown that dependency on the model by the counselee increases the probability of imitation. Therefore, Rose suggests that the therapist can foster counselee dependency early in the relationship through maintaining a high degree of structure, providing physical assistance, and providing direct advice. However, as the counseling or therapy progressed, one would reduce the dependency-inducing behaviors. Bandura also discovered that reinforcement of the model increased the likelihood that the counselee would match the model's behavior, especially when the reward was given in the presence of the counselee. He found, furthermore, that the frequency of the matching response is reduced when the model is directly or vicariously punished. "Far more powerful than any of the above characteristics, however, is the incentive control of observing behaviors (Bandura, 1969, p. 137). For this reason, whenever possible models should be reinforced in the presence of the observer and observers should be reinforced for successful duplication of the modeled behavior" (Rose, 1982a, p. 475).

One other prerequisite for achieving successful modeling appears to be worth citing. Bandura (1969) found that "modeled characteristics that are highly discernible can be more readily acquired than subtle attributes, which must be abstracted from homogeneous responses differing on numerous stimulus dimensions" (p. 136). In other words, Bandura's research suggests that complex behaviors will need to be simplified or divided into related parts to ensure ease and success of imitation.

Even though young children acquire much of what they learn through imitation, Rose (1973) calls attention to the difficulty that younger children (ages 4 to 8) have with imitation. In order to ensure greater success, he suggests the use of matching games in the first meeting (for example, the members imitating a social or task role such as father, mechanic, or baseball player or the leader telling a story with words and actions that the group repeats).

Rose (1982a) contends that the modeling effect is enhanced by three other procedures: behavior rehearsal, coaching, and group feedback.

Behavior Rehearsal

Behavior rehearsal is defined by Rose (1982a) as "the simulated reproduction or role play of modeled or conceptually described behavior by the client" (p. 475).

Sturm (1965) suggests that behavioral rehearsal in comparison to other techniques has "a far greater potential to (1) generate vivid lifelike behavior and cues, thereby maximizing the utility of response and stimulus generalization; (2) condition a total behavioral response—physiological, motoric, and ideational—rather than merely verbal and (3) dispense the powerful reinforcements of enacted models and other characters, who in real life or in fantasy have already dispensed reinforcements" (p. 57).

Behavior rehearsal approximates a real-life experience and appeals to the young child who enjoys role playing, thus facilitating new learning.

Coaching

According to Rose (1982a), Oden and Asher (1977) describe coaching "as a training method that relies heavily on the verbal transmission of cues, concepts, and rules in the performance of a target behavior in a simulated or real stress situation" (p. 475). Rose (1982a) points out that in groups the " 'coach' (the group therapist or a group member) sits behind the actor in a role play and whispers behaviors, rules, or principles that the actor needs to consider during the role play. Occasionally cue cards are used instead of coaches. When coaching is used, it is generally faded in subsequent role plays" (pp. 475–476).

Group Feedback

Rose (1982a) defines group feedback as "a set of verbal responses by group members to a given individual about his or her overt or covert behavior and effectiveness, or other characteristics of handling a given situation" (p. 476). Rose contends that feedback is likely to be facilitative if it provides adequate, but not excessive, amounts of information; if it helps to identify other responsibilities and alternatives; if effective components of performance are pointed out prior to discussing ineffective components; and if clients are trained in the giving and receiving of constructive feedback in practice exercises.

Group feedback usually follows behavioral rehearsal, and occasionally it follows modeling. Group feedback may be used in later sessions to provide counselors with peer impressions of their achievements both in and out of the group (Rose, 1982a).

APPLICATION OF A DEVELOPMENTAL APPROACH TO GROUP COUNSELING FOR CHILDREN 5 TO 9 YEARS OF AGE

The following descriptors (see Appendix A) in the problem-solving/decision-making generic life-skills area have been used in selecting three children for inclusion in play group counseling: "Is able to be goal-directed, understands cause-and-effect relationships, is able to work independently on a task, and tries new methods of problem solving." These children have been assessed by their teachers and counselors, and appear to have deficits and strengths in one or more of these tasks. Each child was selected to serve as a model in one or more of these tasks; in addition, each child also required help in developing age-appropriate skill levels in one or more of the tasks.

Mark is an eight-year-old boy who has difficulty working independently; however, he is goal-directed and is receptive to trying different methods of problem solving. Elaine is an eight-year-old girl who has difficulty understanding the cause-and-effect relationship of her behavior, but is able to work independently. Richard is an eight-year-old boy who is fearful of the future and reluctant to take risks by using creative problem-solving procedures; however, he is goal-directed.

The counselor uses a free-play setting for the first three or four sessions. She meets the group for forty-five minutes and holds the session in a playroom. During this time the children can play with a variety of toys and materials. The counselor shows an interest in each child and makes every effort to establish rapport or build the base of mutual trust and liking for one another. After the base has been established, the counselor begins to structure the last half of each play session. At first she does this through story reading and telling and through the use of puppets. She introduces vicarious models in this way and verbally rewards appropriate behavior. Moving from puppets to dolls, she structures situations and asks the children to use the dolls to work out solutions. She rewards appropriate solutions verbally and asks for replays of inappropriate solutions until they approach appropriate coping behavior for dealing with the tasks.

As the children show progress with vicarious modeling, she also sets up sociodramas and psychodramas revolving around school and family situations for the group to use in modifying their behavior. Finally, the counselor moves into the realm of the here-and-now relationships between herself and each child and those between the children. She models for the children by encouraging their appropriate independence from her and by rewarding appropriate dependence also.

The play and action-selected media are used to promote relationship development and problem resolution and are not, therefore, in themselves the primary focus of the treatment. The counselor is always conscious of the timing of her moves and of the purpose of her techniques. She moves from the least threatening situations in the beginning to the more threatening, but more relevant, procedures as the children show signs of growth. The preceding procedure or model provides ample opportunity for vicarious and real-life modeling and numerous opportunities for implementing other learning principles of desensitization, shaping, operant conditioning, discriminate and assertive training, and reciprocal inhibition. The deliberate use of these principles represents the science of play group counseling, whereas the when and how of implementing them represent the art of this form of treatment.

Although the position in both this illustration and in this text is that play group counseling held in a playroom is the method of choice for children of approximately 5 to 9 years of age, various skills training groups are also encouraged. Most of these groups are structured and time-limited, especially when held in the school setting, but also when held in out-of-school clinics. Success has been demonstrated using structured groups, for example, in elementary school children of divorce in grades 3 to 6 (Anderson, Kinney, & Gerler, 1984), children of divorce (Titkin & Cobb, 1983), for eight and nine-year-old boys with learning and behavior problems (Mishne, 1971), and for children with social skills deficits (Edleson, 1981; Rose, 1982b), to cite only a representative sample. Often, concurrent parent counseling or family counseling groups are held in conjunction with these skills training groups, especially in the case of divorce.

As indicated in Chapter 2, I fully support the use of skills training at all age levels. I especially recommend it in the early school years as a preventive mental health innovation. Larrabee and Terres (1984) contend that counseling in the year 2004 "will be dominated by group experiences that are unprecedented in variety and number" (p. 262). I believe that life-skills/ social skills training will lead that domination as a corollary to group counseling.

SELECTION AND GROUP COMPOSITION

As with other age groups, there is virtually no sound research on preferred ways of selecting and composing a counseling group for the child from 5 to 9. During this period of development, except for the more mature children in the 9-year-old bracket, children rely heavily on the adult or older siblings as their model(s). For this reason, the group counselor has more direct control over what happens in a counseling group with 5- to 9-year-olds than with other age groups. Nevertheless, careful selection and grouping for maximum positive mutual influence is still of prime importance.

The following suggestions are given as guidelines for selecting children for play group counseling:

1. The best predictor of what children will do in a play group is what they in fact do in a similar group such as a trial group similar to the treatment or play group. The best combinations or those who show the greatest mutually therapeutic interactions should be selected as soon as they can be identified for the permanent group.
2. When open-ended groups are conducted, the counselor must try to replace children who have completed treatment with those who can fill the role being vacated. This choice should be based on previous group behavior of the prospective group member, but actual behavior may require removing children from the group if their behavior is detrimental to themselves and the group.

    The concept of role balancing is suggested as a rule of thumb to follow. This means that one should avoid overloading a group with a particular behavior type, such as aggressive, hyperactive children, but rather include a hyperactive or aggressive child in a group including a calm, self-reliant child as well as a withdrawn child and perhaps one other child of a behavioral type that will provide a model for one of the other three. In support of this procedure, Ginott (1968) has stated,

    An effeminate boy needs to identify with more masculine playmates. The dependent child needs the example of more self-reliant groupmates.... Aggressive youngsters need groupmates who are strong but not belligerent. Fearful children need to be placed in a group of more mature youngsters. (p. 177)

3. Slavson (1943) and Ginott (1968) both consider the basic prerequisite for admission to a therapy group the presence or capacity for *social hunger* within the child. This concept would help the play group counselor in screening out only the most antisocial children. Usually these kinds of children are obvious potential "wreckers of groups" and would not be considered for group treatment unless it could be rigidly controlled in a mental hospital or child guidance clinic. Nevertheless, children who show little self-restraint, shallow feelings toward others, and little conscience should be considered lacking in social hunger and poor risks for play group counseling.

4. Age and sex constitute two additional categories that the group counselor must consider when composing a group for treatment by play and action techniques. Ginott (1968) has recommended that preschool children can be placed appropriately in mixed sex groups, whereas school-age children should be separated by sexes. This procedure may prove more appropriate for a clinic population served by Ginott; however, I have found little need to separate the sexes until they approach latency or roughly the age of 9 or 10. At this point the girls are beginning to mature more rapidly than the boys, and their flirtations interfere with treatment when they are placed with less physically mature boys.

   For the most part, children of the same age constitute the most therapeutic grouping. Exceptions are made deliberately to place more aggressive children in older age groups and some immature children in groups with children who are younger than themselves, but not immature. A general practice to follow would be to compose groups in which there is no more than a year's range in the chronological age.

5. Differences in ethnic backgrounds, race, and intelligence do not pose serious problems for young children. However, grouping those with *gross* differences in intelligence, such as inclusion of retarded youngsters with those of average to better than average intellectual ability, should be avoided.

6. Children who have been labeled "unsuitable for group therapy," according to Ginott (1961, p. 27), are children who as infants were deprived of close contacts with their mothers, children with murderous attitudes toward their siblings, sociopathic children, children who have shown accelerated sexual drives, children who have been exposed and/or involved in perverse sexual experiences, those who habitually steal, the extremely aggressive child, and the child who suffers from severe or acute trauma leading to the development of gross stress reactions such as inappropriate terror to a

family pet (following being bitten by a dog) or refusal to enter an automobile (following a recent auto mishap).

GROUP SIZE

The size of a group of young children composed for the purpose of play group counseling should be considered in the light of counselor control. Young children have not developed to any large degree such social graces as listening while others are talking, taking turns, or being considerate of others who may be suffering emotional stress. Since fewer built-in controls exist within each child at this age, the counselor must be prepared to exercise control so that the group does actually function as a facilitative group. In addition to lacking social controls, young children lack adequate controls for their own and others' safety. The counselor must therefore be alert to the safety needs of each child. The fearful child especially requires this kind of safety assurance.

To focus intently on what each child attempts to communicate requires eternal vigilance on the part of the counselor. Since young children depend on their play and nonverbal means for much of their communication, the counselor must control the number of such stimuli so as to be in touch with each child in the group and with the group as a whole. When the counselor moves to structured play and sociodrama and psychodramatic techniques, it is vital to maintain the kind of control over these media that will serve the purpose of counselee growth.

The larger the number in a play group, the fewer the opportunities for the development of close, intimate relationships among the children and between a child and the counselor. Therefore, the larger the number, the slower the development of group cohesiveness; and group cohesiveness appears to be critical in the development of a growth group (Goldstein, Heller, & Sechrest, 1966). Among young children, cohesiveness is especially difficult to achieve since each child is so self-centered. In fact it often appears that in play group counseling, the counseling is individual counseling within the group setting rather than *group* counseling per se.

Another factor that could increase or delimit counselor control is the nature of the counselees in the group. Although this problem should be controlled through role balancing, one or two rather aggressive and/or hyperactive youngsters in a group would necessitate more counselor vigilance and control than a group of less aggressive or hyperactive children. When all the preceding considerations are given to group size, a good practice to follow is not to exceed five, regardless of experience and competence, and to include no more than two or three children if one is just beginning to practice play group counseling. (If co-counseling is practiced, two additional children may be added to these groups.)

FREQUENCY, LENGTH, AND DURATION OF GROUP SESSIONS

Play group counseling (technique) is both prevention and remediation oriented. It is prevention oriented to the degree that a child is having some difficulty acquiring adequate coping behaviors to master successfully a given developmental task. It is remedial to the degree that a child has failed to develop appropriate coping behaviors for a given developmental task and therefore is beginning to experience difficulty in intra- and interpersonal relationships. The counselor, in setting up a play group, should determine the degree to which the group is composed of children who require preventive or remedial treatment. The former usually do not require as intensive treatment or as much counselor intervention as the latter.

When combined with a supportive life-skills training program, preventive play group counseling could be effective on a forty-minute to one-hour-a-week basis over a period from three to twelve months. Play group counseling that is primarily remedial requires greater intensity of treatment, and intensity of treatment, all other variables being equal, varies directly with length and frequency of group sessions. Therefore, two group sessions of forty to sixty minutes equally spaced throughout the week are recommended.

The duration of treatment is difficult to predict; however, periodic evaluations should be made with parents, teachers, and significant others to appraise the child's progress. Usually too much is expected by teachers, parents, and even counselors. Counselors often terminate treatment at the first sign of progress, thus creating a real possibility of a relapse on the part of the child. No minimum time can be set for remedial treatment in play groups, but the counselor should consider six months a reasonable treatment period. At least three months should be allowed for any play group.

For those children who may be able to set their own goals/contracts, the time required for meeting their goals/contracts would determine their length of stay in the group when open-ended groups are used. However, contracting with this age group, other than the upper level of 9-year-olds, is of rather limited value, especially since their presence in the group may not be entirely voluntary.

MEDIA

The purposes for the use of play- and action-facilitating media are

1. To facilitate relationship building or to establish the facilitative base between the children and the counselor.

2. To increase the potential for communication between the child and counselor and among the children themselves by capitalizing on the natural medium of child play.
3. To assist the child in recognizing and/or understanding the difference between appropriate and inappropriate coping behavior—thus providing an opportunity for reality testing.
4. To protect the child's degree of self-disclosure through encouraging a certain degree of vicarious expressiveness and experiencing.
5. To provide occasions for symbolic or vicarious modeling.
6. To facilitate the occurrence of responses that can be rewarded by the counselor, that is, to maximize the opportunity to use the principles of operant conditioning and shaping.
7. To maximize the controlled use of "release therapy" when appropriate.

Much has been written regarding the use of play- and action-producing media with the young child, but virtually no carefully controlled investigations have been done that have demonstrated the superiority of one toy

Table 4–1   Highest ranking toys

Popularity	Communication Value	Fantasy Stimulation	Dynamic Spread	Combined Total
64% doll family	1.41 Nok-Out Bench	55% doll family	11 doll family	Doll family
62% soldiers	1.14 doll family	54% paper and crayon	10 animals	Soldiers
60% gun	1.13 gun	48% clay	9 planes	Gun
55% Nok-Out Bench	1.0 soldiers	46% blocks	8 clay	Clay
51% trucks	0.88 paper and crayons	43% planes	8 trucks	Paper and crayons
50% goose	0.83 clay	39% soldiers	8 gun	Animals
46% telephone	0.79 large baby doll	35% animals	8 Nok-Out Bench	Planes
46% animals	0.65 animals	29% trucks	8 goose	Nok-Out Bench
46% planes		29% furniture		Trucks

Source: H. R. Beiser. (1955). Therapeutic play techniques: Play equipment for diagnosis and therapy. *American Journal of Orthopsychiatry, 25,* 761–770. Copyright © 1955 the American Orthopsychiatric Association, Inc. Reproduced by permission.

over another or one action technique over another. Nor can one expect to find this kind of exacting information, since different toys are likely to be preferred for different problem types. Beiser (1955) studied the free choice of a selected group of toys of 100 children, 79 boys and 21 girls, ranging from 2 to 12 years of age. The range of cases was quite broad, but the cases were of the type referred to the Chicago Institute for Juvenile Research. Each toy was tabulated according to the number of children who played with it (popularity), a ratio of popularity and total dynamic interpretations stemming from play with a toy (communication value), frequency with which the toy stimulated fantasy on the child's part (fantasy stimulation), the breadth or number of dynamic interpretations that a therapist could make from a child's play with an individual toy (dynamic spread), and a combined total ranking of the toys. The highest ranking toys are shown in Table 4–1 and the lowest ranking in Table 4–2. Beiser warned that her finding should be interpreted with caution until further study could relate the influence of degree of disturbance, age, sex, and intelligence to play patterns.

Certain toys and materials are provided for "release therapy." These usually include plastic inflatable figures for punching, pop guns for releasing hostility, finger paint for smearing and messing, and pounding tools and boards for releasing aggression. These media should be used with caution since aggressive children may be stimulated to greater aggression, hostility, and destructiveness if the use of the toy or medium *reinforces* these qualities within them rather than serves as cathartic release.

Pupil personnel workers of the Baltimore County (Maryland) School System (Board of Education, 1963) have categorized play media under these three areas: (1) *toys for release of aggression* (bop bags, guns, soldiers, rubber puppets, finger paints, clay, and play dough); (2) *real-life toys* (doll house, family dolls, animals, medical kits, play money, cars, trucks, chalkboard,

Table 4–2 Lowest ranking toys

Popularity	Communication Value	Fantasy Stimulation	Dynamic Spread	Combined Total
3% pencil	0.0 pencil	0 pencil	0 pencil	Pencil
8% scissors	0.2 crayons (only)	0 ball	1 paste	Paste
9% paste	0.26 furniture	9% Nok-Out Bench	3 scissors	Scissors
13% blocks	0.26 telephone	11% paste	4 blocks	Ball
13% ball			4 ball	

Source: H. R. Beiser. (1955). Therapeutic play techniques: Play equipment for diagnosis and therapy. *American Journal of Orthopsychiatry, 25,* 761–770. Copyright © 1955 the American Orthopsychiatric Association, Inc. Reproduced by permission.

and telephones); and (3) *toys for enhancement of self-concept* (play logs, erector set, puzzles, and maps). Ginott (1961, 1968) has advocated the use of specific toys for the development of the objectives of a therapeutic relationship (catharsis, insight, reality testing, and sublimation). To convey the permissiveness of counselors in their attempt to establish a good *therapeutic relationship*, counselors make heretofore forbidden toys available to the child such as noise-making toys, including drums, pegboards, xylophones, air rifles, and cap guns. Other forbidden toys such as a typewriter, flashlight, and took kit, according to Ginott, serve the purpose of establishing a good relationship. A doll family also serves this end.

Materials included in the playroom for release or *catharsis* must be carefully chosen to fit the child's basic problem. Care should be taken not to include materials that lead to diffuse hyperactivity. Ginott cautions that catharsis in children almost always leads to mobility and acting out and that acting out in and of itself has no curative effects aside from pleasure and release. For hyperactive children, Ginott recommends materials that will focus their energies, such as pegboards, building blocks, rifles for shooting, nails for driving, wood for sawing, construction boxes, and the like. For fearful and fragile children, Ginott recommends materials that can be handled without the aid of tools, such as water, paint, sand, play dough, dolls, chalk, and crayons. These materials also have the added advantage of permitting children to conceal certain of their feelings and to erase or remake or refine certain of their productions.

Toys alone do not provide the child *insight*; therefore Ginott suggests that the counselor structure play situations that will enable children to gain insight into the dynamics of their behavior. This can be done, for example, by providing only one gun, which will likely bring out a conflict. The counselor also might structure a task that requires cooperation of all the children if it is to be accomplished. This might include, for example, preparing puppets for a puppet show. Ginott (1968) cautions the counselor to avoid treating the child suffering from a character disorder with insight methods.

For *reality testing*, toys should be chosen so that the playroom is furnished with those of graded difficulty. Complex puzzles and toys should be excluded from the playroom, especially for the child whose self-image and ego strength is low.

> In order for play therapy to be an experience in social learning, children should be provided with situations and materials that demand exploration of others as well as themselves. Most children at times in their therapy, should be exposed to peers, resistive materials, and planned scarcity of tools, so that they can test themselves in relation to social actualities. (Ginott, 1961, p. 60)

Finally, Ginott recommends sand, water, paint, and clay as essential media for *sublimation* of children's urethral and anal drives. A variety of outlets to promote sublimation are suggested by Ginott. He cites the need for sublimating anger through the punching of dolls or plastic bounce-back toys, as well as the possibility of destroying clay figures or composing critical poems and writing murder mysteries.

In addition to the usual toys included in a typical playroom, consideration should be given to the use of other action-oriented media including sociodrama, child drama, and psychodrama; storytelling and books for the child's use and for the group when read by the counselor; the construction and use of puppets for symbolic or vicarious sociodrama and psychodrama; short films and filmstrips, music, and tape recordings. These media offer the counselor the opportunity to introduce models vicariously through puppet shows, stories, audio tapes and videotapes, and films or filmstrips, which the children can use to imitate. These vicarious models are especially useful when the group is lacking in appropriate peer models. The sociodrama and psychodrama are action techniques that the counselor can structure for the playroom in which the models or participants (protagonist and auxiliary egos) are the group members themselves. (See Appendix E for a list of recommended play therapy materials.)

For the mature 8-year-old and the 9-year-old child, media and techniques appropriate for the preadolescent may be more appropriate than those suggested for the young child. The reader should refer to this section in Chapter 5 for a discussion of appropriate media.

Application of Play Media—An Example

Clinical experience also provides us with certain crude indexes that can guide us in our selection of toys and action media for certain purposes and for certain kinds of children. Based on the rationale developed earlier in this chapter, the first few sessions of play group counseling should be rather unstructured to provide the child opportunities for free play and to enable the counselor to build a facilitative base and to diagnose further the child's problem areas. To build the best facilitative base, the counselor tries to respond on a level that is interchangeable with that expressed verbally and/or symbolically by the child. The counselor communicates understanding of the child by expressing in words and actions a message that is interchangeable with that expressed by a given child. For example, if a young girl begins to punish verbally and/or symbolically a baby brother in a doll play, the counselor expresses verbally that the baby brother can sometimes require so much of Mommy and Daddy's attention that there is little left for sister. Symbolically, the counselor can show understanding by taking the baby brother out of sight of the mother and father doll and putting a little girl doll in their presence.

To follow up this example, the counselor can, through role playing with the dolls and eventually with the child, show how to use appropriate ways of gaining mother's and father's attention without having to resort to the inappropriate and ultimately self-defeating behavior of punishing baby brother. Reinforcement of appropriate coping behaviors in this case can be provided through models who are rewarded by the counselor or story characters if the story is read rather than told. Direct reinforcement can be given when the child's doll play or relationships with other children in the group warrant it.

THE PLAYROOM

The playroom should be located in an area of the school or clinic where the noise will not distract other adults or children. It should be designed so there is complete privacy from onlookers (except for authorized adult observers who are behind a one-way mirror), and it should be soundproof (Meeks, 1967). The playroom should be neither too small nor too large since cramped quarters force children into continuous close contact, which creates occasions for irritation as well as lack of privacy, whereas a room that is too large engenders running and roughhousing. With these considerations in mind, Ginott (1961) recommends a room of 300 to 400 square feet.

The room should be furnished with certain permanent or at least semi-permanent facilities. The room itself and all of its furnishings should be constructed with the physical safety of the children and the counselor in mind. The room should be well lighted and ventilated. Any glass in the windows and light fixtures should be protected by wire mesh. The walls should be easily cleaned and repaintable and the floor also should be easily cleaned, but not treated with wax or other types of polish that would make it slippery. Indoor–outdoor carpeting may be suitable in some cases where safety factors are preeminent.

Each playroom should be equipped with at least one study table and a long wooden bench for use as a table or work area. A chalkboard should be fastened to a wall, and a sturdy easel should be fastened so that it will not fall or collapse. Chairs should be of wood or plastic and noncollapsible. A small area should be set aside for a floor sandbox, including seating space on the edges. A sink with running water should be included in one area of the room. The faucets should be easily controlled by a young child. A large doll house is included as a part of the permanent facilities in a playroom, although it could be portable and stored in a cabinet. Bathroom facilities should be in an easily accessible adjoining room. A large, sturdy cabinet should be set against one wall or in a corner for the storage of supplies and toys, or an adjoining closet should be available for storage. Finally, electrical outlets should be placed above the reach of the children, but accessible to the counselor for the use of items such as tape recorders, slide projectors, and record players.

Beiser (1955) has developed a "portable playroom" that consists simply of a box that includes special toys arranged for a given child. The child can then pick up his or her box and use the toys and materials in a playroom equipped with the permanent fixtures. This portable playroom permits greater individualization of counseling, but incurs the added problem of promoting jealousies among the children.

SUMMARY

This chapter is written to stand on its own. However, for full comprehension, it should be read in conjunction with Chapter 2. In this chapter, I have tried to provide readers with all the information required to develop a rationale for play group counseling with the young child from 5 through 9 years of age. The theoretical approach outlined here is based on the hypothesis that both prevention and remediation of problems in young children can best be served if considerations are given to the developmental stages and coping behaviors appropriate to the given age group.

A further hypothesis has been promulgated in this text: life-skills training is the most economical and efficient means within the area of the *helping relationships* to serve the cause of problem *prevention*. Play group counseling is viewed as a preventive–remedial approach in the helping relationships. It is not promoted as a form of treatment that is preferred over individual counseling. It is presented as a procedure with unique offerings appropriate for some and inappropriate for others, and it is sometimes more efficaciously used in conjunction with individual counseling.

The knowledge and skills appropriate to the following seven developmental areas: psychosocial, physical–sexual, cognitive, vocational, moral, ego, and affective have been subsumed under the four generic life-skills areas described in Chapter 2. The skills appropriate to the child of ages 5 to 9 are listed by age level in Appendix A. Readers are encouraged to use these skills as guides for assessing the appropriateness of a child for inclusion in play group counseling.

A theory and a method of play group counseling consistent with the developmental needs of young children are described in some detail. Play and action techniques are considered the media most consistent with the natural interests and inclinations of young children. The values and limitations of toys and play materials are documented from theoretical and research literature and from personal clinical experiences.

The interventions that appear to be most applicable to changing behavior in the young child are defined and illustrated. Modeling, behavior rehearsal, coaching, and group feedback are presented as interventions most applicable to young children. Sociodrama and psychodrama or role playing and action-oriented procedures are also described.

Selection and group composition, group size, media, and the playroom are separate topics dealt with in this chapter. Each section is developed to be consistent with the theoretical rationale outlined for group counseling in this text and especially for the age group treated in this chapter.

An example of the application of play media to the treatment of young children through group counseling is given to illustrate the development model, including how learning principles can be systematically employed in modifying behavior.

Suggested readings and programs are given at the end of the chapter to assist readers in locating materials for implementation of the play group counseling program. Also, additional theoretical and research references are cited for readers who wish to expand and/or research further the position expounded in this chapter.

REFERENCES ▬

Amster, F. (1943). Differential uses of play in treatment of young children. *American Journal of Orthopsychiatry, 13,* 62–68.

Anderson, R. F., Kinney, J., & Gerler, E. R., Jr. (1984). The effects of divorce on children's classroom behavior and attitudes toward divorce. *Elementary School Guidance and Counseling 19,* 70–76.

Axline, V. M. (1955). Play therapy procedures and results. *American Journal of Orthopsychiatry, 25,* 618–626.

Axline, V. M. (1969). *Play therapy* (Rev. ed.). New York: Ballantine Books.

Bandura, A. (1965). Behavioral modifications through modeling procedures. In L. Krasner & L. P. Ullman (Eds.), *Research in behavior modification.* New York: Holt, Rinehart and Winston.

Bandura, A. (1969). *Principles of behavior modification.* New York: Holt, Rinehart and Winston.

Bandura, A., Ross, D., & Ross, S. (1963). Imitation of film-mediated aggressive models. *Journal of Abnormal and Social Psychology, 66,* 3–11.

Beach, A. I. (1967). The effect of group model-reinforcement counseling on achievement behavior of seventh and eighth grade students. Ph.D. dissertation, Stanford University.

Beiser, H. R. (1955). Therapeutic play techniques: Play equipment for diagnosis and therapy. *American Journal of Orthopsychiatry, 25,* 761–770.

Bender, L. (1955). Therapeutic play techniques: Discussion. *American Journal of Orthopsychiatry, 25,* 784–787.

Board of Education of Baltimore County, Maryland, Guidance Department. (1963). Elementary school counseling. Mimeographed.

Carkhuff, R. R. (1969a). *Helping and human relations.* Vol. 1. *Selection and training.* New York: Holt, Rinehart and Winston.

Carkhuff, R. R. (1969b). *Helping and human relations.* Vol. 2. *Practice and research.* New York: Holt, Rinehart and Winston.

Chittenden, G. E. (1942). An experimental study in measuring and modifying assertive behavior in young children. *Monograph of Social Research and Child Development, 7*(1, Whole No. 31).

Conn, J. H. (1951). Play interview therapy of castration fears. *American Journal of Orthopsychiatry, 25,* 747–754.

Edleson, J. E. (1981). Teaching children to resolve conflict: A group approach. *Social Work, 26,* 488–493.

Frank, L. K. (1955). Play in personality development. *American Journal of Orthopsychiatry, 25,* 576–590.

Ginott, H. G. (1961). *Group psychotherapy with children: The theory and practice of play therapy.* New York: McGraw-Hill.

Ginott, H. G. (1968). Group therapy with children. In G. M. Gazda (Ed.), *Basic approaches to group psychotherapy and group counseling.* Springfield IL: Charles C. Thomas.

Goldstein, A. P., Heller, K., & Sechrest, L. B. (1966). *Psychotherapy and the psychology of behavior change.* New York: Wiley.

Hansen, J. C., Niland, T. M., & Zani, L. P. (1969). Model reinforcement in group counseling with elementary school children. *Personnel and Guidance Journal, 47,* 741–744.

Harms, E. (1948). Play diagnosis: Preliminary considerations for a sound approach. *Nervous Child, 7,* 233–246.

Jack, L. M. (1934). An experimental study of ascendant behavior in preschool children. *University of Iowa studies in child welfare, 9,* 3–5.

Klein, M. (1955). The psychoanalytic play technique. *American Journal of Orthopsychiatry, 25,* 223–237.

Larrabee, M. J., & Terres, C. K. (1984). Group work. *School Counselor, 31,* 257–264.

Lazarus, A. (1968). Behavior therapy in groups. In G. M. Gazda (Ed.), *Basic approaches to group psychotherapy and group counseling.* Springfield, IL: Charles C. Thomas.

Lebo, D. (1955). The development of play as a form of therapy. *American Journal of Psychiatry, 12,* 418–442.

Lowery, L. G. (1955). Therapeutic play techniques: Introduction. *American Journal of Orthopsychiatry, 25,* 574–575.

Meeks, A. (1967). Dimensions of elementary school guidance. *Elementary School Guidance and Counseling, 1,* 163–187.

Mishne, J. (1971). Group therapy in an elementary school. *Social Casework, 52,* 18–25.

Nelson, R. (1972). *Guidance and counseling in the elementary school.* New York: Holt, Rinehart and Winston.

Oden, S., & Asher, S. (1977). Coaching children in social skills for friendship making. *Child Development, 48,* 495–506.

Page, M. L. (1936). The modification of ascendent behavior in preschool children. *University of Iowa studies in child welfare, 9,* 3–65.

Rose, S. D. (1973). *Treating children in groups: A behavioral approach.* San Francisco: Jossey-Bass.

Rose, S. D. (1982a). Group counseling with children: A behavioral and cognitive approach. In G. M. Gazda (Ed.) *Basic approaches to group psychotherapy and group counseling.* (3rd ed.). Springfield, IL: Charles C. Thomas.

Rose, S. D. (1982b). Promoting social competence in children: A classroom approach to social and cognitive skill training. *Child and Youth Services, 5,* 43–59.

Slavson, S. R. (1943). *An introduction to group therapy.* New York: Commonwealth Fund and International Universities Press.

Slavson, S. R. (1945). Differential methods of group therapy in relation to age levels. *Nervous Child, 4,* 196–210.

Slavson, S. R. (1948). Group therapy in child care and child guidance. *Jewish Social Service Quarterly, 25,* 203–213.

Solomon, J. C. (1940). Active play therapy: Further experiences. *American Journal of Orthopsychiatry, 10,* 763–781.

Solomon, J. C. (1955). Play techniques and the integrative process. *American Journal of Orthopsychiatry, 25,* 591–600.

Sturm, I. E. (1965). The behavioristic aspects of psychodrama. *Group Psychotherapy, 18,* 50–64.

Titkin, E. A. & Cobb, C. (1983). Treating post-divorce adjustment in latency age children: A focused group paradigm. *Social Work with Groups, 4,* 15–28.

SUGGESTED READINGS ⎯⎯⎯⎯⎯⎯⎯⎯⎯⎯⎯⎯ ▬

General

Axline, V. (1969). *Play therapy* (rev. ed.). New York: Ballantine Books.

Bandura, A. (1965). Behavioral modifications through modeling procedures. In L. Krasner & L. P. Ullman (Eds.), *Research in behavior modification.* New York: Holt, Rinehart and Winston.

Bender, L. (1955). Therapeutic play techniques: Discussion. *American Journal of Orthopsychiatry, 25,* 784–787.

Bender, L., & Woltmann, A. G. (1936). The use of puppet shows as a psychotherapeutic method for behavior problems in children. *American Journal of Orthopsychiatry, 6,* 341–354.

Blake, R. R. (1955). Experimental psychodrama with children. *Group Psychotherapy, 8,* 347–350.

Brunelle, P. (1949). Action projects from children's literature: An indirect approach to intercultural relations in the elementary school. In R. B. Haas (Ed.), *Psychodrama and sociodrama in American education.* Beacon, N.Y.: Beacon House.

Catterall, C. D., & Gazda, G. M. (1977). *Strategies for helping students.* Springfield, IL: Charles C. Thomas.

Drabkova, S. H. (1966). Experiences resulting from clinical use of psychodrama with children. *Group Psychotherapy, 19,* 32–36.

Frank, L. K. (1955). Play in personality development. *American Journal of Orthopsychiatry, 25,* 576–590.

Ginott, H. G. (1961). *Group psychotherapy with children.* New York: McGraw-Hill.

Ginott, H. G. (1975). Group therapy with children. In G. M. Gazda (Ed.), *Basic approaches to group psychotherapy and group counseling*. (2nd ed.). Springfield IL: Charles C. Thomas.

Haas, R. B. (Ed.) (1949). *Psychodrama and sociodrama in American education*. Beacon, NY: Beacon House.

Harms, E. (1948). Play diagnosis: Preliminary considerations for a sound approach. *Nervous Child, 7,* 233–246.

Henron, R. E., & Sutton-Smith, B. (1971). *Child's play*. New York: Grune & Stratton.

Hosford, P. M., & Acheson, E. (1976). Child drama for group guidance and counseling. In G. M. Gazda (Ed.), *Theories and methods of group counseling in the schools* (2nd ed.). Springfield, IL: Charles C. Thomas.

Jennings, H. H. (1950). Sociodrama as an educative process. In *Fostering mental health in our schools: 1950 Yearbook ASCD*. Washington, D.C.: Association for Supervision and Curriculum Development.

Kawin, E. (1934). *The wise choice of toys*. Chicago: University of Chicago Press.

Keat, D. C. (1974). *Fundamentals of child counseling*. Boston: Houghton Mifflin.

Krise, M. (1952). Creative dramatics and group psychotherapy. *Journal of Child Psychiatry, 2,* 337–342.

Krumboltz, J. D., & Krumboltz, H. B. (1972). *Changing children's behavior*. Englewood Cliffs, NJ: Prentice-Hall.

Krumboltz, J. D., & Thoresen, C. E. (1969). *Behavioral counseling: Cases and techniques*. New York: Holt, Rinehart and Winston.

Landreth, G. (Ed.) (1982). *Play therapy: Dynamics of the process of counseling with children*. Springfield, IL: Charles C. Thomas.

Lebo, D. (1955). The development of play as a form of therapy. *American Journal of Psychiatry, 12,* 418–442.

Lilienthal, J. W., & Tryon, C. (1950). Developmental tasks. II. Discussion of specific tasks and implications. In *Fostering mental health in our schools: 1950 Yearbook, ASCD*. Washington, D.C.: Association for Supervision and Curriculum Development.

Lippitt, R. (1954). Psychodrama in the kindergarten and nursery school. *Group Psychotherapy, 7,* 262–289.

Lott, A. J., Lott, B. E., & Matthews, G. M. (1969). Interpersonal attraction among children as a function of vicarious reward. *Journal of Educational Psychology, 60,* 274–283.

Moreno, J. L. (1949). The spontaneity theory of learning. In R. B. Haas (Ed.), *Psychodrama and sociodrama in American education*. Beacon, NY: Beacon House.

Moustakas, C. E. (1959). *Psychotherapy with children*. New York: Harper.

Muro, J. (1968). Play media in counseling: A brief report of experiences and some opinions. *Elementary School Guidance and Counseling, 3,* 104–110.

Murphy, G. (1960). Play as a counselor's tool. *School Counselor, 8,* 53–58.

Nelson, R. (1967). Physical facilities for elementary school counseling. *Personnel and Guidance Journal, 45,* 552–556.

Norris, J. W. (1974). The use of spontaneous drawing with chromatic colors as a facilitator for group psychotherapy: The development of a technique. Ph.D. dissertation, University of Georgia.

O'Connor, R. D. (1969). Modification of social withdrawal through symbolic modeling. *Journal of Applied Behavior Analysis, 2,* 15–22.

Oden, S., & Asher, S. (1977). Coaching children in social skills for friendship making. *Child Development, 48,* 495–506.

Ohlsen, M. M. (Ed.) (1973). *Counseling children in groups: A forum.* New York: Holt, Rinehart and Winston.

Rose, S. D. (1973). *Treating children in groups: A behavioral approach.* San Francisco: Jossey-Bass.

Rose, S. D. (1982). Group counseling with children: A behavioral and cognitive approach. In G. M. Gazda (Ed.), *Basic approaches to group psychotherapy and group counseling.* (3rd ed.). Springfield, IL: Charles C. Thomas.

Schiffer, M. (1969). *The therapeutic play group.* New York: Grune and Stratton.

Slavson, S. R., & Schiffer, M. (1975). *Group psychotherapies for children: A textbook.* New York: International Universities Press.

Solomon, J. C. (1940). Active play therapy: Further experiences. *American Journal of Orthopsychiatry, 10,* 763–781.

Solomon, J. C. (1955). Play techniques and the integrative process. *American Journal of Orthopsychiatry, 25,* 591–600.

Sturm, I. E. (1965). The behavioristic aspects of psychodrama. *Group Psychotherapy, 18,* 50–64.

Tryon, C., & Lilienthal, J. W. (1950). Developmental tasks: I. The concept and its importance. In *Fostering mental health in our schools: 1950 Yearbook, ASCD.* Washington, D.C.: Association for Supervision and Curriculum Development.

Wells, C. G. (1962). Psychodrama and creative counseling in the elementary school. *Group psychotherapy, 15,* 244–252.

Research

Barnes, L. W. (1977). The effects of group counseling on the self-concept and achievement of primary grade Mexican-American pupils. Ph.D. dissertation, University of Southern California.

Bleck, R. T. (1978). Group counseling using structured play with elementary school disruptive children. Ph.D. dissertation, University of Florida.

Greene, R. L. (1976). The effects of group counseling and consultation on the classroom behaviors and attitudes of selected elementary school children. Ph.D. dissertation, University of Massachusetts.

L'Abate, L. (1979). Aggression and construction in boy's monitored play-therapy. *Journal of Counseling and Psychotherapy, 2,* 137–158.

Moulin, E. K. (1970). Effects of client-centered group counseling on the intelligence, achievement, and psycholinguistic abilities of underachieving primary school children. *Elementary School Guidance and Counseling, 5,* 85–98.

Sabatini, S. G. (1976). An investigation of play group counseling. *Dissertation Abstracts International, 36* (12-A), 7875.

Schiffer, M. A. (1957). Therapeutic play group in a public school. *Mental Hygiene, 41,* 185–193.

Strom, A. Y. (1976). The effects of intensive group play media on the self-concepts of selected second grade children. Ph.D. dissertation, University of Denver.

GROUP RESOURCE MATERIAL ────────────

Preschool and Early School

In order for the reader to be able to obtain detailed brochures and current price lists, materials are listed with reference to the companies that publish them.

Alegra House Publishers
Post Office Box 1443-F
Warren, OH 44482

Divorce Adjustment Bookshelf
A listing of books, workbooks, tapes, and adjustment inventories designed to help children deal with the issues raised by divorce. (Ages 3–15)

American Guidance Service
Publishers' Building
Circle Pines, MN 55014

Small Wonder
A two-part program that encourages the emotional, physical, and intellectual growth of babies and toddlers; special emphasis is on language development.
Level 1: Birth–18 months, remedially to age 3
Level 2: 18–36 months, remedially to age 5

Developing Understanding of Self and Others (DUSO)
Two multimedia programs, each providing a variety of day-to-day activities over a 33-week span.
DUSO Kit, D–1 (Kindergarten–Grade 2)
DUSO Kit, D–2 (Grades 3–4)

Peabody Early Experience Kit
A program of sequenced lessons designed to build cognitive, social, and linguistic skills. (Preschool)

Body Rights
A program to teach children the assertiveness and decision-making skills necessary to protect themselves. (Preschool–Grade 2)

DLM Teaching Resources
One DLM Park
Allen, TX 75002

Peace, Harmony, Awareness
A program consisting of tapes, photographs, and a manual to help adults work with children in developing relaxation techniques and learning to cope with criticism, anger, and stress. (Elementary)

Body and Self-Awareness Big Box
A kit containing 12 individual products that help students establish positive self-concepts and express feelings and reactions to people and situations encountered in their daily lives. (Elementary)

Society for Visual Education, Inc.
1345 Diversey Parkway
Chicago, IL 60614

Lollipop Dragon-Adventures in Self-Awareness
Lollipop Dragon helps youngsters become aware of themselves, their values, and the values of others. (Kindergarten–Grade 2)

Walt Disney
Educational Media Co.
500 South Buena Vista Street
Burbank, CA 91521

Winnie the Pooh
Pooh characters convey (through color filmstrips, cassettes, records, and a

teacher's guide) sensitive and provocative stories in the following areas:

Winnie the Pooh and the Right Thing to Do (Kindergarten–Grade 3)

Back to School with Winnie the Pooh (Kindergarten–Grade 3)

Good Citizenship with Winnie the Pooh Kindergarten–Grade 3)

Donald Duck's Elementary Guidance Series

This filmstrip series helps children develop self-discipline, confidence, and self-respect. (Kindergarten–Grade 6)

CHAPTER 5

Group Counseling for the Preadolescent

The preadolescent is the child in the latency period, with an age range from 9 to 13 years old. During this four-year span the developmental gap between boys and girls is most noticeable, with the normal girl developing secondary sexual characteristics in advance of the normal boy by one to two years. Thus girls in the latter years of the latency period may be better described as early adolescents. The same holds true for more rapidly developing boys. Any of the classifications used to differentiate age groups and developmental levels must be considered only as a norm, with exceptions especially prominent at either end of the age group. Nevertheless, if we are to understand and better assist a given age group, we will need to employ what we know about the *typical* child in a particular age group.

Because boys and girls do vary greatly within the developmental levels, group leaders are encouraged to make use of the guidelines of developmental tasks and appropriate coping behaviors for the age group preceding and also for the age group immediately above the one in which they work. Hence group leaders of preadolescents would need to appraise themselves of the developmental levels of the child 5 to 9 years of age as well as the adolescent above the age of 13.

Children in latency are often neglected children because they have entered into a period of quiescence. Their natural group consists of peers of the *same* sex. They are in the so-called homosexual age of development wherein boys prefer to be with boys and girls prefer to be with girls. Cub and Boy Scouts become important for boys, and girls' clubs, Brownies and Girl Scouts, are important to girls.

The school grades most representative of latency or preadolescence are grades 4, 5, and 6, or the middle school. Junior high school overlaps at least in the seventh grade; but for the early maturing boys and especially for the girls, eighth grade finds them in the early adolescent phase of development. When working with 13-year-olds, therefore, the group leader must use developmental guidelines and group techniques for both the preadolescent and the early adolescent.

The knowledge and skills appropriate to the following seven developmental areas: psychosocial, physical–sexual, cognitive, vocational, moral, ego, and affective have been incorporated into the four generic life-skills areas described in Chapter 2. The skills appropriate to the child of 9–13 are listed by age level in Appendix A. Readers are encouraged to use these skills as guides for assessing the appropriateness of including a child in the activity-interview group counseling described in this chapter.

GROUP COUNSELING

One of the first psychotherapists, if not the first, to recommend the use of activity as a means of creating a therapeutic climate was Moreno (1946). Moreno's activity-oriented approach led to the development of sociodrama and psychodrama. Slavson (1954), however, pioneered and expanded the application of media such as arts and crafts, table games, and outdoor activities such as field trips and excursions in the treatment of adolescents and preadolescents. He referred to this treatment procedure as activity group therapy and activity-interview group therapy. Gabriel (1939), along with Slavson, was one of the first to use activity group work in the treatment of behavioral disorders. She also used field trips, clay, painting, and related activities in treating preadolescents in groups.

Slavson (1945) made the following comment related to the value of activity groups for the preadolescent:

> What little children gain through play and acting out, young children in their latency period and early adolescence achieve through manual activity, creative expression, and free play and interaction with one another. Older adolescents and adults require verbal expression and insight to gain the same results. (p. 202)

Galkin (1937) also contributed to the field of activity group therapy. He used the natural medium of outdoor play and a camp environment of the preadolescent and adolescent in activity group therapy.

Ginott (1961, 1968) followed the lead of Slavson and added additional activity media to the treatment of preadolescents. In addition to the usual arts and crafts, table games, and such, he introduced penny arcade-type machines such as rifle galleries and electric bowling tables and modern communication devices such as the walkie-talkie and typewriter.

An activity group approach within the context of *counseling* has been described by Blakeman and Day (1969). They have borrowed from the activity group therapy literature "the need for communication through a natural and spontaneous activity" and combined this with counseling within a group setting. Their process is defined as follows: "Activity group counseling refers to the group process which improves communication through natural spontaneous activity whereby peers participate in the developmental, behavioral, and attitudinal concerns of the individual members of the counseling group" (Blakeman & Day, 1969, p. 61). Thus activity group therapy has been used as the model for the development of activity-oriented procedures for counseling. Although Blakeman and Day have named their procedure activity group counseling, had they followed Slavson's (1964) lead they might have more appropriately named it activity-interview group counseling *à la* Slavson's activity-interview group psychotherapy, its forerunner. Actually, Blakeman and Day used activities such as darts, basketball, swimming, rifle shooting, and table games such as chess and various card games to generate interaction among the preadolescent boys with whom they worked. The activity was then followed by group discussion of the personally relevant interactions. This method is similar to Slavson's activity-interview group psychotherapy approach.

No single "activity" approach to group counseling seems to include the several options possible. In view of this situation, I have proposed two activity-oriented approaches to group counseling for the preadolescent. Each is developed on the hypothesis that group games, both highly physical and sedentary, are the most natural media and means through which the preadolescent communicates freely and spontaneously.

ACTIVITY-INTERVIEW GROUP COUNSELING ⎯⎯⎯⎯⎯■

Activity-interview group counseling is a composite of activity group therapy *à la* Slavson and interview group counseling. In essence an activity, such as darts, is used to involve the group and to lower the inhibitions and defenses of the group members. The activity itself may provide an opportunity for physical catharsis or a nonsystematized desensitization. It serves the same purpose as systematic desensitization practiced by behaviorally oriented counselors and therapists. In addition to providing a means for tension reduction through physical catharsis, the activity provides an opportunity for interpersonal interactions, which are the concern of the counselor and members in the group "interview" period following the game or activity.

Activity-interview group counseling, like all other variations of group counseling described in this text, is a combination of prevention and remediation. Thus it is intended for preadolescents in particular, but also for adolescents and some adults who are not suffering from debilitating emotional problems.

The activities may be many and varied. They should be chosen by the group counselor according to the needs of the group members. Care should be taken to vary the games or activities in order to provide some success experiences to all members of the group. Athletic preadolescents should have the opportunity to demonstrate their talents in team sports like basketball, touch football, and volleyball. In like fashion, less athletic preadolescents should have an opportunity to experience success in table games such as electric bowling, Ping Pong, chess, checkers, video games and the like. Still other activities such as dancing, swimming, and arts and crafts should be used for those who may have talents apart from the physical or intellective.

Simulation and gaming constitutes a promising medium for use in life-skills training and group counseling for the preadolescent in particular. Games such as the Life Career Game (Varenhorst, 1968) can be adapted for small counseling groups and would provide the less physically competitive preadolescent with a substitute means for showing ability or excellence, such as in decision making. It would also appeal to the group counselor who has less interest and enthusiasm for the more physically active team sports.

Simulating problem resolution can serve as a means of vicariously conditioning preadolescents by rewarding choices or decisions that lead the hypothetical person to success experiences and by not rewarding or vicariously punishing the hypothetical person's inappropriate choices and decisions. Thus this medium could serve much like role playing to protect the real counselee; however, it extends beyond role playing in terms of the complexity of problems, external factors affecting decisions, and such.

Since the activity itself in activity-interview group counseling represents only part of the treatment, those activities that involve simultaneously several if not all the group members should be most used. The discussion or interview group counseling session following the game or activity constitutes the second part of the treatment. During this period the counselor helps the group members focus on the nature of the interactions that occurred during the activity phase of the treatment. The behavior that occurred during the activity is related to the life-style of a given group member in the sequence described in Chapter 3. That is, the counselor builds a strong facilitative base with high levels of empathy, respect, and warmth; only after having established a feeling of mutual trust and caring does the counselor move the group member into the planning and action phase of the treatment through appropriate self-disclosure, genuineness, concreteness, confrontation, and immediacy, à la Carkhuff (1969a, b).

The interview or discussion phase need not be held in a formal setting such as a conference room, although such a room should be available when movement from an activity setting is required. The conference room can also be set up as a dual-purpose room including equipment and materials for group activities as well as chairs for the interview phase.

The following protocol illustrates the dual-purpose setting used with a group of black preadolescent "problem students" ranging in age from 11 to 14. The protocol includes portions taken from the sixth group session. The setting is a dual-purpose room in which six black boys are milling around. Some are reading; others are drawing; one is throwing darts. J. (the subject of discussion) is very active. The counselor is a white male in his early thirties.

Protocol[1]

J.	I'm not gonna' tell anything in the meeting today because every time I do, R. tells Mr. A.
R.	I did not tell!
Co.	Let's hear about this.
J.	I am not going to say anything.
R.	He went and shot off his big mouth, and because I told Mr. A., now he is mad at me.
J.	Ah, Peanut, that isn't either what happened. That isn't the first time you've done this, Peanut. I've been playing with you all day and you've been doing it all along. Every time you touch him he gets mad. Just touch him a little bit and he gets mad; he's a baby.
Co.	How about that Group? How would you handle this?
W.	J. is to blame; he is always to blame. He's a great big bully.
J.	I didn't touch him. I know what I'm gonna' do about it! I'm just not gonna' associate with anybody in this group anymore.
R.	Don't worry; it will pass over.
M.	I think we ought to put them together and let them fight it out.
Co.	It seems to be a lot of buzzing, but no one wants to say anything directly to J. or R. about the situation. I get the idea that all of you would like to, but you're kinda' frightened of what they might say back.
J.	I think the way to settle this whole thing is if I don't associate with R. anymore. When he gets tired of not associating with me, he'll come around and say, "Let's make friends again"; then we'll be friends.
Co.	I'm still puzzled about your saying R. is responsible for all your problems.

1. From J. D. Blakeman, & S. R. Day. (1969). Activity group counseling. In G. M. Gazda (Ed.), *Theories and methods of group counseling in the schools.* Courtesy of Charles C. Thomas, Publisher, Springfield, Illinois.

J.	Yes, he is. And even though you want me to say something, I'm not gonna' say nothing different. He is responsible for all my problems. Let's do something different; I'm tired of this. I don't want to be talking all day long. I'm mad at this group.
Co.	It seems like J. doesn't feel like the group is satisfying him any more. How do the rest of you feel?
Group:	It's great, it's what we want. Let's do it.
W.	Let's get J. out of the group if he doesn't like it.
H.	If he wants out, let's get him out.
L.	Yeah, let's get him out, if he doesn't want to be in the group; let's get him out.
Co.	I guess the boys are saying, J., that the door is open.
J.	Well, one thing about this group is that when we do play basketball or football, we got a sorry bunch of players. None of them really want to play ball. They're just a bunch of goofoffs. We got a sorry bunch of players.
M.	That's what you say. You shoot all the time anyway, how would you know? You never pass it to anyone. Why don't you try to teach some of the boys how to play, rather than chewing at them all the time?
R.	Well, I'd like to say something, I tell you this. When J. has the ball, even if you're wide open, he won't pass it to you. He won't pass it to any little boys. All he wants to do is shoot or pass it to one of the big boys. He keeps on dribbling like he don't even hear. All he does is shoot.
M.	I think J. and I are the best basketball players in here and I think J. doesn't like the other boys. He never passes. I try at least to be good to them.
J.	Yeah, W., L., and T., they're no good. They won't even play. They lose interest in the game, and if you don't keep on them all the time, they won't even play. No sense to pass to them, anyway. They just dribble and lose it. They're no good anyway.
L.	The group wasn't formed just for basketball. There is other reasons, too. Someone else might be good in football. You just want to be the hog in everything you do, J.
Co.	It seems like some of you boys felt like being good in basketball was the main purpose in the group, while others seem to think that there are other purposes in the group.
T.	Yeah, keep us out of trouble.
J.	I'd like to talk now. Now, you say I don't pass the ball, but who in here does pass the ball? Every time I pass to T. or W., they lose the ball. Every time. So why pass to them? Just lose it if I pass it to them.
W.	What are you talking about boy? You don't even know what you are talking about.

J.	Now you answer that, W. Why should I pass it to you? Now . . . if you see somebody that ain't gonna' do no good with something that is given to them, why give it to them? Why do it? Why give it to them?
Co.	It seems like J. sees a different purpose for the group. He wants to be a good basketball player and have a basketball team. Some of the rest of you don't feel that way.
M.	Well, I think anybody that don't know how to play ought to learn, and I think that this is a good place to learn to do things. I think J. is wrong. I think we ought to be teaching boys to learn.
J.	The time to learn is not while you're playing the game. The time to learn is on your own in your own yard. Besides that, you can't teach boys that don't want to learn. Some of these boys would rather play dodge, so go let them play dodge, but when they come on a basketball floor, they ought to play basketball and they ought to try to be good. If they don't show a lot of interest, they shouldn't ought to be out there.
W.	I'm no good at basketball, but I think I'd have a lot of fun playing basketball if J. weren't there.
R.	J. always shoots the ball so when we get back to this meeting, he can just talk all the time and brag about what he did during the game.
Co.	Let's take a look now, boys, at what we are doing. It seems as though everybody is ganging up against J., and it seems like we're trying to tell him that he's not a very good sport when it comes to playing basketball. I think maybe we're being a little hard on him.
J.	Don't worry about me. I don't feel bad.
M.	I think this is good because I think J. needs help. I think he needs help badly not only in basketball but all over.
J.	I don't think I need no help.
M.	Yes, you do need some help. You need lots of help.
J.	You can't help me.
Co.	M., what do you see he needs help in?
M.	He needs to learn how to keep his mouth shut, and he needs help to learn how to act.
J.	I don't need no help from none of you. I don't want any help from anybody.
Co.	You don't want any help, from any of us?
R.	That's his main problem. When somebody tries to help him, he won't let them. It is the same thing he was saying. If he won't help himself, how can we help?
J.	Be quiet. Oh, shut up, Peanut. Peanut, will you shut up! I'm leaving this group. I'm through with this group. This group can't help me. I don't like any of you, and I'm not gonna' be in this group. I am through with you, and I don't want anything to do with you or anybody in this group.

Co.   Sorry you feel that way, J. It sounds like we have been a little hard on you today. It seems like the boys had a lot on their minds.

H.   Yes, it is true.

J.   I'm quitting. I don't want anything more to do with you. I don't want to come to any more of the group meetings. Count me out.

Co.   We'll leave it up to you, J. Whatever you decide is all right with us. I think though that we should leave it open if you would like to come back.

J.   I won't come back, and I won't have any more to do with it.

M.   I hope you do come back, J. I like you. I just think there are some things you need to work on.

W.   Yeah, we like you, J. I'm sorry that you are so mad.

R.   I like you, too, J., even if you are mad at me. And if you don't want to be in the group, I don't think you should have to be.

Meeting ends.   J. says that he is quitting and is very angry. J. comes back to the counselor during the week, however, and apologizes for getting angry. He comes back to the group and is a model group member.

The protocol illustrates a very action-oriented approach on the part of the counselor. He assumed that he had a good base built with J. and the rest of the group. The counselor and the group members showed empathy, warmth, respect, self-disclosure, genuineness, concreteness, immediacy, and confrontation—with a rather heavy emphasis on confrontation. If J. had not previously experienced the counselor and group members as helpful individuals, the result of this session would not have been so positive.

The confrontations of the peer group, though appearing hurtful, were genuine and mixed with expressions of caring. J. was rewarded for his positive behavior and physical attributes, but he was confronted (verbally) for his inappropriate attitudes and behavior. One must be reminded that without a strong base to begin with, confrontation would produce unhealthy responses rather than the healthy response by J.

Application of a Developmental Approach to Activity-Interview Group Counseling

The protocol cited previously highlights a couple of developmental tasks that the preadolescent faces and masters, with help. The principal task is "achieving an appropriate giving-receiving pattern of affection" with the concomitant coping behavior of "accepting one's self as a worthwhile person, really worthy of love." During the latter stages of preadolescence, dramatic physical changes often occur within the individual, and the preadolescent must *find* this apparent new self—learn to love this new self. In the process the preadolescent sometimes becomes very egocentric and preoccupied with self. J.'s egocentricity is characteristic of Kohlberg's Stage 2 of moral development. Right is characterized by that which satisfies one's own needs and occasionally the needs of others. Friendships are used to gain understanding of self (Tryon & Lilienthal, 1950).

Also closely tied with this developmental task are the following tasks: "accepting and adjusting to a changing body" and "managing a changing body and learning new motor patterns." The protocol illustrates how these tasks can be isolated, with both appropriate and inappropriate coping behaviors, and how the peer group can be used to help members through a healthy adult model in the person of the counselor (Tryon & Lilienthal, 1950).

Hargrave and Hargrave (1979) selected twelve fourth through sixth graders for a modified activity-interview group treatment. They selected students who were either shy, withdrawn, and inhibited or aggressive, bossy, and demanding. The group consisted of nine boys and three girls with an average age of 10 years and 10 months. All group members attended at least ten of the fourteen one-and-one-half hour group sessions held weekly. All group members were within the average range of intelligence; however, half of the members were diagnosed as having learning disorders. The treatment group was matched with an equivalent control group. Changes were determined on the Classroom Behavior Inventory (CBI). Teachers completed the CBI before and after treatment.

Group sessions were held immediately after school. Two counseling psychologists and a teacher were the group leaders (the Hargraves). Each treatment session was composed of three parts. The first phase was a one-half hour *discussion phase,* conducted in a lounge area. During this period students discussed problems and events that had occurred during the week between sessions. Focus was on the "here-and-now" social interactions occurring among group members. "A primary emphasis was placed upon the management of attention to individual responses, so that socially inappropriate behavior was not reinforced. Action-oriented techniques such as modeling, role-playing, and behavioral rehearsal were combined with discussion and praise for effective interaction" (Hargrave & Hargrave, 1979, p. 548).

The second phase was the *team sport phase.* This one-half hour was devoted to playing simple games such as kickball and progressed in the course of the program to more difficult sports such as basketball. "Cooperation among teammates within a framework of competition between teams fostered the opportunity for learning the game and for social exchanges in a naturally occurring peer activity. The competitive aspect made the activity comparable to other settings. Group leadership was moved from the therapists to the students as the group progressed." (Hargrave & Hargrave, 1979, p. 548).

The *critique phase* was the concluding one-half hour. It was a relaxed period when soft drinks and cookies were enjoyed. "Problems that occurred during the team sport phase were resolved through discussion and/or role playing; likewise, much praise was given to members who improved their performance, helped others learn the game, displayed good sportsmanship and control, etc. In addition, an effort was made to relate the day's events to other similar situations" (Hargrave & Hargrave, 1979, p. 548).

The results showed a statistically significant change in the teachers' ratings of experimental group members on the Classroom Adjustment variable of the CBI. Narrative statements by teachers also showed positive classroom behavior for the experimental group members. There was no significant change among control students.

> A review of the individual scales that contributed to this change indicates that the students who participated in the group decreased in emotional fluctuation, impulsivity, destructiveness, attention-seeking, rigidity, inappropriate talkativeness, distractibility, and work fluctuation, and increased in obedience, calmness, and passive helpfulness. (Hargrave & Hargrave, 1979, p. 549)

This study represents a modified application of the activity-interview group counseling model described in this chapter insofar as the sexes were mixed in the group and three, instead of two, phases of treatment were employed. Nevertheless the positive results are consistent with the effective application of the activity-interview group counseling model.

Egan (1975) reported the successful use of Activity Discussion Group Therapy (ADGT) for a period of ten years. Egan makes the following five contentions for ADGT:

> (1) ADGT is an ideal therapeutic vehicle to catalyze the attainment of the tasks of latency. (2) Therapy should be based on identification, reinforcement, and insight rather than on any one theoretical principle or technique. (3) Various techniques based on these principles should be employed selectively depending on such variables as maturity, intelligence, degree of deprivation, type and severity of psychopathology, stage of therapy, etc. (4) We should monitor our results and change our methods when we are not getting positive results fast enough. (5) We should develop treatment programs, including involvement of parents and teachers, so that appropriate behavior and development is generalized and maintained in the natural setting without therapy. (p. 199)

The Hargrave and Hargrave (1979) and Egan (1975) studies illustrate the application of activity-interview group counseling to preadolescent groups. Variations of activity-interview group counseling usually include some form of structured groups that incorporates skill training. For example, Schmidt and Biles (1985) used puppetry and role-play situations with middle school students to help them "explore self-perceptions, improve communication skills, make friends, acquire compromising and negotiating skills, and develop healthy relationships with peers" (p. 67). Likewise, Smith, Walsh, and Richardson (1985) organized a Clown Club utilizing "structured fantasy and creative drama for the expression and resolution of conflict" (p. 49) separately with latency-age girls and latency-age boys. Titkin and Cobb (1983) used board games and other exercises as well as skills training for post-divorce adjustment of latency-age children. Chapter 9 describes the application of structured groups for the special population of substance users and abusers. The trend in group counseling is an increased use of structured skills training groups for special populations such as children of divorce, substance abusers, sexually abused children, and so on. See also Chapter 10 on Self-Help Groups; these are rapidly developing for special populations of children, youth, and adults.

ACTIVITY GROUP COUNSELING

Activity group counseling is akin to Slavson's activity group therapy; it is illustrated very well in the film "Activity Group Therapy," directed by Slavson and is available from Columbia University Press. Once again *counseling* is used in this text in lieu of *therapy* because the degree of deterioration or disturbance among the clientele to be served is not so severe as is the case when therapy or "reconstruction of a personality" is involved.

Activity group counseling is different from activity-interview group counseling to the extent that the counselor is much less active on a verbal level. The counselor is present as a catalyst and source of safety or control; but the composition of the group and activities, materials, and other media are chosen more carefully than would be necessary for activity-interview group counseling. Activity group counseling requires a greater skill in social engineering because the group members and the media must be relied on more heavily as agents of change.

The setting and media must accommodate in particular the needs of the overinhibited and the belligerent preadolescent (Ginott, 1968). The engineering requires a careful balance of group members including some overinhibited and some belligerent with some who fall between these two extremes. If the balance is incorrect, the hyperactive and belligerent preadolescents threaten the overinhibited and cause them to withdraw even further. If a group is composed totally of overinhibited preadolescents, there are no assertive peer models for them to imitate, and thus the counselor would be the only model for positive change. Since preadolescents are separated by sex for group treatment, we are describing all-male and all-female groups.

The overinhibited, shy, withdrawn, sexually inadequate preadolescent boy will require media such as fire for fire play, walkie-talkies, tape recorders, video games, and various penny arcade-type machines—rifle gallery, electric bowling table, and the like (Ginott, 1961, 1968). These media are captivating and serve to involve indirectly the overinhibited preadolescent boy with others until he can move to direct personal confrontations. In addition, some of these media permit him to release latent hostility.

On the other hand, the aggressive and belligerent preadolescent boy needs to learn how to sublimate and control his hostile feelings. Fire play, rifle galleries, boxing machines, and the like provide him with acceptable media to release his aggression without infringing on the rights of others. Shop materials include hard substances such as wood for sawing and hammering and similar substances that are thought to serve as media for sublimation for the belligerent preadolescent (Slavson, 1955). Slavson recommends clay, water colors, appropriate molds for making ashtrays, large sheets of paper, and equipment for cooking simple refreshments for the less belligerent. Ginott (1961, 1968) has found it necessary to add to the traditional facilities pioneered by Slavson. He has found that the aggressive and acting-out preadolescent in particular requires media such as fire for fire play, rifle galleries, boxing machines, and the like. These kinds of media appeal to the masculine identification of the aggressive, hostile, and acting-out preadolescent who tends to view water colors, clay, and fine arts material as sissy and to avoid them.

The great attraction of video games for preadolescents and adolescents opens an entirely new medium for use in activity and activity-interview group counseling. Friendly competition among group members may be used productively. Currently the games are not group oriented, though games of this sort may be developed.

Although less is known regarding the media that is suited for aggressive, belligerent, and shy, withdrawn preadolescent girls, some will be comfortable with many of the media used for their counterparts among the boys. Others will prefer to engage in more traditional feminine pursuits, such as styling and setting one another's hair, sewing, cooking, listening to music and dancing, table games, swimming, painting, and handicrafts. It would appear that a balance between sedentary games and active physical games would be preferred. Just as with the preadolescent boys, the use of a variety of activities will permit each girl to be successful at one or more activities.

SELECTION AND GROUP COMPOSITION

The preadolescent age group is the one age group that definitely calls for separation of the sexes in the group treatment plan. There also might be some reason to separate the sexes in the age group from 5 to 9; however, this would most likely be true for those reaching the latency period around age 9. The preadolescent age represents the time when boys prefer to be with boys and girls prefer to be with girls; their *natural* choices are for members of the same sex. This preference should be respected when placing preadolescents in counseling groups.

Activity groups and Life-Skills Training groups, I contend, are the preferred modes of treatment for the preadolescent. The majority of counselees in the age group are boys and games and activities are their most comfortable ways of relating. This tends to be a *masculine* preference, however, and activities, though relevant, are not as necessary in the group counseling of preadolescent girls. Except for the more aggressive preadolescent girls, interview group counseling, the preferred mode of counseling for adolescents and adults, may be used effectively with preadolescent females.

As with other age groups, role balancing and the provision of models for mutual imitation are of prime importance in activity-oriented group counseling. Hansen, Niland, and Zani (1969), in a study of model reinforcement group counseling with elementary school children of low sociometric ratings, had this comment on group composition:

> When none of the students exhibit successful classroom behavior, it is difficult to learn acceptable behavior from each other. This may be true of other group counseling studies using different criteria in which all persons in the group share a common problem. Thus, group composition may be a major reason why so many group counseling studies report null results. (p. 744)

Although proper group composition is important in *activity-interview* group counseling, it is even more critical in the engineering of therapeutic elements for *activity* group counseling because of the greater emphasis of the peer group members on each other and the less active role of the group counselor. The best predictor of the performance or functioning of a preadolescent in a group is some observable behavior during a trial or preliminary group placement (Gazda, 1968).

The preadolescent can be placed in an oversized newly formed group for a trial period of three or four sessions. The best participant combinations, based on direct observation of interaction, can be retained for the duration of the group. The others can be continued on an individual counseling basis until an opening in an open-ended group becomes available or until enough counselees are available for the formation of a new group.

Certain preadolescents do not make good candidates for group treatment. Ginott (1968) has labeled as unsuitable for group treatment (1) preadolescents with accelerated sexual drives such as those with premature and persistent preoccupation with sexual matters; (2) preadolescents who have actively engaged in homosexual activities; (3) psychopathic preadolescents;

(4) destructive preadolescents whose aggressiveness is deep rooted in hostility toward self (masochism) or others (homicidal); (5) preadolescents with long histories of stealing outside the home (preadolescents who steal only at home may be bidding for affection or a temporary act of revenge; these preadolescents may be placed in a group treatment setting); (6) preadolescents who have been involved in a recent trauma or catastrophe; and (7) preadolescents suffering from *intense* sibling rivalry.

The chronological age difference of preadolescents in group treatment should not exceed two years (Ginott, 1968). The social age and the intellectual age of the group members must also be considered in the composition of a group. Since both types of activity-oriented group counseling approaches use the physically active games as well as sedentary games with neither predominating, the socially mature but physically small preadolescents are guaranteed some game or activity in which they have a chance to compete and excel.

The greater the emphasis on activities in the treatment plan (for example, activity group counseling versus activity-interview group counseling), the less the importance of intellectual differences. Nevertheless, "normals" should not be placed in groups with mental retardates, and vice-versa.

Some chronologically younger preadolescents are often deliberately placed in a group with older preadolescents when the younger preadolescent is overly aggressive and requires the control of older groupmates. Similarly, some chronologically older but immature preadolescents are sometimes placed in groups with younger groupmates.

Generally, siblings and close relatives and friends should not be placed in the same group. When siblings are present in the same group, they sometimes feel compelled to look after each other and thus reduce their independent participation. Also, there is the greater possibility of one telling on another, especially when angered or hurt in a family quarrel. The presence of close friends and/or relatives poses the problem of trying to maintain the image that had been developed. This image-maintenance behavior interferes with the counselee's freedom to be real and spontaneous rather than role dominated.

SETTING AND MEDIA

Consistent with the developmental emphasis of this text, all settings, insofar as possible, should be "natural" to the counselee. Activity group approaches to counseling require large rooms and open outdoor areas where a variety of activities by several counselees may be engaged in simultaneously. Schiffer, for example, suggests that a room of approximately 600 square feet is of optimal size (cited by Ginott, 1961). The room should be of sufficient size to accommodate work benches and tables, table tennis, penny arcade-type machines, space for crafts, a meal table, and perhaps a tape deck and tapes. The typical school does not have rooms of this sort. The typical school, however, does have an industrial arts shop, recreation areas, and a home economics suite. These rooms, with their media and materials, can be adapted to the preadolescent.

In addition to the school shop and home economics suite, the gymnasium, swimming pool, and athletic fields and various game courts all provide areas that can be used by the activity group counselor. A small conference room capable of comfortably accommodating six or seven people should be available to the activity group counselor, especially when the activity-interview approach is being used. This room would serve as a place to which to retire for the interview phase following a physical activity. The dual-purpose room described earlier in this chapter could serve equally well for a conference-activity room.

The activity group counselor should view the entire community as the treatment setting. Camping and field trips should be included whenever possible. The therapeutic use of fire building by the preadolescent has been cited by Ginott (1961, 1968), and the camp with its campfire would provide a more natural means of using fire as a treatment medium than the artificial setting of fire building in a sink. Visits to community fairs, penny arcades, and video game rooms may also be more naturally used as treatment media than would be their use in a school setting. Nevertheless, these types of games should be available in one setting or the other and preferably convenient for repeated use.

Gump and Sutton-Smith (1955) hypothesized that certain behaviors (respondent behaviors) were made more likely by given physical settings or, more specifically, that the amount and kind of social interaction is significantly affected by variation of activity settings. Their subjects were twenty-three boys, aged $9\frac{1}{2}$ to $11\frac{1}{2}$ years, who had adjustment difficulties. They had been sent to the University of Michigan Fresh Air Camp. They found that *amount* and *kind* of interaction differed significantly between swimming and crafts. Swimming produced significantly *greater interactions;* however, when compared to counselor involvement, crafts produced significantly *greater involvement* than swimming.

The researchers concluded, "The general implication for recreational and therapeutic work with children is that choice of activities per se is very important; this choice will markedly affect the children's relations to one another and to the leader or therapist" (1955, p. 759). For example, in the swim setting the counselor was more often called on to admire and recognize assertive actions and to settle or supervise conflict interactions and less often asked to be involved in helping interactions, whereas in crafts the opposite tended to be true. According to Gump and Sutton-Smith,

The counselor learns from such data that a "prescription" of swimming will send a child to a "robust" social climate in which total interaction is high and in which assertion and attacking are highly likely. A crafts "prescription," on the other hand will place a child in a "mild" social climate in which total interaction is low, assertive and conflict interaction minimal, and dependency (helping—being helped) interaction high. (1955, p. 759)

Obviously, then, the choice of setting *as well as choice of media used* within the setting should be made carefully to accommodate the needs of the group members. Settings as well as media should be varied to meet the needs of *all* group members.

For the more sedentary games such as card games, chess, and simulator games like the Life Career Game and Family Game, small tables should be available to permit the group to divide into subgroups and to spread out the materials included in the game kit. A sufficient number of chairs should be available for the number involved in the group. With more and more simulation games being produced and with their inclusion of filmstrips and sound films, a filmstrip projector and a movie projector with screens would be appropriate accessories.

GROUP SIZE

Many of the considerations discussed in the section for children from 5 to 9 years of age apply to preadolescent children from ages 9 to 13. Although average children from 9 to 13 have become more socialized than children from 5 to 9 years of age, they still do not have the same degree of self-control that adolescents and adults have mastered. For this reason, group counselors need to limit the number of group participants in this age group so that they can control the therapeutic group processes.

Another consideration given to group size for activity groups is the nature of the activity itself and the possible controlling and/or safety conditions of the activity. Activities such as touch football, softball, and basketball permit physical movement over a wide range or area and detract from the control and resultant safety extended by a group leader, whereas table games such as cards and table tennis localize the group and make it possible for the activity group counselor to retain more overall control of the group members as well as control the safety factor. Activities such as touch football and softball are difficult to play with a small group, and unless another group can be obtained to serve as the opposition, some of the larger team sports would prove inappropriate for activity group counseling.

Providing models for each member in the group is another condition of group counseling that must be considered when determining size for activity groups. If each preadolescent has a model in the group, we can readily see that each time we add a person, we are in fact adding that person plus a model unless certain individuals are serving as models for more than one group member. This, in fact, is quite feasible.

No systematic research has been completed regarding size of preadolescent activity groups; however, I have found five to seven to be an optimum number. Under certain circumstances, especially if a co-counselor is employed, as many as ten may be included in an activity-type counseling group.

FREQUENCY, LENGTH, AND DURATION OF GROUP SESSIONS

The degree of disturbance of the group participants is probably the best indicator of the frequency and duration of treatment through activity group counseling. As with other types of group counseling, activity group counseling, in my opinion, is both prevention and remediation oriented. The degree to which remediation is necessary or the degree to which coping behaviors must be varied or initiated will determine how often and how long a group should meet.

I have found that both activity-interview group counseling and activity group counseling require approximately six months to one year of meeting one-and-a-half to two hours a session at least once a week. Twice-a-week sessions of approximately one-and-a-half hours are recommended especially in the beginning of a group until cohesiveness or esprit de corps has developed. These time periods are only rough guidelines for closed activity groups. Of course, open-ended groups could go on indefinitely just as long as the member turnover was calculated and very gradual—approximately one new member added with the termination of a group member every three months.

SUMMARY

The preadolescent (approximately ages 9 to 13) is the subject of this chapter. Group counseling procedures that are unique to this age group were described. Like the previous chapter, this chapter can be read in conjunction with Chapters 2 and 3, but otherwise is written to stand by itself. The chapter began with a brief description of the preadolescent. Knowledge and skills appropriate for preadolescents are found in Appendix A.

Two types of group counseling for the preadolescent were outlined. Activity-interview group counseling incorporates aspects of activity group therapy à la Slavson and Ginott, plus interview group counseling. Activity group counseling is a modification of Slavson's activity group therapy. It emphasizes the activity or game as part of the treatment procedure more than the combined use of games followed by discussion (activity-interview group counseling). These methods were described as most appropriate for preadolescents, who are game and activity oriented at this age level. A protocol of an activity-interview group was given as an illustration of this approach, and the interactions were explained in accord with the developmental model, including the learning principles operative in behavioral change as well as the core conditions *à la* Carkhuff.

The various types of games, simulations, and media used in the activity approaches were given, and suggestions were made for their utilization within the total treatment program. Both sedentary and more physically active games are recommended.

A defense was provided for separating the sexes in the activity approaches to group counseling and a rationale for selection and group composition was outlined. Essentially, the groups are homogeneous with regard to sex, but heterogeneous with regard to problems of coping behaviors. The behavioral types for whom the activity group approaches are indicated were listed in this section.

Group size for optimum conditions was recommended at between five and seven, depending on the severity of disturbance, appropriate models available for inclusion in the group, and counselor skills. Frequency, length, and duration of group treatment were all related to the same variables considered when determining the size of a preadolescent activity group. For closed groups, six months to one year of one to two sessions of one-and-one-half hours per week were given as rough guides for the prospective practitioner of activity group approaches.

Since the activity group approaches call for settings both within the school and within the community, considerable emphasis was placed on this section. Suggested media were also included in this section. Examples of the settings included swimming pools, athletic fields and courts, gymnasiums, conference rooms, and parks. Examples of media included arts and crafts, card and table games, simulation games, physical activities, and, of course, counselee verbal participation in the interview phase. The chapter concluded with a presentation of research studies that illustrate how the various media have been implemented in activity-oriented group counseling approaches.

REFERENCES

Blakeman, J. D., & Day, S. R. (1969). Activity group counseling. In G. M. Gazda (Ed.), *Theories and methods of group counseling in the schools*. Springfield, IL: Charles C. Thomas.

Carkhuff, R. R. (1969a). *Helping and human relations.* Vol. 1. *Selection and training.* New York: Holt, Rinehart and Winston.

Carkhuff, R. R. (1969b). *Helping and human relations.* Vol. 2. *Practice and research.* New York: Holt, Rinehart and Winston.

Egan, M. H. (1975). Dynamisms in Activity Discussion Group Theory (ADGT). *International Journal of Group Psychotherapy, 25,* 199–218.

Gabriel, B. (1939). An experiment in group treatment. *American Journal of Orthopsychiatry, 9,* 146–170.

Galkin, J. (1937). The possibilities offered by the summer camp as a supplement to the child guidance center. *American Journal of Orthopsychiatry, 7,* 474–483.

Gazda, G. M. (1968). Group counseling: A functional approach. In G. M. Gazda (Ed.), *Basic approaches to group psychotherapy and group counseling.* Springfield, IL: Charles C. Thomas.

Ginott, H. G. (1961). *Group psychotherapy with children.* New York: McGraw-Hill.

Ginott, H. G. (1968). Innovations in group psychotherapy with preadolescents. In G. M. Gazda (Ed.), *Innovations to group psychotherapy.* Springfield, IL: Charles C. Thomas.

Gump, P., & Sutton-Smith, B. (1955). Activity-setting and social interaction: A field study. *American Journal of Orthopsychiatry, 25,* 755–760.

Hansen, J. C., Niland, T. M., & Zani, L. P. (1969). Model reinforcement in group counseling with elementary school children. *Personnel and Guidance Journal, 47,* 741–744.

Hargrave, G. E., & Hargrave, M. C. (1979). A peer group socialization therapy program in the school: An outcome investigation. *Psychology in the Schools, 16*(4), 546–550.

Moreno, J. L. (1946). *Psychodrama.* Vol. 1. *The principle of spontaneity.* Beacon, NY: Beacon House.

Schmidt, J. J., & Biles, J. W. (1985). Puppetry as a group counseling technique with middle school students. *Elementary School Guidance and Counseling, 20,* 67–75.

Slavson, S. R. (1945). Differential methods of group therapy in relation to age levels. *Nervous Child, 4,* 196–210.

Slavson, S. R. (1954). *Re-educating the delinquent.* New York: Harper.

Slavson, S. R. (1955). Group Psychotherapies. In J. L. McCarey (Ed.), *Six approaches to psychotherapy.* New York: Dryden Press.

Slavson, S. R. (1964). *A textbook in analytic group psychotherapy.* New York: International Universities Press.

Smith, J. D., Walsh, R. T., & Richardson, M. A. (1985). *International Journal of Group Psychotherapy. 35* (1), 49–64.

Titkin, E. A. & Cobb, C. (1983). Treating post-divorce adjustment in latency-age children: A focused group paradigm. *Social Work with Groups, 4,* 15–28.

Tryon, C., & Lilienthal, J. W. (1950). Developmental tasks: I: The concept and its importance. In *Fostering mental health in our schools: 1950 Yearbook, ASCD.* Washington, D.C.: Association for Supervision and Curriculum Development.

Varenhorst, B. B. (1968). Innovative tool for group counseling: The Life Career Game. *School Counselor, 15,* 357–362.

SUGGESTED READINGS ⎯⎯⎯⎯⎯⎯⎯⎯⎯⎯⎯⎯⎯⎯⎯⎯⎯⎯⎯⎯ ▬

General

Beker, J. (1960). The influence of school camping on the self-concepts and social relationships of sixth grade children. *Journal of Educational Psychology, 51*, 352–356.

Blakeman, J. D., & Day, S. R. (1969). Activity group counseling. In G. M. Gazda (Ed.), *Theories and methods of group counseling in the schools.* Springfield, IL: Charles C. Thomas.

Boocock, S. S., & Schild, E. O. (Eds.) (1969). *Simulation games in learning.* Beverly Hills, CA: Sage Publications.

Carlson, E. (1969). *Learning through games.* Washington, D.C.: Public Affairs Press.

Epstein, N. (1960). Activity group therapy. *International Journal of Group Psychotherapy, 10*, 180–194.

Ginott, H. G. (1961). *Group psychotherapy with children.* New York: McGraw-Hill.

Ginott, H. G. (1968). Innovations in group psychotherapy with preadolescents. In G. M. Gazda (Ed.), *Innovations to group psychotherapy.* Springfield, IL: Charles C. Thomas.

Green, B. J. (1978). Helping children of divorce: A multimodal approach. *Elementary School Guidance and Counseling, 13*(1), 31–45.

Hansen, J. C., Niland, T. M., & Zani, L. P. (1969). Model reinforcement in group counseling with elementary school children. *Personnel and Guidance Journal, 47*, 741–744.

Hammond, J. M. (1981). Loss of the family unit: Counseling groups to help kids. *Personnel and Guidance Journal, 59*(6), 392–394.

Hargrave, G. E., & Hargrave, M. C. (1979). A peer group socialization therapy program in the school: An outcome investigation. *Psychology in the Schools, 16*(4), 546–550.

Hinds, W. C., & Roehlke, H. J. (1970). A learning theory approach to group counseling with elementary school children. *Journal of Counseling Psychology, 17*, 49–55.

Irvin, A. M. (1960). Regression in children's activity therapy group. *Smith College Studies of Social Work, 31*, 22–37.

Lang, E. F. (1976). The effects of group counseling on selected culturally disadvantaged students. *Dissertation Abstracts International, 37*(5-A), 2638–2639.

Lieberman, F. (1964). Transition from latency to pre-puberty in girls: An activity group becomes an interview group. *International Journal of Group Psychotherapy, 14*, 455–464.

MacLennan, B. W., & Rosen, B. (1963). Female therapists in activity group psychotherapy with boys in latency. *International Journal of Group Psychotherapy, 13*, 34–42.

Moore, L. (1969). A developmental approach to group counseling with seventh graders. *School Counselor, 16*, 272–276.

Moreno, J. L. (1946). *Psychodrama.* Vol. 1. *The principle of spontaneity.* Beacon, NY: Beacon House.

Ohlsen, M. M. (Ed.) (1973). *Counseling children in groups: A forum.* New York: Holt, Rinehart and Winston.

Raser, J. R. (1969). *Simulation and society: An exploration of scientific gaming.* Boston: Allyn and Bacon.

Roberson, A. B. (1979). An elementary school cross-age group counseling program: Changes in self-concept, career goals, and career-related activities preference. *Dissertations Abstracts International, 40* (2-A), 681.

Rosenthal, L. (1957). Limitations of activity group therapy: A case presentation. *International Journal of Group Psychotherapy, 7,* 166–170.

Rotar, F. E. (1979). A group counseling approach using the "Human Development Program" in grades kindergarten through six. Ph.D. dissertation, Kent State University.

Scheidlinger, S. (1965). Three approaches with socially deprived latency-age children. *International Journal of Group Psychotherapy, 15,* 434–445.

Schiffer, M. (1934). *Children's group therapy: methods and case histories.* New York: The Free Press.

Simulation Games. New York: Western Publishing Co., School and Library Department, n.d.

Slavson, S. R. (1945). Differential methods of group therapy in relation to age levels. *Nervous Child, 4,* 196–210.

Slavson, S. R. (1954). *Re-educating the delinquent.* New York: Harper.

Slavson, S. R., & Schiffer. M. (1975). *Group psychotherapies for children: A textbook.* New York: International Universities Press.

Stark, G. K. (1968). A game theory in education. *School and Society, 96,* 43–44.

Sugar, M. (Ed.). (1986). *The adolescent in group and family therapy.* Chicago: University of Chicago Press.

Varenhorst, B. B. (1968). Innovative tool for group counseling: The Life Career Game. *School Counselor, 15,* 357–362.

Webb, A. P. (1964). A group counseling approach to the acting-out preadolescent. *Psychology in the Schools, 1,* 395–400.

Research

Dowing, C. J. (1977). Teaching children behavior change techniques. *Elementary School Guidance and Counseling, 11* (4), 277–283.

Egan, M. H. (1975). Dynamisms in Activity Discussion Group Theory (ADGT). *International Journal of Group Psychotherapy, 25,* 199–218.

Epstein, N. (1960). Activity group therapy. *International Journal of Group Psychotherapy, 10,* 180–194.

Hargrave, G. E., & Hargrave, M. C. (1979). A peer group socialization therapy program in the school: An outcome investigation. *Psychology in the Schools, 16* (4), 546–550.

Poitras-Martin, D., & Stone, G. L. (1977). Psychological education: A skill-oriented approach. *Journal of Counseling Psychology, 24* (2), 153–157.

Runion, K. B. (1975). The effects of activity group guidance on children's self-concept and social power. Ph.D. dissertation, University of Arizona.

Shur, M. S. (1975). A group counseling program for low self-esteem preadolescent females in the fifth grade. Ph.D. dissertation, University of Pittsburgh.

Varenhorst, B. B. (1968). Innovative tool for group counseling: The Life Career Game. *School Counselor, 15,* 357–362.

GROUP RESOURCE MATERIALS ⎯⎯⎯⎯⎯⎯ ▬

In order for the reader to be able to obtain detailed brochures and current price lists, materials are listed with reference to the companies that publish them.

Alegra House Publishers
Post Office Box 1443-F
Warren, OH 44482

Divorce Adjustment Bookshelf
A listing of books, workbooks, tapes,
    and adjustment inventories
    designed to help children deal with
    the issues raised by divorce. (Ages
    3–15)

American Guidance Service, Inc.
Publishers' Building
Circle Pines, MN 55014

Toward Affective Development (TAD)
An activity-centered program designed
    to stimulate psychological and affec-
    tive development. (Grades 3–6)

Transitions
A reassuring program that helps young
    people understand themselves and
    others during the transition from
    childhood to adolescence. (Grades
    6–9)

Argus Communications
One DLM Park
P.O. Box 7000
Allen, TX 75002

Argus Filmstrip and Paperback Programs
Captivating programs that will stimulate
    awareness and understanding of
    self and others.
    Vulture (Grades 6–12)
    Winners and Losers (Grades 5–12)
    I Am Lovable and Capable (Grades
    3–12)

Careers, Inc.
P.O. Box 135
Largo, FL 33540

Attitude Posters
Helpful for stimulating group discus-
    sions. (Grades 4–7)

Center for Applied Research in
    Education Inc.
P.O. Box 430
West Nyack, NY 10995

Coping for Kids
A program of tapes, worksheets and
    activities in twenty-eight lessons
    to help students cope with stress.
    (Grades 4–12)

Research Press
Box 3177 Dept D
Champaign, IL 61821

Skillstreaming the Elementary School Child
A complete and detailed guide on how
    to apply Structured Learning at
    the elementary level. The curricu-
    lum contains: skills for dealing
    with feelings, classroom survival
    skills, alternatives to aggression,
    friendship-making skills, and skills
    for dealing with stress. (Elemen-
    tary)

Social Studies School Service
10,000 Culver Blvd.
P.O. Box 802
Culver City, CA 90232-0802

Innerchoice
A program of self-learning built
    around small group interaction
    and consisting of forty-four
    instructional units covering such
    topics as communication, values,
    risk-taking, decision making, deal-
    ing with alcohol, and the effects of
    smoking. (Grades 6–8)

Time Share
Career Education Division
Box 974
Hanover, NH 03755

My Bread and Butterflies Career Book
Helps develop self-understanding and
  interpersonal skills. (Grades 4–8)

Walt Disney
Educational Media Co.
500 South Buena Vista Street
Burbank, CA 91521

Expectations-A Story About Stress
Film or video designed to help preadolescents recognize and deal
  with stress. Also available in
  filmstrips. (Grades 4–6)

*Decision Making: Critical Thought in
  Action*
Film or video teaching principles of
  critical thinking through a variety
  of dramatizations. Also available
  in filmstrips. (Grades 4–9)

CHAPTER 6

Group Counseling for the Adolescent and Adult

This chapter deals with group counseling for adolescents and adults beginning with age 13 through old age. (See also Chapter 8 for special applications of group counseling with the aged.) The inclusion of adolescents with adults in the application of group counseling may appear to be inconsistent. But when one considers the group medium used most frequently for these age groups, the *interview*, their concurrent treatment is observed to be theoretically sound. Unquestionably the needs of differing age groups will vary, as illustrated in the knowledge and skills appropriate to different age groups found in Appendix A. Group leaders are directed to this Appendix for knowledge and skills appropriate to adolescents and adults.

The typical adolescent and adult have achieved a stage in their development where the most natural and efficient communication medium is language, or verbalizing. Thus, with this age group, *interview group counseling* is the preferred mode of treatment. An overview of the theoretical rationale that applies to all age groups discussed in this text appears in Chapters 2 and 3.

Chapter 4 emphasizes the application of play techniques as the basic medium for change consistent with the developmental readiness of children from ages 5 to 9. Chapter 5 developed the application of a combination of activity and interview group counseling based on the medium of small group activities and games, and was followed by discussion of the interactions produced in the activities, again consistent with the developmental readiness and preferences of children ages 9 to 13. Inasmuch as adolescents 13 and older and adults are developmentally ready and generally prefer to interact through verbal communication, the primary medium for groups at this age is counselee talk.

The counseling/therapy model that is perhaps most consistent with the developmental model of this text and that describes the process of change that occurs in a counseling intervention focusing on counselee verbalization is the Cognitive-Behavior Model of Meichenbaum (1977). Meichenbaum describes his model as an integrative approach inasmuch as he considers insight development as involving both cognitive and affective domains and that frequently the coping response mediated through these domains must be taught. He summarizes his position as follows: "In short, I am proposing that behavior change occurs through a sequence of mediating process involving the interaction of inner speech, cognitive structures, and behavior and their resultant outcomes" (Meichenbaum, 1977, p. 218).

The change process consists of three phases, according to Meichenbaum. These phases, he cautions, are not lockstep, but are interwoven. Phase 1 is self-observation. In this first step, the counselee becomes an observer of his or her own behavior. (In the developmental model this phase is called self-exploration.) Meichenbaum also refers to this phase as "raised consciousness," which is the purpose of self-exploration. Typically the counselee is in a kind of "mental rut" when he or she comes for counseling; his or her thoughts and behaviors are frequently maladaptive and lead to a sense of helplessness and despair. In order to change the maladaptive thoughts and behavior, the counselee must learn to produce thoughts and behaviors incompatible with maladaptive ones. Thus, according to Meichenbaum, the counselee must discover that he or she is no longer a victim of such thoughts and feelings, but an active contributor to his or her own experience.

The counselee usually comes to counseling with some conceptualization of his or her problems. This conceptualization must undergo change if the counselee is to change. This change is mediated by the interaction between counselee and counselor and other counselees. The reconceptualization that takes place is one in which the counselee redefines the problem and as a result gains a sense of control and hope, both necessary if change is to occur. In short, says Meichenbaum, the counselee is changing what he or she is saying to himself or herself about the maladaptive behavior. Mendel (1968) contends that the assignment of meaning is part of every therapist-patient interaction, independent of therapist's theoretical rationale, and, as Lieberman, Yalom, and Miles (1973) discovered, that "meaning attribution" (adding an explanation for behavior or events) was an element significantly related to positive change in their research on small group treatment modalities.

Meichenbaum admits that the manner that a counselor uses to prepare a counselee to accept a particular conceptualization varies considerably from "hard sell" to varieties in between. He, as does this writer, recommends that the counselee and counselor evolve a common conceptualization; that is, that the counselee is an active participant in reaching a reconceptualization of his or her problems. "With skill, the therapist has the client come to view his problem from a different perspective, to fabricate a new meaning or explanation for the etiology and maintenance of his maladaptive behavior" (Meichenbaum, 1977, p. 223).

Phase 2 concerns the counselee's initiating cognitions and behaviors that interfere with the maladaptive ones. Meichenbaum (1977) summarizes this process as follows: "As the client's self-observations become attuned to incipient low-intensity aspects of his maladaptive behavior, the client learns to initiate cognitions and behaviors that interfere with the maladaptive ones. The self-observation signals the opportunity for producing the adaptive thoughts and behaviors" (p. 223).

Meichenbaum hypothesizes that the recognition of the maladaptive behavior triggers an internal dialogue. "However, if the client's behavior is to change, then what he says to himself and/or imagines, must initiate a new behavioral chain, one that is incompatible with his maladaptive behaviors" (Meichenbaum, 1977, p. 224). This new behavioral chain is guided by the translation that has evolved in the counseling process—the counselee's reconceptualization of the cause of his or her problems and his or her part in their continuance. When the counselee uses the new conceptualizations, he or she can follow with different (coping) behaviors, which then serve to consolidate the counselee's emerging structures.

"In summary, the refocusing of the client's attention, the attention in appraisal, and physiological reactions will help change the internal dialogue that the client brought into therapy. In turn, the internal dialogue comes to guide new behavior, the results of which have an impact on the individual's cognitive structures" (Meichenbaum, 1977, p. 224). Meichenbaum's Phase 2, I believe, is similar to the "understanding phase" in the developmental model. However, Phase 2 appears to go further insofar as it appears to involve some trial responses.

Phase 3 of Meichenbaum's model has to do with the counselee's emitting coping behaviors in vivo and what the counselee says to himself or herself about the outcomes of these "experiments." Meichenbaum refers to this third phase as "cognitions concerning change."

Meichenbaum emphasizes that in this phase, it is not enough to produce adaptive acts such as through skill training; rather, what the counselee says to himself or herself about these acts or behaviors and their consequences, especially reactions from others, will determine whether the behavior will persist and generalize. Meichenbaum contends that therapy is not successful until both the counselee's behavior and internal dialogue change.

Insofar as the developmental model also includes teaching new attitudes and behavior based on a consistent model for given life-skills areas, these two models do not appear to be inconsistent with each other. The major difference, in my opinion, is the contribution that Meichenbaum makes to explaining the verbalization process that takes place during counseling and therapy, especially the constructs of internal dialogue and cognitive structures and how the interview counseling process contributes to the formation of these mediating constructs. The developmental model operates on the assumption that the counselee can accept the rationale offered for a given life-skill area. For example, if the life-skill deficit area is Interpersonal Communication/Human Relations, the model that the group leader chooses to teach the counselee in this area must be logical and meaningful to the counselee before he or she will learn it. If it is too esoteric or appears unrelated to the counselee's deficit, the counselee will not expend the necessary effort to learn the model. Once the model is learned, it has within it generalizability.

Although the author uses the descriptors of knowledge and skills in Appendix A as broad indicators of counselee strengths and deficits, it is unlikely that Meichenbaum would use a similar diagnostic approach. Nevertheless, how one organizes one's thinking about these deficits is related to the interview process that prepares a counselee to accept a new model of behavior with its rationale and reject the old nonproductive model with its rationale.

PROTOCOL: ILLUSTRATIVE OF THE APPLICATION OF THE DEVELOPMENTAL MODEL TO INTERVIEW GROUP COUNSELING

The group setting, the nature of each counselee (for example, his or her needs, levels of expectation, and ability to become involved in the helping process), and the person of the group counselor with his or her qualities for helping must be integrated into a model or paradigm for counseling within the group setting. The group setting may be viewed as a potential asset or liability. If the healthy elements within each counselee can be elicited and focused constructively in helping the other group members, then the presence of several individuals maximizes the chance for help. If, however, the unhealthy elements in each individual predominate, the group could be a source of deterioration for each member. Obviously, then, the type of counselees selected for a group will be a significant factor in determining the potential for success or failure. Second, the group counselor's ability to lay a foundation for helping is of primary importance in determining whether counselees grow or deteriorate.

One might assume that when groups are perfectly balanced, there would be very little need for a group leader. Since we are still a long way from being able to set up counseling groups where a perfect or near perfect balance exists, the group leader must be the force that manages the group so as to elicit the best from each member.

I take the position that counselees as individuals and the group as a whole go through recognizable stages or phases during the treatment or helping process, and the group leader is in the position to control the pace and the development of the stages of helping. The phases employed by a group leader who follows the model described here are shown in Figure 3–1. Figure 3–1 also illustrates how these phases are related to the four basic stages that a counseling group typically follows for a given session and over the life of the group.

The protocol that follows illustrates the development of the phases through which a given counselee progresses when the group counselor and the group members use the core conditions of a helping relationship. The core conditions represent the essence of the process goals of the Developmental Group Counseling model and of interview group counseling, in particular.

The following protocol was taken from a group session very early in the life of a group. The protocol illustrates the application of the core conditions by the author to a problem introduced by a group member in *interview group counseling*. Since there was no facilitative base built with the counselee, the group counselor and members were careful to begin with interchangeable responses, especially of empathy. The interaction covered only ten minutes of group time and yet led to a decision that the counselee felt was necessary and appropriate.

The counselee was in her mid-twenties. The group was composed of male and female members from their early twenties to their late fifties. Each statement is numbered to permit easy identification.

Protocol	*Analysis*
Counselee: (1) Every time the phone rings my heart jumps. I stay worried all the time.	*Counselee:* (1) Stimulus 1 was the counselee's initial statement of her problem.
Counselor: (1) You're really pretty sure then that you're going to get some bad news every time the phone rings.	*Counselor:* (1) Response 1 by the group counselor was an attempt to convey an interchangeable response of empathy in that the basic concern of the counselee was communicated regarding the problem at hand.
Counselee: (2) Yes, it seems like that I just wait to hear some upsetting news from home.	*Counselee:* (2) The counselee response showed that she felt understood at least at a minimal level, on the Gazda et al. (1977) Global Scale (see Appendix D).

Protocol	*Analysis*
Group Member A (female): (1) Something then is going on at home that makes you think that something bad is going to happen.	*Group Member A (female):* (1) The group member simply gave another interchangeable level of response conveying understanding at the level the counselee was communicating. Now the counselor and Group Member A had both begun to build a facilitative base with the counselee.
Counselee: (3) Yes, my sister is ill, and they're trying to find out what's wrong with her but they tell me they don't know exactly what it is yet. I feel like maybe I should be there instead of eighty-four miles away, living my own life.	*Counselee:* (3) At this point the counselee feels it is safe to be more concrete or specific about her problem.
Counselor: (2) You feel kind of guilty that in this time of crisis in your family that you're not there to help out.	*Counselor:* (2) Here the counselor detects guilt expressed by the counselee and he responds to it seeking to move to a level beyond what the counselee is revealing explicitly—a 3.5 level (note Global Scale in Appendix D.)
Counselee: (4) Yes, it seems like that every time they've needed me, that I was either away at school or not available. This really has me upset!	*Counselee:* (4) The counselee confirms the feeling of guilt and tells why she feels that way.
Group Member B (male): (1) It is not the first time that they couldn't depend on you to be around? You've been away quite a bit sometimes.	*Group Member B (male):* (1) Another group member responds. He attempts to give an interchangeable-level response, but his choice of words could be perceived as confrontive by the counselee.
Counselee: (5) Yes. Maybe it wouldn't affect me so badly if this were the first crisis, but it seems like it's just been one a minute in the last five years, and I'm really feeling guilty. I'm married now, but I still feel like I have commitments to Mom and Dad.	*Counselee:* (5) The counselee does not misread group member B's response, but uses it to expand on her reasons for her feeling of guilt; therefore his response was slightly better than a level 3 — perhaps a 3.5 or 4 in terms of a gross or overall response on the Global Scale (Appendix D).

Protocol	*Analysis*
Counselor: (3) You feel that during these five years away from home you weren't doing enough to help your Mom and Dad. Now you are married and you're in less position to help them than you were before.	*Counselor:* (3) Here the counselor reenters the interaction and tries to identify the conflict that he perceives regarding the counselee's married state and the dual commitments it introduced. He was trying to go beyond an interchangeable response to get at a source of counselee conflict.
Counselee: (6) Yes. This is it, and then this is the point that confuses me. They wanted me to go away to school and get an education and get a good job. But then being away from home and getting a good education caused me not to be there when they needed me. Now, I've got a good education and am working and I feel like I should be there with them.	*Counselee:* (6) The counselee feels understood and so introduces another source of her conflict and confusion.
Counselor: (4) After they sacrificed for you, you stayed away and now you feel like you owe them something in return, but you haven't been able to pay them back in some way or other.	*Counselor:* (4) Now the counselor shows how well he understands by being concrete and specific about the source of her conflict and feeling of guilt.
Counselee: (7) I guess that's getting to the point. Just marrying and getting your own life, job, house — just how much can you participate in family situations when you are out of school, out of the house, without really feeling like you are giving them less than you really should?	*Counselee:* (7) Counselee senses that the counselor is very closely in tune with her. It is a little threatening perhaps since she comes back trying somehow to justify her current position.
Group Member C (male): (1) You just wish you knew what was a fair return to them (interrupted here by counselee response)	*Group Member C:* (1) Group member C picks up the counselee's struggle over what is fair on her part. He helps her concretize her conflict while still feeling accepted unconditionally.

Protocol	*Analysis*
Counselee: (8) Yes.	*Counselee:* (8) Counselee feels the accuracy of group member C's response and interrupts him with a "Yes."
Group Member C (male): (2) . . . after you're married, and what married people owe their parents.	*Group Member C:* (2) Group member C simply finishes what he intended to say.
Counselee: (9) Yes, especially after they've made sacrifices for me.	*Counselee:* (9) Counselee goes back to counselor's use of the word *sacrifice* in his fourth response. She accepts the fact that her parents did sacrifice for her.
Counselor: (5) I get the feeling that you feel that you do need to do more than you have done.	*Counselor:* (5) At this point the counselor makes the decision to move the counselee into more action levels and introduces for the first time a degree of *conditionality*. Heretofore, as the base was being built, all counselor and other helper responses were unconditional.
Counselee: (10) Yes, but then on the other hand, I'm wondering if I really should.	*Counselee:* (10) The conditionality is sensed by the counselee, and she backtracks slightly as she seeks to justify not doing anything about her guilt feelings — not taking action.
Counselor: (6) Sometimes you think you should, and other times you don't know what a fair return is.	*Counselor:* (6) The counselor senses the threat felt by the counselee and temporarily moves back to an interchangeable response. (unconditionality).
Counselee: (11) Yes, so if I could just work out this problem of not being so — so I wouldn't be so concerned with what's going on at home. If it just wouldn't occupy my mind so much. It really is upsetting me! It seems if I could adjust to the fact that Mom and Dad and my sister have a life, Jack (husband of counselee) and I have a life, and we can just do so much and then function normally.	*Counselee:* (11) The counselee points up (concretizes) the essence of her conflict once more.

Protocol	*Analysis*
Group Member D (female): (1) Somehow if you can just get settled in your own mind that there has to be this separation and that you can feel comfortable about whether you've been fair to your parents.	*Group Member D (female):* Group member D gives an interchangeable-level response showing empathy and unconditionality.
Counselee: (12) Do you think that it's normal to worry about a sister that is sick and ill, and is it normal to the point that you think about it 80 percent of the time and you really spend your time moping and wondering if something is deadly wrong with her? I just don't know what will become of me, nor would I know how to help Mom and Daddy.	*Counselee:* (12) Here the counselee is moving to action by asking if she is normal having the feelings that she does have. She is also indicating a readiness for conditionality on the part of the helpers.
Group Member C (male): (3) You really don't think it's normal to spend that much time worrying about her. You're also feeling quite a bit of guilt about her illness and the fact that you can't do more for her and your parents.	*Group Member C (male):* (3) The group member interprets the counselee's earlier responses as meaning that the counselee felt her concerns to be at the abnormal level. He also aims for a four-level response by an interpretation of guilt feelings over the counselee's sister's illness and then he comes back to her concern with her parents at an interchangeable level.
Counselee: (13) That's why I'm coming and asking for help, because I don't know whether or not it's normal. I kind of feel it is normal, since I do have close ties, and I really do love them — love her and my family. But then I don't have guilt feelings about her illness, 'cause this is something that I did not have anything to do with. I do have a guilt feeling about whether or not I really	*Counselee:* (13) Group member C's response forces the counselee to be more explicit in her feelings toward her sister; otherwise, she reiterates what she has been saying. She also corrects the group member's misinterpretation of the abnormality of her feelings and the fact that she does not feel guilt about her sister's illness.

Protocol	*Analysis*
did help them (parents) enough, or if I'm committing myself to home (when I say home, I mean to Mom and Dad and family) as much as I should. That is the essence of my problem. And then it seems like that because I do have these guilt feelings, and it stays on my mind . . . like I'm always wondering about if something is going to happen. If it is, I say well I should be there. Then if I were there, I wonder how much I really could do.	
Counselor: (7) What could you do? You're kind of torn between the feeling that you need to be there on the one hand, and realistically if you were there, you couldn't do anything anyway to change your sister's health, but you might in some ways be a comfort to your parents.	*Counselor:* (7) The counselor simply tries to communicate at an interchangeable level the nature of her feelings and conflict.
Counselee: (14) Yes. Now what are your views on this?	*Counselee:* (14) Counselee senses her base with the counselor and risks action or a counselor conditional response.
Counselor: (8) I guess all I can tell you Marilyn, is what I hear you telling me—that you're pretty miserable right now the way things are, and it is not getting any better, and that you need to take some kind of action to feel better about this relationship between you and your parents, that you need to do something more than you have done. I don't know what's possible, but that is what I heard you telling me— that you feel like you owe more than you've been giving them back.	*Counselor:* (8) The counselor, not prepared to give specific advice, tries to respond by summarizing for the counselee the overriding message that he had been receiving throughout the short interaction with the confidence that the counselee could translate the message to specific action. Here the counselor showed respect for the counselee's potential for arriving at specific behavioral responses.

Protocol	*Analysis*
Counselee: (15) I do feel that I have to do more. I guess now my next move must be to talk to my husband about my feeling and make plans to do something more for my parents but which will be acceptable to him.	*Counselee:* (15) The counselor was on target, and this was confirmed by the counselee's response. Something that was not known heretofore, the husband's role, was introduced and apparently this was as far as the group could take the counselee until she took the action she herself decided on.

SELECTION AND GROUP COMPOSITION ⎯⎯⎯⎯⎯⎯⎯⎯

The characteristics of a group's composition have been shown to affect the performance and outcome of the group. Shaw (1981) found that groups composed of heterogeneous personalities and member abilities tended to function more effectively. Heslin (1964) reviewed group member characteristics and also showed that the members' ability and adjustment were consistently related to how well the group performed. Jacobs (1974) reported that groups composed of friendly, expressive, and person-oriented members were more productive than groups composed of members lacking these characteristics. Reitan and Shaw (1964) found greater conformity in mixed-sex groups, while Schmitt and Hill (1977) found that racially mixed groups produced greater interpersonal tension than groups composed of one race. Zimpfer and Waltman (1982) observed that expressions of warmth in adolescent groups occurred more often when the groups were socioeconomically and heterogeneously composed.

When composing interview counseling groups of adolescents and adults, I have found that one should be careful not to mix high school freshmen and sophomores with juniors and seniors. Occasionally there can be groupings across more than two grade levels, but this arrangement should be made with care. Within the college age population, there is less of a problem in mixing lower and upper division students than there is in the high school setting; however, undergraduates are not usually easily absorbed into counseling groups of graduate students.

Outside of a school or college setting, I have worked successfully with age ranges of over forty years. Increasingly though, the generation gap has made it somewhat difficult to include the young adult of college age with adults over thirty years of age. Careful screening should be given if exceptions are to be made where the generation gap exists since the primary goal is to provide each individual with cohelpers and models that would best facilitate his or her problem resolution.

Table 6-1 Life-skills criteria and rating scheme for selecting adolescents for a counseling group

Potential Counselees	Fitness/ Health Maintenance	Interpersonal Communications/ Relationships	Identity Development	Problem- Solving/ Decision-Making
David	7	4	7	6
Paul	8	6	5	3
Mike	3	5	3	7
James	4	3	5	3
Bob	4	1	1	2
Karen	7	4	5	5
Sharon	3	5	3	4
Jill	8	6	3	6
Jane	4	3	7	4

Table 6-1 represents an adaptation of a rating system developed by Rose (1973) for selecting individuals for group counseling. The adaptation involves using the tentative generic life skills developed in the Delphi study (Brooks, 1984). By this system, prospective counselees are ranked according to their life-skills strengths and weaknesses. The ranking is done based on an interview with each prospective counselee. The interviewer uses 5 as the criterion of the average adolescent's developmental stage. Each prospective counselee is compared to this assumed mean; 1 represents the lowest point on the scale and 9 represents the highest point.

Table 6-1 illustrates the rankings for the nine prospective counselees. Because Bob was too different from the other group prospects, he would not be selected for placement in this proposed group.

We should look to the life-skills development model as a gross indicator of the type of problems that a person might be experiencing in this age group. Once we have classified the nature of counselee X's problem (perhaps the absence of an appropriate coping behavior), we can be in a position to select a person of approximately the same age (counselee Y) who has developed a successful coping behavior for the specific task of counselee X. In like fashion, we would try to find another counselee who can model for counselee Y, and so on. Matching for purposes of providing at least one good model other than the counselor should be the goal of the group counselor. Selecting two counselees who are having similar coping problems for placement in the same group would be consistent with my position as long as at least one person in the group could model appropriate coping behavior in the task area where the other one is deficient.

In addition to selecting counselees on the basis of their adequate or inappropriate coping behavior for a specific generic life skill, the pretesting of each prospective counselee on the indexes of perceiving and responding (Gazda et al., 1977b) would provide the counselor with levels of counselee functioning on these two dimensions. Since these indexes are loaded on the verbal dimension, they would be especially appropriate for use in predicting a counselee's potential in *interview* group counseling. The index of responding, in particular, is a very good predictor of the ease of difficulty with which a person can be trained systematically in *human relations* skills. These skills are essentially the ability to implement the core dimensions in relating to others. High-level (helpful) responses beget high levels. Thus, counselees will be in a better position to be heard in depth (helped) by both the counselor and other counselees if they can communicate at rather high levels in terms of their ability to be concrete or specific about the nature of their problems, if they can self-disclose in depth (high levels), and if they can be genuine in talking about their troubles. In other words, if a group member self-discloses genuinely and concretely, the counselor and other counselees are more likely to respond with high levels of the core dimensions of empathy, respect, warmth, concreteness, genuineness, appropriate self-disclosure, confrontation, and immediacy. And, conversely, if a counselee can discriminate (perceive) at relatively high levels and can respond at helpful levels as shown on the Global Scale (Appendix D), that group member is likely to be a good counselee and model for other counselees. The higher the communication level of the total group of counselees and counselor, the better the opportunity for the group to receive help and to receive it most efficiently.

GROUP SETTING

The settings for interview group counseling will vary with the age group involved. For the high school and college age groups, a comfortable conference room for seating eight to ten individuals is all that is required. The chairs should be comfortable for both males and females. As a rule, the group should not sit around a table since the table frequently is a barrier to closeness and the resultant opportunity for healthy intimacy. If the room has a rug on the floor, the group may even choose to spend part of the time sitting on the floor as they become more informal and comfortable with each other. Especially important is the necessity for complete privacy and freedom from interruptions.

The setting for adult groups may range, depending on the purpose of the group, from a room in a clinic or industrial setting to a room in a home for the aged. In all cases the room should be large enough to accommodate eight to ten individuals, and the chairs should possess the degree of comfort necessary for the physical condition of the counselee—usually padded or upholstered chairs or couches that can be arranged in a circle. Tables provide the group with an initial feeling of security, but their ultimate effect is to serve as a barrier and therefore they usually should not be included. A rug on the floor makes the room more adaptable to sitting on the floor if the group prefers—especially in the case of marathons.

With the advent of the videotape recorder came theoretical models such as Stoller's (1968) focused feedback, which is compatible with the developmental model outlined in this text. The room for interview group counseling therefore should include space and electrical outlets for a videotape recorder and camera and also for an audiotape recorder, which is standard equipment.

Ideally, the setting for interview group counseling should have a small anteroom adjacent to it and also a bathroom and a small dining area so that it could easily be adapted for a marathon session. The marathon approach is also compatible with the framework of the developmental model.

GROUP SIZE

Size alone as it affects outcome in a therapy (counseling) group is a limited and rather unproductive viewpoint. According to Goldstein, Heller, and Sechrest (1966), "group size as an influence in psychotherapy becomes meaningful only when viewed as an interactional variable" (p. 339). In defense of the preceding issue, Goldstein, Heller, and Sechrest surveyed the group dynamics research in terms of the effects of group size on *member interaction, leadership, and intermember relations*. Although they caution the direct application of their findings to therapy (counseling) groups, we can be guided somewhat by the findings from the group dynamics literature until we have carefully researched studies of the effects of group size on counselees in group counseling.

In terms of *member interaction*, the results of the Goldsten, Heller, and Sechrest review of the literature appear to be exemplified and summarized best by a study of Bales and Borgatta (1955). They studied the interaction effect of problem-solving groups as they increased in size from two to seven. They found that the rate of giving information and suggestions increased with the increase of group size, whereas the rates of asking for opinions and showing agreement decreased. As size increases, there is a tendency toward a more mechanical method of introducing information, less sensitive exploration of the viewpoints of others, and more direct attempts to control others and reach a solution—all of which are associated with the increasing constriction of time available per member (Goldstein, Heller, & Sechrest, p. 340).

When *leadership* is studied as an interacting variable with group size, the findings of Goldstein, Heller, and Sechrest in their review of group dynamics research state that when size increases, more and more of the members address the leader directly and the group becomes more leader centered as the leader in turn begins to address the group as a whole. There is a corresponding increasing acceptance by group members of leader control, and fewer opportunities remain for individual leadership and initiative of group members to emerge.

Intermember relations seem to be quite directly affected by group size. The summary of research on this variable by Goldstein, Heller, and Sechrest (1966) shows that small groups provide the best opportunity for interaction among all members and the greatest opportunity for the development of group cohesion—an important element in the success of a counseling group (see Chapter 3). In problem-solving groups, Goldstein, Heller, and Sechrest found that even-numbered groups seem to be characterized by more disagreements than odd-sized groups and that groups of five are most frequently reported as harmonious problem-solving groups.

One must reiterate the danger of making extrapolations of the research findings on group size of task- and problem-solving groups to counseling and therapy groups; nevertheless, the research *suggests* that we should construct counseling groups based on the knowledge that groups of approximately five to ten provide optimum limits within which we can best function. Odd-sized groups may produce less disagreement (since an even-split polarization is not possible). If our proposed counseling group is to contain reticent members, keeping the group small has an advantage of improving their opportunities for participation and at the same time the disadvantage of introducing greater initial threat to a person who may have expected to hide in a group. Keeping the group small, for example, five members, also could be important in giving the leader control over one or two rather aggressive individuals.

My clinical experience has led me to the development of a rule of thumb for group size based on the type of counselee in the group and the duration and frequency of group sessions. If the duration and frequency is short, such as three months, I prefer small groups of five to seven since this allows for greater intensity of interaction and greater opportunity for growth. If I have from three to six months or a year, I prefer groups of seven to ten. (With groups running beyond six months, one must allow for attrition, for various reasons, of one or two members. Therefore it would be prudent to begin with at least seven members—with other considerations such as degree of life-skills deficits of counselees taken into account.)

The nature of counselees' problems or degree of deficits and duration and frequency of group sessions have a direct bearing on the size of a counseling group. Also, as a rule, the smaller the group, the more frequently it meets, and the longer it meets, the greater the opportunity for intensity of group involvement and growth.

FREQUENCY, LENGTH, AND DURATION OF GROUP SESSIONS

The frequency of the group sessions and also the duration of the counseling sessions are directly related to the intensity of group involvement and growth. In addition to group size, frequency and duration of the group sessions cannot be considered apart from the nature of counselees' problems or number and degree of deficits and also whether a group is open or closed (continues to admit new members as old members complete their treatment—open—or retains all its original members until some agreed-upon termination date—closed). The more severe the counselees' deficits, in general, the more frequently and the longer duration they would meet.

In educational settings, the quarter, semester, and academic school year are natural division points that must be considered in composing groups. Group counselors therefore can be guided somewhat by the likelihood that their group composition might change radically at any one of these division points and thus choose to set termination dates around them. In this regard a quarter arrangement would call for at least two group sessions interspersed during a week, whereas a semester arrangement might call for one session per week of approximately one and one-half to two hours, and the same would be true for an academic school year. When I am faced with a short duration for treatment, I have used one or more marathon sessions in addition to the weekly group sessions to intensify the group involvement and potential for growth.

MEDIA

The primary media employed in *interview* group counseling are, as the name implies, counselee and counselor talk—verbal communication. Of course, this is only complete when nonverbal behaviors are observed in conjunction with verbal communications. Any media, however, that improve communication and lead to increased self-understanding of counselees and improved interpersonal communication are suitable for use in interview group counseling.

Focused feedback (Stoller, 1968) using the videotape recorder (VTR) is recommended as an auxiliary medium to be employed in interview group counseling. When it is employed, the counselor, co-counselor, or group member who is operating the camera and VTR must be selective in focusing on both discrepant and nondiscrepant feedback. In other words, the decision to view and to play back a certain segment or interaction must be made on the basis of whether the interaction helps the counselee(s) understand where they are incongruent with themselves and thus punish (discourage) or, if congruent, reinforce (reward) their responses.

The VTR adds extraneous elements to a group and is not recommended for general application to interview group counseling until the counselor has had practice using the equipment and is very comfortable with it. An audiotape recorder can also be used in a group in much the same manner as the VTR; however it lacks the quality of visual cues that are often very revealing to the counselees and group counselor. The use of galvanic skin response (GSR) in groups has been recommended in a previous work (Gazda, 1968), and it has been used successfully in a pilot study in individual counseling (Michels, Gazda, & Wiggins, 1971).

SUMMARY

Group counseling and life-skills training for the adolescent and adult were the subjects of this chapter. Consistent with Chapters 4 and 5, this chapter focuses on specific age groups (from ages 13 to old age). Tables of developmental tasks and coping behaviors expected of this age group are to be found in Appendix A.

In focusing on group counseling procedures, this chapter refers to interview group counseling as the approach most suitable for adolescents and adults. Within this form variations such as marathons and focused feedback can be adapted to strengthen the treatment program. This chapter gives details that emphasize both relationship and behavioral principles in interview group counseling. Carkhuff's (1969a,b) paradigm is the one most consistent with my current position for relationship counseling via the interview medium. The systematic and cumulative application of the core conditions *à la* Carkhuff of empathy, respect, warmth, concreteness, genuineness, appropriate self-disclosure, confrontation, and immediacy is consistent with the group stages or phases of development that I have postulated. These are Exploratory, Transitional, Action, and Termination. Their relationship to Carkhuff's model was described and also illustrated though the use of a protocol taken from one of my group counseling sessions.

Deemed consistent with the relationship and *behavioral* (life-skills training) features of Developmental Group Counseling is the Cognitive-Behavior Model of Meichenbaum. An overview of Meichenbaum's model is given to provide further explanation of the process of change for interview group counseling previously explained only through the Carkhuff model.

Consistent with Chapters 4 and 5, I have included for the age group of adolescents and adults treated in this chapter sections on selection and group composition, group setting, group size, frequency and duration of group sessions, and media. The concepts of role balancing and the provision of models for each group participant are the key elements stressed for proper selection and group composition. Identifying inadequate coping behaviors of prospective group members is a guideline also recommended to the group counselors for the selection procedure.

The recommended setting for interview group counseling is a conference-type room with comfortable chairs and a rug on the floor (for sitting on the floor when appropriate) capable of seating ten people comfortably in a circle. The setting should guarantee privacy and freedom from interruptions. Also, it should include adjacent bathroom facilities and a small dining area that would be suitable for adapting to a marathon session. Space and electrical outlets suitable for videotaping and playback are recommended facilities.

Group size for interview group counseling ranges from five to ten; however, optimum size is dependent on member interaction, leadership, and intermember relations. Odd-numbered groups seem to be least subject to polarization according to group dynamics research reports.

As a general rule, the severity of the counselees' problems will determine the frequency and duration of treatment. The more frequently a group meets and the longer the sessions (up to about two hours), the more rapid the development of group cohesiveness and positive therapeutic results. Closed groups of a quarter, a semester, or even an entire academic year are quite feasible in educational settings, whereas open groups with no specified group termination date are more practical for clinical settings. Marathon group sessions are recommended to be interspersed to increase the intensity of group involvement as the time limits suggest.

The media most used in interview group counseling are counselee and counselor verbalizations. Nonverbal expressions are basic to full communication, and therefore the group counselor must be proficient in reading nonverbal messages or expressive movements as described in Chapter 11. The use of a videotape recorder with feedback of significant group and individual member interactions and nonverbal expressions was recommended for use in a group counseling setting. Group members or co-counselors can operate the TV camera and VTR.

REFERENCES

Bales, B. F., & Borgatta, E. F. (1955). Size of group as a factor in the interaction profile. In A. P. Hare, E. F. Borgatta, & R. F. Bales (Eds.), *Small groups: Studies in social interaction*. New York: Alfred A. Knopf.

Brooks, D. K., Jr. (1984). A life-skills taxonomy: Defining the elements of effective funtioning through the use of the Delphi technique. Ph.D. dissertation, University of Georgia.

Carkhuff, R. R. (1969a). *Helping and human relations*. Vol 1. *Selection and training*. New York: Holt, Rinehart and Winston.

Carkhuff, R. R. (1969b). *Helping and human relations*. Vol. 2. *Practice and research*. New York: Holt, Rinehart and Winston.

Gazda, G. M. (1968). Group counseling: A functional approach. In G. M. Gazda (Ed.), *Basic approaches to group psychotherapy and group counseling.* Springfield, IL: Charles C. Thomas.

Gazda, G. M., Asbury, F. A., Balzer, F. J., Childers, W. C., & Walters, R. P. (1977a). *Human relations development: A manual for educators* (2nd ed.). Boston: Allyn and Bacon.

Gazda, G. M., Asbury, F. A., Balzer, F. J., Childers, W. C., & Walters, R. P. (1977b). *Instructor's manual to accompany: Human relations development—A manual for educators* (2nd ed.). Allyn and Bacon.

Goldstein, A. P., Heller, K., & Sechrest, L. B. (1966). *Psychotherapy and the psychology of behavior.* New York: Wiley.

Heslin, R. (1964). Predicting group task effectiveness from members' characteristics. *Psychological Bulletin, 62,* 248–256.

Jacobs. A. (1974). Affect in groups. In A. Jacobs and W. Spradlin (Eds.), *The group as agent of change.* New York: Behavioral Publications.

Lieberman, M. A., Yalom, I. D., & Miles, M. (1973). *Encounter groups: First facts.* New York: Basic Books.

Meichenbaum, D. (1977). *Cognitive-behavior modification.* New York: Plenum.

Mendel, W. (1968). The non-specifics of psychotherapy. *International Journal of Psychiatry, 5,* 400–402.

Michels, T. J., Gazda, G. M., & Wiggins, S. (1971). Instrumentation (GSR) and its effects on counselor responses. *Counselor Education and Supervision, 10,* 303–309.

Reitan, H., & Shaw, M. (1964). Group membership, sex, composition of the group, and conformity behavior. *Journal of Social Psychology, 64,* 45–51.

Rose, S. D. (1973). *Treating children in groups: A behavioral approach.* San Francisco: Jossey-Bass.

Schmitt, N., & Hill, T. E. (1977). Sex and race composition of assessment center groups as a determinant of peer and assessor ratings. *Journal of Applied Psychology, 62,* 261–264.

Shaw, M. E. (1981). *Group Dynamics: The psychology of small group behavior.* New York: McGraw-Hill.

Stoller, F. H. (1968). Focused feedback with video tape: Extending the group's function. In G. M. Gazda (Ed.), *Innovations to group psychotherapy.* Springfield, IL: Charles C. Thomas.

Zimpfer, D., & Waltman, D. (1982). Correlates of effectiveness in group counseling. *Small Group Behavior, 13*(3), 275–290.

SUGGESTED READINGS

General

Adams, B. N., Brownstein, C. A., Rennalls, I. M., & Schmitt, M. H. (1976). The pregnant adolescent—A group approach. *Adolescence, 11*(44), 467–485.

Ball, J. D., & Meck, D. S. (1979). Implications of developmental theories for counseling adolescents in groups. *Adolescence, 14*(55), 529–534.

Carkhuff, R. R. (1969). *Helping and human relations*. Vol. 1. *Selection and training*. New York: Holt, Rinehart and Winston.

Carkhuff, R. R. (1969). *Helping and human relations*. Vol. 2. *Practice and research*. New York: Holt, Rinehart and Winston.

Crenshaw, D. A. (1976). Teaching adaptive interpersonal behavior: Group techniques in residential treatment. *Child Care Quarterly, 5*(3), 211–220.

Gazda, G. M. (Ed.) (1976). *Theories and methods of group counseling in the schools* (2nd ed.). Springfield, IL: Charles C. Thomas.

Gazda, G. M. (Ed.) (1982). *Basic approaches to group psychotherapy and group counseling* (3rd ed.). Springfield, IL: Charles C. Thomas.

Goldstein, A. P., Heller, K., & Sechrest, L. B. (1966). *Psychotherapy and the psychology of behavior*. New York: Wiley.

Herstein, N. S. (1977). A group model for residential treatment. *Child Welfare, 56,* (9), 601–611.

Kessler, S., & Bostwick, S. H. (1977). Beyond divorce: Coping skills for children. *Journal of Clinical Child Psychology, 6,* (2), 38–41.

MacLennan, B. W., & Felsenfeld, N. (1968). *Group counseling and psychotherapy with adolescents*. New York: Columbia University Press.

Roskin, G., Kassnove, R., & Adams, J. (1978–1979). Group vocational rehabilitation counseling for drug abusers as an outreach technique in the schools. *Drug Forum, 7*(1), 35–40.

Zakus, G., Chin, M. L., Keown, M., Herbert, F., & Held, M. (1979). A group behavior modification approach to adolescent obesity. *Adolescence, 14*(55), 481–490.

Research

Brewster, R. J. (1976). Group counseling as an alternative to school suspension for high school smoking violators: Help or hindrance? Ph.D. dissertation, Rutgers University.

Garfield, L., & McHugh, E. A. (1978). Learning counseling: A higher education student support service. *Journal of Higher Education, 49*(4), 383–392.

Gatz, M., Tyler, F. B., & Pargament, K. I. (1978). Goal attainment, locus of control, and coping style in adolescent group counseling. *Journal of Counseling Psychology, 25*(4), 310–319.

Gruen, B. J. (1978). Self-concept changes in women through the self-disclosing process in group counseling. Ph.D. dissertation, Fordham University.

Jessum, K. L. (1979). The effects of group counseling on geriatric patients, institutionalized in long-term care facilities. Ph.D. dissertation, Boston University.

Jupiter, B. S. A. (1979). An evaluation of mothers' support groups for returning women students. Ph.D. dissertation, Boston University.

Karpeles, K. (1978). Differential effectiveness of structured and nonstructured group counseling as a function of facilitation for sexual attitude change and sexual behavior change among sexually normal university students. Ph.D. dissertation, University of Southern California.

Kivlighan, R. M., Jr., Hageseth, J. A., Tipton, R. M., & McGovern, T. V. (1981). Effects of matching treatment approaches and personality types in group vocational counseling. *Journal of Counseling Psychology, 28*(4), 315–320.

Klarreich, S. H. (1981). Group training in problem solving skills and group counseling: A study comparing two treatment approaches with adolescent probationers. *Corrective and Social Psychiatry and Journal of Behavior Technology, Methods and Therapy, 27*(1), 1–13.

Lamia, M. C. (1977). A preventive and treatment program for adolescents: Psychological Education. Ph.D. dissertation, California School of Professional Psychology.

Tyler, F. B., & Gatz, M. (1977). Development of individual psychosocial competence in a high school setting. *Journal of Consulting and Clinical Psychology, 45*(3), 441–449.

Whyte, C. B. (1978). Effective counseling methods for high-risk college freshmen. *Measurement and Evaluation in Guidance, 10*(4), 198–200.

Yates, C., Johnson, M., & Johnson, J. (1979). Effects of the use of the vocational exploration group on career maturity. *Journal of Counseling Psychology, 26*(4), 368–370.

GROUP RESOURCE MATERIALS

In order for the reader to be able to obtain detailed brochures and current price lists, materials are listed with reference to the companies that publish them.

American Guidance Service, Inc.
Publishers' Building
Circle Pines, MN 55014

Systematic Training for Effective Parenting (STEP) & STEP/Teen
A multimedia program designed for parent study groups.
STEP: For parents of preschool through middle-school children.
STEP/Teen: For parents of junior high and high-school youth.

Next STEP
This follow-up program to STEP and STEP/Teen offers parents the opportunity to enhance skills they learned in those programs. The focus of this program is on the parents' needs and rights and on helping parents change their own behavior. (Adults)

Strengthening Stepfamilies
A multimedia program designed to deal with the unique issues faced by this type of family. (Adult)

Contemporary Concerns of Youths
Includes discussion topics, activities, and recommended reading on the following topics:
Know Thyself
Relationship with Others
Survival Skills
School-related Concerns
(High School)

You and Your Small Wonder
Two books (Books 1 and 2) of practical, fun-to-do activities that encourage the physical, intellectual, and emotional growth of babies and toddlers. (Adults)

PREP
Program consisting of units designed to help students develop the communication and problem-solving skills associated with parenting. (High School)

Aging: A New Look
A discussion program for midlife and

older adults—and for young people and elders together—exploring the problems and promises of aging. (High School/Adult)

Argus Communications
One DLM Park
P.O. Box 7000
Allen, TX 75002

Argus Filmstrip and Paperback Programs
Captivating programs that will stimulate awareness and understanding of self and others.
Vulture (Grades 6–12)
Winners and Losers (Grades 5–12)
I Am Lovable and Capable (Grades 3–12)

Why Am I Afraid to Tell You Who I Am?
A program in communication which consists of a videotape, a text, a student journal, and a facilitator's guide. (Grades 7–12, College/Adult)

Will the Real Me Please Stand Up
Book and facilitator's guide presenting the basic attitudes and practices that promote effective interpersonal communication. (High School/Adult)

Making Life Choices
Videotape and workbook that present a three-step program of helping young people prepare for life choices. (High School)

Cambridge Career Products
#2 Players Club Drive
Charleston, WV 25311

AIDS Alert
This filmstrip or video answers the most common questions about AIDS through the use of straightforward conversation with physicians, followed by a non-threatening cartoon. (High School/Adult)

Center for Applied Research in Education Inc.
P.O. Box 430
West Nyack, NY 10995

Coping for Kids
A program of tapes, worksheets, and activities to help students cope with stress, consisting of 28 stress control lessons. (Grades 4–12)

Institute for Life Coping Skills, Inc.
Box 138
525 West 120th St.
New York, NY 10027

Adkins Life Skills Program, Employability Skills Series
A program of 10 multi-media units to help teach educationally disadvantaged adults and adolescents how to choose, find, get, and keep a job. (High School and Adult)

LexCom Productions
2720 Sunset Blvd.
W. Columbia, SC 29169

Teenage Suicide: An Approach to Prevention
A two-part video aimed at parents and dealing with the long-term relationship between parents and teens. Part I focuses on common mistakes made by leaders of young people which lead teenagers to believe that the solutions to their problems are out of their hands. Part II focuses on actions that should be taken when suicide is a possibility. (Adult)

McKnight Publishing Company
809 W. Detweiller
Peoria, IL 61615

Exploring Career Decision Making
A multimedia program of fifteen units that helps individuals gain a better understanding of themselves and

the world of work. (Adolescent and Adult)

Research Press
Box 3177 Dept D
Champaign, IL 61821

Skillstreaming the Adolescent
A program which helps the adolescent develop competence in dealing with interpersonal conflicts, in increasing self-esteem, and in contributing to positive classroom atmosphere. Available in book or audiocassettes. (High School)

Singer Education Division
Career Systems
80 Commerce Drive
Rochester, NY 14623

Community Life Skills
A seven-unit multimedia program that encourages citizen involvement in the life of the community. (Grades 7–12)

Interpersonal Life Skills
A multimedia program in eight units that helps develop skills needed to get along with others. (Grades 9–12)

Job Survival Skills
A multimedia approach in fifteen units designed for training individuals in critical personal and interpersonal job behavior. (High School)

Social Studies School Service
10,000 Culver Blvd.
P.O. Box 802
Culver City, CA 90232-0802

Innerchoice
A program of self-learning built around small group discussion and consisting of 47 instructional units dealing with such topics as feelings, communication, decision making, assertiveness, parenting, and the realities of drugs. (Grades 9–12)

Me and Others
A multi-media self-awareness program designed to help students become better acquainted with their strengths and weaknesses, consisting of worktext, filmstrips, relaxation cassette tapes, and a cassette providing 20 role-play situations. (Grades 9–12)

Studies for Urban Man, Inc.
P.O. Box 1039
Tempe, AZ 85281

Work and Leisure Satisfaction
A program to encourage understanding the person–job relationship and to aid in applying this understanding to oneself and one's own situations. (High School/Adult)

Time Share
Career Education Division
Box 974
Hanover, NH 03755

Finding Your First Job
A workbook that helps individuals learn about finding their first full-time job. (Grades 9–12)

Career Opportunities
Filmstrips or cards describing career opportunities in several major academic areas. (Grades 9–12)

Walt Disney
Educational Media Co.
500 South Buena Vista Street
Burbank, CA 91521

Before It's Too Late–A Film On Teenage Suicide
This film (or video) can be used to teach students how to spot suicidal behavior in their friends and how to save a life by being a supportive friend. (High School)

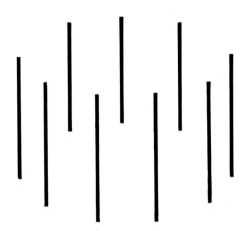

PART TWO

Part Two consists of four chapters that were selected to represent the most important application of group procedures to specialty groups. Three chapters that were in the third edition have been updated and revised: Family Group Counseling, Group Counseling with the Elderly, and Group Counseling with Substance Users and Abusers. A fourth chapter on Self-Help Groups has been added because of the rapid growth of self-help groups in our society.

C H A P T E R 7

Family Group Counseling[1]

FROM PSYCHE TO SYSTEM

Although marital and family therapy was developed in a similar milieu to group counseling and shares some members with that community, currently it is a separate entity with a separate knowledge base and an additional set of skills. Both group and family treatments seem to have their roots in Adlerian psychology. Adler's individual psychology paradoxically suggested that social connectedness is essential for healthy emotional development (Ford & Urban, 1963). Exploring family relationships was an important element in treatment. Peer interactions were also essential. This seedbed fostered both family and group movements tangentially away from individual therapy.

In the 1940s, both movements became more visible. Kurt Lewin (1948, 1951) promulgated group dynamics into a zeitgeist. In 1942 the Association of Marriage Counselors (AAMC) was founded. Both of these variants from traditional counseling explained behavior through changes in the relationship systems. More was involved in treatment than just intrapsychic issues.

Both group and family therapeutic communities enlarged, experienced successes, and gained identity over the next two decades. Details on the development of group counseling are provided in Chapter 1. Marital and family therapies merged under the common interest in conjoint therapy and a systems orientation to treatment (Olson, 1970).

---

1. Authored by Jerry A. Mobley, Ph.D. a private practitioner in Macon, Georgia who is licensed as both a Professional Counselor and Marriage/Family Therapist.

By the end of the 1970s, the situation had changed. Cartwright and Zander's *Group Dynamics* (1968) did not need another edition. No significant new breakthroughs had emerged. The lamentation was evident in the *Journal of Applied Behavioral Sciences* when some leaders of the group movement expressed "What Never Happened" in small group work (Bednar & Kaul, 1979). Another suggested the movement was only "sleeping" and would hopefully awaken (Back, 1979). At best the situation was as Alvin Zander (1975, p. 281) expressed it: "The innovativeness of research in group dynamics has been on a plateau for a few years." Although group dynamics does not include everything that is involved in group counseling, the contrast with the tone in marriage and family work is dramatic.

In their review of the 1970s, Olson, Russell, and Sprenkle (1980) state that "marital and family therapy has emerged as a significant and separate mental health field." They support that claim with the following indicators:

First, there have been over 1,500 articles and 200 books on marital and family therapy published between 1970–1979. The number of journals on this topic has increased from two in the early 1970's to more than 10 in 1979. (p. 239)

Amid economic difficulties, organizations like the National Council on Family Relations and Family Service Association of America have become established forces. Ackerman (1967), Bowen (1966), Framo (1970), Haley (1963), Jackson (1959), Minuchin (1974), Satir (1967), and Zuk (1972) have become standard-bearers for the movement by vigorously suggesting new concepts for evaluation. The past decade of vigor in marital and family counseling is a contrast to developments in other treatment modes. (Short, reasonably detailed histories of marital and family therapy are Olson, 1970; Guerin, 1976; and Kaslow, 1982.)

I believe the perceived distance between the new body of marital/family literature and techniques and other approaches, even small group work, widened over the 1970s. I construe the American Association of Marriage and Family Counselors' (AAMFC) name change to the American Association for Marriage and Family Therapy (AAMFT) as evidence of this cleavage. That significant organization separated itself from individual and group work in that 1978 name change. I believe the difference to be more than semantic.

Although some theories are applied to individual, group, and family situations, marital and family therapy more often is conceptually different from individual or group work. Levant (1978) and Ellis (1978) apply their individual oriented client-centered and rational-emotive skills, respectively, to the family and are probably justified in doing so. These approaches, however, are not in the mainstream of family therapy.

Most group counseling books, such as this one, include a chapter on the special group, the family. That inclusion is justified, but minimizes the differences between the two areas. The situation was graphically displayed in Sager and Kaplan's (1972) *Progress in Group and Family Therapy*. The first fifteen chapters consider group therapy, while the next eleven explore family therapy. Group counseling was one thing, family was another. The twain did not meet then and still do not meet.[2]

SYSTEMS THEORY

People live in systems. Daily they are involved in personal settings or *microsystems*, including family, friendship groups, immediate work settings, and classrooms; a network of personal settings or *mesosystems*; the larger institutions of society or *exosystem*, such as governmental agencies, the economic system, the business world, and religious organizations; and the culture or *macrosystem* (Egan & Cowan, 1979, pp. 70–71). The family may well be the most important microsystem and has been conceptualized in the marital and family literature as a system.

The idea of a system involves several basic concepts taken from the physical sciences and introduced into family therapy by Jackson (1959), Haley (1963), and Watzlawick, Beavin, and Jackson (1967). These characteristics include wholeness, nonsummativity, homeostasis, and boundaries. *Wholeness* suggests that a change in one part of the system will cause an adjustment in the rest of the family's structure; therefore the entire family unit becomes the focus of therapy. Even when only one family member is actually in therapy, the focus is still on the family because the total family will embrace or resist the changes that therapy produces. What one person in the family system does structures the behavior of the other family members.

From this perspective the family itself has an identity beyond the individuals. It is *not* the sum of mother, father, and children (*nonsummativity*). The family, as a unit with the marital dyad as the architects of that unit, has unwritten rules and balancing mechanisms that tend to keep the family structure and events in equilibrium or homeostasis. Thus a self-regulating function occurs within the family unit. These mechanisms resist change. Part of the duties of the therapist is to identify these mechanisms as they occur in the family. The orientation of counseling is therefore away from the specific content of the information offered by the family in favor of analyzing the transactions or the process of interaction.

The component members within a family system are different from each other and not perfectly integrated; however, the underlying rules by which they operate provide for order and predictability. In more healthy

---

2. Many of these ideas were clarified for me by Karen S. Wampler, associate professor at the University of Georgia.

families, adaptibility occurs more creatively. These rules defining who participates and how they participate are called *boundaries:*

> For proper family functioning, the boundaries of subsystems must be clear. They must be defined well enough to allow subsystem members to carry out their functions without undue interference, but they must allow contact between the members of the subsystems and others. Some families turn upon themselves to develop their own microcosm, with a consequent increase of communication and concern among family members. As a result, distance decreases and boundaries are blurred. Other families develop overly rigid boundaries. These two extremes of boundary functioning are called enmeshment and disengagement. . . . Most families fall [between these extremes] within the wide normal range. (Minuchin, 1974, p. 54)

Different-ness can be the disguised issue involved in boundary confusion. According to Satir (1967), being different in problem families is seen as a thing to be avoided because it can lead to disagreement, conflict, and eventually separation. The destructive self-protection that occurs as a reaction against "different-ness" can be powerfully expressed in "the deep reluctance to acknowledge that the marriage is in trouble" (Mace & Mace, 1976). Like any other self-protection, these efforts are antigrowth oriented and counterproductive to the marital or family relationships. Additionally, this issue acts to keep the family from seeking assistance with their difficulties.

From a systems perspective, the family is a dynamic unit; the members operate together along prescribed patterns to maintain an overall balance. As will be illustrated in the case study at the end of this chapter, to change any member, to imbalance the system from its familiar interactions, forces changes on all of the member components.

FAMILY AND GROUP COUNSELING COMPARISONS

Family and group counseling meaningfully contrast with each other. They are alike in many ways, but they differ on several important points. When the focus is predominantly skill development, either for family members or for individuals, the differences between them disappear.

Similarities

In an enlightening discussion between the author/editor of this volume and two of his peers, many commonalities between family group counseling and group counseling emerged: an active, controlling leadership, the benefit of understanding the individuals in either group, the importance of recognizing the groups' respective structures, and the validity of assessing the group as a whole (Ritter, West, & Trotzer, 1987). These four areas summarize the similarities I believe exist in both formats.

First, both counseling processes require the leader to lead. Unlike the traditional counseling group, a family in counseling is probably ready to share its distresses and enact them prematurely in the session. The counselor needs to slow the family down. The traditional group has safety needs, and desires the support of a counselor who communicates a clear direction and control over the session. Overall, the group counselor needs to speed the group up. While the needs are different, the requirement on the group leader is the same for either group. The counselor must exercise administrative control over the sessions and keep them moving at an appropriate pace.

Second, some awareness of the individuals in the group is essential. Families and counseling groups are, after all, made up of people, who may have been created equal, but do not function that way in groups. The counselor particularly needs to know if the individuals have been able to master age-appropriate skills during various developmental stages. (See the next section on Family Development.) For example, when parents are having difficulty with their 14-year-old, I immediately check the parents' sexual adjustment and leaving home issues. The parents' deficits in developing skills around sexuality and launching could be impacting their successful parenting of an adolescent through these issues. In non-family groups the counselor also addresses the members' deficit skill areas. The deficit might be in an emotional area, and the task of group counseling would be to improve their reaction to anxiety. If the need were in a social skill area, the counselor could utilize the group to encourage experimentation by a shy group member. In either the family group or the traditional group, the leader's knowledge of developmental success(es) and limitation(s) among its members is essential. I find family counseling the richer perspective because of the inclusion of the parent generation.

Third, a hierarchy among group participants evolves and patterns of communication are established among them. Whether the group is a family unit with a long history or a counseling group with a limited history, specific roles emerge to which the counselor in either setting should attend. The most precocious group members typically have more skills and are given more power in their group. The less skilled are often scapegoats for their group. Members of similar power recognize each other. Alliances form: children join with one parent against the other parent in much the same manner that a less skilled member might join with a stronger member against the group leader, or an almost endless variety of combinations. The leader would do well to recognize these situations and the roles that are being played. What the counselor does with these awarenesses may be different for the two counseling groups, but the leader needs to know not only the individuals' skill development, but also their place in the group.

Finally, some holistic assessment of the counseling group is going to occur in effective family counseling as well as in group counseling. I particularly like to comment on the group's progress—especially when the group has indeed progressed. "You have worked hard and are not where you were just a few weeks ago" equally encourages family and non-family groups. Similarly, the recognition of a gestalt or mood can be facilitative. Successfully negotiating the group's defenses, timing interventions, and terminating the treatment depend on this sense of where the group is. The group will recognize, on some level, the effectiveness of the leader who can respond to these group issues. In family work the counselor must ally with the parent who caused the counseling to occur, but the alliance is not an invitation to co-therapy. The leader cannot frustrate the group-as-a-whole while looking after any one part or subgroup. If that individual or subgroup is sufficiently needy, then conjoint therapy or group work may not be the best choice for treating them. In either type of group work, recognizing the condition of the total group is important for the group leadership.

Differences

As has been alluded to earlier, significant differences occur in family group counseling compared with group counseling. Ritter et al. (1987) summarized a couple of major variances and mentioned a third in the body of their text (p. 299): epistemology, history, and the difference between rehearsal and real life.

In his discussion of epistemology Hansen said:

> The most crucial difference between group and family counseling has to do with the epistemology. The real issue relates to the thought process. Most of individual and group counseling is based on a linear thought process of causation. When working with clients in a group, the presumption is that each person has a problem and that is the reason he or she is there. People are going to develop insight, which in turn leads to change in behavior. That's a linear thought process. In a family systems approach, the assumption is that the family has a problem and that the person identified as a client is only a symptom bearer of that system. The family is a system, and each person is connected to each other person. It's like having a mobile; you flick any part of the mobile and the entire mobile moves. It takes a change in one's thought process to believe that symptoms come out of a system. Systemic rather than linear thinking, then, is the critical difference between group and family counseling. (Ritter et al., 1987, p. 296)

Since the entire family sits before the family counselor, the interrelationships among family members can be conceptualized and treated. Group counselors lack comparable resources and are therefore limited in their conceptualizations and interventions compared with family counselors.

Another difference involves the histories of the respective groups. The counseling group is an artifact created by the counselor. This group's existence is a result of the counselor's choices. The beliefs, norms, and meeting times are shaped by the leader. Outside the counseling office the group does not even exist. Almost none of these points are true for families.

Families arrive with long, substantial histories firmly in place. The relationship to the counselor is only a recent event. The group is the given; the counselor, chosen. The belief system is not negotiable: The family members will live by their values (or reactions against their values) down to the last scapegoat. About the only aspect family counselors have control over is meeting time and place and possibly some norms about how the sessions will proceed. When the family counseling is over, not only do the members see each other, *they live together!* It is little wonder that family counselors needed the additional conceptualizations that systemic thinking has provided.

Note that family history continues to be written in the counseling sessions. Unlike counseling groups where the relationships function *as if* they were the old parent–child patterns, family groups *are* the old parent–child patterns. Change during sessions is not rehearsal; change is writing a new history in life's most significant relationships.

Family and Group Education

The focus of this volume has been to minimize the differences between family and group counseling—and that focus is probably correct since family education is more like a structured group experience than family counseling. These group experiences have structure, but allow for a level of interaction that facilitates group development. (See the section on Marital Enrichment and Family Life Education.) The group leader in this environment clearly exhibits two roles: the counselor who facilitates self-exploration and the educator who imparts essential information. The group process person stimulates interaction among the members. The academic normalizes the group members' experience with information.

The family members who most often attend an educational experience come from one generation, the parent generation. They might be learning parenting skills, divorce adjustment, or how to tell their children about AIDS prevention. Since only one generation is present, even when both parents attend, the group counseling model, rather than family counseling model, best applies.

1. A linear, not systemic change is being attempted. The parents are striving to gain insight that will lead to a change in their behaviors.
2. The dynamics of the group will depend more on the history of the families participating in the group.

Because of these issues, family themed group experiences are more accurately described as group counseling sessions rather than family counseling. Significant subgroups, marital couples, make up the group and are therefore important considerations, but they do not change the group from group counseling to family group counseling.

DEVELOPMENTAL THEORY

Family histories are studies in change. Individuals grow, relationships develop, families ameliorate, communities decay or improve, and societies evolve. The way families change follows predictable patterns.

Family Life Cycle

For years family practitioners have said that the family goes through definable stages, but worthwhile adaptations have been made in Duvall's (1957, 1971) developmental sequence. Carter and McGoldrick (1980) have added a preliminary stage before coupling, young children, and so forth, which they call the Unattached Young Adult (Table 7–1). They have also adapted the cycle to consider the special development of divorced, postdivorce, and remarried families (Tables 7–2 and 7–3).

    The gain or loss of members or ability by those members typically forces an adjustment within the family system. When family members are added through birth, marriage, or adoption or lost through death, divorce, or departure from home, the entire family enters an awkward time of stress. With the increase of status such as job promotion, the arrival of new capacity such as puberty, the loss of status through retirement, or the decrease of capacity through illness, the family enters into a time of transition (Minuchin, 1974).

Table 7–1   Stages of the family life cycle

Family Life Cycle Stage	Emotional Process of Transportation: Key Principles	Second-Order Changes in Family Status Required to Proceed Developmentally
1. Between families: unattached young adult	Accepting parent offspring separation	a. Differentiation of self in relation to family of origin b. Development of intimate peer relationships c. Establishment of self in work
2. Joining of families through marriage: newly married couple	Commitment to new system	a. Formation of marital system b. Realignment of relationships with extended families and friends to include spouse

Family Life Cycle Stage	Emotional Process of Transportation: Key Principles	Second-Order Changes in Family Status Required to Proceed Developmentally
3. Family with young children	Accepting new members into the system	a. Adjusting marital system to make space for child(ren) b. Taking on parenting roles c. Realignment of relationships with extended family to include parenting and grandparenting roles
4. Family with adolescents	Increasing flexibility of family boundaries to include children's independence	a. Shifting of parent–child relationships to permit adolescent to move in and out of system b. Refocus on midlife marital and career issues c. Beginning shift toward concerns for older generation
5. Launching children and moving on	Accepting a multitude of exits from and entries into the family system	a. Renegotiation of marital system as a dyad b. Development of adult-to-adult relationships between grown children and their parents c. Realignment of relationships to include in-laws and grand-children d. Dealing with disabilities and death of parents (grandparents)
6. Family in later life	Accepting the shifting of generational roles	a. Maintaining own and/or couple functioning and interests in face of physiological decline; exploration of new familial and social role options b. Support for a more central role for middle generation c. Making room in the system for wisdom and experience of the elderly; supporting the older generation without overfunctioning for them d. Dealing with loss of spouse, siblings, and other peers and preparation for own death. Life review and integration.

Source: From E. A. Carter and M. McGoldrick (Eds.). (1980). *The family life cycle: A framework for family therapy.* New York: Gardner Press, Inc. Reproduced by permission.

Table 7–2 Dislocations of the family life cycle requiring additional steps to restabilize and proceed developmentally

Phase	Emotional Process of Transition Prerequisite Attitude	Developmental Issues
Divorce		
1. Decision to divorce	Acceptance of inability to resolve marital tensions sufficiently to continue relationship	Acceptance of one's own part in the failure of the marriage
2. Planning breakup of system	Supporting viable arrangements for all parts of the system	a. Working cooperatively on problems of custody, visitation, finances b. Dealing with extended family about divorce
3. Separation	a. Willingness to continue cooperative coparental relationship b. Work on resolution of attachment to spouse	a. Mourning loss of intact family b. Restructuring marital and parent–child relationships; adaptation to living apart c. Realignment of relationships with extended family; staying connected with spouse's extended family
4. Divorce	More work on emotional divorce: overcoming hurt, anger, guilt, etc.	a. Mourning loss of intact family; giving up fantasies of reunion b. Retrieval of hopes, dreams, expectations from the marriage c. Staying connected with extended families
Post-divorce family		
1. Single-parent family	Willingness to maintain parental contact with ex-spouse and support contact of children with ex-spouse and family	a. Making flexible visitation arrangements with ex-spouse and family
2. Single-parent (non-custodial)	Willingness to maintain parental contact with ex-spouse and support custodial parent's relationship with children	a. Finding ways to continue effective parenting relationship with children b. Rebuilding own social network

Source: From E. A. Carter and M. McGoldrick (Eds.). (1980). *The family life cycle: A framework for family therapy.* New York: Gardner Press, Inc. Reproduced by permission.

Table 7–3 Remarried family formation

Phase	Prerequisite Attitude	Developmental Issues
Entering new relationship	Recovery from loss of first marriage (adequate "emotional divorce")	Recommitment to marriage and to forming a family with readiness to deal with the complexity and ambiguity
Conceptualizing and planning new marriage and family	Accepting one's own fears and those of new spouse and children about remarriage and forming a stepfamily; accepting need for time and patience for adjustment to complexity and ambiguity of 1. Multiple new roles 2. Boundaries: space, time, membership, and authority. 3. Affective issues: guilt-loyalty conflicts, desire for mutuality, unresolvable past hurts	a. Work on openness in the new relationships to avoid pseudomutuality b. Plan for maintenance of cooperative coparental relationships with ex-spouses c. Plan to help children deal with fears, loyalty conflicts, and membership in two systems d. Realignment of relationships with extended family to include new spouse and children e. Plan maintenance of connections for children with extended family of ex-spouse(s)
Remarriage and reconstitution of family	Final resolution of attachment to previous spouse and ideal of "intact" family; acceptance of a different model of family with permeable boundaries	a. Restructuring family boundaries to allow for inclusion of new spouse-stepparent b. Realignment of relationships throughout subsystems to permit interweaving of several systems c. Making room for relationships of all children with biological (non-custodial) parents, grandparents, and other extended family d. Sharing memories and histories to enhance stepfamily integration

Source: From E. A. Carter and M. McGoldrick (Eds.). (1980). *The family life cycle: A framework for family therapy.* New York: Gardner Press, Inc. Reproduced by permission.

The first time any of these transitions occurs, the more pronounced the effects (Carter & McGoldrick, 1980, p. 41). The second child is not as difficult to adjust to as the first. Nor is the second child going off to college. The second career change is not as upsetting. In general the same applies to most second-time experiences.

Carter and McGoldrick (1980, p. 41) also have categorized "normative" events "arising directly from the procreative and child bearing functions" and "paranormative" events that occur "frequently but not universally." Normative events are marriage, birth of child, child enters school, child enters adolescence, child launched into adulthood, birth of grandchild, retirement, and senescence. Paranormative events are miscarriage, marital separation and divorce, illness, disability, and death, relocations of household, change in economic status, and extrinsic catastrophe with massive dislocation of family unit.

Application and Support for Family Development

The importance of normative data on family development concerns the perennial twin issues of prediction and control. Ultimately, the prevention of misdevelopment and facilitation of appropriate transition for individuals, groups, or families is bound up in these two issues.

> A developmental approach allows for the programming that can be implemented *prior* to the onset of potentially damaging transitions in family process. Thus, by knowing beforehand what changes are going to occur and what skills are necessary to meet those changes most effectively, families might better be able to respond constructively to change. (Smith & Knight, 1978, p. 202)

Using developmental guidelines, individuals, groups, and families could be prepared for the next facet of their experience. This assumption applies equally well to the three groups. Missed preparation would create deficit areas requiring remediation or therapy. Actualizing people and groups are able to pass through stages of development without difficulty because they have the appropriate skills. The "clinical" population, whether they are individuals, groups, or families, probably have missed the appropriate life-skill development.

Two recent studies demonstrate the impact of developmental life events on family members as well as the family. In one of these studies, Barnhill and Longo (1978) suggest regression and fixation as potential concepts in the treatment of acute distress in families. They use those terms in a family development context: "Our work with families in acute distress suggests the need to increase the specificity with which our assessments and interventions are tailored, by incorporating the family developmental view" (p. 469). They supported Duvall's stages, saying her work is a "relatively sound framework" (p. 470). Similarly, Gartner et al. (1978) are able to describe a typology of troubled family constellations "in terms of the stress families experience during developmental crises involving structural change" (p. 47). The following four constellations are described:

> Families in the sample studied came into treatment following difficulty forming a marital relationship (Constellation A); raising children and allowing them to leave the family (Constellation B); dealing with the death or departure of a parent (Constellation C); and coping with the loss of a supportive familial network in later life (Constellation D). (p. 57)

Their results are consistent with Hadley et al.'s (1974) correlation between a developmental crisis and the onset of symptoms in family members.

Since many family events are predictable and some inevitable, a thorough knowledge of these events might frame a useful context for considering families. If these events are predictable, then they might become a source for preventing difficulties.

MARITAL ENRICHMENT
AND FAMILY LIFE EDUCATION

The concepts of family systems and predictable family development can be applied usefully in numerous ways. Two of the more popular stereotypes use these concepts to label illness or to suggest strengths to be developed. The first is remedial, therapeutic, and, unfortunately, expensive. The latter is proactive, educational, and less expensive. The issues of human frailty, personal limitations, and death in the medical model are contrasted with human potential, growth, and health in the enrichment model. Small group work and family education incorporate many of the same purposes, strategies, processes, and techniques when attempting to actualize human potential.

Explanation and Description

The humanistic movement that spawned the concept of human potential actualization is also the source of enrichment in marriage and family relationships (Otto, 1976). "The underlying hypothesis, therefore, is that marriage (and families) fail in many instances because the couples are unable to capitalize their existing resources" (Mace & Mace, 1976, p. 323). Rather than give a medical label of illness to a particular family member or the family unit, enrichment assumes that "no one or any relationship is fully functioning to its capacity. Therefore, there is always room for growth" (L'Abate, 1978). Within a variety of formats, enrichment programs seek to teach on a performance basis the skills that are basic to healthy human beings.

On a continuum from marriage and family education to therapy, marriage and family enrichment is somewhere between the two. While enrichment is educative, or more accurately, "reeducative" in nature, it is "experimental" and "process" oriented rather than "content" oriented (L'Abate, 1978).

> At the same time enrichment differs from therapy in that it is structured, prearranged, can be administered to non-clinical couples and families, and can be applied by individuals with a lower level of training than a therapist. The model is basically a preventive one. (L'Abate, 1978, p. 2)

For me the distinction between enrichment and education in the context of a Structural Group Experience (SGE) is minimal. I am attempting through the preplanned exercises to provide live experiences for the participants to illustrate and add meaningfulness to the issues I am exploring with them.

An important distinction is whether the experience is to help a group of individuals (parents) or a group of couples. With a group of individuals, I would use an activity to enhance their personal growth as evidenced in their relationships to others in the group. More honesty, vulnerability, and acceptance of their behavior in the group might be indicators of this progress. With a group of couples, the activity instead should increase the couple's growth. That progress may or may not become directly evident to the group leader or group members. Indirect evidence, such as couples smiling at each other, will make the group a pleasant place to be but not necessarily produce stimulating discussion. Nor should it. (See Mace and Mace, 1976.) My leadership of the group seems to be different depending on the difference in these two groupings.

A variety of marital enrichment and family life education are available today. Many religious and secular enrichment programs are described in Otto (1976), Miller (1975), and L'Abate (1978). The Family Service Association of America provides numerous workshop models for family life education, including *Aging Parents—Whose Responsibility, Career Planning for Women, Couples Communication and Negotiation Skills, Parent-Child Communication, Parenting Children of Divorce, Separation and Divorce, Stress Management,* and *Training Leaders for Family Life Education.*

Families and Health

Recent studies concerning the relationship between health and the family provide support for a skill-oriented family health model. The reactions of individuals to life stress events are based on their perceptions of themselves, the quality of their relationships with their immediate and extended family, the availability of other social support, and the defined problem (Caplan, 1976; Lewis et al., 1976; Neser, 1975; Nuckolls, 1975; Pratt, 1976; Prendergast, 1975). Of particular significance in the maintenance and prevention of illness as well as the recovery from or adjustment to ill health is the functioning of the family unit (Lewis et al., 1976) and its developmental stage (Crawford, 1972).

Beavers (1981) has expressed the results of his and several of his colleagues (Lewis et al., 1976) as a systems model for family health and illness. He asserts that certain forces hold family members together in much the same way that gravity pulls people toward earth. In physical science, those gravitational forces are also called *centripetal forces*. At the same time, forces exist that force family members away from the family unit. Like rocket power, these *centrifugal forces* overcome gravity (the pull of the family) and allow members to have autonomy from the family.

Both forces can be beneficial and are present in healthy families. But they can be overwhelming when they occur without the balance of the opposing force. (See Figure 7–1 and Table 7–4.) If everyone in the family is doing his or her own thing (centrifugal forces), the parents work and pursue their hobbies and the children manage themselves, the attractiveness of being a family (a centripetal issue) is minimized and will produce a

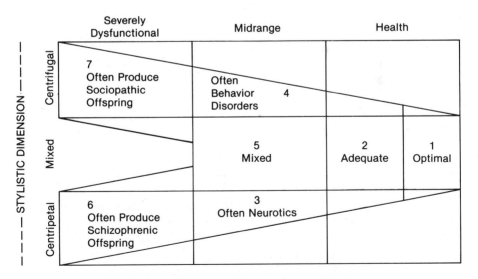

Figure 7–1 Beavers's systems model of families

Source: From W. R. Beavers. (1981). A systems model of family for family therapists. Reprinted from Volume 7 (pp. 299–307) of *Journal of Marital and Family Therapy.* Copyright © 1981 American Association for Marriage and Family Therapy. Reprinted by permission.

Table 7–4   Colón's elaborations of Beavers's family systems model

Level of Family Organization	Low	Middle	High
	Severely Disturbed	Moderately Disturbed	No Disturbance
(1) View of reality	Sameness No differentiation	Black/white Good/bad	Shades of grey Differentiated
(2) Nuclear and extended family organization	Fusions Cut-offs Fluidity Overt breakdown Overt cross-generational collusions	Limited extended family contact not enough to absorb stress Rigidity Covert cross-generational collusions	Active extended family contact Enought to absorb N.F. stress Spouse unit dominant Sib subunit different from spouse unit
(3) Sense of time	Sense of timelessness Time does not seem to pass Things don't change	Distorted Passage of time not fully accepted	Passage of time is accepted Time changes are celebrated
(4) Vulnerability to stress	Very high Multiproblems	Are subject to stress There are unresolved problem areas	Less subject to stress Can resolve problems
(5) Parental control	Intrusive Tell kids what to think and feel	Criticism is frequent Attempt to control what kids think and feel Rigid rules	Accept kids' thoughts and feelings Try to shape kids' behavior Clear, flexible rules
(6) Communication	Unable to complete communication sequences Reactive response to one another Unable to resolve conflict	Able to complete some communication sequence Able to achieve partial resolutions Rules more rigid	Able to complete communication sequences Able to achieve full resolutions All are to be listened to and responded to

Level of Family Organization	Low	Middle	High
	Severely Disturbed	Moderately Disturbed	No Disturbance
(7) Affect	Negative Chaotic Without variety	Negative Some variety Competitive	O.K. to express both positive and negative Cooperative
(8) Reaction to separation, loss, death	Very disorganized Refuse to accept or mourn Denial of death	Frozen reaction Limited acceptance Partial mourning	Do accept loss Do let go Do mourn
(9) Physical context	Impoverished Substandard housing Inadequate food and clothing	More options Adequate food, clothing, and housing	Many options Abundance of food, clothing, and housing
(10) Employment context	None or very limited No sense of the future being better	Usually employed on regular basis Jobs tend to be routine Limited opportunity to advance	Regularly employed Interesting jobs Opportunities to advance
(11) Social context	Isolated Alienated Fragmented	Less alienation Some connection and cohesiveness	Not alienated Active, viable Social contact Many options

Source: From F. Colón. (1980). The family cycle of the multiproblem poor family. In E. A. Carter and M. McGoldrick (Eds.), *The family life cycle: A framework for family therapy.* New York: Gardner Press, Inc. Reproduced by permission.

somewhat predictable affect. On the other extreme, if the parents do not allow their children (or each other) to explore a life away from home and appropriately leave the nest without guilt, the gravity becomes repressive to the emotional well-being of children (or spouse). Health includes a balance of identification with and support from the family unit (centripetal forces) and at the same time encouragement and recognition for efforts toward self-sufficiency (centrifugal forces).

In general Types 1 and 2 in Beavers's (1981) scheme refer to healthy, balanced families. The individuals are capable of managing their lives. Parents and children have mastered the appropriate developmental skills. At the same time they are each contributing to their family relationships and the family as a whole. They are recognizable as a family unit.

The fourth and seventh types, more centrifugally imbalanced, are also powerful individuals. They seem to be able to look after themselves. In the more extreme case, Type 7, this appearance is the result of overcompensation. Violent males have often been forced to take too much responsibility too soon in their development (Weitzman & Dreen, 1982). Thus they overcompensate for their lack of development and take on a pseudo-power. These people also tend to be drug abusive. A milder form of this process, Type 4, includes people who are defensive and hide behind blaming behaviors. While individually the family members appear to be well defined, the family lacks identity as a unit. It does not resemble the healthy family because it lacks this sense of being a group (Beavers, 1981, pp. 303–304).

Types 3 and 6 are the inverse of Types 4 and 7. The family is well defined, but the members are indistinct. The individual members in Types 3 and 6 are not capable of taking responsibility for themselves in numerous ways and can become tremendously dependent. Neither type can accept their hostile feelings and tend to repress them. In the extreme (Type 6), schizophrenia is the child's solution to the dilemma of emotional ambivalence (Beavers, 1981, pp. 303–304). Incest seems to follow this blurred individual interpretation: the qualities of the marriage become attributed to someone who is not the marital partner (Finkelhor, 1978, p. 45).

Type 5 families usually have one parent in Type 3 and the other in Type 4. Many times spouse abuse involves the dependency of the centripetal style coordinated with the hostility of the centrifugal style (Hendricks-Matthews, 1982).

Families can be entrenched in their centripetal or centrifugal styles to greater or lesser degrees. Numerous issues appear to be involved (Table 7–4). The family's view of reality includes their relationship to their extended families; their sense of time; their vulnerability to stress; the amount and quality of parental control; their communication patterns and problem resolution; their range of expressed affect; how they respond to loss; their physical environment; their employability; and their social context (Colón, 1980). More functional families are more highly skilled individuals who are better at networking within their families and their communities. The least functional families tend to be impoverished on several important issues. More typically families will have strong areas and deficits.

This conceptualization might help professionals to recognize family needs and attempt to help people within their relationship systems. The primary system we probably should consider is the family.

FAMILY LIFE EDUCATION RESOURCES

A number of programs have been popularized to improve marriages and family living. Over 800 different approaches and organizations have been catalogued by the Family Resource Coalition.[3] The following selective programs form a background for some generalizations that will be made about Family Life Education (FLE).

FLE programs can be designed to improve marital or parenting skills. Several programs are available in the area of couples enrichment: the ACME Marriage Enrichment Program (Mace & Mace, 1976), the Conjugal Relationship Modification Program (Elliot & Saunders, 1982), Marriage Encounter (Bosco, 1973), and Minnesota Couples Communication Program (Miller, Nunnally, & Wackman, 1976). Some of these programs have developed to the point that they include leader certification and follow-up programs.

Most of my experience in Family Life Education has been in parent education and involved either Family Service America[4] or the American Guidance Service.[5] FLE has been part of the mission of Family Service America's approximately 300 member agencies for decades. They publish manuals for programs in the following areas: *Training Leaders for Family Life Education, Parent-Child Communication, Parenting Children of Divorce, The Single Parent Experience, Parents of New Borns,* and *Effective Stepparenting.*

The American Guidance Service's material includes excellent audio cassettes, which contain dramatized situations that illustrate the point being taught, along with manuals, colorful charts, and posters. Their holdings include *PREP for Effective Family Living* (a pre-parenting program for teens), *Systematic Training for Effective Parenting (STEP)* (also available in Spanish), *STEP/Teen* (STEP skills applied to parents of teen-agers), and *Strengthening Stepfamilies.*

Two other programs seem worthy of mentioning: Gordon's (1970) time-honored *Parent Effectiveness Training* (P.E.T.)[6] and Bavelok and Comstock's (1983) abuse prevention *Nurturing Program.*[7,8] The basics from P.E.T. are often included in other parenting programs. Unlike all of the other programs mentioned here, the *Nurturing Program* has components for both

3. Family Resource Coalition, Suite 1625, 230 North Michigan Avenue, Chicago, Illinois 60601. (312) 726-4750.

4. Family Service America, 11700 West Lake Park Drive, Milwaukee WI 53224. (800) 221-2681.

5. American Guidance Service, Publisher's Building, Circle Pines, MN 55014. (612) 786-4343

6. Effectiveness Training, Inc., 531 Solana Beach, California 92075. (612) 481-8121.

7. Family Development Resources, Inc., 767 Second Avenue, Eau Claire, WI 54703. (715) 833-0904.

8. National Committee for Prevention of Child Abuse, 332 South Michigan Avenue, Suite 950, Chicago, IL 60604-4357. (312) 663-3520.

parents and children. While the parents are getting support and direction in one room, children are being given age-appropriate activities teaching family life and child abuse prevention.

SELECTION OF MEMBERS
AND COMPOSITION OF GROUPS

Marital and family enrichment programs operate on a principle that is indigenous to the selection process. Enrichment is *not* therapy. Participants are attempting to make satisfying relationships even better, rather than working to rehabilitate dysfunctional relationships. The educational and experiential components in these programs build on already existing strengths in the individuals and couples. They are typically motivated to change and are able to assimilate information without much difficulty.

With this principle in mind, individuals or couples who are over-whelmingly lacking in strengths to build on or lacking in motivation are probably not good candidates for either a marital or a parenting enrichment program. This rule would include most of the general screening issues that are covered in Chapter 2 of this book.

Having provided the rule, consider the exceptions. I prefer the motto: "Proceed with courage." I take an optimistic view of who can get help from groups; in most situations I prefer that people prove they cannot benefit from the group, rather than have me eliminate them.

If the leader has included a few questionable group members, several other changes could be considered. A coleader would be my first adjust-ment if the group were less than ideal. One leader could help in processing what is occurring in the group, while the other continues the program. Without much interruption a leader could even remove a person or couple if the situation became problematic. Remember: in family work the leader would have two problem people, husband and wife, not just one. There-fore some extra consideration about a co-facilitator might be prudent.

Also, another way to protect against the negative influence of a prob-lem individual or couple is to provide off-setting positive group members. I have utilized a policy of *never* charging people who want to retake a course, in order to recruit members who have had experience with the concepts in the course. These members become peer facilitators and role models for the group. Special care can be made to pair the potential problem person(s) with the potential support person(s) during specific activities.

The enrichment process is nevertheless set to operate around certain norms and motivation. Reality often operates in opposition to these norms. Juvenile courts and state social workers frequently refer needy people to parenting groups for help. Getting enough health in the group to have something to build on is not easy. As Parent's Anonymous sponsor, I struggled with this problem and found a solution.

The support group met weekly and was interrupted three times a year for parent education. The combination of family enrichment and ongoing support provided an environment in which the peer facilitators could be developed and resistance could be worked through. With both processes operating, virtually no screening of clients has been necessary for several years.

GROUP SETTING

Almost any place can be a meeting place for a couples or family enrichment program. FLE most often occurs in professional offices, schools, churches, and community centers. Retreat facilities are particularly popular for couples enrichment programs because they isolate the participants from outside distractions.

To repeat the obvious, care should be taken to establish the location/setting for couples/family treatment. The location can determine who attends. If you meet at the county health department, your clientele will probably come from those who use its services. A clear marketing decision needs to be made about who is being targeted for services.

Whatever location is used, can it be secured? Is the room available 30 minutes before and after the sessions? In a hospital or hotel, can the paging system be controlled? What is happening in the next room? A rowdy meeting or wedding party with a band can be devastating. Can the temperature be controlled?

The quality of the room is important. Is it comfortable and well-lighted? Does the furniture move? Pews will *not* work for enrichment. The furniture has got to move or the people need to be comfortable sitting on the floor.

The too-large room is as bad as the too-small room. A sense of needing more people or having an echo is a real distraction. In a perfect world, the just-right room would be found. Most are still looking for it.

Even if the perfect place were found, another issue would still need to be considered: confidentiality. Industries are beginning to use pro-health, prevention programs. They have excellent training facilities in many cases. Group leaders need to be sensitive and to protect the identities of those employees who want to remain anonymous. Thus, meeting in the front office conference room will not work. In the same regard, some places in the community may be too visible to allow the confidentiality of some group members.

GROUP SIZE

The size limit that most often occurs with enrichment programs seems to be 20 participants. My experience confirms that when an educational program that could have some therapeutic qualities gets beyond this number, the group becomes an audience. Having fewer than 20 participants may be desirable from the perspective of group dynamics, but it handicaps both the income of the leader(s) and the outreach attempts of the program.

Smaller groups require more participation from each group member. Pressure will bear upon a group of 8 to have everyone share. If the members are introverted, the group will become uncomfortable in a way that does not occur with 12 or more members. Having more participants protects both the group and the group leader from this discomfort.

When couples are involved, starting a multi-week program with 8 or fewer members has additional complications. If someone cannot attend, two participants will be missing that night. Should two families be affected by sickness or transportation problems, half the group may be absent. A group of four is not interesting to lead and is poor utilization of most leaders' time. By arranging a larger group and cancelling smaller groups, the family group counselor manipulates the size of the group to produce a functional group.

FREQUENCY, LENGTH, AND DURATION OF GROUP SESSIONS

Family Life Education programs are paced into 15 to 20 hour lengths that can be weekend intensive or can meet weekly for as many as 12 weeks. To imagine that any significant change would occur for an individual or couple in less time is not realistic; however, shorter programs can be useful and might be necessary.

Marriage enrichment retreats are most often single-weekend events that start on Friday night and conclude on Sunday. The vulnerability and communication learned in one session can be immediately applied to the remainder of the time. Having a week between meetings would probably distract the couple, rather than give them time to apply what they had learned.

In contrast, parent enrichment almost never uses this weekend marathon format. The time between sessions is perceived as a positive aspect. The parents can take the information and insights gained from their group and attempt applications in their world, and then return the next week for additional coaching. This process is continued for months—until the new behaviors are firmly established and the couples' resistance no longer exists.

Asking adults to give up an hour-and-a-half or two hours every week for several months seems to minimize the reality of baseball, music lessons, single parenting, vacations, and a host of other middle-class experiences. Furthermore, great segments of our communities need some help, but their situations are too chaotic to be able to commit to meeting for months. If they could predict and control their family experience for several months, they would have achieved a great deal.

By scaling down the goal of enrichment from changing a life to altering a specific response, a shorter time period can be utilized with meaningful results. Industry is offering its employees "smart lunches," where single topics like active listening or the family council can be discussed without reference to all of the related parenting issues. Each presentation is a surprise from a group dynamics perspective, but can be useful without the other months of meetings. It is also helpful if these presentations are tied to some other activity like the company's Employee Assistance Program, an ongoing educational program in the community, or a city-wide emphasis on children or child abuse.

After years of frustration from trying to coerce court referrals to finish the months of FLE in the standard format, I reorganized for success. Several professionals and I experimented with four, two-hour sessions of Systematic Training for Effective Parenting—and had great success. Once again, our goals had to be reduced, but it was better to present a program in which participants could be successful than one that they could only partially attend, which would produce feelings of failure. My motto again was "Proceed with courage."

MEDIA

The entire range of media is being used in family group enrichment. Written and electronic material in every form is available. The western world has gotten sophisticated to the point that these media are compulsory. The most typical media include books, audiotapes, flipcharts, and tests. One particular testing procedure is discussed in a case study at the end of this chapter.

Family counseling has also created the *genogram* (Bowen, 1966) and *performed sculpting* (Satir, 1967) that are sometimes used in Family Life Education. The genogram recreates the family's family tree on paper. Included are intergenerational issues that seem to intrude in the current generation's functioning. Sculpting is another way to clarify family issues. The counselor physically recreates the relationship patterns occurring within the family, using the family members themselves or stand-ins. Physical positioning is assumed for family members to illustrate their relationships to each other. Repositioning occurs until an "ideal" or consensus arrangement is reached.

FAMILY COUNSELING: A CASE EXAMPLE

While family counseling might be the recommended treatment method, in many settings family counseling is not possible or practical because too few family members can be present on a regular basis. School psychologists and counselors in the school system often are unable to meet with parents and surely cannot meet with all the siblings and/or extended family for conjoint counseling, even when a tremendous need is present. Much the same situation exists for institutionalized family members. Knowledge of the family system could be critical, but the opportunity for obtaining that information might be lacking.

That problem was exemplified in the following case study. A nine-year-old Spanish-American, whom I will call Dan Ortego, illustrates what can happen if the skilled counselor attempts to help without some awareness of the family system. It also demonstrates one way that the counselor could identify some of the family dynamics without conjoint counseling.

The family's structure was monitored using a multidimensional scaling computer program from the Bell Laboratories, Individual Differences Scaling (INDSCAL) (Carroll & Chang, 1970). The process for gathering the information was the same as Mobley and Gazda (1981) have described, with one exception: the results were *not* taken into consideration until *after* termination with the family. The dimensions were interactively named by the family at that time. INDSCAL was *not* used to shape the treatment, only to record the effects of it.

Problem

Dan's mother expressed concern over the difficulty Dan was having in school and reported that his younger brother (approximately one year younger) was having many of the same difficulties. Both were taking 75mg of Cylert® per day to manage their "hyperactivity." She was also concerned that Dan did not have a "positive male influence" since her divorce from his Mexican father.

Although Dan had improved in the past year and was having a successful year at elementary school, his mother wanted to assess the difficulties of having moved the children across cultures (from Mexico) and to learn what she could do to help them make the transition. Unlike the male children, the older daughter had done well in school and had pleased her mother by gaining proficiency in English prior to moving to the United States.

Procedure

During the first three sessions, a variety of psychological instruments were administered, as well as the computer-assisted sociometric, INDSCAL. The latter was given pre- and post to assess the family's dynamics at the beginning and ending of counseling, respectively.

Dan manifested several behaviors during testing that persisted to varying degrees throughout the three months he was in counseling: (1) a concern over the quality of his performance, (2) a lack of realistic self-evaluation, (3) an enjoyment of personal attention, and (4) a variety of off-task behaviors that seemed designed to control the sessions. Although his test performances indicated essentially normal abilities, the above aspects of his social-emotional life had become familial issues and needed to be amended.

Since the problem areas suggested by Dan's behavior involved the entire family unit and the children's sex-role models, the INDSCAL ratings were performed including all possible models: the former husband, two female maids, and mother's present male friend. This task was accomplished using only the perceptions of the mother and three children.

Counseling

A relationship-building form of counseling was begun to develop the positive relationship with Dan that his mother had suggested. His shortcomings were not discussed in favor of his frustrations. He expressed confusion at times, hostility toward his mother, admiration of his father's exciting style, and impatience with his sister.

In a consultation with the mother, the counselor suggested that Dan was working hard to get her attention. She might be able to avoid his energetic intrusions into her personal time if she gave him special time first. No mention was made of the other children since she had asked for help with only Dan.

Also, in reviewing the test results, it was suggested that she encourage Dan's effort rather than his results. At present he might not be experiencing many successes, and he could become more discouraged without additional intervention from her. The medication was continued.

Pretest Results

In Figure 7–2, the former husband (number 1) is isolated from the family unit and diagonally opposite from the mother, daughter, and male friend. In this contrast of opposites, the new male friend is farther away from the origin—more different from the former husband—than anyone else in the lower left quadrant. At the same time, both boys are in the upper left quadrant and opposite the second housekeeper a little and the first housekeeper a lot. The boys and the housekeepers seem to be adversaries.

Several important issues seem to be summarized in this picture: (1) the people falling below the line, with only one exception, are female while those above are male, and (2) those who are currently in the family unit are on the left while those who are absent are on the right. The counselor might make several hypotheses about this particular family based on these arrangements:

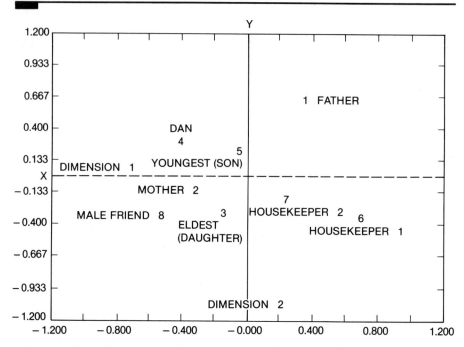

Figure 7–2   INDSCAL graph of family dynamics—precounseling

1. Some of the qualities in her sons, particularly the eldest, over which the mother might be concerned are probably related to the boys' similarity to their father.
2. Since the father was not perceived as a contributing part of the family and was ultimately excluded, being like the father could produce an internal tension in the boys to perform "better" than the father did. Failures would have a tremendous impact on them.
3. Being female (different from the father) in this family does not produce the stress that being male (like the father) does.
4. The x-axis might be a continuum from most to least important people in terms of significance to this family. Dan is perceived by the family (since this graph is a composite of everyone's ratings) as more important than even the mother. Misbehavior pays off.
5. The boys seem to be allied together to weather being torn between their images of their father on the one hand (upper right) and their mother, or worse still, the male friend on the other hand (lower left).[9]

9. For additional information concerning the development of these hypotheses, see Mobley and Gazda (1981).

These hypotheses of family values and interrelationships are similar in kind to that which would have come out of conjoint family therapy. This type of information provides a larger context in which to understand the nuclear family's needs for sexual identity and personal accomplishment.

Posttest Results

After three months the INDSCAL analysis was repeated (Figure 7–3) and many changes were noted: (1) the daughter was an isolate; (2) the youngest child was identified with his father; and (3) Dan was in alliance with his mother and her male friend. Significant changes had occurred in this family's structure. The additional time the mother had spent with Dan had achieved its goal of closeness with her and possibly identification to a "positive male influence" (and away from his father); however, the rest of the system changed too. The daughter was now an isolate, and the youngest child had become almost completely identified with the father. Mother had exchanged her problem with Dan for a problem with the younger brother and had lost much rapport with her daughter. The operation (counseling) was a success, and the patient died (family got worse).

Dan had developed significantly as a person and family member, and those changes were reflected in the INDSCAL printout. His schoolwork

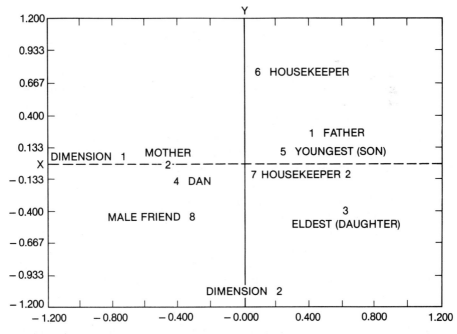

Figure 7–3   INDSCAL graph of family dynamics—postcounseling

had continued to improve; he was able to be involved in peer play without his brother; and he more consistently contributed to the family (for example, he washed dishes and kept his room clean), while being less demanding. Yet, although the time and attention given to Dan by the single parent was valuable, the impact of these efforts was negative for the rest of the family system. Special time was extended by the mother to all of the children on a regular schedule, and the siblings' discouragement almost immediately diminished.

Discussion

Often the treatment that counselors, psychologists, and therapists would like to offer clients involves the entire family system; however, the circumstantial realities may allow only a parental conference at best. Effecting change in part of the system without providing for changes in the entire system can generate repercussions that will either invalidate the counseling or create problem situations as detrimental as the ones being overcome.

The discouragement that occurred in the system with the two other children while Dan was being encouraged is explainable in terms of systems theory. If there are a fixed number of reinforcements within the system to go around, when one person gets them, the others are forced to do without. This effect of Dan's counseling is both predictable and reasonable. Being able to monitor or even use these results of counseling is an important part of conjoint family therapy/counseling.

In this case an alternative to conjoint counseling, a powerful computer-assisted sociometric, was used. While for exploratory purposes the results were not applied in treatment, INDSCAL could have provided the counselor with feedback from the entire family unit while he worked with predominantly one person from that unit. Not only might INDSCAL prove to be a "technological breakthrough for family therapy" (Mobley & Gazda, 1981), but also it might offer an alternative to conjoint family therapy/counseling where the need is for family, not just individual, therapy/counseling, but family therapy/counseling is not possible or practical.

SUMMARY

This chapter begins by pointing out the conceptual difference between marital and family therapy and group counseling and therapy. Next the family as a system is explored. From a systems perspective, the family is a dynamic unit in which the members function together along prescribed patterns to maintain an overall balance.

The developmental sequence of families is illustrated by Carter and McGoldrick's (1980) developmental family life cycle and related to the developmental theory espoused in this text.

Beavers's (1981) system for classifying functional/dysfunctional family types is illustrated and discussed.

The chapter next addresses the topics addressed in each of the applied chapters in this text: selection and composition of members; group setting; group size; frequency, length, and duration of sessions; and media employed.

The chapter concludes by presenting the unique application of multidimensional scaling to the diagnosis and treatment of a broken family.

REFERENCES

Ackerman, N. W. (1967). *Expanding theory and practice in family therapy*. New York: Family Service Association of America.

Back, K. W. (1979). The small group: Tightrope between sociology and personality. *Journal of Applied Behavioral Science, 11,* 283–294.

Barnhill, L. R., & Longo, D. (1978). Fixation and regression in the family life cycle. *Family Process, 17,* 469–478.

Bavolek, S. J., & Comstock, C. (1983). *Nurturing program*. Eau Claire, WI: Family Development Resources.

Beavers, W. R. (1981). A systems model of family for family therapists. *Journal of Marital and Family Therapy, 7,* 299–307.

Bednar, R. L., & Kaul, T. J. (1979). Experimental group research: What never happened! *Journal of Applied Behavioral Science, 11,* 311–319.

Block, D. A. (1973). The clinical home visit. In D. A. Block (Ed.), *Techniques of family therapy: A primer*. New York: Grune & Stratton.

Bosco, A. (1973). *Marriage encounter: A rediscovery of love*. St. Meinrad, IN: Abby.

Bowen, M. (1966). The use of family theory in clinical practice. *Comprehensive Psychiatry, 7,* 345–374.

Caplan, G. (1976). The family as a support system. In G. Caplan & M. Killilea (Eds.), *Support systems and mutual help*. New York: Grune & Stratton.

Carroll, J. D., & Chang, J. J. (1970). Analysis of individual differences in multidimensional scaling via an N-way generalization of "Eckert-Young" decomposition. *Psychometrika, 35,* 238–319.

Carter, E. A., & McGoldrick, M. (Eds.) (1980). *The family life cycle: A framework for family therapy*. New York: Gardner Press.

Cartwright, D., & Zander A. (1968). *Group dynamics: Research and theory*. New York: Harper & Row.

Colón, F. (1980). The family life cycle of the multiproblem poor family. In E. A. Carter & M. McGoldrick (Eds.), *The family life cycle: A framework for family therapy*. New York: Gardner Press.

Crawford, C. O. (1972). *Health and the family: A medical-sociological analysis*. New York: Macmillan.

Duvall, E. (1957). *Family development*. Chicago: Lippincott.

Duvall, E. (1971). *Family development*. Philadelphia: J. B. Lippincott.

Egan, G., & Cowan, M. (1979). *People in systems: A model for development in the human-service professions and education*. Belmont, CA: Brooks/Cole.

Elliott, S. S., & Saunders, B. E. (1982). The systems marriage enrichment program: An alternative model based on systems theory. *Family Relations, 31* (1), 52–60.

Ellis, A. (1978). Family therapy: A phenomenological and active directive approach. *Journal of Marriage and Family Counseling, 4,* 43–50.

Finklelhor, D. (1978). Psychological, cultural and family factors in incest and family sexual abuse. *Journal of Marriage and Family Counseling, 4,* 41–49.

Ford, D. H., & Urban, H. B. (1963). *Systems of psychotherapy: A comparative study.* New York: Wiley.

Framo, J. (1970). Symptoms from a family transactional viewpoint. In N. Ackerman, J. Lieb, & J. Pearce (Eds.), *Family therapy in transition.* Boston: Little, Brown.

Gartner, R., Fulmer, R., Weinshel, M., & Goldklank, S. (1978). The family cycle: Developmental crises and their structural impact on families in a community mental health center. *Family Process, 17,* 47–58.

Gordon, T. (1970). *P.E.T.: Parent effectiveness training.* New York: Peter H. Wyden.

Guerin, P. J. (1976). Family therapy: The first twenty-five years. In P. J. Guerin (Ed.), *Family therapy and practice.* New York: Gardner Press.

Hadley, T., Jacobs, T., Milliones, J., Caplan, J., & Spitz, D. (1974). The relationship between family developmental crisis and the appearances of symptoms in a family member. *Family Process, 13,* 207–213.

Haley, J. (1963). *Strategies of psychotherapy.* New York: Grune & Stratton.

Hendricks-Matthews, M. (1982). The battered woman: Is she ready for help? *Journal of Contemporary Social Work, 63,* 131–137.

Jackson, D. D. (1959). Family interaction, family homeostasis and some implications for conjoint family psychotherapy. In J. J. Masserman (Ed.), *Individual and family dynamics.* New York: Grune & Stratton.

Kaslow, F. W. (1982). History of family therapy in the United States: A kaleidoscopic overview. In F. W. Kaslow (Ed.), *The international book of family therapy.* New York: Brunner/Mazel.

L'Abate, L. (1978). *Enrichment: Structural introventions with couples, families, and groups.* Washington, D.C.: University Press of America.

Levant, R. (1978). Family therapy: A client-centered perspective. *Journal of Marriage and Family Counseling, 4,* 35–42.

Lewin, K. (1948). *Resolving social conflicts.* New York: Harper.

Lewin, K. (1951). *Field theory in social science.* New York: Harper.

Lewis, J., Beavers, W., Gossett, T., & Phillips, V. (1976). *No single thread: Psychological health in family systems.* New York: Brunner/Mazel.

Mace, D. R., & Mace, V. (1976). Marriage enrichment—A prevention group approach for couples. In D. H. Olson (Ed.), *Treating relationships: Bridging theory and practice.* Lake Mills, IA: Graphic Publishing Co.

Miller, S. (Ed.) (1975). *Marriage and families: Enrichment through communities.* Beverly Hills, CA: Sage Publications.

Miller, S., Nunnally, E. W., & Wackman, D. B. (1976). A communication training program for couples. *Social Casework, 57,* 9–18.

Minuchin, S. (1974). *Families and family therapy.* Cambridge: Harvard University Press.

Mobley, J. A., & Gazda, G. M. (1981). Multidimensional scaling: A technological breakthrough for family therapy. *Journal for Specialists in Group Work, 6,* 52–60.

Neser, W. (1975). Fragmentation of black families and stroke susceptibility. In B. Kaplan and J. Cassel (Eds.), *Family and health: An epidemiological approach.* Chapel Hill, NC: Institute for Research in Social Service.

Nuckolls, K. (1975). Life crises and psychosocial assets: Some clinical implications. In B. Kaplan and J. Cassel (Eds.), *Family health: An epidemiological approach.* Chapel Hill, NC: Institute for Research in Social Sciences.

Olson, D. H. (1970). Marital and family therapy: Integrative review and critique. In C. B.. Broderick (Ed.), *A decade of family research and action,* Minneapolis, MN: National Council on Family Relations.

Olson, D. H., Russell, C. S., & Sprenkle, D. H. (1980). Marital and family therapy: A decade of review. In F. M. Berardo (Ed.), *Decade review: Family research, 1970–1979.* Minneapolis, MN: National Council on Family Relations.

Otto, H. A. (Ed.) (1976). *Marriage and family enrichment: New perspectives and programs.* Nashville: Abingdon.

Pratt, L. (1976). *Family structure and effective health behavior: The energized family.* Boston: Houghton Mifflin.

Prendergast, T. (1975). Parent-child behaviors associated with health-related behaviors. In B. Kaplan and J. Cassel (Eds.), *Family and health: An epidemiological approach.* Chapel Hill, NC: Institute for Research in Social Sciences.

Rappaport, A. F. (1976). Conjugal relationship enhancement program. In D. H. Olson (Ed.), *Treating relationships.* Lake Mills, IA: Graphic Publishing Company.

Ritter, Y., West, J., & Trotzer, J. (1987). Comparing family counseling and group counseling: An interview with George Gazda, James Hansen, and Alan Hovestat. *Journal of Counseling and Development, 65,* 295–300.

Sager, C. J., & Kaplan, H. S. (Eds.) (1972). *Progress in group and family therapy.* New York: Bruner/Mazel.

Satir, V. (1967). *Conjoint family therapy: A guide to theory and technique.* Palo Alto, CA: Science and Behavior Books.

Smith, P. A., & Knight, S. (1978). Family group counseling. In G. M. Gazda, *Group counseling: A developmental approach* (2nd ed.). Boston: Allyn and Bacon.

Watzlawick, P., Beavin, J. H., & Jackson, D. D. (1967). *Pragmatics of human communication.* New York: W. W. Norton.

Watzlawick P., Weakland, J., & Fisch, R. (1974). *Change.* New York: Norton.

Weitzman, J., & Dreen, K. (1982). Wife beating: A view of the marital dyad. *Journal of Contemporary Social Work, 63,* 259–265.

Zander, A. F. (1975). The study of group behavior during four decades. *Journal of Applied Behavioral Science. 11,* 272–282.

Zuk, G. (1972). *Family therapy: A triadic-based approach.* New York: Behavioral Publications.

SUGGESTED READINGS ▬

Ackerman, N. W. (1967). *Expanding theory and practice in family therapy.* New York: Family Service Association of America.

Back, K. W. (1979). The small group: Tightrope between sociology and personality. *Journal of Applied Behavioral Science, 11,* 283–294.

Beavers, W. R. (1981). A systems model of family for family therapists. *Journal of Marital and Family Therapy, 7,* 299–307.

Bowen, M. (1966). The use of family theory in clinical practice. *Comprehensive Psychiatry, 7,* 345–374.

Carter, E. A., & McGoldrick, M. (Eds.), (1980). *The family life cycle: A framework for family therapy.* New York: Gardner Press.

Colón, F. (1980). The family life cycle of the multiproblem poor family. In E. A. Carter & M. McGoldrick (Eds.), *The family life cycle: A framework for family therapy.* New York: Gardner Press.

Duvall, E. (1957). *Family development.* Chicago: Lippincott.

Duvall, E. (1971). *Family development.* Philadelphia: J. B. Lippincott.

Framo, J. (1970). Symptoms from a family transactional viewpoint. In N. Ackerman, J. Lieb, & J. Pearce (Eds.), *Family therapy in transition.* Boston: Little, Brown.

Haley, J. (1963). *Strategies of psychotherapy.* New York: Grune & Stratton.

L'Abate, L. (1978). *Enrichment: Structural introventions with couples, families, and groups.* Washington, D.C.: University Press of America.

Minuchin, S. (1974). *Families and family therapy.* Cambridge: Harvard University Press.

Mobley, J. A., & Gazda, G. M. (1981). Multidimensional scaling: A technological breakthrough for family therapy. *Journal for Specialists in Group Work, 6,* 52–60.

Olson, D. H., Russell, C. S., & Sprenkle, D. H. (1980). Marital and family therapy: A decade of review. In F. M. Berardo (Ed.), *Decade review: Family research, 1970–1979.* Minneapolis, MN: National Council on Family Relations.

Otto, H. A. (Ed.) (1976). *Marriage and family enrichment: New perspectives and programs.* Nashville: Abingdon.

Pratt, L. (1976). *Family structure and effective health behavior: The energized family.* Boston: Houghton Mifflin.

Sager, C. J., & Kaplan, H. S. (Eds.). (1972). *Progress in group and family therapy.* New York: Brunner/Mazel.

Satir, V. (1967). *Conjoint family therapy: A guide to theory and technique.* Palo Alto, CA: Science and Behavior Books.

Zuk, G. (1972). *Family therapy: A triadic-based approach.* New York: Behavioral Publications.

C H A P T E R 8

Group Counseling with the Elderly[1]

This chapter deals with group counseling with the elderly, particularly those in the upper range of the young–old, 55 to 75, and the lower range of the old–old, 75 and older (Neugarten, 1975). It may be adapted to serve the interests of those not yet retired, but who have concerns in regard to retirement planning and retirement.

A brief historical overview featuring some ideas and opinions on aging precedes a focus on group counseling for the aged. This will be followed by a discussion of some of the characteristics of the elderly. Next, developmental tasks and implementation of group counseling will be considered.

HISTORICAL OVERVIEW

The needs and concerns of the aged have received particular attention since World War II. Little was done in the early part of the twentieth century because of the influence of Freud's pessimism with regard to treating the aged. (The average life expectancy in the United States at the turn of the century was 45 years of age.) Since this period, great contributions have been made by those in the medical profession, the helping professions, and the interdisciplinary field of gerontology. An excellent review of the literature in regard to psychotherapy with the elderly is that of Sparacino (1978–1979), itself following an earlier review of Rechtcshaffen (1959).

---

1. Written by Francis G. Hendrix, Ph.D., and Charlalee Sedgwick, M.A.

Gotestam (1980) reported comprehensively on behavioral and dynamic psychotherapy with the elderly.

Lillian J. Martin is credited with providing the first report on psychotherapy with the aged in 1931. After her own retirement Martin founded the San Francisco Old Age Counseling Center, a comprehensive program, and directed it until her death at age 92. An encouraging movement is in evidence today with the establishment of such programs as the Lieff and Brown multispeciality program (1981), which features a problem-oriented rather than a diagnosis-centered program, and the multispeciality program of Riefler et al. (1981), in which treatment includes the elderly and their families. Lawton (1980), Lacy (1981), and Montgomery (1980) are among those who have been concerned with the physical environment of the elderly. Butler (1963), Butler and Lewis (1977), and others have done a great deal of work with life review and reminiscence.

The problems of the elderly have been of interest to the counseling profession for some time. However, this interest is not reflected in the curriculum of institutions that feature counselor education training programs; courses on counseling the elderly are few and far between. Salisbury (1975), in a national survey of such programs, found that most institutions indicate a great need for such courses. Out of this report grew the American Personnel and Guidance Association (now American Association of Counseling and Human Development) Special Training Project on counseling the aged (Ganikos, 1979). The increasing body of literature in the field reflects the growing interest in counseling the elderly.

Currently a very small percentage of the elderly receive outpatient treatment. Busse and Pfeiffer (1973) have suggested that the elderly either receive long-term psychiatric treatment or none at all, unlike treatment that is available to others; they have also shown that the elderly are less likely to receive intermediate forms of treatment such as counseling. Several writers suggest that therapists and the elderly have a mutual aversion to each other because of several factors, including cohort effect on the elderly and ageism on the part of some in the helping professions. Currently fewer than 4 percent of the clients of community mental health clinics are 65 and older. With more emphasis in training programs today and more exposure of the elderly to counseling services, this picture appears to be changing.

CLIENT CHARACTERISTICS

Probably the most accurate statement to be made in regard to client characteristics is that there is a *lack* of universal characteristics. Variability is very evident in the elderly. Individual differences in all areas appear to be even more pronounced than in other age divisions of the population. Nevertheless it is still possible to enumerate some prevalent characteristics.

The elderly in general have lowered incomes compared to previous incomes, but the majority are not poor as defined by government poverty standards. Seventy percent of those over 65 years of age own their homes. The old–old widows are the less well off financially. The aged are thought of in general as being more conservative (Glamser, 1974). The educational level of the elderly is lower than will be that of succeeding generations. Sexuality remains throughout the life span. Society tends to focus on decline, and this attitude carries over to some degree to the older individuals' views of themselves. However, there is evidence that a particular elderly individual may not feel that the stereotypes apply to him or her, even though they may describe others his or her age. Goebel (1982, p. 466) reported: "This study did not give evidence that a negative stereotype of age is held by older adults." With the developing body of knowledge about aging, increased public awareness regarding the aged, and the increasing numbers and percentage of the aged in the population, it seems reasonable to think that societal attitudes, as well as attitudes of the aged, will be somewhat modified.

Heart disease, cancer, stroke, and arthritis are more common conditions in the aged population than in the younger. There is a high probability of chronic disease of some degree in the elderly, particularly among the old–old. Some of these conditions are associated with past and present life-style such as medical care, diet, exercise, rest, psychological stress, and habits such as smoking. While the current cohorts of the elderly did not have access to the present level of health care information, succeeding cohorts will have had this advantage and probably will be socialized toward using it. There is increasing awareness of the concept of wellness, evidenced by the proliferation of workshops and clinics devoted to health care.

Generally the senses decline in function somewhat. The sense organs become less able to discriminate or less sensitive to the small differences in presented stimuli. Some elderly people may have difficulty in hearing lower- or higher-pitched sounds. Sensory problems, just as more obvious physical ones, need a medical evaluation. In some cases of deafness, a hearing aid is indicated and helpful. Reaction time may be slower, and the elderly person may attempt to compensate. Exercise is helpful in maintaining gross and fine motor movement.

In general the intellectual functions most often used tend to be maintained and sometimes improve slightly throughout the life span—for example, word knowledge (Barry, 1977, p. 117). Learning appears to be more selective. The consensus in regard to personality seems to be that it remains more or less stable over time, although individual traits may become stronger or somewhat modified. Some elements of aging need to be taken into account, however, because they can have an effect on personality. A person with a substantial hearing problem may become suspicious that others are talking about him or her when he or she cannot understand the conversation.

In regard to the elderly and work, several studies have shown that the elderly are more dependable in that they are absent less and are punctual. Also, when the elderly are presented with new tasks, given that they are motivated, they will learn well when not under time pressure.

Numerous studies have investigated the predictors and correlates of life satisfaction. Writers in the field of aging have emphasized the importance of having at least one confidant as a correlate to life satisfaction (Snow & Crapo, 1982). This is a significant point for consideration in group counseling for the elderly. The stage theorists refer directly or inferentially to the developmental task of forming close relationships and maintaining them. In the elderly population, a widow, for example, has lost her spouse, who was her primary confidant. Focusing on the importance of reestablishing a confidant relationship can be, for the group, a very purposeful aim.

In his study of the relationship of family background variables to locus of control in the elderly, Cicirelli (1980) found that cohesiveness among siblings and children of the elderly was related to greater internality. Greater activity, self-confidence, and adaptability are associated with an internal locus of control in the elderly. Interestingly, the number of brothers one has was associated with greater externality in this study. An external locus of control includes the feeling that what happens to one is because of chance, fate, or powerful others; an internal locus of control is based on the feeling or belief that one's own actions are responsible for events in one's life.

In her study of age preferences of older adults in relationships important to their life satisfaction, Goebel (1982) reported that older adults preferred middle-aged and older individuals, especially in independent relationships (more distant). In interdependent relationships (including friends and relatives), age preference was less pronounced.

Most elderly people, 88 to 90 percent, have family, close relatives, or other support systems. As far back as 1959, the World Health Organization attempted to put the myth of uninvolvement or abandonment to rest in their report, *Mental Health Problems of the Aging and Aged*. They stated that the lasting devotion of children for parents had been amply demonstrated. They based this statement on data from careful studies carried out in several industrialized countries. Nevertheless the myth of abandonment persists. Shanas (1968) points to the two groups she thinks perpetuate this belief: the elderly themselves, particularly the childless elderly, and professional workers whose case loads consist primarily of the childless elderly. Not only do adult children not abandon their elderly parents, but Shanas has shown that the relationship is reciprocal. Elderly parents help their adult children in times of trouble, and adult children help the parents.

Family support systems have received some attention in regard to their function when the elderly are not institutionalized. Increasing attention is being accorded support for family members with parents who are geriatric patients. The focus is twofold: (1) to help the adult children so that they may better help parents and (2) to lower the anxiety level of the adult children. The second focus is just now receiving more attention. Shore (1964), Manaster (1967), Silverstone and Hyman (1976), Hausman (1979), and Hendrix (1982) are among those who have focused on the needs of adult children in regard to their elderly parents. York and Calsyn (1977) conducted a needs assessment study in regard to the needs of families with patients in nursing homes, and Hendrix based a program on their findings with the goal of lowering the anxiety level of the primary family member caretakers of geriatric patients in nursing homes; with those results, Hendrix created a program that is intended to lower the anxiety level in people who have a family member in a nursing home.

Johnson and Bursk (1977), Johnson (1978), and Johnson and Spence (1982) investigated relationships between adult children and elderly parents in general and between adult daughters and older mothers specifically, with a resulting intervention program aimed toward supporting adult children concerned about their aging parents. The 1977 study showed both health and attitude toward aging to be significant in the relationship between adult children and elderly parents. The 1978 study of mothers and daughters indicated that living environment and attitude toward aging directly affected relationships.

Snow and Crapo (1982) investigated emotional bondedness, subjective well-being, and health in 205 elderly male Veterans Administration outpatients who were not actually ill and found that emotional bondedness has a direct effect on both subjective well-being and health. These investigators used a new scale, the Emotional Bondedness Scale (Snow, 1980), in conjunction with scales for measuring subjective well-being and health status. Socioeconomic variables were also considered. Snow and Crapo found that at least one confidant is of prime importance for subjective well-being. The quantity of social interaction is less crucial. Emotional bondedness can also predict health.

Beckman and Houser (1982) studied the consequences of childlessness on the sociopsychological well-being of a large sample of older women and summarized their results:

> Widowed childless older women had lower psychological well-being than did widowed mothers. However, among married women childlessness had no significant effects on well-being. Results also show that physical capacity, religiosity, quality of social interaction, and strength of social support are all positively associated with well-being among older women. (p. 243)

Harel, Sollod, and Bognar (1982) investigated predictors of mental health among semirural aged. Their findings supported earlier research indicating that health, finances, social resources, and social interaction are important predictors of mental health in the elderly.

Butler (1963) and Butler and Lewis (1977) contend that elderly people review their lives spontaneously and that sometimes they need assistance in working through unresolved conflicts. This view is congenial to Erikson's formulations (1950, 1963) in regard to attaining ego integrity, his eighth stage, in which one's life is seen as having had meaning and order.

The physical environment is of crucial import to the elderly both in and out of institutions. Lawton and Nahemow's Ecologic Model (Lawton, 1980) states in effect that the greater the disability or the less the environmental competence of the elderly person, the more he or she is controlled by the environment. For environmental mastery, the physical setting needs to be barrier-free for the disabled. Lawton and others consider optimal a physical environment that is neither too difficult nor too easy for the individual, but is suited to his or her level of competence. Montgomery (1980), in referring to the continuum of life from dependence through independence to some degree of dependence, states that as the old grow older, the life space shrinks, and it is logical to assume that the physical environment becomes increasingly important. Lacy (1981) in writing about the interior design of institutions states as one positive goal that they must not be monotonous. Lacy also advocates the use of the resident's personal belongings and their choice of furniture arrangement to help reduce frustration and a sense of helplessness.

DEVELOPMENTAL TASKS OF THE ELDERLY

Developmental Group Counseling with the elderly is approached here with the framework for intervention based on the tasks/stages of concern to those in this age group and their appropriate stage development. The premise for intervention rests on the need for mastering earlier developmental tasks when indicated before proceeding to developmental tasks that are related to the present age/stage of the individual members.

Erikson's (1950, 1963) developmental theory of personality focuses equally on the earlier and later stages of life. He hypothesizes that socialization is lifelong and that socialization of adults is different from that of children; that is, the social context has more bearing on adult development. Erikson's eighth psychosocial developmental task, that of late maturity, concerns a sense of ego integrity versus a sense of despair: a basic acceptance of one's life as having been inevitable, appropriate, and meaningful versus a fear of death as Neugarten interprets it. This eighth stage is further delineated by Peck (1956) into tasks for middle age and for old age. Peck emphasizes the fact that the time sequence may vary according to the individual. His goals for middle age may be applied to the young–old, whose mastery of these tasks leads into those of late maturity. These tasks include valuing wisdom versus physical powers, socializing versus sexualizing in human relationships, cathetic flexibility versus cathetic impoverishment, and mental flexibility versus mental rigidity. These tasks generally arise in some form in group counseling with the elderly and can be explored within the group. For example, valuing wisdom versus valuing physical powers is sometimes presented problematically in a statement such as, "I used to help my daughter with her Sunday dinners, but lately I just go and make no contribution."

Peck's tasks for old age include ego differentiation versus work-role preoccupation, body transcendence versus body preoccupation, and ego transcendence versus ego preoccupation. The first task specifically in regard to retirement role often surfaces in counseling groups in this form: "I ran a business for forty years. I haven't yet found anything to replace that responsibility."

Havighurst (1953, 1972) offers seven psychosocial development tasks of adjustment and adaptation, which overlap and complement those of Erikson and Peck. The difficult task of adjusting to the death of one's spouse or the task of adopting and adapting social roles in a flexible way roughly parallels Peck's task of attaining cathetic flexibility. A group member involved with this task may state this quite specifically after the initial grief fades somewhat when a spouse has died as, "I am so lonely and I can't think what to do about it."

Loevinger (1976) cautions that numbering stages is misleading. Further, she states, "Though stage names suggest characteristics that are usually at a maximum at that stage nothing less than the total pattern defines a stage" (p. 15). The Autonomous Stage has as tasks acknowledging and coping with conflicting needs and duties. A person exhibits coping behavior by recognizing problems and seeing situations as complex, as well as developing strategies to the problem. Someone who is able to cope has a high tolerance for ambiguity. The autonomous person recognizes others' need for autonomy and sees emotional interdependence as inevitable. Coping includes appreciating the need for interdependence and simultaneously respecting others' need for autonomy. Self-fulfillment is a goal that supplants achievement. In coping, achievement is seen as only part of a successful life; fulfillment becomes more important. The concept of various roles broadens, and coping is accomplished when the individual behaves differently according to role.

Loevinger's highest, and rarest, stage is the Integrated Stage, which encompasses the Autonomous Stage characteristics plus a consolidation of a sense of identity. Coping includes a more specific sense of identity. The Integrated Stage person is more likely to be at peace with himself or herself.

Dupont's (1979) highest and rarest stages are the Autonomous and Integritous stages. Characteristically, the Autonomous person sees himself or herself as in control of his or her own destiny. Coping includes internalized standards; external standards are resisted. The Integritous person has a fully developed philosophy of life, and his or her integrity is invested with affect. Coping includes development of a prized feeling of wholeness. Integrity is highly valued, sometimes more than life. Dupont refers to integrity as a feeling of prized wholeness concomitant with consistent conduct in accordance with principle.

Kohlberg (1973) delineates three levels in moral development, each of which has two stages, across the life span. Familiarity with all of his stages is desirable because a given individual may or may not have completed earlier stages. These levels are preconventional, conventional, and postconventional. The fifth and sixth stages constitute the postconventional level.

Kohlberg's last stage, the stage that might be reached in the last part of one's life, is the highest in moral reasoning. At this stage, an individual finds himself or herself putting universal principles of justice first in his or her evaluations; he or she supports ethical principles that are more universal: "At heart, there are universal principles of justice, of the reciprocity and equality of human rights, and of respect for the dignity of human beings as individual persons" (Kohlberg & Turiel, 1971, p. 416). Coping behaviors include great sensitivity to and concern about others. A stage 6 person would seek revocation of laws that were not universally applicable or were discriminatory.

Developmental tasks in the physical–sexual area in this age group include, but are not limited to, medical care, diet, exercise, rest, and psychological stress level. The elderly person copes by attending to these tasks on a regular and productive basis. The elderly individual needs to know the changes that are likely to occur in his or her sexual life. Even though sexuality continues to be a viable form of expression throughout life the form of that expression becomes different; response time, for example, changes. (Pfeiffer & Davis, 1972) On the other hand, the need to be touched never diminishes.

Super et al. (1975), in regard to vocational development, includes in his tasks that of "declaration." His guidelines for this developmental stage include a slowing of pace—working fewer hours, for example, or turning to a part-time job. Peck (1956) includes the stage of ego differentiation versus work-role preoccupation. Carp suggests (1977) that the period of retirement itself should be considered a developmental phase. Retirement means different things to different people on a continuum from refusal to retire from the work force to a highly developed approach to utilization of leisure. This may include volunteer activities, as well as expanded family roles and other hobbies and interests. With the increasing present and probable future leisure time both during employment and after formal retirement, more options will be available. Returning to school in post-retirement or semiretirement either because of interest or retraining is already possible and recognized by the number of administrative units set up in several universities to attend to the interests and needs of this group of students.

In regard to cognitive developmental tasks and coping behaviors, Schaie (1980) writes in his article on intelligence and problem solving:

> Most of what we know about intelligence and problem solving in the elderly has been learned using instruments and techniques developed for children and young adults. We are only at the beginning of charting adult functioning with techniques which are truly indigenous to the elderly. It is quite possible, therefore, that what appears as disadvantage when compared with the young, may simply represent a regrouping and reexpression of function which might be quite appropriate and adaptive for the old. Research now in progress in a number of laboratories will hopefully shed light on this major issue. (p. 280)

IMPLEMENTATION

Developmental group counseling with the elderly is approached here following the developmental model outlined earlier in this book. The framework for intervention is based on tasks/stages of concern to those in the later phases of age development and their appropriate stage development, à la stage theorists. These coping behaviors are delineated in Appendix A. The premise for intervention rests on the need for mastering earlier developmental tasks when indicated before proceeding to developmental tasks related to the present age/stage of the individual members.

SELECTION AND GROUP COMPOSITION

The groups referred to here are those composed of residents of retirement and nursing homes, participants in senior center programs, day care programs, and other counseling groups. The chronological age of the group members would be in the upper range of Neugarten's (1975) young–old, 55 to 75, and the lower range of the old–old, 75 and older. This approach is appropriate for those with reality orientation intact and without major hearing impairment. People with difficulties like these need separate, special groups. A pregroup screening interview aids in placing those with some degree of commonality in the same group. This interview also serves as a time for introduction to the group ground rules.

Generally it is desirable for the group members to be of the same or overlapping cohorts because much of their interaction with others, when living in a group residence, is with cohorts. An individual's willingness to share concerns with others he or she feels to be similar to him or her is important for a person at this time in his or her life. The importance of being around people who are of like mind and who offer social support is obvious for the elderly when most of them have had to face losses of long-time relationships. With cohorts, the elderly person not only has general support, but also the chance to develop deep and close relationships that can fill the gap those other losses have made.

When there are conflicts between generations, it is a good idea to include other ages in the group. For example, one might offer group counseling to the elderly and staff or to the elderly and adult children. The counseling group allows a supportive climate for resolution of conflict. Also needed are groups for elderly married couples with unresolved conflicts. It seems reasonable to assume that as the life space shrinks somewhat, the marital relationship becomes even more important. My observation is that in a considerable percentage of marriages of forty to fifty years duration, there is some degree of perceived pain because of unresolved emotional conflicts with the spouse. The typical resident group is composed of widows in the 70- to 80-year range, because of the present life expectancy for this group of women and the fact that these widows were, on the average, four years younger than their husbands.

GROUP SETTING

Ideally the group counseling room would be situated away from loud noises and interruptions. An example of a room that does *not* lend itself well to the group sessions is the central dining room in a nursing home because of the adjacent kitchen equipment and activity and the fact that people are accustomed to walking in at any time.

Comfortable seating for this population includes upholstered chairs, straight chairs with arms, and room for wheelchairs. The seating should be high enough to allow ease for standing. Overstuffed chairs are particularly difficult for some in this age group. Temperatures should be in the 75-degree range and the room free of floor drafts because members of these groups frequently suffer from poor circulation.

GROUP SIZE

Optimally these counseling groups should range in size from 6 to 8 members. The smaller group setting allows for greater development of interaction among the members and cohesiveness. Goldstein, Heller, and Sechrest (1966) reviewed the group dynamics research in view of optimum group size when size is viewed as an interactional variable. They found that the research suggests that as size of group increases, the group becomes more leader centered and more slanted toward members giving information and suggestions and less toward asking for opinions and agreement. We prefer a group of 6 to 8, which allows for occasional absences without considerable reduction in group size.

FREQUENCY, LENGTH, AND DURATION OF GROUP SESSIONS

Customarily counseling groups for the aged meet weekly, preferably around 3:00 P.M. for one-and-one-half hours for six weeks with a five- to ten-minute break at midpoint preceded, if feasible, by a fifteen-minute break for refreshments. Generally the groups are closed; the membership remains constant throughout its duration. The reason for this is in the service of developing greater intimacy and providing a greater probability for building confidant relationships. The option is available to the members of choosing to join a future group after termination of the present one. Often these experienced group members add significantly to the growth of a new group by the behaviors they model, such as active listening and empathic responding, and, in some cases, serving as an effective cotherapist. LaWall (1981) suggested this latter concept in regard to conjoint couples' therapy with the elderly. A disadvantage of this option is that one who joins the second group may exhibit superfluous activity or directiveness. This can best be handled in advance by another pregroup screening interview, prior to the second group membership, in which such issues are sensitively discussed.

MEDIA

While the primary medium is talk coupled with observations of nonverbal behaviors in these groups, five-minute taped presentations of relevant material on such issues as health, role changes, and relations with children are advantageous at the outset of each session. A sample protocol of a taped presentation follows:

> The premise underlying this tape concerns your treatment of and attitude toward yourself and the relationship of these factors to emotional well-being. It appears to be generally accepted that these behaviors and attitudes we might discuss today are included among those contributing to a sense of well-being. Again, the matter of individual differences is a prime consideration in how you choose to handle these ideas.

In line with these thoughts, we might consider three relevant areas: (1) support system, (2) activities, and (3) attention to health care. The first two are closely related in the present context, and to some degree we might consider them jointly. Support system here refers to the network of people with whom you are in close contact and on whom you depend for some degree of encouragement, understanding or pleasant company. This network may consist of family, friends, co-workers, or others associated with your outside activities such as church groups for example. Some questions posed in regard to these matters are:

1. How strong do you make your support system? This question may be better answered in terms of less global questions. For example:
   (a) With whom would you like to be on better terms? Immediate family, extended family, friends, others?
   (b) How might you accomplish this?
   (c) Is it time now?
   (d) With whom would you like to be better acquainted? When?
2. Which kinds of activities including others do you enjoy?
3. What do you really like to do in the line of a hobby or interest? Do you make time for this?

Several general health care questions are posed for your consideration.

1. When did you last see your doctor, dentist, ophthalmologist, or other medical professional for "check-ups"?
2. Did you ask your doctor about an exercise program suitable for you?
3. Are you nutrition-conscious?

You have probably thought of many of these ideas in this tape already. Won't you share your thoughts and feelings with us today?

These tapes are usually developed by the group counselor and serve two purposes. First, they serve as stimulus statements for discussion. Second, since the duration of the group sessions is less than the average fourteen hours spent in counseling groups (Gazda, 1975), it is felt that they give a degree of focus that engenders group growth in the short-term groups. After the initial taped presentation at the beginning of each session, an attempt is made to adhere to that definition of Developmental Group Counseling formulated by Gazda et al.

In addition, at the beginning of the first session, a copy of group ground rules, which are part of group structuring, is given to each group member and presented for discussion by the group leader. The prospective group members are introduced to the group ground rules initially during the screening interview.

COUNSELOR ROLE(S)

The role the counselor plays in the group reflects his or her philosophy as well as parameters that are set by the structure and orientation of the group itself. In summary, the functions of the group include: being effective in building expectancy states for being liked and liking the other group members, stressing the hard work involved, stressing the screening that went into the selection of members, and distinguishing group activity as different from regular social life in that personal concerns are discussed in the group in a consistent and appropriate way. Counselor leadership provided is more active at the outset, with increasing focus toward group centeredness as the sessions progress. Two considerations are of particular relevance here. First, Pfeiffer (1971) prefers more therapist activity, or directiveness, with elderly psychiatric patients. It appears that the ground rules, building of positive expectancies, and setting of goals, along with the taped presentations, provide adequate focus for this elderly population in counseling groups with reality orientation intact and major hearing impairment absent. Thus the group leader can operate within the permissive framework for counseling groups. Second, Pfeiffer and others stress the need for considering how losses can be replaced. Examples of these losses range from developing confidant relationships to exploring options for arranging the physical environment so that it is suited to the individual's level of competence.

The topics of taped presentations are gleaned from the expressed needs of earlier group members and the literature. Among the topics are health, finance, attitudes of self and others toward aging, widowhood, reminiscence, role changes, and relationships with spouse, peers, adult children, grandchildren, siblings, staff, or other significant relationships. (I do not present a taped presentation on death and dying unless the group consensus is that the topic should be explored because members are typically at diverse stages in dealing with this topic and may not have come to these sessions prepared to deal with this topic.) Occasionally unresolved conflicts from the past may be better dealt with at length in private sessions and then shared with the group at the discretion of the leader and the individual member.

A general goal in therapeutic encounters is to help the client/patient feel more in control of his or her life. Specific focus is in order at this time on the members' controlling those variables that they can influence. The counseling group setting provides a supportive climate for exploring options and alternatives and, sometimes, making decisions in regard to the future. It is important to follow the pace of the members. Some have planned the way they would like to be, given several circumstances, until death. Others may like only to begin consideration of alternatives in regard to remaining time.

The leader may set a weekly time when he or she is available for private sessions. Often the topic arises spontaneously on such occasions as when a hallmate in the retirement home became ill and was taken to a nursing home on the morning after having "played a good hand of bridge last night." The apparent inference is " . . . and this could happen to me."

It is important for the group leader to be available for further exploration or to make an appropriate referral when feasible. Sometimes a joint session with a distressed member and his or her family after the group sessions end is useful. When the results of decision making will affect others, it is advisable to suggest to the group member a joint session with the others involved.

SUMMARY

Consideration of intervention specifically geared to the elderly has received increasing focus since its beginning about fifty years ago. Yet today a disproportionately small number of this population receive or seek professional help in this area. Explanations offered include a mutual aversion concept, both on the part of some counselors/therapists and some elderly people because of cohort effect. However, changes are occurring that might remedy the situation, including more focus on counseling the elderly in training programs and more exposure of the elderly to the ideas of individual and group work in various programs geared to promoting physical and emotional well-being. This chapter has offered an approach specific to a population of those from the upper range of the young–old to the lower range of the old–old with reality orientation intact and without major hearing impairment.

This approach may be applied to the elderly in several settings. It encompasses a developmental orientation with tasks/stages in the various aspects of the elderly and suggested coping behaviors.

REFERENCES

Barry, J. (1977). The psychology of aging. In J. and C. Wingrove (Eds.), *Let's learn about aging: A book of readings*. New York: Wiley.

Beckman, L., & Houser, B. (1982). The consequences of childlessness on the social-psychological well-being of older women. *Journal of Gerontology, 37* (2), 243–250.

Busse, E. W., & Pfeiffer, E. (Eds.), (1973). *Mental illness in later life*. Washington, D.C.: American Psychiatric Association.

Butler, R. N. (1963). The life review: An interpretation of reminiscence in the aged. *Psychiatry, 119*, 721–728.

Butler, R. N., & Lewis, M. T. (1977). *Aging and mental health: Positive psychosocial approaches* (2nd ed.). St. Louis: C. V. Mosby.

Carp, F. M. (1977). The life span development context. In J. Barry and C. Wingrove (Eds.), *Let's learn about aging: A book of readings*. New York: Wiley.

Cicirelli, V. G. (1980). Relationship of family background variables to locus of control in the elderly. *Journal of Gerontology, 35*(1), 108–114.

Dupont, H. (1979). Affective development: Stage and sequence. In R. L. Mosher (Ed.), *Adolescents' development and education*. Berkeley, CA: MuCutchan.

Erikson, E. H. (1950). *Childhood and society*. New York: W. W. Norton.

Erikson, E. H. (1963). *Childhood and society*. (2nd ed.). New York: W. W. Norton.

Ganikos, M. (1979). Project on Counseling Older Adults. American Association for Counseling and Development, 599 Stevenson Avenue, Alexandria, Virginia 22304.

Gazda, G. M. (1975). Group counseling: A developmental approach. In G. M. Gazda (Ed.), *Basic approaches to group psychotherapy and group counseling* (2nd ed). Springfield, IL: Charles C. Thomas.

Glamser, F. D. (1974). The importance of age to conservative opinions: A multivariate analysis. *Journal of Gerontology, 29*, 549–554.

Goebel, B. L. (1982). Age preferences of older adults in relationships important to their life satisfaction. *Journal of Gerontology, 37*(4), 461–467.

Goldstein, A. P., Heller, K., & Sechrest, L. B. (1966). *Psychotherapy and the psychology of behavior*. New York: Wiley.

Gotestam. K. G. (1980). Behavioral and dynamic psychotherapy with the elderly. In J. E. Birren & R. B. Sloane (Eds.), *Handbook of mental health and aging*. Englewood Cliffs, NJ: Prentice-Hall.

Harel, Z., Sollod, R., & Bognar, B. (1982). Predictors of mental health among semi-rural aged. *Gerontologist, 22*(6), 499–504.

Hausman, C. P. (1979). Short-term counseling for people with elderly parents. *Gerontologist, 19*(1), 102–107.

Havighurst, R. J. (1953). *Developmental tasks and education* (2nd ed.). New York: David McKay.

Havighurst, R. J. (1972). *Developmental tasks and education* (3rd ed.). David McKay.

Hendrix, F. G. (1982). The effect of structured group counseling on the anxiety level of the primary caretaker of geriatric patients. (Dissertation Abstracts International, *42*(10), 4300-A. No. DA8206269.)

Johnson, E. (1978). "Good" relationships between older mothers and their daughters: A causal model. *Gerontologist, 18*(3), 301–306.

Johnson, E., & Bursk, B. (1977). Relationship between the elderly and their adult children. *Gerontologist, 17*(1), 90–96.

Johnson, E., & Spence, D. (1982). Adult children and their aging parents: An intervention program. *Family Relations, 31*(1), 115–122.

Kohlberg, L. (1973). Continuities and discontinuities in childhood and adult moral development revisited. In P. B. Baltes & K. W. Schaie (Eds.), *Life-span development and psychology: Research and theory*. New York: Academic Press.

Kohlberg, L., & Turiel, P. (1971). Moral development and moral education. In G. Lesser (Ed.), *Psychology and educational practice*. New York: Scott, Foresman.

Lacy, M. (1981). Creating a safe and supportive treatment environment. *Hospital and Community Psychiatry, 32*(1), 44–47.

LaWall, J. (1981). Conjoint therapy of psychiatric problems in the elderly. *Journal of the American Geriatrics Society, 29*(2), 89–91.

Lawton, M. P. (1980). *Environment and aging*. Monterey, CA: Brooks/Cole.

Lieff, J. D., & Brown, R. A. (1981). A psychogeriatric nursing home resocialization program. *Hospital and Community Psychiatry, 32*(12), 862–865.

Loevinger, J. (1976). *Ego development*. San Francisco: Jossey-Bass.

Manaster, H. (1967). The family group therapy program at Park View Home for the Aged. *Journal of the American Geriatrics Society, 15*(3), 302–306.

Montgomery, J. E. (1980). Living environments of the elderly: "Hard architecture." *Presentations on Aging*. Faculty of Gerontology/Gerontology Center, University of Georgia.

Neugarten, B. L. (1975). The future and the young-old. *Gerontologist, 15*(1), 4–9.

Peck, R. (1956). Psychological developments in the second half of life. In J. Anderson (Ed.), *Psychological aspects of aging: Proceedings of conference planning on research*. Washington, D.C.: American Psychological Association.

Pfeiffer, E. (1971). Psychotherapy with elderly patients. *Postgraduate Medicine, 50*, 254–258.

Pfeiffer, E., & Davis, G. (1972). Determinants of sexual behavior in middle and old age. *Journal of the American Geriatrics Society, 20*(4), 151–158.

Rechtcshaffen, A. (1959). Psychotherapy with geriatric patients: A review of the literature. *Journal of Gerontology, 14*, 73–84.

Reifler, B., Larson, E., Cox, G., & Featherstone, H. (1981). Treatment results at a multi-specialty clinic for the impaired elderly and their families. *Journal of the American Geriatrics Society. 29*(12), 579–582.

Salisbury, H. (1975). Counseling the elderly: A neglected area in counselor education. *Counselor Education and Supervision, 14*, 237–238.

Schaie, K. (1980). Intelligence and problem solving. In J. Birren & R. Sloane (Eds.), *Handbook of mental health and aging*. Englewood Cliffs, NJ: Prentice-Hall.

Shanas, E. (1968). *Old people in three industrial societies*. New York: Atherton Press.

Shore, H. (1964). Relatives of the resident. In M. Leeds & H. Shore (Eds.), *Geriatric institutional management*. New York: G. P. Putnam & Sons.

Silverstone, B., & Hyman, H. K. (1976). *You and your aging parent*. New York: Pantheon Books.

Snow, R. (1980). Middle-aged persons' perceptions of their intergenerational relations. Ph.D. dissertation, University of Chicago.

Snow, R., & Crapo, L. (1982). Emotional bondedness, subjective well-being and health in elderly medical patients. *Journal of Gerontology, 37*(5), 609–615.

Sparacino, J. (1978–1979). Individual psychotherapy with the aged: A selective review. *International Journal of Aging and Human Development, 9*(3), 197–220.

Super, D. E., Crites, J., Hummel, R., Mosher, H., Overstreet, C. B., & Warnath, C. (1957). *Vocational development: A framework for research*. Monograph No. 1. New York: Bureau of Publications, Teachers College, Columbia University.

World Health Organization. (1959). *Mental health problems of the aging and the aged*. Technical Report Series, No. 171. Geneva: World Health Organization.

York, J., & Calsyn, R. (1977). Family involvement in nursing homes. *Gerontologist, 17*(6), 500–505.

SUGGESTED READINGS ━━━━━━━━━━━━━━━━━━━━━━━━━ ▬

Barry, J. R., & Wingrove, C. R. (1977). *Let's learn about aging: A book of readings.* New York: Wiley.

Birren, J. E., & Sloan, R. B. (Eds.) (1980). *Handbook of mental health and aging.* Englewood Cliffs, NJ: Prentice-Hall.

Botwinick, J. (1978). *Aging and behavior.* (2nd ed.). New York: Springer.

Burnside, J. M. (1978). *Working with the elderly: Group process and techniques.* North Scituate, MA: Duxbury Press.

Busse, E. W., & Pfeiffer, E. (Eds.), (1973). *Mental illness in later life.* Washington, D.C.: American Psychiatric Association.

Butler, R. N., & Lewis, M. I. (1977). *Aging and mental health: Positive psychosocial approaches* (2nd ed.). Saint Louis: C. V. Mosby Company.

Erickson, E. H., Erickson, J. M., & Kivnick, H. Q. (1986). *Vital involvement in old age: The experience of old age in our time.* New York: W. W. Norton.

Hendricks, J., & Hendricks, C. D. (1979). *Dimensions of aging: Readings.* Cambridge, MA: Winthrop Publishers.

Kra, S. (1986). *Aging myths: Reversible causes of mind and memory loss.* New York: McGraw-Hill.

Lawton, M. P. (1980). *Environment and aging.* Monterey, CA: Brooks/Cole.

Perlmutter, M., & Hall, E. (1985). *Adult development and aging.* New York: John Wiley & Sons.

Pifer, A., & Bronte, L. (1986). *Our aging society: Paradox and promise.* New York: W. W. Norton.

Poon, L. W. (Ed.) (1980). *Aging in the 1980's: Psychological issues.* Washington, D.C.: American Psychological Association.

See also the following journals and APGA Project on Counseling Older Adults:

Educational Gerontologist

Geriatrics

Gerontologist

Journal of Aging and Human Development

Journal of Counseling Psychology

Journal of Gerontology

Journal of the American Geriatrics Society

Ganikos, M. Project on Counseling Older Adults. Write American Association for Counseling and Development, 559 Stevenson Ave., Alexandria, VA 22304.

Schlossberg, N. (1984). *Counseling adults in transition.* New York: Springer.

Skinner, B. F. & Vaughan, M. E. (1983). *Enjoy old age: A program of self-management.* New York: W. W. Norton.

CHAPTER 9

Group Counseling with Substance Users and Abusers[1]

Substance use and consequent abuse has been and continues to be a prevalent aspect of civilized society. In recent years, increased awareness apparently has reached the public's conscience, which has resulted in a subsequent increase in treatment and prevention programming. A compelling reason motivating this movement seems to be the strong relationship between motor vehicle accidents and deaths, and intoxicated drivers. For instance, 51,077 people died in motor vehicle crashes in 1980 (NHTSA, 1981). When blood alcohol concentration (bac) was measured for drivers killed, it was found that between 40 and 55 percent had bac's of at least 0.10, which is legally drunk. In fact, the average bac of fatally injured drivers was found to be 0.20. (NHTSA, 1978). (One may be charged with alcohol-impaired driving at a bac of 0.05.) These bac's take on additional meaning when considering a twelve times greater chance of being involved in a fatal crash with a bac of 0.10 and a twenty times greater incidence of crashes with a bac of 0.15 (Jones & Joscelyn, 1978, p. 22).

Since auto crashes precipitated by drunkenness are only one part of the price society pays for substance abuse, the total cost of recreational and addictive use of alcohol and other drugs is many times greater. Considering other major areas of loss—worker productivity, increases in illness and injury, incarceration and legal costs, family and psychological stress, and crime and violence—the extent of related damage is staggering. A recent

---

1. Written by Michael Kavkewitz, Ph.D., Director of Psychological Services, Private Hospital, Chattanooga, Tennessee

Gallup poll (*Alcoholism,* January and February 1983) indicated that 33 percent of families surveyed admitted that drinking has been a cause of trouble in their family. When one realizes that 33 percent of the drinking-age population (those fourteen and older) are abstainers (*Alcoholism,* January and February 1983), the pervasive scope of substance use and abuse becomes obvious.

Many people, however, use mood-changing substances with no ill effect. Thus, it is not simply the substances that cause problems but how they are used.

CAUSES OF CHEMICAL DEPENDENCY

In attempting to understand why some people become substance abusers, research has documented various reasons. Social factors include legal availability (Terris, 1967), peer group influence (Jessor & Jessor, 1975), and occupation (Plant, 1979). Psychological factors include affective disorders (Winokur, Clayton, & Reich, 1969), childhood behavioral problems (Vaillant & Milofsky, 1982), and individual attributions and expectations concerning alcohol use (Marlatt & Rohsenow, 1980). Furthermore, Vaillant and Milofsky (1982) pointed to ethnicity and family history of alcoholism, while Glueck and Glueck (1950) found marital conflict, lack of maternal supervision, and no attachment to father as predictors of alcoholism.

Despite Vaillant and Milofsky's (1982) study finding cultural attitude of primary importance, a preponderance of studies that contrasted heredity and environment have shown that biological relatives, even when physically absent, were more of a risk factor for alcoholism in children than alcoholics in the environment (Bohman, 1978; Goodwin, 1979). The genetic factor of high tolerance for the effects of alcohol may explain these results in part. Thus, alcoholism may be viewed as caused by interactions of a number of factors unique for each individual in patterns common to all those so afflicted.

Although factors such as peer group pressure, expectations, and attributions seem reachable through in-school prevention programs; others like occupation, ethnicity, and family background seem hard to affect. However, in this respect, Vaillant and Milofsky (1982) found what may be a common thread. They found children in ethnic groups with low alcohol dependency being taught appropriate drinking habits within families that did not tolerate adult drunkenness. In high dependency groups, a combination of intolerance for nonadult drinking and tolerance for adult drunkenness was present. Also, the normally highly relevant factor of family history of alcoholism was much less predictive of alcoholism in offspring in high alcohol-dependent ethnic groups and considerably more predictive with ethnic groups low in alcohol dependency. Thus, appropriate modeling, early instruction, and prohibitions based on consequence instead of age appear to be factors related across causes and addressable in prevention programming.

CHEMICAL DEPENDENCY AND ADOLESCENCE

A difference in dynamics between drug use and the use of alcohol and tobacco is that many drug users' parents never used drugs. This assertion is supported by marijuana arrest records, which have increased from 18,815 in 1965 to 420,000 in 1973, and 457,000 in 1977. The estimated number of heroin-dependent persons has increased from 100,000 in 1960 to 700,000 in 1975 (Schroeder, 1975, 1980). By 1979, the government declared that the number of heroin addicts had declined to 450,000 (Schroeder, 1980). This pattern is reflected in adolescent usage. The National Institute on Drug Abuse (NIDA) (cited in Rice, 1978) reported 14 percent of all youths 12 to 17 had tried marijuana in 1971, while 23 percent had tried it by 1974. By 1977, according to a survey for the National Institute on Drug Abuse, more than 50 percent of high school seniors had smoked marijuana at least once and more than 25 percent used it at least once a week (Schroeder, 1980).

However, as the sixties generation has grown up, there have been changes in patterns of substance usage. In San Mateo County, California, the department of Public Health and Welfare (cited in Rice, 1978) reported an increase from 27 percent to 49 percent of ninth-graders admitting one or more uses of marijuana from 1968 to 1974, but a leveling off to 48 percent in 1977. Also, ninth-graders admitting to ten or more uses increased from 14 percent to 30 percent from 1968 to 1974 and decreased to 27 percent in 1977, while ninth-graders admitting to fifty or more uses decreased from 20 percent to 16 percent from 1974 to 1977. Although more twelfth-graders admitted to use than did ninth-graders, across-the-board trends were similar. These results, along with McKillip et al.'s (1973) study of Chicago high school students, where 39.5 percent admitted to trying marijuana with 39 percent trying tobacco and 59.9 percent trying alcohol, show a trend of marijuana use beginning to approximate that of alcohol and tobacco.

The Second Report of the National Commission on Marijuana and Drug Abuse (1973) also indicates greater proportionate increases in marijuana use over tobacco and alcohol for both high school and junior high school students from 1967 to 1972. In 1969, 42 percent of junior high school students admitted to trying alcohol, with 41 percent trying tobacco and 10 percent trying marijuana. By 1972, 56 percent admitted to alcohol use, 51 percent to use of tobacco, and 16 percent to marijuana. The proportionate increase for marijuana was even greater for high school students. In 1967,

62 percent admitted to alcohol use, 50 percent to tobacco use, and 15 percent to marijuana use; by 1972, 74 percent admitted to alcohol use, 66 percent to tobacco use, and 40 percent to marijuana use.

Based on NIDA's Seventh Annual Report to Congress on Marijuana and Health for the period up to and including 1977, Schroeder (1980) reported that marijuana used by persons ages 12 to 17 had increased 25 percent in a single year. Among high school seniors, one in eleven used marijuana on a daily basis as compared to one in twelve in 1976 and one in seventeen in 1975.

Although statistics vary from study to study, national norms in the fall of 1974, as reported in the White Paper on Drug Use (1975), indicated close to 60 percent of 12 to 17-year-olds having denied use of alcohol and tobacco, with slightly greater than 20 percent having tried marijuana.

This chapter was written in 1983, and since then there has been an increase in public awareness and action regarding the dangers of substance abuse. Along with this awareness, there has been a significant decline in the use of marijuana, amphetamines, stimulants (speed), Methaqualone (Quaaludes), barbiturates, and tranquilizers (Johnson et al. 1987). Still, cocaine use has remained strong and thus has become the second most prevalent illicit drug behind marijuana. With the well publicized dangers of "crack," this trend is especially significant. Furthermore, teenage cigarette use has been stable in the eighties and alcohol use has declined only slightly to 65.3 percent of high school students admitting use within thirty days prior to the survey. Thus, although inroads have been made with the drugs of the sixties, new dangers have arisen, especially with cocaine/crack. Still, chemical dependency, especially including alcohol and tobacco use, remains an issue of pervasive scope and high impact.

The proportionate increase in marijuana use in the sixties and early seventies and cocaine use in the eighties are not the result of family history. Thus, other factors need to be explored in understanding its prevalence. Such factors include curiosity, sensual pleasure, social pressure, tension relief, and attempts at gaining increased awareness (Center of Counseling and Psychological Services, 1970; New England Learning and Research, 1970; Salisbury & Fertig, 1968; Sallan, Zinberg, & Frei, 1975). These environmental factors may be seen as interacting with sociological and hereditary factors. Finally, developmental identity crises need to be faced in preparation for effective group work.

PREVENTION OF ADOLESCENT SUBSTANCE ABUSE

In presenting an overview of prevention efforts, Evans et al. (1979) emphasize that fear-based approaches focusing on future costs, such as lung cancer and heart disease, are ineffective since young people are more present than future oriented. Bland, Bewley, and Day (1975) support this conclusion, finding that many school boys who smoked did not even perceive themselves as smokers. Thus, McGuire's (1973) emphasis on the importance of programs providing regular checks as to whether students are both paying attention to and comprehending the message presented addresses Bland's finding.

In focusing on factors influencing the initiation and maintenance of habitual behavior, Sherif and Sherif (1964) and Hill (1971) support the widely held assumption of the powerful influence that peer pressure exerts. Palmer (1970) found that the second most predictive factor in student smoking was parental smoking habits. In both cases, the apparent influence of role models imparts a major impact on adolescent habit choice and maintenance. Reviews of health education campaigns also support the learning-by-example dynamics of modeling. Leventhal (1970) suggests that public health campaigns are most successful when they show how to comply rather than when they attempt to convince their audience that one ought to comply. Similarly, McGuire (1973) attributes the limited success of education programs to "failure to show the way to overcome" (p. 49) various drugs. In addition, Evans et al. (1970) found that by the seventh grade, despite the fact that almost all students believe smoking to be dangerous, about 20 percent had already started, confirming the adolescent's tendency to be influenced by modeled behavior rather than words.

Although adolescents learn substance use through modeling, they may continue it because it serves a purpose or addresses an otherwise neglected area of need. Fodor, Glass, and Weiner (1968) comment on this issue stating, "Smoking education must in fact become health education, taking into consideration the multiplicity of factors relating to smoking and health— physical, mental and social" (p. 94). Furthermore, the more and the longer one turns to substance use to address unfulfilled needs, the harder one finds it to break the habit and replace it with more appropriate skills. Thus, the adolescent who has productive skills that address basic need areas is least likely to be prone to chronic substance abuse.

Peer Facilitation

In communicating a prevention-oriented message, Horowitz (1966) emphasizes the importance of credibility, maintaining that adolescents should be told all of the facts as honestly as possible. To do so, he suggests enlisting the aid of student leaders and students themselves. This use of peers to facilitate treatment is supported by Hilgard et al. (1969), who found this approach useful in influencing behaviors and attitudes of other adolescents in group therapy. Similarly, Goodman (1967), Hamburg and Varenhorst (1972), and Feuerstein, Hanegbi, and Krasilowky (1970) have successfully used peers to help maladapted adolescents. Furthermore, Fine, Knight-Webb, and Vernon (1977) found their volunteer peer-counselor format to be benefited by having several training sessions in order to communicate expectations and to let peer counselors get the "feel" of group participation.

Use of Groups

In using groups as the modality for prevention and treatment of adolescent substance abuse and for the treatment of adult alcoholics, several criteria have been considered. First, especially with adolescents, there is the strong influence of peer modeling of both appropriate behavior and attitudes. Next, research over thirteen studies has shown that individual psychotherapy was no more effective than therapy in group (Luborsky, Singer, & Luborsky, 1975). Thus, the cost efficiency of group treatment appears advantageous. Furthermore, Emrick (1975), in reviewing studies from 1953 to 1972, found that the factor that seemed most related to improvement in alcoholics was staying in treatment. However, in analyzing studies with control groups, it was found that between 19 and 75 percent of outpatients attending noncompulsory groups dropped out by the fourth session (Baekeland, Lundwall, & Kissin, 1975). Dropout rate was particularly high among low socioeconomic status people, of whom only 5 percent came to group-based or emergency room referrals (Chafetz & Blane, 1963). Chafetz and Blane and others have found this rate to increase dramatically when follow-up help is given. Because of budget limitations, such help may be more readily available when group rather than individual treatment is used. Furthermore, since low socioeconomic status people are more likely to be apprehended as adolescents, the trend seems applicable to the treatment of adolescents, as well as adult substance abusers.

The following sections deal with conducting substance abuse prevention groups with adolescents in a secondary school environment, life-skills treatment groups with adolescents apprehended by authorities for substance-abuse-related behavior, and various types of treatment groups for adult alcoholics. These populations were chosen since they were thought to be representative of group treatment interventions currently operative and also since they represent different aspects of related treatment issues.

ADOLESCENTS

The roots of substance abuse may be conceptualized as addictive behavior patterns. Such patterns develop from an interaction between inherited and learned factors. When focusing on adolescence, these factors may be thought to form predispositions that may be actualized into varying degrees of addictive behavior. As such, these predispositions characteristically face the developmental "storm and stress" of strong peer group influence, limit testing, rebelliousness, new exploratory behaviors, and rapid physiological and psychological change.

When teenagers depend on drugs to cope with developmental changes, they risk not learning healthy, adult coping skills. Thus addiction may take root, and it may be twenty years before treatment is sought. Then the individual may be faced with major deficits and limited life options.

As with adult substance abuse, including alcoholism, adolescents rarely voluntarily seek early treatment. Thus, an issue in doing group work with this population is under what auspices one's group will be organized and what the characteristics of its membership will be. An area where group counseling is generally not applied and may potentially be most useful is with adolescents who are moderately heavy substance users, but who function adequately in society. Individuals in this cross-section may be well enough adjusted to use group counseling effectively but, tragically, may never get referred since there is no obvious problem.

Adolescents who generally fit this profile often do get referred to groups when their substance use leads to confrontations with limit-setting authorities. In recognition of the waste in human potential of substance abusers, there has been a recent increase in substance-abuse prevention efforts. Often these interventions have been attempted through educational group work in secondary school systems. Thus both the general school population as well as substance users who have been apprehended are targeted by such group interventions.

CHEMICAL DEPENDENCY LIFE-SKILL GROUPS

Selection and Composition

Education-based substance-abuse prevention groups may be used with students as early as the first grade. (Emphasis will be on adolescent groups in this chapter.) At about age 14, many youth have experimented with alcohol and/or other drugs, principally marijuana. Few, however, have formed adult addictive patterns. All students in a given high school grade may be included in drug education groups. Individuals would be excluded only if unable or unwilling to function effectively in a normal classroom. Some retarded, learning disabled, and/or highly disruptive individuals would thus require more individualized prevention training.

Length, Duration, and Size

Length of groups can be tailored to fit within the length of a school term. They may be run weekly or biweekly and meet typically for one class period. A class period would be set aside before and after the group sessions for preevaluation and postevaluation of student attitudes and factual knowledge concerning substance use issues. Ideally, group size would be limited to twelve to twenty members to allow for adequate time for both small group experiential exercises with whole group feedback, plus individual questions and answers.

Leader Role

This group may be led by teachers assisted by mature students of typically the next grade level (referred to here as peer facilitators). Because of the great importance of the modeling influence of teachers and peer facilitators, leadership positions would best be restricted to those not currently substance abusers. All leadership positions ideally would be selected from volunteers. Peer facilitators would be older students who have demonstrated successful leadership roles.

Leadership training is provided to faculty and peer facilitators. It is conducted by professionals and emphasizes human relations training skills such as recognizing and reflecting feelings, listening, role playing, and group involvement. Both teachers and peer facilitators undergo similar training based on the premise that effective relationship skills will enhance possibilities of effective leadership.

The group curriculum consists of professionally written outlines with adaptations for particular school system and community needs (see Appendix B for examples of session outlines). Teaching life skills that provide positive alternatives to substance use in the face of stress and peer group pressure is the essence of substance-abuse prevention. An approach emphasizing honesty and concreteness, while taking into account the adolescent's typical, "What's in it for me now!" perspective, are keys to group effectiveness. Thus, telling teenagers not to smoke pot because statistics indicate a somewhat higher rate of male infertility among heavy users will likely backfire. The essence of a substance-abuse prevention program consistent with Developmental Group Counseling is the teaching of life skills such as physical fitness/health maintenance, interpersonal communication/human relations, problem-solving/decision-making, identity development, and purpose-in-life, that stress positive learnings. Providing information about legal penalties for possession and sales of illegal drugs and obvious physical risks can be included in life-skills training, but primarily as possible problems when life skills are not learned.

The impact of the group will be facilitated when trust is increased. In establishing this trust, it may be helpful to acknowledge not only the deficits but the benefits of substance use. Denying the felt euphoria and temporary feelings of well-being stemming from the identity and rituals of this pleasure-seeking life-style may communicate ignorance or dishonesty to adolescents. They may then define themselves in opposition to authority by themselves denying the benefits of a nonsubstance-use-related life-style. This attitude is exemplified by the street saying, "Being straight is for those who can't handle drugs!" Thus, the leadership role instead will acknowledge and attempt to respond to the adolescent's *adult* reasoning capacity and decision-making responsibility. Transactional Analysis supports this approach as an appropriate avenue for eliciting *adult ego state* responses. Therefore, the role of leadership is not to tell students never to use drugs or alcohol, but to provide them necessary skills, knowledge, and the acknowledgment of their responsibility and capacity for adult decisions and accountability. Use of a peer facilitator to assist in this process further supports responding to the adolescent's developmental transition toward adulthood by serving as a concrete example of a teenager with adult responsibility.

An additional leadership role is the assessment of the degree of mastery of knowledge and skills ascertained by the end of the life-skills training period. Students achieving sufficient mastery will advance to new groups, while others would continue the same theme for the new term. Grades would not be used since emphasis is on learning rather than ranking who learns best.

Media and Setting

Ideally life-skills groups taught for prevention are groups conducted at school in rooms with chalkboards, movable furniture and carpeted floors. Audiovisual equipment such as slide projectors, tape recorders, videotape units, and movie projectors can be useful. These media can stimulate and help in maintaining group interest through providing concrete examples of group themes. Movable furniture and a carpeted floor can provide flexibility for seating arrangements, including informal comfortable seating on the floor.

Ethics

Issues. Some ethical issues arising from educational life-skills training groups for the prevention of substance abuse may include the following:

1. A member tells the leader after group how his alcoholic father beats him and his mother and that his mother is too scared to seek help.
2. A school administrator wants the group leader to name members who are probable substance users so that disciplinary action can be taken.
3. A school administrator tells the leader that the police are using undercover agents posing as students to break up drug dealing.

4. A probation officer calls and asks the leader to evaluate progress of a member so that this information could be used in deciding whether the member is to be incarcerated.

Responses

1. At issue when violence is reported is determination of the degree to which a risk of imminent harm exists. If such an outcome seems inevitable, prompt notification of authorities will be necessary. If harm appears unlikely, finding help for the member reporting home violence may be most appropriate. Although it appears that this entire family needs help, noncrisis intervention without parental assent may have the side effect of a sense of intrusion that could undermine helping efforts. If the adolescent is not in danger, more effort directed toward gathering more information and finding an appropriate way to help the family would be recommended.

2. At issue for a leader being asked to reveal identities of substance abusive members for disciplinary review is the maintenance of the member's confidentiality. To compromise this commitment would likely alienate the attempted alliance with members in establishing an open, caring group atmosphere. Thus, the group's effectiveness would be severely compromised. However, the school has some parenting responsibilities. Thus, if a member bragged of selling drugs and alcohol to other students, the harm caused by this illegal action would be implicitly supported if no countermeasures were taken. To avoid conflict between confidentiality and school parenting responsibility, a leader may spell out group rules, especially concerning limits of confidentiality when laws are being broken, in a pregroup interview and at the start of the first session.

3. Having knowledge of an undercover operation again speaks to the issue of confidentiality. Thus, not saying anything while conducting discussions on drug use may be seen as complicity in the entrapment of members. On the other hand, exposing the presence of a spy in the school may constitute interference with a police investigation. A compromise may be to dissuade members from revealing self-damaging confessions by indicating that you as group leader could not guarantee confidentiality.

4. At issue again in responding to the inquiries of a probation officer concerning a member's group participation is confidentiality. The member needs to be aware of the arrangement in which he or she is being reported on as a matter of informed consent. To deny the probation officer access might promote either undeserved incarceration or undeserved freedom. An alternative may be, with the

member's informed consent, to report solely on attendance so the member might have the opportunity to learn with a minimum of coercion.

SUBSTANCE ABUSE UNSTRUCTURED INTERVIEW COUNSELING GROUPS

The life-skills chemical dependency prevention program may be appropriate for almost all adolescents. However, for adolescents who have already been charged with substance abuse and related behavior, a different group approach may be valuable. Such an approach may function as an unstructured interview counseling group. In this type of group, members are given the opportunity to explore their life-styles and feelings with the goal of developing insight and commitment to change their life-styles. At the point where members identify their life-skill strengths and deficits and make a commitment to change, they are ready to be referred to a remedial life-skills training group to learn skills where deficits exist.

Selection and Composition

In starting the unstructured interview counseling group, a pregroup interview is strongly recommended. Those present at this interview will include, if possible, the group leader, the prospective member, his or her parents or guardians, and a representative of the authority who has mandated group involvement. The leader begins by having all present share their perspectives on the circumstances precipitating referral to group. From this, the leader will work with the prospective member toward establishing an individualized service contract. This written document shall outline the prospective member's responsibilities: short-, intermediate-, and long-term goals; and a time line indicating duration of treatment. This contract may be reviewed periodically and revised when necessary. To the extent that group membership is part of the contract, a guarantee by the leader to maintain confidentiality is needed, including a list of possible exceptions. Typical exceptions include a record of attendance for, say, a probation officer and situations where irreversible harm would seem imminent. Other group rules such as no weapons, fighting, drugs, or alcohol in group and the respecting of the rights of other members would also be made clear at this time. Thus, from the pregroup interview, a system defining responsibilities and support may be established.

Group membership is restricted to those age 12 to 17 who have the capacity for independent or semi-independent functioning and can interact in a group setting without being highly disruptive. There are advantages and disadvantages in having same sexes versus mixed membership. However, it may be helpful to avoid a situation where, in a mixed group, either the males or the females are greatly outnumbered.

Length and Duration

In accord with the adolescent's typical commitments and needs, including school transportation, athletic practices, and part-time jobs, limiting the length of group to one hour may be necessary for practical purposes. Ideally one and one-half hours could foster more in-depth progress; however, a shorter group may be worthwhile because of reduced fidgeting and requests for excused absences. The group may typically meet weekly for ten to twelve weeks, although twice-a-week meetings, when feasible, may enhance continuity and cohesiveness.

Leader Role

The group may be led by a counselor familiar with substance-use issues and the community in which members live. The leadership role includes acting as a facilitator, a model, a mentor, and a community liaison person. As a model, the leader will be faced with the adolescents' testing of limits and questioning of authority. Firm, caring, and consistent responding will allow eventual building of trust from which may spring members' efforts toward reevaluation of their often turbulent life-styles. Going the extra mile, such as by taking members who have met their contracts for a hike or to a ballgame or movie, can further facilitate the leader's efficacy. Use of a peer facilitator must be cautiously approached since this level of group may be open to legal and emotional issues for which even a sophisticated teenager may be hard pressed to handle.

Size

Because of the intense personal exploration and possible crisis management aspects of unstructured interview counseling groups, a maximum of 8 members is recommended. However, since it is usually helpful to have a minimum of 6 members present per session for group continuity, a roster as large as 12 plus a waiting list may be used to offset sporadic attendance. Attendance may be affected by teenagers' "now"-oriented perspective. Thus, having incentives and provisions for leverage to facilitate and maintain attendance can prove valuable.

Media and Setting

Since adolescents' options for independent transportation are often limited, a setting convenient to public transportation is appropriate. A location convenient to the community's secondary school(s) may be equally useful. It can also be helpful when the group's facility is not aligned with limit-setting agencies such as juvenile court or the school system. The adolescents' possible unpleasant associations with these entities may generalize to activities conducted in their facilities. Instead, a community center such as a library or public recreation center or private office may be more facilitative. Movable furniture, nearby snack and drink machines, a nearby water fountain, and a bathroom may also be helpful in maintaining a relaxed atmosphere. The group room per se may be set up as follows:

1. Comfortable, roughly equivalent chairs set up in a circle (avoid swivel or reclining chairs).
2. Window shades kept closed to avoid distractions and maintain privacy.
3. No furniture (tables or ottomans) inside the circle.
4. All members have a front row seat.
5. A consistent specific procedure set up for
   a. controlling room temperature
   b. smoking, eating, and drinking (preferably none)
   c. telephone calls, or other emergency/non-emergency interruptions
   d. monitoring attendance (e.g. signing a sheet passed around at the beginning of the session)

Ethics

Issues. Although many of the ethical issues for groups with adolescents who have been in trouble and who require exploration and identification of life-skills deficits and commitment to change are similar to those for adolescents referred to life-skills training groups, difficult situations that are more likely to occur in the former type groups include:

1. A leader catching a member in group with a bag of marijuana.
2. Two members having a knife fight in group.
3. A member admitting that his or her parent(s) is(are) supplying him or her with drugs.

Responses

1. Catching a member with marijuana points to a core conflict regarding the leader's adult authority, the member's right to confidentiality, and the leader's role as a model. If the leader attempts to confiscate the marijuana, the member may resist, causing possible injury and/or group resentment and loss of trust. To take no action

implicitly supports the member's illegal drug use, and to tell the member to go home may give the member an excuse to substitute being in group with getting high. To tell a parent or authority may be breaching the member's confidentiality, while to use this incident as a focal point risks reinforcing acting out with attention. A possible solution could be to have prior agreement of a rule specifying consequences for such action, for instance, telling a parent or probation officer.

2. If a knife fight erupts, the primary issue is how to limit bodily injury to all present, including the leader. After the violence is stopped, following through with legal ramifications will supersede the members' rights to confidentiality because of the life-threatening nature of such an incident. If payback violence is anticipated, probable targets need to be alerted.

3. When a member is given illegal drugs by his or her parents, the leader must determine how to help the member most effectively. Tipping off the police could be a violation of confidentiality and may shake group trust. Condemning the parents' actions in front of the group may instigate resentment, especially since many members may feel these parents are good. Ignoring or minimizing this report risks modeling avoidance of the group's basic purpose. It is possible, however, through careful exploration of this member's relationship with his or her family, to identify areas where changes are needed. Although such recognition will not necessarily condemn the drug-sharing aspect of this family, it may serve to deromanticize it, potentially aiding members in seeing the price they may pay for maintaining substance-dependent life-styles. If the member in question is deeply disturbed and in crisis over his or her home situation, group probing may be too threatening. Caring for his or her present pain through group and or individual support may take priority. The issues of (1) whether the member needs placement outside the home and the relative quality and effectiveness of available alternatives plus (2) how the group can stay effective in light of undermining outside factors need to be addressed.

GROUPS FOR ADULT ALCOHOLICS

Adult alcoholics typically have been drinking for a considerable period of time before starting treatment. For instance, the alcoholic adult may have been a moderate to heavy drinker who adequately handled drinking as an adolescent, but faltered as the years passed. The cumulative effects of drinking often progress to produce a dysfunctional adult.

Since drinking dulls the pain and awareness of facing progressive stagnation and deterioration, the problem drinker is caught in a vicious cycle. Consequently, immediate relief of alcohol becomes increasingly important. As dependence on alcohol increases, the individual's rate of emotional and personal development decreases or even backslides. Regression occurs as the individual fails to practice and thus loses competency in sober coping strategies and instead attempts to maintain equilibrium through self-sedation.

When alcoholics are first seen in treatment, their coping mechanisms are already beginning to fail. Unfortunately, the alcoholic at this point more often than not denies his or her problem. This continues typically until the point at which the alternatives to treatment are strong immediate penalties.

Thus, when conducting groups with alcoholics, it is important to have the group meet the alcoholic at the point at which his or her personal development has stopped. Through matching group agenda with the alcoholic's changing needs in his or her slow steps toward recovery, chances for effective treatment can be maximized. Because of the great needs of the alcoholic and limits of available support systems, all too often treatment ends with premature termination and subsequent recidivism.

In response to this problem, this section attempts to speak to the ways in which various types of alcoholism treatment groups may be used. Effective usage will allow the alcoholic to deal with developing needs as he or she begins recovery.

Selection and Composition

When considering selection and composition for groups in which alcoholics are treated, it is important to weigh specific group functions relative to community resources and members' needs. This may be understood in the light of different types of groups offered. Groups in which alcoholism is treated cover issues including detoxification, support, counseling, alcohol education, life-skills training, family living, women's roles, homosexuality, adolescence, young adulthood, and recovering. Some issues like counseling and skills training are facilitated by pregroup selection interviews. These interviews can be used to assess the prospective member's appropriateness while also providing the opportunity to communicate group rules and/or expectations. Typically, rules that may differ from general counseling groups may be requirements of minimum lengths of sobriety for group membership. Similarly, a treatment program offered to groups such as the Salvation Army may require members to take Antabuse®, a drug that causes violent illness if mixed with alcohol, as a prerequisite for admission.

A widespread selection criterion is that the prospective member has had or is having trouble associated with alcohol use. However, those currently drinking alcoholically and quite often those admitting to drinking at all will be deemed unacceptable for membership. While it is obvious that people who stay drunk all the time will not be able to use the group effectively and probably will disrupt other members, recovering alcoholics admitting current normal social drinking will also characteristically be excluded. Despite some research indicating recovering alcoholics becoming successful social drinkers, the majority of treatment professionals agree the risk of returning to pathological drinking patterns is so great that any possible sanction of renewed drinking behavior is countertherapeutic. Furthermore, troubled individuals such as hard drug addicts and the emotionally disturbed are not encouraged and may not be allowed to join alcoholism treatment groups. This may be understood in that alcoholics, through being stigmatized by society, develop a group cohesion and identity. Although this identity seemingly includes many negative connotations, it also provides a familiarity and safety beneficial to beginning group process.

Typical groups for adult alcoholics are composed mostly of men over 35 years old. Adolescent and young adult alcoholics are less likely to be seen in treatment and when involved more often pick groups specific to their age group. Similarly, female alcoholics sometimes form women's groups. Thus, although alcoholism provides a common bond and subsequent cohesion among group members, groups are often organized in reference to members' backgrounds and characteristics, although not necessarily any more so than groups focusing on mental health or drug addiction or other related areas.

Length, Duration, and Size

The varying needs of alcoholics at different stages of recovery will likely influence the length and duration of groups at any particular stage. An alcoholic's initial contact with groups may be when going through a detoxification center as an inpatient. In this level of group, a key theme to be addressed is that of stabilization. Implications of this theme help define optimal group length and duration within the context of the members' physical, psychological, and practical needs. Since members typically are under sedation and are at least somewhat disoriented, a meeting time of fairly brief duration, about forty-five minutes, would be appropriate. Basic orientation should be given, including the effects of the medicines, issues of coping with physical distress, fears and complaints, procedures that need to be followed, outside arrangements that need to be made, and options for further treatment. Since a member may attend such a group only up to ten times and usually for only three to five meetings, treatment of these issues necessarily has to be brief. This group would typically meet on a daily basis. The size of an inpatient stabilization group optimally will be small—five or six members. In a small group, individual crises can be addressed, and individual discomfort and alertness can be assessed.

A second stage in the recovery process may be entering a thirty-day or six-week residential treatment program. Since acceptance into such a program will be contingent on basic physical stabilization, members now will probably be better able to maintain longer periods of concentration in a group. Therefore, the group's length may be increased from forty-five minutes to one-and-one-half hours. One way of keeping to an hour-and-a-half is to have the group scheduled to meet for one hour and fifteen minutes, with a range of from one hour to one-and-one-half hours based on the leader's discretion. Having a ritual of a consistent starting and ending time with some flexibility with reference to issues of immediacy is seen as desirable.

When considering outpatients, the parameters may again change. For example, Alcoholics Anonymous has a program in which new members are assigned to attend ninety meetings in their first ninety days of sobriety. This use of groups serves as a replacement for the members' previous dependency on alcohol. When counseling groups are used in the initial stages of the recovery process or by those who use the group to maintain sobriety, but not to emphasize much self-searching, frequent attendance—two to four times weekly—can be useful. In such a group, up to twenty members may be efficacious since simply assembling a large nondrinking gathering may provide cause for optimism. Also, in such a crowd a member may feel more comfortable in that there is likely to be less social pressure to speak. The weakness in these groups is that members have less opportunity to speak, and involvement may be limited.

When general psychotherapy is the theme of the group, having 6 to 8 patients, a leader, and a coleader offers the opportunity for both a sense of group as opposed to individual relationship, plus a chance for daily participation for all members. When the theme is more of a structured psycho-educational one, a larger size, say 10 to 14 patients, is workable since typically less time will be focused on individuals' intense emotional issues. Risks in working on intense personal issues in larger groups include having less assurance of confidentiality and not being able to adequately check on reactions of members, especially quieter ones. Thus, modulations of size, amount of structure, and intensity of issues approached can strongly influence group effectiveness.

When groups focus more on insight development and commitment to personal change, a smaller ongoing group with a closed roster that meets for longer sessions on a weekly basis may function best. Thus, a limit of 8 members (12 with a coleader) meeting for a one-and-one-half to two-hour session, with an optional mid-group ten-minute break can provide adequate time for more in-depth personal exploration, plus an opportunity to get to know other members on a more intimate basis. When counseling groups focus more on skills training, frequent attendance, open rosters, and larger membership are functional.

The life-skills training groups for alcoholics who are stable and have adequate support systems are education-oriented and theme-specific groups. These groups optimally will be limited to 12 members (15 with the presence of a coleader). They would typically run from 6 to 12 weeks and have a closed roster. A pregroup interview would be used in which group rules such as committing to attend all sessions, to participate actively in training exercises, and to do homework would be spelled out. Group sessions would run from one to one-and-one-half hours, and meetings would typically be on a weekly basis.

Members of life-skills training groups would ideally be concurrently involved in both counseling groups and A.A. Such a schedule raises the issue of where lies the limit on how many groups is too many. While members best limit themselves to one counseling/therapy group at a time so as not to work at cross-purposes when self-exploring, the need for support and for learning new coping skills and strategies may be enhanced by concurrent involvement in other levels of groups. However, concurrent participation in life-skills training groups may best be limited, since addictive personalities may become "groupaholics." Let us keep in mind that a basic goal of group participation is a healthy, well balanced life-style.

Limiting attendance of support and A.A. type meetings must be approached carefully. When a member is suspected of attending groups to the extreme exclusion of other more basic life tasks, it may be that the member is struggling and doing the best he or she can do now. If so, a suggestion to come to fewer meetings may precipitate a drinking episode.

Media and Setting

A key issue concerning media for alcoholism treatment groups is how to attract the people who can be most helped by them. Since the alcoholic is often the last to acknowledge that a problem exists, media efforts need to be aimed at affected others, such as family members and employers. Television and radio ads, educational programs, and workshops for employers, church, and civic groups may provide appropriate coverage. When the alcoholic arrives for treatment, media can be important in sensitizing him or her to the implications of the disease, while providing hope that choosing treatment will lead to recovery. Lectures, slide presentations, films, question-and-answer sessions, and literature are methods of communicating these messages. Graphic illustrations such as slides of car wrecks, diseased livers, and accompanying statistics have been used, but not very effectively, in attempting to portray risks. Autobiographical data have been used to acknowledge hope. For instance, testimonials from recovering alcoholics who have had the courage to admit to their illness in public have helped change the image of the alcoholic from that of skid row bum to that of people found in all walks of society.

A basic aspect of a setting conducive to group work with alcoholics is the presence of ashtrays and coffee mugs. Although some groups prohibit smoking or drinks as unwise distractions, they may also be seen as replacements for oral needs once met by drinking. Thus, although the recovering alcoholic risks distraction with smoking and drinking rituals, the enforced delay of these rituals can risk considerably greater distraction. Accordingly, an appropriate setting for a group with alcoholics may include a well-ventilated room with comfortable chairs, a coffee urn, ashtrays, and reasonably close access to a bathroom.

Leader Role

Alcoholics often have learned to trust the bottle as the one sure thing in life. By the time it fails them, they are likely to be faced with deficits in their physical, emotional, psychological, and spiritual functioning. In beginning the recovery process, the group leader can be an important guide when able to model successful, nonsubstance-abusive functioning. In addition to modeling, the leader may guide by teaching basic facts of the addictive cycle and life skills necessary in developing alternate options. Finally, the leader needs a willingness and capacity for sharing empathy and patience with members of a patient population known for marked recidivism.

A difficult attitude that leaders are faced with is denial. Members not fully recovered from their last binge often proclaim, "I'll never drink again!" In addressing this "It can't happen here!" type of attitude, the leader can help the client explore positive and negative aspects of alcoholic versus abstinent life-styles so that such members are faced with how drinking benefited them. Thus, they may see that they may risk drinking again if unable to attain equivalent benefits through a sober life-style. The leader may help members learn to recognize how the addictive cycle's immediate reinforcement trades short-term gain for an overall deficit. When this is recognized, the leader can begin to model and teach the alcoholic life skills where deficits, usually multiple, have been identified.

Members often confront a new leader by asking if he or she is an alcoholic. If he or she is not, the belief that the leader cannot possibly understand the feelings of an alcoholic may follow. Such a confrontation can be seen as both a manipulation and a sincere plea for understanding. This writer, a moderate drinker, has responded by stating that "I do understand suffering, anger, fear, and sadness through my own experience and I hope we can work together so that my admittedly incomplete understanding can help in a meaningful way." In overcoming manipulation, leaders are faced with accepting without resentment that they can and will be "taken." Modeling genuineness without resentment allows members to see a successful life-coping skill based on a value of human relationships and delayed gratification.

Ethics

Issues.   Some ethical issues typical of counseling groups with alcoholics arise in situations when:

1. A member comes to group obviously intoxicated.
2. A member comes to group who *may* be intoxicated.
3. A member dangerous to himself or herself or others when drinking misses a group session without notice.
4. A member who is an A.A. sponsor describes a "helping" intervention he or she made when it is obvious that the intervention made was highly inappropriate.
5. An A.A. member admits to being involved in a sexual relationship with his or her sponsor.
6. A staff peer who is a recovering alcoholic is quoted by members as saying, "Only an alcoholic can understand another alcoholic!"
7. An alcoholic member is urged by family members to go back to drinking.
8. An alcoholic member risks losing a job by not drinking.
9. A recovering alcoholic is living with a practicing alcoholic.
10. A member takes the risk of revealing his or her homosexuality and is not supported, but instead condemned by members.

Responses.   In attributing ethical responsibility in these situations, there is no one right course of action. Input from group members and circumstances particular to any given situation may have a strong bearing on the relative effectiveness of alternate interventions. Therefore, what will be attempted are some guidelines in reasoning that attempt to respond to basic issues in the preceding situations.

1. When dealing with an obviously drunk member, the basic issue is his or her disruptive influence on the group. Thus, tell the member that he or she must leave and offer assistance if necessary, such as transportation to a detoxification unit or helping contact an A.A. sponsor. Usually this action will result in minimal disruption for the group. The message attempted is that drunkenness in group will not be tolerated, but that it also will not be reinforced by punishment.
2. In the case that one suspects a member of being intoxicated and one is not sure, one must be cautious not to accuse a member wrongly. However, when one suspects a member, this is likely based on observation. Thus, without accusing, one may share one's impression of differences noted in the member's behavior and/or appearance. For instance, one might say, "You seem less talkative than

usual; is there anything about being here this evening that is different?" Since many members have extensive experience observing inebriated behavior, their reactions may be the key factor in this situation.

3.   When, say, a suicidal or homicidal member is uncharacteristically absent without notice, one must ask, "Is the member in imminent danger, and what can be done to help?" A simple potentially effective intervention is attempting to telephone the member before starting the group. If contact cannot be made, the options of continuing attempts, calling authorities, or waiting until after group to make further inquiries may be weighed against perceived risk to the member. Although attempting to contact the member will delay the start of the group, it may be less of a disruption than worry that may be fed by having done nothing. Also, if an attempt has been made, rescue may be facilitated and potential guilt at having realized the possibility and done nothing will have been allayed.

4.   When a member who is an A.A. sponsor shares his or her engagement in highly inappropriate behavior with sponsorees, the issue becomes the potentially conflicting responsibilities of the leader. The leader has responsibility to the group, the sponsor, and the affected sponsorees. The leader risks facing condemnation regardless of which tack he or she chooses. However, if through group the sponsor can be helped to avoid the potentially destructive consequences of his or her actions, everyone may gain. This approach may be pursued when the sponsor makes both a commitment and progress toward improvement.

5.   A sponsor having sex with his or her sponsoree is a specific example of situation 4. An additional issue is why this generally private, potentially destructive issue has surfaced in group now.

6.   When members quote another staff member as proclaiming only a recovering alcoholic can help an alcoholic recover, the issue becomes how to support one's staff as an effective, unified treatment team without negating one's own effectiveness as leader. (Let us assume the leader is neither a recovering alcoholic nor does he or she believe that it takes one to cure one.) The leader may approach the issue by pointing out the concern for effective treatment the other staff member is expressing and that he or she shares that concern, but differs in treatment philosophy. The leader may also offer members the opportunity to check out working with the other staff member and to pick the one who suits them.

7, 8, 9.   In considering a member whose family or whose boss does not want him or her to stop drinking or one who is living with a practicing alcoholic spouse, a common issue is whether recovery can be effectively facilitated within the member's current system. When the spouse plays the roles of victim, rescuer, and persecutor, the dynamics of such a system are not conducive to growth. In these systems, the roles reverse, and the payoff is bad feelings. If the system is so rigid that the alcoholic's recovery will necessitate its dissolution, the group's role may be in helping the member recognize this and supporting him or her in finding an alternative system where he or she can function as a more successful, sober individual. Such support does not mean pressuring the member to jump at the first opportunity to leave, since he or she is surviving in the current system and may need a relatively supportive alternative to make such a major change.

10. In considering destructive systems, unfortunately, a group may provide an overall negative influence. For instance, a member after gaining trust and consequently revealing his or her homosexual preference may be condemned by other members as a disgusting pervert. Core issues in this situation include the gay member's right to effective treatment and the group members' rights to their own values. Even though condemnation may well stem from some members' own conflicted sexuality, with the gay member possibly having the healthiest sexual adjustment of any other member, other members have a right not to deal with threatening personal issues. The leader would be responsible not only for helping the condemned member deal with rejection, but also in aiding other members deal with their threatened sexuality. The condemned member may be helped by first having him or her leave the group. This decision would be based on whether the member could continue productive participation. Logically a greater understanding and acceptance of sexual mores would be gained. However, if this gap is too great, the leader is responsible for assisting in further treatment or appropriate referral. The leader also has the responsibility to help members unsettled by this incident. If these members are receptive, it may be an opportunity for them to explore and challenge their values; however, if they are not ready, responsibility may lie in helping the group adjust to functioning on the level at which it can be productive.

SUMMARY

This chapter has explored substance-abuse issues as they pertain to doing group work with adolescents, adolescents in trouble, and adult alcoholics. Although many of the dynamics of working with these populations in groups are similar, there also are differences, which are demonstrated in each population's self-identity. Thus, alcoholics, even though they may use mood-changing drugs, often do not identify themselves as drug users. Also, adolescent drug users who drink often see little similarity between themselves and, say, their alcoholic parents or relatives. Therefore, in providing group functions, including support, skills training, and facilitation of self-understanding, knowing both facts regarding substance use and the attitudes and feelings of group members are basics in conducting effective group counseling. In conclusion, for group work that focuses on substance-use issues to accomplish effective group counseling, it may well not only address negative aspects of abuse, but it also needs to take into account major systems affecting members' life-styles.

REFERENCES

Alcoholism: The National Magazine (1983). (3).

Baekeland, F., Lundwall, L., & Kissin, B. (1975). Methods for the treatment of chronic alcoholism: A Critical Appraisal. In R. Gibbons et al. (Eds.), *Research advances in alcohol and drug programs*. New York: Wiley.

Bland, J. M., Bewley, B. R., & Day, I. (1975). Primary schoolboys: Image of self and smoker. *British Journal of Preventive Social Medicine, 29*, 262–266.

Bohman, M. (1978). Some genetic aspects of alcoholism and criminality. *Archives of General Psychiatry, 35*, 269–276.

Center for Counseling and Psychological Services. (1970). *Survey of drug usage: Preliminary report*. Report No. 2. Orono, ME: University of Maine.

Chafetz, M. E., & Blane, H. T. (1963). Alcohol-crisis treatment approach and establishment of treatment relations with alcoholics. *Psychological Reports, 12*, 862.

Emrick, C. D. (1975). A review of psychologically oriented treatment of alcoholism: II. The negative effectiveness of treatment versus no treatment. *Journal on Studies on Alcohol, 37*, 1055–1060.

Evans, R. I., Henderson, A. H., Hill, P. C., & Raines, B. E. (1979). Current psychological, social and education programs in control and prevention of smoking: A critical methodological review. In A. M. Gotto and R. Paoletti (Eds.), *Atherosclerosis Reviews*. New York: Raven Press.

Evans, R. I., Rozelle, R. M., Lasater, T. M., Dembrowski, T. M., & Allen, B. P. (1970). Fear arousal, persuasion and actual versus implied behavior change: New perspective utilizing a real-life dental hygiene program. *Journal of Personality and Social Psychology, 16*, 220–227.

Feuerstein, R., Hanegbi, R., & Krasilowsky, D. (1970). The corrective object relations (COR) theory and treatment group techniques. *Psychosocial Process, 1*, 29–46.

Fine, S., Knight-Webb, G., & Vernon, J. (1977). Selected volunteer adolescents in adolescent group therapy. *Adolescence, 12*(46), 189–197.

Fodor, J. T., Glass, L. H., & Weiner, J. M.(1968). Smoking behavior, cognitive skills and educational implications. *Journal of School Health, 38*, 94–98.

Glueck, S., & Glueck, E. (1950). *Unraveling juvenile delinquency*. New York: Commonwealth Fund.

Goodman, G. (1967). An experiment with companionship therapy: College students and troubled boys—Assumptions, selection and design. *American Journal of Public Health, 57,* 1772–1777.

Goodwin, D. W. (1979). Alcoholism and heredity. *Archives of General Psychiatry, 36,* 57–61.

Hamburg, B. A., & Varenhorst, B. B. (1972). Peer counseling in the secondary schools: A community health project for youth. *American Journal of Orthopsychiatry, 42,* 566–581.

Hilgard, J., Straight, D., & Moore, U. (1969). Better adjusted peers as resources in group therapy with adolescents. *Journal of Psychotherapy, 73,* 75–100.

Hill, D. (1971). Peer group conformity in adolescent smoking and its relationship to affiliation and autonomy needs. *Australian Journal of Psychology, 23,* 189–199.

Horowitz, M. J. (1966). Psychological aspects of education related to smoking. *Journal of School Health, 36,* 281–286.

Jessor, R., & Jessor, S. L. (1975). Adolescent development and the onset of drinking. *Quarterly Journal of Studies on Alcoholism, 36,* 27–51.

Johnson, L. D., O'Malley, P. M., & Bachman, J. G. (1981). Psychotherapeutic, licit and illicit use of drugs among adolescents: An epidemiological perspective. *Journal of Adolescent Health Care, 8,* 36–51.

Jones, R. K., & Joscelyn, K. B. (1978). *Alcohol and highway safety 1978: A review of the state of knowledge, summary volume.* U.S. Department of Transportation Pub. No. DOT HS 803–764. Washington, D.C.: National Highway Traffic Safety Administration.

Leventhal, H. (1970). Findings and theory in the study of fear communications. In L. Berkowitz (Ed.), *Advances in experimental social psychology.* Vol. 5. New York: Raven Press.

Luborsky, L., Singer, B., & Luborsky, L. (1975). Comparative studies of psychotherapies. *Archives of General Psychiatry, 32,* 995–1008.

Marlatt, G. A., & Rohsenow, D. J. (1980). Cognitive processes in alcoholic use: Expectancy and the balanced placebo design. In N. K. Marlow (Ed.), *Advances in substance abuse: Behavioral and biological research.* Greenwich, CT: Jai Press.

McGuire, W. J. (1973, October 22–25). Models for drug education: Experimental findings on the communication of drug education. Unpublished. Toronto, Canada.

McKillip, J., et al. (1973). Patterns and correlates of drug use among urban high school students. *Journal of Drug Education, 3,* 5.

National Highway Traffic Safety Administration. (1978). *1978 Alcohol and Highway Safety Review.* U.S. Department of Transportation. Washington, D.C.: U.S. Government Printing Office.

National Highway Traffic Safety Administration. (1981). *Fatal accident reporting system 1979.* U.S. Department of Transportation Pub. No. DOT HS 805 570 Washington, D.C.: U.S. Government Printing Office.

New England Learning and Research. (1970). *A survey of drug use in a cross-section of Maine communities.* Augusta, ME: Author.

Palmer, A. B. (1970). Some variables contributing to the onset of cigarette smoking in junior high school students. *Social Science Medicine, 4,* 359–366.

Plant, M. L. (1979). *Drinking careers.* London: Tavistock.

Rice, F. P. (1978). *The adolescent: Development, relationships and culture* (2nd ed.) Boston: Allyn and Bacon.

Salisbury, W. W., & Fertig, F. R. (1968). The myth of alienation and teenage drug use: Coming of age in mass society. *California School Health, 4*(1), 29–39.

Sallan, S. E., Zinberg, N. E., & Frei, D. (1975). Antiemitic effect of delta-9-tetrahydrocannibinol in patients receiving cancer chemotherapy. *New England Journal of Medicine, 293,* 795–797.

Schroeder, R. C. (1973). *The politics of drugs.* Washington, D.C.: Congressional Quarterly.

Schroeder, R. C. (1980). *The politics of drugs* (2nd ed.). Washington, D.C.: Congressional Quarterly Press.

Sherif, M., & Sherif, C. W. (1964). *Reference groups: An exploration into conformity and deviation in adolescent groups.* New York: Harper and Row.

Terris, M. A. (1967). Epidemiology of cirrhosis of the liver: National mortality data. *American Journal of Public Health, 57,* 2076–2088.

Vaillant, G. E., & Milofsky, E. S. (1982). The etiology of alcoholism: A prospective viewpoint. *American Psychologist, 37,* 494–503.

White paper on drug abuse: A report to the president from the Domestic Council Drug Abuse Task Force. (1975). Washington, D.C.: U.S. Government Printing Office.

Winokur, G., Clayton, D. J., & Reich, T. (1969). *Manic depressive illness.* St. Louis, Mo.: Mosby.

SUGGESTED READINGS ────────────────────────────── ▬

Beauchamp, D. E. (1980). *Beyond alcoholism.* Philadelphia: Temple University Press.

Gitlow, S. E. & Peyser, H. S. (Eds.) (1980). *Alcoholism: A practical treatment guide.* New York: Grune & Stratton.

Hilgard, J., Straight, D., & Moore, U. (1969). Better adjusted peers as resources in group therapy with adolescents. *Journal of Psychotherapy, 73,* 75–100.

Jessor, R., & Jessor, S. L. (1975). Adolescent development and the onset of drinking. *Quarterly Journal of Studies on Alcoholism, 36,* 27–51.

Marlow, N. K. (Ed.) (1980). *Advances in substance abuse: Behavioral and biological research.* Greenwich CT: Jai Press.

Mendelson, J. H., Mello, N. K., & Lex, B. W. (1986). Alcohol and marijuana: Concordance of use by men and women. *National Institute on Drug Abuse: Research Monograph Series,* No. 68, 117–141.

Morris, J. (1986). Interdisciplinary treatment of alcoholism. *Alcoholism Treatment Quarterly, 3* (4), 125–131.

Rice, F. P. (1978). *The adolescent: Development, relationships and culture* (2nd ed.). Boston: Allyn and Bacon.

Schroeder, R. C. (1980). *The politics of drugs* (2nd ed.). Washington, D.C.: Congressional Quarterly Press.

Vaillant, G. E., & Milofsky, E. S. (1982). The etiology of alcoholism: A prospective viewpoint. *American Psychologist, 37,* 494–503.

C H A P T E R 10

Self-Help Groups[1]

The self-help group is a unique group modality that presents its own special challenge to the helping profession. By definition, *self-help groups* are groups in which members assume primary responsibility for the organization, functioning, and leadership of the group. The role of the professional in self-help groups is not the typical role of organizer and leader that he or she assumes with counseling groups.

The contemporary helping professional, however, cannot afford to ignore the presence and importance of self-help groups. The self-help group is becoming a major delivery system in the mental health field. In the last twenty years we have witnessed a striking increase in the number and variety of self-help groups. In 1982 Katz estimated that well over a half million self-help groups existed and that at least 14 million people were members of self-help groups (Katz, 1982). The groups deal with a range of issues so diverse as to almost defy classification. Issues of parenting, life transition, handicap, addiction, and disease are among the concerns addressed by the groups. As new societal concerns emerge, self-help groups are formed to help those affected. For instance, the rise in the divorce rate and changes in child custody have led to the formation of self-help groups for mothers without custody. In response to the recent rise in incidence of AIDS, support groups have been formed for the various groups of people affected by the disease, including groups for AIDS victims, their parents, and their spouses.

1. Written by Inese Wheeler, Ph.D. candidate, University of Georgia.

The challenge for the mental health profession is to find a way to deal with self-help groups that will incorporate the expertise of the professional without destroying the autonomy that is the essence of the self-help movement.

HISTORY

Self-help is by no means a new phenomenon. In the broadest sense, the activity of self-help is as old as human society (Pancoast, Parker, & Froland, 1983). In the early twentieth century Kropotkin (1914/1972) traced cooperative groups to prehistoric times and suggested that the very condition of civilization lay in the early development of habits of cooperation through food gathering and the maintenance of group safety. In the narrower sense of groups formed for mutual aid in dealing with a specific issue, self-help can be traced to two different roots. One is economic and is typified by the emergence of the English Friendly Societies, an early form of trade unions (Katz & Bender, 1976a). The other is religious and was first expressed in the Methodist group founded by John Wesley in the 1700s (Rodolfa & Hungerford, 1982).

In twentieth century America self-help has developed expressions that have been responsive to the demands of the times. The early part of the century saw the growth of unions and ethnic self-help associations. The first anonymous groups were formed in the early 1930s, coinciding with the Depression and the repeal of Prohibition, and continued to develop through the 1950s. Some of these groups, such as Alcoholics Anonymous and Gamblers Anonymous, established national organizations that still exist today. In the 1950s self-help became increasingly politicized with the emergence of the civil rights movement, the women's movement, and consumer groups (Pancoast, Parker, & Froland, 1983). Throughout the century and continuing to the present self-help groups have become less economic and more personal in emphasis (Remine, Rice, & Ross, 1984).

CLASSIFICATION

Defining and classifying a phenomenon with such a long history and such diverse forms of expression is not a simple task. Killilea (1976) has suggested that self-help might not be a single, unitary movement. According to her, self-help groups could be seen as support systems; as social movements; as spiritual movements and secular religions; as systems of consumer participation; as alternative care-giving systems adjunct to professional helping systems; as intentional communities; as subcultural entities that represent a way of life; as supplementary communities; as expressive social influence groups; and as organizations of the deviant and stigmatized.

Katz and Bender (1976b) proposed a classification of self-help groups that includes the whole range of the phenomenon. Their classification consists of the following categories: (1) groups that focus primarily on individual self-fulfillment or personal growth (e.g. Recovery, Inc.); (2) groups that focus primarily on social advocacy (e.g. the Committee for the Rights of the Disabled); (3) groups whose primary focus is to create alternative patterns for living (e.g. gay rights and women's liberation groups); (4) groups that provide refuge (usually residential) for desperate people who are seeking protection from the pressures of life and society (e.g. addicts or ex-addicts); (5) mixed types of groups that arise from shared life situations (e.g. bereavement, divorce, or Vietnam veterans).

Katz (1972) made a distinction between groups whose primary purpose is to change society and those that work for adjustment of their members within the existing framework. Gay rights organizations and women's rights groups have a political and societal orientation, whereas groups such as A.A. and Parents Without Partners focus on individual adjustment. Katz and Bender (1976b) label the societal orientation as an *outer* focus and the individual orientation as an *inner* focus.

Within the context of the self-help group with an inner focus, we find different systems of classification. Bean (1975) suggests three types of groups: crisis, permanent, and addiction. Crisis-oriented groups address problems resulting from major life transitions. The focus of these groups is to provide emotional support and educational information. Membership may be temporary. Permanent self-help groups focus on long-term problems that carry a stigma and mark the individual as different. Groups for dwarfs, former prisoners, or mental patients fall into this category. The goals of these groups are to improve members' self-esteem and combat prejudice. Addiction-oriented self-help groups are geared toward people with destructive habits such as drugs, alcohol, gambling, overeating, and smoking. The focus is on helping members learn new behaviors.

Borman (1979) categorized self-help groups with an inner focus according to how they deal with change. One type of group works toward effecting change within its members. The other type seeks to help members adapt to life changes. The first type of group centers on the need to modify member behavior and attitude. The anonymous groups and Recovery, Inc., are examples of this type. These groups often specify clear and concrete guidelines through which to obtain the desired change. The second type of group focuses more on adapting to and coping with life changes. These groups provide a variety of helping methods for their members, but do not specify concrete guidelines. Parents Without Partners, Widowed Persons Service, and Survivors of Suicide Victims are examples of this category.

It is the self-help group oriented toward helping the individual, rather than changing society, that is of interest to the mental health professional. The groups whose primary role is social advocacy (e.g. National Organization of Women and National Gay Task Force) tend to have large, powerful national organizations. The individual-oriented groups may have national organizations that perform some advocacy functions, but the heart of these organizations lies in the face-to-face interaction of the individual members at the local level. These groups provide services similar to those provided by the mental health profession and could be considered to be adjuncts or alternatives to psychotherapy (Levy, 1976).

SPECIAL CHARACTERISTICS

Despite their diversity, self-help groups share underlying characteristics that embody the essentials of the self-help phenomenon. Katz and Bender (1976b) suggested a definition that has gained wide-spread acceptance:

> Self-help groups are voluntary, small group structures for mutual aid and the accomplishment of special purpose. They are usually formed by peers who have come together for mutual assistance in satisfying a common need, overcoming a common handicap or life-disrupting problem, and bringing about desired social and/or personal change. The initiators and members of such groups perceive that their needs are not, or cannot be, met by or through existing social institutions. Self-help groups emphasize face-to-face social interactions and the assumption of personal responsibility by members. They often provide material assistance, as well as emotional support; they are frequently "cause"-oriented, and promulgate an ideology or values through which members may attain an enhanced sense of personal identity. (p. 9)

The definition suggests that self-help groups share the following characteristics: a peer orientation, a problem focus, an estrangement from societal norms, and an ideological base. Peer orientation is the central characteristic of the self-help groups. Most self-help groups are organized and maintained by persons who share a common condition, situation, symptom, or experience. The role of the professional is minimized. It is the fact of sharing a problem that defines membership status in the groups. A peer in a self-help group thus has a commonality or mutuality of problems with other members.

The problems faced by members of self-help groups differentiate them from society as a whole. At times individuals faced with particular problems have not been able to get help within the existing system. The emergence of the present self-help group movement occurred in the 1930s when two groups with stigmatizing conditions—mental retardation and alcoholism—began to create mechanisms for those affected by the conditions to help one another, as opposed to relying on professional help (Steinman & Traunstein, 1976). The self-help movement is based on an outsider orientation. The degree of this orientation differs among the particular groups. Some groups are composed of members who are stigmatized by society and considered deviant: alcoholics, addicts, gamblers, transvestites, ex-convicts, dwarfs, and mental patients (Sagarin, 1969). Other groups deal with conditions which, although not considered stigmata, are not shared by other members of society: serious illnesses, disabilities, and losses. Members of self-help groups are out of step with society.

Perhaps because they are out of step with society, self-help groups develop ideologies to counteract the stigma and isolation. The groups have teachings about the causes and cures of the particular problem. These teachings, or ideologies, are guidelines that serve to sustain and inspire the person afflicted with the problem. Ideologies can be written and specific, as in the case of the Alcoholics Anonymous' 12-step program, or an informal oral tradition passed on from member to member (Borman, 1982).

COMPARISON TO OTHER GROUPS

Although self-help groups possess unique characteristics, they also share characteristics with other helping groups. They are similar to counseling groups in structure and broad goals. Both types of groups emphasize face-to-face interaction among their members. The overall goal of both is to bring about personal change. Lakin (1985) has suggested a number of characteristics that self-help groups share with traditional therapy groups. According to him, both emphasize emotional expression and catharsis. Both encourage support among their members, although self-help groups put a greater emphasis on this support. Finally, both self-help and therapy groups work toward implementing behavior change and more effective coping strategies.

A recent study by Toro, Rappaport, and Seidman (1987) suggests some possible differences between self-help groups and psychotherapy groups. Members of the self-help group studied (GROW International) perceived that their group had more active leaders, greater group cohesion, more structure and task orientation, and fostered more independence than did members of the psychotherapy groups. Members of psychotherapy groups perceived that their groups encouraged more expression of negative and other feelings and showed more flexibility in changing the group's activities than did members of the self-help groups. However, since little research has been done comparing self-help and psychotherapy groups, the results need to be interpreted cautiously (Toro, Rappaport, & Seidman 1987).

The most significant difference between self-help and counseling groups is in the leadership patterns. Most self-help groups are organized and led by non-professionals. Distrust of the professional is not uncommon (Back & Taylor, 1976). In fact, assumption of responsibility for change by the members is the essence of the self-help group. From their perspective, the know-how and expertise lies with those who have struggled with and overcome the problem, not the professional. Thus, peer leadership is an important aspect of the helping power of the self-help group.

Peer leadership is also the characteristic that distinguishes self-help groups from another type of group—the support group. The support group shares some important characteristics with the self-help group. Members of the support group share the same problem and that problem becomes a criterion for membership. The problem is often perceived as a stigmatized attribute. As with the self-help group, the basic goal of the support group is to increase the members' coping abilities. Support groups also value the dissemination of information on all aspects of the particular problem as an important function of the group, as do self-help groups (Rosenberg, 1984). The two types of groups even share the same population at times. Both types of groups can be found for the bereaved, victims of abuse, and those with handicaps.

Pearson (1986) suggests that the distinction to be made between self-help groups and support groups is not related to whom they are *for*, but whom they are *by*. The leader of a self-help group usually is experiencing or has experienced the same situation as the group members and this experience with the problem constitutes the authority necessary to lead the groups. Some self-help groups, moreover, have no designated leader and therefore no one person is responsible for the efficient functioning of the group (Rosenberg, 1984). In support groups the leader is a professional group worker who claims knowledge of and assumes responsibility for the group process.

Support groups provide a form of self-help to populations who are unwilling or unable to organize themselves. For instance, children are not able to form their own self-help groups and yet might benefit from interaction with peers who share their experience. Support groups have been formed for bereaved children, siblings of handicapped children, and children who have been sexually abused (Gitterman & Shulman, 1986).

DYNAMICS

The self-help group, like other small groups, has its own characteristic dynamics. These dynamics are the result of the interplay of the following factors: its leadership patterns, the characteristics of its membership, the norms that develop within the group, and the stages that characterize the group over time. Since self-help groups are a grassroots phenomenon and typically not under the influence of professional direction, the dynamics vary from group to group. Nevertheless, general patterns are discernible (Napier & Gershenfeld, 1985).

As stated previously, the expertise required of a self-help group leader is experience with the issue around which the group is organized (Katz, 1970). Authority is shared by peers. Leaders may emerge in the groups, but they are seen as peers willing to assume responsibility, not as experts set apart from other members (Napier & Gershenfeld, 1985). Some groups, in fact, deliberately exclude professionals from leadership roles (Katz, 1970). In a self-help group it is possible to enter as a new member desperately in need of help and in time rise to a position of leadership. Some self-help groups even specifically adopt a rotation of membership in order to discourage dominance by a few.

Peer leadership is rarely found in group work outside of the self-help movement. Berzon and Solomon (1964), in their study of self-directed therapy groups, found the groups to be ineffective. The participants would not, over an extended period of time, assume responsibility for what happened in the group. Berzon and her colleagues have developed audiotapes to be used by self-directed encounter groups. They have found that planned program materials can be used by self-directed groups to facilitate personal growth for the individual members (Berzon, Solomon, & Reisel, 1972). Some self-help organizations provide materials and guidelines to facilitate the emergence of peer leadership.

Membership in self-help groups is voluntary. People who join a self-group must identify themselves as having a problem and needing help from others (Gartner & Riessman, 1980). Since the group members share a focal concern not shared by the rest of society, the self-group becomes a powerful reference group for the individual. By serving as a reference group with which members strongly identify, self-help groups facilitate changes in self-perception and empower the individual member (Napier & Gershenfeld, 1985).

The norms of the self-help group reflect the unique characteristics and function of the group. They vary widely from group to group, and reflect the ideology embodied by the group. They may be expressed in formal documents or unspoken assumptions. They may be fixed and entrenched or open to revision. As with norms in all groups, they serve to direct and control member behavior.

Napier and Gershenfeld (1985) believe that there are two group norms that serve as the underpinnings for many self-help groups: mutual aid and activity as means of solving one's problems. Mutual aid implies that assistance is a reciprocal process. Group members are expected to support each other in recovery. They are being helped, but are also helping. Long-time members guide the beginners, who in turn will eventually guide others. The norm of activity focuses on active coping. People are urged to face their handicap or problem and to continue functioning. A.A. exhorts its members to take it "one day at a time." Groups for bereaved parents, children, and spouses are encouraged to mourn, but also to re-engage in life.

Like other groups, self-help groups follow a pattern of growth. Katz (1970) outlined a model for group development consisting of five stages: Origin, Informal Organization, Emergence of Leadership, Formal Organization, and Professionalization.

The Origin stage is characterized by the presence of a founder or founders. At times the founder is a professional who is in disagreement with the accepted treatment or service for the problem and who has a vision of how the problem can be rectified. The founder carries out the work of planning and conducting the initial meeting.

In the next stage, Informal Organization, the group continues to add new members. At this point few rules exist to govern the activities of the members. Leadership and responsibility is shared informally. During this stage the role and authority of the founder is significantly reduced (Napier & Gershenfeld, 1985).

As the group develops a history and sense of identity, new leadership emerges from the group. Eventually a division of labor appears and certain functions become identified with certain individuals. Activities become more routinized and defined at this point. This is the Emergence of Leadership stage.

In his more recent writings, Katz (1981) admits that many self-help groups do not develop beyond the emergence of leadership. In fact, he has found that some groups (e.g. women's consciousness-raising groups) never develop a leadership structure. Other groups, however, responding to increasing size and complexity, continue to develop through the final stages.

In the next stage, Formal Organization, the overall organizational structure is developed and codified into rules or bylaws. The roles of the leaders, strategy-planners, and members-volunteers are more clearly defined and established through practice and trial-and-error. As activities are increased, an administrative structure is needed to direct them. The organization becomes more defined and rigid.

Finally, in the Professionalization stage, the leadership group finds it necessary to give up some of its function to paid staff members. As increasingly professional activities are undertaken, professionally qualified staff members may enter the organization. Volunteer activities, the hallmark of the self-help group, still exist, but are supplemented by paid activities.

A DEVELOPMENTAL PERSPECTIVE

By definition self-help groups are autonomous and self-governing. Consequently, they are groups geared toward adult concerns. One way to look at the groups is from an adult development perspective. According to this perspective, psychic growth does not end with adolescence, but continues through an individual's life span. Increasingly, adulthood is being viewed as a time of active change and transition (Schlossberg, 1981; Wortley & Amatea, 1982). In one conception of adult development, adults are seen as progressing through stages. These stages are characterized by psychological issues that need to be resolved in order for the individual to advance to the next stage (Erikson, 1963) or tasks to be accomplished (Havighurst, 1953). Some authors believe that stage transitions are age related (Levinson, 1978). Others suggest that life context is more important than chronological age (Lowenthal, Thurnher, & Chiriboga, 1975). Alternatively, some theorists and researchers in adult development reject the notion of stages and take a "life-course perspective" (Schlossberg, 1981). According to this perspective, life events play the pivotal role in adult development. Life events include events considered normative, such as getting a job, marriage, transitions to parenting, retirement, and events considered nonnormative, such as divorce, unemployment, health problems, and death.

What the various approaches to adult development have in common is the assumption that adulthood has its own set of tasks and challenges. Adulthood is seen as a time of transition. Transitions, whether because of internal psychic pressures or events outside the individual, present a challenge to the individual. Schlossberg (1981) writes: "A transition can be said to occur if an event or non-event results in a change in assumptions about oneself and the world and thus requires a corresponding change in one's behavior and relationships" (p. 5).

When a life event and its consequent transition is on time and expected, it can be considered normative. The individual experiencing a normative life event has access to peers who are experiencing a similar event. However, when a life event is off-time and unexpected—nonnormative—the individual might find himself or herself isolated from peer support. Neugarten (1968) believes that there exists a socially prescribed timetable for the ordering of major life events. To be off-time, whether early or late, carries penalties. The individual finds himself or herself in a deviant position. Widowhood late in life constitutes a normative, although stressful transition. Early widowhood complicates the transition, making it more difficult to negotiate.

A life event can also turn into a crisis. The birth of a child is an important and challenging transition. The birth of a handicapped child, however, will probably add further strains and difficulties to the transition.

Some self-help groups deal with normative life transitions. The La Leche League for nursing mothers, the National Organization of Mothers of Twins Clubs, and retirement groups are examples. Silverman (1985) suggests that self-help groups are one of the few places in contemporary society where expertise in coping with transitions can be found. Members can obtain information from others who have had similar experiences, legitimize their feelings, and find role models.

Most self-help groups do not deal with normative transitions, however. They deal with deviations from expected life experiences. Examples of such deviations are single parenthood, divorce, serious illness, and early widowhood. Or they may be the absence of expected, normative events (Danish, Smyer, & Nowak, 1983). Remaining childless once married, not launching one's children, and remaining single are examples of such nonevents.

A partial listing of self-help groups related to parenting may illustrate the numerous ways in which a normative life transition can turn into a nonnormative event. There are groups for parents of premature babies (Premature and High Risk Infants); for parents whose children die at birth (Aiding a Mother Experiencing Neo-Natal Death), or in the first year (National Foundation for Sudden Infant Death Syndrome); for adopted children seeking their natural parents (Adoptees' Liberty Movement Association), and for parents who have surrendered children for adoption (Concerned United Birth Parents); for single parents (Parents Without Partners), mothers (Association of Professional Women Who Are Mothers) or fathers (Fathers' Rights); for parents with handicapped children (groups for every disability), or children who are dying (the Candlelighters); for parents who abuse their children (Parents Anonymous) and for children who have been abused (Daughters and Sons United); and at the other end of the life-span for those whose parents (or relatives) are institutionalized (Friends and Relatives of the Institutionalized Aged) (Gartner & Riessman, 1984).

The special characteristics of the self-help group make it particularly appropriate for dealing with transition. Since the groups are problem oriented, a person undergoing a nonnormative transition finds himself or herself in the majority, not the minority. Peer support, not available in society as a whole, can be found within the context of the self-help group.

HOW SELF-HELP GROUPS WORK

The issue of how self-help groups function, or to put it simply, how self-help groups help, is still very much an open question. Some rudimentary attempts have been made to develop theories specific to self-help groups (Antze, 1979; Levy, 1979). Most theoretical approaches derive from existing sociological and psychological theory (Katz, 1981). The following change mechanisms have been proposed: mutual support (Katz, 1981; Silverman, 1980); helper therapy (Riessman, 1965); and the role of ideology (Antze, 1979).

The role of mutual support in self-help groups seems almost axiomatic. Self-help is often termed *mutual aid*. Self-help groups are alternately called *support groups.* There seems to be a tacit assumption in the literature on self-help groups that a mutual support process is operating and that this process is positive. Silverman (1985) suggests that it might be important to look at the specific type of mutual support at work in the groups.

There is a body of considerable research that indicates that social support buffers the adverse psychological impact of stressful life events and ongoing life strains (Thoits, 1986). Thus, the value of social support is recognized as a positive force for individuals under stress. Since self-help is directed at people in stress, social support is likely to be one of the helping processes in the self-help group (Silverman, 1985).

Recent writings and research on social support have stressed the variety that exists in social support since there is increasing evidence that differing types of support have varying effects (Kessler, Price, & Wortman, 1985). The source of the social support seems to be crucial in the effectiveness of the support. For instance, women with breast cancer may be more likely to accept emotional support from someone who has had the same experience than from an uninformed friend (Dunkel-Schetter & Wortman, 1982).

The self-help group may provide a particularly effective form of social support for individuals experiencing unique situations or problems. Schacter (1959), reporting on a study of affiliative tendencies of college students during periods of anxiety, observed that students first chose to be with others in the same situations. Silverman and Smith (1984), in a study of three self-help groups, found that people who joined the groups did so out of a need to find someone else who had a similar experience. Peers who have gone through a similar experience seem to be unique sources of help for people in stress.

Not only may the opportunity to find someone like oneself be central to learning to cope with stress, but also the opportunity to change roles and become a helper may be important as well. Riessman (1965) has called this "the helper therapy principle." He suggests several ways in which helping might be beneficial to the helper. Doing something worthwhile to help someone in need may give the helper a sense of adequacy and effectiveness. The helper may also benefit from the status associated with the role. In addition, in the process of helping, the helper may be learning through teaching and acquiring a broader perspective of his or her predicament. Rappaport (1985) calls this process *empowerment*: gaining psychological control over oneself and extending the positive influence to others.

There is some evidence for the positive effects of the helping process. In a study of Mended Hearts, a self-help group for heart surgery patients, Lieberman and Borman (1979) found significant differences between two groups of men who had undergone open-heart surgery. Only those who were active in the organization and could be considered helpers made better adjustments than non-members. Rappaport (1985) reports a study of groups of multiple sclerosis sufferers, Compassionate Friends, and Overeaters Anonymous. The investigators found that the individuals who both provided and received social support obtained more benefits and satisfaction from their participation.

Both mutual aid and helper therapy are helping processes that operate to a greater or lesser extent in other types of groups. Antze (1979) has proposed a theory of how self-help groups work, based on a unique feature of the groups. According to him, each group has an ideology—a specialized system of teachings that members consider to be the key to recovery. These teachings are the cumulative wisdom of member experiences. Ideology may be explicit or implicit, but in all cases it guides the purpose of the group and structures the self-help process (Suler, 1984).

Antze believes that ideologies are systems of meaning that function as a "cognitive antidote" to the basic features of a condition shared by everyone who joins the group. The ideology of the group counteracts the maladaptive beliefs of the members, undermining the problematic aspects of their lifestyle. In time, new attitudes and values replace the dysfunctional ones. Suler (1984) suggests that "the groups construct a social reality that acts as a shared basis for perceiving and acting in the world" (p. 30).

Antze developed his theory from observation of groups whose objectives are behavioral control of members: Alcoholics Anonymous, Recovery, Inc., and Synanon. These groups have explicit, well-developed ideologies. However, the concept has also been applied to the groups that emphasize adaptation and coping with stressful situations (Sherman, 1979; Suler, 1984). The goal of most behavioral control groups is to eliminate or control problematic behavior. The ideology attempts to counteract habitual self-destructive attitudes and beliefs held by an individual that contribute to the behavior. Stress-coping groups, on the other hand, do not seek to eliminate behavior, but to reconceptualize it and place it in an adaptive perspective (Sherman, 1979). The ideology of these groups is not as carefully delineated as that of the behavioral control groups.

Each group, whether oriented toward behavioral change or coping, develops its own unique ideology based on the problem shared by its members. As an illustration, Antze (1979) contrasts the ideology of Alcoholics Anonymous and Recovery, Inc. According to Antze, alcoholism is perpetuated by the alcoholics' belief that they are omnipotent. The ideology of A.A. encourages the individual to accept alcoholism as a disease that is beyond his or her control and to rely on a "higher power." The ex-psychiatric patients of Recovery tend to prolong their symptoms by attributing them to sickness beyond their control. Recovery's ideology encourages them to believe that they could overcome their symptoms if they try hard enough to act as if they are healthy. The various stress-coping groups encapsulate and transmit the essence of what has worked for others who have previously faced that specific problem or situation.

In emphasizing the role of ideologies, Antze (1979) is arguing for the existence of another helping process in the self-help group. He calls this the *persuasive function* of the group. According to him, the process works because the groups are fixed communities of beliefs. The beliefs are perpetuated by activities characteristic of the groups: sharing of experience and offering of advice. Both can be subtle forms of indoctrination. Because self-help groups deal with specialized problems, members tend to be alike in some ways. Festinger (1954) has suggested that individuals are more likely to be influenced by groups of persons whom they perceive as similar to themselves. Finally, many self-help groups address difficult conditions. New members often arrive in states approaching despair. With their former lives in disarray, they may be more ready to embrace a new system of ideas that promises relief.

ROLE OF THE PROFESSIONAL

The helping processes that seem to be most central to the effectiveness of self-help groups, mutual aid, helper therapy, and the role of ideology, are processes in which the professional plays a peripheral role. When professionals take a primary role in self-help groups, they run the risk of tampering with the intrinsic helping process of the groups. There are roles for the professional in the self-help group, but they are not the traditional roles that the professional has assumed in other helping groups (Silverman, 1986).

As long as the professionals screen members, convene the groups, and retain responsibility for running the program, the process is not a self-help experience. Aspects of mutual help exist in any group therapy experience (Yalom, 1985), but not to the degree found in self-help groups. The therapy group leader does not relinquish his or her control and authority. Maintaining dependence on the professional in a self-help setting limits the effectiveness of helper therapy and interferes with the "empowerment" of the individual (Rappaport, 1985).

Antze (1979) has suggested that professional involvement runs the risk of tampering with group ideologies. The mere presence of a professional may weaken the meaning of certain teachings (e.g., "Only a drunk can help another drunk."). If the professional points out that a belief runs against medical or psychological knowledge, the effect is certain to be negative. Antze recommends that the first rule for a professional working with a self-help group should be a scrupulous respect for its teachings.

Most, although not all, writers in the self-help area stress the need for collaboration between the groups and professionals. However, they also note the obstacles to collaboration. For example, self-help groups have been observed to have a strong bias against professional help (Barish, 1971) and to distrust professionals (Back & Taylor, 1976). These attitudes, along with a strong emphasis on anonymity, would make collaboration difficult.

In spite of the difficulties, professionals are becoming involved in self-help groups and some groups welcome the involvement (Wollert, et al., 1980). One of the factors in effective collaboration seems to be a knowledge of the specific goals and workings of the self-help group. Another is the establishment of rapport. In their report on the development of a collabora-tive model between professionals and Make Today Count, a self-help group for individuals dealing with life-threatening illness, Wollert, Knight, and Levy (1980) suggest that professionals need to convey respect for the group in order for the alliance to work.

Several "avenues for collaboration" (Wollert & Barron, 1983) exist that could enhance the effectiveness of self-help groups. Among these are: referrals to and from the self-help groups (Rodolfa & Hungerford, 1982; Silverman, 1986); shared leadership (Yoak & Chesler, 1985); organizational development services; consultation services (Wollert & Barron, 1983; Silver-man, 1986); and ongoing service roles (Wollert & Barron, 1983).

Mutual referral between self-help groups and professionals can be bene-ficial to the individual in need of help. The self-help group can provide valuable information and affiliation that can serve to augment professional services. When making a referral to a self-help group, a professional should have an awareness of the goals and workings of the group (Rodolfa & Hungerford, 1982). Some individuals who join a self-help group may be functioning at a significantly lower level of adaptation than other members and might need more than the group is able to offer. The self-help group can refer the individual to professional sources of help in the event partici-pation in the group becomes too stressful (Rodolfa & Hungerford, 1982).

Yoak and Chesler (1985) suggest shared leadership as a method of collaboration. In a study of 43 self-help and support groups for parents of children with cancer, they found three forms of leadership: the profession-als as primary leaders, the parents as primary leaders, and leadership shared between parents and professionals. The shared leadership groups had a greater longevity, tended to retain parents of deceased children, and had more varied approaches to organizational structure and activities. York and Chesler suggest that the shared leadership model may incorporate both a lack of dependence on the professional and the continuing access to professional resources.

The type of service that professionals have most commonly provided to self-help groups is some form of organizational assistance during the early stages of development (Wollert & Barron, 1983). In a study of 10 well-known self-help groups, including Alcoholics Anonymous, Recovery, Inc., and Parents Anonymous, Borman (1979) found professional encourage-ment in the formative stages of all the groups. The type of services provided by professionals varies widely in terms of their level of assumed responsibility. The positive outcomes for this type of collaboration include learning group interaction skills from observation of the professional and bolstering of confidence, which comes from the interaction (Wollert & Barron, 1983).

Consultation is another service that professionals may render to self-help groups. Consultative services are typically time-limited and intermittent. They may have either an organizational focus or a case focus. The case focus is useful when questions arise concerning issues of psychological diagnosis, medical screening, or crisis intervention (Wollert & Baron, 1983).

Professionals may also adapt roles of an ongoing nature. Sponsorship is one of these roles. Sponsorship provides professional acknowledgment of the group and contributes to the group's credibility in the community. Sponsors, however, ideally leave the leadership of meetings to a group member, although they may influence the process through advice to the leaders or through emergency intervention. Wollert and Barron (1983) suggest the advocator-mediator role for the professional. The responsibilities of the advocator-mediator are to observe the group, identify conflicts, clarify alternatives for resolution, and negotiate compromises acceptable for all those involved.

APPLICATION

The variability and diversity of self-help groups make it difficult to describe the form that a typical group might take. Since groups are formed in response to the needs of a particular group of people, they take on the structure that is best suited to meet those needs. On the other hand, self-help groups are small, face-to-face groups and thus are limited in form and expression.

Selection and Composition

The selection process for self-help groups cannot be as formal and controlled as for counseling groups. Open access is a key characteristic of self-help groups. Membership is available to anyone suffering from the particular condition addressed by the group. Self-help groups typically do not screen members. New groups often have to campaign actively for members in order to continue to function. Established groups depend on both professional referrals and informal word-of-mouth networks.

Since the sole requirement for membership in a self-help group is a particular problem or characteristic, the groups tend to be both homogeneous and heterogeneous. The shared problem provides a common identity for a membership that often varies greatly in age and socio-economic status.

Size

Silverman (1985) suggests that a typical self-help group has between 10 and 20 members. However, this figure does not give the complete picture. The range of group size is extensive, from the few members of a beginning group to more than 50 in some well-established groups. The larger groups tend to have a formal structure and emphasize information dissemination, while the smaller ones offer more opportunities for interaction among members. Some groups with large memberships split into smaller segments during parts of their meeting time in order to encourage member-to-member interaction.

Setting

Typically self-help groups hold meetings in church halls, public buildings, or other no-rent or low-rent facilities. Many small groups meet in members' homes. Since most self-help groups are financed by minimal dues or voluntary contributions, economy often becomes the primary consideration in choosing a setting.

Frequency and Duration of Sessions

Frequency of sessions depends on the goals of the self-help group. Addiction groups tend to have more frequent meetings than crisis groups. These groups may meet more than once a week, whereas a typical life-transition group might meet once a month. In addition, most self-help groups also offer services to supplement group sessions. Newsletters published by both national organizations and local groups offer information about the group's concerns. Some groups maintain a hotline service so that those in need have constant access to information and to an understanding listener. Others, particularly those dealing with addictive behavior, use a "buddy-system" so that members can count on one-to-one encouragement between meetings.

Theoretically, a self-help group can continue to function indefinitely. The group is always open to new members. In fact, recruiting new members is an important function of the group. As older members leave, they are replaced by the new ones. In actuality, some self-help groups are not successful in maintaining continuity. Borman and Lieberman (1979) believe that the less successful groups fail to recruit new members, thus becoming closed systems and eventually dying out.

Media

Self-help groups seem to be bound by few rules in their use of media. Most of the groups allow for member-to-member interaction for some portion of the meetings, but also include a variety of educational and therapeutic components. Programs for meetings can include visiting speakers, group discussions, study groups, films, and skills training.

Information is highly valued by self-help groups and is delivered through a variety of media. Groups often maintain lending libraries of books and pamphlets dealing with the issue they address. Newsletters published by the group are also used to disseminate information.

EVALUATION

The rapid growth of self-help groups would seem to be a testimony to their effectiveness. However, the research on their efficacy and how they function has been limited (Toro, Rappaport, & Seidman, 1987; Powell, 1985).

Research on self-help groups presents some particular difficulties. Self-help groups vary in focus, type, structure, meaning to participants, member characteristics, ideology, and so on. Research designs and methods are complicated by the need to study the groups in their natural settings (Katz, 1981). In addition, few self-help groups have any doubts about their effectiveness and thus find no need to collaborate in research (Levy, 1984). Those that might be willing to collaborate often question the appropriateness of outcome criteria set by outsiders.

Powell (1987), in his review of studies on autonomous self-help organizations, concludes that they showed positive effects. However, he cautions that these findings come from quasi-experimental designs and thus are not as powerful as they would be if experimental designs had been employed. Moreover, the positive evaluations are related to active participation over an extended period of time. There seem to be few benefits for the occasional or passive participants.

Levy (1984) suggests that self-help group research has a unique contribution to make to psychotherapy. According to him, self-help groups have much to recommend them as sources of information about the nature of therapeutic process, social support systems, and small groups. The groups are characterized by a pragmatic attitude toward their operation. Group procedures are likely to reflect what has been found to be effective. Levy believes that, "by observing the operation of self-help groups, we have a unique opportunity to gain insight into the natural psychotherapeutic processes of everyday life" (1979, p. 159).

Various authors have stressed the positive contributions of self-help groups to the mental health field. Some consider the growth of self-help a revolution in mental health services (Gartner & Riessman, 1984). They view the formal service structure as too big, bureaucratized, inaccessible, costly, and often ineffective. For them self-help represents a major shift in health care from an emphasis on the professional service giver to an emphasis on the consumer. Others (Lieberman & Borman, 1979) view self-help as a welcome addition to the existing mental health delivery system that can be used to alleviate some of the strain on the system. In spite of the differences in philosophic orientation, writers in the field agree that self-help has important practical implications. It is inexpensive, highly responsive, and accessible. The positive quality of self-help groups cited most by proponents is *empowerment*. According to them, self-help groups do not encourage dependency, as does the traditional model of professional service delivery.

Self-help groups have not escaped criticism, however. Lakin (1985) has suggested that the procedures of certain behavioral control groups (e.g. Recovery, Inc., A.A., and Synanon) may be inappropriate and even harmful for some people. Frew (1986) believes that because of a lack of professional leadership, self-help groups do not progress past the initial, inclusion phase, of their development and thus cannot reach their full potential as therapeutic groups. Powell (1987) cites the problems that plague self-help groups: the tentative and uncertain goals and activities of the beginning group; leadership struggles within groups that sap their effectiveness; and the groups' continued need to struggle for resources.

SUMMARY

Self-help in groups is one of the oldest forms of care for human problems. Yet, its power and potential have only recently been rediscovered by scholars and mental health professionals. Today, it is an increasingly utilized and rapidly growing mental health service.

The self-help groups that interface with the mental health profession are those oriented toward helping the individual achieve either behavioral change or adjustment to a life change. The groups are characterized by the following: a peer orientation, a problem focus, an estrangement from societal norms, and an ideological base. These characteristics distinguish self-help groups from other psychotherapy groups and contribute to their unique effectiveness. Individuals who share a common, often stigmatizing, problem come together and find support and hope. Peer leadership provides opportunities for "helper" therapy and member empowerment. Group ideologies serve as powerful, persuasive systems that provide a "cognitive antidote" to the condition addressed by the group.

The optimal role for professionals in self-help groups seems to be one that will preserve their unique helping processes. Recent research is beginning to delineate the effectiveness of the self-help process. Further research has the potential of increasing our understanding of how humans attempt to help each other cope with the stresses of everyday life.

REFERENCES ⸻

Antze, P. (1979). The role of ideologies in peer psychotherapy groups. In M. A. Lieberman & L. D. Borman (Eds.), *Self-help for coping with crisis* (pp. 272–304). San Francisco: Jossey-Bass Publishers.

Back, K. W., & Taylor, R. C. (1976). Self-help groups: Tool or symbol? *Journal of Applied Behavioral Science, 12*(3), 295–309.

Barish, H. (1971). Self-help groups. In *The encyclopedia of social work, 2*(16th ed.). New York: The National Association of Social Workers.

Bean, M. (1975). Alcoholics anonymous, part I. *Psychiatric Annals, 5,* 7–61.

Berzon, B., & Solomon, L. N. (1964). The self-directed therapeutic group: An exploratory study. *International Journal of Group Psychotherapy, 14,* 366–369.

Berzon, B., Solomon, L. N., & Reisel, J. (1972). Audio-taped programs for self-directed groups. In L. N. Solomon & B. Berzon (Eds.), *New perspectives of encounter groups* (pp. 211–223). San Francisco: Jossey-Bass.

Borman, L. D. (1979). Characteristics of development and growth. In M. A. Lieberman & L. D. Borman (Eds.), *Self-help groups for coping with crisis: Origins, members, processes, and impact,* (pp. 13–42). San Francisco: Jossey-Bass.

Borman, L. D. (1982). Kalmuk resettlement in America. In G. H. Weber & L. M. Cohen (Eds.), *Belief and self-help* (pp. 31–74). New York: Human Sciences Press.

Borman, L. D., & Lieberman, M. A. (1979). Conclusion: Contributions, dilemmas, and implications for mental health policy. In M. A. Lieberman & L. D. Borman (Eds.), *Self-help groups for coping with crisis* (pp. 406–430). San Francisco: Jossey-Bass.

Danish, S. J., Smyer, M. A., & Nowak, C. A. (1983). Developmental intervention: Enhancing life-event processes. In P. B. Baltes & O. G. Brim, Jr. (Eds.), *Life-span development and behavior* (Vol. 3, pp. 339–366). New York: Academic Press.

Dunkel-Schetter, C., & Wortman, C. B. (1982). The interpersonal dynamics in cancer: Problems in social relationships, and their impact on the patient. In H. S. Friedman & M. R. Dimatteo (Eds.), *Interpersonal issues in health care* (pp. 69–100). New York: Academic.

Erikson, E. H. (1963). *Childhood and society* (2nd ed.). New York: Norton.

Festinger, L. (1954). A theory of social comparison processes. *Human Relations, 7,* 117–140.

Frew, J. E. (1986). Leadership approaches to achieving maximum therapeutic potential in mutual support groups. *Journal for Specialists in Group Work, 11* (2), 93–99.

Gartner, A., & Riessman, F. (1980). *A working guide to self-help groups.* New York: New Viewpoints/Visions Books.

Gartner, A., & Riessman, F. (Eds.). (1984). *The self-help revolution.* New York: Human Sciences Press.

Gitterman, A., & Shulman, L. (Eds.). (1986). *Mutual aid groups and the life cycle.* Itasca, IL: F. E. Peacock Publishers.

Havighurst, R. J. (1953) *Human development and education.* New York: Longmans, Green.

Katz, A. H. (1970). Self-help organizations and volunteer participation in social welfare. *Social Work, 15* (1) 51–60.

Katz, A. H. (1972). Self-help groups. *Social Work, 17,* 120–121.

Katz, A. H. (1981). Self-help and mutual aid: An emerging social movement. *Annual Review of Sociology, 7,* 129–155.

Katz, A. H. (1982). Self-help and human services. *Citizen Participation, 3* (3), 22–23.

Katz, A. H., & Bender, E. I. (1976a). Self-help groups in western society: History and prospects. *The Journal of Applied Behavioral Science, 12* (3), 265–282.

Katz, A. H., & Bender, E. I. (1976b). *The strength in us: Self-help groups in the modern world.* New York: Franklin Watts.

Kessler, R. C., Price, R. H., & Wortman, C. B. (1985). Social factors in psychopathology: Stress, social support and coping processes. *Annual Review of Psychology, 36,* 531–72.

Killilea, M. (1976). Mutual help organizations: Interpretations in the literature. In G. Caplan & M. Killilea (Eds.), *Support systems and mutual help: Multidisciplinary explorations* (pp. 37–94). New York: Grune & Stratton.

Kropotkin, P. (1972). *Mutual aid: A factor of evolution.* New York: New York University Press. (Original work published 1914)

Lakin, M. (1985). *The helping group.* Reading, MA: Addison-Wesley.

Levinson, D. J. (1978). *The seasons of a man's life.* New York: Knopf.

Levy, L. H. (1976). Self-help groups: Types and psychological processes. *The Journal of Applied and Behavioral Science, 12,* 311–322.

Levy, L. H. (1979). Processes and activities in groups. In M. A. Lieberman & L. D. Borman (Eds.), *Self-help groups for coping with crisis: Origins, members, processes and impact* (pp. 234–271). San Francisco: Jossey-Bass.

Levy, L. H. (1984). Issues in research and evaluation. In A. Gartner & F. Riessman (Eds.), *The self-help revolution* (pp. 155–172). New York: Human Sciences Press.

Lieberman, M. A., & Borman, L. D. (Eds.). (1979). *Self-help groups for coping with crisis: Origins, members, processes, and impact.* San Francisco: Jossey-Bass.

Lowenthal, M., Thurnher, B., & Chiriboga, D. (1975). *Four stages of life: A comparative study of men and women facing transitions.* San Francisco: Jossey-Bass.

Napier, R., & Gershenfeld, M. (1985). *Groups: Theory and experience.* Boston: Houghton Mifflin.

Neugarten, B. L. (1968). *Middle-age and aging.* Chicago: University of Chicago Press.

Pancoast, D., Parker, P., & Froland, C. (Eds.). (1983). *Rediscovering self-help: Its role in social care.* Beverly Hills: Sage.

Pearson, R. E. (1986). Guest editorial. *Journal for Specialists in Group Work, 11* (2), 66–67.

Powell, T. J. (1985). Improving the effectiveness of self-help. *Social Policy, 16,* 22–29.

Powell, T. J. (1987). *Self-help organizations and professional practice.* Silver Springs. MD: National Association of Social Workers.

Rappaport, J. (1985). The power of enpowerment language. *Social Policy, 16,* 15–21.

Reissman, F. (1965). The "helper" therapy principle. *Social Work, 10,* 27–32.

Remine, D., Rice, R. M., & Ross, J. (1984). *Self-help groups and human service agencies: How they work together.* New York: Family Service America.

Rodolfa, E. R., & Hungerford, L. (1982). Self-help groups: A referral resource for professional therapists. *Professional Psychology, 13* (3), 345–353.

Rosenberg, P. P. (1984). Support groups: A special therapeutic entity. *Small Group Behavior, 15* (2), 173–186.

Sagarin, E. (1969). *Odd man in: Societies of deviants in America.* Chicago: Quadrangle Books.

Schacter, S. (Ed.). (1959). *The psychology of affiliation*. Stanford, CA: Stanford University Press.

Schlossberg, N. A. (1981). A model for analyzing human adaptation to transition. *Counseling Psychologist, 9*(2), 2–36.

Sherman, B. (1979). Emergence of ideology in peer psychotherapy groups. In M. A. Lieberman, & L. D. Borman (Eds.), *Self-help groups for coping with crisis: Origins, members, processes, and impact* (pp. 272–304). San Francisco: Jossey-Bass.

Silverman, P. (1980). *Mutual help groups: organization and development*. Beverly Hills: Sage.

Silverman, P. (1985). Tertiary/secondary prevention: Preventive intervention, the case for mutual self help groups. In R. K. Conyne (Ed.), *The group worker's handbook: Varieties of group experience* (pp. 237–257). Springfield, IL: Charles C. Thomas.

Silverman, P. (1986). The perils of borrowing: Role of the professional in mutual help groups. *Journal for Specialists in Group Work, 11* (2), 68–73.

Silverman, P., & Smith, D. (1984). Helping in mutual help groups for the physically disabled. In A. Gartner, & F. Riessman (Eds.), *The self-help revolution* (pp. 73–94). New York: Human Science Press.

Steinman, R., & Traunstein, D. M. (1976). Redefining deviance: The self-help challenge to the human services. *Journal of Applied Behavioral Science, 12* (3), 347–361.

Suler, J. (1984). The role of ideology in self-help groups. *Social Policy, 14*, 29–36.

Thoits, P. A. (1986). Social supports as coping assistance. *Journal of Consulting and Clinical Psychology, 54*, 416–423.

Toro, P. A., Rappaport, J., & Seidman E. (1987). Social climate comparison of mutual help and psychotherapy groups. *Journal of Consulting and Clinical Psychology, 55* (3), 430–431.

Wollert, R., & Barron, N. (1983). Avenues of collaboration. In D. Pancoast, P. Parker, & C. Froland (Eds.), *Rediscovering self-help: Its role in social care* (pp. 105–123). Beverly Hills: Sage.

Wollert, R. W., Knight, B., & Levy, L. H. (1980). Make today count: A collaborative model for professional and self-help groups. *Professional Psychology, 11*, 130–138.

Wortley, D. B., & Amatea, E. S. (1982). Mapping adult life changes: A conceptual framework for organizing adult development theory. *The Personnel and Guidance Journal, 60*, 476–482.

Yalom, I. (1985). *The theory and practice of group psychotherapy* (3rd ed.). New York: Basic Books.

Yoak, M., & Chesler, M. (1985). Alternative professional roles in health care delivery: Leadership patterns in self-help groups. *Journal of Applied Behavioral Science, 21*, 427–444.

SUGGESTED READINGS

Gartner, A., & Riessman, F. (1980). *A working guide to self-help groups*. New York: New Viewpoints/Visions Books.

Mallory, L. (1984). *Leading self-help groups*. New York: Family Service America.

Silverman, P. R. (1980). *Mutual help groups: Organization and development*. Beverly Hills, CA: Sage Publications.

SELF-HELP CLEARINGHOUSES ⎯⎯⎯⎯⎯⎯⎯⎯⎯⎯⎯

For help in finding and forming self-help groups:

California 1-800-222-LINK (in CA only)
Connecticut (203) 789-7645
Illinois 1-800-322-M.A.S.H. (in IL)
Kansas (316) 686-1205
Massachusetts (413) 545-2313
Michigan 1-800-752-5858 (in MI)
Minnesota (612) 642-4060
Missouri–Kansas City (816) 361-5007
Nebraska (402) 476-9668
New Jersey 1-800-FOR-M.A.S.H. (in NJ)
New York State (518) 474-6293
N.Y.–New York City (718) 788-8787
N.Y.–Long Island (516) 348-3030
N.Y.–Westchester (914) 347-3620
Oregon–Portland (503) 222-5555
Pennsylvania–Pittsburgh (412) 247-5400
Pennsylvania–Scranton (717) 961-1234
South Carolina (803) 791-2426
Texas–Dallas (214) 871-2420
Vermont 1-800-442-5356
Greater Washington, DC (703) 536-4100

For national U.S. listings and directories:

Self-Help Clearinghouse, NJ (201) 625-7101
Self-Help Center, Illinois (312) 328-0470
National Self-Help Clearinghouse, N.Y. City (212) 840-1259

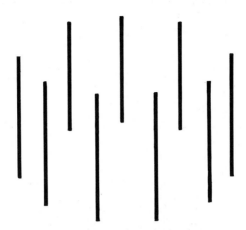

PART THREE

The three chapters contained in Part Three were included in the third edition. They have been revised and updated for this fourth edition. These chapters complete the gestalt of Developmental Group Counseling. They are Nonverbal Communication in Group Counseling, Ethical and Legal Issues in Group Counseling, and An Analysis of Group Counseling Research Literature.

C H A P T E R 11

Nonverbal Communication in Group Counseling[1]

The topic of nonverbal communication is like the old story of the six blind men of India and their perceptions of the elephant—it means different things to different people. And, like the elephant, the topic is broad, complex, and interesting. For our purposes, *nonverbal communication* can be defined as any human behavior that is directly perceived by another person and that is informative about the sender. This definition is a liberal one for two reasons. First, the message does not have to be one the sender had intended to send, and second, an unlimited variety of behaviors can be regarded as communication if they are useful as such.

Words (verbal communication) and other behavior (nonverbal communication) interweave and influence each other. The nonverbal component may influence the verbal in several ways—it may modify, enrich, illustrate, or even substitute for the word. Of the two components, nonverbal communication is often the more significant. The nonverbal component is so potent that Birdwhistell (quoted by Davis, 1973) states that "no more than 35% of the social meaning in any conversation is embedded in the words that are spoken" (p. 22).

Nonverbal communication is a wide-ranging subject. Substantial contributions to the literature have come from anthropology, sociology, psy-

1. This chapter was written by Richard P. Walters, Ph.D., a counseling psychologist working in Boulder, Colorado.

chology, psychiatry, speech and communication arts, drama, dance, and ethology. Until recent years, most of the literature has been descriptive. There are hundreds of accounts of human behavior as observed in various situations or cultures. Although many of these reports are quite interesting, they frequently have not added to our understanding of the motivation of behavior, which is of considerable importance to the counselor. Only in recent years have reasonably successful attempts been made to develop a general theory of nonverbal communication behavior, aided by innovations in methodology for observation and analysis.

The purpose of this chapter is to help counselors apply knowledge of nonverbal communication to the practice of group counseling. First, some of the basic characteristics and uses of nonverbal behavior will be reviewed. Then this general information will be applied to processes in group counseling. Emphasis will be placed on skills for the counselor and on the counselor's effective use of the nonverbal cues given by the group members. Recommended readings for further study appear at the end of the chapter. Some nonverbal activities that may form part of counseling or psychotherapy will be excluded from consideration. The excluded activities are dance, art and music therapies, guided fantasy, relaxation training, play or activity therapies, and nonverbal encounter exercises such as the "blind walk." Also excluded from this chapter is consideration of nonverbal behavior in psychiatric inpatient populations. References for further reading on nonverbal communication in hospitalized populations appear at the end of this chapter.

Many thousands of different nonverbal behaviors can be identified and labeled. The following list only hints at the number and diversity. The nonverbal behaviors are categorized to make it easier for the reader to become aware of them. Because their meaning is so greatly influenced by context, culture, and idiosyncratic factors, only minimal information on possible interpretations is included within the list. Additional information about interpreting nonverbal cues follows in this chapter.

1. Nonverbal communication behaviors using time
    a. Recognition: Promptness or delay in recognizing the presence of others or in responding to their communication
    b. Priorities
        (1) Amount of time another is willing to spend communicating with a person
        (2) Relative amounts of time spent on various topics
2. Nonverbal communication behaviors using the body
    a. Eye contact (important in regulating the relationship)
        (1) Looking at a specific object
        (2) Looking down
        (3) Steady to other person

        (4) Defiantly ("hard" eyes) glaring
        (5) Shifting eyes from object to object
        (6) Looking at other person but looking away when looked at
        (7) Covering eyes with hand(s)
        (8) Frequency of looking at another

  b. Eyes
        (1) "Sparkling"
        (2) Tears
        (3) "Wide-eyed"
        (4) Position of eyelids

  c. Skin
        (1) Pallor
        (2) Perspiration
        (3) Blushing
        (4) "Goose bumps"

  d. Posture (often indicative of physical alertness or tiredness)
        (1) "Eager," as if ready for activity
        (2) Slouching, slovenly, tired looking, slumping
        (3) Arms crossed in front as if to protect self
        (4) Crossing legs
        (5) Sits facing the other person rather than sideways or away from
        (6) Hanging head, looking at floor, head down
        (7) Body positioned to exclude others from joining a group or dyad

  e. Facial expression (primary site for display of affects, thought by many researchers to be subject to involuntary responses)
        (1) No change
        (2) Wrinkled forehead (lines of worry), frown
        (3) Wrinkled nose
        (4) Smiling, laughing
        (5) "Sad" mouth
        (6) Biting lip

  f. Hand and arm gestures
        (1) Symbolic hand and arm gestures
        (2) Literal hand and arm gestures to indicate size or shape
        (3) Demonstration of how something happened or how to do something

  g. Self-inflicting behaviors
        (1) Nail biting
        (2) Scratching
        (3) Cracking knuckles
        (4) Tugging at hair
        (5) Rubbing or stroking

  h.   Repetitive behaviors (often interpreted as signs of nervousness or restlessness; may be organic in origin)
- (1) Tapping foot, drumming or thumping with fingers
- (2) Fidgeting, squirming
- (3) Trembling
- (4) Playing with button, hair, or clothing

  i.   Signals or commands
- (1) Snapping fingers
- (2) Holding fingers to lips for silence
- (3) Pointing
- (4) Staring directly to indicate disapproval
- (5) Shrugging shoulders
- (6) Waving
- (7) Nodding in recognition
- (8) Winking
- (9) Nodding in agreement; shaking head in disagreement

  j.   Touching
- (1) To get attention, such as tapping on shoulder
- (2) Affectionate, tender
- (3) Sexual
- (4) Challenging, such as poking finger into chest
- (5) Symbols of camaraderie, such as slapping on back
- (6) Belittling, such as a pat on top of head

  k.   Grooming
- (1) Degree of cleanliness
- (2) Scent
- (3) Makeup
- (4) Hair color (especially if noticeably altered) and style

3. Nonverbal communication behaviors using vocal media

  a.   Tone of voice
- (1) Flat, monotone, absence of feeling
- (2) Bright, vivid changes of inflection
- (3) Strong, confident, firm
- (4) Weak, hesitant, shaky
- (5) Broken, faltering

  b.   Rate of speech
- (1) Fast
- (2) Medium
- (3) Slow

  c.   Loudness of voice
- (1) Loud
- (2) Medium
- (3) Soft

    d. Diction
- (1) Precise versus careless
- (2) Regional (colloquial) differences
- (3) Consistency of diction

4. Nonverbal communication behaviors using the environment
    a. Distance
- (1) Moves away when the other moves toward
- (2) Moves toward when the other moves away
- (3) Takes initiative in moving toward or away from
- (4) Distance widens gradually
- (5) Distance narrows gradually

    b. Arrangement of the physical setting
- (1) Neat, well ordered, organized
- (2) Untidy, haphazard, careless
- (3) Casual versus formal
- (4) Warm versus cold colors
- (5) Soft versus hard materials
- (6) Slick versus varied textures
- (7) Cheerful and lively versus dull and drab
- (8) "Discriminating" taste versus tawdry
- (9) Expensive or luxurious versus shabby or spartan

    c. Clothing (often used to tell others what a person wants them to believe about oneself)
- (1) Bold versus unobtrusive
- (2) Stylish versus nondescript

    d. Position in the room
- (1) Protects or fortifies own position by getting objects such as a desk or table between self and other person
- (2) Takes an open or vulnerable position such as in the center of the room, or side-by-side on a sofa, or in simple chair with nothing between self and other person
- (3) Takes an attacking or dominating position (for example, by blocking the exit from the area or by maneuvering the other person into a boxed-in position
- (4) Movement about the room
- (5) Moving in and out of the other person's territory
- (6) Stands when other person sits, or gets position higher than the other person

People send thousands of signals daily. And, whether it is fair to do so or not, one makes hundreds of interpretations of the signals of others, whether his or her interpretations are valid or not and regardless of whether the interpretations are meaningful, even if accurate. The net effect of these exchanges of nonverbal communication can, however, be beneficial to both parties if it is understood how one uses these channels effectively.

It is not possible to accomplish fully the understanding of nonverbal communication in one chapter. Readers are urged to consult the recommended readings cited at the end of the chapter and to use the suggested exercises for further study.

CHARACTERISTICS OF NONVERBAL COMMUNICATION

This section describes some general characteristics of nonverbal communication behaviors. Later sections deal with behaviors related more specifically to the leader, to the member, and with the use by the leader of observations of the members' behaviors.

Nonverbal Behaviors are Difficult to Interpret

Nonverbal communication has become a popular subject in recent years. It would be easy, and fun, to treat it simplistically. Several books would have one believe that by learning a few simple rules one can be an instant wizard in reading other persons' hidden motives. But it is not that simple. There has been a distinct lack of success in attaching definitions to nonverbal behaviors. The prominent scholars studying nonverbal communication today agree that it is not possible to compile concrete, consistently accurate explanations of the meaning of nonverbal behaviors. Several factors seem to preclude it:

1. *Idiosyncrasy of nonverbal behavior.* A given act or gesture may have opposite meanings for two persons. For example, a frown might mean concentration when displayed by one person; annoyance, when displayed by another. Scheflen (1964) points out that variations related to differences in personality, gender, age, status, position, and health may occur.
2. *Cultural differences.* There are no truly universal meanings. Darwin (1872) began a popular and long-lived misconception that there are basic nonverbal behaviors that have the same meaning the world around. There are none. For example, in our society a simple up-and-down head nod means "yes" and a side-to-side shake means "no," but in Bulgaria and among some Eskimos, these signals mean the opposite. Counselors should make every effort to become aware of the nonverbal cues used by the persons with whom they

interact. (For more on cultural differences, see Hall, 1955; LaBarre, 1947, Morris et al., 1979.)

3. *Situational differences.* Arms folded across the chest is often interpreted as a sign of defensiveness or rigidity. That is true *part of the time.* But it may also occur because a person finds it comfortable, is cold, is covertly scratching, is hiding a blemish or tattoo on the arms, or is hiding dirty hands. Similarly, tears may come from joy, relief, anguish, guilt, or self-pity. Silence may be generated out of spite, embarrassment, confusion, feelings of being at an impasse, or overwhelming gratitude. Gottman (1980) found less consistency in the nonverbal communication of positive affect than negative. Making and acting on snap interpretations is likely to get one into trouble, so always set nonverbal behavior in context.

4. *Differences among observers.* Osgood (1966) believes that the meaning of a nonverbal behavior may be based on the experiencing of the signal. His view suggests that attempts to apply lexical labels to nonverbal behaviors may actually decrease the accuracy of interpretation.

Making and acting on snap interpretations of the meaning of nonverbal behavior is likely to get one into trouble, so always set nonverbal behavior in context. It is possible to get some useful clues by observing nonverbal behavior, but it is not possible at this time and probably will never be possible to interpret nonverbal behaviors with precision and certainty. Some general rules can supply guidelines, but no attempt will be made to supply a dictionary of meanings of nonverbal behaviors.

Nonverbal Behaviors Become Habits

Nonverbal behavior patterns become habituated (Davis, 1973, p. 130; Deutsch, 1949). As they do with most habits, individuals are likely to lose conscious awareness of how they do things. Try this experiment to demonstrate the existence of gestural habits: Place your hands in front of you, palms together, and clasp your hands with your fingers intertwined. Note how natural it feels. Notice which thumb is on top. Place the other thumb on top and reposition the fingers so they are again intertwined. This will probably feel quite awkward because the way you did it the first time is the way you always do it. You have a habit of clasping your hands together in a certain way. If you did it with equal frequency the two ways, they would feel equally natural. You may wish to repeat this experiment by folding your arms over your chest, then reversing the position.

Changing habituated nonverbal patterns is a long and difficult process. Even so, if counselors find themselves using nonverbal behaviors that reduce their ability to be helpful to others, it may be worth the effort required to change them.

Nonverbal Behaviors are Usually Honest

Since nonverbal behaviors are habits, it is difficult to deceive another person with words—nonverbal gestures reveal the true feelings even though an individual may seek to disguise those feelings with words. Novelists had known it for years, but Freud (1963) set it down for clinicians when he wrote that "no mortal can keep a secret. If his lips are silent, he chatters with his fingertips; betrayal oozes out of him at every pore" (pp. 77–78).

Studies by Mehrabian (1971), Mehrabian and Wiener (1967), and Ekman and Friesen (1960a, 1972) have shown experimentally that persons cannot mask all signs of feeling from view. Those studies affirm the old folk saying, "Truth will out." This certainly is a practical argument in favor of verbal and emotional congruence on the part of the group leader.

It can be useful and legitimate to mask or modify our display of emotion. For example, it is better to not show anger to an angry person or fear to a frightened person during crisis, not to avoid the realities, but to help them keep their emotions under control until the stressors are dealt with.

Behaviors that are frequently associated with deception are: more speech errors, shorter responses, longer hesitations, less smiling, more eye contact, covering mouth with hand, and touching nose. This list was synthesized from reports by Heilveil and Muehleman (1981), Kraut (1976), Mehrabian (1971), Morris (1977), and Sitton and Griffin (1981).

People give nonverbal communication greater validity than verbal communication. When there is a discrepancy between verbal and nonverbal messages, people believe the nonverbal message even though they may not consciously be aware of the nonverbal signals. A study by Kaul and Schmidt (1971) found that an "interviewer's manner had a greater impact upon his perceived trustworthiness than did the words he used" (p. 546).

The same effect applies to perceived discrepancies in group members' behavior. A female group member denied hostility toward another member, but refused to look at him when he spoke to her. The discrepancy between her words and behavior was obvious to every person in the group. Faced with the discrepancy, the group members chose to believe her nonverbal signals. Prodding by the group eventually resulted in her opening up and working through strong hostility toward the man (whose mannerisms had reminded her of a former boyfriend).

Nonverbal Behaviors Anticipate
Subsequent Verbal Disclosure

Strong internal emotional content is often observable in behavior before it has been expressed verbally for the first time. This behavior is often symbolic, but it still offers useful clues about the sender to the group leader and other members. For example, a young man in a group removed his sandals on entering the session. He sat cross-legged on a chair and was attentive but passive during the first half of the session. He appeared sullen. Rather suddenly he put his sandals on and sat erect on the edge of his seat. A group member interpreted this as a sign of his wanting to leave the group, an impulse the young man denied. He was encouraged to get in touch with and to disclose his feelings. Further work revealed that he was faced with a complex decision between two attractive alternatives. He recognized that he had a strong desire to escape (run from) the necessity of making a decision. The group member's interpretation was a reasonable one and, though wrong in the literal interpretation, had touched symbolic meaning. It facilitated involvement by the young man toward resolving a conflict.

A traditional psychoanalytic view is that emotional conflicts are often expressed in symbolic actions instead of conscious thought. Mahl (1968) points out that Freud provided specific examples of such behavior in each of four major clinical reports (Dora, Little Hans, the Rat Man, and the Wolf Man). See Dunbar (1960) for further reading on this subject.

Nonverbal Behaviors Arise from Genetic and Environmental Sources

There is strong support in literature for the belief that nonverbal behaviors are genetic. Ethologists point to human behavior in rage (such as the prolonged hostile stare), surprise (widening of the eyes and dropping of jaw), or happiness (smile) that are found in similar form among various mammals. Cultural anthropologists show evidence that these behaviors are found to have had the same meaning among almost all groups of people around the world for centuries. These widespread and enduring similarities are usually interpreted as supporting a hereditary origin.

Yet there are divergent meanings for many nonverbal behaviors. For example, touching the ear is a superlative in Portugal, protection against the evil eye in Turkey, a sign of skepticism in Scotland, denotes jeering at effeminancy in Yugoslavia and southern Italy, and warns of imminent punishment to Greek children (Morris et al., 1979). Clearly nonverbal behaviors are not solely genetic in origin.

Nonverbal Behaviors are More Accurately Decoded by Women

Judith Hall summarized seventy-five studies that reported accuracy for males and females at decoding nonverbal cues of emotion (Hall, 1978). Her analyses revealed that more studies showed female advantage than would occur by chance and that women seem to be more accurate in this task regardless of sex or age of sender. She suggests that this is because of early learning, added motivation to relate to others expressively, and practice at attending to interpersonal expression.

What is the practical significance of these findings for the group counselor? First, many women counselors deserve a high level of self-confidence in this area (without becoming complacent). Second, males should double-check their level of competence. Third, it strengthens the rationale for male-female cotherapy teams. We should all continue to work toward the highest possible level of skill in the decoding of nonverbal cues from others.

PURPOSES OF
NONVERBAL COMMUNICATION

Nonverbal communication has several purposes. These are intermingled and are usually not given conscious attention by the sender. Still, it will be helpful to consider them in general terms before specific attention is given to nonverbal behavior in group counseling.

To Express Emotion

Consideration of the nonverbal component of communication is essential for adequate understanding of the person speaking. A study by Haase and Tepper (1972) concluded that "to rely solely on the verbal content of the message reduces the accuracy of the judgment by 66%" (p. 421). Statistical analysis of communication in both verbal and nonverbal channels by Mehrabian and Ferris (1967) resulted in coefficients for each of the main effects: .07 for verbal components, .38 for vocal components, and .55 for facial components. These data suggest that the impact of nonverbal behaviors is very great indeed. Unless the counselors can receive the information conveyed through nonverbal behavior—intentional communication or not—they will miss essential information about group members. (For detailed treatment of this topic, see Watzlawick, Beavin, & Jackson, 1967.)

To Illustrate, Modify, or Enrich the Words

Nonverbal communication may be used to denote shape, size, direction, spatial relationships, movement, and bodily action. How tall is my daughter? This high. I can show you, but I cannot tell you. It would be much easier for me to demonstrate a golf swing to you than to write a description. Try this experiment: Stop any person on the street and ask directions to a nearby place. In all probability, the first thing the person will do—even before speaking—is raise a hand to point.

A single bit of nonverbal communication is rarely meaningful. Still, the pieces add up and for the perceptive helper, nonverbal cues add color, richness, and depth to the understanding of the other person. The words "I don't like him" may be said in a mild tone of voice; they take on intensity if shouted or if, even with a mild tone of voice, the speaker's fists are clenched. By paying attention to the messages in all channels, trends can be detected, intensity of feelings may be more fully experienced, and underlying conflicts and motives may be recognized before they are expressed in words.

To Regulate Participation

What do you do when you cannot get a word in edgewise? Two-year-olds jump up and down and say "Mommy! Daddy! Look at what I can do!" Older person have more methods to use in getting into or out of communication. Some are more subtle than a screaming 2-year-old; some are not.

Conventional signals to show that a person wants to communicate include: eye contact, moving closer, "ahem" or other vocalizations to attract attention, and touching. Common signals to communicate desire to close a conversation include: fidgeting, rising from chair, moving away, and looking at one's watch. Any of these can be styled to insult or control, or to affirm, the other person.

To Deceive

One of the classic Broadway show tunes includes the phrase " . . . so, put on a happy face." At times everybody does this. People manipulate their nonverbal behavior. It is not always inappropriate, but it is usually difficult because of the "leakage effect" mentioned earlier.

Morris (1977) points out that the demands and context of some vocations foster the skill of deception. He states that successful actors, actresses, politicians, lawyers, confidence tricksters, magicians, and used-car salesmen polish the skill of lying through nonverbal channels to the point that "it sparkles so brightly that the rest of us, most of the time, actually enjoy being taken in by it" (1977, p. 45).

It may be useful to disguise our emotion. For example, in the process of resolving a conflict with another person, it may be helpful to mask one's feelings of anger so as to lessen the arousal of anger in the other person. This is not to avoid dealing with the roots of the conflict, but to reduce the chance of aggravating the situation; playing down the feelings is constructive, not a manipulative deception.

To Shape Feeling

It is interesting to notice what one's hands do when one has trouble explaining feelings. Often the speaker reaches outward as if to catch the elusive thought or rubs his or her head as if to dislodge the message from its hiding place.

Nonverbal behaviors not only communicate, but also shape thought and feeling. The behaviors mentioned, through proprioceptive feedback, increase determination to understand fully and express openly. The muscle tension of frowning has been shown to increase the subjective feeling of anger (Izard, 1975), and we can recall from personal experience occasions when "putting on a happy face" was the predecessor to subjective happiness.

To Offer Feedback About the Relationship

One group member sits on the edge of his chair, taps his foot quickly, drums his fingers on his knee, looks at his watch frequently, and occasionally exhales heavily and audibly. Another group member sits erect, but in a comfortable posture, maintains good eye contact with all other group members, nods her head affirmatively to something being said, and changes facial expression as emotions within the group change. You do not need to be told which group member is bored and wants to leave and which member is actively involved. Nonverbal behaviors are a language of relationship. They give almost continuous feedback on the meaningfulness of the relationship and the effectiveness of helping.

NONVERBAL BEHAVIORS
OF THE GROUP COUNSELOR

Group members are influenced by the nonverbal behaviors of the leader and other members. Noted anthropologist Edward Sapir (1927) wrote that "we respond to gestures with extreme alertness and, one might also say, in accordance with an elaborate secret code that is written nowhere, known by none, and understood by all" (p. 137). Nonverbal cues are noticed by and affect all group members. Siegel and Sell (1978) demonstrated that the failure to perform expert nonverbal behaviors during counseling leads to the client's perceiving the counselor as unexpert. Studies by Fretz et al. (1979), Haase and Tepper (1972), LaCrosse (1975), and Strong et al. (1971) also show relationship between counselor nonverbal behavior and client perception of expertise. Therefore it is imperative that the group leader's nonverbal behavior and verbal message complement one another rather than compete or be incongruent. The nonverbal component should contribute to more complete and more accurate understanding and depth of relationships if the group is to achieve optimal success.

Some group leader behaviors are ambiguous. For example, the leader may show signs commonly associated with anxiety (excessive perspiration, wavering voice, trembling) when actively involved during "peak" periods of a session. If group members notice these behaviors, they may interpret them negatively (as a result of leader inexperience or fear of failure) or positively (as a result of the leader's complete emotional involvement with a complex and difficult job at hand). Other nonverbal behaviors, such as an absence of change in amount of eye contact, proximity, or degree of congruence during emotionally charged periods during a session, may be interpreted as competence and comfort (which may or may not be true) or lack of involvement. Webbink (1986) describes the importance of assertive eye contact in maintaining discipline in the classroom and in other leadership roles (p. 45). Research by Van Houten, et al. (1982) showed that eye contact and a firm grasp of the student's shoulder enhanced the effectiveness of verbal reprimands. The interpretations made by group members influence their perceptions of the leader's self-confidence or the quality of the leader's involvement.

Rate of speech is another nonverbal behavior that may be interpreted in different ways. A slow rate with a weak, faltering tone may be perceived as lack of confidence. The same slow rate with a full, steady tone may be interpreted as meaning that the leader is carefully thinking about what he or she is saying, something very respectful of the group members. Persons who speak fluently and fairly fast, with variation in pitch and volume, are perceived as high in competence (Street & Brady, 1982).

This section describes both preferred and undesirable nonverbal behaviors for the group leader. Even though group counselors do not consciously control many of their nonverbal behaviors, they can become consciously aware of them and learn to control some of them. At the least, counselors should develop an awareness of their nonverbal style and become sensitive to its effect on other persons. Remember that the essence of good communication lies in the quality of the message and not in the style of delivery. It is not necessary to be a silver-tongued orator to be an effective group leader. Tyler (1969) says, "One of the rewards of continuing counseling experience is the realization that what one says need not be fluent or elegantly phrased in order to be effective" (p. 41).

Attending Behaviors

Attending behaviors are nonverbal behaviors used while listening to another person. They include such modes of communication as posture, eye contact, and facial expression. These behaviors frequently communicate the listener's attitude toward the speaker or the topic. Attending behaviors may be effective or ineffective. Effective attending behaviors communicate that one is interested in the other person and facilitate the growth of a helping relationship. Ineffective attending behaviors give an impression of disinterest or rejection and tend to discourage the other person from genuineness and self-disclosure.

Table 11-1   Attending behaviors

Ineffective Use (doing any of these things will probably close off or slow down the conversation)	Nonverbal Modes of Communication	Effective Use (these behaviors encourage talk because they show acceptance and respect for the other person)
Spread among activities	Attention	Given fully to talker
Distant; very close	Space	Approximate arms length
Away	Movement	Toward
Slouching; rigid; seated leaning away	Posture	Relaxed but attentive; seated leaning slightly toward
Absent; defiant; jittery	Eye contact	Regular
You continue with what you are doing before responding; in a hurry	Time	Respond at a first opportunity; share time with them
Used to keep distance between the persons	Feet and legs (in sitting)	Unobtrusive
Used as a barrier	Furniture	Used to draw persons together
Does not match feelings; scowl; blank look	Facial expression	Matches your own or other's feelings; smile
Compete for attention with your words	Gestures	Highlight your words; unobtrusive; smooth
Obvious, distracting	Mannerisms	None or unobtrusive
Very loud or very soft	Voice; volume	Clearly audible
Impatient or staccato; very slow or hesitant	Voice: rate	Average or a bit slower
Apathetic; sleepy; jumpy; pushy	Energy level	Alert; stays alert throughout a long conversation
Sloppy; garish; provocative	Dress, grooming	Tasteful

Source: Richard P. Walters, (1980). *Amity: Friendship in action.* Kentwood, Michigan: Published by the author, p. 31. Reproduced by permission.

There are no clear-cut rules to follow, but some general principles will help group counselors use effective behaviors and avoid ineffective ones. Table 11-1 lists a number of modalities of nonverbal communication and describes in general terms effective and ineffective behaviors in those modalities.[2] The guidelines for attending behaviors will allow counselors to be effective, but still express their own uniqueness as persons.

Four important benefits of using good attending behaviors are the following:

1. They make it easier for counselors to listen and to remember accurately. Listening can be hard work. Good attending behaviors are physically comfortable. Being natural and comfortable makes it easier to stay emotionally and intellectually alert and involved over a period of time.

2. They enhance the other person's self-respect. Giving fully of one's own energy, time, and attention is a compliment to the other person, contributing to a sense of worth and helping to build a good relationship.

3. They facilitate self-exploration by the person talking. By making it easy and worthwhile for the group member to talk, they reinforce openness and self-disclosure.

4. They model appropriate behavior. The counselor's example teaches preferred behavior to group members.

Ineffective attending behaviors tend to close off conversation or prohibit a helping relationship from developing. If one's attention begins to lapse after listening to someone talk for a few minutes, it will probably result in some changes in that person's behavior. When speakers suspect that the listener's attention is waning, they are likely to try to recapture attention. There are many ways this may be attempted (such as by talking louder or in a more animated way, by talking faster, by changing the subject to something that may be of more interest to the listener, by moving closer to the listener, or, if the listener is looking in another direction, by moving into his or her field of view so that eye contact cannot be avoided). These are signs that the listener-counselor's attending behaviors are deficient at that time and that the speaker is not satisfied with the level of attention. Group counselors may observe this during interaction between members, in which case they may wish to point out what is happening so that the dynamics can be understood by the group.

2. The four tables in this chapter are similar in purpose and in the way in which they were developed. They should be used with discretion. Do not overapply the information in the tables (for example, do not rigidly follow each suggestion about effective attending skills shown in Table 11–1 or jump to conclusions on the basis of information in the other tables). Use the tables as general guidelines to increase your awareness of nonverbal behaviors and to shape your own optimal nonverbal style.

The data that are tabulated are supported either by frequency of appearance in the nonverbal communication literature or by particularly thorough and convincing research findings. Hundreds of pieces of literature have been consulted in the preparation of these tables; because of space limitations, it is not possible to identify all the sources.

Wiens, Harper, and Matarazzo (1980) showed that the one interviewer behavior they controlled, response time to interviewee speech, did affect the behavior of the interviewee. The work of Hill et al. (1981) also shows that attending skills do make a difference.

Yet counselor nonverbal behavior is not rigidly proscribed. Young (1980) shows that when client attitude and global impression of the counselor are favorable, the counselor's nonverbal style can be less effective without harm to the counseling process. Still, it will be a great advantage to the counselor to present the best possible nonverbal behaviors to all clients at all times.

Communication of Core Conditions

Recent research shows that several conditions of communication facilitate the counseling process. These core conditions have been isolated from research and specify the common factors present when the helping relationship is successful. (See Gazda et al., 1977; and Gazda, Childers, & Walters, 1982, for further study of the core conditions.)

Table 11–2 summarizes some of the behaviors frequently associated with high or low levels of the core conditions. Several clusters of behavior are described by a common stereotype in place of a lengthy behavioral description. Only those of unique importance to a particular condition are listed. These behaviors, along with good eye contact and effective attending behaviors, must usually be present to attain helpful levels of a given condition. The table may be used to assess one's own level of functioning on the various conditions.

The condition of warmth depends on nonverbal media for complete and clear communication more than does any other core condition. Concreteness uses nonverbal media the least.

Nonverbal Behavior Associated With Leader's Styles

Different patterns of nonverbal behavior appear in association with various group leader styles. Table 11–3 lists several group leader styles and describes clusters of nonverbal behaviors that are likely to appear with each. The leadership style of a group counselor may change from time to time, even changing within a single session. The style may have no relationship to the leader's theoretical or methodological orientation.

It is possible and useful—if done with caution and in a spirit of honest inquiry—to look at group leaders' nonverbal behaviors and make some tentative inferences about their individual leadership styles. Group counselors may find it helpful for their self-improvement to check their own behavior (videotaping is ideal). Counselors should analyze the motivation that may underlie their use of these behaviors, especially if they note that

Table 11–2   Nonverbal communication of the core conditions

Core Conditions	Undesirable Leader Nonverbal Behaviors— Likely to be Associated with Low Levels	Desirable Leader Nonverbal Behaviors— Likely to be Associated with High Levels
Empathy	Frown resulting from lack of understanding	Positive head nods; facial expression congruent with content of conversation; "mm-hms";
Respect	Mumbling; patronizing tone of voice; engages in doodling or autistic behavior to the point of appearing more involved with that than with the interaction	Spends time with other person; fully attentive
Warmth	Apathy; delay in responding to approach of other person; insincere effusiveness; fidgeting; signs of wanting to leave	Smile; appropriate physical contact; close proximity; leaning toward; attentiveness; relaxed but concerned voice tones (see Table 11–4)
Genuineness	Low or evasive eye contact; lack of congruence between verbal and nonverbal; drop in frequency of movement; excessive smiling	Congruence between verbal and nonverbal behavior
Concreteness	Vague gestures used as a substitute for gestures or words with specific meaning (for example, shrugs shoulders when other person is vague instead of asking for clarification)	Draws diagram to clarify an abstract point; clear enunciation
Self-disclosure	Bragging gestures; points to self; covers eyes or mouth while talking	Gestures that keep references to self low key (for example, a shrug accompanying the words, "It was no big deal," when talking about a personal incident)
Immediacy	Turning away or moving back when immediacy enters the conversation	Enthusiasm
Confrontation	Pointing finger or shaking fist at group member; tone of voice that communicates blame or condemnation; loudness of voice that is intimidating; wavering quality of voice; unsure of self	Natural tone of voice; confidence

Source: Gazda, G., Asbury, F., Balzer, F., Childers, W., Walters, R. (1977). *Human relations development: A manual for educators,* 2nd ed. (Boston: Allyn and Bacon). Reproduced by permission.

Table 11–3   Nonverbal behavior associated with various group leader styles

Group Leader Styles and Goals	Characteristics and Examples of Nonverbal Behavior
Inadequate/ingratiating Goal: to buy the friendship of group members	Seductive behaviors (intimate proximity, quasi-sexual touching); excessive effusiveness (back slapping, "ho, ho, ho" style, exaggerated handshaking); seeks to establish "happy family" atmosphere (chairs close, serves others by pouring coffee, hanging up coats, and so forth)
Timid/nonassertive Goal: to get through the session without conflict	Faltering voice; use of furniture as barrier; little eye contact when speaking; may use nonverbal mode to send controversial messages; keeps group members distant from one another; inappropriate cheerfulness; pacifying and appeasing behaviors (ignores observable conflict or inappropriateness; minimizes disagreement); autistic mannerisms; fidgeting; frequently looks at watch; protective posture; backs away if other person moves toward
Hostile/aggressive Goal: to release own anger	Defiant eye contact; ignores other persons or delays responding to them; arrives late and/or holds group beyond closing time; touches with thumps or symbolic hitting; "ready to pounce" posture; backs other persons into corner; physiological changes associated with anger; intrudes on space of another; tries to cause other person to back up and then pursues by moving toward (symbolic hunt)
Authoritarian/controlling Goal: to gain self-esteem by dominating group members	Intrusive proximity; stands when others are seated; low congruence; task-oriented use of time; gestures of command (pointing, holding fingers to lips for silence, touching to get attention); has special chair (fancier, higher); frequent looks of disapproval
Confident/competent Goal: to help others	Uses behaviors listed in Table 11–1 as effective attending skills, behaviors in Table 11–2 that are associated with high levels of the core conditions, and clearly communicates warmth (see Table 11–4)
Neophyte/leader in training Goal: to learn the practice of group conseling	It is to be expected that the nonverbal behavior of the inexperienced group leader will need to improve and develop, as will other aspects of leadership; common characteristics of the beginning leader include anxiety symptoms; reduced eye contact, especially while talking; eye contact unevenly distributed among group members; closed and/or rigid posture; vocalization lacking incisiveness

they use several behaviors within a single category of leader style. These styles of interpersonal relationship may also be observed in group member behavior.

Nonverbal Communication of Warmth and Acceptance

Of all the core conditions, warmth is the most dependent on nonverbal behaviors for full expression. The impact of nonverbal cues is so important that the absence of certain nonverbal behaviors is interpreted as the absence of warmth.

The communication of counselor warmth has been shown to have a powerful effect on clients. LaCrosse (1975) found that counselors communicating with an affiliative manner were rated as more attractive and persuasive than counselors with an unaffiliative manner. Wright (1975) found counselor warmth associated with favorable outcomes. Sherer and R. Rogers (1980) found counselors whose nonverbal behaviors communicate warmth to be rated as more effective. Carl Rogers (1957), describing it as *unconditional positive regard,* included it as one of his necessary and sufficient conditions for therapeutic personality change. Studies by Mehrabian (1969) and Reece and Whitman (1962) showed that greater warmth produced more words from the participants. Gibb (1972) stated that warmth is "significant, necessary, therapeutic, and enhancing for personal learning. The expression of warmth is self-fulfilling. Warmth feeds on itself and breeds new warmth" (p. 471). Findings such as these suggest that warmth, adequately communicated by the group leader, may perpetuate itself and spread, bringing benefits such as greater disclosure by group members, greater responsiveness to the leader, and facilitation of the growth processes.

In a study of the behavioral cues of interpersonal warmth, Bayes (1972) pointed out that the cues are elusive and varied, but enough studies have been done to offer a consensual behavioral description of the components of nonverbal warmth.

The findings of nine research studies (Bayes, 1972; D'Augelli, 1974; Duncan, Rice, & Butler, 1968; Kelly, 1972; LaCrosse, 1975; Mansfield, 1973; Mehrabian, 1969; Shapiro, 1972; Strong et al., 1971) that examined the behavioral correlates of client perceptions of counselor warmth are summarized below.

1. Smiling.
2. General positive affect, especially as communicated through facial expression.
3. Verbal fluency and absence of filled pauses (for example, "um" or "ah").
4. Movement, with greater movement being interpreted as alertness.

5. Posture in which counselor's trunk is leaning forward.
6. Voice tones that are normal to soft in loudness, open, and normal to low in pitch; vocal quality described as relaxed, serious, and concerned.
7. Attentive listening.
8. Maintenance of eye contact.
9. Absence of fidgeting.
10. Face-to-face orientation.
11. Closer proximity (39" versus 55" or 80").

Modeling Congruence and Other Preferred Behaviors

When there is incongruence between verbal and nonverbal behaviors, the nonverbal behaviors are believed. For example, a counselor greeted a counselee arriving for an appointment by saying, "It's nice to see you." The counselee replied, "You always say that, but I wonder if you mean it. I see we are starting late again. It looks to me like you give other people extra time, but I get cut short." The use of time nonverbally communicated the truth that the counselor actually disliked seeing the counselee. Faced with the discrepancy, the counselee believed the behavior.

Bugental, Kaswan, and Love (1970) examined the effects of incongruence on children. They found that messages in which the speaker smiled while making a critical statement were interpreted more negatively by children than by adults and that, faced with a contradiction, children resolve the incongruity by assuming the worst. They caution that the effects can be very disturbing.

Graves and Robinson (1976) demonstrated that judged counselor congruence is significantly less when verbal and nonverbal cues are inconsistent. LaRusso (1978), based on research findings, underscores the importance of counselor congruence when working with paranoid patients. The group leader needs to model congruence. Without it, there is ambiguity in the relationship and no adequate basis for trust. The group leader should also model other behaviors that are consistent with effective functioning as a person. Modeling, as has been mentioned earlier in this book, is a potent method of training and persuasion.

MANAGEMENT OF THE GROUP ENVIRONMENT

The facilities and the counselor's use of them contribute to or detract from therapeutic effectiveness. Several elements are relevant.

Furniture. My personal preference is for lightly padded fiberglass shell chairs that tilt, swivel, and have casters. These are comfortable, but more important they give freedom for full nonverbal expression. On the other hand, the very independence of one unit from another and their egalitarian uniformity do not create rivalry for "choice" seats or avoidance of "sitting next to that turkey," as may happen in a room with hard-to-move furniture mixed between single seats and couches. The more active group leader depends less on conflict generated by the environment as a source of therapy material.

Room. Keeping the same room is advantageous because the place can become identified with acceptance, stability, security, and success in personal growth. Possessiveness may be noted by reluctance to leave the room at the end of a session or by territorial protectiveness if a new group member is added. These generally are signs of group health, while providing immediate material to process.

Size. A room that seems cavernous to group members may evoke a sense of insignificance and anxiety; a small room may heighten sexual or aggressive feelings and anxiety. Opt for the larger room and cluster the furniture into a cohesive unit if faced with this choice.

Decor. Simply from personal preference, I choose impressionistic paintings or graphics that evoke low-key joy or contentment, earth-toned pastel colors, and live plants. Realistic scenes evoke less specific moods; abstracts may be jarring and aversive to the confused client.

Leader/coleader position. We are most likely to be in a circle, without tables. As leader I'll sit at "6 o'clock" and my coleader at "1 or 2 o'clock." Since group members have the greatest interaction with those opposite them in the circle, this arrangement makes uniform attention to group members and verbal and nonverbal communication between therapists rather easy.

If we sit adjacent we may be perceived as huddled together protectively or, more likely, as mobilized for a united assault on the group (another good example of the divergence of interpretations possible as we look at nonverbal communication). Adjacent seating usually gives therapists greater power and is appropriate for groups who need the security of strong leadership or in which strong control must be exercised.

NONVERBAL BEHAVIORS OF GROUP MEMBERS

Group members' nonverbal behaviors can help the counselor better assess and understand their affective and attitudinal states. Table 11–4 lists some

Table 11–4 Behaviors frequently associated with various group member states

	Head	Face	Mouth	Eye Contact	Hands	Posture	Position	Proximity	Level of Arousal	General
Despair/depression	Down	Sad frown (eyebrows down at outer ends)	Tightness	Little or none; may cover eyes with hand	Autistic behaviors; body-focused self-stimulating movements	Approaches fetal position	Withdrawing movements; moves away from others	Distant	Apathy; indifference	Avoidance of others
Excitement/euphoria	Mobile movement	Mobility of expression	Smiling; laughing	Tries to capture and to hold eye contact of all other persons ("Look at me.")	Sweeping, expansive movements	Frequent change; seductive	Movements toward others	Close; pushes into personal space of others	Hyperactivity	Grandiose, exaggerated nonverbal behaviors
Fear/anxiety	Stiff movement; chin down	Flushing	Tightness; clenching teeth	Darting glances to others; wants to keep watch on others, but not meet their gazes ("I'll watch you.")	Tightness; gripping; sweaty palms ("clenched and drenched")	Frequent movement; crouching; hunching shoulders	Angled away; protective	Moderately distant	Watchful alertness	Jerking movements, mannerisms; fear-related physiological changes; carefully guards a small territory

Behavior	Head	Face/Eyes	Lips	Gaze	Hands/Gestures	Posture	Orientation	Proximity	Tension	Other
Hostility/ rejection of another person (Active/Overt)	Head, and often chin, thrust forward and/or tilted upward	Angry frown (eyebrows down at center)	Lips tensed and pushed forward slightly	Defiant	Clenching; fist; thumping (symbolic hitting)	Poised on edge of chair	Face to face	Moves boldly into personal space of others	High	Acting out such as slamming door or shifting chair noisily
(Passive/ covert)	Head down; turned away slightly	Squinting of eyes	Closed; normal	Aversion; blank staring	Body-focused movements; self-inflicting behaviors	Infrequent change	Angled or sideways ("cold shoulder")	May gradually and unobtrusively encroach on personal space of others	High, but effort to disguise it; real or feigned sleep	Efforts to control movement and disguise affect; sneezing, coughing, wheezing
Dependency/ attraction toward another	Head slightly down while making eye contact ("poor me")	Mirrors expression of other	Frequent smiling	Frequent	Reaching motions	Quasi-courtship	Beside and angled toward	Close	Typically high, but may vary	Real or feigned fatigue
Resistance to learning	Turned; rolled back	Rigidity of expression	Tightness	Avoidance	Clenched; looking at watch; body-focused movements	Held in; stiffness of limbs	Turns away from stimulus	Increases distance; moves back	Mirroring of behavior	Silences; absences from or lateness to sessions; behaviors that break the group's social norms; sudden onset of physical symptoms

clusters of nonverbal behaviors likely to accompany several specified client states. When several of the behaviors associated with a particular state are seen, the counselor may infer a reasonable probability of the existence of that state. But always remember that the presence of the behaviors does not *prove* the state. Use the inferences (hunches) derived from the nonverbal behaviors of group members as part of a total approach toward understanding them. Follow up by checking for further evidence that helps to support or to reject the inferences.

Group members may resist personally relevant involvement with group process. They may experience this as an approach-avoidance conflict, knowing that it is necessary to learn more about one's self, yet fearing to face new information or risk sharing one's self fully with others. This ambivalence may result in a confusing array of nonverbal behaviors, including those usually associated with anger and fear.

In this situation, the balance between therapeutic progress and regression or departure from the group is precarious. It is a time for the group leader to exercise accurate judgment, yet it is a time when it is most difficult to be certain about the group's "real" status—thus the earlier caution about being gentle in confronting the group member on the basis of interpretation of nonverbal signs.

I once assumed leadership of a therapy group that had been meeting with the same membership for many months. One member had a particularly long history of group experience and was quite knowledgeable about group process. She was always quite actively involved with the concerns of others and, indeed, was quite effective in helping others gain greater self-understanding. But when attention turned toward her own needs, she suddenly shifted into a full-fledged "poor me" syndrome. She would become teary-eyed, with a woebegone expression, her body drooping lifelessly. Her voice would become a weak, faltering, whiney monotone as she recited her fears and failures of the previous week. The recital seemed to exhaust her last bit of energy—she would grip her head in her hands and bend over in her chair, complaining of dizziness. She would occasionally look up to receive the pity of the other group members. If pressed for further involvement, she would complain of weakness and/or numbness in the legs, a severe headache, and of feeling cold. The other group members would console her and then move on to other topics.

After ten to fifteen minutes she would perk up. The recovery usually happened in this sequence: darting glances, raising head, resumption of eye contact with members, straightening posture to sitting erect in chair, and speaking. Eye contact with the leader was the last behavior to be resumed. It seemed clear from the context and from the quick onset and dissipation of physical symptoms that her nonverbal behaviors were part of a pattern of resistance. The other group members were not only allowing it, but also rewarding her by offering sympathy for her melodramatic tales.

The pattern was broken by pointing out several things to her in the following sequence: how it appeared she felt, that this seemed to be a sudden change, that the same pattern had occurred the previous two weeks, and that her recoveries occurred quite quickly. "How can this be?" she was asked.

She replied by admitting that she knew it was a defensive maneuver and asked that she not be allowed to get away with it in the future. She had always known, I presume, that her game playing was obvious to the rest of the group and to the leader. Confronting her gently made it easier for her to "confess." Had she been "accused" of resistance, she might have made one of her typical retreats or have become unproductively hostile.

Seating patterns can be informative. A group member may sit next to a therapist to feel protected or to avoid the more direct involvement that sitting face to face with the leader entails. Position may signal support for or identification with the leader.

Chair position pushing outside the perimeter of the group is disassociation from the others stemming from hostility, fear of conflict, a sense of rejection, or some other significant dynamic you would want to identify. A group member's shift to a new position within the group may signal important intrapsychic developments. For example, moving to a position opposite the leader may coincide with a decision to assert self-control, to confront issues (and, quite likely, the leader) head on.

GROUP LEADER'S USE OF OBSERVATIONS OF MEMBER BEHAVIOR

The group counselor should be continuously observing group members' nonverbal behaviors. The purpose is to understand more fully and accurately the members as individuals and in their relationship with other persons. This information is used to facilitate their growth and change.

There are many things to see in a counseling group session, but it is difficult to know the exact meaning of what is seen. *Nonverbal behaviors must always be judged in context and their meaning considered tentative.* A simplistic, cocksure approach to interpretation of nonverbal behavior is hazardous under any circumstances, but especially so in counseling.

Observe nonverbal behavior in the group as completely as possible before using the observations with the counselee(s). Use perceptions of the counselee's nonverbal behaviors as clues to possible hidden attitudes or motives rather than as proof that they exist. Formulate hunches about possible meanings and look for other behavior or words that confirm or disprove the hunches.

Careful observation may penetrate deception by the group member who, for whatever reasons, wishes to communicate that things are different than they really are. Table 11–5 shows several nonverbal behaviors found

Table 11–5   Behaviors concomitant with deception

Hestitates longer[a]

More speech errors[a,b,c]

Shorter responses[a,b,c]

Less smiling[a]

More eye contact[d]

Covering mouth with hand[e]

Touching nose[e]

[a]Heilveil and Muehleman, 1981.
[b]Kraut, 1976.
[c]Mehrabian, 1971.
[d]Sitton and Griffin, 1981.
[e]Morris, 1977.

to be associated with deception. The comparison is within the individual—that person's behavior when attempting deception in contrast with the same person when not attempting deception. If these behaviors are seen, it does not mean that the person is attempting to deceive, but deception is more likely than when those behaviors are not seen.

Paul Ekman and Josph Hager report new research demonstrating that deliberate expressions are generally stronger on the left side of the face, but spontaneous expressions tend to be symmetrical (Goleman, 1981). They quickly caution against drawing conclusions from just one or two nonverbal cues, stressing the importance of using all available cues, as well as the person's subjective reports.

Fairbanks et al. (1982) concluded that the cluster of nonverbal behaviors that includes eye contact avoidance, postural rigidity, and nonfunctional nervous movements is likely to correlate strongly with lack of receptivity to effective counseling. Karpf (1980) also states that muscular rigidity usually indicates resistance. The group leader who sees nonverbal cues that suggest resistance might direct attention to that issue before pursuing other matters.

Desmond Morris (1977) points out that some behaviors are more under control than others. He says that facial expression is most easily controlled because it occurs to us to control it and there are conventional expressions to use. Posture and body movements are least well controlled, he says, because we are less aware of what we are doing through those channels than through the face, and the definitions of expression are less well defined. The conclusion from all of this is that we should gather as much information as we can, but we must be cautious in our evaluation of the meaning.

One way to evaluate hunches about the meaning of group member behavior is offered by Fromm-Reichmann (1950). She suggests that by assuming the posture or other physical experiencing of another, one may "gain understanding of their cryptic communication of it" (pp. 93–94). Group counselors wait until they have enough information to have a high probability that their hunch is accurate before sharing the idea with the group member. It is usually better to ask for clarification of the meaning of nonverbal behaviors than to offer interpretations, especially early in a relationship. A simple remark, delivered in warmth, is often successful in encouraging the group member to tell more (for example, "You have been very quiet today" or "You seem to be pretty excited about something").

If the counselor is calling attention to some potentially significant nonverbal behavior, it is best to phrase it tentatively (for example, "I notice that you are gripping the arm of the chair tightly. I wonder if that means something," or "You haven't been looking at any of us during the past several minutes. Are you into something that you want to share with the rest of us?"). Beginning gently in this way is less threatening to the counselee, who may easily deny the significance of the nonverbal behavior if he or she so chooses. The group leader can accept the counselee's denial or pursue and intensify attention on the behavior, as professional judgment dictates. If counselors act prematurely or too harshly on the basis of their interpretations of nonverbal behavior, they run the risk of hurting the relationship and possibly losing the opportunity to help.

A recent session included a young woman who had joined the group, as she put it, "to learn to get along with people better." As attention focused on her, she appeared relaxed and was sitting rather conventionally with legs crossed and arms at her side. When the subject of her attitude toward her father-in-law was approached, she maintained that there were no problems in that relationship. As she spoke, I noticed an abrupt change in her behavior—her right foot began shaking vigorously and quickly from side to side and she clasped her arms across her chest, clenching her elbows with her hands. I pointed those behaviors out to her and added, "Maybe there is a lot of energy and a lot of feeling inside that would like to get out, and you are trying hard to keep it in." At that point she reported that she had bitter and overwhelmingly strong feelings of anger toward her father-in-law. During the session, she was able to acknowledge and partially to resolve that significant conflict.

By asking her about her external behavior, she had a choice of responding or not responding in terms of the internal conflict that she knew about and others could only suspect. Inquiring about observable behavior is much less risky than making "pot-shot" interpretations of what may or may not be going on inside. Another advantage is that "any interpretation which a patient is able to unearth for himself is more impressive to him, hence more likely to produce an immediate and lasting curative effect, than any interpretation offered by the therapist." (Fromm-Reichmann, 1950, p. 128). Offer group members a chance to help themselves; if that fails there will still be other chances to be more directive.

There may be occasions to observe and to discuss group members' nonverbal behaviors that affect their functioning in society (for example, poor eye contact, a tendency to intrude on another's personal space, crude or obnoxious behaviors). Group counseling affords more opportunities for observation of and feedback on such behaviors than does individual counseling, and optimal use should be made of the opportunities.

Changes in nonverbal behavior over a period of time may indicate a group member's progress. The following case history illustrates changes in nonverbal behavior during the course of counseling. The counselee was a 34-year-old woman involved in group counseling for a period of four months. The paragraphs below describe behaviors that were typical for her at different stages of treatment.

First session: Seated erect in chair, always facing straight ahead. Legs together with feet flat on floor and legs never crossed. Hands folded in lap. She blushed when spoken to. Her only eye contact was with darting glances.

Middle sessions: Posture varied from time to time during session. Varied placement of arms and legs. Blushed only when disclosing new information or expressing anger. Eye contact when being spoken to, but looked away when speaking.

Last session: Used a variety of postures. Turned toward person speaking to. Gestured with arms and hands. Did not blush, even when confronting others or being confronted. Open eye contact.

Are you, the reader, interpreting these changes in external behavior as signs of an internal freeing up of constraints and as manifestations of increased self-confidence? That's the way *she* interpreted them! Observing behavioral changes such as these gives the counselor clues to the counselee's progress. They are useful to the extent that they are accurate—and the accuracy of interpretation is something that can be validated with the person.

Generally, counselors should be patient in gathering information about a group member and gentle in giving initial confrontations, especially when they are based on interpretation of nonverbal behaviors. This approach will be most effective and efficient in the long run.

WORKING TOWARD COMPETENT USE OF THE NONVERBAL DOMAIN

There are three major goals to work toward in order to make optimal use of the nonverbal domain in group counseling practice. This section suggests some ways of working toward each of the three goals:

1. Achieve a high awareness of nonverbal cues. To work toward this goal, use the exercises that appear next.
2. Be able to form reasonably accurate, tentative inferences from group members' nonverbal behaviors. Work toward this goal by studying this chapter, especially Table 11–4, and by studying the recommended readings cited at the end of this chapter.
3. Be able to apply inferences. They can help counselors learn more about the group members and can be used to help group members better understand themselves and their interpersonal styles. The processes of applying inferences are described above in the Group Leader's Use of Observations of Member Behavior section. Work toward this goal by studying that section and practice using the methods described. If counselors have difficulty sharing their inferences with group members, they may need to improve their confrontation or assertion skills.

Exercises in Awareness of Nonverbal Communication

Awareness is the first step in gaining full use of the nonverbal domain. The following exercises will help counselors become more aware of nonverbal signals.

1. Observe nonverbal communication used by other persons around you or on television. Note examples of specific behaviors that you particularly like or dislike. List nonverbal behaviors that seem to interfere with and/or terminate conversations between two persons. List other nonverbal behaviors that seem to cause a conversation to move ahead and that might indicate a relationship of mutual trust and caring is beginning to develop.
2. Observe your own nonverbal communication behaviors. Study the list at the beginning of this chapter to become more aware of nonverbal behaviors you use. List nonverbal behaviors you wish to modify. List any you think might be misinterpreted by others.
3. Keep a list of ways in which nonverbal behaviors are used and give examples of each. The following classification system for nonverbal behaviors was adapted from Ekman and Friesen (1969b):
    a. Those that make complete nonverbal statements (for example, to beckon by curling the index finger or signals by athletic officials). Nonverbal behaviors of this type come the closest to having definite and widely understood meanings.
    b. Those that modify verbal communication by accentuating qualifying, or masking the meaning of the words (for example, saying, "I'm not angry" through clenched teeth).

   c.   Those that illustrate verbal communication (for example, to demonstrate size or shape of an object or the motion of swinging a tennis racket).
   d.   Those that regulate the interaction (for example, to look frequently at a watch as a way of saying, "I'm in a hurry" or "I would like to leave" or to remove sunglasses as a way of saying, "I'm willing to be myself and to let you see me as I really am").
   e.   Those that display emotions (for example, facial expressions or pounding the fist or stamping a foot).
4.   Evaluate the quality of your attending behaviors. With a partner, take turns talking about anything of interest. Your partner talks, you listen. An observer should assess your attending behavior, using Table 11–1 as a checklist to note effective and ineffective behaviors. For assessment under less contrived circumstances, have a coleader rate you during a group session or have a friend observe you in casual social situations. If you can be videotaped in spontaneous interaction, you can do your own assessment, which can be quite enlightening.

SUMMARY

This chapter began with a definition of nonverbal communication. The definition was followed by a categorization of nonverbal behavior according to communication through the following media: time, the body, voice, and the environment.

In the next section, some general characteristics of nonverbal communication were reviewed. Nonverbal expressions convey emotion; they are habits; they tell the truth when words may lie; they enrich the meaning of words; they are a clue to verbal behavior to follow; and they provide clues about a relationship.

The appropriate use of nonverbal behavior by the group counselor was explored through a table of appropriate and inappropriate attending behaviors and by means of a table and discussion illustrating the nonverbal communication of empathy, respect, warmth, concreteness, genuineness, self-disclosure, confrontation, and immediacy. This section was followed by an example of a group counselor's understanding of and assistance to a group member by his accurate utilization of nonverbal cues.

A comprehensive table of nonverbal behaviors frequently associated with various group-member states was included to assist the group counselor in understanding the complex nonverbal behaviors of the group members. Following this table, exercises were included to help the group counselor implement the three goals for competent use of nonverbal communication, which are to achieve a high awareness of nonverbal cues, to be able to form reasonably accurate, tentative inferences from group members' nonverbal behaviors, and to be able to apply the inferences effectively. The chapter closes with a list of suggested readings.

REFERENCES

Bayes, M. A. (1972). Behavioral cues of interpersonal warmth. *Journal of Consulting and Clinical Psychology, 39,* 333–339.

Bugental, D. E., Kaswan, J. W., & Love, L. R. (1970). Perception of contradictory meanings conveyed by verbal and nonverbal channels. *Journal of Personality and Social Psychology, 16,* 647–655.

Darwin, C. (1872). *The expression of the emotions in man and animals.* New York: Appleton Press.

D'Augelli, A. R. (1974). Nonverbal behavior of helpers in initial helping interactions. *Journal of Counseling Psychology, 21,* 360–363.

Davis, F. (1973). *Inside intuition: What we know about nonverbal communication.* New York: McGraw-Hill.

Davitz, J. R., & Davitz, L. (1959). The communication of feelings by content-free speech. *Journal of Communication, 9,* 6–13.

Deutsch, F. (1949). Thus speaks the body—An analysis of postural behavior. *Transactions. New York Academy of the Sciences,* Series II, *12,* 58–62.

Dunbar, F. (1960). Interpretation of body behavior during psychotherapy. In J. H. Masserman (Ed.), *Science and psychoanalysis.* Vol. 3. *Psychoanalysis and Human Values.* New York: Grune & Stratton.

Duncan, S. D., Jr., Rice, L. N., & Butler, J. M. (1968). Therapists' paralanguage in peak and poor psychotherapy hours. *Journal of Abnormal Psychology, 73,* 566–570.

Ekman, P., & Friesen, W. V. (1969a). Nonverbal leakage and clues to deception. *Psychiatry, 32,* 88–106.

Ekman, P., & Friesen, W. V. (1969b). The repertoire of nonverbal behavior: Categories, origins, usage, and coding. *Semiotica, 1,* 49–98.

Ekman, P., & Friesen, W. V. (1972). Hand movements. *Journal of Communication, 22,* 353–374.

Fairbanks, L. A., McGuire, M. T., & Harris, C. J. (1982). Nonverbal interaction of patients and therapists during psychiatric interviews. *Journal of Abnormal Psychology, 91,* 109–119.

Fretz, B. R., Corn, R., Tuemmler, J. M., & Bellet, W. (1979). Counselor nonverbal behaviors and client evaluations. *Journal of Counseling Psychology, 26,* 304–311.

Freud, S. (1963). *Dora: An analysis of a case of hysteria.* New York: Collier Books.

Fromm-Reichman, F. (1950). *Principles of intensitive psychotherapy.* Chicago: University of Chicago Press.

Gazda, G. M., Asbury, F. R., Balzer, F. J., Childers, W. C., & Walters, R. P. (1977). *Human relations development: A manual for educators* (2nd ed.). Boston: Allyn and Bacon.

Gazda, G. M., Childers, W. C., & Walters, R. P. (1982). *Interpersonal communication: A handbook for health professionals.* Rockville, MD: Aspen.

Gibb, J. R. (1972). TORI theory: Nonverbal behavior and the experience of community. *Comparative Group Studies, 3,* 461–472.

Goleman, D. (1981). The 7,000 faces of Dr. Ekman. *Psychology Today, 15* (2), 43–49.

Gottman, J. M. (1980). Consistency of nonverbal affect and affect reciprocity in marital interaction. *Journal of Consulting and Clinical Psychology, 48,* 711–717.

Graves, J. R., & Robinson, J. D. (1976). Proxemic behavior as a function of inconsistent verbal and nonverbal messages. *Journal of Counseling Psychology, 23,* 333–338.

Haase, R. F., & Tepper, D. T. (1972). Nonverbal components of empathic communication. *Journal of Counseling Psychology, 19,* 417–424.

Hall, E. T. (1955). The anthropology of manners. *Scientific American, 192,* 84–90.

Hall, J. A. (1978). Gender effects in decoding nonverbal cues. *Psychological Bulletin, 85,* 845–857.

Hayduk, L. E. (1978). Personal space: An evaluative and orienting overview. *Psychological Bulletin, 85,* 117–134.

Heilveil, I., & Muehleman, J. T. (1981). Nonverbal clues to deception in a psychotherapy analogue. *Psychotherapy: Theory, Research and Practice, 18,* 329–335.

Hill, C. E., Siegelman, L., Gronsky, B. R., Sturniolo, F., & Fretz, B. R. (1981). Nonverbal communication and counseling outcome. *Journal of Counseling Psychology, 28,* 203–212.

Izard, C. (1975). Patterns of emotion and emotion communication in hostility and aggression. In P. Pliner, L. Krames, & P. Alloway (Eds.), *Advances in the study of communication and affect* (Vol. 2). New York: Plenum.

Karpf, R. J. (1980). Nonverbal components of the interpretive process in psychoanalytic psychotherapy. *American Journal of Psychotherapy, 34,* 477–486.

Kaul, T. J., & Schmidt, L. D. (1971). Dimensions of interviewer trustworthiness. *Journal of Counseling Psychology, 18,* 542–548.

Kelly, F. D. (1972). Communicational significance of therapist proxemic cues. *Journal of Consulting and Clinical Psychology, 39,* 345.

Kraut, R. R. (1976, September). Verbal and nonverbal cues in the perception of lying. Paper presented at the annual meeting of the American Psychological Association, Washington, D.C.

LaBarre, W. (1947). The cultural basis of emotions and gestures. *Journal of Personality, 16,* 49–68.

LaCrosse, M. B. (1975). Nonverbal behavior and perceived counselor attractiveness and persuasiveness. *Journal of Counseling Psychology, 22,* 563–566.

LaRusso, L. (1978). Sensitivity of paranoid patients to nonverbal cues. *Journal of Abnormal Psychology, 87,* 463–471.

Lothstein, L. M. (1978). Human territoriality in group psychotherapy. *International Journal of Group Psychotherapy, 28,* 55–71.

Mahl, G. F. (1968). Gestures and body movements in interviews. In J. Shlien (Ed.), *Research in psychotherapy.* Vol. 3. Washington D.C.: American Psychological Association.

Mansfield, E. (1973). Empathy: Concept and identified psychiatric nursing behavior. *Nursing Research, 22,* 525–530.

Mehrabian, A. (1969). Significance of posture and position in the communication of attitude and status relationships. *Psychological Bulletin, 71,* 359–372.

Mehrabian, A. (1971). Nonverbal betrayal of feeling. *Journal of Experimental Research in Personality, 5,* 64–73.

Mehrabian, A., & Ferris, S. R. (1967). Inference of attitude from nonverbal communication in two channels. *Journal of Consulting Psychology, 31,* 248–252.

Mehrabian, A., & Wiener, M. (1967). Decoding of inconsistent communication. *Journal of Personality and Social Psychology, 6,* 109–114.

Morris, D. (1977). *Manwatching: A field guide to human behavior.* New York: H. N. Abrams.

Morris, D. (1977). Nonverbal leakage: How can you tell if someone's lying. *New York, 10*(2), 43–46.

Morris, D., Collett, P., Marsh, P., & O'Shaughnessy, M. (1979). *Gestures.* New York: Stein and Day.

Osgood, C. E. (1966). Dimensionality of the semantic space for communication via facial expressions. *Scandinavian Journal of Psychology, 7,* 1–30.

Reece, M. M., & Whitman R. N. (1962). Expressive movements, warmth, and verbal reinforcement. *Journal of Abnormal and Social Psychology, 64,* 234–236.

Rogers, C. R. (1957). The necessary and sufficient conditions of therapeutic personality change. *Journal of Consulting Psychology, 21,* 95–103.

Sapir, E. A. (1927). *Language: An introduction to the study of speech.* New York: Harcourt, Brace.

Scheflen, A. E. (1964). The significance of posture in communication systems. *Psychiatry, 27,* 316–331.

Shapiro, J. G. (1972). Variability and usefulness of facial and body cues. *Comparative Group Studies, 3,* 437–442.

Sherer, M., & Rogers, R. W. (1980). Effects of therapist's nonverbal communication on rated skill and effectiveness. *Journal of Clinical Psychology, 36,* 696–700.

Siegel, J. C., & Sell, J. M (1978). Effects of objective evidence of expertness and nonverbal behavior on client-perceived expertness. *Journal of Counseling Psychology, 25,* 188–192.

Sitton, S. C., & Griffin, S. T. (1981). Detection of deception from client's eye contact patterns. *Journal of Counseling Psychology, 28,* 269–271.

Street, R. L., Jr., & Brady, R. M. (1982). Speech rate acceptance ranges as a function of evaluative domain, listener speech rate, and communication context. *Communication Monographs, 49,* 290–308.

Strong, S. R., Taylor, R. G., Bratton, J. C., & Loper, R. G. (1971). Nonverbal behavior and perceived counselor characteristics. *Journal of Counseling Psychology, 18,* 554–561.

Tepper, D., & Haase, R. (1978). Verbal and nonverbal communication of facilitative conditions. *Journal of Counseling Psychology, 25,* 35–44.

Tyler, L. E. (1969). *The work of the counselor.* (3rd ed.). New York: Appleton-Century-Crofts.

Van Houten, R., et al. (1982). An analysis of some variables influencing the effectiveness of reprimands. *Journal of Applied Behavior Analysis, 15*(1), 65–83.

Watzlawick, P., Beavin, J., & Jackson, D. (1969). *Pragmatics of human communication.* New York: Norton.

Waxer, P. (1974). Nonverbal cues for depression. *Journal of Abnormal Psychology, 83,* 319–322.

Webbink, P. G. (1986). *The Power of the Eyes.* New York: Springer Publishing Co.

Wiens, A. N., Harper, R. G., & Matarazzo, J. D. (1980). Personality correlates of nonverbal interview behavior. *Journal of Clinical Psychology, 36,* 205–215.

Wright, W. (1975). Counselor dogmatism, willingness to disclose, and clients' empathy ratings. *Journal of Counseling Psychology, 22,* 390–395.

Young, D. W. (1980). Meanings of counselor nonverbal gestures: Fixed or interpretive? *Journal of Counseling Psychology, 27,* 447–452.

SUGGESTED READINGS

Beakel, N. G., & Mehrabian, A. (1969). Inconsistent communications and psychopathy. *Journal of Abnormal Psychology, 74,* 126–130.

Beier, E. (1966). *The silent language of psychotherapy.* Chicago: Aldine.

Berger, M. M. (1958). Nonverbal communications in group psychotherapy. *International Journal of Group Psychotherapy, 8,* 161–177.

Davis, F. (1971). *Inside intuition: What we know about nonverbal communication.* New York: Signet.

Ekman, P., & Friesen, W. V. (1968). Nonverbal behavior in psychotherapy research. In J. Shlien (Ed.), *Research in psychotherapy.* Vol. 3. Washington, D.C.: American Psychological Assoc.

Engebretson D. E. (1973). Human territorial behavior: The role of interaction distance in therapeutic interventions. *American Journal of Orthopsychology, 43,* 108–116.

Gladstein, G. A. (1974). Nonverbal communication and counseling/psychotherapy. *The Counseling Psychologist, 4,* 34–57.

Grant, E. C. (1972). Nonverbal communication in the mentally ill. In R. A. Hinde (Ed.), *Non-verbal communication.* London: Cambridge University Press.

Harper, R., Wiens, A., & Matarazzo, J. (1978). *Nonverbal communication: The state of the art.* New York: Wiley.

Harrison, R. P. (1974). *Beyond words: An introduction to nonverbal communication.* Englewood Cliffs, NJ: Prentice-Hall.

Hill, D. (1974). Non-verbal behavior in mental illness. *British Journal of Psychiatry, 124,* 221–230.

Horowitz, M. J. (1968). Spatial behavior and psychopathology. *Journal of Nervous and Mental Disease, 146,* 24–35.

Katz, M., & Katz, V. T. (Eds.). (1983). *Foundations of nonverbal communication.* Carbondale: Southern Illinois University Press.

Knapp, M. L. (1972). *Nonverbal communication in human interaction.* New York: Holt, Rinehart and Winston.

Leathers, G. (1986). *Successful nonverbal communication.* New York: Macmillan.

Malandro, A., & Barker, L. (1983). *Nonverbal communication.* Reading, MA: Addison-Wesley.

Meerloo, J. A. M. (1967). Contributions of psychiatry to the study of human communication. In F. E. X. Dance (Ed.), *Human communication theory.* New York: Holt, Rinehart and Winston.

Pederson, D., & Shears, L. M. (1973). A review of personal space research in the framework of general systems theory. *Psychological Bulletin, 80,* 367–388.

Ruesch, J., & Kees, W. (1971). *Nonverbal communication: Notes on the visual perception of human relations* (2nd ed.). Berkeley: University of California Press.

Scheflen, A. E. (1963). Communication and regulation in psychotherapy. *Psychiatry, 26,* 126–136.

Scheflen, A. E. (1973). *How behavior means.* New York: Gordon and Breach.

Scheflen, A. E., & Scheflen, A. (1972). *Body language and the social order: Communication as behavioral control.* Englewood Cliffs, NJ: Prentice-Hall.

Weitz, S. (1979). *Nonverbal communication* (2nd ed.). New York: Oxford University Press.

Winick, C., & Holt, H. (1961). Seating position as nonverbal communication in group analysis. *Psychiatry, 24,* 171–182.

Winick, C., & Holt, H. (1961). Some external modalities of group psychotherapy and their dynamic significance. *American Journal of Psychotherapy, 15,* 56–62.

C H A P T E R 12

Ethical and Legal Issues in Group Counseling[1]

This chapter provides the reader with current information concerning ethics and legal issues involved in group counseling. While some of these issues relate to the training of group leaders, the majority of concerns are about establishing and leading various types of groups including, but not limited to, therapy groups, growth groups, self-help groups, groups for couples, and support groups. The information contained in this chapter is based, in part, on an extensive literature review and analysis of current ethical standards and legal issues in the helping professions (Gazda, Childers, & Brooks, 1987), and the information obtained in Gazda et al.'s (1973) study of twenty-six professional associations, societies, and individuals representing these associations in which group procedures were a part of the functions employed by the membership.

The literature reflects a fair degree of agreement on a number of basic issues or topics especially relevant to group work. Thus, for the most part, the material contained in this chapter is relevant to all of the varied group procedures as practiced in the related disciplines in the helping professions. Issues that are unique to a particular type of group or style of leadership will be especially noted.

As was noted in the previous edition of this text, ethical considerations in group work are receiving greater attention in the current literature. As a result of the increased focus in this area, ethical issues are continuously being clarified and refined. The Association for Specialists in Group Work

1. Coauthored with R. Ernest Taylor, J. D., Ph.D., Athens, Georgia and Tina Stern, Ph.D., Oxford College, Oxford, Georgia.

(1980) has published *Ethical Guidelines for Group Leaders,* which is reproduced as Appendix F (now under revision). These guidelines have been elaborated in *A Casebook of Ethical Guidelines for Group Leaders* by Corey, Corey, and Callanan (1982). The Association for Specialists in Group Work also dedicated the September 1982 issue of *Journal for Specialists in Group Work* to ethical issues in group work.

Legal issues, as decided in courtrooms in state and federal jurisdictions, provide us with another means of clarification and formulation of ethical issues. For example, while confidentiality was originally an ethical concern, that issue has become increasingly the focus of legal battles in our nation's courts (e.g., *Tarasoff* v. *Regents of the University of California,* 1974). Our legislatures have also sought to settle issues such as confidentiality by prescribing the limits of therapist/client privacy (Denkowski & Denkowski, 1982). This issue, along with others of equal importance, will be elaborated on later in this chapter.

Gazda, Childers, and Brooks (1987) have cited numerous other professional issues that have been the subject of lawsuits. These include sexual relationships between therapist and client, informed consent, clients' right to treatment, improper use of somatic therapies, and other unethical practices. Whenever ethical issues are contested in courts of law, it has important implications for group work. There is hardly any issue in private, individual therapy that cannot be applied to the practice of group therapy. In the same way, there is no issue that one could raise concerning small group therapy or counseling that could not also be applied to the various other types of group work. Thus, in this chapter, except where particular circumstances dictate special ethical/legal guidelines, the discussion will center on small group work for personal growth (group counseling) rather than on other types of groups (e.g., task accomplishment groups). In that light, *group work refers to the dynamic interaction between collections of individuals for prevention or remediation of difficulties or for the enhancement of personal growth/enrichment through the interaction of those who meet together for a commonly agreed-on purpose and at prearranged times.* A number of people meeting in this purposeful way have the potential to become a group if they succeed in clarifying their goals, agree on ways to accomplish them, and maintain the committed participation of all involved.

When a group is formed, it is important for all to recognize it as such and to understand that there are certain ethical guidelines that apply to its functioning. *Ethics of group work are those agreed-on practices consistent with our broader ethical commitments (political, moral, and religious) that we think are reasonable and that responsible practitioners and clients will generally support.*

It is important to understand that, while there are specific ethical guidelines that we can rely upon in group work (e.g., *Ethical Guidelines for Group Leaders,* 1980), ethics are not absolutes. They inevitably change both as new scientific evidence dictates new approaches and as our culture changes. Rarely, however, can ethics lead the way; rather, they must reflect the changes that take place in the moral, religious, and political arenas or else they would become prejudicial barriers that restrict growth, rather than serving as guidelines within which professional and counselee growth can proceed with some order, confidence, and security.

It is recognized that, because there are few unchanging, universal absolutes in the field of human relations, ethical codes or guidelines are seldom equally acceptable to all responsible practitioners at the same time. At present, commonalities of beliefs are emerging in group work, and these commonalities will be the emphasis of most of the remaining portions of this chapter.

GROUP LEADERSHIP

The subject of group leadership (and the group leader) is the primary item of interest with regard to ethics and legal issues. This is as it should be since the group leader's competency, style, and behavior are the most important variables in determining the overall ethical behavior of the group. The ethical issues concerning the group leader can be related to the *Ethical Guidelines for Group Leaders* (1980) (hereinafter referred to as the *Guidelines*) by reference to Section and Item number. For example, the group leader's responsibility for providing group services to clients can be referred to Section B, Item 7 in the *Guidelines*. As the discussion touches on the various individual guidelines, the section letter and item number will be placed in parentheses following that discussion. (As mentioned earlier, the *Guidelines* are reproduced as Appendix F.)

The first set of ethical issues concerning the group leader falls under the general rubric of *professional responsibility*. The leader should not only have been adequately trained to engage in group practice (A–1), but also should have adopted a generally accepted code of ethics (C–1). The *Guidelines* require the group leader to either display the *Guidelines* or to make them available to the group members. In addition to the *Guidelines*, the group leader should also be able to meet acceptable standards of professionalism such as is called for by the Association for Specialists in Group Work's *Professional Standards for Group Counseling* (1983) (see Appendix G). These standards provide detailed competencies expected of any person engaging in the practice of group counseling. A group leader who does not possess professional credentials must function under the supervision of a professionally qualified person (B–7). Also, the group leader should have established a clear set of ground rules by which he or she and the other group members are guided in their interactions with one another both in and out of the group setting.

One of the quickest ways for a group leader to get into legal trouble is by engaging in practices for which he or she has received inadequate preparation. Many prospective group members are already fearful of what might happen once they have joined a group. If the leader is not well trained and prepared to deal with these fears, or neglects, for example, to protect each group member from unnecessary and unreasonable intrusions into his or her privacy, some member of the group might suffer emotional harm and be in a position to bring legal action against the group leader.

Legal action, as discussed here and later in this chapter, most often refers to a malpractice suit. The word "malpractice" means *bad practice* and such a lawsuit is usually brought against a professional for failing in his or her responsibility to the client (called "breach of duty"). Generally speaking, the claim against the professional is made by a "plaintiff" who seeks a monetary award based on a specified amount of damages. These damages may be physical, financial, and/or emotional.

For example, if a group member were allowed to be verbally abused by other members of the group, he or she might become emotionally upset and even fearful for his or her physical safety. This would give rise to a cause of action sufficient to sustain a lawsuit against the group leader for malpractice. An inexperienced group leader could get caught up in the emotional surge of something happening in the group and be quite unaware of the effects of the group's behavior on any particular member of the group.

The group leader should also ensure that group members are aware of certain rights that each of them has with regard to group activities. Prospective group members should be told that their participation must be voluntary (A–7) and that they have freedom to leave the group at any time they choose (A–7). There are individuals who can feel trapped in a group setting; often they become confused and are helpless to extricate themselves from what appears to be, at least for them, a threatening environment. An untrained group leader might neglect to tell prospective members about this particular right and that might lead to trouble. It should be noted that there may be instances where a group member might be compelled to attend group therapy, such as in child custody matters where the court has ordered parents to attend a group on parenting as a condition to their maintaining custody of their children. If that is the case, the group leader must carefully and fully document such participation.

Another right that all group members have involves the freedom to resist following the suggestions or prescriptions of the group members or the leader (B–1). Left unattended or without proper guidance, a group can easily leave the realm of listening and supporting to engage in advice giving. Group leaders who have not been properly trained could fall into the same trap. A group member who, for instance, did not possess a sufficiently strong sense of self and was not previously informed of his or her right to ignore the group's suggestions or prescriptions, might feel compelled to act in the prescribed way. This behavior could well lead to disastrous results.

Before leaving the topic of leadership, it is important to note several other issues that relate to the group leader's overall sense of responsibility toward the group membership. Before beginning any group work, and even with adequate training and professional preparation, the group leader should have developed a well-conceptualized model for explaining behavioral change. The leader needs to be able to explain such change not only to himself or herself but also, from time to time, to group members as well. People want to know how change occurs and they will look to the group leader for an explanation.

Also, the group leader should have a clear understanding, developed from the professional and legal literature, of group members' rights, in general, and know how these rights can be protected in a group setting. Leaders must be able to protect individual members from physical threats, intimidation, coercion, and peer pressure (B–1). In this same vein, group leaders should abstain from inappropriate personal relationships with group members during the group's existence and in any following professional involvement (B–5).

RECRUITMENT OF GROUP PARTICIPANTS

Once a professional has developed the idea for a group project, the process of participant recruitment begins. It should be kept in mind that professional standards, as detailed by the group leader's discipline, should be adhered to at all times during the recruitment phase. Often these guidelines are more explicit for professionals in private practice than for those in public, institutional settings such as schools, mental health facilities, businesses, and industrial organizations. There are some guidelines, such as those listed below, that apply to both settings:

1. Announcements should include an explicit statement of the group's purpose, length and duration of sessions, and the number of participants that will be accepted (A–1).
2. Announcements should include an explicit statement regarding the leader's qualifications for leading the proposed group.
3. Announcements should include an explicit statement regarding the leader's fee (if any) that specifies the amount for professional services rendered; any amounts for meals, lodging, materials, and so forth that each group member would be responsible for; and, the amount (if any) for follow-up services.

4. Group members should not be coerced to join the group by superiors or the group leader (A–7).
5. Claims that cannot be substantiated by *scientific* evidence should not be made.
6. Prospective group members should be informed ahead of time that, unless the prescribed minimum number of group participants is attained, the group will not be formed.

For more information concerning public advertisements or announcements for psychological services, see the American Psychological Association's "Ethical Principles of Psychologists," the reference for which is listed in the Suggested Readings section at the conclusion of this chapter.

SCREENING OF GROUP PARTICIPANTS

Since there is evidence that not everyone can benefit from a group experience, the leader has an obligation to institute some form of screening procedures to ensure that prospective members understand what will be expected of them and to allow the leader to select only those members likely to benefit themselves and other participants.

Some general guidelines designed to ensure that the preceding conditions prevail include appraising prospective group members of their ability to achieve specific benefits from the group experience. High-risk members ordinarily should be excluded from group treatment. The American Medical Association's Council on Mental Health describes the following types of persons who "run a risk of [experiencing] adverse reaction[s] from sensitivity training: (a) persons who are frankly psychotic and those with impaired sense of reality; (b) persons with a significant degree of psychoneurosis; (c) those with a history of marked emotional lability; (d) those who react to stress with psychological decompensation or psychosomatic illness; and, (e) persons in a crisis situation" (1971, p. 1854). Except for category (b), these individuals would also be poor risks for counseling, therapy, and quasi-therapy group (A–2).

During the screening process, prospective group members should be told candidly what will be expected of them, the risks they will incur, and what techniques the leader will employ (A–6). This information, along with other information about the group process, should be included in a document provided to each prospective member. This document would be titled, "Informed Consent Statement" and should be read, discussed where necessary to clarify any confusing statements, and signed by those group members electing to participate in the group activity.

Informed consent is a very important concept. Without such consent, the leader is vulnerable to a lawsuit from any group member who feels he or she "got more than was bargained for" or that the group process was not what was expected and caused the participant "undue emotional stress." There are three elements to informed consent: the client's ability to give consent, the client's truly being informed, and the voluntariness of the consent.

The prospective group member, in order to be considered by the courts as being capable of giving consent, must not exhibit any behavior indicative of mental incompetence, nor have been declared mentally incompetent by a court of law. Also, if the person is a minor, then the parent or legal guardian must give consent. However, with any incompetent person, it is probably more ethical to obtain his or her consent as an indication of voluntariness (A–7).

In order to ensure that the group member's consent is an informed one, the leader should explain (preferably in writing) the following points:

1. The procedures and basic approach to be used and why they will be used (A–6).
2. The leader's role in the group's process (A–7).
3. The members' roles in the group's process and the risks they might incur should they join the group (A–6).
4. Any discomforts that group members might experience (A–6).
5. What group members can expect in the way of outcome(s) from engaging in the group process.
6. What other methods are available that the group member might consider as an alternative to participating in the group.
7. Assurance that group members can ask questions about the group process at any time.
8. Assurance that group members can withdraw from the group at any time or refuse to participate or be a part of any portion of the group process (A–7). For example, the group leader may have planned some activities that require the group members to engage in physical contact with each other (e.g., hugging and the "trust lift,") and, without prior informed consent, some members might become offended and/or very threatened by these exercises.

While it is not essential to provide an informed consent statement in writing to group members, it would provide more protection to both the group members and the group leader. The members are allowed to see and study the issues involved at their leisure and can thus make a more careful decision about joining the group. The leader, on the other hand, can reduce his or her professional liability by eliminating the question of failure to adequately inform the group members.

The third element of informed consent is the voluntariness of the member's consent. The member must be afforded true freedom of choice. Prisoners, for example, who are required to participate in group therapy are not doing so voluntarily. Persons ordered by a court to participate in some group process cannot be said to be participating voluntarily. Students who join in group processes at the "request" of their principal or teacher, cannot be engaged in voluntary behavior either because they are feeling coerced or are a minor or both. When these conditions exist, it is important that the leader make careful note of every aspect of the situation and decide for himself or herself whether to accept responsibility for the group or refuse to accept that particular person into the group.

Some final actions the group leader needs to take before accepting an applicant into the group include inquiring of the prospective member whether he or she is currently in similar treatment with another group or with an individual counselor or therapist. If such is the case, the leader is ethically bound to obtain clearance from the other professional who is treating the potential group member.

The group leader should inform prospective members that they will be removed from the group if, in the opinion of the leader, they are being harmed by the group or are harming others in the group (B–1). Also, the leader should investigate the prospective member list to ensure that superiors are not placed in groups with subordinates unless both are fully aware of the risks involved in such an arrangement and both give free, informed consent. Likewise, students/trainees should not be *required* to be in therapy/counseling groups with their teachers or with others who may have evaluative control over them (A–7). Lastly, the group leader should discuss, in detail, the concept of confidentiality with each prospective member and be assured that the applicant understands the importance of this issue.

CONFIDENTIALITY

There is general acceptance among group leaders that confidentiality is a prerequisite for the development of group trust, cohesion, and productive work in counseling, therapy, and quasi-therapy groups. The importance of this concept should be discussed fully with prospective group members during the screening process. It is discussed separately here to specify in detail the various dimensions of confidentiality in group work. The leader should also reiterate the main objectives of confidentiality during the first group session and, thereafter, be aware of a continuing need to remind the group of the confidentiality issue where and when it is felt necessary.

What follows is a general discussion of the issues involved in confidentiality along with some guidelines that should serve to fill the basic needs of any group leader. However, it is most important that the group leader, before he or she engages in the practice of group work, become *thoroughly* familiar with *all* aspects of the confidentiality issue. The leader should be informed of the statutes and case law governing confidentiality and know the circumstances under which confidentiality must be broken. The leader should also know the demands and expectations of the institution in which the group is being conducted (if such is the case) regarding confidentiality and loyalty. Recall, for example, the circumstances discussed earlier concerning groups held in schools, prisons, and public mental health clinics.

During the screening process, the leader should inform prospective members whether confidentiality is a requirement of group membership. Confidentiality is generally required in therapy, counseling, and other experiential groups, although it must be pointed out very clearly to each prospective member that complete confidentiality cannot be guaranteed by the leader.

Prospective group members should be informed that legally privileged communication generally does not extend to group members (A–5). This means that the concept of privilege, whereby the courts have recognized that the client has a right to require the therapist to maintain complete confidentiality as to any and all communications between the two unless specifically waived by the client, does not apply or extend to group members (A–3). As such, group members are under no legal obligation to maintain confidentiality among themselves, nor can they refuse to divulge information about the communications between them if ordered to do so by a court of law (Cross, 1970).

Also during the screening process, the leader should inform prospective members explicitly of areas or instances in which the leader may be required to break confidence (A–3). The group leader should have already developed a clear plan for identification of and intervention with suicidal and dangerous group members. Such a plan should meet the legal requirements of the state in which the leader practices. For example, most states require therapists to inform an appropriate state-level department if it is discovered that a client is either being abused or is abusing a minor. The therapist must divulge such information or face civil and, in some states, criminal sanctions.

Case law and ethical principles call upon the therapist/group leader to either control the client (group member) who is considered suicidal or inform the appropriate officials or family members or both. When it is discovered that a client/group member is potentially dangerous and is posing a threat to another person or persons, the leader is obligated to either control the client by involuntary admission to a hospital for evaluation and observation (see *Bradley Center, Inc.* v. *Wessner et al.*, 1982) and/or warn the potential victim (see *Tarasoff* v. *The Regents of the University of California*, 1976).

Other confidentiality issues that should be covered during the screening process include informing prospective members of any research that might be carried out concerning that group and each group member must give written permission to be included in such research. Also, if the group sessions are to be tape or video recorded, prospective group members need to be so informed and provide their written consent for such recording. Furthermore, the group members should be informed that they have the right to stop the recorder at any point they choose if they feel that the recording is restricting their participation (A–8). The leader should ensure that all audio and video tapes are erased as soon as they are no longer needed and should assure group members of this procedure.

If the group is composed of couples, family members, or groups of family members, the group leader should make sure that each group member understands the leader's position vis-a-vis confidentiality. Usually one of two positions is taken by the group leader. Either the leader treats each member of the group as a separate client and thus treats all communications, whether made in or outside the group's meeting time, as confidential. Or the leader treats the group as a whole as "the client" and refuses to maintain confidences with any individual group member. The important point here is that the group leader must tell all of the group members, during the screening process, his or her position concerning this matter.

Lastly, if the group is to be composed of minors, the group leader should be thoroughly familiar with the statutes and case law regarding the need for obtaining parental or legal guardian consent and any special status a particular minor group member might enjoy (e.g., emancipation granted due to marriage). Parental consent should also be considered for purely ethical reasons as well, and any minor agreeing to join a group should be made aware of the extent of confidentiality the leader can promise to him or her as a minor.

There are a number of administrative procedures regarding confidentiality, both with record keeping for purely administrative reasons (client files and insurance filings) and as required for research. Some general guidelines regarding confidentiality in record keeping are as follows:

1. The group leader shall refrain from revealing unnecessary identifying data of group members when seeking professional consultation. The leader should discuss the group or individuals within the group for professional purposes only.
2. All data collected from group participants for research purposes must be obtained only after group members have given their written permission.
3. The group leader must disguise all data that identify group members if they are used in publications and/or instruction (A–3).
4. The group leader should know how client records are handled, by whom, how long they are stored, where they are stored, who has access to the records, and what will happen to the records over time.

5. The group leader should know if clients have access to written records and what the procedure is for clients to obtain records.
6. Records should not be released to anyone without the informed consent of the client.
7. If computers are used for record storage or in any way in which group members are identified, precautions should be taken to ensure limited access to the data bank. The threats to confidentiality posed by the use of computers should be thoroughly understood by the group leader.
8. If third-party (insurance) reimbursement is being used, the leader should provide the minimum amount of information necessary. The leader should never send whole records to an insurance company and should inform group members of the extent of information being provided to insurance companies.

Before leaving the subject of confidentiality, there is, perhaps, need to make special note of an ethical dilemma that has only recently arisen. One of the growing needs in the area of group counseling is the provision of support groups for persons who have the AIDS virus. There are, as yet, no definitive legal precedents to guide the group leader insofar as confidentiality with this group is concerned. Thus, our ethical guidelines and standards are of critical importance to those who choose to provide such group services. Of course, since this issue is quite new, our ethical standards/ guidelines have not been adjusted to reflect a specific position on this matter. It is even more important, therefore, that the group leader have a firm grasp of the general intent of those guidelines he or she has adopted and be able to apply an understanding of the general ethical position on confidentiality to that of dealing with persons with the AIDS virus.

There have been a number of articles and editorial positions taken on the issue of confidentiality with AIDS patients. In editorials published in the *Journal of Sex and Marital Therapy* (Kaplan, Sager, and Schiavi, 1985, 1986), three professionals advocated very specific and strong procedures they felt necessary to prevent further spread of the AIDS virus. Gray and Harding (1988) reported that in a recent professional dialogue, published in *Sexuality Today* (1986), participants contended that therapists have an obligation to warn any known sexual partner of the client who has been tested positive for the AIDS virus. This warning should be made, they argued, regardless of the AIDS client's level of cooperation. This position obviously borrows from the ruling in the *Tarasoff* case concerning the duty to warn potential victims of the possibility of being harmed by the therapist's client.

Gray and Harding (1988) call for the use of a process of educating the AIDS client, consulting with the AIDS client's primary health care provider, and actively supporting the AIDS client's efforts to communicate difficult messages to his or her sexual partners. Failing this, should the

AIDS client continue having sexual relations with unsuspecting partners, Gray and Harding agree that the confidential relationship between the therapist and the client be breached.

Another issue related to group members who have been infected with the AIDS virus can be found in support groups and therapy groups for cancer patients and their families. The incidence of AIDS infection with patients receiving multiple blood transfusions is higher in the cancer patient population than with most other groups. Should a group leader who knows that a potential group member has been so infected with the AIDS virus breach the confidential relationship established with the potential member and inform the other group members of the situation?

Perhaps the informed consent statement should indicate the group leader's position on this matter and all potential group members be required to read and understand the informed consent statement *before* disclosing any medical information. The medical literature on the method of infection of the AIDS virus clearly points to only a few methods of transmission of the virus. A group setting would hardly seem to be one that would pose a threat of acquisition of the virus. Nevertheless, we must not ignore our duty to *all* group members. Perhaps using Gray and Harding's (1988) approach might help resolve this issue without the group leader having to force the disclosure.

TERMINATION AND FOLLOW-UP ⎯⎯⎯⎯⎯⎯⎯⎯⎯ ▬

Termination and follow-up become ethical issues more because of errors of *omission* rather than errors of *commission*. All too often group leaders neglect this phase of group work and termination of the group is abrupt and without much processing of termination issues. More often than not, this problem is observed when the group is of the short-term, weekend encounter variety where there is no follow-up period built into the process. This problem frequently arises when the group leader is from out-of-town and conducts a combination training–therapy workshop.

Since the leader is present only for the workshop, he or she is unfamiliar with the local professional resources and is not able to make a satisfactory referral for a group member when it is needed. And since the leader often does not plan a return trip for a follow-up session, the group participants are left on their own to secure follow-up assistance. Should a member or members feel neglected by this process, the group leader could be in for some rough legal rides. At the very least, a member could legitimately make a complaint to the ethics board or appropriate state agency concerning the professional's lack of proper care for the group members' welfare.

The ethical group leader always provides for a termination process whether that be a two- or three-session decompression and winding up process, as would be the case with long-term groups, or merely one or two hours of dealing with termination issues at the conclusion of a weekend workshop/group session. The group needs to have closure of its activities. Members of the group need to take care of unfinished business and the leader should ensure that their efforts are not frustrated because of a poorly planned termination process.

Young and Rosen (1985) have made several suggestions for the leader of short-term or weekend type group sessions. They believe it is helpful for the leader not only to try to clear up any misunderstandings, apprehensions, and confusions *before* the session ends, but also to provide the members with his or her telephone number so as to avert post-retreat crises. The member can then contact the group leader if, at a later time, he or she feels that some additional support or counseling is needed.

As to follow-up, the group leader should plan for short-term time-limited groups (B–10). The group leader should either make himself or herself available or be acquainted with and have a commitment from a qualified professional who agrees to accept referrals from the group whenever the group leader cannot continue his or her professional involvement with the group or any particular member of the group (B–10). The group members should be informed of competent referral sources to whom they will have access, provided such assistance is needed (B–10).

Lastly, the group leader should have a method for obtaining evidence of the effectiveness of his or her leadership of the group. A post-treatment questionnaire, to be answered anonymously by the group members at the conclusion of the group, together with some longer-range follow-up data in the form of a letter to each member, on group members' functioning relative to the expressed purposes of the group, should help illustrate the level of benefit each member has obtained from participation in the group. This type of information is difficult to obtain unless the leader has secured each member's knowledge and acceptance of its value during the screening process.

LEADERLESS GROUPS

Self-help or leaderless groups are proliferating despite concerns over insufficient research support. It would seem that, until greater supportive research evidence becomes available, therapy and quasi-therapy groups should arrange for consultation with professional leaders. The practice of establishing therapy groups that are directed by audiotaped instruction should not be permitted unless a professionally trained leader is monitoring the group's progress.

There have been some valid arguments put forward as to the rationale for self-help groups. Corey, Corey, and Callanan (1988) point out that "[t]he growth of self-help groups reflects the idea that people who have encountered and resolved certain difficulties possess unique resources for helping others like themselves (p. 76)." Groups such as Recovery Incorporated, Overeaters Anonymous, Synanon, and others have proliferated and generally prospered.

It is, as Corey et al. (1988) suggest, difficult for a group leader who has not shared the experiences of the group to work effectively with the group. However, that should not suggest that a group leader turn away from the opportunity to be of valuable assistance to such a group. The formation of a focused group, *facilitated* by a trained group leader, can be a very useful entity. The leader need not have shared the experiences of the group as long as he or she understands the dynamics of group processes and can help guide the group in achieving its fullest potential.

The leader can serve as a guide and resource person to the group and can become a respected and valued member of the group without having shared the experiences of the group. The leader must, at all times, bear in mind his or her role and not overstep the boundaries of common sense that limit his or her interaction with the other members of the group. In this way the leader can fulfill his or her ethical obligation to the group and, at the same time, not limit the group's effectiveness in any way.

GENERAL PROCEDURES FOR HANDLING UNETHICAL ACTIONS

There are generally accepted procedures established by most professional associations for policing their members. The various codes of ethics and professional standards also serve as legal criteria for courts who are engaged in civil and criminal trials of professionals accused of misconduct. It is very important, therefore, that professional group leaders become very familiar not only with the ethics and standards of their association (e.g., *Ethical Guidelines for Group Leaders*, 1980), but also they should be intimately aware of the general ethical guidelines of their profession (e.g., American Psychological Association's *Ethical Principles of Psychologists*, 1981).

Most ethical codes indicate the procedures to be followed when a person has evidence of unethical practice or behavior by a professional. The group leader should not fail to make such procedures available to each group member so that the member will have knowledge of recourse should he or she feel aggrieved by the group leader's handling of the group.

In the case of one professional determining that there is a need to complain about another professional's conduct, in general, one should first protect the clients affected by the unethical actions. Assuming that the client is in no immediate danger, the "accused" should be informed of his or her unethical actions and should be given the opportunity to correct the situation, if possible. If the "accused" refuses to correct the problem, the complaining professional is bound by his or her ethics to report (with proper regard to accuracy of details, fairness, and discretion) the incident to the appropriate professional association's ethical practices committee and/or to the "accused's" superior or institutional representative. A professional who ignores the unethical practice or behavior of other professionals is equally guilty of unethical conduct in the view of the associations within the helping professions.

Of course, if the complaining party is a non-professional group member or client of the "accused," he or she would take the same steps as outlined earlier unless he or she has not been made aware that such a process is available. Otherwise, the person will most likely seek legal advice from an attorney. It would seem in the professional's best interest, therefore, to make sure that his or her clients are aware of the ethical complaint process. Of course, the client can and sometimes does seek redress via both routes—the ethics committee and in court.

Ethical Guidelines for Group Leaders, published by the Association for Specialists in Group Work (ASGW) specifies actions to be taken when apparent violations of ethical guidelines have occurred. The guidelines provide for an investigation by the ASGW ethics committee and the possible recommendation for a hearing before the same committee. The hearing would be in accordance with the American Association for Counseling and Development's Policy and Procedures for Processing Complaints of Ethical Violations.

SUMMARY

This chapter attempts to review basic guidelines for the ethical practice of group workers, especially for those who lead counseling, therapy, and quasi-therapy groups. The guidelines are based on a careful review of the literature and on a questionnaire survey sent to appropriate professional associations and societies within the helping professions. Wherever a consensus was found concerning ethical practices, these were emphasized. It was also recognized that not every detail of ethical practice could be covered in this chapter. The reader is urged to make use of the references and suggested readings listed at the end of this chapter.

REFERENCES

American Medical Association's Council on Mental Health. (1971). Sensitivity training. *Journal of the American Medical Association, 217,* 1853–1854.

Association for Specialists in Group Work. (1980). *Ethical guidelines for group leaders.* Falls Church, VA: Author.

Association for Specialists in Group Work. (1983). *Professional standards for group counseling.* Falls Church, VA: Author.

Bradley Center, Inc. v. Wessner et al., 250 Ga. 199 (1982).

Corey, G., Corey, M. S., & Callanan, P. (1982). *A casebook of ethical guidelines for group leaders.* Monterey CA: Brooks/Cole.

Corey, G., Corey, M. S., & Callanan, P. (1988). *Issues and ethics in the helping professions* (3rd ed.). Pacific Grove, CA: Brooks/Cole.

Cross, W. (1970). Privileged communications between participants in group psychotherapy. *Law and Social Order, 2,* 191.

Denkowski, K. M., & Denkowski, J. C. (1982). Client-counselor confidentiality: An update of rationale, legal status and implications. *Personnel and Guidance Journal, 60,* 367–371.

Does Tarasoff obligate therapists to warn sexual partners of their clients who test positive for AIDS? (1986). *Sexuality Today, October 26,* 1.

Gazda, G. M., Bretcher, R., Kissiah, W., Kuckleburg, R., Lackey, H. Jr., Norris, J., Saylor, J., Seidenschur, P. P., & Steele, R. (1973). Recommended changes and additions to APGA Code of Ethics to accommodate group workers. *Counselor Education and Supervision, 13,* 155–158.

Gazda, G. M., Childers, W. C., & Brooks, D. K., Jr. (1987). *Foundations of counseling and human services.* New York: McGraw-Hill.

Gray, L. A., & Harding, A. K. (1988). Confidentiality limits with clients who have the AIDS virus. *Journal of Counseling and Development, 66,* 219–223.

Journal for Specialists in Group Work. (1982). Special issue: *Ethical issues in group work, 7*(3).

Kaplan, H. S., Sager, C. J., & Schiavi, R. C. (1985). Editorial: AIDS and the sex therapist. *Journal of Sex and Marital Therapy, 11*(4), 210–214.

Kaplan, H. S., Sager, C. J., & Schiavi, R. C. (1986). Editorial: Preventing the spread of AIDS. *Journal of Sex and Marital Therapy, 12*(3), 159–164.

Tarasoff v. *Regents of the University of California,* 529 P.2d 553 (1974).

Young, M. E., & Rosen, L. S. (1985). The retreat: An educational growth group. *Journal for Specialists in Group Work, 10*(3), 157–163.

SUGGESTED READINGS ⸺

American College Personnel Association. (1976). The use of group procedures in higher education: A position statement by ACPA. *Journal of College Student Personnel, 17,* 161–168.

American Group Psychotherapy Association. (1978). *Guidelines for the training of group psychotherapists.* New York: Author.

American Medical Association's Council on Mental Health. (1971). Sensitivity training. *Journal of the American Medical Association, 217,* 1853–1854.

American Personnel and Guidance Association. (1978). *Ethical standards: American Personnel and Guidance Association.* Washington, D.C.: Author.

American Personnel and Guidance Association Ethics Committee. (1982). *Selected bibliography: Ethics and legal issues.* Falls Church, VA: Author.

American Psychiatric Association (1970). *Task force report 1: Encounter groups and psychiatry.* Washington, D.C.: Author.

American Psychological Association. (1967). *Casebook on ethical standards of psychologists.* Washington, D.C.: Author.

American Psychological Association (1973). *Ethical principles in the conduct of research with human participants.* Washington. D.C.: Author.

American Psychological Association (1973). Guidelines for psychologists conducting growth groups. *American Psychologist, 28,* 933.

American Psychological Association (1981). Ethical principles of psychologists. *American Psychologist, 36*(16), 633–638.

American Psychological Association (1981). Specialty guidelines for the delivery of services by counseling psychologists. *American Psychologist, 36*(6), 652–663.

Association for Specialists in Group Work. (1980). *Ethical guidelines for group leaders.* Falls Church, VA: Author.

Berzon, B., & Solomon, L. (1966). The self-directed therapeutic group: Three studies. *Journal of Counseling Psychology, 13,* 491–497.

Biggs, D., & Blocher, D. (Eds.). (1987). *Foundations of ethical counseling.* New York: Springer.

Birnbaum. M. (1969, November 15) Sense about sensitivity training. *Saturday Review,* 82ff.

Callis, R. (Ed.) (1976). *APGA Ethical standards casebook* (2nd ed.). Washington, D.C.: American Personnel and Guidance Association Press.

Carkhuff, R., & Truax, C. (1965). Lay mental health counseling: The effects of lay group counseling. *Journal of Consulting Psychology, 29,* 426–432.

Corey, G., & Corey, M. S. (1987). *Groups: Process and practice* (3rd Ed). Monterey, CA: Brooks/Cole.

Corey, G., Corey, M., & Callanan, P. (1979). *Professional and ethical issues in counseling and psychotherapy.* Monterey, CA: Brooks/Cole.

Corey, G., Corey, M., & Callanan, P. (1982). *A casebook of ethical guidelines for group leaders.* Monterey, CA: Brooks/Cole.

Davis, K. (1980). Is confidentiality in group counseling realistic? *Personnel and Guidance Journal, 59,* 197–201.

Gazda, G. M. (1971). *Group procedures in education.* Washington, D.C.: American Personnel and Guidance Association Press.

Gazda, G. M., Bretcher, R., Kissiah, W., Kuckleburg, R., Lackey, H. Jr., Norris, J., Saylor, J., Seidenschur, P. P., & Steele, R. (1973). Recommended changes and additions to APGA Code of Ethics to accommodate group workers. *Counselor Education and Supervision, 13,* 155–158.

Gazda, G. M., Duncan, J. A., & Meadows. M. E. (1967) Group counseling and group procedures—Report of a survey. *Counselor Education and Supervision, 6,* 305–310.

Gazda, G. M., Duncan, J. A., & Sisson, P. J. (1971). Professional issues in group work. *Personnel and Guidance Journal, 49,* 637–643.

Gazda, G. M., & Mack, S. (1982). Ethical practice guidelines for group work practitioners. In G. M. Gazda (Ed.), *Basic approaches to group psychotherapy and group counseling* (3rd Ed.). Springfield, IL: Charles C. Thomas.

Glenn, C. (1980). Ethical issues in the practice of child psychotherapy. *Professional Psychology, 11*(4), 613–616.

Golann, S. E. (1969). Emerging areas of ethical concern. *American Psychologist, 24,* 454–459.

Gumaer, J., & Scott, L. (1985). Training group leaders in ethical decision making. *Journal for Specialists in Group Work, 10,* 198–204.

Hopkins, B. R., & Anderson, B. S. (1985). *The counselor and the law.* Alexandria, VA: AACD Press.

Jacobs, E. E., Harvill, R. L., & Masson, R. L. (1988). *Group counseling: Strategies and skills.* Pacific Grove, CA: Brooks/Cole.

Jenkins, D. (1962). Ethics and responsibility in human relations training. In I. Weschler and E. Schein (Eds.), *Issues in human relations training,* (pp. 108–113). Washington, D.C.: National Training Laboratories, National Education Association.

Kearney, M. (1984). Confidentiality in group psychotherapy. *Psychotherapy in Private Practice, 2*(2), 19–20.

Kelman, H. S. (1968). *A time to speak—On human values and social research.* San Francisco: Jossey-Bass.

Lakin, M. (1969). Some ethical issues in sensitivity training. *American Psychologist, 24,* 923–939.

Lakin, M. (1972). *Experiential groups: The uses of interpersonal encounter, psychotherapy groups, and sensitivity training.* Morristown, NJ: General Learning Press.

Lakin, M. (1986). Ethical challenges of group and dyadic psychotherapies: A comparative approach. *Professional Psychology: Research and Practice, 17*(5), 454–461.

Lakin, M. (1988). *Ethical issues in the psychotherapies.* New York: Oxford University Press.

McMillan, M. (1979). Conflicting loyalties: A literature review. *Personnel and Guidance Journal, 58,* 97–100.

Melton, G. (1981). Children's participation in treatment planning: Psychological and legal issues. *Professional Psychology, 12*(2), 246–252.

Meyer, R., & Smith, S. (1977). A crisis in group therapy. *American Psychologist, 32,* 638–643.

Moreno, J. L. (1957). Code of ethics of group psychotherapists. *Group Psychotherapy, 10,* 143–144.

Moreno, J. L. (1962). Code of ethics for group psychotherapy and psychodrama: Relationship to the Hippocratic Oath. *Psychodrama and Group Psychotherapy Monograph No. 31.* Beacon, NY: Beacon House.

Mullan, H. (1987). The ethical foundations of group psychotherapy. *International Journal of Group Psychotherapy, 37*(3), 403–416.

National Training Laboratory Institute. (1969). *Standards for the use of laboratory method.* Washington, D.C.

Olsen, L. C. (1971). Ethical standards for group leaders. *Personnel and Guidance Journal, 50,* 288.

Patterson, C. H. (1972). Ethical standards for groups. *Counseling Psychologist, 3,* 93–102.

Pope, K. S., Tabachnick, B. G., & Keith-Spiegel, P. (1987). Ethics of practice: The beliefs and behaviors of psychologists as therapists. *American Psychologist, 42*(11), 993–1006.

Sampson, J., & Pyle, K. R. (1983). Ethical issues involved with the use of computer-assisted counseling, testing, and guidance systems. *Personnel and Guidance Journal, 61*(5), 283–287.

Schutz, B. (1982). *Legal liability in psychotherapy.* San Francisco, CA: Jossey-Bass.

Schwitzgebel, R., & Schwitzgebel, R. (1980). *Law and psychological practice.* New York: Wiley.

Shostrom. E. L. (1969). Group therapy: Let the buyer beware. *Psychology Today, 2,* 37–40.

VanHoose, W., & Kottler, J. (1977). *Ethical and legal issues in counseling and psychotherapy.* San Francisco: Jossey-Bass

C H A P T E R 13

An Analysis of the Group Counseling Research Literature

The number of group counseling and therapy published articles has been decreasing since the mid-1970s. However, Dies (1979) found that the percentage of group *research* publications has been steadily increasing in the last twenty years from approximately 5 percent in the mid-1950s to close to 20 percent in the mid-1970s (Stockton & Morran, 1982). Although Dies included all types of group research, especially group psychotherapy, this chapter limits its review to group counseling research articles and those closely related to that subject.

The purpose of this review and analysis is to acquaint readers not only with the strengths and deficits of past and current research, but also, because of the variables focused on, to acquaint readers with the different types of groups (clientele being served), the length and duration of group sessions, the most popular instruments used to evaluate changes, goals, and outcome criteria, and general effectiveness of group counseling.

Over the years, group counseling and group psychotherapy have been defined in many ways. One of the most popular differentiations between the two terms is that *group psychotherapy* usually occurs in a hospital or similar institutional setting. On the other hand, *group counseling* usually occurs in an educational setting and generally involves clients with less acute symptoms or less disruptive behavior than those seen in group psychotherapy. More recently, popular use, based on reports in the literature, indicates that psychotherapy occurs in most settings, as does group counseling. (The implication is that the definitions seem to be based largely on the professional bias of the author.) For the purpose of this analysis, studies in the literature were included that expressly use the words *group counseling* in the title or explicitly refer to group counseling in the text. This analysis is meant to supplement earlier reviews of the literature by Gazda and Larsen (1968), Gazda (1971), and Gazda and Peters (1973, 1975). The analysis includes 641 group counseling research studies from 1938 through June 1987. Although the review is not exhaustive, it is intended to be comprehensive, not just representative. Studies analyzed include dissertations and published investigations in various professional journals; however, for the 1976 through 1987 period, in addition to dissertations, only the following journals were reviewed: *Journal for Specialists in Group Work, Journal of Counseling Psychology, International Journal of Group Psychotherapy, Small Group Behavior,* and *Journal of Group Psychotherapy, Psychodrama and Sociometry.*

VARIABLES USED

The analysis of the 641 counseling studies that follows is based on the following variables: type of controls, treatment period, instruments used, test statistics employed, experimental designs used, type of study (outcome or process), type of group (nature of participants involved), group size (*N* of the study), and criteria and outcomes or nature of the results obtained. The second half of this chapter includes a comparison of these variables for the 641 studies with earlier analyses of the same variables for the time periods 1938–1970, 1970–1973, 1973–1976, 1976–1982, and 1983–1987. Trends for these periods on the variables are also indicated. The chapter closes with a list of recommendations for future group counseling research.

Nature of the Study

An analysis of the combined 641 articles and studies reviewed since 1938 indicates that about 69 percent are classifiable as outcome, 6 percent as comparison or descriptive (also a type of outcome), and 20 percent as process studies. Because of a lack of classifiable characteristics or a combination of factors such as outcome and process variables, 5 percent were classified as miscellaneous studies. A trend among studies within the past few years is toward an increase in the number of *outcome* studies. Process and outcome studies increased only slightly, and the number of comparison and descriptive studies decreased.

Type of Group

More than 90 percent of the studies reviewed used students in an educational setting as group participants. The remaining 10 percent of the studies involved, for example, groups composed of adults, ethnic groups, inmates, mental retardates, and mental patients. However, during the 1983–1987 time period, less than 70 percent of the studies reviewed used students in an educational setting. The studies during the past few years indicate the growing use of more of a diversity of participants who were actively involved in ongoing group psychotherapy than in the past (for example, female alcoholics, black female college students, female graduate students, pregnant teenagers, mental retardates, first offenders, incest victims, military personnel, battered women, and many other individuals).

Inasmuch as type of group also can be analyzed on the basis of type of intervention strategy employed and insofar as there is a definite trend toward the use of structured group strategies versus the more traditional unstructured or interview models, 61 studies between 1976 and 1982 were analyzed according to structured versus unstructured interventions employed. Table 13–1 shows these findings and suggests that there is a definite trend in favor of effectiveness of structured (usually some sort of skills training) strategies/models over unstructured intervention strategies/models.

Table 13–1 Comparison of structured versus unstructured intervention strategies for counseling groups based on predicted positive changes ($N = 61$)

Age Level	Structured	Unstructured	Comparison Strategies
Elementary school	4S*	1PS*, 3NS*	0
Junior high school	1S, 2PS, 2NS	3PS, 4NS	0
Senior high school	3S, 3PS, 1NS	1S, 4PS, 11NS	1
College	2S, 2PS, 1NS	1S, 1PS, 7NS	2
Adult		1NS	0
TOTAL	10S, 7PS, 4NS	2S, 9PS, 26NS	3

*Note: S = significant, PS = partial significance (some positive predicted changes), NS = nonsignificance, comparison studies compared one type of intervention vs another type, but not structured versus unstructured.

Group Size

It is important to realize that the group size figure refers to the total N reported in each study. It does not indicate the actual size of the counseling or experimental group. For example, a study could report an N of 40. However, only 20 of the 40 may actually be in the counseling (experimental) group. The other 20 may constitute a control group that receives no treatment. In the literature, group size ranges from a process study with an N of 3 to an outcome study with 266 experimentals. The average group size for the 1938–1976 period was 50. The average size for the 1983–1987 period was 56. The average 1976–1982 was 62. The decrease may be due in part to the increasing number of studies in recent years that have used no contact control group as well as placebo groups.

Controls

Some form of control group was used in 80 percent of the studies prior to 1970. From 1970 through 1976, some form of control group was used in over 95 percent of the studies and from 1976 through 1982, 91 percent used some form of control group. During the 1976 to 1980 period, more rigorous studies used both a no contact control group and a placebo group, although these well-designed studies were in the minority. From 1983 to 1987, some form of control group was used in 70 percent of the studies. This decrease may be due in part to research utilizing a variety of experimental designs that do not necessitate a defined control group.

Treatment Period Duration

The typical treatment was calculated by averaging the number and the duration of the experimental sessions for all studies that used treatment groups. The average treatment was approximately 15 hours over a duration of 9 weeks for the period 1938–1976. From 1976 through 1982, the average treatment was 19 hours over 10 weeks. From 1983 through 1987, the average treatment was 20 hours over a 10 week period. It is important to realize that these figures are greatly affected by researchers who employed a behavior modification or a marathon format. Behavior modification studies tend to involve a minimum number of treatment sessions spaced over a few days. Researchers who employed a marathon format tended to schedule a large number of treatment hours over a few days (for example, 25 hours of treatment over one weekend). In recent years, the number of studies utilizing a marathon format has decreased (less than 2 percent). This decrease does not suggest that therapists are not conducting marathon groups, but that few studies are published or are suitable for publication.

Instruments

This category refers to measures used to evaluate process and outcome variables. The majority of the studies reviewed incorporated more than one instrument. To minimize distortion, frequency rather than percentage of use will be discussed.

The relative ranking of the instruments was fairly stable over the 1938–1976 period. Grade-point average was used about 52 times, but its use decreased considerably during the 1970–1982 period and continued to decrease during the 1983–1987 period. Self-reporting techniques other than those included in standardized tests were used 59 times. Their use has declined significantly in recent years. On the other hand, researcher-devised questionnaires and scales were used 236 times. The 1970–1982 period revealed a significant increase in the use of researcher-devised questionnaire scales that continued to increase through the 1983–1987 period. Achievement and ability tests were used 43 times throughout the 1938–1982 period. However, a review of recent studies (1983–1987) indicates that the use of achievement and ability tests decreased, as did the number of studies using students in educational settings as group participants. Interviews as evaluative instruments declined in use, especially since 1970.

Instruments reported used between 15 and 20 times include the Tennessee Self-Concept Tests, the Semantic Differential, and Personal Orientation Inventory, the FIRO-B, and Rotter's I-E Scale. Instruments used at least 5 times include the Hill Interaction-Primary Rating Scale and Beck Depression Scale.

Most process studies reported the use of some form of interaction analysis based on researcher-designed instruments. Other popular instruments were the Hill Interaction Matrix, the Bales Interaction Process Analysis, leadership scales, peer ratings, role playing, nonverbal classifications, and other similar instruments.

Test Statistics

As was the trend with instruments, the use of multiple statistics is more prevalent than the use of a single statistic, especially in more recent years. Again, rather than report the results in percentages, which could be distorting, the frequency of use will be presented. For the overall 1938–1987 period, over 20 different test statistics were employed in varying degrees. The analysis of variance, in one form or another, was used 265 times. The t-test was used 210 times. These figures suggest a significant increase in use of the analysis of variance and a significant decrease in the use of the t-test in the eleven-year period from 1976 to 1987. Correlation coefficients in one form or another were used 98 times. Some form of descriptive statistics was used over 75 times. Chi-square, used 71 times, shows a decrease during the same eleven-year period. Analysis of covariance was used 90 times. This suggests a significant increase in use during the 1976–1987 period. Factor analysis was used about 21 times. Each time, this statistical procedure was used in conjunction with other statistics. The most salient trend in recent years is toward multiple statistical analysis of data.

Experimental Designs

The classification system for the experimental designs of the studies reviewed in the 1938–1987 period is described by Campbell and Stanley

(1963). The various experimental designs are classified under three major headings: preexperimental designs, true experimental designs, quasi-experimental designs, and a fourth or "other" design, including process (see Tables 13–2 and 13–3).

Over the entire 1938–1987 period, approximately 73 percent of the outcome studies were classified as true experimental designs, which means that some form of control group was used. About 58 percent of the total studies reviewed were classified in the category of true experimental designs. Process and unclassifiable studies made up the bulk of the "other" designs category, representing 20 percent. A notable trend within recent years is the high percentage of investigations using a true experimental design. Well over 93 percent of the authors of recent dissertations that were reviewed employed a control group. Both a no contact control group and a placebo group were employed in some of the dissertations and in a few of the reported studies.

Comparing data from the earlier review of the research literature (Gazda & Peters, 1975) indicates that process studies increased significantly

Table 13–2 1983–1987 Experimental Design

True Experimental Designs	Preexperimental Designs	Quasi-Experimental Designs	Other Designs
Pretest–posttest control group	One-shot case study	Equivalent material	Descriptive one group pretest–posttest
$N = 71$	$N = 3$	$N = 0$	$N = 3$
Solomon four-group	One group pretest–posttest	Nonequivalent control group	Descriptive simple survey
$N = 3$	$N = 20$	$N = 1$	$N = 15$
Pretest only control group	Static group comparison	Separate sample pretest–posttest	Process
$N = 1$	$N = 0$	$N = 23$	$N = 6$
			Unclassifiable
			$N = 33$
Factoral		Recurrent cycle	Qualitative
$N = 17$		$N = 1$	$N = 3$

Note: Total $N = 198$

Table 13–3 1983–1987 Combined Data

True Experimental Designs	Preexperimental Designs	Quasi-Experimental Designs	Other Designs
Pretest–postest control group	One-shot case study	Equivalent material design	Descriptive one group pretest–posttest
$N = 320$	$N = 8$	$N = 8$	$N = 9$
Solomon four-group	One group pretest–posttest	Nonequivalent control group	Descriptive simple survey
$N = 6$	$N = 37$	$N = 12$	$N = 27$
Pretest only control group	Static group comparison	Separate sample pretest–posttest	Process
$N = 29$	$N = 4$	$N = 26$	$N = 26$
			Unclassifiable
			$N = 63$
Factoral		Recurrent cycle	Qualitative
$N = 17$		$N = 1$	$N = 3$

Note: Total $N = 641$

in frequency from 36 between 1938 and 1973 to 65 from 1938 to 1982, an increase of 21 from 1973 to 1982. The majority of process studies were initiated within the 1970–1982 period. However, the number of process studies decreased within the last six years to approximately 39 studies.

Criteria and Outcomes

About 50 percent of the studies reviewed and analyzed in the 1938–1970 period showed significant gains (Gazda, 1971). A closer look at some of these studies revealed that often only one of several variables was significant in studies employing multiple measures. Frequently the variable found to be statistically significant was more transient as to permanence of behavior than were some of the other variables. In the 1970–1976 period, more than 88 percent of the studies reviewed indicated significant change in the predicted direction.

During the periods 1976–1982, the percentage of studies reviewed that showed significant change in the predicted direction dropped significantly from 88 to 70 percent. This decrease continued through the 1983–1987 period. This significant decrease cannot be fully explained, although it may represent a change in attitude of journal editors of accepting more research studies that do not show significant change. This percentage, however, would be higher if it were not for the number of dissertation abstracts included in the review where there were no significant results obtained. On the other hand, the combined effect of multiple hypotheses and more sophisticated analyses may increase the likelihood of detecting less apparent, yet still statistically significant, differences.

SUMMARY ANALYSIS
OF GROUP COUNSELING RESEARCH

The next part of this analysis is a comparative summary of the group counseling literature.

Nature of the Study: Purpose

Of the studies and dissertations reviewed during the 1970–1976 period, about 84 percent were investigations of outcome variables, 9 percent were concerned with both process and outcome, and 7 percent were directly concerned with process variables. During the 1983–1987 period, about 69 percent were outcome studies, 20 percent process, and 35 percent were in the process and outcome areas.

In the 1970–1976 period, many outcome studies showed an increased use of more behaviorally diversified variables. Some of the more unique outcome variables include problem-solving competency, self-disclosure, personal and social skills, weight reduction, vocational development, feminine values, fear of death, increase in healthier behavior, religious attitudes, satisfying sexual activity, and more assertive behavior. Recent outcome studies have included such variables as interpersonal attraction, trusting behavior, self-disclosure and self-help skills.

Type of Group

Undergraduates participated as counselees in the greatest number of studies. However, the use of undergraduates as counselees appeared to slightly decrease over the past 6 years. Adolescents ranked third in terms of frequency of involvement as counselees. Adults ranked second, followed by elementary and secondary school students and graduate students. In recent years, there has been a trend to use a more diversified clientele. Group counseling participants in recent studies have included brain-damaged mental patients, imprisoned former drug users, imprisoned felons, learning disabled children, pregnant teenagers, parents, geriatric patients, divorcees, nurses, black female college students, incest victims, delinquent boys, theology students, music students, and children of divorce as well as the more typical clients. This may mean that some investigators are bringing group counseling procedures to populations having unique characteristics in an attempt to investigate the efficacy of group counseling in coping with the problems unique to these populations.

In spite of the emphasis on more diversified clientele, an important variable neglected in most studies was group composition. The majority of the investigators appeared to select the participants with little or no discussion of the implications of group composition. In many studies, the group composition was not ascertainable. There is evidence that group composition has a significant effect on the outcome (Gazda, 1971; Peters, 1972; Yalom, 1985). An encouraging development in recent years is the increasing use of instruments to aid in selecting group participants.

After reviewing the research on group composition, cohesion, and attraction, Stockton and Morran (1982) concluded:

> We have learned that attraction to the group can be enhanced by the manipulation of pregroup training, composition, and leader reinforcement and by a variety of interventions such as feedback and self-disclosure. At the present time, researchers have learned some interesting, although preliminary, information. We believe that future attention to cohesion and attraction to the group offer the interested researcher a number of useful areas for investigation into ways to enhance outcomes in small groups. (p. 58)

Group Size

The overall average treatment sample size of the 1938–1976 period was 36. Prior to 1970, the average treatment sample size was 29. In the 1970–1973 period, the average treatment size increased to 47. However, for the 1973–1976 period, it decreased to 35, and for the period 1976–1982, it again increased to an average of 62. The 1983–1987 time period saw a slight decrease in sample size to 56.

Despite this fluctuation in average sample treatment size over the years, the research designs of recent investigations tend to be more methodologically sophisticated and rigorous. This increase in rigor is evidenced by an increase also in the use of more sophisticated instruments and statistics. (See Campbell and Stanley, 1963, for a discussion on research designs.)

Controls

In the 1938–1970 period, approximately 80 percent of the researchers included some form of controls in their studies. From 1970 to 1976, controls were used in one form or another in more than 95 percent of the investigations, 91 percent of the studies used controls for 1976–1982, and 76 percent of the investigations in 1983–1987 used controls. There has been an increasing number of studies that employed both a no contact control group and a placebo control group when contact groups are employed. The two control groups differed in terms of attention received by the participants. Usually the no contact control group received no attention. It is strongly recommended that both types of control groups be employed when feasible.

Only a few investigators used some form of follow-up assessment. Unfortunately, this procedure is most neglected in dissertation investigations. Perhaps the lack of follow-up procedures as an intrinsic part of an investigation indicates the tacit assumption that if change is going to occur, it will occur over a short period of time. A more reasonable assumption is that periodic follow-up assessments can be quite tedious for the investigator. Nevertheless, follow-up assessment would be a valuable source of data concerning permanence of change.

Treatment and Process

For the period of 1938–1976, the average length of time of the experimental treatment was 15 hours extended over an average period of eight-and-one-half weeks. Although the average increased to 10 weeks for a total of 19 hours during the 1976–1982 period, and 20 hours in 1983–1987, this time period is probably too short to expect significant behavioral changes with any kind of permanence. It is important to realize that these figures are affected by marathon and behavior modification studies that tend to mass considerable treatment hours over a short period of time or employ only a few treatment sessions. Probably just by increasing the average duration of the experimental treatment, increasing the average per-session time of treatment, and using some systematic follow-up procedure, many studies would have shown increased significant behavior changes.

Instruments

Instruments included standardized psychological tests such as the MMPI and Beck Depression Scale, a large variety of self-report instruments, including standardized and nonstandardized; researcher-devised-questionnaires, scales, and inventories; achievement and intelligence tests; grade point averages; and observer ratings, check-lists and behavioral observations. Although over 140 different instruments/evaluation procedures were used during the 1976–1987 period, only 30 were used two or more times and only 9 were used five or more times. Essentially this means that the majority of instruments and evaluative devices are designed specifically for a given study and therefore usually have little data on validity and reliability.

A notable trend in recent years is the increased use of multiple measures. Perhaps some investigators are beginning to think of behavior in terms of clusters of individual behaviors that interface with each other. Another noticeable trend is that many investigators are developing their own questionnaires, and administering them as preposttests. The inherent weakness in this approach is the lack of validity of the instrument.

Statistics

Consistent with earlier trends (Gazda & Peters, 1975), there remains a strong trend toward using multiple statistics. It is now the rule rather than the exception to use at least two complementary statistics to analyze the data. For the 1976–1982 period, 42 percent of the studies used more than one test statistic. During this 1983–1987 time period, over 70 percent of the studies used multiple statistics. At the same time, many researchers are increasing the number of hypotheses used. Consequently, there may be a link between multiple statistics, multiple hypotheses, and the increased number of statistically significant results.

Experimental Design

Overall, about 73 percent of the outcome studies for the period 1938–1987 were classified as true experimental designs according to the criteria of Campbell and Stanley (1963). This means that some form of control group, as well as quantification methods, were used. Process studies account for approximately 10 percent of all the studies analyzed. A recent trend in the past four years is an increased use of quasi-experimental design and descriptive survey.

Criteria and Outcome

A significant majority of published studies in recent years have reported at least one statistically significant result consistent with predictions. For the periods 1976–1982, and 1983–1987, 70 percent reported significance in the predicted direction. This source rate may be artificially high because of several factors (for example, journal editors are quite reluctant to publish studies that do not achieve some level of statistically significant results). Although there is an overall increase in rigor and sophistication of research methodology, most of the investigations reviewed did not explicitly state the theory or model on which the investigation was based.

Replications of prior investigations have not generally increased within the past few years, perhaps because replications are not considered as respectable as primary investigations. It is important to realize that an essential step in the identification of causative variables in group counseling is the replication of studies (that is, applying the same treatment levels to different treatment groups).

On the basis of the studies reviewed, group counseling research is making considerable progress toward identifying major causative variables. Research methodology shows a dramatic increase in overall sophistication and rigor. Control and/or placebo groups are generally being used, and observable behaviors are being used as dependent variables. However, there are still considerable gaps in group counseling knowledge and weakness in the methodology that can be overcome.

RECOMMENDATIONS

The following recommendations are based on the deficiencies that exist in the reviewed group counseling research literature.

1. There is a need to state explicitly the model or theory on which the investigation is built and to describe the group experience. The ultimate goal is to predict general principles of behavior and not just to locate bits and pieces of correlated activity.
2. Characteristics of group participants should be described in order to allow comparison of the effects of different treatment interventions and to make possible generalization and/or detailed replication to occur (Stockton & Morran, 1982).
3. The appropriate unit of analysis for parametric statistical purposes is the group itself rather than individual members within the group because it better meets the assumptions of random and independent distribution of the variance associated with the error terms. Alternative methodological approaches such as nonparametric procedures, complex correlational techniques, and naturalistic or qualitative studies offer promise for this field (Stockton & Morran, 1982).
4. Length of experimental treatment should be increased when possible, and some form of systematic follow-up of the participants should be used to allow for assessing permanence of change.
5. Replication of studies should be encouraged to permit greater validation of results.
6. More diversified treatment groups should be used to increase generalizability of the process.
7. Important process variables, such as group composition and level of leader skills, have been largely neglected. Attempts should be made to investigate these areas.

8. "Variables chosen for assessment purposes should be clearly related to the stated goals of the group. Probably the approach with the most potential is one in which dependent variables are selected from the cognitive, emotional, and behavioral perspectives. The exclusion of any of these may obscure significant treatment effects and unnecessarily limit research findings" (Stockton & Morran, 1982, p. 75). "Choices for appropriate assessment of group process and outcome variables require the utilization of multiple measures that are based on meaningful conceptual formulations. . . . It is important to administer process instruments with which one can analyze the group interaction" (Stockton & Morran, 1982, p. 75).

9. Greater emphasis on nonreactive measures, such as videotape equipment, should be used as an adjunct to evaluation.

10. When possible, both a control group *and* a placebo should be used to heighten the degree of validity of the research. Commenting on this issue, Stockton and Morran (1982) stated, "Perhaps the most notable shortcoming in this area has been the failure to provide a viable treatment that elicits the same degree of expectancy and commitment as the experimental treatment" (p. 74).

11. More frequent application of the time series design (Campbell & Stanley, 1963) that allows the counselee to be his or her own control and avoids matching errors (sometimes at the risk of lowered evaluation instrument reliabilities), should be implemented.

12. Jacobs (1975) contends that the complexity of the variables involved in group counseling research necessitates programmatic research (sequence studies). Furthermore, these complex variables also necessitate, according to Jacobs (1975), two types of replication: use of at least two groups per experimental condition and repetition of parts of earlier studies in later studies with somewhat different procedures and objectives to try to determine whether the results are durable over different exercises or procedures.

13. Hill (1975) contends that an underlying problem of current group research is the difficulty of comparing findings because of the absence of a widely accepted format for conducting and reporting group research. Hill proposes that all group research studies should specify the conditions obtaining within the group studied in regard to specific variables that are expressed in a standardized fashion and with standardized measurement. The variables or group conditions proposed by Hill are as follows: group size, time (length of sessions), expectation of duration of therapy, group composition (for example, diagnostically homogeneous, sociologically homogeneous, interaction styles homogeneous or heteroge-

neous—advantages and disadvantages of each), therapist attributes (personal interaction style, professional experience, and theoretical orientation), population involved, group roles (three roles—patient, therapist, spectator—are engaged in by members and leaders, interrelationships and time spent in each role are significant variables), and feedback (effect of feedback modalities and content).

14. The application of multidimensional scaling to groups holds considerable promise for selecting members and evaluating group progress and outcome (Gazda, Evans, & Kaltenbach, 1975).

SUMMARY

This chapter contained a report and analysis of 641 group counseling studies reported since 1938. Each study was analyzed on the following variables: type of controls, treatment period (length and duration), type of group, instruments used for assessment of change, test statistics employed, type of study, experimental designs employed, size of the research sample, and nature of the results obtained. Since the same variables had been used in analyzing group counseling research for the periods 1938–1970, 1970–1973, 1973–1976, 1976–1982, and 1983–1987, trends for each of the variables were noted for these time periods.

The chapter closed with a list of recommendations derived from an analysis of the 641 studies. The list represents suggestions for improving group counseling research based on my review and recommendations from Jacobs, Hill, and Stockton and Morran who have also given serious consideration to this issue.

REFERENCES

Campbell, D., & Stanley, J. (1963). Experimental and quasi-experimental designs for research. In N. L. Gage (Ed.), *Handbook of research in teaching.* Chicago: Rand McNally.

Dies, R. R. (1979). Group psychotherapy reflections of 3 decades of research. *Journal of Applied Behavioral Science, 15*, 361–374.

Gazda, G. M. (1971). *Group counseling: A developmental approach.* Boston: Allyn and Bacon.

Gazda, G. M., Evans, L. P., & Kaltenbach, R. F. (1975, April). *Instrumentation in group research.* Paper presented at the University of Indiana Invitational Conference on Experimental Small Group Research: Perspectives on Current Issues and Future Directions, Bloomington.

Gazda, G. M., & Larsen, M. J. (1968). A comprehensive appraisal of group and multiple counseling research. *Journal of Research and Development in Education, 1*, 57–132.

Gazda, G. M., & Peters, R. (1973). An analysis of research in group procedures. *Educational Technology, 13*, 68–75.

Gazda, G. M., & Peters, R. (1975). An analysis of research in group psychotherapy, group counseling and human relations training. In G. M. Gazda (Ed.), *Basic approaches to group psychotherapy and group counseling*. Springfield, IL: Charles C. Thomas.

Hill, W. F. (1975, April). *A master plan for group therapy research.* Paper presented at the University of Indiana Invitational Conference on Experimental Small Group Research: Perspectives on Current Issues and Future Directions, Bloomington.

Jacobs, A. L. (1975, April). *Research on methods of social intervention: The study of the exchange of personal information in brief personal growth groups.* Paper presented at the University of Indiana Invitational Conference on Experimental Small Group Research: Perspectives on Current Issues and Future Directions, Bloomington.

Peters, R. (1972). The facilitation of change in group counseling by group composition. Ph.D. dissertation, University of Georgia.

Stockton, R., & Morran, D. K. (1982). Review and perspective of critical dimensions in therapeutic small group research. In G. M. Gazda (Ed.), *Basic approaches to group psychotherapy and group counseling*. (3rd ed.). Springfield, IL: Charles C. Thomas.

Yalom, I. (1985). *The theory and practice of group psychotherapy.* (3rd ed.). New York: Basic Books.

SUGGESTED READINGS ⸻

Bednar, R. L., & Kaul, T. J. (1969). Experiential group research: Current perspectives. In S. L. Garfield and A. E. Bergin (Eds.), *Handbook of psychotherapy and behavior change: An empirical analysis*. New York: Wiley.

Bednar, R. L., & Lawlis, F. (1971). Empirical research in group psychotherapy. In A. E. Bergin, and S. L. Garfield (Eds.), *Handbook of psychotherapy and behavior change*. New York: Wiley.

Campbell, D., & Stanley, J. (1963). Experimental and quasi-experimental designs for research. In N. L. Gage (Ed.), *Handbook of research in teaching*. Chicago: Rand McNally.

Cartwright, D., & Zander, A. (Eds.) (1968). *Group dynamics: Research and theory*. (3rd ed.). New York: Harper and Row.

Dies, R. R. (1979). Group psychotherapy reflections on 3 decades of research. *Journal of Applied Behavioral Science, 15*, 361–374.

Erickson, F. & Schultz, J. (1982). *The counselor as gatekeeper: Social interaction in interviews*. New York: Academic Press.

Garfield, S. L., & Bergin, A. E. (1978). *Handbook of psychotherapy and behavior change*. (2nd ed.). New York: Wiley.

Glass, G. V. (1976). Primary, secondary and meta-analysis of research. *Educational Researcher, 5*, 3–8.

Goetz, J., & LeCompte, M. (1984). *Ethnography and qualitative design in educational research*. New York: Academic Press.

Goldstein, A. P., Heller, K., & Sechrest, L. B. (1966). *Psychotherapy and the psychology of behavior*. New York: Wiley.

Henry, S. E., & Kilman, P. R. (1979). Student counseling groups in senior high school settings: An evaluation of outcome. *Journal of School Psychology, 17*(1), 27–46.

Luborsky, L., Auerback, A. H., Chandler, M., & Cohen, J. (1971). Factors influencing the outcome of psychotherapy: Review of quantitative research. *Psychological Bulletin, 6,* 371–388.

Moos, R. (1974). *Evaluating treatment environments.* New York: Wiley.

Moscovici, S., Mugny, G., & Van Auermaet, E., (Eds.) (1985). *Perspectives on minority influence.* Cambridge: Cambridge University Press.

Russell, E. W. (1978). The facts about encounter groups: First facts. *Journal of Clinical Psychology, 34,* 130–137.

Stockton, R., & Morran, D. K. (1982). Review and perspective of critical dimensions in therapeutic small group research. In G. M. Gazda (Ed.), *Basic approaches to group psychotherapy and group counseling.* (3rd ed.). Springfield, IL: Charles C. Thomas.

Van Houten, R., et al. (1982). An analysis of some variables influencing the effectiveness of reprimands. *Journal of Applied Behavior Analysis, 15*(1), 65–83.

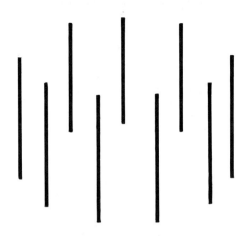

PART FOUR

Part Four represents a departure from the Developmental Group Counseling model. It consists of seven chapters selected to represent the major theoretical positions of group counseling and therapy, in addition to the developmental model upon which this text is based. These chapters have been carefully selected to be representative of the major theories applied to group counseling and therapy, but they are not intended to be exhaustive. They can be grouped according to the following classifications:

Analytic/ Dynamic	Existential/ Experimental	Behavioral/ Cognitive-Behavorial
Group Analysis (Group Analytic Psychotherapy) (M. Pines, L. E. Hearst, & H. L. Behr—*à la* S. H. Foulkes)	Person-Centered Group Therapy (J. Woods, *à la* C. Rogers)	Multimodal Group Therapy (A. Lazarus)
Adlerian/Teleolanalytic Group Counseling (M. Songstegard, R. Dreikurs, & J. Bitter — *à la* A. Adler)	Existential: Logotherapy (D. A. Williams & J. Fabry —*à la* V. Frankl)	Cognitive-Behavorial (C. Sedgwick—*à la* D. Meichenbaum)
	Gestalt Therapy in Groups J. S. Simkin—*à la* E. Berne)	

C H A P T E R   14

Group Analysis[1]
(Group Analytic Psychotherapy)

INTRODUCTION ━━━━━━━━━━━━━━━━━━━━━━ ▬

Group analytic psychotherapy is the term applied by S. H. Foulkes to the form of psychotherapy he developed from 1938 onwards. As a psychoanalyst trained in a classical tradition, Foulkes brought to his work a knowledge of an adherence to many of the basic principles of psychoanalysis, combined with a deep appreciation of the social nature of humans and the profound importance of socialization processes in the development of the personality. The combination of these two viewpoints led him to the logical application of these principles to small group psychotherapy in a formal setting. Many of his fundamental ideas were derived from and confirmed by the experience of working as an army psychiatrist at Northfield, a psychiatric military hospital, during World War II, where he laid down many of the fundamental principles of the therapeutic community (Bridges, 1946; Main, 1946). This experience of larger groups as well as the small formal psychotherapeutic group laid the foundations for the application of group analytic principles and methods to settings other than the small group. Group analytic principles therefore have been influential in the development of large group psychotherapy and of the therapeutic community and family therapy.

The work of S. H. Foulkes is described in four volumes of his own writings (Foulkes, 1948, 1964, 1965, 1975 a & b) and in those of his colleagues

---

1.   Abstracted from Pines, M., Hearst, L.E., & Behr, H.L. (1982). Group analysis (Group analytic psychotherapy). In G.M. Gazda (Ed.), *Basic approaches to group psychotherapy and group counseling* (pp. 132–178). Springfield, IL: Charles C. Thomas.

(Abse, 1974; de Mare, 1972, 1977; Kadis, Krasner, Weiner, Winick, & Foulkes, 1974; Pines, 1978a, 1978b, 1981a, 1981b; Skynner, 1969). The journal *Group Analysis* founded by S. H. Foulkes in 1967 acts as an international forum for those sympathetic to group analytic psychotherapy based on this model.

THEORETICAL FOUNDATIONS

The theory of group analysis rests on the premise that the essence of human beings is social, not individual. The individual organism is the basic biological unit; the basic psychological unit is the group (Hooper, 1980; Napolitani, 1980). The individual is an artificial, though plausible, abstraction; each person is basically and centrally determined by the world in which he or she lives, by the group, by the community of which he or she forms a part. Inside and outside, individual and society, body and mind, fantasy and reality, cannot be opposed: All separation is artificial isolation. The individual is a part of a social network, "a little nodal point as it were," and can only artificially be considered in isolation, like a fish out of water.

It follows from this that the neurotic position is in its very nature highly individualistic. It is group-destructive in essence, for it is genetically a result of an incompatibility between the individual and his or her original group. Because of this incompatibility, instead of being a nodal point in his or her network, he or she becomes a focal point of disturbed interpersonal processes.

The neurotic symptom is a disturbed expression of the patient's conflicts, never experienced in articulate language and therefore inaccessible to memory or to expression. Via a symptom, the patient communicates fundamental and unconscious conflicts.

The proper study of the individual is within his or her natural group, particularly the family. If the psychiatrist were to go out into the patient's life, he or she would find that the patient's problems represent only one aspect of an intricate group problem and he or she would also see different aspects of the patient to those seen in the consulting room. The psychiatrist would discover the *location* of the disturbance in some aspect of the patient's life situation and interpersonal relationships. Psychological disturbances are *located*, that is, take place between persons, and can never be wholly confined to a person in isolation.

In the group analytic situation, disturbances can be located and traced in their effects on the dynamic processes of the group. For instance, if a patient overcomes silence for the first time when the therapist is absent, the speech inhibition is partly located in the therapist. However, if the patient can speak when alone with the therapist, the problem is that he or she cannot share the therapist with others.

The therapeutic process itself is identical with working towards an ever more articulate form of communication. This is achieved by (a) the group process—the patient's active participation in a mutual process, that of making himself or herself understood and of understanding the attempted communication of others, and (b) the therapist seeing "meaning in action" in the dynamic events of the group and taking them as his or her frame of reference. The medium through which he or she works is communication with words, and the ultimate aim is expression in articulate verbal language that can be understood and shared by all.

The main aims of therapy are insight and adjustment. ("Adjustment should be seen as the equivalent of 'adaptation' in the psychoanalytic sense"; Hartmann, 1958.) "There is a relationship between the two: Insight promotes adjustment, adjustment facilitates insight, insight without adjustment does not go very far, adjustment without insight is incomplete but it can work. Adjustment seems to be the more fundamental from a therapeutic, insight from a scientific point of view." (Foulkes, 1964, p.87). By adjustment, Foulkes means the process of inner psychological change, the restructuring of the inner world, derived from and reflected in character and interpersonal relationship. He does not mean compliance with the therapist's authority, and his or her norms, or merely "fitting in" with the group's current attitudes. He warned therapists against undervaluing the enormous power of their authority, that the group unconsciously strives to supply what they want. The therapist, as in other analytic situations, has to recognize and to work through the unconscious compliance of the patients (Foulkes, 1971).

The therapist's first aim is to facilitate participation on the part of the group's members. He or she recognizes and accepts their dependency needs but does not collude with them. The therapist's aim is to "wean" them, that is to work through these needs. Interpretations should come from the group itself; the group is the instrument to be used whenever possible. The therapist's activity must be discriminating, encouraging the liberation of the group from passivity and dependency. If patients are brought into a situation they are continually helping to create and to shape they become more aware of their own reactions and their contradictions. They meet themselves in the situation they have helped to create and for which they now have to accept some responsibility. The less structured the therapeutic situation, the more the patients must extend themselves and become engaged in order to cope with it.

The Group Analytic Situation

The group analytic situation can usefully be considered in the following manner.

1. *Structure.* Patterns of relationships that are relatively stable and continuous arise out of the interactions of the members of the

group. These patterns of relationships take shape as habitual roles taken up by the individuals, as configurations between several members of the group. Alliances, subgroups, and divisions are examples of these. (Psychic structuring represents processes with a slow rate of change; Rapaport, 1960.)

2. *Process.* There are processes with a more rapid rate of change representing the dynamic component of the group, which is in constant flux, and this manifests as the interaction of all the elements of the situation, including the reciprocal relationships, the communications, verbal and nonverbal.

3. *Content.* It is through the analysis of this manifest content, transmitted through structure and process, that latent content emerges, which is necessarily determined by the structure and process already described. The group analyst pays as much attention to structure and process as to content.

The patterns of relationship that are relatively stable and continuous, i.e., the structure of a group, can be altered by planned and deliberate interventions, as by Moreno's use of the sociogram, which shows the participants the nature of their relationships. The Group Analytic method, however, facilitates the gradual evolution of awareness of the ongoing patterns of relationships by the members of the group themselves.

Individuals in the group will inevitably participate against the background of the total network of communications that has evolved in the group. This total network of communications is what Foulkes called the group matrix (Abraham, 1973). The matrix is a slowly developing, specific group phenomenon, in which the meaning of individual neurotic responses can be mapped out against the group context. This brings in the dimensional aspect of foreground and background, a phenomenon that Foulkes emphasized from the perspective of Gestalt psychology. The individual's contributions and participations stand out against the background of the group as a whole and represent his or her unique style of participation.

Thus, in group-specific terms, individual and group resistance manifest as attempts to break the mandatory framework of the group analytic situation, for instance by late-coming, absenteeism, irregular attendance, socializing outside the group, and so on. Transference resistance in the group situation by virtue of its repetitiveness and exclusiveness tends to block group processes and thus becomes an issue for the group as a whole.

THERAPEUTIC FACTORS

Many factors are similar to those of psychoanalysis and psychodynamic psychotherapy: greater consciousness of what were previously unconscious forces, catharsis, working through, insight and analysis of defense mechanisms. Besides these, there are therapeutic factors that are group-specific, arising out of the group situation in itself with all its social factors and forces.

Therapeutic factors in the group analytic situation can be differentiated from group specific factors. Therapeutic factors are as follows:

Socialization. Through the process of sharing, through the experience of group acceptance and belongingness, the patient is brought out of his or her isolation into a social situation in which he or she can feel adequate. "He is a fellow being on equal terms with the others" (Foulkes, 1964, pp.33–34).

Mirror Phenomena. The patient can see aspects of himself or herself reflected in the image, behavior, and problems of the other members of the group. Through this he or she is enabled to confront various aspects of his or her social, psychological, and body image through identification with and projection onto the other members of the group.

Condenser Phenomena. Even deep unconscious material is expressed more readily and more fully in the group through the loosening and stimulating effects that the persons have upon one another. Symbolic meanings of dreams or symptoms that manifest themselves through such formations as phobias can be more readily understood and worked with collectively, through the pooling of associations in the group. It is as if what the group members hold in common through their dreams and symptoms can suddenly be understood, the symbol having acted as a "condenser."

Exchange. The members of the group often have a lively exchange of information with each other that leads to understanding both of self and of the meaning of emotional interactions and problems; this also can lead to chain phenomena and resonance. Each member of the group will reverberate to a group event according to his or her currently displayed level of development. Thus, for example, if a theme evolves in a group that has to do with violence, one can see how some members withdraw defensively, others display a marked interest in the behavior of the other persons, i.e., sharing the use of projection, while others can be self-revelatory about their own fantasies. Group themes around issues such as parting, loss, grief, mourning, etc., are rich sources of information as to the prevailing fixation and developmental level of group members and of the group as a whole.

Group as Support. In any therapeutic situation there will always be a balance between the integrative and analytic forces at work. Analysis and interpretation inevitably arouse anxiety and can lead to further defensive activity on the part of the individual. The individual's awareness that he or she is not alone in his or her attempt to resist, as well as to uncover his or her inner world, both gives him or her support and lessens some of the inevitable narcissistic mortification that arises through acceptance of interpretation. The group members will support each other through painful periods and actively help each other towards the integration of their conflicts. Often one sees patients accepting interpretations and comments from other members of the group that they would resist accepting from a therapist. This is because the person giving the interpretation or the confrontation will often offer himself or herself as a person to be identified with, as if saying "I know from my own experiences, I say this as one who has the same experiences as yourself and this is how and why I understand you so well."

Communication. "Working towards an evermore articulate form of communication is identical to the therapeutic process itself" (Foulkes, 1948, p.169).

The therapeutic process "from symptom to conflict" is synonymous with a growing capacity for communication. The therapist's role is to facilitate the processes of communication in the group; the process of *analyzing* takes precedence over that of *interpretation.*

"Neurotic and psychotic disturbances are always linked with blockage of the system of communication, socialization, of the patient and the aim of analysis is precisely to translate the autistic symptom into a problem which can be verbalized" (Foulkes, 1964, p.112). Each patient benefits through working towards a freer expression of conflicts within the group situation, both his or her own and those of his or her peers. "The language of the symptom, although already a form of communication, is autistic. It mumbles to itself secretly, hoping to be overheard; its equivalent meaning conveyed in words is social" (Foulkes & Anthony, 1965, pp.259–260). "The group has to go downwards and to deepen its understanding of the lower levels of the mind by broadening and deepening its vocabulary until every group member also understands these levels" (Foulkes & Anthony, 1965, p.263).

SELECTION OF GROUP MEMBERS

The group analytic situation can accommodate a wide range of persons and problems, provided that they can meet the minimal requirements of the analytic approach. The prospective group member will be required to reflect upon and react to the interpretive interventions made by the therapist and the manifold communications emanating from the group members. The person under consideration must possess a minimal ability to tolerate confrontation, the forced interaction of a relatively closed environment, and the frustration of slow, gradual, and oscillating change. There must be a willingness and ability to enter into the treatment contract, that is, to attend regularly—once or twice weekly sessions over a two to three years' period—and to keep the "rules" of the group (see below).

In the selection interview, the therapist will attach less significance to traditionally psychiatric categories, such as psychosis, neurosis, or personality disorders, and pay more attention to the ability to communicate in a group and the capacity to develop insight and motivation for change (Foulkes, 1964). However, sometimes even the apparently unmotivated patient who nevertheless stays in the group may derive considerable benefit from it.

Contraindications

Patients with severe character disorders whose symptoms are ego-syntonic would not only fail to benefit from group-analytic psychotherapy but might well be destructive to the group itself. Certain socially very isolated individuals, without the necessary supportive network outside the group to sustain them in the intervals between group sessions, do not do well in group analysis. Other patients who are doubtful candidates are those with grossly unrealistic expectations of the group, the therapist, and the therapeutic processes: They perceive the group as powerfully destructive or as magically healing. Patients with overwhelming attachment needs, such as drug addicts or alcoholics, would be excluded from the typical heterogeneous group-analytic therapy group, but they might do well in a homogeneous group, often within a hospital or ambulant clinic setting (Arroyave & Pangbourne, 1976). Generally speaking, the earlier and deeper the psychogenic trauma, and the more disorganized the personality, the more cautious will the group therapist be when considering such a patient's inclusion. Some group analytic therapists consider that severe early deprivations such as prolonged hospitalization, maternal depression, institutional upbringing, etc., warrant prolonged individual preparation or a combination of individual and group therapy. Such patients experience the group as yet another depriving experience (Wolff & Solomon, 1973).

COMPOSITION

The notion of the optimal composition of the group-analytic therapy group is based on the Foulkesian concept that the therapeutic process is identical with an ever-widening and increasing communication process. The benefit each person receives from working towards a free expression of his or her conflict in a group is closely linked with the level of communication such a group can comprehend.

The group that best promotes such communication is one with the widest possible span between personality types, "a mixed bag of diagnoses and disturbances" (Foulkes, 1975, p.66). In this atmosphere of lively diversity, the all-important cross-transferences, mirror-reactions, and other group-specific phenomena occur and manifest themselves freely and clearly. The limiting factor here is the therapist's and the group's ability to contain the tensions created in such a group, without endangering its cohesion and integrity. It can also be said that the more diverse the group in its composition, the more necessary does it become for one variable to be held in common—such as intelligence, or educational background (Foulkes, 1975).

In composing a group with optimal diversity, it becomes important to avoid isolation, for whatever reason, of any one of its members: For example, the inclusion of an elderly patient in a group with an age span of between 25 to 45 years of age would not be indicated; similarly a person who holds extreme religious or political convictions would likely be isolated in a group of people with broader-based views.

If the therapist works with the model of a closed group, the decisions as to composition will be accomplished at the group's formation. If, on the other hand, the model is the slow-open group, the important problem of the group's composition remains throughout its life. The aim is to hold the size fairly steady, to synchronize carefully both departures and arrivals of patients, and thus maintain the richness and diversity of the group's experience and the highest degree of flexibility. In such a group, there is a remarkable capacity to allow the emergence and expression of bizarre thinking and borderline and psychotic manifestations; these are received, held, and eventually modified, thereby moving from the idiosyncratic to the "common sense" of the group as a whole (Foulkes, 1964).

The composition of specialized more homogeneous groups follows similar principles. These include groups for adolescents, adoptive parents, psychotic patients, phobic patients, alcoholics, sexual deviants. These groups, although homogeneous in the diagnostic sense allow for a wide latitude in such variables as personality attributes, modes of expression of conflict, and defensive organization. Patients in this category with sufficient ego-strength and initiative may well be better placed in a heterogeneous group, which may benefit from their inclusion. There is some evidence that the inclusion of one or two patients with borderline personality organization in a group of neurotic patients has mutual benefit for both parties. The borderline patients activate strong responses in the neurotic patients and the neurotic patients help the borderline patients to modulate the intensity of their affective swings and to strengthen their capacity for secondary processes (Pines, 1975, 1978a).

SIZE

Most group analysts find that they work comfortably with six to eight patients in a group, since both patient and therapist are able to encompass eight to nine persons within their visual field. Thus the group can remain a face-to-face group. While the group as a whole is seen to provide the therapeutic momentum, it is always the individual who is the object of the therapy. Too large a group militates against intimacy and the feeling of containment and reduces the impact of each individual contribution. Face-to-face contact also becomes more difficult in a larger group, and the constraints of time may not allow each member sufficient opportunity for self-presentation.

Too small a group, say one of four or five participants, lacks the vital function of representing the social norm and emotional normalcy from which each individual in the group deviates. There is also a sense of lack of group identity, and therapy in very small groups of three and four members takes on the quality of individual psychotherapy *in* the group (Gosling, 1981).

For the group members, the field of action in which the ever-increasing and deepening communicative processes take place, the matrix, is well served by the size of a group of eight. Such a group offers a favorable environment in which to experience, partake of, and influence both intrapsychic and interpersonal phenomena. The group of eight facilitates what Foulkes called "ego training in action" (Foulkes, 1964, p. 82).

From the therapist's point of view, a group of eight makes it possible for him or her to pay attention to the totality of the group and its communicative processes. At the same time it allows the therapist to attend to the individual's contributions, both verbal and nonverbal, and to locate them in the context of the group communications.

GROUP SETTING

The group-analytic setting is the physical environment within which the group's therapeutic task takes place. The therapist as the "dynamic administrator" supplies, creates, and maintains the setting throughout the group's life. He or she guards the group boundaries and negotiates between it and the wider social environment. The setting provided will differ with the wider system within which the group functions: a hospital, a therapeutic community, a clinic, or private practice. In every case the therapist should, if possible, provide a reasonably sized, quiet room free from outside interference, with an identical chair for each member arranged in a circle. The chair should be comfortable and allow for a full view of the occupants. A central table small enough not to obscure the view of the group members acts as the group's center, while the circle of chairs represents the group boundaries. The table, or the group itself, may come to signify a transitional object (Koseff, 1975), supplied as it is by the therapist and invested with meaning by the group. Sometimes the group culture prescribes that the therapist's seat be fixed, and the patients group themselves in a more or less permanent order every time. In other groups the therapist and the group members choose different positions in the circle each session. In either case, the choice of neighbor, and the proximity from the therapist, are significant communications that are subject to translation from the nonverbal into the verbal, the unconscious into the conscious modality of experience. By keeping the setting as steady as possible, the significance of changes within it becomes available to the group members. In a hospital setting, the maintenance of the group room, its availability for the sessions on the appointed day and hour, are signs of the nature of the dynamic forces surrounding the group that can work towards its integrity or destruction. It is the task of the therapist as the administrator to guard the boundaries and negotiate between the group and its environment.

The room itself should be entirely free of interruption from extraneous sources for the duration of the session. It is surprising how often this is difficult to achieve, yet it is vital for the success of the therapy. Colleagues have to be worked with and their understanding and cooperation won. The wider network in which the therapy takes place is potentially both enriching and depleting of the therapeutic process. A closed group meeting regularly in an institutional setting generates its own institutional dynamics, and the therapist, both as administrator and in his or her role as guardian of the boundary, has to ensure that the wider network accepts the existence of the group. It is the therapist's responsibility to create the venue for the group, prepare it for the sessions, and protect it from intrusions.

In groups of young adolescents the group-analytic process is often facilitated by introducing paper and drawing or modelling materials. The way in which these materials are used provides additional opportunities for communication and gives to young people who have difficulty in verbalizing the chance to involve themselves more actively in the group process.

Children's groups typically have play materials built into their structure. The circular table is divided into parts, each of which becomes the child's own territory. In this way the autistic play of a child can progress into shared play, providing something of the equivalent of the adult group communicative process.

FREQUENCY, LENGTH, AND DURATION OF GROUP SESSIONS

Group-analytic sessions of 90 minutes are held once or twice a week, over a period of two to three years and often longer. Group analysis is therefore prolonged, thorough, and demanding on the patient, the group, and the group analyst since reliability and continuity are of its very essence. The aim is a deep and lasting change in internal object constellations and the resulting external relationships and perception of the environment. It is by its nature slow and the investment in time and committment is considerable. At the other end of the scale there is the danger of "group addiction," that is "group analysis interminable" with resulting loss of independence, self-reliance, and ego integrity. Foulkes likened the treatment to a spiral staircase with exits: Where termination takes place will depend on the individual's personal aims and expectations. This is one reason why the preferred pattern of groups is the *slow-open* one: Individual members leave in their own time; the group as such continues, often over a very long time. It develops a long and detailed history that is part of the group's culture and enters the matrix and thus the individual's internal group life. The *closed group* is one that starts and finishes together. Intense work can be done in such a group, which achieves an idiosyncratic group culture and strong interpersonal relations. It is left to the therapist and to external circumstances whether the slow-open or the closed group is the preferred medium of therapy. The open group usually forms in hospitals with a rapid turnover of patients and in universities and other institutions (Bramley, 1977) in which the comings and goings are determined by the nature of the institution rather than the therapeutic needs of the individual. However, it is a group pattern that attracts interest and invites experimentation exactly because of its community-oriented structure. Clinical experience and research are needed to validate the open group's therapeutic potential.

MEDIA EMPLOYED

Group analytical psychotherapy employs no other medium than the verbal and nonverbal interaction of the group members. Structured exercises play, video feedback etc., are not an intrinsic part of the technique. The introduction of these parameters, although they might activate and focus certain processes within the group, is considered to be an interference with the gradual evolution and unfolding of the group developmental processes and the therapeutic factors mentioned above. Play and recreation have been referred to in relation to adolescent and children's groups where they are a natural part of the therapy.

THE FUNCTION OF THE THERAPIST

Two distinct functions pertain: (1) *Dynamic Administration:* See section on "Setting." (2) *Therapeutic Activity:* We distinguish between leadership, analysis, and interpretation.

As a *leader* the therapist is not primarily concerned with the formation of a "good, efficient" group. The therapist is not out to create a team, to encourage good morale, friendship, and bonhomie. As a leader, he or she puts the group as a whole into the center of his or her attention; the leader tries to let the group speak, to bring out agreements and disagreements, repressed tendencies, and resistances against them. The leader activates and mobilizes that which is latent in the group and helps in the analysis and interpretation of process and content and of interpersonal relationships. The leader encourages the active participation of the members of the group and uses the contribution of the members in preference to his or her own. Inevitably the leader has a powerful effect on the evolving culture of the group. He or she emphasizes the "here and now" aspect of the situation and stands for an attitude of tolerance and appreciation of individual differences. The leader helps the members of the group become active participants in the process of group maturation through which individual change takes place.

Inevitably the group will first look to the therapist as to an omniscient and omnipotent figure from whom they expect magical help. In that sense the group may experience the therapist as a father figure, or when in a regressed state, as the primordial mother. Foulkes did not go far into the discussion of the symbolism of differences between the therapist as the father and the group as the mother (see for instance the writings of Walter Schindler, 1951, 1966 and Philip Slater, 1966). What he did pay much attention to is the process of maturation that occurs as the group is gradually weaned from its dependence upon the therapist as leader. As Foulkes put it, one cannot be weaned from something that has not previously been there or been powerfully established. To begin with, therapists should accept the "exalted" position into which the group puts them, not because it gratifies their own wishes for power but because from this position they can lead the group into a process of analysis, insight, and more appropriate adult behavior. Leaders first accept the positions the group chooses to confer on them, realizing that this gives the group security. It is a position they accept in order eventually to relinquish, to change from being a leader *of* the group to being a leader *in* the group. Eventually, the group replaces the leader's authority by that of the group itself. Thus, there is a modification of the individual superegos. The power of the leader is based upon projections of such superego components of each person's personality. Gradually, as the group weans itself from dependence upon the leader and as he or she uses his or her power not destructively or coercively, leadership becomes an ego-based activity rather than a superego one.

Interpretation is one of several interventions available to the group conductor. The therapist attempts to foster the group's abilities to understand and to interpret their own situations, reactions, and behavior and to develop the self-analytic functions of the group. The therapist waits until

he or she has evidence that the group is not able on their own to understand the dynamic processes and unconscious meanings of the events of
the session; if the therapist waits sufficiently long he or she will, more often
than not, find that the group can themselves evolve or resolve the dynamic
issues of the session. Often what the therapist says is to elucidate what has
not yet been said by any one member of the group. This rather humble
activity that often does not rank as "interpretation" may be a crucial element in the therapy. The therapist's actions may be subsumed under the
heading of "activity." This may include reflection on group events; bringing events from the background into the foreground of the group's attention; linking communications, clarifications, and confrontations with
individuals; drawing the group's attention to events that are being ignored,
such as the silence or withdrawal of a previously active member; pointing
out the configurations that are developing within the group, of which
subgrouping, pairing and scapegoating are examples. Often the therapist
will feel that his or her most appropriate role is to remain silent, thereby
becoming the projective and containing element of the group situation.

"Interpretation is used when analysis fails." Complementing this activity, the therapist may interpret his or her understanding of the unconscious
processes to the group as a whole or to individuals within the group. As the
group matrix develops and as the modes of communication that the group
members make with each other become more sensitive and deeper, so the
therapeutic process proceeds *pari passu* with these processes. The process of
therapeutic change is therefore in a sense silent, that is, it is not solely based
upon interpretations. What may be fundamental for the individuals in the
group is the way in which their relationships to each other alter and
develop over time. The members of the group are often extremely sensitive
to this and they develop keen awareness and insight into these often very
subtle developments. Frequently in a group, patients will comment that
they are now able to say things to each other that they would not have been
able to say previously. The alteration in these role-relationships and interpersonal relationships in the group provides the "moveable context" of
the group analytic situation that de Mare (1972) has contrasted to the
"unchanging context" of the psychoanalytic situation. In psychoanalysis
the relationship aspects are kept constant so that transference will appear
against the unchanging context. In the group analytic situation transference relationships are explored and analyzed in order to free the individuals from the transference-bound repetition and thus enable them to develop
more sensitive, less distorted, and more mature forms of relationship. Thus
a good deal of the therapeutic processes that have been called "ego training
in action" represent the silent working through in the new situation of
previously pathological and unresolved conflicts.

The therapist allows the interpretation to come to him or her from the
contributions of his or her patients. Basically, the therapist's interpretative

activities can be differentiated into the following three types: (1) interpretation that enables unconscious processes to become more conscious, (2) interpretation of resistance and defense, (3) interpretation of transference reactions.

The group members' interpretative contributions as cotherapists to one another are essential components of the therapeutic processes, although if and when this interpretative culture becomes a manifestation of resistance it has to be dealt with as such. The culture slowly evolves, partly based on identification with the therapist but, as Foulkes emphasized from the start, group members' reactions to one another often represent unconscious interpretations that need to be made conscious.

The group analyst is free to make interpretations to individuals as well as to the group as a whole, as interpretations are always significant for the group as a whole as well as for the individual. Thus, they can be addressed to any particular individual, can refer to any configuration of relationships within the group, or between the group and the therapist, can be concerned with the "here and now" or range over the whole history of the group. They should preferably be based upon the available experience of the moment and on the level at which the emotion is most active.

The therapist directs his or her interpretation towards the following:

1. Ongoing group interactive processes, such as group regressions, fantasies, subgroupings, pairing, mirroring, etc.
2. Repetitive conflict situations.
3. An understanding of the past experiences that spring to the mind of the patient in association to the group situation.
4. Current experiences in the life of the patient both within and without the group.
5. "Boundary incidents," events taking place at the interface between the ongoing group and the outside life of the individuals comprising it.

There are no essential distinctions between processes inside the group and those going on outside, for inside and outside are false dichotomies. Boundary incidents therefore can involve the relationship of a patient to any member of his or her own social group and even to his or her body, as manifested in illness, psychosomatic or otherwise.

Transference

It should be clear from what has been said so far in this article that in group analytic theory and practice, therapists do not confine their activities to interpretations nor are their interpretations always directed to transference or particularly towards themselves as the central figures of the group. To do this would be to maintain the therapist in the role of the central figure, as a projection of superego fantasies on the part of the individuals. The therapist in the group being in a face-to-face situation and being both part of the group as well as being "outside" the group, is far more visible to the group members than is the unseen analyst in the psychoanalytic situation. By virture of this situation, *who* he or she is, his or her personality, and his or her responses to the group situation will affect the group processes (Foulkes, 1964). *What* he or she is, is intrinsically part of what he or she does. The mutative changes are therefore not confined to the effects of transference interpretations; the mutative experiences may arise out of confrontations between members of the group or between the group as a whole and the therapist, and not solely from interpretative activities. Foulkes therefore opposed the argument that only transference interpretations are mutative, and because he did not draw a rigid distinction between events occurring within the group situation itself and those occurring outside, he felt free to pay attention to these "external" events. For him the equation for therapy was $T = (t + X)$, where T stands for the total therapeutic situation, t for the transference, and X for the current interpersonal and life situation of the patient outside the group. In Foulkes' view a situation had developed within psychoanalysis where "the transference can swallow up the neurosis" (Foulkes, 1975a). By this he meant that the transference process, which should be the main vehicle of liberation for the individual from his or her neurotic conflicts, can become so powerful and so resistant to change that it largely replaces the illness and does not give way to a healthy resolution (Cortesao, 1974; Leal, 1968). This could arise from a faulty technique, that of exclusive attention to the transference, that can have the effect of infantilizing the patient and maintaining him or her in a dependent, neurotically gratifying position and one which also gratifies the therapist's unconscious countertransference. It was in response to this faulty development that Foulkes developed his therapeutic equation.

GROUND RULES

There are a few basic rules to which the prospective group analysand is expected to adhere. Members are expected to attend every session, to arrive on time, and to stay for the entire session unless unavoidable circumstances arise that prevent this. Individuals are expected to inform the group of their intended absence in advance, or in the case of unexpected absence they should let the therapist know. The therapist prepares the individual at the outset for the possibility of departure from the group, by imposing the expectation that he or she should give advance notice of his or her intention to leave the group at least a month before he or she plans to do so. This allows for a period of working through the termination of therapy and preempts a disruptive departure that may have repercussions on both the group and the departing member.

Group analysis carries with it an implicit expectation that significant events and experiences in the individual's life situation should be honestly disclosed to the group. No subject, topic, or theme is proscribed and all expressions of feeling are invited. Events that the individual feels to be important should be shared with the group in a time and manner determined by the individual's own level of comfort and spontaneity. The rule of honest disclosure fosters a respect both for the individual and the group. By virtue of regular, full, and sustained participation in the group, members gradually introduce into the group all facets of their personalities, and in this way they develop a pool of material that contributes to the formation of the group matrix.

A minimum of activity is preferred, as this is felt to detract from symbolic expression through the spoken word of the strong feelings that emerge. It is the translation of early primitive modes of expression into interpersonal terms by talk that makes change possible and through which the corrective emotional experience of the group occurs. For this reason group members remain seated throughout the session, expected to communicate through both minimal activity and talk. They do not touch one another as a rule, except for an occasional neighborly gesture of comfort or consolation in moments of distress. Abstinence from physical contact provides the momentum to overcome emotional blocks verbally, or to remain with the feelings that have been mobilized in this way until an understanding of their meaning can be reached.

For similar reasons, anxiety-reducing activities like smoking, drinking, and eating during sessions are not accepted as a constructive part of the group culture. While there may be no blanket prohibition on these activities at the outset, when they do occur, the therapist intervenes in order to create a group climate that will lead the group towards an explanation of the defensive significance of these activities, both for the individuals engaging in them and for the group as a whole.

Members are asked not to socialize with one another outside the group. When this does happen they are generally encouraged, through the open atmosphere of the group, to examine the significance of such extra-group contact by telling of it in the group and reflecting on its meaning.

Strict confidentiality and respect for the privacy of disclosed material is asked of all the members, as it is only in an atmosphere of mutual trust that therapy can take place.

Generally, it is the therapist who decides on matters pertaining to the composition of the group, such as introduction of a new member. However, he or she is careful to prepare the ground by mentioning in the group any proposed changes in the structure of the group. He or she does this in advance and listens carefully to the response from the group at both the manifest and latent level; he or she regards the feelings generated by these changes as important material for therapeutic work in the group.

A decision to leave the group is taken by the individual member, but again the therapist and the group play an active part in helping the individual towards this decision, by examining the significance for the individual and the group of his or her departure. The breaking of ground rules is in itself an important communication, albeit on a primitive level, that will be offered for the process of translation in the group.

REFERENCES ▬

Abraham, A. (1973). Individual and group matrix. *Group Analysis, 6*(2), 105–110.

Abse, D. W. (1974). *Clinical notes on group-analytic psychotherapy.* Bristol, England: John Wright & Sons Ltd.

Arroyave, F., & Pangbourne, J. (1976). Group methods in the treatment of alcoholics. *Group Analysis, 9*(1), 32–33.

Bion, W. R. (1961). *Experiences in groups and other papers.* London: Tavistock Publications.

Bramley, W. (1977). A group-analytic approach to training. *Group Analysis, 10*(1), 32–39.

Bridges, H. (1946). The Northfield experiment. *Bulletin of the Menninger Clinic, 10*(3), 71–78.

Brown, D. (1979). Some reflections on Bion's basic assumptions from a group-analytic view point. *Group Analysis, 12*(3), 204–210.

Burrow, T. (1927). *The social basis of consciousness.* New York: Harcourt, Brace and Co.

Cortesao, E. L. (1974). Transference neuroses and the group-analytic process. *Group Analysis, 7*(3). 4–10. (supplement)

de Mare, P. B. (1972). *Perspectives in group psychotherapy.* London: George Allen and Unwin Ltd.

de Mare, P. B. (1977). Group-analytic principles in natural and stranger groups. *Group Analysis, 10*(1), 16–21.

Elias, N. (1978). *The civilizing process.* Oxford: Blackwell Publishers.

Ezriel, H. (1973). Psychoanalytic group therapy. In L. R. Wolberg & E. K. Schwartz (Eds.), *Group therapy: An overview.* New York: Intercontinental Medical Books Corporation.

Foulkes, S. H. (1948). *Introduction to group-analytic psychotherapy.* London: William Heinemann Medical Books Ltd.

Foulkes, S. H. (1964). *Therapeutic group analysis.* London: George Allen and Unwin Ltd.

Foulkes, S. H. (1971). Access to unconscious processes in the group analytic group. *Group Analysis, 4*(1), 4–14.

Foulkes, S. H. (1975a). *Group-analytic psychotherapy, method and principles.* London: Gordon and Breach Science Publishers Ltd.

Foulkes, S. H. (1975b). Qualification as a psycho-analyst as an asset as well as a hindrance of a future group analyst. *Group Analysis, 8*(3), 180–182.

Foulkes, S. H., & Anthony, E. J. (1965). *Group psychotherapy* (2nd ed.). London: Pelican Books.

Gosling, R. H. (1981). A study of very small groups. In J. S. Grotstein (Ed.), *Do I dare disturb the universe? A memorial to Dr. Wilfred Bion.* California: Caesure.

Hartmann, H. (1958). *Ego psychology and the problem of adaption.* New York: International Universities Press.

Hooper, E. (1982). Discussion on paper by Marie Jahoda, Individual and group. In M. Pines & L. Rafaelsen, (Eds.), *The individual and the group: Boundaries and interrelations* (Proceedings of the 7th International Congress of Group Psychotherapy held Aug. 1980, at the University of Copenhagen and sponsored by the International Association of Group Psychotherapy). New York: Plenum Press.

James, D. C. (1980). W. R. Bion's contributions to the field of group therapy: An appreciation. In L. R. Wolberg & M. L. Aronson (Eds.), *Group and family therapy: An overview.* New York: Brunner/Mazel, Inc.

Kadis, A. L., Krasner, J. D., Weiner, M. F., Winick, C., & Foulkes, S. H. (1974). *Practicum of group psychotherapy* (2nd ed). New York, Harper & Row.

Koseff, J. W. (1975). The leader using object-relations theory. In Z. A. Liff & J. Aronson (Eds.), *The leader in the group.* New York: J. Aronson.

Leal, M. R. M. (1968). Transference neurosis in group analytic treatment. *Group Analysis, 1* (2), 101–109.

Lewin, K. (1951). Field theory in social science. In *Selected theoretical papers.* D. Cartwright (Ed.), New York: Harper Brothers.

Main, T. F. (1946). The hospital as a therapeutic institution. *The Bulletin of the Menninger Clinic, 10* (3), 66–70.

Napolitani, D. (1980, August). Beyond the individual: The relationship between subject and group in a group-analytic perspective. Paper presented at the VII International Congress of Group Psychotherapy, Copenhagen. New York: Plenum Press.

Napolitani, D. (1982). Structure de groupe en psychoanalyse et analyse du groupe. [Group structure in psychoanalysis and group analysis.] (Fren.) *Connexions, 37* 145–193.

Pines, M. (1975). Group psychotherapy with 'difficult' patients. In L. Wolberg, M. Aronson, & A. R. Wolberg (Eds.), *Group therapy: An overview.* New York: Stratton Intercontinental Medical Book Corp.

Pines, M. (1978). The contributions of S. H. Foulkes to group-analytic psychotherapy. In L. R. Wolberg, M. L. Aronson, & A. R. Wolberg (Eds.), *Group therapy: An overview.* New York: Stratton Intercontinental Medical Book Corp.

Pines, M. (1978a). Group-analytic psychotherapy of the borderline patient. *Group Analysis, 11* (2), 115–126.

Pines, M. (1978b). Psycho-analysis and group analysis. *Group Analysis, 11* (1), 8–20.

Pines, M. (1981a). The fundamentals of group-analytic therapy. In M. Pines (Ed.), *The evolution of group analysis.* London: Routledge, Kegan and Paul.

Pines, M. (1981b). Introduction to the work of S. H. Foulkes. In M. Pines (Ed.), *The evolution of group analysis.* London: Routledge, Kegan and Paul.

Rapaport, D. (1960). The structure of psycho-analytic theory: A systematizing attempt. *Psychological Issues 6.* (Monograph)

Rickman, J. (1957). *Selected contributions to psychoanalysis.* London: Hogarth Press.

Schindler, W. (1951). Family pattern in group formation and therapy. *International Journal of Group Psychotherapy, 1,* 100–105.

Schindler, W. (1966). The role of the mother in group psychotherapy. *International Journal of Group Psychotherapy, 16,* 198–202.

Skynner, A. C. R. (1969). A group-analytic approach to conjoint family therapy. *Child Psychology and Psychiatry, 10,* 81–106.

Slater, P. E. (1966). *Microcosm.* New York: Wiley.

Sutherland, J. D. (1952). Notes on psychoanalytic group therapy. *Psychiatry, 15,* 111–117.

Wolff, H. H. & Solomon, E. C. (1973). Individual and group psychotherapy: Complementary growth experience. *International Journal of Group Psychotherapy, 23*(2), 177–184.

SUGGESTED READINGS _____ ▬

Abse, D. W (1979). Trigrant Burrow and the inauguration of group analyses in the U.S.A. *Group Analysis, 12*(3), 218–229.

Anthony, E. J. (1971). The history of group psychotherapy. In H. I. Kaplan & B. J. Sadock (Eds.), *Comprehensive group psychotherapy.* Baltimore: The Williams and Wilkins Co.

Behr, H. L. (Ed.). *Group Analysis.* London: Institute of Group Analysis, Various issues.

de Mare, P. B. (1972). *Perspectives in group psychotherapy.* London: George Allen and Unwin Ltd.

Foulkes, S. H. (1964). *Therapeutic group analysis.* London: George Allen and Unwin Ltd.

Foulkes, S. H. (1975). *Group-analytic psychotherapy, methods and principles.* London: Gordon and Breach Science Publishers Ltd.

Kreeger, L. (Ed.). (1975). *The large group: Dynamics and therapy.* London: Constable and Co., Ltd.

Pines, M. (1978). The contributions of S. H. Foulkes to group-analytic psychotherapy. In L. R. Wolberg, M. L. Aronson, & A. R. Wolberg (Eds.), *Group therapy, an overview.* New York: Stratton Intercontinental Medical Book Corp.

Pines, M. (1981). Introduction to the work of S. H. Foulkes. In M. Pines (Ed.), *The evolution of group analysis.* London: Routledge, Kegan and Paul.

C H A P T E R 15

The Existential Approach
Logotherapy[1]

INTRODUCTION

Logotherapy was chosen as representative of existential therapy because it is a direct offshoot of modern existential philosophy, which originated from the Danish theologian Soren Kierkegaard. Although the word "existentialism" did not come into usage until 70 years after Kierkegaard's death, he laid the foundations of a philosophy that was further developed in Germany by Martin Heidegger and Karl Jaspers, and in France by Jean Paul Sartre, Albert Camus, and Gabriel Marcel.

The basic tenet of existential philosophy is contained in the sentence "existence precedes essence," which means that one's essence, one's essential being, is the result of one's existence, namely, what one does with one's life. To put it more succinctly, what people do determines what they are. The emphasis is on choice and responsibility for one's choices. Further, emphasis is placed on personal uniqueness and the importance of meaning.

While meaning is central for both the German and the French branch of

1. Abstracted from Williams, D. A., & Fabry, J. (1982). The existential approach: Logotherapy. In G. M. Gazda (Ed.), *Basic approaches to group psychotherapy and group counseling* (pp. 179–212). Springfield, IL: Charles C. Thomas.

existential philosophy, there is a significant difference. The French existentialists assume that life has no meaning in itself, but human beings have an innate need to find meaning; therefore people have to "invent" meanings that make sense to them. The German existentialists assume that life, existence itself, does have meaning, and that it is not up to people to "invent their own" but to discover the meanings their lives hold.

The first person to use the principles of existential philosophy in therapy and counseling was the Swiss psychiatrist Ludwig Binswanger, who was a follower of Sigmund Freud but broadened Freud's ideas in the direction of existentialism. He called his system *Daseinsanalyse*.

Viktor Frankl, the founder of logotherapy, was a student of Alfred Adler, whose individual psychology was in turn an offshoot of Freud's psychoanalysis. Frankl was greatly influenced by the philosophy of the German existentialists Heidegger and Jaspers, and the phenomenologist Scheler. Frankl rejected the French existentialists' contention that life has no meaning and people have to arbitrarily "give" meaning to their existence. To assume that, he said, would make life a meaningless blotch like a Rorschach test into which each person can read his or her own individual meanings. Rather than being comparable to Rorschach blots, Frankl sees meanings as being analogous to embedded figure puzzles. In solving such puzzles one usually turns the picture in many different ways before suddenly having the "aha!" experience of discovering the object hidden in the picture.

Frankl's whole life and work is testimony of his attempts to prove that life does have intrinsic meaning. Such proof can be found only "existentially," by living as if life had meaning and not as if everything were chance. In his practice, and in the practice of his followers, he found proof that the assumption of a meaningful life is the precondition of health. The therapy he developed was originally (in the 1920s) "logo-therapy" and later (in the 1930s) the alternative term "existential analysis" was used. When his books began to be translated into English, the confusion with Binswanger's *Daseinanalyse*, which also was translated as "existential analysis," prompted Frankl to change the name of his therapy to "logotherapy" to avoid confusion. The Greek word *logos*, which signifies "the unifying principle of the universe," was translated by Frankl as "meaning," thus logotherapy is "therapy through meaning."

Logotherapy differs from other existential treatment modes in that it alone has successfully developed what can properly be called psychotherapeutic techniques (Ungersma, 1961). Logotherapy also differs from other current existential modes in that it places more emphasis on what Frankl calls objective meanings to be fulfilled in the world. The other existential modes are much more subjectively based.

THEORETICAL FOUNDATIONS

The Human Condition: Its Three-Dimensional Nature

In logotherapy the human being is seen as a totality in three dimensions: the biological, the psychological, and the spiritual or noëtic. To see human beings only in their biological or psychological dimensions is to see them only as animals, the victims of their drives and instincts, or as machines that can be manipulated. To see a human being as devoid of the spiritual dimension is to reduce the person to a caricature. To use a simile introduced by Frankl, just as an airplane while it taxies on the ground shows no uniqueness until it rises above the ground and flies, so does the human being exemplify true humanness only when rising beyond the physical and psychological dimensions into the specifically human phenomena.

The Will to Meaning

In logotherapy the *will to meaning* is the central force in human motivation. The will to meaning is seen as stronger than Freud's "will to pleasure" and Adler's "will to power." In the Nazi death camps Frankl was able to observe firsthand the strength of this motivator. He witnessed how, under equal circumstances, those individuals who were more oriented toward a meaning to be fulfilled were more likely to survive the rigors of camp life. According to logophilosophy the human will to meaning is not in vain, for, according to its precepts, life offers a meaning in all circumstances. Whether one chooses to search for the meaning is another matter.

Dimensions of Meaning

Logotherapy recognizes two types of meaning: the meaning of the moment and ultimate meaning. Fabry (1980) defines *ultimate meaning* as "the premise that order exists in the universe despite apparent chaos; that each person is part of that order and that he can decide whether and how to participate in that order" (pp. 11–12). This definition allows for several interpretations of that order, including God, life, nature, science, the great spirit, and others. The acid test for ultimate meaning is whether it is adequate in the face of tragedy. If it is, then one can presume that the meaning is, indeed, ultimate.

The *meaning of the moment* refers to the transitory meanings that present themselves to the individual literally moment by moment. The significance of the meaning of the moment ranges from the mundane to the heroic, with the former being far more frequent. Crumbaugh (1973) has pointed out that the perception of the moment-by-moment meanings requires a gestalt process. Frankl thinks that while in a gestalt perception we perceive a so-called "figure" against a "background." In the specific case of meaning perception we become aware of a possibility against the background of reality, that is, we suddenly become aware of what we can do about a given situation. In every moment we choose from the gestalt of life, from the totality of all potential choices, one possibility and make it a reality.

Regarding the general question as to what is the meaning of life, Frankl refuses to answer. In his opinion this is a senseless question, just as senseless as the question, "What is the best move in chess?" The answer to this question, naturally, is that there is no *best* move; it depends on one's position on the board, one's individual strategy, the personality of one's opponent, the possibility for the unexpected, and so on. Likewise, there is no such thing as *the* meaning of life—at least it would not be accessible to the limited intellectual capacities of a finite being such as a human; or, as Frankl puts it, "the more comprehensive meaning is, the less it is comprehensible."

Pathways to Meaning

Logotherapy suggests three major routes to meaning: (1) creativity and achievement, (2) experiencing, and (3) attitude. The meaning derived from creativity and achievement is usually obvious; it is equally obvious that this source of meaning is a powerful motivator of human behavior. Experiential meaning refers to the meaning derived through the experience of that which is aesthetically pleasing (e.g., the experience of truth or beauty in nature or art or music) or the experience of love. Attitudinal meaning is most important in logotherapy. It refers to the meaning potential inherent in a situation in which the individual freely chooses an attitude (seeing the opportunity to learn from a crisis, for example) in the face of unavoidable circumstances. One can take a meaningful attitude toward a situation that in itself is meaningless.

Self-transcendence

Self-transcendence refers to the human ability to reach beyond one's own person toward causes to serve or people to love. This concept occupies a central position in logotherapy. Frankl (1978) states, "I thereby understand the primordial anthropological fact that being human is being always directed, and pointing, to something or someone other than oneself: to a meaning to fulfill or another human being to encounter, a cause to serve or a person to love. Only to the extent that someone is living out this self-transcendence of human existence, is he truly human or does he become his true self" (p. 35). Frankl holds that even one's identity is dependent upon self-transcendence; he quotes one of his existential mentors, Karl Jaspers, in support of his position. Jaspers observed that "What man is, he ultimately becomes through the cause which he has made his own" (cited in Frankl, 1967, p. 9). Frankl also takes the position that self-actualization cannot occur except as a consequence of self-transcendence. According to logophilosophy the more one aims directly for self-actualization, the more one will miss it. Only by investing one's time and energy in causes and people beyond one's self can self-actualization occur. Frankl claims that even Maslow eventually accepted this notion.

Freedom

Logotherapy places a great deal of emphasis on human freedom. However, it is clearly restricted; human beings are never free *from* conditions, but they are always free to choose their attitude *toward* the conditions. Environment and heredity both have a great impact on one's life but neither influence can ever take away one's freedom to take a stance toward those conditions. To say it another way, attitudinal meaning is an ever-present possibility regardless of the tragedy or devastation that may befall one. Freedom of attitude is, therefore, seen as unconditional.

Responsibility

Frankl has referred to logotherapy as education to responsibility. In logotherapeutic terms *responsibility* refers to the ability and willingness to respond to the meaning potentials offered by life. Responsibility also carries the traditional meaning of owning the outcomes of human choices and behavior. Logotherapy treats freedom and responsibility as if they were a single phenomenon with freedom constituting the negative portion and responsibility constituting the positive portion. Frankl (1978) has facetiously remarked that the United States need a Statue of Responsibility on the west coast to counterbalance the Statue of Liberty on the east coast.

Choice

The issue of *choice* is most important from an existentialist standpoint. Jaspers (1932) said it poignantly when he stated, "So far as I choose, I am; if I am not, I do not choose" (p. 182). In a sense, then, a person *becomes* his or her choices. Frankl's view of human choice is consistent with Jaspers's. In *Psychotherapy and Existentialism* (1967) he states, "Man makes decisions every moment, even unwittingly and against his will. Through these decisions man decides upon himself. Continually and incessantly he shapes and reshapes himself" (p. 35). In the concentration camps Frankl saw that despite the horror of the conditions, many free choices remained. Through their own choices some inmates behaved "like swine while others behaved like saints" (1967, p. 35).

Some individuals shrink from the issue of choice-making. Their reason for doing so is obvious enough—anxiety. To choose one alternative over another is often to condemn one alternative into permanent nonbeing. Permanently condemning an alternative that may, itself, be very attractive can cause anxiety and depression through a feeling of loss. These feelings of loss are particularly acute for obsessive-compulsive individuals. Some people believe they can escape choice-making situations by diligently working to keep their options open at all times. Frankl (1967) warns that these efforts are in vain, however, "for wherever [a person] turns he is confronted with the exigencies of life and the demand to make meaningful and valuable and, thus, existential commitments" (p. 47).

Action

Meaningful choice implies the implementing of the appropriate action. The existential position has little regard for reflection and intentions that are not followed up with substantive action. Sartre and Frankl are largely in agreement on the issue of action. Sartre (1957) states, "He [the human being] exists only insofar as he realizes himself. He is, therefore, nothing else but the sum of his actions, nothing else but what his life is" (p. 37). Frankl's emphasis on action is equally clear. In *The Unconscious God* (1975) he states, "Human existence exists in action rather than reflection" (p. 30).

The Tragic Triad

Logotherapy refers by this term to three inescapable conditions of human life; namely, suffering, guilt, and death. Although the inescapability of these conditions is patently obvious to most people, it does not in any way prevent them from attempting to escape via comforting illusions. Frankl notes that progressivism and scientism are extensively used as tools for creating such illusions. The naive notion that "science will save us" has been promoted with a great deal of success. This belief has been especially evident in the United States. Rather than burying the reality under illusions, logotherapy urges that these inescapable conditions be faced and accepted. This acceptance, once it has occurred, becomes the source of great strength.

Suffering

Logotherapy does not view suffering as the great menace of humankind. According to logotherapeutic doctrine, suffering offers the sufferer the possibility of experiencing the highest value, the deepest meaning. Animals can suffer, but only human beings can perceive a meaning in their suffering. Often the meaning of the suffering is not readily apparent. In such cases the sufferers may find meaning in their predicament by choosing an attitude of courage and resolve in the fact of their tragedy. Only because humans are endowed with what Frankl calls "the defiant power of the human spirit" is this attitude of courage possible. The assumption of such an attitude has the effect of ennobling the sufferers, for their suffering has become an achievement. Attitudinal meanings remain, therefore, as a possibility right up until the last breath. The suffering referred to here is, of course, unavoidable suffering. To suffer needlessly is simply masochism.

Guilt

Like suffering, guilt should be avoided when possible, but there always remains a profound guilt that is inescapable. Frankl even goes so far as to assert that becoming guilty is a human *right*. Just as it is the right of human beings to feel guilty, it is also their obligation to overcome guilt. The obligation to overcome guilt can serve as a powerful incentive to initiate healthy changes.

Finiteness and Death

Breisach (1962) considers human finiteness to be the central challenge of Sartre and Kierkegaard and the central pillar of Heidegger's philosophy. Frankl is in agreement with this mainstream existential concept. He (1967) speaks of the need of human beings to become reconciled with their finiteness. When they come to grips with their limited time and capacities, they will likely begin to ask what meanings life has to offer in the time remaining. The asking of such questions has the effect of projecting them out of the superficial comfort that life offers and into the more important meanings that remain to be realized.

The most significant aspect of human finiteness is our own death, and perhaps, we most desperately need to come to terms with this. Frankl (1967) states that only in the face of death is it meaningful to act. So long as one soothes oneself with the illusion of endless time, decisive action is meaningless or even fanatical. Kaufman (1976) captures this view in the following: "Lives are spoiled and made rotten by the sense that death is distant and irrelevant. One lives better when one expects to die, say, at forty . . . " (p. 214).

The logotherapist's preoccupation with death is in no way morbid. The acceptance of one's own death allows individuals to place the petty concerns of their lives into proper perspective and to begin to take action on those larger issues they have been intending to begin "tomorrow" for the past many years.

Once, however, that one has taken action and actualized a meaning potential, there is no need to be concerned with the transitoriness of life. For, as Frankl points out, when fulfilling a meaning we are, as it were, rescuing it into the past. Frankl (1963) states, "In the past, nothing is irrecoverably lost but everything irrevocably stored" (p. 191).

Commitment

The logotherapist considers *commitment* to be an essential life task. Individuals must risk committing themselves to causes even though those causes may, in the end, prove to be unworthy of their commitment. As Allport (1950) has pointed out, commitments force a person into the difficult position of being half-sure and whole hearted at one and the same time. The difficulty of making commitments does not, in any way, however, excuse one from this venture. Crumbaugh (1979) considers commitment to be both the most important and the most difficult step in logotherapy.

Sources of Neurotic Disturbance

Frankl takes the position that neurotic disturbances may contain an existential conflict, but not every existential conflict is seen as neurotic. Some of the existential conflicts that can cause neuroses will be mentioned here.

The way in which one handles choice-making situations has important implications for the development of neurosis. Persons who refuse to make choices with decisiveness in the hopes of keeping all of their options open are inviting neurotic disturbance. As Salzman (1968), Shapiro (1965), and Laughlin (1967) have pointed out—and Frankl had phenomenologically analyzed in 1955—the inability to decide is a hallmark of the obsessive personality.

Regarding obsessional disorders Frankl further observes that obsessive patients are intolerant of the tension between what is and what they think ought to be. Their world view is one of "hundred-percentness, or a search for the absolute, a striving for absolute certainty in cognition or decision" (1955, p. 191). Since such aspirations are impossible to achieve, obsessive patients will concentrate their efforts in a specific area; but even here they can succeed only partially, and then only at a great price.

Closely related to the existential conflict with choice-making is the consistent attempt to escape the awareness of life's task. Alfred Adler has shown that persistent flight from one's tasks can end in neurosis.

Logotherapy maintains that the acceptance of one's finiteness is a precondition for mental health, and the inability to accept it is characteristic of the neurotic personality. Inability to accept one's finiteness is implicated in the anxiety neuroses. Behind neurotic anxiety there is existential anxiety, in particular, fear of death, which is simultaneously fear of life.

A special type of neurosis that logotherapy alone recognizes is called noögenic neurosis. Noögenic neuroses are seen not as arising from the psyche or the soma but from the noös, the dimension of the human spirit, in the presence of a conflict. Noëtic conflicts, which are referred to here, are conflicts between competing values that pull the patient in two opposing directions, thereby causing existential frustration. Absence of a healthy spiritual tension opens up what Frankl calls the existential vacuum. Logotherapeutic research has shown that about 20 percent of today's neuroses are noögenic.

Frankl has observed that excessive focusing of one's attention on uncomfortable symptoms has the effect of worsening those very symptoms. Stutterers, for example, inevitably stutter more when they focus their attention on their stuttering rather than on the content of their speech. The same is true for neurotic symptoms. For example, the more the obsessives concentrate their attention on their obsessive thoughts, the more intense these unwanted thoughts become. Frankl has termed this excessive attention to symptoms *hyperreflection.*

In the pleasurable domain the counterpart of hyperreflection is hyperintention. Hyperintention is characterized by excessive striving for pleasurable goals such as orgasm, potency, relaxation, and sleep. Paradoxically, the more one focuses direct attention on these goals, the more elusive these goals become. The consequence of hyperintending pleasurable events is only more and more frustration. Hyperintention may exacerbate neurotic problems already present by adding such problems as impotency, frigidity, insomnia, and anhedonia.

TREATMENT OVERVIEW

Logotherapy is neither a panacea nor a therapy in competition with other therapies. It often serves as an important complement. Frankl is of the opinion that many of today's therapies overlook the uniquely human (i.e., spiritual) dimension in their approaches. He sees the task of "rehumanizing" psychotherapy as one of logotherapy's main tasks.

The renowned physician Paracelsus proclaimed that diseases originate in the realm of nature, but healing comes from the realm of the spirit. It is this spiritual realm that logotherapy seeks to bring to the forefront. One might say that all good doctors have been aware of this spiritual dimension and unknowingly or otherwise have practiced logotherapy. Cousins (1979) attributes to Albert Schweitzer the belief that the two best medicines were (a) knowledge of a job to do and (b) a good sense of humor. Ungersma (1961) reports that Frankl has said, in effect, that if logotherapy did nothing more than bring to the general awareness what previously had been practiced intuitively by good doctors, that alone would be a worthwhile goal.

Within the human spiritual dimension, logotherapy maintains that a certain amount of tension is not only ineradicable but highly desirable. This stance is in contrast with the psychoanalytic school of thought, which perceives the individual as striving for tension reduction. Frankl sees healthy tension as that "between being and becoming." The prolonged absence of such a tension can result in an existential vacuum.

A good understanding of Frankl's concept of healthy tension is required in order to understand logotherapeutic treatment philosophy. This he illustrates with a metaphor from architecture. If an architect wants to strengthen a decrepit arch, he *increases* the load that is laid upon it and in so doing joins the parts together more firmly. Therefore the goal of the logotherapist is often to bring clients into full awareness of their life task. By so doing the therapist allows them to feel the full weight of their burden, but they now have a much better chance of overcoming their neurosis. Sometimes clients can be helped by asking them what they have to *offer* life rather than what they want to *get* from life. This is an attempt to engage the clients' altruistic motivations. Yalom (1975) strongly concurs with this approach as he has found altruism to be one of the major curative factors.

The therapeutic benefit of bringing the clients to awareness of their life task is spelled out with clarity in a remark by Nietzsche: "He who has a *why* to live for can bear almost any *how*" (cited in Frankl, 1963, p. xi).

Frankl's own life bears testimony to the truth of Nietzsche's remark. A person with adequate meaning can withstand and even defy the most inhumane conditions imaginable. As mentioned earlier, logotherapy refers to the quality that allows one to defy the seemingly unbearable, as the defiant power of the human spirit. In logotherapy the facts are not so important as the *attitude* taken toward the facts. Included here under the term *facts* are also neurotic symptoms. From a logotherapeutic standpoint the symptoms themselves are not so important as the attitude taken toward the symptoms. It may well be that clients are totally unable by conscious means to alter their symptoms. Despite their inability to change their symptoms, they retain responsibility for their attitude toward the symptoms. This applies even for the psychoses, which Frankl sees as having physiological etiologies. In the arena of attitude one retains the freedom of choice and with the freedom there is, of course, the attendant responsibility.

Weisskopf-Joelson (1980) sees considerable healing benefits in the use of the defiant power of the human spirit, stating, "By far the most healing value proposed by logotherapy is the value of shouldering inescapable suffering courageously" (pp. 5–6).

Sahakian (1980) has shown that logophilosophy, itself, is therapeutic. Fabry (1980), also, considers logophilosophy to have therapeutic benefits, primarily in terms of its protection of the individual against reductionism. That the individual is a battleground for conflicting drives is an accepted reality in logotherapy. That the individual is *nothing but* a battleground for such forces would never be accepted. The notion that the human brain functions like a computer is in no way foreign to logophilosophy. On the other hand, the notion that the individual is *nothing but* a computer is viewed as anathema. Frankl (1978) sees logophilosophy as a means of protecting the individual from the new nihilism of today, the philosophy of "nothingbutness." This philosophy denies us the feelings of inherent dignity that is so necessary in order to withstand such inevitables as guilt, suffering, and death.

Logophilosophy teaches that the acceptance of pain, guilt, and death is a necessary step we all must take. Frankl (1967) states that "The more the neurotic tries to deny them (guilt and death), the more he entangles himself in additional suffering" (p. 88). To prevent further entanglement in this needless suffering, logotherapy advocates confrontation with finality. Frankl (cited in Fabry, 1977), with tongue in cheek, has termed this psychotherapeutic confrontation with death "last-aid." Last-aid is considered an important aspect of the logotherapeutic endeavor. Effective application of last-aid has several valuable outcomes. The acceptance of one's own death can lead to authentic decisions and decisive action in the here and now. It also has the effect of widening one's perspective, helping to differentiate more easily those activities that are relatively meaningless from those that are meaningful.

Frankl has referred to logotherapy as "height" psychology as opposed to psychoanalytic "depth" psychology. Logotherapy is height psychology because it includes in its view the higher aspirations of human beings (such as their will to meaning) rather than reducing them to the merely physiopsychological level. Logotherapy could also be referred to as "width" psychology in that it endeavors to widen the clients' perspective, to broaden their world view.

Another aspect of logophilosophy considered to have therapeutic effects is its emphasis on individual uniqueness. To help clients discover otherwise unseen meanings in their lives, a logotherapist will often draw their attention to certain relationships in which they are irreplaceable. Some critics of logotherapy have pointed out that such interpretations foster grandiosity. There are two replies to this. This interpretation is simply pointing out facts that may have passed out of a depressed client's awareness. Another reply to this criticism is that while there might be some danger in overrating humankind, underrating is even more dangerous. Frankl is fond of quoting Goethe's admonition: "If we take man as he is, we make him worse; but if we take him as he should be, we help him become what he can be."

Paradoxical Intention

Paradoxical intention is one of the major psychotherapeutic techniques of logotherapy. Here the therapist is called upon actually to *encourage* clients to intensify their neurotic symptoms. The method is called *paradoxical intention* because, if properly applied, the clients will find much to their surprise that if they consciously attempt to manufacture the symptoms, they will be unable to do so.

Frankl practiced paradoxical intention as early as 1929 and published his findings in 1939. Persons with phobias, obsessions, and compulsions have been successfully treated by his technique.

An understanding of paradoxical intention is perhaps best afforded by example. Frankl (1963) reports a case in which he successfully treated a physician who had a phobia about excessive perspiring. Whenever the physician expected that the circumstances for perspiring were present, great beads of perspiration would pop out on him. The harder he tried to stop, the wetter he became! Frankl's advice took the client by surprise. Next time the physician was faced by a situation prompting an outbreak, he was to intend paradoxically to show those around him just how much he *could* perspire. If he had perspired only one quart on the previous occasion, he should really outdo himself and try for 10 quarts! After only one week the physician was able to free himself of a phobia that had a four-year history.

To explain the effectiveness of paradoxical intention, Frankl utilizes the concept of anticipatory anxiety—the anxiety about recurrence of a symptom, The notion that the fear of fear is itself very dangerous is quite ancient, going back as far as Seneca, 2000 years ago. Frankl has observed that anticipatory anxiety precipitates the very condition that is so greatly feared. To neutralize this anticipatory anxiety, he found a sense of humor the most effective tool. As soon as clients can laugh at their symptoms, the anticipatory anxiety is deflated and can no longer precipitate the feared event. As Allport (1950) has written, "The neurotic who learns to laugh at himself may be on the way to self-management, perhaps to cure" (p. 92).

Logotherapy promotes the use of paradoxical intention, moreover, because it engages the person's spiritual dimension, the sense of humor, and the capacity for self-detachment. Self-detachment is understood as the capacity peculiar to humankind that allows individuals to step away from themselves and arbitrarily choose a new attitude toward their symptoms.

Further explanations of the effectiveness of paradoxical intention are to be found in its implicitly antinarcissistic and antiegocentric properties. Both narcissism and egocentrism have been shown to be widely implicated in emotional disorders. As Williams and Patrick (1980) have pointed out, paradoxical intention is pointing the client away from self-adoration by encouraging clients to laugh at their symptoms. It is difficult to imagine an egocentric attitude in a situation with this new perspective entering in and previously unavailable to them. As a result, the old world view is broadened when logotherapy is functioning in "width."

Dereflection

Dereflection is the second major therapeutic technique of logotherapy whereby clients are encouraged to cease focusing on their symptoms and instead to focus on meaning potentials. This technique has been shown to be the therapy of choice in cases where the client is fighting for pleasure but experiencing only frustration (i.e., situations in which the client is hyperintending). With regard to orgasm, for instance, the more a woman focuses on her orgasm, the less likely it is to occur; the same applies in the case of potency in the male.

Again, an example from Frankl's files illustrates the use of dereflection. He reports the case of a 24-year-old woman who came to him complaining of being unable to experience orgasm. Frankl told her that he would not be able to see her for a couple of months but in the meantime she should forget about orgasm entirely and think only of giving pleasure to her husband, seeking to make herself as lovable as possible. The woman returned after a couple of days to report that she had just experienced her very first orgasm!

The explanation of why dereflection works is, again, found in the spiritual realm. As Frankl (1978) points out, clients are able to forget themselves only if they give of themselves. To give of oneself is to engage in self-transcendence, a uniquely human capacity in the realm of spirit.

A further explanation of the effectiveness of dereflection is to be found in its antinarcissistic properties. As Williams and Patrick (1980) have pointed out, the forgetting of oneself is the important ingredient in dereflection, and this is antithetical to narcissism.

THE GROUP PROCESS

Logotherapy was originally conceived as individual therapy, but for 20 years, as group therapy in general became more accepted, logotherapy too has been practiced increasingly in a group setting. That the mechanics of the logotherapeutic group process are perhaps more flexible than in most other approaches lies in the nature of logotherapy. Logotherapy emphasizes the uniqueness of each human being and the unique relationships between counselor and client, or in a group the unique relationships among all participants including the counselor as one of them. These relationships cannot be operated by any kind of "mechanics," which would reduce the participant to a machine that can be manipulated or to an animal that can be trained. Logotherapy must remain a relationship between human beings, creative, imaginative, highly improvisational, but its improvisations are based on the philosophy underlying logotherapy.

To be sure, a certain element of mechanics—concerning selection of members, group composition, size and frequency of meetings—is necessary. These considerations depend on the purpose of the group.

By and large, logogroups serve two different purposes—therapy and problem-solving. Therapeutic groups are those for patients who have been diagnosed as suffering from a mental illness physically or psychologically based. Problem-solving groups are for participants who have no disease but merely a feeling of general uneasiness, doubt, frustration, emptiness, a feeling of being trapped by life, an anxiety about decisions to be made in transition periods of their lives. Included in this group are also people facing unavoidable suffering in the normal crises of life: incurable illness, old age, the death of a significant person, or those who feel anguish or despair.

SELECTION OF GROUP MEMBERS

Since the goal of logotherapy is to help people find focus and direction in their lives, logogroups can be helpful to almost anyone and, properly handled, harmful to no one. Nevertheless, there are considerations as far as the selection of group members is concerned.

One consideration pertains to the distinction between logogroups for the sick and those for participants with human problems. The distinction is not always clear; there is a no-man's-land between the two areas. Some clients could be diagnosed as "sick" or merely as struggling with problems that are, or seem to be, too large to be borne without outside help. Ideally, a psychiatrist would be the one to make the diagnosis and assign the participant to one type of group or the other. This procedure is practical only where the logogroups are held in a clinic or an institution in which a psychiatrist is in charge, or when the patient is referred to a logogroup by a psychiatrist.

In most cases, however, the selection is made by the group leader who generally is a psychologist, a counselor, or a social worker trained in the field of logotherapy. The assignment to one type of group or the other can, by itself, have therapeutic effects. A Catholic nun, for example, who suffered from endogenous depressions suffered less from these somatically caused depressions than from guilt feelings that her faith in God should have been strong enough to overcome her depressions—that she must have done something to deserve this punishment. By assigning her to a group with other endogenously depressed patients she was given the message: your depression is caused by a biological dysfunction, you need not feel responsible for it and therefore need suffer no guilt. Her placement in this setting did not relieve her original endogenous depression but freed her from her additional depression over being depressed. (Frankl speaks of "piggyback depressions," a noëtic depression sitting on top of the somatic one.)

Prospective group members who belong to the no-man's-land between the sick and those merely having human problems will, in turn, gain by being admitted to the problem-solving logogroups. If such persons are assigned to therapy groups for the sick, they will consider themselves sick, intensify their hyperreflection on sickness, and make it more difficult to achieve the first goal of logotherapy: to gain distance from their symptoms.

Instead of saying to themselves: I *am* sick, I *am* depressed, I *am* a failure, they are led to see themselves as persons with many potentials who *have* a symptom, a depression, or failures, but are also persons with the resources of the human spirit to take a stand against these drawbacks. They can rid themselves of what they *have* and stop feeling that they are stuck with what they *are*. Often, assigning clients to logogroups for people who are not sick but "merely" have problems will serve a self-fulfilling purpose: they will no longer consider themselves sick and thereby become healthier.

Most of today's logotherapy groups are problem-solving groups. These groups span a wide range of human problems—career, family, old age, the struggle to find meaning in a chaotic world. In such general groups, participants are accepted who respond to such wordings as "This group is not for the mentally ill but for the mentally searching," or "This group is for those who feel empty, frustrated, trapped, in transition, or in need of direction, purpose."

During the past years, logogroups have been established that concentrate on certain problems mentioned above. Special intergenerational groups have been held and researched in Chicago (Eisenberg, 1980), with members ranging from the upper teens to the eighties. Eisenberg (1979) reports that

> the long-living see themselves in the middle-aged and young group members, evoking powerful memories. . . . They also see their own children and grandchildren in the other two age groups, with forceful reemergence of joys and sorrows, gratifications and guilt feelings. . . . The middle-aged members look, as it were, into a two-way mirror: in one they see themselves in the older members, their own parents, and the parents in themselves; in the other they see themselves in their children and children's children who will be like them. . . . The young experience confrontation with "parents" in a nonthreatening atmosphere of trust and support, with permission and invitation to communicate openly, and voice negative emotions freely.

In the volume *Logotherapy in Action* (Crumbaugh, 1979) several logotherapists discuss group therapy for juvenile delinquents, the aged, addicts, minorities. Elisabeth Lukas has started "dereflective" logogroups, with the purpose of steering the attention of the participants away from their problems and toward goals and commitments. James C. Crumbaugh has for years held logogroups for problem drinkers. Naturally, the selection of members for special type groups has to be geared to their stated purpose.

GROUP COMPOSITION, SIZE, AND SETTING

Except for groups selected for a specific purpose, and even within the special-purpose groups, logogroups will do best with a variety of participants in age, sex, race, social and educational backgrounds. This consideration, too, is in line with the logophilosophy that emphasizes the human spirit where most people are similar because they are human. The physical part is influenced by genes, upbringing, sickness, or injuries; the psychological part with each group member will differ with childhood experiences, past traumas, and conflicts. However, logotherapy is based on the belief that the dimension of spirit contains such universally human resources as the will to meaning, the freedom to make choices (at least in attitude), goal orientation, the capacity for self-transcendence, and self-detachment; the ability to be creative, a sense of humor, and the defiant power of the spirit even, or especially, in people who are handicapped in their physical or psychological dimension.

The universality of the resources of the human spirit becomes evident in a group comprising a variety with their diverse problems and backgrounds. Thus, the lesson of universality of spirit comes across without ever having to be mentioned. By listening to the concerns of others, many participants are surprised that they can identify with so many aspects brought up even though their own situation of age, sex, and background may be different. The unspoken message of the mixed group is that we are all human beings, let's make use of our human resources.

The recommended *size* for problem-solving logogroups is from 8 to 12—large enough to get the benefits of a group interchange, and small enough for each participant to feel the personal impact of the group. Crumbaugh (1973) stated that individuals, to find meaning, must feel that they are *someone*, and that they are *useful*. In a group up to 12, these feelings are fostered.

Logogroups for patients under medical care, and especially those led by psychiatrists, may be smaller, often as small as three or four, if the small framework serves the purpose of the psychiatrist.

The *group setting* will allow the participants as much freedom as is possible within the stated purpose. Private homes are not suited unless the group can function free from all distractions such as telephone, pets, music that is not part of the group process, children or other people whose presence is in any way felt, even if they are not seen. A comfortable seating arrangement on chairs or cushions arranged in a circle is preferable, with the leader as part of the circle. It is advisable to have a kettle on and instant tea and coffee available. Advance agreement on time and place for smoking is also advisable.

FREQUENCY, LENGTH, AND DURATION OF GROUPS

Logogroups concerned with human problems are held as a rule once a week, for 2½ to 3 hours each time, and for eight weeks, but every conceivable variation is possible. Crumbaugh (1980), working with problem drinkers, has found four two-hour sessions a week, for three weeks, most successful. Eisenberg (1980), in her intergenerational groups, met in weekly sessions, 1½ hours long for eight consecutive weeks. Robert Wilson (1985), working with junior high students, supervised teachers meeting with the young people in logogroups for about ½ hour twice a week during one school quarter. Fabry has led an openended group, once a week, each session lasting 2½ hours. Participants can join by committing themselves for at least one month. This commitment can be renewed from month to month. Participants drop out when they feel they do not get what they expected or when they feel that they now have the ability to solve their problems on their own. This group has averaged nine participants. One has remained throughout the entire period and considers himself greatly improved, one dropped out because he did not find the help he was looking for, three moved away, nine "graduated" and most of these keep in contact with the leader or some group members with whom they had formed a friendship. Present group members have been with the group from two to nine months.

Logogroups have also been held as weekend workshops (Friday night, Saturday, and Sunday) or as daylong workshops, lasting about seven hours, with time out for lunch. Such workshops are either demonstrations of what logotherapy can accomplish, or they are supplementations of ongoing weekly sessions. Day-long or weekend groups afford the opportunity to apply the creative methods of logotherapy in depth, such as work with art and music, and list-making, dreams, and fantasies as ways to make conscious the unconscious parts of the human spirit: the repressed meanings, frustrated directions, and ignored values. These long sessions also foster friendships among group members, which is considered a significant part of the process. Weekend sessions, however, are *not* used as "marathons" whose purpose it is to weaken the defenses of the participants so that they will reveal things they otherwise would not have. Marathons are in contradiction to the principle of logotherapy that places free choice and responsibleness at the center of the therapy.

MEDIA EMPLOYED

Because logotherapy is based on the Socratic dialogue (discussed by Frankl, 1967) the most important medium employed is the spoken word. The main purpose of the Socratic dialogue is to help group members make conscious their repressed will to meaning (similar to the way psychoanalysis helps patients make conscious their thwarted psychological drives). According to logotherapeutic beliefs, we all know in our unconscious who we are, who we still can become, and what our meaningful goals are. Just as Socrates believed that the role of the teacher is not to pour information into the students but to help them bring out the knowledge that is already there, so Frankl believes that the role of the logotherapist is not to provide meaning but to make conscious the meanings that clients already hold.

Although the Socratic dialogue is the centerpiece of logotherapy, many media can be applied to help clients get in touch with their noëtic unconscious. Among the supplementary means that have been applied by various logotherapists are list-making, journal writings, drawing, sculpture, dance and movement, logodramas, biofeedback, tapes used in autogenic training, and video feedback. These are supplementary tools which the leaders of logogroups may apply whenever they seem to serve a purpose. These are always applied in accordance with the principles of logotherapy and must not be used in a manipulative manner, which reduces the clients to something lower than their full humanness.

THERAPIST'S ROLE

The most important qualification for logotherapy leaders is their familiarity with the basic principles of this therapy so they can impart and apply them to the group. Some leaders spend the first few minutes of each session in a minilecture of some aspect of logotherapy. Others have no set time for "teaching" but explain certain facets of logotherapy whenever an opportunity presents itself, and rely in general on books on logotherapy the group members are expected to read. Books on logotherapy have been termed "bibliotherapy" because their reading itself provides therapy.

Leaders must also be trained in applying the methods of logotherapy, especially the Socratic dialogue, paradoxical intention, and dereflection. They must also be familiar with a variety of supplementary methods they can apply by improvisation when they seem to serve a purpose.

Although leaders of logogroups must be superior in knowledge to the other group members on principles and methods, they must be equals on the human level. They must participate fully in the discussions, relate incidents from their lives, illustrate a point at hand, and share their problems. They must act as role models for the other members of the group. Logoleaders will be most successful in being genuine, caring human beings struggling with the problems of life as everyone else but who have found a philosophy that has helped them and that they are willing to share with the group members.

Robert Leslie, professor of pastoral counseling at the Pacific School of Religion in Berkeley, and a student of Frankl, sees the following functions of a logoleader:

> *Structuring:* Starting and ending at the appointed time, providing support for each person's contribution, protecting members against destructive attack.

Mirroring: Making observations about what is happening, observing incongruities between words and actions, pointing out behavior patterns.

Focusing: Helping the group move from social chitchat into greater depth, from impersonal, peripheral issues to personal involvement in significant concerns.

Modeling: Actively participating as one of the group, according to the agreed rules.

Nudging: Encouraging participants toward change: "Where do you go from here? What are you going to do about it?"

Linking: Tying together disconnected statements, picking up unfinished business.

Sharing: Not only participating in the group process but also allowing members to participate in leadership.

These functions may seem similar to those of other groups, especially those of existential or humanistic hue. But logotherapy group leaders have an additional function, in challenging a person from where he or she is to where he or she wants to be, to see the learning opportunity behind a failure, to spot the growing edge of a crisis, to divine meaning possibilities behind frustrations, to be aware of the escape hatches of traps, the chance to reach out beyond the present limitations toward a vision yet unrealized.

Perhaps the most important function of the logoleader is to be aware of the unconscious decisions that become apparent during the group discussion, even though they may not be apparent to the person concerned. Some word, some gesture, some cue may give an indication of a decision that has taken place in the unconscious—a "logohook" on which the principles of logotherapy can be attached. The leader is not authorized to "give" meaning to the participants but once a logohook has become visible, the leader is justified to throw his or her support behind it, to say "yes" to a direction the group member has chosen, however tentatively and unconsciously. The leader will not automatically say "yes" to all the decisions of individual members. He or she will say "no" to decisions that are reductionistic (reducing the person below his or her humanness), pandeterministic (expressing the belief that one's actions are completely determined by forces beyond one's control), or nihilistic (denying that meaning can be found).

A final role of the leader is assistance in the establishment of group norms that are consistent with logophilosophy. Listed below are some of the more important norms and some suggestions as to how such norms can be promoted.

1. Norm of assuming responsibility for one's attitude toward unavoidable circumstances. The leader's modeling of this norm is

highly desirable, if not essential. To promote this norm, it should be made clear to all that they have the right to gently confront those who may wish to deny that choice exists in the realm of attitude.

2. Norm of self-transcendence. Self-transcendent behavior, especially when evidenced in the group, should be generously rewarded. Further reinforcement of this norm can be obtained by soliciting testimonials of the benefit derived from this behavior.

3. Norm of challenging those who systematically evade making choices. When it becomes obvious that a group member is attempting to keep all of his or her options open in order to avoid decisive choice, the right to challenge this person on this issue should be clear.

4. Norm of disdain for reductionism, pandeterminism, and nihilism. Comments or interpretations that smack of these "isms" should be challenged.

5. Norm of opposing hyperreflection. Catharsis is highly desirable. However, if the focus on one particular problem becomes inordinate (in the subjective judgment of the leader), the group should be encouraged to move on to another issue, perhaps treating the hyperreflected issue via paradoxical intention before doing so.

GROUND RULES

Leslie (1971) outlined the following general guidelines for logogroups which, with variations, have been tested under differing conditions:

Each group member accepts responsibility for the group life. Group members are encouraged to participate, interact, not wait for the group leader to straighten out difficulties as they arise. Perhaps the one major rule that should be stressed from the beginning is: You always have the right to refuse to answer a question or decline to discuss a certain subject until you are ready, but if you speak, be honest.

Communication is sought on a deeper than socializing level. Participants are challenged to remain on a personal level. When quoting books, referring to television programs, or relating the experiences of others, they are questioned as to how they personally relate to the quoted passages or stories.

Group members are to make the present situation the focus of their attention, without ignoring the past. They learn not to use the past as an excuse for present failure but as a challenge to learn from mistakes as well as achievements from the past.

The emphasis is on personal sharing, not on diagnostic probing. Participants are not here to solve each other's problems but offer illustrations from their own life experiences in which *they* solved similar problems for themselves. Any suggestion of how someone else can solve his or her problem is likely to arouse a "yes but" reaction. Participants are advised to remain in the area where they are the greatest expert: the area of their own feelings and experiences.

Observations are welcome but attacks are discouraged. Instead of saying, "You have a very annoying way of interrupting me," the annoyed person can put it this way: "I find myself getting annoyed whenever I am interrupted."

REFERENCES

Allport, G. W. (1950). *The individual and his religion.* New York: Macmillan.
Allport, G. W. (1956). *The participant citizen.* Durban: Natal Technical College.
Allport, G. W. (1962). Psychological models for guidance. *Harvard Educational Review, 32,* 373.
Breisach, E. (1962). *Introduction to modern existentialism.* New York: Grove Press.
Cousins, N. (1979). *Anatomy of an illness as perceived by the patient.* New York: Norton.
Crumbaugh, J. C. (1973). *Everything to gain: A guide to self-fulfillment through logoanalysis.* Chicago: Nelson Hall.
Crumbaugh, J. C. (1979). Exercises of logoanalysis. In J. B. Fabry (Ed.), *Logotherapy in action.* (pp. 151–160.) New York: Aronson.
Eisenberg, M. (1979). The logotherapeutic intergenerational communication group. *The International Forum for Logotherapy, 2,* 23–25.
Eisenberg, M. (1980). Logotherapy and the college student. *The International Forum for Logotherapy, 3,* 22–24.
Fabry, J. B. (Ed.). (1977). Victor Frankl—Festival of meaning. *Uniquest* (Berkeley), *7,* 1–44.
Fabry, J. B. (1980). *The pursuit of meaning: Viktor Frankl, logotherapy, and life.* San Francisco: Harper and Row.
Frankl, V. E. (1955). *The doctor and the soul: From psychotherapy to logotherapy.* New York: Random House.
Frankl, V. E. (1963). *Man's search for meaning.* New York: Simon and Schuster.
Frankl, V. E. (1967). *Psychotherapy and existentialism: Selected papers on logotherapy.* New York: Simon and Schuster.
Frankl, V. E. (1975). *The unconscious god: Psychotherapy and theology.* New York: Simon and Schuster.
Frankl, V. E. (1978). *The unheard cry for meaning: Psychotherapy and humanism.* New York: Simon and Schuster.
Jaspers. K. (1932). *Philosophie.* Berlin: Springer.
Kaufman, W. (1976). *Existentialism, religion and death.* New York: New American Library.
Laughlin, H. P. (1967). *The neuroses.* Washington: Buttersorths.
Leslie, R. C. (1971). *Sharing groups in the church.* Nashville: Abingdon Press.
Sahakian, W. S. (1980). Philosophical therapy: A variation on logotherapy. *The International Forum for Logotherapy, 3,* 37–40.

Salzman, L. (1968). *The obsessive personality: Origins, dynamics, and therapy.* New York: Science House.

Sartre, J. P. (1957). *Existentialism and human emotion.* New York: Philosophical Library.

Shapiro, D. (1965). *Neurotic styles.* New York: Basic Books.

Ungersma, A. J. (1961). *The search for meaning: A new approach in psychotherapy and pastoral psychology.* Philadelphia: Westmoreland Library.

Weisskopf-Joelson, E. (1980). The place of logotherapy in the world today. *The International Forum for Logotherapy, 3,* 41–43.

Williams, D. A., & Patrick, S. (1980). A new remedy for narcissism. *The International Forum for Logotherapy, 3,* 41–43

Wilson R. J. (1985). *Modal salient beliefs towards environmental action strategies of groups displaying differing levels of action behavior.* (Doctoral dissertation. Southern Illinois University at Carbondale). *Dissertation Abstracts International, 46,* 3312A.

Yalom, I. D. (1975). *The theory and practice of group psychotherapy.* New York: Basic Books.

SUGGESTED READINGS

Crumbaugh, J. C. (1973). *Everything to gain: A guide to self-fulfillment through logoanalysis.* Chicago: Nelson Hall.

Fabry, J. B. (1980). *The pursuit of meaning: Victor Frankl, logotherapy, and life.* San Francisco: Harper and Row.

Fabry, J. B., Bulka, R. P., & Sahakian, W. S. (1979). *Logotherapy in action.* New York: Aronson.

Frankl, V. E. (1955). *The doctor and the soul: From psychotherapy to logotherapy.* New York: Random House.

Frankl, V. E. (1963). *Man's search for meaning.* New York: Simon and Schuster.

Frankl, V. E. (1967). *Psychotherapy and existentialism: Selected papers on logotherapy.* New York: Simon and Schuster.

Frankl, V. E. (1975). *The unconscious god: Psychotherapy and theology.* New York: Simon and Schuster.

Frankl, V. E. (1978). *The unheard cry for meaning: Psychotherapy and humanism.* New York: Simon and Schuster.

C H A P T E R   16

Person-Centered
Group Therapy[1]

INTRODUCTION

On the 11th of December, 1940, in a speech at the University of Minnesota, Carl Rogers aroused a furor among scholars and mental health professionals by sketching a radically different therapeutic approach. He tentatively outlined *Newer Concepts in Psychotherapy*, which rely "much more heavily on the individual drive toward growth, health, and adjustment." Therapy becomes "a matter of freeing (the client) for normal growth and development." This new approach, Rogers announced, "places greater stress upon . . . the feeling aspects of the situation than upon the intellectual aspects." It stresses "the immediate situation" rather than "the individual's past," emphasizing "the therapeutic relationship itself as a growth experience" (Rogers, 1974, p. 8). In the next 20 years, through empirical studies, the conditions for realizing the ambitions of this "newer therapy" were meticulously formulated in theory and practice. Client-centered therapy is still dedicated to discovering the conditions that favor the activation of healing and growth within the person.

In the 1970s the term *person-centered* won favor over *client-centered*. The term is used to reflect the therapist's attitude toward the person. The therapist does not see a *patient* who is sick, nor a *client* who is a customer.

---

1. Abstracted from Wood, J. K. (1982). Person-centered group therapy. In G. M. Gazda (Ed.), *Basic approaches to group psychotherapy and group counseling* (pp. 235–275). Springfield, IL: Charles C. Thomas.

The therapist centers attention not on a theory, nor on himself or herself, but on the other, the *whole person*.

The "small" person-centered therapy group consisting of 8 to 12 persons with one or two therapists revolutionized the practice of psychotherapy. With the advent of the encounter group, it was no longer possible to make a sharp distinction between "therapy" and "growth." In 1968 the La Jolla Program (an institute of the Center for Studies of the Person) began an education program for group facilitators featuring brief groups of 50 to 100 persons. In 1973 Rogers and other colleagues initiated a new form of person-centered group work: more than 100 persons live together for about two weeks in a group-directed *community for learning*; their only planned activity, besides meals, is to gather in one large meeting where all plans and decisions of the group are made. Person-centered approach workshops have been convened in North and South America, Asia, and Europe.

This person-centered approach to group psychotherapy (though not denying disorder) relies on the natural ordering tendencies of life. The approach respects mystery while it yearns for knowing. Ambitiously searching, reaching deeply into speculations and theories, straining for a wisdom just beyond conscious awareness, it continues to return to essential life processes for perspective. Person-centered group therapy recognizes not a theory but the "unique, subjective, inner person as the honored and valued core of human life" (Rogers, 1974, p. 9).

THEORETICAL FOUNDATIONS

The theoretical foundation of *person-centered group therapy* is emerging from practice, research, and from theory of client-centered individual therapy. Client-centered therapy grew out of continuing work with persons in psychotherapy. Feedback from research, itself stimulated from hypotheses and speculations springing from experience, revised and sharpened both the approach to therapy and the concepts used to formulate a theory. Refinements in practice led to new statements and suggested new research avenues. Presented here is material from which new formulations of theory are emerging.

It will be convenient for this discussion to think of individual therapy— one therapist with one client—as a group of two persons. A theoretical statement will then be formulated that applies to two classes of events: the two-person group, the small group (up to 20 persons).

Two-Person Group

By the early 1960s, a theory was well established on one fundamental axiom, a view of human nature that emerged from practical experience.

This axiom (a corollary of the formative tendency) states that *each person is capable of experiencing the incongruence between the self-concept and his or her total organismic reality; also within the person is a natural tendency to reorganize the self-concept to a closer congruence with the totality of experience.*

This natural tendency has no form and may take many forms. For one person, moving toward becoming the totality of his or her experience might mean changing a relationship partner or a career; for another it might mean living more committedly in the present life-style. One person may work harder for material advancement or increase responsibilities; another may reduce responsibilities or minimize efforts to earn more, following simpler pursuits. One is more expressive, another more receptive.

What conditions do not impede, perhaps even encourage, this actualizing tendency? Nearly half a century of groping experience and painstaking research have concentrated on this question.

For answers, person-centered therapists and researchers sifted for clues in the delicacies of the interaction between persons. By studying the quality and tone of voice, verbal behavior, posture, and gestures, researchers were able to assess the accurate and sensitive empathy of the therapist in his or her relation with the client. Similarly, researchers assessed the warmth and unconditionality of positive regard toward the client, and the match between the experience going on within the therapist and his or her outward behavior. The client's perceptions of these qualities in the therapist were assessed by self-report. It was found that when these four qualities were present in the therapist, and perceived by the client, the client was more likely to move away from "oughts," pleasing or meeting the expectations of others, and toward self-direction and complexity, openness to and trusting experience, and more acceptance of others.

Entering the 1960s the main theorem of the theory of person-centered (group) therapy was formulated: *The inherent healing capacities and the actualizing tendency are released in an interpersonal relation where the therapist is congruent in the relationship, is experiencing unconditional positive regard toward the client, and is experiencing an empathic understanding of the client's internal frame of reference, and when the client perceives, at least minimally, the unconditional positive regard and the empathic understanding of the therapist for him or her* (see Rogers, 1959).

Small Groups

The person-centered psychotherapy group (Coulson, 1970, 1972; Rogers, 1970) consisting of 8 to 12 persons and a therapist is not just a bigger version of the two-person group; it must be understood and studied on its own natural terms. The small group possesses all the capacities for healing and self-knowing as the dyadic situation as well as other significant features.

Direct interactions between the therapist and client are less frequent and appear less important in the small group than in dyadic therapy. Another group member may be even more facilitative than the therapist in a given instance. Sometimes a person, sitting silently, not directly involved in the interaction, is profoundly affected. As the individual grows in awareness, working consciously with the natural inner wisdom, the formative tendency also is operating in the collection of individuals. Occasionally, from the chaos a wisdom unexpectedly arises to provide solutions to "unsolvable" problems. Of course, at times the group must endure the frustration of no solution. In other instances, with no solution articulated, the group acts as one body on a felt sense of purpose and direction.

In the small group the therapist is also required to give up his or her professional role and the security, respect, and whatever helpfulness might be achieved from a position of authority. The therapist's name is changed to *facilitator*, reflecting the importance of interactions between group members and allowing greater genuineness in all group relationships. Though speaking is not required, participants in the group insist on honest, feelingful (verbal or nonverbal) expression from all members, including the designated facilitator.

To enter the personal world of the individual client, the therapist had to surrender fixed concepts of "the" world. To appreciate and follow the person's experiencing, without forcing change, the therapist had to surrender reliance on theories or opinions of how things "should" be for how things really *are* for the client. Of the small group facilitator even further surrendering is required. The group expands personal exploration to here-and-now "real life" relationships. The group setting includes self-knowing, healing, and a social therapeutic aspect—understanding of others and improving effective communications with others—as potential benefits. The small group facilitator must be fluent in the moment-to-moment action of persons in relationship without resorting to speculations and explanations of process.

The skillful group facilitator begins to surrender to his or her own personal experiencing as well, opening to feeling and discovering unexpected aspects of himself or herself as part of new learnings in the relationship with the group and its members.

With changing persons and changing societies, with what was once possibility now reality, and with new possibilities for human development, new therapeutic forms continue to emerge. Likewise, the consciousness of the therapist has been required to grow over the years; over time we see the effect of the formative tendency on the lives of therapists as well as clients.

Figure 16–1 illustrates some trends in person-centered group development. It can be seen that each level of group work requires more of the therapist/facilitator/convenor. The pattern of consciousness developing in

TRENDS IN HALF CENTURY OF PERSON-CENTERED THERAPY

Year	Location	Method	Group	Role	Description
1935	Rochester (New York)			Patient (Therapist)	Surrender of role of expert.
1940	Ohio (State)	Nondirection (two-person)			Take guidance from client.
1945			Two-person group: Psychotherapy		Relationship more personal.
1950				Client (Facilitator)	Surrender of rigid theories.
1955	(Chicago) Illinois				
1960		Reflection (two-person)			Trust in own feelings.
	Wisconsin		Small group: Psychotherapy & social therapy		Congruent with own experience.
1965		Experiencing (two-person) (applications)			Therapist experience enters relation.
1970		Encounter (small group)			Surrender control of intellect.
1975	California (Center for Studies of the Person)		Large group: Psychotherapy, social therapy & create, heal & surpass culture	Person (Convenor)	Trust more intuitive processes.
1980		Community for Learning (large group)			Surrender theories to rely on experience.
					Greater trust in group for organic decisions, self-knowing beyond the personal.
					Surrender to being more than doing.
	Rogers moves west—organizing radius expands	Increased involvement of therapist as a genuine person with larger numbers of persons—closer to "real" life	Increased complexity of therapeutic effort	"Other" viewed more holistically	Therapist's deepening surrender to increased complexity

Figure 16–1   Trends in person-centered group development.

the convenor seems to be a deepening of the surrender of roles, even "helping," of fixed concepts of the world, or reliance on only rational thought, of knowledge from previous experiences, of reliance on spoken information, to trusting more the creative tendencies of life, trusting more completely the whole organism—reason, intuition, feelings, the body—as a source of guidance. The historical pattern of consciousness reflects a "letting go" of possibilities to make way for the emergence of "impossibilities." The increasing complexity of this approach to group therapy demands, of the convenor, a greater openness to live in the freshness and surprise of the moment, awakened and changed by that living.

A Current Theoretical Statement

The accumulation of clinical experiences in small and large groups and findings from research of one-to-one therapy suggest the need for a generalized theoretical formulation. Running through the development of person-centered group therapy from the beginning has been an increasing willingness (without denying the destructive forces of life) to trust and follow formative events in others, in oneself, and in groups of persons. The formative tendency may be seen moving forward the experiencing of a client in the presence of another who is perceived as empathic, genuine, and warm. It can be seen in the process of the small group where the formative tendency sharpens and obscures outlines of individuality and reorganizes the collection into a new complexity. It can be seen in the larger group or community in organic decisions that surpass the group's rational abilities, moving madness toward health, even surpassing the organization of culture itself. In each of these forms we see a tendency operating within to awaken the person to a consciousness of his or her own evolution. Surviving the changing forms of therapy over the years there remains in the person-centered "therapist" an inner constancy: the desire to be engaged (in a facilitative way) in the "client's" struggle for liberation *and* the willingness to be changed by his or her own experiencing in the relationship with the "client."

A current theoretical statement that takes into account years of research and clinical observations in two-person groups, small groups, and large groups may now be formulated.

The foundation of the theory of person-centered group therapy is the formative tendency of the universe. The fundamental theorem of this theory may be stated: *When persons (some called, at times, therapist, facilitator, convenor and some called client, group member, participant) bring a certain readiness to their meeting the formative tendency is allowed to reorganize more complex capacities and perceptions within the individuals and within the collective.*

The *readiness* in the person called therapist is characterized by the ability to translate easily between feelings and ideas, to be congruent in the relationship with others, to experience unconditional positive regard toward others, and to experience an empathic understanding of the others' internal frame of reference and to follow it intuitively without necessarily "understanding." It is further characterized by the capability of living in the moment, in uncertainty and even doubt, to follow intuitively the expressions of the "collective organism," with every expression to be able to follow, to lead, to remain still in cooperation with the creativity of the moment's mysterious dictates. This readiness is also characterized by the willingness to trust the formative tendency as it organizes the other person's experiencing. There is a willingness, in this readiness, to be guided and *changed* by the therapist's own inner experiencing in the relationship(s).

In the person called client this *readiness* includes the willingness to be changed by his or her direct experience and to develop the ability to focus within his or her inner world and the inner world of others. Thus, this person allows the operation of the actualizing tendency and perceives the other's unconditional positive regard and empathic understanding for him or her.

More *complex capacities and perceptions* include the increased awareness and heightened receptivity of the total organismic reality and reduction of the incongruence between self and experience—becoming a complete person, as an individual and a member of the human species. These capacities may also include self-healing, "psychic" abilities, and "spirituality," as well as "practical" knowledge by which individual and collective human life may benefit.

SELECTION OF GROUP MEMBERS

There are no rules for the selection of group members for a person-centered group. Meetings convened for certain populations, such as women's groups or men's groups, or for specific themes, of course select members accordingly.

Generally speaking the person's readiness and his or her own choice are the primary factors in group membership. The congruence between the person's goal in attending and what the convenor believes is possible to achieve from attending the group is assessed by the prospective participant and convenor. Together they decide. The person with realistic expectations who believes he or she may benefit from the group experience and will be able to contribute to the group process is usually accepted. In ongoing therapy the group members are usually consulted before admitting a new member.

GROUP COMPOSITION

Doubtless, the attitudes and skills of the facilitator, the attitudes and learning capacities of group members, conditions of the environment, the composition of persons, and the interaction generated all influence the outcome, for better or worse, of group therapy. It is not known, at present, just what the composition of group members should be for optimum results. Probably, just as a good soup contains surprising and (when taken alone) irritating ingredients, the best composition would follow a "taste" for the benefits of the experience rather than logic.

It is customary for group convenors to attempt, if possible, a balance between male and female, old and young, in the composition of groups. In large residential programs, the many small groups are balanced "geographically" as well. Of course, if certain persons, such as married couples, wish to be together or separate, their wishes are respected. In support of this diverse composition for groups, Bruce Meador (1980), one of the directors of the La Jolla Program, says, "We don't feel we are playing god by composing groups as much as possible like the world." Having member whose personal experiences are very different is also thought to increase the creative possibilities of the group in releasing the formative tendency and enriching each person's learning.

GROUP SIZE

The customary size for the intensive small person-centered group is between 8 and 12 persons.

In recent years there has been a definite trend toward development of a form of larger person-centered group. The La Jolla Program conducts daily meetings consisting of from 50 to 150 participants in its facilitator training program. These large group events, which meet for an hour or so in the mornings, have many of the qualities of the small group encounter.

Communities for learning, consisting of from 100 to 250 persons, have been convened in many parts of the world. These programs govern themselves from beginning to end through group-centered processes. Often small group meetings and two-person groups are employed along with other activities.

It was thought from work in dyadic therapy that each person needed individual time for self-explorations; therefore, the ratio of total time for group meetings to individual "air time" dictated the group size. Such a formula is no longer followed. In the larger groups, for example, although relatively few persons are able to speak, benefit may, and often does, come to those who are silent as well. The group size seems not as important as the quality of the therapeutic environment established in the group.

GROUP SETTING

Groups have been convened in a rambling old coffee plantation in Brazil, a resort hotel in the Philippine Islands, a marbled monastery outside of Rome, university courtyard and residence halls, television studios, and countless other settings.

There are probably physical qualities in the environment that foster healing, but they are unknown at this time. Generally, person-centered group meetings are held in an airy, carpeted room with space enough for movement, a comfortable and quiet setting where there will be few interruptions. Every effort is made to create an environment, both physically and psychologically, that will not impede the person's "natural growth."

FREQUENCY, LENGTH, AND DURATION OF GROUP SESSIONS

Ongoing groups customarily meet 3 or 4 hours weekly for an unspecified duration. Participants join and leave the groups at will. In groups with a specified duration, all participants begin together and remain throughout the group. For the weekend group, the meetings are usually held from Friday evening until Sunday afternoon, with time out for meals and sleep. These groups meet a minimum of 16 hours. Communities for learning customarily meet for 10 days to two weeks. In every instance, the group members influence the frequency, length, and duration of group sessions.

MEDIA EMPLOYED

Media are not specified or prohibited from person-centered groups. Traditionally, person-centered therapists have preferred verbal interaction and use no media in their groups. Of course, tape recordings, films, and video tapes have been made of person-centered therapy for research and educational purposes (McGaw, 1968, 1971; McGaw & Rice, 1973).

In this, as in all that happens in the group, it is up to the convenors and the group members; some have used video, art, dance, creative writing, and various nonverbal exercises, among other media, at their own discretion. In the communities for learning, since persons with a wide range of interests and abilities are meeting together, it is likely that all of these media will be employed spontaneously.

THERAPIST'S ROLE

That each participant be provided an opportunity to live consciously in harmony with the wisdom and intentions of the formative tendency, as it creates the human species, is the goal of person-centered group therapy. The person-centered approach trusts the potency of natural life forces and attempts to establish a group climate that does not interfere with their intent.

The role of the facilitator (or therapist) is to be facilitative in the creation of this climate. An ideal atmosphere is one where he or she and each other participant may enter into a creative process, living his or her own complex wholeness, whether the person is in direct interaction with the designated facilitator, another member, or even in silence.

Participants are asked to bring a readiness and reasonable expectations to the meeting of persons in the group. For his or her part, the facilitator is asked to bring, first of all, an *alertness* to each other person, to himself or herself, and to the group as a single entity or process. This alertness includes the sensitivity to who might be the most facilitative person at any time in the group. The facilitator listens sensitively, carefully, and as accurately as possible to each other person and the feelings on the edge of the person's awareness. He or she listens in such a way as to sense the meaning and feelings aroused by the person's expressions (verbally and nonverbally), in the group, and internally. The facilitator accompanies the person, sifting through complications (in the person or within the group), keeping the communication on the track of the significance it has for the person. The goal of this listening is not just to "get in touch with feelings," it is to follow the person's discovery of the moment's rich labyrinth of experiencing and to facilitate the expression of one grand unclear internal "this" in a present meaning.

Do anything you want, Gendlin (1974) advises facilitators, as long as you "stay in touch at all times with the person's directly felt concrete experiential datum—and help the person also to stay in touch with that, and get into it. (If doing that is the baseline, every other procedure and idea can also be tried out, and one returns quickly again to finding out, listening, and responding to where it leaves the person)" (p. 220).

Although, through directing attention to one's inner self, a person may become more self-centered, it is not the purpose of group therapy to bring about a self-preoccupation. The climate of the group is intended to allow the participant to focus inwardly, not to the exclusion of effective life in the world but solely to contact and unite with the formative tendency.

The facilitator is asked to bring to the meeting not an obligation but a *willingness* to live within a creative environment the group may construct together (at times in ways he or she would not be able to predict or perhaps even understand). Though not blindly acceptant, he or she is asked to trust the group and be willing to "live" the theory, doing what is implicitly demanded of other participants.

The facilitator, cooperating with the inner forces of his or her own actualization, listens within with the same sensitivity and alertness he or she affords others. From the facilitator's point of view, the attention paid toward himself or herself, toward another person in the group, or to the "mood" or "climate" of the group is more of an a-tension, a melting of tension, of role, analysis, or evaluative capacities in favor of an intuitive following of his or her inner world, the other's inner world, and the organic wisdom of the group. The facilitator's *willingness* to be changed by the experience characterizes, and perhaps distinguishes, this approach from other approaches to group therapy.

The facilitator trusts his or her own total organism: body, sensations, emotions, reasoning, and intuitive faculties, to live in the moment, to be guided by new principles developed out of increased awareness. The other group members will come to know who the facilitator genuinely is and what he or she is feeling. They know that the facilitator will respond to the moment, not from learned techniques, even if that means saying or doing something risky, unpopular, or even "untherapeutic." Although he or she will not impede the process with personal problems, the character of the group will be influenced by the *person* of the facilitator as much as by the individuality of the group members, to the extent that he or she feels comfortable, just as the others.

Finally, the facilitator is asked to bring an attitude of nonevaluative caring for the group members. This attitude grows out of the trust in the individual's capacity to know himself or herself and find the pace and direction of personal change. This kind of acceptance applies to the group as well and the ability of a group of persons together to mobilize a healing capability. Of this trust, Rogers (1970) says:

> I trust the group, given a reasonably facilitating climate, to develop its own potential and that of its members. For me this capacity of the group is an awesome thing. . . . This is undoubtedly similar to the trust I came to have in the process of therapy in the individual, when it was facilitated rather than directed. To me the group seems like an organism, having a sense of its own direction even though it could not define the direction intellectually. . . . I have seen the "wisdom of the organism" exhibited at every level from cell to group. (P. 44)

Each group—the collection of unique individuals, at a particular time, in a particular setting—is approached by the facilitator on its own terms. Not suffocating everyone with a single approach, he or she attempts to understand and (within the limits of existing conditions) operate within the group on its own terms. The facilitator interacts with each other member in an authentic way and keeps in consciousness the whole, paying attention to the overall "music" of the group.

The best facilitator is not, necessarily, the one with the most training or the one with the most credentials. In one encounter group project (Bebout, 1976), for example, four out of five professionally trained therapists were not acceptable as group leaders. The best group facilitators are the ones who facilitate best.

The facilitator is not *trying* to be the best or even, strictly speaking, trying to be empathic, or genuine, or nonpossessively warm. He or she simply brings these capacities to the meeting. The designated person does not decide in advance to direct the person or the group in a particular way, as this is not of the creativity of life. The designated facilitator, likewise, does not decide in advance to be nondirective, or unstructured, as this does not come from the creativity of the moment either. The facilitator surrenders impatience and easy answers for a creative state of waiting—alert to follow *or* to lead. He or she is willing to live unattached to a particular form of outcome, to be surprised by the unique creation of each group of persons. Like Keats's (1899) Shakespeare he or she possesses a *"negative capability . . . capable of being in uncertainties, mysteries, doubts, without any irritable reaching after fact and reason"* (p. 277).

Success is not marked by how well the facilitator shines in presenting the cardinal attitudes but in how well the group's creative, growthful wisdom is released and the benefits of growth afforded its members. If the group can create a facilitative climate, the formative tendency will do the rest. Members will move from being remote or unaware of feelings toward acknowledging and expressing feelings as they change and flow inside; from remoteness from inner experiencing toward trusting and using inner experiencing as a referent for behavior; from dogmatism to flexibility of constructs; from finding the cause of problems "out there" to owning part in creating problems; from fearful, hesitant, closed relationships with others to more open, expressive, personal relationships; from separateness to a oneness in feeling, cooperation, and creative problem solving.

GROUND RULES

There are no stated ground rules for person-centered groups. When persons meet together, bringing a readiness for growth, they formulate together the rules for their own meetings. Each group is unique, and explicit and implicit agreements vary widely. Generally speaking, the groups usually prohibit physical violence, they adopt policies around meeting times, the admittance of new members, and a procedure for terminating the group. Group members usually feel they owe each other an explanation for any behavior outside of the meetings that affects the group.

Although arrived at by exhausting consideration of everyone's feelings and opinions, these policies change frequently.

Often the group will insist that each member attend each complete meeting of the group. This rule varies widely, depending on the culture. In Brazil, for example, it is not uncommon for a person to join a group in the middle of a session, become intensely involved, and leave before the conclusion of the meeting. In many parts of North America, on the other hand, this behavior would not be tolerated by the group.

Of course, the norms established by low-structure events can become a set of ground rules to the uninitiated. Expressions of feelings, being "real," closeness, not accepting authority outside of oneself are examples of behaviors that may become "rules" followed by the group. These implicit agreements vary not only with the culture but change from time to time within a culture, being modified from generation to generation and according to popular social movements of the era and the amount of experience the members possess in group processes.

REFERENCES

Bebout, J. (1976). Basic encounter groups: Their nature, method, and brief history. In H. Mullan & M. Rosenbaum (Eds.), *Group psychotherapy: Theory and practice.* New York: Macmillan.

Coulson, W. R. (1970). Major contribution: Inside a basic encounter group. *The Counseling Psychologist, 2,* 1–34.

Coulson, W. R. (1972). *Groups, gimmicks and instant gurus.* New York: Harper & Row.

Gendlin, E. T. (1974). Client-centered and experiential psychotherapy. In D. A. Wexler & L. N. Rice (Eds.), *Innovations in client-centered therapy.* New York: John Wiley & Sons.

Keats, J. (1889). *The complete poetical works of Keats.* Boston: Houghton Mifflin.

McGaw, W. H., Jr. (Producer). (1968). *Journey into self* (documentary film). La Jolla, Calif.: Western Behavioral Science Institute, 1150 Silverado, La Jolla, CA, 92037.

McGaw, W. H., Jr. (Producer). (1971). *Because that's my way* (documentary film). Pittsburgh: WOED National Educational Television, G.P.N. Films, Box 80669, Lincoln, Neb., 68501.

McGaw, W. H., & Rice, C. P. (Producers). (1973). *The steel shutter* (documentary film). La Jolla, CA: Center for Studies of the Person, 1125 Torrey Pines Rd., La Jolla, CA, 92037.

Meador, B. S. Personal communication, June 29, 1980.

Rogers, C. R. (1959). A theory of therapy, personality, and interpersonal relationships, as developed in the client-centered framework. In S. Koch (Ed.), *Psychology: A study of science* (Vol. 3, *Formulations of the person and the social context*). New York: McGraw-Hill.

Rogers, C. R. (1970). *On encounter groups.* New York: Harper & Row.

Rogers, C. R., & Wood, J. K. (1974). Client-centered theory. In A. Burton (Ed.), *Operational theories of personality.* New York: Brunner/Mazel.

SUGGESTED READINGS

Bowen, M., Miller, M., Rogers, C. R., & Wood, J. K. (1979). Learnings in large groups: Their implications for the future. *Education, 100* (2), 108–116.

Bozarth, J. D. (1981). Large group therapy via the community group. In G. Gazda (Ed.), *Innovations to group psychotherapy* (2nd ed.). Springfield, IL: Charles C. Thomas.

Frank, J. D. (1961). *Persuasion and healing: A comparative study of psychotherapy*. Baltimore: John Hopkins Press.

Gendlin, E. T. (1978). *Focusing*. New York: Everest Hourse.

Gendlin, E. T., Beebe, J., Cassens, J., Klein, M., & Oberland, M. (1968). Focusing ability in psychotherapy, personality, and creativity. In J. M. Schlein (Ed.), *Research in psychotherapy*. (Vol. 3). Washington, D.C.: APA.

Rogers, C. R. (1961). *On becoming a person*. Boston: Hougton Mifflin.

Rogers, C. R. (1979). The foundations of the person-centered approach. *Education, 100*(2), 98–107.

C H A P T E R 17

Teleoanalytic (Adlerian) Group Counseling[1]

INTRODUCTION

The group approach pursued by the writers has been called adlerian psychology, individual psychology, and the teleoanalytic approach. Alfred Adler was one of the first, if not the first, to use group approaches and as far as can be determined, the first to use group methods in a school setting, counseling parents and children before groups of teachers in the schools of Vienna. The psychological formulation, which Adler called *individual psychology* to denote the holistic concept of the human organism, resides in the philosophic belief that understanding human behavior necessitates understanding the entire field in which the individual operates.

Individual psychology, therefore, indicates a socioteleological approach to the understanding of human motivation. In this context, all people are perceived as social beings, and behavior is viewed as goal directed and purposeful (Dreikurs, 1957).

THEORETICAL FORMULATIONS

Before proceeding to a discussion of group counseling, it seems appropriate first to describe the teleoanalytic approach to counseling in general. The

1. Abstracted from Sonstegard, M., Dreikurs, R., & Bitter, J. (1982). The teleoanalytic group counseling approach. In G. M. Gazda (Ed.), *Basic approaches to group psychotherapy and group counseling* (pp. 507–551). Springfield, IL: Charles C. Thomas.

technique of counseling or psychotherapy practiced by teleoanalytic psychologists can be described as an uncovering and interpreting form of therapy with a characteristic method of exploration, interpretation, and guidance. Like any specific approach to counseling, it has its own theoretical framework.

Humans, in this theoretical framework, are perceived as social beings for whom every action has a purpose. The holistic view of humanity is reflected in the name *individual psychology*. It was meant to indicate the indivisibility of the person, who is more than the sum total of all physical, mental, and emotional processes and functions. In contrast to prevalent mechanistic, deterministic theories, Adler recognized creative ability through which individuals set their own goals and determine their own movements, expressing the total personality, past experiences, present attitudes, and ideas about one's future. The teleological concept implies self-determination. It does not matter whether the individual is aware of his or her decisions. Consciousness is not required for most functions, whether they are physical or psychological. Humans operate on an economy principle; they are consciously aware only of what they need or what they want to know. All abilities and faculties are in the service of personal intentions. The mind and body, the ability to think and feel, are available without the requirement of consciousness, which often would impede rather than assist the individual.

Human beings are primarily motivated by a strong desire to belong. Only within the group can individuals fulfill the potentialities that they possess. All human qualities are then conceived as expressions of social interaction; they indicate movement toward others. Social interest, a feeling of belonging, permits and stimulates full social interaction; it is restricted by feelings of inferiority. When individuals feel inadequate or inferior to others, they doubt their place in the group. Then, instead of moving toward participation, they defend themselves against social demands. Maladjustments and dysfunction result from partial or total discouragement. Manifest symptoms of maladjustment are safeguards. They ensure against loss of prestige and against open admission of antisocial or asocial intentions.

Self-deception about one's intentions is part of normal human experience. We cannot know ourselves; we can never be sure of our motives or our intentions. We need subjectivity to participate in social living. We need a biased apperception to move forcefully in a self-chosen direction. Our whole personality is based on a subjective interpretation of life, developed during our formative years. Personality is the result of training and growth that is less stimulated by heredity and environment than by the child's own interpretation, conclusions, and decisions. The individual's basic concept of self and life, a personal orientation toward social participation, forms a fixed pattern: the life-style or the personality. Fundamental notions, convictions, and logical assumptions underline the life-style and form the "private logic" on which the individual operates.

Making group counseling an effective therapeutic agent depends to a certain extent upon the theoretical formulation of the counselor. From the teleoanalytic point of view, an improvement of group members depends upon reorientation and a better understanding of the principles of social living and cooperation. Of primary importance is the modification of one's mistaken motivation, the mistaken notions that each person develops and maintains. The reorientation means a change in the group member's attitude toward a present life situation and problems. This reorientation is an educational experience, a *re*education and a *re*learning.

Group counseling is learning. If learning is to take place, there must be action; group participation is the action that is necessary. Without participation by members, no therapy can result. The participation can be of nonverbal as well as a verbal nature. Even though a member of the group merely listens without comment, that person may go away with some clarification of a problem. Witnessing disclosures made in a group and hearing the group assessment or "feedback," guided and stimulated by the counselor, can supply the listener with new insights. While participation is necessary, verbal expression is never forced or required from a group member.

Group techniques are more imperative in a democratic society where the authority of the individual has been replaced by the authority of the group. Society puts a premium upon prestige, while the group minimizes its significance. The group attempts to eliminate vanity and anxiety about status; it helps to free the group member from the vertical movement of personal glory by which a person constantly measures him- or herself against others. In this way, group counseling attempts to replace detrimental social values. This again characterizes group counseling as primarily an educational process, promoting new values.

Group counseling must have structure. This is easily discernible in individual counseling, but less so in the group. Certain dynamics of individual counseling apply also to the group counseling process: (1) establishment and maintenance of proper relationships; (2) examination of the purpose of the group members' actions or behaviors; (3) revealing to the individual the goals being pursued, called *psychological disclosure;* and (4) reorientation and redirection. In contrast to individual counseling, however, certain specific dynamics are essential in group counseling.

Relationship

The counselor becomes established as the group leader, even though a democratic atmosphere must prevail. The effective group counseling relationship is based on mutual respect. This does not mean that group members may do anything they please. Firmness and kindness are necessary in all group counseling.

As perceived by the authors, relationship requires more than a mere establishment of contact and rapport. Winning the client's cooperation for the common task is a prerequisite for counseling, individually or in groups. The group facilitates cooperation. Maintaining it requires constant vigilance.

A sense of social connectedness is naturally fostered through group counseling. Often as an individual listens to someone else discuss a personal problem, some insight or understanding is promoted in the listener, a unique phenomenon of group counseling. A bonding of shared difficulties or shared experiences follows. The group members identify with others and come to understand their feelings and accept their ideas. This encourages participation. Universalization is the cementing element in achieving group cohesiveness.

Assessment

A discovery of the purpose motivating behavior and a sociopsychological understanding of the individual is always the focus of assessment. Teleoanalytic group counselors make use of any number of assessment techniques, most of which were developed as the foundation of individual psychology. Process assessments of group members' family constellation, relational difficulties, early recollections, dreams, and art work produce clues to each individual's life goal and life-style. Each of these techniques reveal the individual member's interpretation of self and life as well as any mistaken notions that may be connected to these interpretations.

Dreikurs (1940) first organized and described the mistaken goals of children. Examining or discovering the child's goals can be done in individual counseling as well as in a group situation. The child's goals and movements, however, become more obvious in interaction with others in the group, in contrast to the limited interaction experienced with the counselor in individual sessions. The counselor no longer depends exclusively on the child's verbal reports of interactions with others; rather, the counselor sees the child in action during the session. Often the child acts differently in a group than when alone with the counselor. Much of the veneer that the child uses to cover up may be stripped away in the group, as the true personality in openly revealed.

Insight

Groups are more effective than individual counseling in helping people to gain insight and redirect their mistaken goals and mistaken notions. Many would not be able to learn about themselves except for the interaction taking place in the group; the sense of social connectedness established within groups helps members see themselves in others. Thus the psychological disclosures and interpretations during the group sessions are not only valuable for the person to whom they are directed but also to other group members who learn from these disclosures. This is especially true of children.

The reactions of the group members make *the* significant difference in the group process of insight and redirection. Group members accept each other more in their redirective efforts, because they feel the equality that exists among them. The counselor will always be able to develop more insight and exert more corrective influence when the active support of the group has been won.

The insight that a counselor helps to develop in the group sessions is not limited to the individual. Very few persons, if any, understand their own behavior. Even though Socrates admonished people to "know thyself" centuries ago, that task is still largely unfulfilled; in reality, it may never be accomplished by any single individual. Yet, people can and will learn about human behavior in general. So it is that children and adults in groups learn something about themselves and even more about humanity in general. Indeed, it is through this understanding of human nature that people begin to understand themselves. Group counseling is (in reality) a learning process. Experience shows that the group enhances learning, and that group counseling as a learning process is enhanced by the group.

Disclosure or insight often becomes an end product in individual counseling as well as in group counseling. Insight, however, is not an end in itself; it is merely a means to an end. It may not be the basis for a change in motivation, but it is always a step in that direction.

Reorientation

The end product is reorientation. Children are helped to redirect their mistaken goals. Adults can learn to give up erroneous concepts of self, life, and dealing with others. Parents and teachers often give up mistaken practices and find more effective methods of influencing children. When parents and teachers change their approach, the child's relationships improve—with peers, adults, and siblings; even a more realistic concept of self can be adopted. The group becomes an agent in bringing about these changes because of the improved interpersonal relationships in the group. There is a greater possibility for each group member to see himself or herself accurately and to recognize a faulty self-concept or a mistake in the goals being pursued.

In the action and interaction between the members of the group, each expresses goals, intentions, and a personal social orientation. Looking for deep and unconscious psychological processes in children and many adults is not necessary and is often detrimental. Such introspection usually eschews the real problem that exists in the social field in which the individual operates.

Many youngsters are not only socially isolated but also develop negative concepts of themselves that no amount of effort on the part of teachers and counselors can eliminate. The group as an educational medium increases one's receptiveness to different ideas, to new facts or concepts. It goes beyond this, however. It helps each member integrate and really accept new ideas previously completely foreign to one's own thinking.

Peer encouragement often plays the significant role in a reorientation process. The impact of group members focusing upon an individual's strengths and appreciating each other's efforts is tremendous. Members begin to help each other; participating in a group almost automatically evokes mutual help. In contrast, most classrooms are highly competitive— with each student interested, for the most part, in personal elevation. Under these conditions, there is little chance to assume responsibility for one another or to counteract the social isolation in which each student exists.

It is generally assumed that children in the same classroom know each other. On the contrary, many are as isolated as a hermit. Group counseling helps to dissolve the social wall within which many children live.

Recognizing that the problems of all children are essentially social gives group counseling its special significance in regard to both the assessment of the child's problems and the solutions to the problems. The group provides a social situation with real meaning. Some youngsters have never had an opportunity to test themselves in a real social situation. They may never have adequately found their place in a family group or been assured a place in the school group. In group counseling each member has a place and feels it, despite the various attitudes and ideas presented by peers. Under the guidance of the counselor, members learn how to contend with individual differences and disagreements; they develop coping devices which are used to advantage when each member returns to the family and to the classroom.

Since the problems of each youngster reveal themselves in the group, they must be solved in the group. It is in group counseling that youngsters find they are equal to others. In counseling groups, deficiencies lose their stigma. Paradoxically, deficiencies may be the necessary qualification for membership in counseling groups, as is the case in group counseling for underachievers. Thus, in a group, deficiencies do not lessen social status, but rather serve as a basis for equality for all group members.

In a democratic society, as contrasted with an autocratic society, an atmosphere of equality is developed. As has been pointed out above, the potentiality for establishing socially positive attitudes is not found in the community or in the school, but it is possible in well-directed counseling groups. The group thus becomes a value-forming agent. Individual counseling does not lend itself to bringing about necessary value changes. The normal family and classroom experiences of a youngster are not usually conducive to correcting an already established, faulty value system. They may even fortify useless values. Since all human values are of a social nature, group counseling cannot avoid dealing with values. Social participation in one way or another affects the value system of the individual. The impact of social experiences in group counseling is bound to be beneficial. It is of extreme importance that teachers and counselors and even neighbors take a more dynamic role in value formation. Adults have largely abdicated their rightful position in serving as norm setting and value forming agents. Because of this, value formation and norm setting have become a prerogative for subgroups in which the youngster attempts to find his or her place.

The effects of successful outcomes of group counseling, regardless of the method and the theoretical basis on which the counselor operates, must be evident in the encouragement and increased self-confidence of the group members, permitting them to participate in the life tasks more forcefully and candidly. Reorientation denotes the ability to establish and maintain proper human relationships based on self-confidence and respect for others.

SELECTION OF GROUP MEMBERS

As in other areas of group counseling (e.g., regarding size, setting, length and frequency of sessions, etc.), research is almost nonexistent or has not clearly demonstrated sound criteria for the selection of group members. Neither has research indicated an optimal group composition for obtaining maximum motivation modification through group counseling. Most of the criteria, lacking adequate research, have been drawn from the practitioner's personal experience with groups.

Groups may be formed in any number of ways. Selection processes differ from setting to setting and according to the needs of the situations within settings. In the writers' experience, groups have been formed on the basis of court referrals of first-time offenders, from clinical referrals of children and adolescents experiencing psychosomatic disorders, within community family education centers, and from various populations within schools.

Within schools, for example, teachers may select students they feel will profit from group counseling. Groups are frequently formed with children suggested by the principal or vice principal. Parents have asked to have their children included in a group. If the child is receptive to the idea, he or she may invite other children to form a group. Children already in a group frequently ask if they may invite a classmate who is having trouble, because "we may be able to help him." Sometimes children form their own groups and ask a counselor to lead them. Quite often, a counselor will suggest to children with whom he or she works individually that they might profit from group counseling.

In recent years, some writers (Ohlsen, 1977; Wattenburg, 1953) have suggested that the counselor select only those individuals who will be successfully helped by given group counseling methods. While the intake procedures associated with this selection process provide excellent preparation for group members, the selection process, itself, too often fails to offer help to those individuals who need it most. No one is compelled to join a group. Once they become members, they may leave when they no longer benefit from the counseling. Whatever the manner of group formation, however, no one who wishes to join is turned away; refusing an individual the opportunity to become a member of a group is contrary to democratic premises (Sonstegard & Dreikurs, 1973).

GROUP COMPOSITION

As with group selection procedures, research offers little guidance in the area of group composition. Yalom (1975) does suggest that a certain type of homogeneity will promote group cohesiveness, but he also notes that group cohesiveness and positive "therapy outcome" are not necessarily the same. It has been suggested above that there is some advantage in forming groups of individuals with common difficulties. Teleoanalytic counselors have run successful groups for underachievers, school dropouts, problem parenting, criminal offenders, couples, depressed clients, and chemical abusers. Experience suggests that a homogeneity of concern lessens the stigma that is often attached to a given problem.

While no one is denied access to group counseling, several considerations should be kept in mind. It is advisable to have an even number of males and females in a group whenever possible. Such an arrangement provides support for each gender within the group and allows for the development of equality between the sexes. Too divergent an age range among children and adolescents should be avoided. While there is no set age range for group composition, generally a maximum spread of three to five years is acceptable. Children and adolescents who are closer in age have similar life experiences and often find it easier to relate to each other. Temperament and activity-level need not be an issue in group composition. Extremely withdrawn children, for example, can be mixed in the same group with aggressive, acting-out, and attention-getting youngsters, to some advantage for all.

GROUP SIZE

Ten to 12 has usually been accepted as a maximum group size. Many counselors seem to prefer groups numbering 6 to 8. Generally, the lower limit on group size is determined by the need for group functioning; the upper limit depends to a great extent upon the skills and experience of the counselor, the amount of available time for group sessions, and to some extent, the nature and the purpose of the group.

Yalom (1975) suggests that five is the lower limit for effective group functioning. These writers concur. Although the number "5" is arbitrary (and certainly some groups of three have been beneficial to the members), group interaction, motivation modification, and peer encouragement processes are all increased with a larger number of participants.

As the group gets larger, more time is needed if each individual is to have an opportunity to focus upon personal difficulties. It has already been mentioned, however, that much growth and learning can take place in groups when members identify with each other (whether or not they focus individually on their own concerns); of greater importance, therefore, is the skill and experience of the counselor. Some teleoanalytically oriented counselors have held group discussions with parents and children numbering 25 to 30 and with a whole classroom numbering 30 or more pupils.

The nature and the purpose of the group has some effect on group size. Adlerian family group counseling has been used with as many as 100 people at a time. Some Adlerian counselors using psychodramatic techniques have practiced with 40 to 50 people in attendance. Some of the more recent group processes for adults include structured activities and tasks; the group size is therefore limited to about 20. In each of these cases, the processes used allow larger numbers to participate without diminishing the educational purposes of the group.

GROUP SETTING

While the atmosphere of the meeting room can support and augment the enjoyment of the group experience, it is not a crucial factor in group effectiveness. Some institutions simply cannot supply ideal space. The authors, faced with crowded school conditions, have held counseling sessions with youngsters in boiler rooms, auditorium stages, storage rooms, and isolated corridors, without excessive handicaps. The group sits in a circle with the counselor. When furniture is provided, the size needs to be appropriate to the age of the group. Sitting around a table is avoided.

An ideal meeting room should have a carpeted floor for both comfort and sound insulation. It should be well lighted and of sufficient size to allow four to five feet of space between the circle and the walls of the room. It should also be devoid of distractions such as noise from intercoms, music, hallways and corridors, and in schools from shop and physical education classes.

FREQUENCY, LENGTH, AND DURATION OF GROUP SESSIONS

The time factor in groups has been used in a number of different ways, including successful experiences with weekend groups and week-long groups. Many groups in schools, community agencies, and correctional facilities have been continuous and open to changing membership. The most common format, however, has been the weekly group session extending about 12 to 14 weeks; in schools, the duration is often established by the amount of time left in a semester or school year.

In practice, a consistent time, place, and day of the week can be established through a discussion with members of the group (and parents and teachers, if appropriate). In the authors' experience, 30 minutes seems appropriate for elementary school children, 50 minutes for junior high and high school students, and about 90 minutes to 2 hours for adult populations. It is especially vital in schools to adhere to the time schedule rather carefully. In the first place, the group members develop a serious and business-like attitude toward the sessions, and second, the teachers are in a position to plan classroom procedures without undue disruption. This is vital where the support and participation of the faculty are indispensable to the success of the group counseling program.

MEDIA EMPLOYED

There in nothing inherent in the teleoanalytic psychological formulation that is inimical to the employment of various media, especially in individual counseling. The teleoanalytic counselor, however, proceeds with group counseling primarily through verbal interaction, which permits a candid examination of each group member's difficulties. Next, the objective elements are assessed; namely, member's relationships to parents and siblings, the family constellations, how members view their positions in their families, and individual early recollections. The interpretations of life-style are presented either by group members or the counselor. Frequently, the counselor may employ structured activities or psychodrama with the group, dramatizing a situation; role playing is employed by the teleoanalytic counselor more frequently than play therapy.

It is practical and simple to move into "playing out" an incident rather than talking it out: "show us what happened." Especially if it is a situation that requires a solution, such as a conflict situation, the counselor may ask, "Does anyone have a better idea of what could be done?" (Grunwald, 1969, p. 36). If several different situations are depicted, the counselor discusses with the group the solutions they consider to be the best.

Play therapy would likely be used more often and with effectiveness if facilities were provided. The writers have used play therapy as a medium in application of the teleoanalytic psychological formulation in a school setting. The availability of necessary space and equipment for play therapy in a school setting, however, often presents difficulties. The school administration is likely to consider this an unproven frill. In only the most affluent schools will the approach be accepted without adequate data to substantiate its efficacy.

Those counselors who have musical skills often apply another medium, music therapy. Music therapy as a therapeutic process may appeal not only to the counselors but also the group members in intensifying the corrective effectiveness of the group counseling process (Dreikurs, 1954). A similar use has been made of art therapy (Dreikurs, 1969).

COUNSELOR'S ROLE

A discussion of group counseling would be incomplete without some attention given to the role and training of the counselor. What kind of person does it take to be a group counselor? What are the characteristics? Must a certain personality be possessed?

The writers maintain that there are no unique characteristics a group counselor must possess. It would be difficult to visualize, however, a shy, reticent person achieving any measure of success. Group counseling, especially as applied to children, requires a certain degree of outgoingness. The counselor must have a genuine liking for people, feel comfortable in company with them, and enjoy mutual give-and-take (interaction), whether it be congenial or controversial.

Group counselors must have self-confidence and feel that others, too, can be justified in having confidence in them. This projection of confidence is especially important when working with children. The counselor must have faith in an acquired ability of knowing what to do; most importantly, the counselor must put away any fear of being tested or defeated by children.

Group counselors always need the courage of their convictions. Here a certain amount of caution is indicated, for counselors with courage and conviction may be inclined to play God. Without conviction, however, they will not command respect. Unless counselors have respect for themselves, they cannot expect the same from members of the group. A conviction in the soundness of the group process leaves counselors free to listen, relaxed and calm, while they observe the dynamics of the group interaction and the verbal and nonverbal participation. Counselors can be firm and kind in their interpersonal relationships. They can be friendly without the destructiveness of familiarity.

Basic to the theoretical formulation set forth early in the chapter, the group counselor must assume the responsibility of serving as an interpreter and a guiding agent in the psychological process of change. It is a role function to direct, when necessary, the group's interaction into meaningful channels through an understanding of what is taking place. If a counselor fails to assume this proper role, an entire session may be spent in innocuous shop talk. Here, the counselor must put into play every skill that has been mastered. He or she must be a true "leader," not an imposing autocrat. The counselor must know when to permit group members to proceed undirected in their exploration, as well as when direction is required. Being attuned to the appropriate moment, making the right statement, and asking a significant question are all skills a group counselor must develop. There are statements and questions that turn off group interaction as well as ones that open necessary discussions.

Sensitivity to both adults and children, their actions and reactions, can be learned. Once it is acquired as a working tool, the professionally growing counselor improves and perfects the skill through continuous practice. Actually, group members will often help a less-experienced group counselor to grow as a leader and to acquire effective techniques.

GROUND RULES

Ground rules for the group are usually established at the beginning of the first meeting. The counselor will often initiate the discussion, but it is the group's responsibility to reach an agreement about rules. A typical set of rules will protect the basic rights of individuals and enhance the flow of interaction among group members. To be effective, the number of ground rules established should be rather small, and they should be stated and defined clearly.

In the authors' experience, a few ground rules seem to surface in discussions regularly. (1) One may talk freely about anything one wishes, but one must also respect others' rights to talk freely. This ground rule often includes an individual's right *not* to talk and not to be forced to talk. (2) All discussions are confidential. It is often wise to note that confidentiality is the avoidance of discussions outside the group that would disclose either names or group concerns in a mischievous way, possibly hurting someone. (3) One must attend the group sessions regularly. Needless to say, a regularly scheduled meeting is necessary for this ground rule. Sometimes, group members will also discuss and reach an agreement about what will happen if someone decides to leave the group. In addition, the discussion may include a decision about whether the group membership is open or closed.

REFERENCES

Dreikurs, R. (1940, December; 1941, January). The importance of group life. *Camping Magazine, 12,* 8–9; *13,* 1.

Dreikurs, R. (1953). The dynamics of music therapy. In M. Bing (Ed.) *Music therapy.* (pp. 15–26). Lawrence: The Allen Press.

Dreikurs, R. (1957). Group psychotherapy from the point of view of Adlerian Psychology. *International Journal of Group Psychotherapy, 7,* 363–375.

Dreikurs, S. (1969). Art therapy for psychiatric patients. *Perspectives in Psychiatric Care, 7* (3), 134–143.

Grunwald, B. (1969). Role playing as a classroom group procedure. *The Individual Psychologist, 6* (2), 34–38.

Ohlsen, M. (1977). *Group counseling* (2nd ed.) New York: Holt, Rinehart & Winston.

Sonstegard, M., & Dreikurs, R. (1973). The Adlerian approach to group counseling of children. In M. Ohlsen (Ed.), *Counseling children in groups: A forum.* New York: Holt, Rinehart, & Winston.

Wattenburg, W. (1953). Who needs counseling? *Personnel and Guidance Journal, 32,* 202–205.

Yalom, I. (1975). *The theory and practice of group psychotherapy* (2nd ed.). New York: Basic Books, Inc.

SUGGESTED READINGS

Croake, J. (1970). Group counseling. *Psychology in the Schools, 7* (1), 32–36.

Dreikurs, R. (1956). Adlerian psychotherapy. In F. Reichman & J. L. Moreno (Eds.), *Progress in psychotherapy.* New York: Grune.

Dreikurs, R. (1957). Group psychotherapy from the point of view of Adlerian psychology. *The International Journal of Group Psychotherapy, 7,* 363–375.

Dreikurs, R. (1957). *Psychology in the classroom.* New York: Harper.

Dreikurs, R. (1958). Group dynamics in the classroom. *Proceedings of the Thirteenth Congress of the International Association of Applied Psychology.* Rome: Tip. Ferri.

Dreikurs, R. (1959). Early experiments with group psychotherapy. *American Journal of Psychotherapy, 13,* 882–891.

Dreikurs, R. (1960). *Group psychotherapy and group approaches.* Chicago: Alfred Adler Institute.

Dreikurs, R. (1961). *Adult-child relations: A workshop on group discussions with adolescents.* Eugene: University of Oregon Press.

Dreikurs, R., Corsini, R., Lowe, R., & Sonstegard, M. (1959). *Adlerian family counseling.* Eugene: University of Oregon Press.

Kern, R., Matheny, K., & Patterson, D. (1978). *A case for Adlerian counseling: Theory, techniques, and research evidence.* Chicago: Alfred Adler Institute.

Seidler, R. (1936). School guidance clinics in Vienna. *International Journal of Individual Psychology, 2*(4), 75–78.

Sonstegard, M. A. (1964). A rationale for interviewing parents. *School Counselor, 12,* 72–76.

Sonstegard, M. (1968). *The basic principles and rationale of group counseling.* Moravia, N.Y.: Chronicle Guidance Publications.

Sonstegard, M. (1968). Mechanisms and practical techniques in group counseling in the elementary school. In J. J. Muro & S. L. Freeman (Eds.), *Readings in group counseling.* Scranton, PA: International Textbook Co.

Sonstegard, M., Bitter, J., & Hagerman, H. (1975). Motivation modification: An Adlerian approach. *The Individual Psychologist, 2,* 17–22.

Sonstegard, M., & Dreikurs, R. (1973). The Adlerian approach to group counseling of children. In M. Ohlsen (Ed.), *Counseling children in groups: A forum.* New York: Holt, Rinehart, & Winston.

Stormer, E. (1967). Milieu group counseling in elementary school guidance. *Elementary School Guidance Counselor, 1*(3), 240–254.

Sweeney, T. (1975). *Adlerian counseling.* Boston: Houghton Mifflin Co.

Zarski, J., Bitter, J., & Sonstegard, M. (1977). Training parents as functional professionals in a community setting. *The Individual Psychologist, 2,* 36–45.

C H A P T E R 18

Multimodal
Group Therapy[1]

INTRODUCTION

Many systems of psychotherapy may be said to rest on a *blockage model* of human disturbance. Different terms are used to describe this process—repression, inhibition, barrier, fixation—but the implication is that emotional difficulties are a product of inimical circumstances that generate conflicts or create traumatic upheavals within the person. Therapy then becomes a process of restoring the person to more adaptive functioning by releasing, or derepressing, or disinhibiting these intrapsychic elements. This view is exemplified by psychoanalytic and Rogerian therapies.

Many people suffer emotionally because their learning histories failed to provide them with necessary coping skills. Their maladaptive reactions do not stem from blockages or barriers that, if released, will permit them to utilize their adaptive capacities. Poor role models and other impoverished learning experiences have left them with *deficits* rather than "blockages."

No amount of insight or unpossessive caring is likely to fill the hiatuses resulting from insufficient learning. Teaching, training, coaching, modeling, shaping, and directing are necessary. The multimodal view of personality development and problem solving considers *both* the blockage model and the insufficiency model to be valid and relevant. Most clients suffer

---

1. Abstracted from Lazarus, A. (1982). Multimodal group therapy. In G. M. Gazda (Ed.), *Basic approaches to group psychotherapy and group counseling* (pp. 213–234). Springfield, IL: Charles C. Thomas.

from conflicts in the aftermath of unfortunate experiences *and* are hampered by various deficits in their social and personal repertoires.

Can a model of *faulty learning* (the acquisition of needless worries, fears, miseries, and other maladaptive thoughts, feelings, and actions) be combined in a schema of *deficient or nonexistent learning* (missed opportunities, or no occasions for acquiring coping or adaptive skills) without succumbing to eclectic muddles? Many theorists and therapists recognize the need for multidimensional and multifactorial approaches, but their attempts at fusion lead only to confusion.

We need a coherent model of human functioning that generates efficient and effective treatment strategies, one that considers the *whole person* and yet provides precision without sacrificing comprehensiveness. As the present chapter will attempt to show, the multimodal orientation satisfies these criteria.

THEORETICAL FOUNDATIONS ⎯⎯⎯⎯⎯⎯⎯⎯⎯⎯

Essentially, we are biological beings who move, feel, sense, imagine, think, and relate to one another. Our "personalities" are composed of seven modes—behavior, affect, sensation, imagery, cognition, interpersonal relationships, and our biological make-up. If we take the first letters from each of these functions, we have BASIC IB. If we refer to the biological mode as "drugs" (as a convenient shorthand term to denote that many interventions in this area consist of tranquilizers, antidepressants, and other medications, without forgetting that by the D or "drug" modality we are also concerned with nutrition, hygiene, exercise, and the panoply of medical diagnoses and treatments), a more compelling acronym emerges: BASIC I.D.*

In the same way that music arises from the interaction of seven notes–ABCDEFG—human personality is composed of the BASIC I.D. Sociocultural and political factors fall outside of the BASIC I.D. While there is reciprocity between objective and subjective events, sociological variables are not part of "temperament" and "personality." Nevertheless, it is imperative to appreciate the cultural heritage of any person before endeavoring to assess or modify his or her BASIC I.D.

The involvement or activation of one modality will, to a greater or lesser extent, influence every other modality. Indeed, any significant life event will have an impact on the entire BASIC I.D. For example, given that Mr. Smith, aged 65, has just retired from work, a multimodal therapist would ask: *How will this influence his ongoing behaviors?* (What acts and perfor-

---

*We used to use BASIC ID, but I.D.—as in *identity*—is preferred over the ambiguous "ID."

mances will be dropped, added, increased, and decreased?) *What impact will his retirement have on his affective responses?* Will he be anxious or suffer from depression, or develop some other dysphoric state? Will he be happy, contented, and calm?) *Will his sensory inputs undergo changes?* (Will he spend more time relaxing, reading, sightseeing, listening to music, having sex, sampling different foods? Will he be more inclined to dwell on aches, pains, and physical tensions?) *What changes will occur in his imagery?* (Will his "self-image" undergo a change? What mental pictures will he have about his immediate and long-range future?) *Will there be noticeable cognitive shifts?* (Will his philosophy and outlook on life change substantially? Will there be any modification of his decision-making and problem-solving capacities?) *How will interpersonal relations be affected by his retirement?* (Will he spend more time with relatives, friends, and acquaintances? Will he develop new social contacts?) *Will his new status have positive or negative repercussions on the state of his health?* Thus, the BASIC I.D. serves as a compass or cognitive map to ensure that every vector of "personality" receives direct attention.

A thorough knowledge of human personality from a multimodal perspective hinges on two main factors. First, one acquires a comprehensive list of the main ingredients across the client's BASIC I.D. Next, an appreciation of the interactions among the different modalities is necessary. Let us elaborate on these two aspects.

Phase One

Initially, a multimodal assessment includes the following types of questions:

Behavior: What do you regard as some of your main strengths or assets? What behaviors are getting in the way of your happiness? What would you like to stop doing? What would you like to start doing? What behaviors would you like to increase or decrease?

Affect: Are you troubled by anxiety, guilt, anger, depression, or any other negative emotion? What makes you laugh? What makes you cry? What makes you sad, mad, glad, scared?

Sensation: What do you especially like and dislike seeing, hearing, tasting, smelling, or touching? What stimuli facilitate or inhibit sexual arousal? Do you suffer from unpleasant sensations (aches, pains, dizziness, tremors, etc.)?

Imagery: What do you picture yourself doing in the immediate future? What is your body image like? How would you describe your self-image? What mental pictures do you have of the way you would like your future to be?

Cognition: What are your main "should's, ought's, and must's?" (Ellis, 1977). What are some of your most cherished values and beliefs? What are your major intellectual interests and pursuits?

Interpersonal: Who are the most important people in your life? What do you expect from significant others? What do they expect from you? What do you give to and get from them?

Drugs: Are you taking any prescribed or self-prescribed medicines? Do you have any concerns about the state of your health? What are your habits pertaining to diet, exercise, and other health-related areas?

The foregoing is by no means intended as an exhaustive list of questions across the BASIC I.D. In therapy, these preliminary questions are followed by a detailed life history questionnaire (a 14-page printed booklet covering the BASIC I.D.) and by anamnestic interviews. Nevertheless, even a fairly cursory inquiry into a person's BASIC I.D. will elicit central and significant information.

Phase Two

For illustrative purposes, it is simpler to start with examples that apply to individuals, and then to describe specific group applications.

After obtaining the main ingredients of a person's BASIC I.D., the next step is to examine the interactions among the different modalities. When a person behaves in a particular way, what impact (if any) does this activity have on the other modalities? Likewise, when a person is experiencing a sensory delight, or a strong affective reaction, or an interpersonal confrontation, how is this influencing, and being influenced by, inputs from each of the other modalities? To understand and appreciate the major interactions among the various modalities is to achieve a level of prediction and control that leaves little to chance. For example, the following two descriptions of "anxiety attacks" suffered by two people with different *modality firing orders* yield distinctive portraits of their respective afflictions.

> *Case A.* "I now realize that my anxiety and panic attacks begin with certain thoughts and images. I may be feeling fine when, for no apparent reason, I start thinking, 'What if I faint?' This is rapidly followed by unpleasant images: passing out, hitting my head on the ground, other people staring at me, and so forth. Immediately after these negative thoughts and frightening images, I experience very unpleasant sensations, usually heart palpitations and dizziness. I then start feeling that I must escape and I usually look for the nearest exit.

From a multimodal perspective, this narrative yields an important insight into the sequence of modalities that trigger and sustain this individual's anxiety reactions. Note the order: C-I-S-B (the cognitions and images lead to unpleasant sensory reactions that are followed in turn by escape or avoidance behavior, the whole sequence culminating in a full-blown anxiety or panic attack).

> *Case B.* A client who was well-schooled in multimodal concepts stated: "My anxieties are usually triggered by my sensations. First, I become aware of a weird feeling somewhere in my body: a peculiar odor, a metallic taste in my mouth, or perhaps a shimmering in my eyes, or some other unusual sensation. When this happens, I may start thinking that something is the matter with me, and I picture myself dying or going crazy or something horrible. I then try to get away and I start looking for my husband. Usually he can calm me down pretty fast."

While Case A and Case B both suffer from anxiety and panic attacks, even a brief outline of the respective modality sequences (or *firing order*) demonstrates distinctive differences. Case A's Cognitive-Imagery-Sensory-Behavior sequence suggests different therapeutic interventions from Case B's Sensory-Cognitive-Imagery-Behavior-Interpersonal pattern. The essence of multimodal therapy is to attend to specific problems within all relevant modalities, as well as to the interactive effects of each individual modality with every one of the other six. We refer to the assessment of modality firing orders as *tracking*.

Since multimodal therapists heed Occam's razor (the view that explanatory principles should not be needlessly multiplied), we are opposed to jargon, neologisms, and much of the "psychobabble" (Rosen, 1977) that has arisen. Since certain technical terms are necessary for rapid and shorthand communication, we talk about the *BASIC I.D.*, we refer to the *different modalities,* and we talk about *modality firing orders.* In accounting for disturbances in human conduct, in the broadest sense, we are all products of our genes, our physical environment, and our social learning history. Our fundamental concern is how the myriad of influences to which we are heir finally coalesce and impact throughout each person's BASIC I.D. A basic theoretical proposition is that people are troubled by a multitude of specific problems that call for a wide range of particular treatment strategies. After familiarizing group members with the BASIC I.D. concept, we find that most of them have little difficulty constructing *modality profiles* (i.e., a chart or list of specific problems in each modality), which then serves as a "blueprint" for therapy.

How does a person acquire his or her specific inputs across the BASIC I.D.? Since association plays a key role in all learning processes, many elements are the result of *classical and operant conditioning.* When using these traditional learning theory concepts, we need not fall prey to the controversies that surround them. When someone says, "I never drink orange juice because my mother used to put bitter medicines in the juice to disguise their taste," one may explain the avoidance mechanism in terms of classical conditioning. When a person with numerous aches and pains has a spouse who is unusually attentive to these complaints, operant conditioning may be invoked to account for the problem. In therapy, one attempts to overcome "classically conditioned problems" by deliberately introducing new associations (as in desensitization procedures, where coping images and feelings of serenity are employed to counterpose anxiety). Problems that are engendered or maintained by "operant conditioning" call for a reorganization of consequential behaviors.

The content of one's BASIC I.D. is derived also from *modeling and vicarious processes*. Human survival is greatly facilitated by the fact that we can acquire new responses by watching someone else perform an important sequence of behavior and then doing it ourselves (Bandura, 1969, 1977). *Private events* (thoughts, images, and sensations) are influenced by, and reciprocally affect, the other modalities. Many experts have stressed the fact that people do not respond to some *real* environment but rather to their own *perceived* environment. Thus, the ideas to which we are exposed, the values we acquire, our use of language and semantics will all influence our selective attention and will determine which stimuli are noticed, how they are noticed, how much they are valued, and how long they are remembered (Bandura, 1978).

In the same way that an artist works from a base of three primary colors—red, yellow, and blue—the multimodal therapist keeps the BASIC I.D. constantly in mind. The skillful painter knows exactly how to obtain specific shades of green, orange, pink, purple, violet, etc., and an expert multimodal therapist is aware of the interactions within the BASIC I.D. that lead to particular reactions. In addition to identifying the major assets and liabilities in each modality, we often find it useful (especially for generating productive group discussions) to obtain *structural profiles*. This is achieved by pointing out, in everyday terms, that some people are primarily "doers," whereas others are "thinkers," or "feelers," or people-oriented "relators," and so forth. On a 10-point scale for each modality of the BASIC I.D., clients are asked to rate the extent to which they perceive themselves as doing, feeling, sensing, imagining, thinking, and relating. The "D" modality will reflect the extent to which they observe and practice "health habits"—regular exercise, good nutrition,—and avoid cigarettes, drugs, excessive alcohol, et cetera. Simple bar diagrams may be constructed.

Figure 18–1 reflects a person who is clearly highest in the behavioral and interpersonal modalities. Such a "doer" and "relator" may be expected to be highly active socially. He or she would place a premium on *doing things with other people*. Imagine obtaining a structural profile from this individual's spouse showing very high self-ratings in affect and imagery, and low scores in behavior and interpersonal areas. This "feeler and

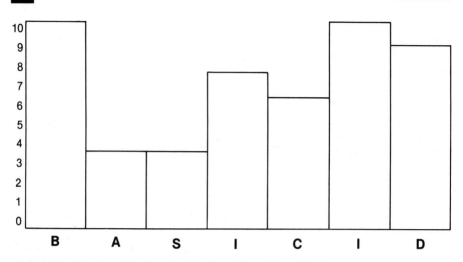

Figure 18–1 A sample BASIC I.D. bar diagram.

dreamer" might react negatively to marriage with a person who is exceptionally active and gregarious, and vice versa.

In addition to their obvious value in marriage therapy, these structural profiles generate meaningful discussions in general group therapy settings. Often a distinction emerges between the degree of emotion that people *feel* and how much affect they *express:* A person may rate 10 for subjective feeling and 2 for objective expression of these feelings.

Our fundamental assumption is that there is no problem, no achievement, no personal nor interpersonal event that cannot be subsumed under the BASIC I.D. We maintain that every condition to which the psyche and human flesh is heir can be accounted for by the BASIC I.D. Joy, optimism, love, disgust, adoration, awe, failure, achievement, hope, faith, greed, ambition, sex, aggression, disappointment, anticipation, fear, grief, ecstasy, contempt, surprise, motivation, boredom, or whatever other action, feeling, sensation, image, idea, personal bond, or physical factor a person may experience resides in the BASIC I.D. Since every modality is present, to a greater or lesser extent, in every other, this is truly a "dynamic" theory of personality.

There is one additional concept or tactic that merits attention: *second-order BASIC I.D. profiles.* After drawing up the initial modality profile, listing specific problems in each modality, the client and therapist discuss particular treatment options for each difficulty. For example, let's say that in the affective mode we have the following entry: "Gets extremely upset in the face of criticism and rejection." Initially, desensitization may be considered a likely treatment for this hypersensitivity. However, if the client fails to respond to this procedure, one might ask him or her more detailed questions about "criticism and rejection" and construct a specific BASIC I.D. profile that focuses on these issues.

The initial BASIC I.D. profile is a macrocosmic overview of an individual's psychological functioning. Second-order BASIC I.D. profiles magnify specific facets of the person's problem areas and permit the clinician to understand the client more fully and to devise effective coping strategies. Some of my colleagues have constructed third-order BASIC I.D. profiles, but I have not found it necessary to go beyond second order assessments.

SELECTION OF GROUP MEMBERS

The easiest groups to conduct are those that are relatively homogeneous and have clear-cut goals. These include smoking-cessation groups, groups of men and women with sexual dysfunctions, weight-reduction groups, assertiveness training groups, and couples' groups for enhancing marital interaction. The formation of therapy groups has often been a matter of propinquity. For example, at present, I am seeing four agoraphobic women and two agoraphobic men who have many similar problems and reactions. A group may very well facilitate their progress by enhancing their motivation through mutual support and encouragement.

Generally, the choice of group therapy over individual therapy is made when there is reason to believe that the presence of other people will augment the processes of learning, unlearning, and relearning. Thus, when a BASIC I.D. assessment reveals several *interpersonal difficulties*, that individual is considered a likely candidate for multimodal group therapy. Similarly, clients with negative self-images and feelings of inadequacy often derive rapid benefit from multimodal groups. People who are likely to have a disruptive effect are not invited to join any groups (e.g., deeply depressed, or extremely hostile, paranoid, or deluded individuals). Highly obsessional clients locked into severe rituals are also seen individually or in a family context rather than in groups.

While many of my colleagues conduct multimodal groups with children and adolescents, my own expertise is limited to adults. The majority of my clients span a 30-year age range—from their twenties to their fifties. Some years ago I would see some clients individually as well as in a group. Since this tended to create some confusion and conflict, I now prefer to have my group members exclusively committed to their group meetings. (Clients who receive individual as well as group therapy are inclined to hold back in group meetings and save sensitive material for their individual sessions, which tends to undermine group morale.)

GROUP COMPOSITION

The most productive and effective groups appear to have been those with an equal distribution of men and women, with an age range of no more than 10 to 15 years. When a clear imbalance arises (e.g., women are in the minority, there are far fewer blacks than whites, there is one Jewish or Catholic member in a group of Protestants, and so forth), the group is often sidetracked into unproductive concerns. When forming a group, I strive to achieve "balanced matching." I select people who are not too discrepant in terms of their socioeconomic backgrounds, levels of education, and what Adlerians might call their overall "life-style." In multimodal vernacular, I look for compatible BASIC I.D.s. People, for instance, who are high on affect and imagery (emotional dreamers) are unlikely to resonate to those who are more cognitive and action-oriented (thinkers and doers). The aim is to avoid extreme differences. On the other hand, those who are relatively impoverished in imagery or sensory modalities can learn much from those whose imagery and sensory outputs are rich and vivid.

Unlike Slavson (1959), multimodal groups are never selected on the basis of some diagnostic classification. Instead, specific problems in specific modalities are evaluated for their amenability to group interaction.

GROUP SIZE

I have found that multimodal groups are best conducted with 4 to 10 members. It seems to me that one of the many reasons for working in groups is simply that if two heads are better than one, 10 heads may be still better. When there are more than 10 group members, the multimodal format becomes watered down—the participants do not receive the amount of individual attention they may require. When there are fewer than four in the group, there is insufficient diversity and a lack of balanced interchange. I am generally most comfortable and effective working with a group of about eight. Whenever possible, I prefer conducting groups with a cotherapist.

GROUP SETTING

Two important ingredients in the group setting are physical comfort and the absence of distractions. For our aims and purposes, it is pointless to herd clients into a small room, crowd them into uncomfortable chairs, while loudspeakers intermittently disrupt the proceedings with calls and announcements. (As an intern, I had to conduct my first group in a hospital under these conditions.) My present group room is a 12-by-25 foot rectangular area that is carpeted, well soundproofed, with indirect adjustable lighting, simply furnished with comfortable couches and chairs. Various plants, abstract paintings, and some pieces of sculpture add a warm touch to the ambience.

FREQUENCY, LENGTH, AND DURATION OF GROUP SESSIONS

Our group meetings take place weekly and last 1½ to 2 hours. This interval seems most suitable for clients to practice new behaviors, carry out homework assignments, and consolidate whatever learning took place in the previous group session. When there are six or fewer members in a group, a 90-minute time span is usually sufficient; with more than six members, two hours seems necessary. Some years ago, I used to have 3-hour group meetings, but I found this span too long. Many people became bored and restless, bathroom breaks disrupted the ongoing activities, and some clients paced themselves accordingly and tended to regard the first hour as a warm-up period.

I have experimented with several different formats for conducting multimodal groups (Lazarus, 1975a, 1975b). Time-limited groups appear to be the most effective. Group members are informed at the first meeting that the group will meet for 20 sessions and then disband. Clients who so desire may then enter individual therapy or join a different group. I have found that this makes most clients more responsive to the active learning, unlearning, and relearning that lies at the foundation of multimodal methods.

MEDIA EMPLOYED

The educational emphasis that underlies the multimodal orientation makes the group setting most reminiscent of a comfortable classroom. My cotherapist and I will often "leap to the blackboard" in order to underscore a point. Clients are encouraged to have notepads and writing materials at hand. Some bring tape recorders to the sessions. Excerpts from books may be shared, sections from relevant psychoeducational cassette recordings may be presented, and the use of videotapes sometimes affords significant learning experiences. Most groups, however, center on discussion, role playing, relaxation exercises, behavior rehearsal, and feeling identification. (For a full discussion of these procedures see Lazarus, 1981.) Since we believe that most substantial changes occur outside the group, we devote considerable time to the implementation of homework assignments (Shelton & Ackerman, 1974). There is persuasive evidence that performance-based methods are far superior to purely verbal or cognitive procedures (Wilson, 1980).

THERAPIST'S ROLE

In multimodal groups, the therapists are educators, trainers, leaders, and helpers who provide information, instruction, feedback, and serve as role models. By modeling assertive (nonaggressive) behaviors, disputing irrational ideas, offering positive reinforcements, engaging in constructive criticism, and self-disclosing various abilities and disabilities, the multimodal group therapist tends to be quite active. There are times, however, when the demand characteristics of the group call for a more passive-reflective stance; the sensitive clinician will heed these requirements and respond accordingly. Thus, recently, during the seventh or eighth group meeting, a member complained that he found the group too structured and too task-oriented. He suggested that a few meetings be devoted simply to trading information and providing honest impressions of one another in the group. Most of the other members agreed with his suggestion, whereupon he assumed leadership for the next two sessions. Members then requested more specific problem-solving maneuvers, but by that time the group atmosphere had become much more cohesive and the clients seemed to show enthusiasm for the more structured BASIC I.D. assessment and therapy. If there is one single most important element in the process, it is *flexibility* on the part of the therapists.

GROUND RULES

The first ground rule is confidentiality. At the outset, clients are informed that information revealed during group meetings is to be viewed as privileged. Members are free to talk about the group and its activities provided that individuals remain anonymous and outsiders obtain no identifying leads. The next ground rule is that people are never to be criticized or attacked *as people*. The goal is to create a helpful, constructive, and safe environment where people are willing to self-disclose, and where they are free from the sarcasm, slights, and innuendoes that are so prevalent in social circles. When a group member violates this rule, he or she is first asked the constructive intent behind his or her remarks, whereupon the therapists usually model or suggest a more effective way of communicating and interacting.

At the beginning of the group, clients are given a photocopy of the following *Five Basic Group Principles:*

1. What transpires in the group is strictly confidential.
2. Outside of the group, members are required not to share feelings or information with other group members that they are unwilling to disclose to the group as a whole.
3. If any group member has negative reactions pertaining to the group, it is important to air these complaints inside and not outside the group.
4. Withholding feelings and observations—whether positive or negative—diminishes one's own role in the group and retards group progress in general.
5. Constructive criticisms are those that are directed at negative or offensive behaviors, not at people per se.

Film

A 48-minute film titled, "Multimodal Behavior Therapy" shows the author conducting an initial interview with a young woman. It demonstrates the assessment-therapy linkage across the client's BASIC I.D. This film is Part III of *Three Approaches to Psychotherapy II*, in which Carl Rogers presents "Client-Centered Therapy" in Part I and Everett L. Schostrom conducts an initial interview of "Actualizing Therapy" in Part II.

These films are available as 16 mm films or 3/4" videocassettes (color). Rental prices are $40 for each film or $400 for the purchase of each film (plus shipping and handling). They may be ordered from Psychological Films, Inc., 110 N. Wheeler Street, Orange, California 92669.

REFERENCES

Bandura, A. (1969). *Principles of behavior modification*. New York: Holt, Rinehart and Winston.

Bandura, A. (1977). *Social learning theory*. Englewood Cliffs, New Jersey: Prentice-Hall.

Bandura, A. (1978). The self-system in reciprocal determinism. *American Psychologist, 33,* 344–358.

Brunell, L. F., & Young, W. T. (Eds.) (1981). *A multimodal handbook for a mental hospital: Designing specific treatments for specific problems*. New York: Springer.

Ellis, A. (1977). The basic clinical theory of rational-emotive therapy. In A. Ellis & R. Grieger (Eds.), *Handbook of rational-emotive therapy* (pp. 3–34). New York: Springer.

Gazda, G. M. (1971). *Group counseling: A developmental approach*. Boston: Allyn & Bacon.

Lazarus, A. A. (1975a). Group therapy and the "BASIC I.D." in C. M. Franks & G. T. Wilson (Eds.), *Annual review of behavior therapy, 3,* 721–732.

Lazarus, A. A. (1975b). Multimodal behavior therapy in groups. In G. M. Gazda (Ed.), *Basic approaches to group psychotherapy and group counseling* (2nd ed.). Springfield, IL: Charles C. Thomas.

Lazarus, A. A. (1981). *The practice of multimodal therapy.* New York: McGraw-Hill.

Rosen, R. D. (1977). *Psychobabble.* New York: Atheneum.

Shelton, J. L. & Ackerman, J. (1974). *Homework in counseling and psychotherapy.* Springfield, IL: Charles C. Thomas.

Slavson, S. R. (1959). Parallelisms in the development of group psychotherapy. *International Journal of Group Psychotherapy, 2,* 451–461.

Wilson, G. T. (1980). Toward specifying the "nonspecific" factors in behavior therapy: A social learning analysis. In M. J. Mahoney (Ed.), *Psychotherapy process.* New York: Plenum.

SUGGESTED READINGS

Brunell. L. F. (1978). A multimodal treatment model for the mental hospital: Designing specific treatments for specific problems. *Professional Psychology, 9,* 570–579.

Brunell, L. F., & Young, W. T. (Eds.) (1981). *A multimodal handbook for a mental hospital: Designing specific treatments for specific problems.* New York: Springer.

Fay, A., & Lazarus, A. A. (1981). Multimodal therapy and the problems of depression. In J. F. Clarkin & H. Glazer (Eds.), *Depression: Behavioral and directive treatment strategies.* New York: Garland Press.

Keat, D. B. (1979). *Multimodal therapy with children.* New York: Pergamon.

Lazarus, A. A. (1981). *The practice of multimodal therapy.* New York: McGraw-Hill.

Roberts, T. K., Jackson, L. J., & Phelps, R. (1980). Lazarus' multimodal therapy model applied in an institutional setting. *Professional Psychology, 11,* 150–156.

C H A P T E R   19

Gestalt Therapy in Groups[1]

INTRODUCTION

Gestalt is a German word meaning whole or configuration. As one psychological dictionary puts it: " . . . an *integration* of members as contrasted with a summation of parts" (Warren, 1934, p. 115). The term also implies a unique kind of patterning. Gestalt therapy is a term applied to a unique kind of psychotherapy as formulated by the late Frederick S. Perls, his coworkers, and his followers.

Dr. Perls began, as did many of his colleagues in those days, as a psychoanalyst, after having been trained as a physician in post World War I Germany. In 1926 he worked under Professor Kurt Goldstein at the Frankfurt Neurological Institute for brain-injured soldiers where he was first exposed to the tenets of Gestalt psychology but "was still too preoccupied with the orthodox approach to assimilate more than a fraction of what was offered" (Perls, 1947, p. 5). Later Perls was exposed to the theories and practice of Wilhelm Reich and incorporated some of the concepts and techniques of character analysis into his work.

1. Abstracted from Simkin, J. S. (1982). Gestalt therapy in groups. In G. M. Gazda (Ed.), *Basic approaches to group psychotherapy and group counseling* (pp. 179–212). Springfield, IL: Charles C. Thomas. Revision by Paula Bickham, Ph.D. candidate, University of Georgia.

THEORETICAL FOUNDATIONS

Much of what human beings need to live in the world is contained outside of the ego boundary. In order to bring what is needed within the organism from the world outside of the ego boundary it is necessary for the organism to (a) be *aware* of a need and (b) expend the necessary energy to bring the needed substance through the ego boundary. The process of getting something through the ego boundary is called *contact*.

Perls believed that the basic drive in the human organism is *dental aggression*. During the first several months of life the infant as a suckling is totally dependent on its environment for survival. At this early stage its only self-supportive mechanisms are basic physiological survival systems such as respiration, metabolism, assimilation, and elimination, etc.

With the eruption of teeth and the development of the ability to crawl and then perambulate a marked change occurs, or at least potentially can occur, with a gradual switch from almost complete environmental support to more and more self-supportive possibilities.

The young child, if permitted, can now begin to explore and discriminate, discover what is nourishing (palatable) and what is toxic (unpalatable).

This developmental phase during which dental aggression allows the child to destructure (primarily food, but also the beginning possibilities of ideas, values, etc.) and through contact restructure, integrate, make part of oneself, is crucial. To the extent that the child is interfered with during this developmental phase it is forced to *introject* (swallow whole) rather than destructure and reintegrate. If the child is continuously forced to take in without chewing and tasting, it will form the habit of becoming more and more dependent on environmental support, behaving like an automaton and gradually losing the capacity for creativity.

A human being is considered a total organism functioning as a whole, rather than an entity split into dichotomies such as mind and body. With the philosophical background of humanism, *à la* Otto Rank, the organism is seen as being born with the capacity to cope with life. This is opposed to what the author calls the original sin theory of human development—that the organism must learn to repress or suppress its instinctual strivings in order to become "civilized." The emergence of existential philosophy coincided historically with the development of gestalt therapy. Wilson Van Dusen (1960) believes that there is only one psychotherapeutic approach that unites the phenomenological approach with existential theory, and that is gestalt therapy.

The theoretical model of the psychodynamic schools of personality—chiefly the Freudian school—envisions the personality like an onion consisting of layers. Each time a layer is peeled away, there is still another layer until you finally come to the core. (Incidentally, in the process of "analysis" of the onion, you may have very little or nothing left by the time you come to the core!) The author envisions the personality more like a large rubber ball, which has only a thick outer layer and is empty inside. The ball floats or swims in an environment so that at any given moment only a certain portion is exposed while the rest is submerged in the water. Thus, rather than inventing an unconscious or preconscious to account for behavior that we are unaware of, it is suggested that the unaware behavior is the result of the organism not being in touch with its external environment because of being mostly submerged in its own background (internal environment) or in contact with (usually preoccupied with) fantasies.

Perls, trained as a psychoanalyst and strongly influenced by the philosophy of Sigmund Friedlander, also conceptualized personality as being multilayered. The outer layer he described as the *cliché layer*. There is little, if any, genuine self invested in the polite sentences such as "How are you?" or asking others questions about themselves or their family without any real interest. Beneath the cliché layer is a second, which is called the *role-playing layer*. Originally when learning these roles there was a lot of self invested. However, at present, role-playing is frequently automatized and masks the genuine self. These learned roles may be that of father or mother, son or daughter, teacher or student, and the like. Beneath the role-playing layer Perls described the *impasse layer*. Sometimes called the death layer by the Russians, this layer is experienced as a feeling of emptiness or no-thingness in the Zen sense. For many people the subjective experience of being without clichés or roles is extremely frightening. If one passes through the impasse, the fourth layer, the *implosive-explosive layer*, is reached. At this level a person is closely aware of emotions that are either expressed or imploded. The last layer is the genuine personality stripped of all the learned (usually phoney) ways of being in the world (Simkin, 1979).

Perls posited a hierarchical need system in expanding his personality theory. He believed that "from the survival point of view the most urgent situation becomes the controller, the director takes over" (Perls, 1976, p. 33). An example of the hierarchical need system would be an emergency when there is a sudden outbreak of fire. If one ran from the fire and depleted his oxygen supply, one would stop to breathe because breathing would now take precedence over running (Simkin, 1979).

Yontef (1971) summarized the theory of gestalt therapy. He reasoned that organismic needs lead to sensory motor behavior. Once a configuration is formed that has the qualities of a good gestalt, the organismic need that has been foreground is met and a balance or state of satiation or no-need is achieved.

When a need is met, the Gestalt it organized becomes complete and it no longer exerts an influence—the organism is free to form new gestalten. When this gestalt formation and destruction are blocked or rigidified at any stage, when needs are not recognized and expressed, the flexible harmony and flow of the organism/environment field is disturbed. Unmet needs form incomplete gestalten that clamor for attention and, therefore, interfere with the formation of new gestalten (Yontef, 1971, p. 3)

As Perls, Hefferline, and Goodman (1951) put it, "The most important fact about the figure-background formation is that if a need is genuinely satisfied, the situation changes" (p. xi).

In order to bring about the possibility of closure, the completion of earlier unfinished situations, patients are encouraged to deal with past events as if they were occurring in the present. A specific technique for bringing past events into the now is asking the person to describe the event in the first person present tense as if it were occurring at the moment. The theoretical basis for this technique is rooted in the belief (and experience) that emotions which were overwhelming at the time they occurred were dealt with through the ego defenses of projection, retroflection, and introjection. By encouraging a person to reexperience rather than talk about a past event the avoided affect may, and frequently does, surface through the support of the patient's adult ego as well as the presence of a sympathetic nonjudgmental gestalt therapist.

According to Beisser, change occurs paradoxically by continuing a behavioral pattern rather than attempting to alter or change that pattern. "Change can occur when the patient abandons, at least for the moment, what he would like to become and attempts to be what he is. The premise is that one must stand in one place in order to have firm footing to move" (Beisser, 1970, p. 77).

From another theoretical vantage, Perls claims that all that is needed for behavioral change to occur is *awareness*. The primary therapeutic tool in gestalt therapy is awareness, which may be defined as being in touch with one's own existence. This ability to focus on what is actual defines a person's immediate subjective reality. Learning to focus one's awareness allows that person to discover that what is, is. There is no right or wrong reality.

Perls suggested the possibility of "universal awareness." "With the hypothesis of universal awareness we open up to considering ourselves in a living way rather than in the aboutisms of having a mind, ego, superego and so forth" (Perls, 1975, p. 69). In order to establish good contact with the environment it is necessary to risk discovering one's own contact boundaries through experiencing what is "me" and "not me." Adequate contact requires adequate *support*. Focus in gestalt therapy frequently is on developing appropriate support for desired contactfulness. Support systems may include knowledge, interest, concern for others, breathing, the undercarriage of one's body, etc. Invariably gestalt therapists become cognizant of faulty support systems as they deal with their patients' inability to be contactful.

A basic assumption in gestalt therapy is that the way in which the patient deals with his or her world is reenacted in the way he or she deals with the therapist. Based on this assumption, stress is placed on the I-Thou interaction that occurs between therapist and patient. Gestalt therapists aim for transparency of self rather than cloaking themselves in the mantle of therapist and encouraging transference reactions. This is not to say that transference does not occur in gestalt therapy. Rather, an attempt is made to minimize rather than to maximize transference reactions by dealing with what is ongoing at the moment in the therapist-patient interactive process.

SELECTION OF GROUP MEMBERS

Based on this writer's 30 plus years of experience, the most useful single criterion in the selection of group members is heterogeneity.

When forming a group, care is taken to include as wide a range as is practicable of age and type of psychopathology. Attempts are also made to have equal numbers of male and female participants.

All potential group members are first seen in individual therapy to determine the nature and degree of disturbance and to explore the person's attitudes and extent of willingness to participate in a group. Inasmuch as group attendance involves less flexibility as to time of appointment, more time spent during each treatment session and the reduced cost of each treatment session, these issues are addressed and explicated.

Whenever there is overwhelming evidence that the potential group member is or will become a monopolist within the group, he or she is excluded from consideration. This frequently involves evidence of extreme narcissism and/or severe characterological defects.

Although this writer has successfully included borderline patients in his groups, he has excluded patients who were actively hallucinating and/ or delusional.

An additional criterion used in the selection of group members has been the degree of acceptance by the other group members when introducing a potential new member to an established group. If several members of an ongoing group feel negatively toward the prospective new member, experience has shown that attempting to bring in someone under these circumstances frequently becomes disruptive to both the group process and the therapy of the new member as well.

GROUP COMPOSITION

During the period from 1960 through 1970, this writer had a wide variety of ongoing groups. These were psychotherapy groups, psychotherapy groups for couples, and training groups in gestalt therapy. All of the patients in the therapy groups were previously patients in individual gestalt therapy. The range of time that a person was in individual treatment prior to entering a group was anywhere from a few sessions to two or three years. Each therapy group was balanced with an equal number of male and female patients. Attempts were made to ensure the heterogeneity of the groups by bringing in as wide a range of age, occupation, presenting problems, etc., as possible from the sources available.

GROUP SIZE

Typically, groups meeting at the author's Beverly Hills office consisted of eight members. During a two-hour period, usually three or four members had an opportunity to do extended work and all eight could participate in the interaction. Experimenting with both larger and smaller numbers eventuated in eight being the optimum number in terms of comfortably utilizing the size of the office, sharing the hourly costs of group therapy, and forming a group with which the author felt most compatible. Training groups, which were co-led, and the couples group were usually limited to 12 people.

GROUP SETTING

Most of the psychotherapy groups met in the author's Beverly Hills office in a room about 15 feet by 15 feet with wood panelled walls. The couples group and the training groups, as well as a Wednesday morning group, met in the living room of the author's home. The room was about 18 feet by 24 feet in size, with a large number of upholstered chairs, couches, thick rug, pillows, et cetera.

Preference for meeting in the home of the author was based on the larger physical setting, convenience and appropriateness for meeting with training groups and the couples group. The greater informality of a living room setting was believed to be facilitative of less formal barriers for both of these types of groups.

FREQUENCY, LENGTH, AND DURATION OF GROUPS

Therapy groups met once a week for a two-hour session. Occasionally the larger groups, such as the couples group or training group continued beyond two hours. All of the above-mentioned groups were open-ended with the exception of the couples group, which was a closed group.

Approximately one-third of the group patients were also seen in individual therapy on a once-a-week basis or less frequently. None of the couples were in individual therapy concurrently and none of the therapists in training groups were in regular individual treatment.

The typical group patient had about 70–80 hours of group treatment over a period of eight months to a year. Some group members were able to terminate treatment within three to six months (25–50 hours of therapy). Others had been in group as long as three years when the author discontinued practice in Beverly Hills. Average attendance for couples groups is 25 sessions (50–60 therapy hours), over approximately eight months.

MEDIA EMPLOYED

Although this writer has routinely been using videofeedback in individual gestalt therapy with fixed-focus cameras since 1968, he has found this medium cumbersome with groups. In some training groups, one of the trainees will volunteer to "play cameraman" while the group is in process, with mixed results. Frequently the lack of experience on how and where to focus makes the videofeedback difficult to understand. Using experienced cameramen and sound technicians becomes economically prohibitive, except for producing training tapes or films.

Many gestalt therapists use structured exercises. Frequently, at the beginning of a group session, each member including the therapist(s) will make a here-and-now statement of what their foreground is and whether or not they intend to explore a particular issue or problem area during the group session. If several members announce their intention to work during the group session, time is taken to arrange for an equitable ordering of who will be first, second, and so on.

At times, this writer has asked group members to imagine that the group session had ended and, in retrospecting about the group, to see if they can get in touch with any regrets, unfinished resentments or appreciations, and the like. This fantasy exercise, when used judiciously, can serve to enliven a group that appears to have a low energy level and in which participants are relatively inactive.

During some group sessions, spontaneous group movement such as dance or forming a circle, etc. may evolve. This writer usually discourages the use of stereotyped exercises of any kind and prefers to reinforce natural, creative expressions.

THERAPIST'S ROLE

The gestalt therapist primarily acts as a facilitator in the group whose function is to use his or her awareness to feed back to the group members their perceptions, attitudes, and feelings while interacting within the group.

By concentrating on what is going on (the process) rather than what could be (fantasy) or should be (moralizing), the person is encouraged to take responsibility for what he or she is doing. Assuming members desire to change how they are, they are encouraged to be how they are in the present in order to change. Being in contact with one's own potentially nourishing or toxic behavior enables one to assimilate or reflect that behavior. This is also true for one's being in contact with the behavior of others. Giving permission to self to experience and taste everything, but to swallow only what is nourishing and to spit out what is toxic empowers the individual to make choices that are right for the here-and-now moment. Choice and growth are thus enhanced through organismic self-regulation.

All gestalt therapists, in keeping with the I-Thou philosophy, see themselves as models who will relate in a horizontal fashion with the rest of the group members.

In addition to the role of facilitator, some gestalt therapists will also engage in dyadic exchanges with one member of the group. Frequently this is perceived as individual therapy within a group setting even though the other group members may be influenced by witnessing this dyadic interchange.

In co-therapy situations, usually one of the gestalt therapists is available to work with any member of the group wishing to explore an issue, while the other will attend to the rest of the group members as the work proceeds. Occasionally co-leaders will agree to be equally available to work with one person within the group or will alternate focusing on the one person.

New concepts in gestalt group therapy integrate the intrapersonal, interpersonal, and group process dynamics. As the group progresses through developmental stages of trust and safety, establishing norms, exploration, confrontation, confluence, and working, the group members develop awareness of themselves as individuals as well as members of the group.

This new synthesis of gestalt therapy and group process was developed by the teaching faculty at the Gestalt Institute of Cleveland. Even though this group acted in many ways as a team, special note is given to Edwin Neviw, Carolyn Hirsch Lukensmeier, Leonard Hirsch, and Richard Wallen as having been highly important and influential in the process (Kepner, 1980).

For every event in the gestalt group process there is a cycle: centering → sensation → awareness → energy → action → contact → resolution → withdrawal (Zinker, 1977). Figure 19–1 illustrates this group process cycle.

Centering oneself facilitates the growth of awareness. Centering is done by relaxing the mind and body and focusing on the breathing. By first

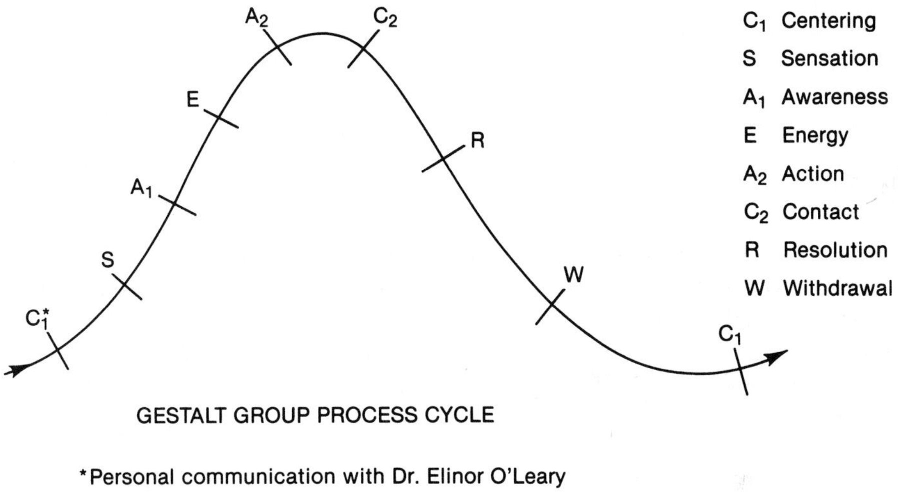

C_1 Centering
S Sensation
A_1 Awareness
E Energy
A_2 Action
C_2 Contact
R Resolution
W Withdrawal

GESTALT GROUP PROCESS CYCLE

*Personal communication with Dr. Elinor O'Leary

Figure 19–1 Gestalt Group Process Cycle

letting go and emptying oneself to the deepest part of the self, one is able to stop "doing" and return to experiencing and being. One makes contact with the group in a centered state; members are more fully present to one another and the group process as they wait for the figural image to emerge.

Group members are now free to attend to sensations emerging through their ability to see, hear, touch, taste, smell, think, and move. Paying attention to the sensory data that the body provides is a rich resource for communication. Members are invited to share how their sensations are related to others in the group, moving toward new awareness of interpersonal dynamics. As personal awareness is shared between members, a theme develops to mobilize group energy. The group leader may suggest different here-and-now experiments to guide group members to greater understanding and learning. As the group engages in the self-selected experiment, contact is made which leaves the group feeling satisfied. During resolution, group members process their experience and new learnings. After the group members integrate their new findings, they withdraw, which creates a space for new figural images to emerge. The group member once again consciously becomes centered, focusing on breathing and relaxing the body as the process of the gestalt group cycle continues.

As change occurs and the group becomes a safer place for the member to explore interpersonal, intrapersonal, and group process dynamics, boundaries become more permeable and flexible, allowing increased sensation to enter into awareness. The gestalt group cycle becomes more fluid as the group progresses through the developmental stages (Figure 19–2). The individual is now able to take more risks in becoming more fully human, more congruent and centered. New learning is applied to group interactions and in turn is generalized to everyday situations.

GROUND RULES

A universal ground rule in gestalt therapy is no gossiping. Frequently group members who are in training will want to use tape recorders. This author permits the use of tape recording after every person in the group has agreed to allow such recording. When any individual is working in the group setting on his or her own issues, he or she may tape record his or her

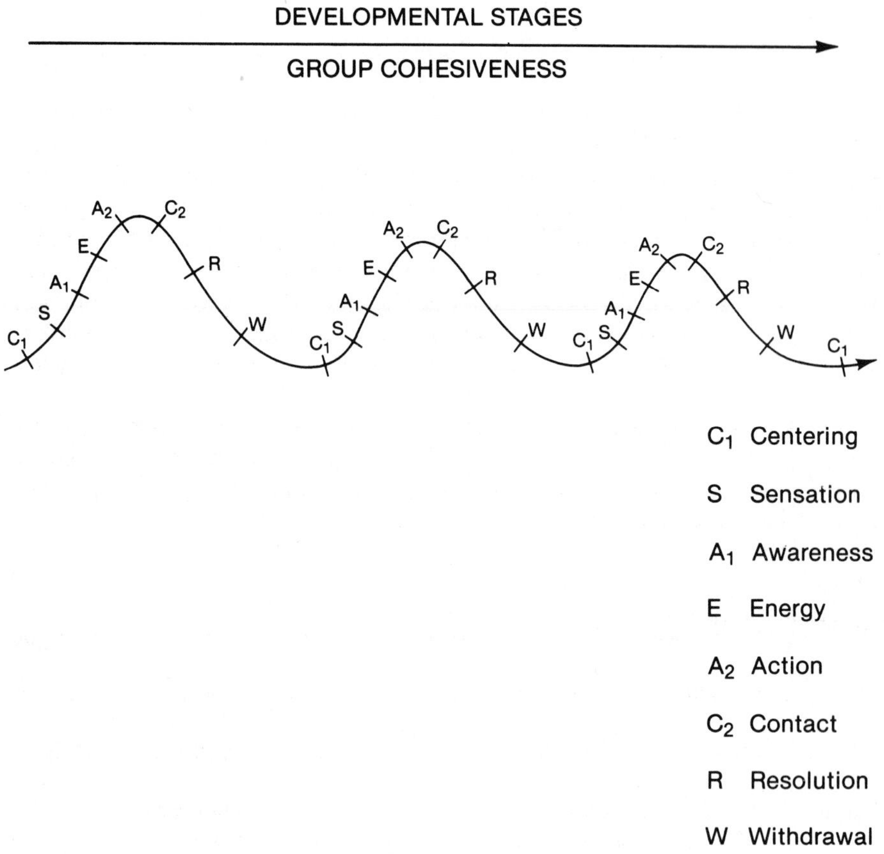

DEVELOPMENTAL STAGES

GROUP COHESIVENESS

C_1 Centering

S   Sensation

A_1 Awareness

E   Energy

A_2 Action

C_2 Contact

R   Resolution

W   Withdrawal

Figure 19–2   Developmental Stages

own material. Tape recording of another person's work without their expressed permission is a violation of professional ethics and is not allowed.

At times specific ground rules are consensually agreed to in a particular group as the need for these rules becomes apparent, for example, if some people within a group are using alcohol or drugs and this interferes with their effectiveness within the group. Occasionally two people will form a confluent dyad. Usually this will result in their draining off anxiety and/or issues that properly belong in the group. In such a case the group leader and/or group members will confront the confluent pair within the group.

On the basis of extensive experience, people who are related in some fashion (husband and wife, lovers, office coworkers, etc.) are discouraged from participating in the same group. This author takes responsibility for setting this condition. On rare occasions where people have agreed in advance to a nonconfluent contract, he has made exceptions.

SUMMARY

Gestalt group therapy has gone through its own development of working with one person in a "hot seat" to integrating intrapersonal, interpersonal, and group dynamics. It is a powerful therapy that facilitates individuals' and group's awareness in the here-and-now through experiments. When the leader of the group possesses the core facilitative conditions of empathy, unconditional positive regard, and genuineness, and relates to others in an I-Thou manner, the experiments are perceived by the group members as the therapist trying to clearly communicate understanding of the person. The facilitator's task is to help members learn more about themselves step-by-step.

Gestalt therapy offers one an opportunity to be in touch with the connection of the mind and body. Furthermore, it teaches individuals a process of developing internal support to encounter and make contact with self and the environment.

REFERENCES

Beisser, A. R. (1970). The paradoxical theory of change. In J. Fagan & I. L. Shepherd (Eds.), *Gestalt therapy now*. Palo Alto, CA: Science and Behavior Books.

Feder, B., & Ronall, R. (1980). *Beyond the hot seat: Gestalt approaches to group*. New York: Brunner/Mazel.

Kepner, E. (1980). Gestalt group process. In B. Feder, & R. Ronall (Eds.), *Beyond the hot seat: Gestalt approaches to group*. New York: Brunner/Mazel.

Perls, F. S. (1947/1969). *Ego, hunger and aggression*. London: Allen and Unwin. New York: Random House.

Perls, F. S. (1967). Workshop vs. individual therapy. *Journal of the Long Island Consultation Center, 5*(2), 13.

Perls, F. S. (1975). Resolution. In J. O. Stevens (Ed.) *Gestalt is.* Moab, UT: People Press.

Perls, F. S. (1976). Gestalt therapy verbatim: Introduction. In C. Hatcher, & P. Himelstein (Eds.). *The handbook of Gestalt therapy.* New York: Jason Aronson.

Perls, F. S., Hefferline, R. D., & Goodman, P. (1951/1965). *Gestalt therapy.* New York: Julian Press. (New York: Dell).

Simkin, J. S. (1979). Gestalt therapy. In R. J. Corsini, & Contributors. *Current psychotherapies* (2nd ed.). Itasca, IL: F. E. Peacock Publishers.

VanDusen, W. (1960). Existential analytic psychotherapy. *American Journal of Psychoanalysis, 20*(1), 310.

Warren, H. D. (1934). *Dictionary of psychology.* New York: Houghton-Mifflin.

Yontef, G. M. (1971). *A review of the practice of Gestalt therapy.* Los Angeles: Trident Shop, California State College.

Zinker, J. (1977). *Creative process in gestalt therapy.* New York: Vintage Books.

SUGGESTED READINGS

Fagan, J., & Shepherd, I. L. (Eds.). (1970). *Gestalt therapy now.* Palo Alto, CA: Science and Behavior Books.

Perls, F. S. (1969). *Gestalt therapy verbatim.* Moab, UT: Real People Press.

Polster, E., & Polster, M. (1973). *Gestalt therapy integrated: Contours of theory and practice.* New York: Vintage Books.

Stevens, B. (1970). *Don't push the river (it flows by itself).* Lafayette, CA: Real People Press.

Van De Riet, V., Korb, M., & Gorrell, J. (1980). *Gestalt therapy: An Introduction.* New York: Pergamon Press.

C H A P T E R 20

Cognitive-Behavioral Group Therapy[1]

INTRODUCTION

Cognitive-behavior modification as a therapeutic treatment addresses itself primarily to changing how a client thinks. It is a therapy that utilizes metacognition as a means to an end, and encourages clients to think about their thoughts as a way of changing those thoughts. Such a procedure for change reflects the cognitive-behavioral belief that cognitions, as events, processes, and structure, direct and guide behavior.

How the cognitions of the client are approached describes the differences between cognitive therapies. Albert Ellis, for example, would confront the underlying cognitive structures of the client; that is, his or her beliefs. Aaron Beck, as his research with depressives reveals, would look at the behavior of the client to provide a roadmap into the inner world of his or her cognitions. He would then encourage the client to try new behaviors for the purpose of analyzing the self-talk that would occur as a result of the change (Meichenbaum, 1977). Donald Meichenbaum would address himself primarily to changing the inner speech clients make to themselves. He believes that the inner speech, or the internal dialogue, affects both the underlying cognitive structures and the behavior at the same time. Thus, cognitive behaviorists recognize a division of three when considering mental processes—cognitive structures, inner speech, and behavioral acts— and they differ according to which of these processes they hold *a priori*.

1. Written by Charlalee Sedgwick, Ph.D. candidate, University of Georgia.

Cognition, as Meichenbaum (1977, 1986) presents it, can be understood in three different ways: as event, as process, as structure. Mental events, the raw material of cognition, include what Beck (1976) calls *automatic thoughts*, which basically are available consciously and can be called up to the forefront of one's mind. Attributions, expectancies, and task-irrelevant thoughts can be automatic, as can be non-verbal events such as images, symbolic "words," and gestures. For instance, an imagined scenario can run at a rapid pace through one's mind without a word appearing. The effect is the same—the individual is left mentally "placed," as it were, set up to expect certain actions or events as a result of having been visited by the fantasy, which came unbidden.

Cognitive behaviorists believe that cognition is intimately linked with affect (Beck, 1970, 1976; D'Zurrila & Goldfried, 1971; Ellis & Grieger, 1978; Meichenbaum, 1977), so much so that the two are difficult to separate. Cognitive events that are laden with affect are called, according to Zajonc (1980), "hot," as contrasted with those that are "cold." Meichenbaum (1977) suggests that affect is "stored" in the same way facts are, and that which stimulates a set of concepts (a schema) into conscious action will also release associated affect. It is a cognitive-behavioral view that insight cannot be experienced by a client unaccompanied by a joint movement of affect and cognition.

In a description of automatic thoughts, Beck (1976) mentions that this kind of thinking is not vague and unformulated, but is specific. Automatic thoughts occur in "a kind of shorthand . . . only the essential words in a sentence seem to occur." The person sees such thoughts as "plausible, reasonable"; this characteristic explains why they are idiosyncratic. Thirdly, these thoughts "just happen . . . they seem to be relatively autonomous in that the patient made no effort to initiate them . . . " (Beck, 1976, pp. 36–37). The label "automatic thoughts" speaks mainly to the random kind of thinking people do, which guides their behavior and can for the most part be called scripted and habitual. Such unintentional thinking, insofar as it is maladaptive, is one target of cognitive-behavioral therapy.

Meichenbaum, referring back to Plato, calls such unintentional thinking the *internal dialogue*, which describes verbal and non-verbal events. He means "dialogue" instead of "monologue" for the purpose of conveying the fact that one listens to oneself as well as speaks to oneself. This "self-communication system," insofar as it describes a process, has within it the potential for change (Meichenbaum, 1977, p. 212).

A concept of cognition ought to reflect an understanding of how people process information. The rubric "cognitive processes" means, according to Meichenbaum, the way in which an individual selectively picks what he or she wants to think about as well as the meaning he or she will attribute to it. It is important to recognize here that a person is not usually aware of how he or she processes information; it is much like driving a car, walking, or breathing. Only when an individual becomes aware of what he or she is doing (or thinking), is there some hope for changing those actions or thoughts.

Cognitive structures, Meichenbaum's third dimension of cognition, include tacit assumptions a person makes about his or her world; in other words, his or her beliefs. By self-observation the clients learn to see their beliefs as hypotheses open to testing, not as unassailable facts. The client begins to recognize his or her overgeneralizations, magnifications, arbitrary inferences, dichotomous reasoning, and the like as faulty thinking. Supported by the strength of the client's collaboration with the therapist, the client learns to see new meanings in his or her behaviors and is encouraged to translate his or her manner of living differently.

The emphasis in Meichenbaum's approach is placed on *how* to think rather than on *what* to think; that is why his problem-solving training focuses more on coping than mastery of problems. Teachers, for example, rarely model to their students how they handle frustration and failure while setting out to perform a certain task; they seldom demonstrate to students the cognitive step-by-step procedure involved in problem-solving (Meichenbaum, 1986). A coping model who falters in the face of an anxiety-producing problem but goes on to exhibit coping, thereby becoming a mastery model, is the most persuasive model for effecting change (Bandura, 1976).

PRINCIPLES OF CHANGE ⎯⎯⎯⎯⎯⎯⎯⎯⎯⎯⎯⎯ ∎

After having learned new skills and approaches, the client experiments with what he or she has learned, in vivo. This client is likely to find that the outcomes of such experiments were not as he or she expected. The client's task then becomes one in which he or she makes efforts to fit the fact of these results into previously existing expectations, i.e., his or her cognitive structures. Meichenbaum builds on the "incompatible" findings to raise the consciousness of the client. That client is like the scientist; his or her awareness moves to a kind of new frontier, motivated by curiosity, which puts him or her in a particular state of readiness to receive new information.

Meichenbaum (1977) uses the analogue of the scientist and his or her activities to describe the chain reaction of the behavior change process. It is, for example, the scientist's cognitive structures (his or her beliefs) and the internal dialogue that these structures stimulate that make him or her perceptually aware of certain phenomena; i.e., it governs what he or she is looking for. The activity of the internal dialogue sparks a heightened awareness which makes the scientist sensitive to new data. As the scientist collects that new data, he or she is realizing that it is consistent with or anomalous with his or her prior beliefs. These results, insofar as they are inconsistent, activate the internal dialogue, which now becomes preoccupied with assimilating the new information.

What scientists then say to themselves in response to the results of their actions will determine whether their beliefs (the cognitive structures) will be held intact or will be changed (Meichenbaum, 1977, p. 214).

In the example of the scientist, Meichenbaum illustrates his paradigm of change. Like a rippling effect, deliberate and conscious change that first occurs in the internal dialogue is felt both in the underlying cognitive structures and outwardly in behavior. There is a loop of activity that is implied in Meichenbaum's model which has changes again occurring in the domain of the internal dialogue before changes in the cognitive structure and behavior become permanent. It is important to understand Meichenbaum's vision of cognitive change to grasp why he addresses the internal dialogue of the client and wins the client's collaboration in the effort to understand self-talk.

GROUP PROCEDURE

Groups that are formatted to be cognitive-behavioral are essentially insight-oriented. According to Meichenbaum (1971), group insight-oriented psychotherapy provides the members a chance to discuss the self-verbalizations they make while behaving in a negative and non-functional way. For example, in a 1971 group study on anxiety, Meichenbaum encouraged each member to become aware of (gain insight into) the self-verbalizations and self-instructions which he or she emitted in anxiety-producing interpersonal situations. As each member reports on such self-statements, the other members strengthen the beginning tendency to become aware by voicing shared common experiences. In this process the group members begin to become acquainted with the irrational, self-defeating, and self-fulfilling nature of such statements. Secondly, the group members learn, by way of the style the group leader models, to make both incompatible self-instructions and incompatible behavior. Encouraged by one another, they individually not only try to behave in accord with the new self-instructions, but also learn to take note of the internal dialogue that comes as a result of confronting the inconsistent results of one's own new behavior.

Turk, Meichenbaum, and Genest (1983) have described the above as a behavior-analytic assessment approach consisting of three stages—problem identification, response enumeration, and response evaluation. In other places Meichenbaum (1985, 1986) has called the phases conceptualization, skills acquisition and rehearsal, and application and follow-through.

GROUP METHODS

Cognitive-behavioral group efforts involve some elements of didactic teaching, Socratic discussion, problem solving, cognitive restructuring, behavioral and imaginal rehearsal, self-monitoring, self-instruction, self-reinforcement, efforts at environmental change, imagining practice, and as the case may be, relaxation training. In the initial phase of group therapy four procedures are completed: (1) assessment, (2) group discussion, (3) situational analysis, and (4) homework assignments. In the initial group session, the therapist explores the intensity and duration of the members' presenting problems. In an effort to describe the problem fully, a client may be asked to rehearse an imagery procedure—"run a movie through his head"—reporting on thoughts and feelings as well as behaviors. A behavioral assessment may be done as an adjunct; for example, the group members assembled for the treatment of anxiety may meet in an office or laboratory, or *in situ* where they would be asked to cope with certain anxiety-producing situations. Subsequently, the group will gain cohesiveness and identity as the group members later discuss their reactions to such an assessment (Meichenbaum, 1977).

In keeping with the exploration of self-statements, homework may be assigned which has the clients become aware of how their thought processes contribute to how they feel and behave. Meichenbaum and Genest (1977) point out that therapists differ as to how structured such homework assignments should be.

A client's behavior in the group will illustrate much of his or her self-talk, which can lead to a beneficial exploration by the group. As reconceptualization begins, and each client starts to use his or her maladaptive behaviors as cues for the coping procedure taught in therapy, much of what had been said by the group previously will come back. Inasmuch as negative self-talk is acted out and discussed in the group, and is in fact worked in as a therapy procedure by the leader, generalization of treatment is ensured (Meichenbaum & Genest, 1977).

Coping and reinforcing self-statements are introduced to the group at each phase of therapy. For instance, one might say to oneself in the face of being overwhelmed: "Keep the focus on the present; what is it I have to do?" or "This is the anxiety that I thought I might feel. It's a reminder for me to cope." Reinforcing self-statements could be as follows: "It's working. I can control how I feel." or "I made more out of my fear than it was worth." (Meichenbaum, 1977, p. 12).

Making self-statements helps an individual to

a) assess the reality of the situation; b) control negative, self-defeating, anxiety-engendering ideation; c) acknowledge, use, and possibly relabel the anxiety they are experiencing; d) "psych" themselves up to perform the task;

e) cope with any intense anxiety they might experience; and f) reinforce themselves for having coped. (Meichenbaum & Genest, 1977, p. 11)

Imagery procedures, as in desensitization, are effective in later stages of therapy as ways of rehearsing coping responses. Coping imagery procedures have also been found to enhance change substantially (Kazdin, 1973; Meichenbaum, 1972). Inasmuch as the imagined situation is similar to a real-life situation, the chances are greater for treatment generalization.

THERAPIST'S ROLE ━━━━━━━━━━━━━━━━━━━━━━━━━━━━━━━━━━ ■

Even though the cognitive-behavioral therapist acts primarily like a guide and consultant, Meichenbaum (1971, 1977, 1985, 1986) stresses the importance of the relationship the therapist fosters with his or her clients. The therapist makes efforts to see that each client's viewpoint is being adequately addressed. Meichenbaum speaks to the collaboration the therapist and client develop as being a prerequisite for the learning that is to follow. Basically the client-trainer relationship is a "framework in which coping skills are nurtured"; it is the quality of the relationship, usually established by the third session that determines outcome (Meichenbaum, 1985, p. 28).

Despite the theoretical orientation of the therapist, it is the collaboration between therapist and clients that begins the process of reconceptualization. The quality of this therapeutic relationship will have a bearing on how well clients hear the therapist, and how willing they will be to make the effort to assign new or different meanings to their experiences.

In the initial phase of therapy, the therapist is trying to assess each client's presenting problem correctly. For example, the therapist is distinguishing whether the problem is a "can't" or a "won't"; "can't" problems indicate a difficulty with responses, suggesting the need of behavioral rehearsal and coping skills training. A "won't" problem implies that the client's problem is born out of the internal dialogue, creating negative self-statements that interfere with adaptive behaviors (Meichenbaum & Genest, 1977, p. 6). Indication that the problem is a "won't" points to the fact that the client already knows the adaptive responses, but will not do them because of situations he or she interprets as being too threatening.

The group leader is more Socratic than didactic. Meichenbaum (1985) uses the example of Colombo, a TV character who demonstrates how as an interviewer he uses his own befuddlement as a way of not only soliciting information, but also as a means of having others "try on" a particular perspective or conceptualization.

The cognitive-behavioral therapist also begins the reconceptualization process by reinforcing the idea that one is not alone in his or her emotional distress; in other words, it is the therapist's job to amplify the normalizing process already common to good group activity.

GROUP SIZE AND COMPOSITION

Cognitive-behavior groups are generally kept small, namely because, in a small group, it is easier for the group members to "brainstorm." In addition, members in a small group more carefully clarify one another's problems, interact more efficiently in the planning of action, and closely monitor each other's implementation (Rose, 1982). Meichenbaum (1988) suggests that a group number from 6 to 12, and that each session run from 75 to 90 minutes. With anxious students (1971), Meichenbaum took care to have both sexes represented in each group numbering on the average, 6. Cognitive-behavioral training programs, on the other hand, have been administered to classroom-size groups. Meichenbaum (1986) has indicated how readily classroom procedures can be adapted to fit self-instructional training.

Meichenbaum's groups have mainly been homogeneous, focusing on people with specific problems like test-anxious students or fear-avoidant phobics. Homogeneity is recommended because the treatment is usually short-term—a heterogeneous mix would not facilitate focusing on coping skills and "target-specific conceptualizations" in a short period of time (Meichenbaum, 1988).

GROUP SETTING

According to Rose (1982), cognitive-behavioral groups adhere to two main principles in reference to the group setting: they attempt to make the setting resemble as closely as possible the setting in which the problems originated, and they make the setting attractive to the group. Fortunately, cognitive-behavior modification is very adaptable to natural settings. For example, Deikis presented Stress Inoculation Training didactically to scuba divers (supplemented with in vivo rehearsal in the pool) having problems with panic (Meichenbaum, 1985). There are many opportunities for building Meichenbaum's model of stress management into work settings as on-the-job experience. Usually, however, groups meet in a quiet, comfortable place where the members can be reflective about their thoughts. The conditions are basically comfortable, quiet, and private—conditions in which the group members can relate to each other supportively.

MEDIA EMPLOYED

The media of cognitive-behaviorism is primarily verbal, as the therapeutic emphasis is on the client's learning how to consciously grasp his or her self-talk and voice this aloud to others. Homework is given as an activity to embellish and make consistent the individual's reflective efforts away from the group. In the sessions, cognitive modelling and overt self-instructional material are components of this kind of therapy.

Other procedures are the use of film; for example, shy children were taught how to be more active socially by watching a film where children modeled interacting (Meichenbaum, 1977). Meichenbaum (1977) also recommends supplemental media such as videotape feedback and subjects' prerecorded self-statements. Operant techniques, like social and token reinforcement can be combined with cognitive self-instruction. Self-instructional packages have been found to be effective with procedures that use desensitization, imagery, and modeling (Meichenbaum, 1977).

LENGTH AND DURATION OF TREATMENT

Cognitive-behavioral therapy is short-term; on the average treatment lasts about 8 to 22 sessions, with a group numbering anywhere between 6 to 12 (Meichenbaum, 1988). Meichenbaum's (1971) anxiety groups consisted of 8 sessions, with a follow-up battery of anxiety self-report scales given three months later. There is more variation in length with the larger classroom groups. Meichenbaum (1986) reported on a group of hyperactive boys undertaking self-instructional training that continued for 24 sessions—2 one-hour periods a week for 12 weeks. The members of the young hyperactive children's group, who were learning by imagery how to slow down (they practiced acting like turtles), had a life of 3 weeks for 15 minutes each day (Meichenbaum, 1986).

Stress Inoculation Training (SIT) groups such as the one led by Sarason, Johnson, Berberich, and Siegal (1979) may be provided with fewer sessions; these police academy trainees had 6 two-hour training session. Nurses meeting for SIT were administered the training twice a week for 60 minutes over a 4-week period (Meichenbaum, 1985).

Lately (1988), Meichenbaum has said that the length of group therapy finally depends on the needs of the group members and should be based on performance. A follow-up, in the form of assessments, should be part of the procedure; booster sessions and follow-through interventions are also recommended.

GROUND RULES

Commitment to attending the group sessions regularly is a very basic rule of this approach, as each session builds on what has been taught in previous sessions (Sank & Shaffer, 1984). Also, regular attendance takes into account the fact that the members come to count on one another for support and feedback.

Group members are asked to be prompt to avoid repeating the beginning for latecomers. Promptness also ensures that there is no delay in getting started; this rule underlines the importance of the initial instructions as well as homework review, both of which occur at the beginning.

Homework is an essential part of the cognitive therapy group treatment. Clients are given assignments at the end of each session that are to be completed by the beginning of the next. Homework is much of the content of the session itself; therefore those who do not complete the homework cut down on their potential involvement in the group.

A high premium is put on participation because of the belief that more active group members receive greater benefits from the group experience. Participation, as is the keeping of confidences, is seen as the individual's responsibility. Fostering that individual's responsibility is one of the goals of the group, the idea being that each person is expected to be developing into his or her own therapist by learning the new skills taught in the group (Sank & Shaffer, 1984).

SUMMARY

Thought processes operate automatically unless they are interfered with. Cognitive behaviorism, as exemplified in the work of Meichenbaum, seeks to make these interruptions in the name of correcting old, maladaptive patterns of thinking. Semantic theorists believe that thought that works behind the scenes, so to speak, drives behavior. The therapist cultivates a way in which he and the client can both hold that client's faulty concepts up to the light and examine them for flaws.

In the same way that cognitive-behaviorism respects the interdependent nature of affect and cognitive functioning, so too does this theory respect that interrelation between the unconscious and conscious mind (Meichenbaum, 1984). In the same way that metacognitions represent the interface between the unconscious and conscious, so do semantic therapists represent guides who seek to lead their clients through this area, acquainting them with both that aspect of mind that is automatic and another aspect of mind that is accessible to assessment, research, and therapy.

REFERENCES

Bandura, A. (1976). Effecting change through participant modeling. In J. D. Krumboltz, & C. Thoresen (Eds.) *Counseling methods*. New York: Holt Rinehart and Winston.

Beck, A. (1970). Cognitive therapy: Nature and relation to behavior therapy. *Behavior Therapy, 1*, 184–200.

Beck, A. T. (1976). *Cognitive therapy and the emotional disorders*. New York: International Universities Press, Inc.

D'Zurilla, T., & Goldfried, M. (1971). Problem-solving and behavior modification. *Journal of Abnormal Psychology, 78*, 107–126.

Ellis, A., & Grieger, R. (1978). *RET: Handbook of rational emotive therapy*. New York: Springer.

Kazdin, A. (1973). Covert modeling and the reduction of avoidance behavior. *Journal of Abnormal Psychology, 81*, 87–95.

Meichenbaum, D. (1972). Cognitive modification of test anxious college students. *Journal of Consulting and Clinical Psychology, 39*, 370–390.

Meichenbaum, D. (1977). *Cognitive behavior modification: An integrative approach*. New York: Plenum.

Meichenbaum, D. (1985). *Stress inoculation training*. New York: Pergamon Press.

Meichenbaum, D. (1986). Cognitive-behavior modification. In F. H. Kanfer, & A. P. Goldstein (Eds.) *Helping people change*. New York: Pergamon Press.

Meichenbaum, D., & Deffenbacher, J. L. (1988). Stress Inoculation Training. *The Counseling Psychologist, 16*, p. 69–90.

Meichenbaum, D., & Genest, M. (1977). Treatment of anxiety. In G. Harris, *The group treatment of human problems: A social learning approach*. New York: Grune & Stratton.

Meichenbaum, D., & Gilmore, J. B. (1984). The nature of unconscious processes: A cognitive-behavioral perspective. In K. S. Bowers & D. Meichenbaum (Eds.), *The unconscious reconsidered*. New York: John Wiley & Sons.

Meichenbaum, D., Gilmore, B., & Fedoravicius, A. (1971). Group insight versus group desensitization in treating speech anxiety. *Journal of Consulting and Clinical Psychology, 36*, 410–421.

Piaget, J. (1954). *Construction of reality in the child*. (Trans. M. Cook). New York: Basic Books.

Rose, S. D. (1982). Group counseling with children—a behavioral and cognitive approach. In G. M. Gazda (Ed.), *Basic approaches to group psychotherapy and group counseling*. Springfield, IL: Charles C. Thomas.

Sank, L. I., & Shaffer, C. S. (1984). *A therapist's manual for cognitive behavior therapy in groups*. New York: Plenum Press.

Sarason, G., Johnson, J. H., Berberich, J. P., & Seigel, J. M. (1979). Helping police officers to cope with stress: A cognitive-behavioral approach. *American Journal of Community Psychology, 7*, 593–603.

Turk, D., Meichenbaum, D., & Genest, M. (1983). *Pain and behavioral medicine*. New York: Guilford Press.

Zajonc, R. (1980). Feeling and thinking: Preferences need no inferences. *American Psychologist, 35*, 151–175.

SUGGESTED READINGS ⎯⎯⎯⎯⎯⎯⎯⎯⎯⎯⎯⎯ ■

Beck, A. (1976). *Cognitive therapy and the emotional disorders*. New York: International Universities Press.

Frank, J. (1974). *Persuasion and healing*. New York: Schocken.

Goldfried, M., Decenteceo, E., & Weingerg, L. (1974). Systematic rational restructuring as a self-control technique. *Behavior Therapy, 5,* 247–254.

Kelly, G. (1969). Personal construct theory and the psychotherapeutic interview. In B. Maher (Ed.), *Clinical psychology and personality: The selected papers of George Kelly.* New York: John Wiley.

Laqarus, R., Averill, J., & Opton, E. (1970). Towards a cognitive theory of emotions. In M. Arnold (Ed.), *Feelings and emotions.* New York: Academic Press.

Luria, A. (1961). *The role of speech in the regulation of normal and abnormal behaviors.* New York: Liveright.

Meichenbaum, D. (1975). Enhancing creativity by modifying what subjects say to themselves. *American Educational Research Journal, 12,* 129–145.

Novaco, R. (1975). *Anger control: The development and evaluation of an experimental treatment.* Lexington, MA: D. C. Heath.

Polanyi, M. (1958). *Personal knowledge: Towards a post critical philosophy.* Chicago, IL: University of Chicago Press.

Appendix A

Knowledge and Skill Descriptors by Age Level for the Four Generic Life-Skill Areas of Interpersonal Communication/Human Relations, Problem-Solving/Decision-Making, Physical Fitness/Health Maintenance, and Identity Development/Purpose in Life

The items in this appendix are taken from the national Delphi study that identified life-skills descriptors for childhood, adolescence, and adulthood and grouped these descriptors into generic categories. The list is not exhaustive, but it is comprehensive in its coverage. The following descriptors were judged by panels of experts, who then assigned them to the categories. Where possible, normative age ranges are attached to the descriptors that indicate the approximate time in a person's life when the skill is usually acquired.

INTERPERSONAL COMMUNICATION/ HUMAN RELATIONS SKILLS ⎯⎯⎯⎯⎯⎯⎯⎯⎯⎯ ▬

Definition: Skills necessary for effective communication, both verbal and nonverbal, with others, leading to ease in establishing relationships; small and large group and community membership and participation; manage-

From D. K. Brooks, Jr. (1984). A life-skills training: Defining elements of effective functioning through the use of the delphi technique. Unpublished doctoral dissertation, University of Georgia, Athens, Georgia. Copyright © D. K. Brooks, Jr. (1984). Reprinted by permission.

ment of interpersonal intimacy; clear expression of ideas and opinions; giving and receiving feedback; and so forth.

Descriptor

In childhood, the individual:

Functions with age-appropriate independence outside the home (ages 2 through 4).

Understands and acts on established rules of conduct (ages 2 through 4).

Masters social tasks within one's immediate environment (ages 2 through 5).

Interacts with age-mates (ages 2 through 5).

Communicates affect through language expression (ages 2 through 7).

Differentiates positive and negative feedback (ages 2 through 7).

Accords equal justice to one's peers and oneself (ages 2 through 7).

Gives and receives affection in appropriate ways (ages 3 through 6).

Follows or leads in a group depending upon the circumstances.

Develops meaningful relationships with age-mates.

Maintains relationships with peers.

Relates to members of both sexes in play situations (ages 4 through 6).

Responds with affect to peers and adults in an age-appropriate fashion (ages 4 through 10).

Develops and nurtures peer relationships (ages 4 through 10).

Recognizes other points of view (ages 4 through 10).

Meets personal goals through cooperative play (ages 5 through 7).

Works and plays cooperatively with peers (ages 6 through 8).

Uses interpersonal skills in social situations (ages 6 through 14).

Values personal privacy and respects that of others (ages 7 through 8).

Applies abstract principles such as fairness to interpersonal relations (ages 7 through 9).

Values democratic processes in group decisions (ages 7 through 11).

Understands and follows rules in games (ages 7 through 11).

Views interpersonal relations from the perspective of others (ages 7 through 12).

Establishes primary identification with peers (ages 8 through 10).

Values others for their own sake.

Listens attentively to others.

Responds empathetically to others.

Resolves interpersonal disputes through negotiation.

Finds "no-lose" solutions to conflicts.

Differentiates assertiveness from aggression.

Differentiates competition from conflict.

Differentiates leadership from dominance.

In adolescence, the individual:

Responds with empathy to the problems of others (ages 8 through 10).

Is able to initiate, maintain, and, when appropriate, terminate friendships (ages 8 through 10).

Understands and accepts as healthy the interpersonal communication of sexual attraction (ages 8 through 11).

Utilizes language to represent complex concepts with increasing accuracy (ages 9 through 13).

Employs perspective-taking in interpersonal situations (ages 10 through 13).

Understands that accomplishment of group goals may require compromise and reevaluation of personal goals (ages 10 through 13).

Forms interpersonal relationships based on mutuality and respect for individual identity (ages 10 through 15).

Relates positively with significant persons in one's immediate environment (ages 10 through 15).

Undertakes cooperative enterprises involving individual responsibility (ages 11 through 12).

Is independent in many relationships (ages 11 through 14).

Shows reasonable respect for legitimate authority (ages 11 through 14).

Understands the value of social order (ages 11 through 14).

Appreciates diversity in personalities and activities (ages 11 through 15).

Is able to resolve conflicting loyalties.

Tolerates differences of opinion without being afraid of holding to a divergent view.

Appreciates a sense of community with peers (ages 11 through 15).

Relates comfortably with members of the opposite sex (ages 12 through 14).

Is able to be objective about relationships (ages 12 through 16).

Responds reciprocally in interpersonal relationships (ages 13 through 16).

Appreciates laws as necessary for the maintenance of order while questioning those that are unjust (ages 14 through 16).

Understands and resolves ambiguity in peer-group values (ages 14 through 18).

Understands and acts in accordance with situationally appropriate social customs (ages 14 through 18).

Is open to the opinions and actions of others.

Is assertive in interpersonal relationships.

Copes successfully with peer pressure.

Selects appropriately from one's repertoire of interpersonal skills as situations and groups change (ages 15 through 17).

Recognizes the feelings and motives behind interpersonal actions.

Conducts oneself in social group situations with poise and confidence.

Appreciates the problems and uniquenesses of one's parents.

Understands to some degree the problems and difficulties of others.

Responds to the feelings of others and is able to express one's own feelings.

Develops support from peer relationships (ages 16 through 18).

Initiates and nurtures mutually satisfying sexual relationships (ages 17 through 20).

Appreciates one's similarity to others (peers) rather than feeling one is an outsider.

[NOTE: In the following items age ranges become much less normative than is the case for childhood and adolescence. The systematic study of adult development and aging is a much newer branch of the behavioral sciences than the life periods that precede it. The literature is therefore much less specific about when certain life-skills are acquired.]

In adulthood, the individual:

Relates to others with appropriate openness (young adulthood).

Manages intimacy with close friends (young adulthood).

Uses one's peer group for support while still maintaining one's individual autonomy (young adulthood).

Chooses relationships that are based on more than physical attractiveness (young adulthood).

Maintains continuous satisfying relationships with family members (young adulthood).

Is able to commit to a long-term relationship with a partner (young adulthood).

Forms close relationships based on interdependence (young adulthood).

Gets along with both superiors and peers on the job (young adulthood).

Communicates one's wants and needs effectively (young adulthood).

Identifies and forms relationships with potential mentors (young adulthood).

Utilizes interpersonal skills to expand the circle of one's relationships (young adulthood).

Is able to listen so well to another that one's response reflects the original statement in both content and affect (young adulthood).

Tolerates and respects those of different backgrounds, habits, values, and appearance (young adulthood).

Behaves in a marriage relationship so as to balance giving and getting (young adulthood).

Utilizes one's personal freedom to make judgments and decisions that are harmonious with the public good (young adulthood).

Assumes responsibility as a community member (young adulthood).

Manages conflicts on the job and at home (young adulthood).

Is able to give and take (young adulthood).

Is able to engage in a mentoring relationship (young adulthood).

Is able to establish and enjoy relationships within social groups (young adulthood).

Undertakes adult civic and social responsibilities (young adulthood).

Maintains intimacy with partner during child-rearing years (young adulthood).

Relates effectively with one's aging parents (young adulthood).

Contributes to the welfare of others (young adulthood).

Relates empathetically and effectively to one's children (if any) at all developmental stages (early middle age).

Recognizes and respects the individual rights, personal worth, and uniqueness of others (early middle age).

Copes effectively with the possible dependence of one's aging parents (early middle age).

Draws on one's reservoir of experiences in understanding broad social issues and community concerns (middle age).

Is able to be at peace with others (middle age).

PROBLEM-SOLVING/ DECISION-MAKING SKILLS

Definition: Skills necessary for information seeking; information assessment and analysis; problem identification, solution, implementation, and evaluation; goal setting; systematic planning and forecasting; time management; critical thinking; conflict resolution; and so forth.

Descriptor

In childhood, the individual:

Is able to develop and carry out a complex intention.

Employs fantasy and role playing regarding future vocational aspirations.   ·

Chooses activities suited to interests.

Expands cognitive and sensory understanding by exploring the immediate environment (ages 2 through 4).

Makes perceptual judgments involving one variable (ages 2 through 7).

Utilizes intuition in making judgments (ages 4 through 7).

Utilizes objective data in making judgments (ages 4 through 7).

Anticipates possible consequences of actions through personal reflection (ages 4 through 10).

Understands and relates tasks to goal achievement (ages 5 through 7).

Formulates future plans on a limited basis (ages 5 through 9).

Is able to be goal-directed (ages 5 through 9).

Sticks with tasks to completion (ages 6 through 7).

Makes choices that take personal abilities into account (ages 6 through 10).

Understands age-appropriate cognitive tasks (ages 7 through 8).

Evaluates one's actions and those of others by the perceived intentions, not just by the consequences (ages 7 through 11).

Follows directions in situations involving multiple tasks (ages 7 through 11).

Is able to read for pleasure.

Chooses and participates in activities that are fun.

Tries new methods of problem solving (ages 8 through 9).

Utilizes logical thinking in investigations (ages 8 through 10).

Understands cause and effect relationships (ages 8 through 10).

Is able to work independently on a task (ages 9 through 10).

Is able to reverse cognitive operations (ages 9 through 10).

Uses cognitive and perceptual processes in problem solving (ages 9 through 10).

In adolescence, the individual:

Makes logical deductions in problem solving (ages 9 through 13).

Can manipulate and apply abstract ideas in problem solving (ages 9 through 13).

Analyzes and applies multiple reference systems to problem-solving tasks (ages 11 through 12).

Learns and uses an effective approach to decision making.

Maintains balance between awareness of one's own opinions and those of others in making decisions (ages 11 through 14).

Uses role models to learn about occupations (ages 11 through 17).

Identifies and defines personal problems and goals (ages 14 through 18).

Develops personal talents and considers implications for life planning (ages 14 through 18).

Takes directions and follows through on tasks.

Gathers reliable information about occupations (ages 14 through 18).

Is able to compare and analyze patterns of thought (ages 14 through 18).

Is able to analyze multiple variables in problem solving (ages 14 through 18).

Systematically explores a broad range of potential occupational choices (ages 14 through 18).

Distinguishes between supported opinions and those without support (ages 14 through 18).

Is able to do critical task analysis as an initial step in problem solving (ages 15 through 16).

Narrows one's range of potential occupational choices after having engaged in thorough exploration (ages 16 through 18).

Makes and implements informed educational decisions (ages 16 through 19).

Demonstrates personal values as the basis for making decisions.

Is able to dispute irrational beliefs or ideas.

Generates alternative problem solutions based on pertinent information (ages 17 through 19).

Is flexible in decision making (ages 17 through 19).

Anticipates consequences of actions and decisions affecting occupational choice (ages 17 through 19).

Utilizes experiences in trial, simulated, and part-time work in analyzing tentative occupational choices (ages 17 through 19).

Makes appropriate educational and occupational plans and decisions at critical points in one's career (ages 18 and over).

Makes tentative plans and action steps toward implementing occupational choices (ages 18 and over).

Plans and implements occupational choice (ages 18 and over).

[NOTE: In the following items age ranges become much less normative than is the case for childhood and adolescence. The systematic study of adult development and aging is a much newer branch of the behavioral sciences than the life periods that precede it. The literature is therefore much less specific about when certain life-skills are acquired.]

In adulthood, the individual:

Makes personally appropriate educational and occupational decisions (young adulthood).

Applies information-seeking skills to a job search (young adulthood).

Is able to manage one's finances (young adulthood).

Is able to be confident in one's decisions (young adulthood).

Balances mutual needs and plans long-term goals with one's partner (young adulthood).

Establishes one's own home with constructive parental support (young adulthood).

Establishes one's own home without financial dependence on parents (young adulthood).

Is able to envision one's future (young adulthood).

Assesses evidence with detachment and objectivity (young adulthood).

Is able to think clearly and solve problems, even in a crisis (young adulthood).

Sees multiple perspectives about issues of theoretical and practical importance (young adulthood).

Understands how emotions influence decisions and actions (young adulthood).

Resolves conflicts, makes decisions, and encounters new situations through effective problem-solving strategies (young adulthood).

Is able to think creatively (young adulthood).

Decides and acts based on one's best judgment (young adulthood).

Sets personal goals and plans for their implementation (young adulthood).

Decides how one wants to be involved with children (young adulthood).

Makes choices that lead to a satisfying lifestyle (young adulthood).

Assesses and analyzes one's commitments on an ongoing basis and orders one's priorities and goals accordingly (early middle age).

Realistically assesses one's future career prospects while valuing one's career accomplishments (early middle age).

Maintains satisfactory performance in one's occupation (early middle age).

Sets goals and applies personally chosen performance standards to their achievement (early middle age).

Balances security and risk-taking in occupational decisions, taking one's personal goals and family commitments into account (early middle age).

Analyzes one's relationship with one's partner on an ongoing basis and plans responsibly in light of that analysis (early middle age).

Incorporates a realistic awareness of one's aging into decision making (early middle age).

Maintains one's sense of occupational competence in the face of competition from young workers (middle age).

Values one's achievements while realistically planning for achieving one's remaining goals (late middle age).

Plans for retirement alternatives (late middle age).

PHYSICAL FITNESS/
HEALTH MAINTENANCE SKILLS

Definition: Skills necessary for motor development and coordination, nutritional maintenance, weight control, physical fitness, athletic participation, physiological aspects of sexuality, stress management, leisure activity selection, and so forth.

Descriptor

In childhood, the individual:

Demonstrates muscle control and coordination (ages 2 through 4).

Acquires self-help skills requiring muscular coordination (ages 2 through 4).

Learns to set reasonable and safe limits on physical activities (ages 6 through 8).

Understands the nature of physical maturation (ages 8 through 9).

Performs fine motor skills with greater consistency (ages 8 through 10).

Can relate the function of sexual organs to one's understanding of reproduction (ages 9 through 10).

Can maintain a high level of energy and stamina.

In adolescence, the individual:

Understands what is normal and natural about sexual arousal and expression.

Participates in competitive, cooperative, and/or individual sports.

Can understand and decide how to control one's rapidly changing body in positive ways.

Understands how body and emotions combine to affect human behavior.

Understands menstruation as a normal physical phenomenon (ages 11 through 13).

Accepts as normal various physiological changes associated with puberty (ages 12 through 13).

Copes with occasionally undesirable side effects of physical maturation (ages 13 through 15).

Copes positively with increased sexual arousal and activity (ages 13 through 15).

Understands masturbation as normal sexual activity (ages 14 through 16).

Applies principles of good grooming and personal hygiene in daily living (ages 14 through 16).

Incorporates avocational and recreational interests into one's lifestyle (ages 15 through 19).

[NOTE: In the following items age ranges become much less normative than is the case for childhood and adolescence. The systematic study of adult development and aging is a much newer branch of the behavioral sciences than the life periods that precede it. The literature is therefore much less specific about when certain life-skills are acquired.]

In adulthood, the individual:

Selects and enjoys satisfying leisure-time activities (young adulthood).

Promotes physical fitness through appropriate regular exercise and dietary habits (young adulthood).

Incorporates appropriate health and fitness activities into one's lifestyle (young adulthood).

Conceptualizes one's health in terms of wellness rather than simply the absence of illness (middle age).

Maintains positive body image as physical changes occur (middle age).

Copes with age-related physical decline and illness (late middle age).

IDENTITY DEVELOPMENT/ PURPOSE IN LIFE SKILLS

Definition: Skills and awareness necessary for ongoing development of personal identity and emotional awareness, including self-monitoring, maintenance of self-esteem, manipulating and accommodating to one's environment, clarifying values, sex-role development, developing meaning of life, establishing moral/value dimensions of sexuality, and so forth.

Descriptor

In childhood, the individual:

Identifies with parent or parental surrogate (ages 2 through 4).

Describes emotional, social, mental, and personal characteristics in self and others (ages 2 through 4).

Expresses appropriately the emotions of anger, fear, happiness, and sadness (ages 2 through 7).

Forms gender identity.

Stabilizes gender identity.

Identifies with same-sex peers.

Focuses on development of special talents (ages 3 through 5).

Achieves balance between dependence and independence as a result of maturation (ages 3 through 6).

Carries out age-appropriate family responsibilities (ages 3 through 6).

Understands that one's perspective is often different from that of others (ages 3 through 6).

Performs age-appropriate tasks for oneself (ages 3 through 7).

Understands one's place within one's immediate environment (ages 4 through 6).

Obeys rules in the absence of authority (ages 4 through 6).

Uses self-control, willpower, and cooperation (ages 5 through 7).

Accepts moral responsibility for one's actions (ages 5 through 9).

Takes responsibility for appropriate household chores (ages 6 through 9).

Assumes responsibility for one's actions (ages 6 through 9).

Understands that individual differences are normal and acceptable (ages 8 through 10).

Understands and applies age-appropriate concepts of right and wrong (ages 8 through 10).

Understands differences between child and adult roles (ages 8 through 10).

Understands the differences between absolute and relative standards and values (ages 8 through 10).

Utilizes a variety of coping strategies to express anger (ages 8 through 10).

Deals with ambiguity in unfamiliar situations (ages 8 through 11).

Utilizes intrinsic motivation to avoid punishment.

Faces problems with confidence in one's ability to solve them.

Achieves reasonable, age-appropriate control over emotions (ages 9 through 13).

Has a sense of humor.

Accepts limitations in sports.

Accepts limitations in academics.

Accepts limitations in physical stature.

Is content when alone.

Can overcome the need for immediate gratification.

Identifies with humanity in general, not just parents or peers.

Acts according to humanistic, cooperative, and altruistic values.

Is able to express personal ownership of one's emotions.

Can differentiate losing from failing.

In adolescence, the individual:

Understands and accepts the development of secondary sex characteristics (ages 10 through 11).

Accepts uncertainty without being threatened by it (ages 11 through 13).

Is able to analyze one's thoughts and feelings (ages 11 through 13).

Is able to identify the role of personal feelings in one's values (ages 12 through 15).

Incorporates feelings about one's maturing body with other elements of one's emerging self-image (ages 13 through 15).

Is able to develop a clearer and more realistic self-identity (ages 13 through 15).

Examines and reformulates one's values and beliefs on an ongoing basis (ages 14 through 16).

Deals with one's emerging needs for independence through constructive ways (ages 14 through 16).

Appreciates one's own development and that of one's peers as representative of a broad range of individual differences (ages 14 through 18).

Appreciates the uniqueness of one's identity and expresses it with confidence (ages 14 through 18).

Develops and utilizes a set of personal standards as guides to action (ages 14 through 18).

Synthesizes current developmental processes into a positive self-image (ages 14 through 18).

Expresses one's emotions appropriately (ages 14 through 18).

Acts responsibly in decisions, actions, and relationships (ages 14 through 18).

Incorporates one's life experiences and resources into an independent lifestyle (ages 14 through 18).

Achieves an appropriate balance between dependence and independence (ages 15 through 16).

Utilizes introspection in understanding oneself (ages 15 through 17).

Incorporates a variety of learnings about oneself into one's self-image (ages 15 through 18).

Follows rules through reason and conscious choice rather than through blind adherence.

Examines and utilizes one's value system in resolving personal moral issues (ages 16 through 18).

Is able to analyze sex roles and to assess their applicability to oneself (ages 16 through 19).

Applies one's concept of personal identity in decision making and interpersonal relationships (ages 17 through 19).

Demonstrates positive work attitudes.

Deals with uncertainty in relations with authority.

Understands the significant meaning of a real love relationship and the part sex plays in this.

Understands the difference between physical sexual attraction and real emotional love and/or friendship.

Formulates and reformulates identity and values, taking peer values into account, without being governed by them.

Can laugh at oneself and develop a sense of humor.

Accepts responsibility for one's actions.

Is able to conceive of oneself in a special occupational role.

Understands the place of work, homemaking, leisure, and other roles in self-realization.

[NOTE: In the following items age ranges become much less normative than is the case for childhood and adolescence. The systematic study of adult development and aging is a much newer branch of the behavioral sciences than the life periods that precede it. The literature is therefore much less specific about when certain life-skills are adopted.]

In adulthood, the individual:

Examines and resolves differences between personal beliefs and social norms (young adulthood).

Defines one's identity in terms of personal ideals and values (young adulthood).

Fully participates in intimate sexual relationships (young adulthood).

Identifies values implicit in particular occupations (young adulthood).

Deals effectively with frustration and failure (young adulthood).

Expresses anger in a constructive way (young adulthood).

Maintains excitement and enthusiasm for living (young adulthood).

Manages one's emotions in constructive ways (young adulthood).

Experiences and encourages mutuality in sexual relationships (young adulthood).

Tolerates ambiguous circumstances (young adulthood).

Acts with independence and an awareness of likely outcomes (young adulthood).

Creates a coherent set of personal values (young adulthood).

Expresses one's emotions appropriately (young adulthood).

Integrates one's values and goals into an independent lifestyle (young adulthood).

Learns selectively from models, not just mentors (young adulthood).

Adjusts to change and loss (e.g., moving away, death) in close relationships (early middle age).

Is aware of self and creates personal meaning through one's own efforts (early middle age).

Understands the meaning of dependence, independence, and interdependence, and how to strike a balance among the three (early middle age).

Views objectively the aspirations one has for one's children (early middle age).

Assesses objectively one's strengths and weaknesses for various life roles (early middle age).

Synthesizes elements of personal values and societal norms into a consistent personal morality (early middle age).

Takes risks and seeks to grow in new ways (early middle age).

Can affirm oneself (early middle age).

Understands how one's values are affected by external influence (early middle age).

Achieves a sense of personal identity through translating one's commitments into actions (early middle age).

Copes effectively with grief at the death of one's parents (early middle age).

Maintains an integrated and positive sense of self as one moves through the life span (middle age).

Acts consistently with personally chosen moral values (middle age).

Maintains one's sense of occupational competence in the face of competition from younger workers (middle age).

Realizes that all life is change and that few choices are final (middle age).

Incorporates one's experiences, values, and goals into a personally relevant philosophy of life (middle age).

Is comfortable with one's physical and mental capacities independent of age (middle age).

Adjusts to changes in family role responsibilities (middle age).

Accepts and copes with irreversible effects of aging (late middle age).

Maintains one's identity and self-esteem as occupational involvement changes (late middle age).

Finds purposeful and satisfying activities in all stages of life (late middle age).

Appreciates, copes with, and uses times of solitude (late middle age).

Balances mental, physical, and emotional resources in maintaining effective functioning (later maturity).

Balances the need to maintain independence with the reality of one's resources, asking for help when necessary (later maturity).

Copes effectively with grief at the death of loved ones (later maturity).

Accepts changing commitments as one grows older (later maturity).

Faces death with composure (later maturity).

Appendix B
Sample of Life-Skills Training Materials for High School Age Group

I. Generic Life Skill: Communication
II. Unit I: Introduction
III. Session 3: Barriers to Communication
IV. Learner's Objectives:
   The student will learn to recognize ineffective communication styles.
   The student will assess his/her own ineffective communications.
   The student will begin to develop a repertoire of effective communication habits.
V. Activity A—Introduction

Teacher's instructions: 5 min.

State the following or convey the same message in your own words:

To have friendships, you need good communication. You need it to get friendships started and to keep them going. Good communication means understanding the other person and the other person understanding you. That doesn't happen all by itself. It takes some effort.

There are several things that make it hard to have good communication. These are things that get in the way of having clear and complete communication with other persons. They are barriers to good communication. If we know what the barriers are, we can learn how to get around them so that communication can be full and complete.

Some styles of communication do not help friendship develop. In fact, these styles can be hurtful. Some of these styles are useful in special situations, but when it comes to meeting new people and getting along with them, they are a disaster.

We will call these hurtful styles "Verbal Villains." They bite and they sting and they burn! Not that they always intend to, but when used at the wrong time, they do. You see, good intentions are not enough! (Gazda, Walters, and Childers, p. 15)[1]

As you are watching this filmstrip, look for yourself and your friends.

VI.   Activity B—Filmstrip

20 min.

Teacher's instructions:
    Show the filmstrip "Verbal Villains."[2]

VII.   Activity C—Discussion of filmstrip

20 min.

Teacher's instructions:
    Discuss the filmstrip. You may want to use some of these questions:
    What verbal villains have you encountered?
    How did you feel when someone said things like that to you?
    How would you have preferred the person to have responded to you?

[1]See Resources list at end of unit.
[2]See Resources list at end of unit.

Homework Assignment: During the next twenty-four hours, listen for verbal villains and write down examples in your workbook. You may find yourself making some of these same mistakes. Make note of these.

Resources Needed:

Filmstrip projector and tape player

Filmstrip "Verbal Villains" available from:

Life Enchantment

8000 East Girard

Suite 601

Denver, Colorado 80231

Real Talk by G. M. Gazda, R. P. Walters & W. C. Childers, 1981

Humanics Limited

P. O. Box 7447

Atlanta, Georgia 30309

Learning Styles: Auditory, visual

Hierarchy of Learning: Knowledge, application, evaluation

I.   Generic Life-Skill: Personal Identity
II.   Unit: 1 Title: Values
III. Session: 11 Title: Values and Advertising
IV.   Learner's Objectives:
      The student will become cognizant of the subtle values in advertising.
      The student will become aware of the ways these values are made
          appealing.
V.   Activity 1: Values in American Advertising

Teacher Instructions: 35 min.
    Divide into groups of six. Have the students work with their
magazines and the Worksheet "Values in American Advertising."
Each should choose (1) a product they have bought, (2) a product
their family has bought, and (3) an ad that especially appeals to them.
Analyze each ad according to the worksheet. Share results in small
groups.

VI.   Activity 2: Summarizing Values in Ads

Peer Facilitator Instructions: 10 min.
    Bring the whole group back together. As a group endeavor to
make a values list for the advertising industry in America, listing
values on chart paper (to be used later).

Homework Assignment: Students are to take the "Values in Ameri-
    can Advertising" worksheet home, watch television commercials,
    and analyze three of them.
Resources Needed: Chart paper, felt-tip marker, magazines (stu-
    dents will bring these), copies of the worksheet "Values in Amer-
    ican Advertising"
Learning Styles: Auditory, visual, kinesthetic
Hierarchy of Learning: Translating skills, analysis, synthesis, evalua-
    tion

WORKSHEET

Values in American Advertising

1. Name of product
2. Approximate cost of product. Is this product something everyone can have? . . . half of our society could get? . . . only a few could get?
3. Describe what you notice when you look at the ad.
4. What are the advertisers telling us about their product?
5. What are the advertisers telling us about ourselves?
6. How is this product supposed to make a difference in our lives?
7. What is *valued* in the ad?
8. Additional insights and comments.

I.   Generic Life-Skill: Personal Identity
II.   Unit: 1
III. Session: 5 Title: Values and Rewards
IV.   Learner's Objectives:

The student will understand intrinsic and extrinsic rewards.
The student will be aware of his/her choices, consequences, and values
   in making decisions.

Activity 1

10 min.	Teacher Instructions: Give mini-lecture in your words or as given below.

Mini Lecture

Much of what we do we do because we have learned that certain
behaviors get certain rewards. When you were small your mother may
have taught you to say "please" by only giving you a cookie when you did
say please. Your teachers reward good school work with good grades. You
may have learned to do good school work because you get a feeling of
satisfaction from doing well or because you like to learn or because its
necessary to achieve another goal.

Rewards or consequences of behavior may be thought of as fitting into
two categories: extrinsic, coming from outside; and intrinsic, coming from
within. Some of us value one kind of reward more than another. As young
people mature intrinsic rewards generally are valued more. There is always
some combination of extrinsic and intrinsic rewards functioning in even the
most mature person. Your parents may work because they enjoy their jobs,
because they consider their contribution important, and becuase they want
the money they earn.

See if you can determine the reward and its origin in the following examples:

1.   A student cleans her room on Saturday before going out with friends.

     Reward   _____
     Origin   _____
     Why do you think so?

2.   John trips Daniel as he walks into the room.

3.   Steven plays ball with his little brother.

4. Jennifer spends hours shopping for just the right outfit.

5. Jim and Susan cut school to spend the day at the lake.

It is not always possible to determine another person's rewards or origin. It may not be easy to determine our own. Let's consider some decisions and see if we can determine the expected rewards.

Activity 2

5 min	Teacher Instructions: Divide the group into four. Give each student the sheet entitled: "Values and Rewards Worksheet." Have them consider all possible options for each situation, and the probable consequences for each option. Try to decide whether a particular consequence involves intrinsic or extrinsic reward, and which would be more important to each of them.
10 min.	Bring group back together for discussion of activity 2.

Homework Assignment

During the next 3 days be aware of choices you make and what the rewards are. Write four of these down, listing the options you had, the consequences, and which rewards were intrinsic, which were extrinsic.

Resources Needed: "Values and Rewards Worksheet"
Learning Styles: auditory, visual
Hierarchy of Learning: knowledge, translating skills, application, evaluation

WORKSHEET

Values and Rewards

1. You have a new job working in a toy store at the mall. You've been
    working there three weeks. Your cousin has invited you to come up
    for a weekend of skiing. Consider whether you would ask off from
    work or not, and what the consequences would be.
    Examples
    1. You decide to ask off.
    Possible Consequences
         1. You feel scared
         2. Your boss fires you
         3. Your boss agrees to let you off
    2. You decide to call in sick.
    Possible Consequences
         1. You go skiing and have a great time
         2. Your boss finds out and fires you
         3. Your parents get involved, tell you they're disappointed in
             you, make you apologize and restrict you
    3. You decide not to ask off
    Possible Consequences
         1. You miss a great weekend
         2. You feel cheated
         3. You feel responsible and mature

2. You've been going with Robin most of the school year. You have
    not promised to see each other exclusively. You have fallen into
    that pattern. You're going to spend a weekend with a friend from
    camp. He wants to know what you want to do about going out with
    a girl there. What are your choices?
3. You're playing number three on the tennis team. Your game is
    getting much sharper, and you think you could get to play number
    two with a little more practice time and a little more concentration.
    To do that you're going to have to give up something else—time for
    studying, hanging out, helping at home, other commitments.
4. Susan is your best friend and would do anything for you. She's just
    found out that she's failing math and will be put on restriction if
    she doesn't pull her grades up quickly. You've just had the test
    she's having tomorrow. Susan asks you to help her study tonight.

5. You and your mother are shopping for a new jacket. She's found one on sale that fits, is warm, and exactly what you don't want. You want one like the other guys are wearing. This one you'd be embarassed to be seen in.

6. Your ten-year-old brother got in a fight after school today. Some older kids were picking on him. You want him to talk to your parents about those kids. He doesn't want to.

Appendix C
Developmental
Schema Chart

THE TODDLER AND PRESCHOOL AGE (UNDER 5 YEARS)

Tasks in Process

Child

To reach physiologic plateaus (motor action, toilet training.)

To differentiate self and secure sense of autonomy.

To tolerate separations from mother.

To develop conceptual understandings and "ethical" values.

To master instinctual psychological impulses (oedipal, sexual, guilt, shame).

To assimilate and handle socialization and acculturation (aggression, relationships, activities, feelings).

To learn sex distinctions.

Mother

To promote training, habits and physiological progression.

To aid in family and group socialization of child.

To encourage speech and other learning.

To reinforce child's sense of autonomy and identity.

To set a model for "ethical" conduct.

To delineate male and female roles.

Source: Senn, Milton, J. E., & Solnit, Albert J. (1968). *Problems in child behavior and development* (Philadelphia: Lea & Febiger). Reproduced by permission.

Acceptable Behavioral Characteristics

Child	*Mother*
Gratification from exercise of neuromotor skills.	Is moderate and flexible in training.
Investigative, imitative, imaginative play.	Shows pleasure and praise for child's advances.
Actions somewhat modulated by thought; memory good; animistic and original thinking.	Encourages and participates with child in learning and in play.
Exercises autonomy with body (sphincter control, eating).	Sets reasonable standards and controls.
Feelings of dependence on mother and separation fears.	Consistent in own behavior, conduct, and ethics.
Behavior identification with parents, siblings, peers.	Provides emotional reassurance to child.
Learns speech for communication.	Promotes peer play and guided group activity.
Awareness of own motives, beginnings of conscience.	Reinforces child's cognition of male and female roles.
Intense feelings of shame, guilt, joy, love, desire to please.	
Internalized standards of "bad," "good"; beginning of reality testing.	
Broader sex curiosity and differentiation.	
Ambivalence toward dependence and independence.	
Questions birth and death.	

Minimal Psychopathology

Child	*Mother*
Poor motor coordination.	Premature, coercive, or censuring training.
Persistent speech problems (stammering, loss of words).	Exacting standards above child's ability to conform.
Timidity toward people and experiences.	Transmits anxiety and apprehension.
Fears and night terrors.	Unaccepting of child's efforts; intolerant toward failures.
Problems with eating, sleeping, elimination, toileting, weaning.	

Child	Mother
Irritability, crying, temper tantrums.	Overreacts, overprotective, overanxious.
Partial return to infantile manners.	Despondent, apathetic.
Inability to leave mother without panic.	
Fear of strangers.	
Breathholding spells.	
Lack of interest in other children.	
Destructive tendencies strong; temper tantrums.	
Inability or unwillingness to do things for self.	
Moodiness and withdrawal; few friends or personal relationships.	

Extreme Psychopathology

Child	Parent(s)
Extreme withdrawal, apathy, depression, grief, self-destructive tendencies.	Extreme depression and withdrawal; rejection of child.
Complete failure to learn; speech difficulty, especially stuttering.	Intense hosility; aggression toward child.
Extreme and uncontrollable antisocial behavior (aggression, destruction, chronic lying, stealing, intentional cruelty to animals).	Uncontrollable fears, anxieties, guilts.
	Complete inability to function in family role.
Severe obsessive-compulsive behavior (phobias, fantasies, rituals).	Severe moralistic prohibition of child's independent strivings.
Inability to distinguish reality from fantasy.	
Excessive sexual exhibitionism, eroticism, sexual assaults on others.	
Extreme somatic illness; failure to thrive, anorexia, obesity, hypochrondriasis, abnormal menses.	
Complete absence or deterioration of personal and peer relationships.	

PUBERTY AND EARLY ADOLESCENCE
(12 TO 15 YEARS)

Tasks In Process

Child	*Parent(s)*
To come to terms with body changes.	To help child complete emancipation.
To cope with sexual development and psychosexual drives.	To provide support and understanding.
To establish and confirm sense of identity.	To limit child's behavior and set standards.
To learn further about sex role.	To offer favorable and appropriate environment for healthy development.
To synthesize personality.	
To struggle for independence and emancipation from family.	To recall own adolescent difficulties; to accept and respect the adolescent's differences or similarities to parents or others.
To incorporate learning to the gestalt of living.	
	To relate to adolescents and adolescence with a constructive sense of humor.

Acceptable Behavioral Characteristics

Child	*Parent(s)*
Heightened physical power, strength and coordination.	Allow and encourage reasonable independence.
Occasional psychosomatic and somatopsychic disturbances.	Set fair rules; are consistent.
Maturing sex characteristics and proclivities.	Compassionate and understanding; firm but not punitive or derogatory.
Review and resolution of oedipal conflicts.	Feel pleasure and pride; occasional guilt and disappointment.
Inconsistent, unpredictable, and paradoxical behavior.	Have other interests besides child.
Exploration and experimentation with self and world.	Marital life fulfilled apart from child.
Eagerness for peer approval and relationships.	Occasional expression of intolerance, resentment, envy, or anxiety about adolescent's development.
Strong moral and ethical perceptions.	

Child

Cognitive development accelerated; deductive and inductive reasoning; operational thought.

Competitive in play; erratic work-play patterns.

Better use of language and other symbolic material.

Critical of self and others; self-evaluative.

Highly ambivalent toward parents.

Anxiety over loss of parental nurturing.

Hostility to parents.

Verbal aggression.

Minimal Psychopathology

Child

Apprehensions, fears, guilt, and anxiety toward sex, health, education.

Defiant, negative, impulsive, or depressed behavior.

Frequent somatic or hypo-chondriacal complaints; or denial of ordinary illnesses.

Learning irregular or deficient.

Sexual preoccupation.

Poor or absent personal relationships with adults or peers.

Immature or precocious behavior; unchanging personality and temperament.

Unwillingness to assume the responsibility of greater autonomy.

Inability to substitute or postpone gratifications.

Parent(s)

Sense of failure.

Disappointment greater than joy.

Indifference to child and family.

Apathy and depression.

Persistent intolerance of child.

Limited interests and self-expression.

Loss of perspective about child's capacities.

Occasional direct or vicarious reversion to adolescent impulses.

Uncertainty about standards regarding sexual behavior and deviant social or personal activity.

Extreme Psychopathology

Child	*Parent(s)*
Complete withdrawal into self, extreme depression.	Severe depression and withdrawal.
Acts of delinquency, asceticism, ritualism, overconformity.	Complete rejection of child and/or family.
Neuroses, especially phobias; persistent anxiety, compulsions, inhibitions, or constrictive behavior.	Inability to function in family role.
	Rivalrous, competitive, destructive, and abusive to child.
Persistent hypochondriases.	Abetting child's acting out of unacceptable sexual or aggressive impulses for vicarious reasons.
Sex aberrations.	
Somatic illness; anorexia, colitis, menstrual disorders.	Perpetuation of incapacitating infantilism in the preadolescent.
Complete inability to socialize or work (learning, and so forth).	Panic reactions to acceptable standards of sexual behavior, social activity, and assertiveness.
Psychoses.	Compulsive, obsessive, or psychotic behavior.

Appendix D
Global Scale for Rating Helper Responses

Level 1.0   Not Helpful: Hurtful

A response in which the helper:

> ignores what the helpee is saying,
> ridicules the helpee's feelings,
> seeks to impose his or her beliefs and values on the helpee,
> dominates the conversation,
> challenges the accuracy of the helpee's perception,
> or uses problem-solving dimensions in a way that damages the relationship.

Level 2.0   Not Helpful: Ineffective

A response in which the helper:

> communicates a partial awareness of the helpee's surface feelings,
> gives premature or superficial advice,
> responds in a casual or mechanical way,
> reflects total content but ignores the feelings of the helpee,
> uses problem-solving dimensions in a way that impedes the relationship,
> or offers rational excuses for withholding involvement.

Level 3.0   Helpful: Facilitative

A response in which the helper:

> reflects accurately and completely the helpee's surface feelings and communicates acceptance of the helpee as a person of worth.

Level 4.0   Helpful: Additive

A response in which the helper:

> demonstrates willingness to be a helper and accurately perceives and responds to the helpee's underlying feelings (empathy),
> appropriately uses one or more of the problem-solving dimensions to:
> assist the helpee to move from vagueness to clarity (concreteness),
> reveal perceptions of the helpee in their entirety (genuineness),
> share similar experiences (self-disclosure),
> suggest things the helpee might do (expertise),
> point out discrepancies in the helpee's words and/or actions (confrontation),
> or talk about present feelings between the helpee and helper (immediacy).

Table D–1   Global scale (short form)

Level	Key Word	Results	Helper Actions Characterized by	Helper's Goal
1.0	harmful	not helpful	criticism	inappropriate; to gratify self by dominating the helpee
2.0	ineffective	not helpful	unsuitable advice	inappropriate; stated goal to help; real goal is to be a hero
3.0	facilitative	helpful	relationship building	to earn the right to help
4.0	additive	helpful	problem solving	to help

Source: Gazda, G. M., Asbury, F. A., Balzer, F. J., Childers, W. C., & Walters. R. P. (1977). *Human relations development: A manual for educators,* 3rd ed. (Boston: Allyn and Bacon.) Reproduced by permission.

Appendix E
Recommended Play Therapy Materials

The following materials have been found to be useful in facilitating a wide range of children's expressions in a fully equipped playroom.

small table and two chairs
dollhouse
doll furniture
bendable doll family
ironing board
iron
chalkboard and chalk
colored chalk and eraser
dart gun and suction darts
dart board
suction throwing darts
stove (wooden)
dishes (plastic or tin), pans, silverware
dishpan
empty fruit and vegetable cans, etc.

egg cartons
broom
dolls
rag doll
doll bed, clothes, etc.
doll buggy
purse and jewelry
Bobo®
trucks, cars, airplane
tractor, boat
bus (Fisher Price type)
pounding bench and hammer
xylophone
drum
toy solders and army equipment
straw hat, fireman's hat
pine log, hammer and nails

Source: Landreth, G. L. (Ed.) (1982). *Play therapy: Dynamics of counseling with children.* Springfield, Ill.: Charles C. Thomas. Reproduced by permission of Charles C. Thomas, Publisher.

sandbox, large spoon, funnel, sieve, pail

miniature farm animals and barn

rubber knife

handcuffs

toy pistol

balls (large and small)

nursing bottles (plastic)

telephone (two)

toy machine gun

blunt scissors

construction paper (several colors)

crayons, pencils, paper

Scotch* tape, paste

rubber snake, alligator

toy watch

building blocks (different shapes and sizes)

tempera paints, easel, newsprint, brushes

finger paint

Play-Doh*

Lone Ranger type mask

pipe cleaners

tongue depressors

Gumby* (bendable nondescript figure)

medical kit

ATV* (multiwheel type vehicle for riding—scooting around on)

play money and cash register

rags or old towels

plastic fruit

hand puppets—doctors, nurses, policeman, mother, father, sister, brother, baby alligator, wolf

Appendix F
Ethical Guidelines for Group Leaders[1]

PREAMBLE

One characteristic of any professional group is the possession of a body of knowledge and skills and mutually acceptable ethical standards for putting them into practice. Ethical standards consist of those principles which have been formally and publicly acknowledged by the membership of a profession to serve as guidelines governing professional conduct, discharge of duties, and resolution of moral dilemmas. In this document, the Association for Specialists in Group Work has identified the standards of conduct necessary to maintain and regulate the high standards of integrity and leadership among its members.

The Association for Specialists in Group Work recognizes the basic commitment of its members to the Ethical Standards of its parent organization, the American Association for Counseling and Development, and nothing in this document shall be construed to supplant that code. These standards are intended to complement the AACD standards in the area of group work by clarifying the nature of ethical responsibility of the counselor in the group setting and by stimulating a greater concern for competent group leadership.

1. Approved by the ASGW Executive Board, November 11, 1980

Source: Association for Specialists in Group Work. Alexandria, Va.: Author, 1980. Reproduced by permission of the AACD.

The following ethical guidelines have been organized under three categories: the leader's responsibility for providing information about group work to clients, the group leader's responsibility for providing group counseling services to clients, and the group leader's responsibility for safeguarding the standards of ethical practice.

A. Responsibility for Providing Information about Group Work and Group Services

A–1. Group leaders shall fully inform group members, in advance and preferably in writing, of the goals in the group, qualifications of the leader, and procedures to be employed.

A–2. The group leader shall conduct a pre-group interview with each prospective member for purposes of screening, orientation, and, in so far as possible, shall select group members whose needs and goals are compatible with the established goals of the group; who will not impede the group process; and whose well-being will not be jeopardized by the group experience.

A–3. Group leaders shall protect members by defining clearly what confidentiality means, why it is important, and the difficulties involved in enforcement.

A–4. Group leaders shall explain, as realistically as possible, exactly what services can and cannot be provided within the particular group structure offered.

A–5. Group leaders shall provide prospective clients with specific information about any specialized or experimental activities in which they may be expected to participate.

A–6. Group leaders shall stress the personal risks involved in any group, especially regarding potential life-changes, and help group members explore their readiness to face these risks.

A–7. Group leaders shall inform members that participation is voluntary and that they may exit from the group at any time.

A–8. Group leaders shall inform members about recording of sessions and how tapes will be used.

B. Responsibility for Providing Group Services to Clients

B–1. Group leaders shall protect member rights against physical threats, intimidation, coercion, and undue peer pressure insofar as is reasonably possible.

B–2. Group leaders shall refrain from imposing their own agendas, needs, and values on group members.

B–3.   Group leaders shall insure to the extent that it is reasonably possible that each member has the opportunity to utilize group resources and interact within the group by minimizing barriers such as rambling and monopolizing time.

B–4.   Group leaders shall make every reasonable effort to treat each member individually and equally.

B–5.   Group leaders shall abstain from inappropriate personal relationships with members throughout the duration of the group and any subsequent professional involvement.

B–6.   Group leaders shall help to promote independence of members from the group in the most efficient period of time.

B–7.   Group leaders shall not attempt any technique unless thoroughly trained in its use or under supervision by an expert familiar with the intervention.

B–8.   Group leaders shall not condone the use of alcohol or drugs directly prior to or during group sessions.

B–9.   Group leaders shall make every effort to assist clients in developing their personal goals.

B–10.   Group leaders shall provide between-session consultation to group members and follow-up after termination of the group, as needed or requested.

C.   Responsibility for Safeguarding Ethical Practice

C–1.   Group leaders shall display these standards or make them available to group members.

C–2.   Group leaders have the right to expect ethical behavior from colleagues and are obliged to rectify or disclose incompetent, unethical behavior demonstrated by a colleague by taking the following actions:

(a) To confront the individual with the apparent violation of ethical guidelines for the purposes of protecting the safety of any clients and to help the group leader correct any inappropriate behaviors.

(b) Such a complaint should be made in writing and include the specific facts and dates of the alleged violation and all relevant supporting data. The complaint should be forwarded to:

> The Ethics Committee
> c/o The President
> Association for Specialists in Group Work
> 599 Stevenson Avenue
> Alexandria, Virginia 22304

The envelope must be marked "CONFIDENTIAL" in order to assure confidentiality for both the accuser(s) and the alleged violator(s). Upon receipt, the President shall (a) check on membership status of the charged member(s), (b) confer with legal counsel, and (c) send the case with all pertinent documents to the chairperson of the ASGW Ethics Committee within ten (10) working days after the receipt of the complaint.

(c) If it is determined by the Ethics and Professional Standards Committee that the alleged breach of ethical conduct constitutes a violation of the "Ethical Guidelines," then an investigation will be started within ten (10) days by at least one member of the Committee plus two additional ASGW members in the locality of the alleged violation. The investigating committee chairperson shall: (a) acknowledge receipt of the complaint, (b) review the complaint and supporting data, (c) send a letter of acknowledgement to the member(s) of the complaint regarding alleged violations along with a request for a response and relevant information related to the complaint and (e) inform members of the Ethics Committee by letter of the case and present a plan of action for investigation.

(d) All information, correspondence, and activities of the Ethics Committee will remain confidential. It shall be determined that no person serving as an investigator on a case have any disqualifying relationship with the alleged violator(s).

(e) This charged party(ies) will have not more than 30 days in which to answer the charges in writing. The charged party(ies) will have free access to all cited evidence from which to make a defense, including the right to legal counsel and a formal hearing before the ASGW Ethics Committee.

(f) Based upon the investigation of the Committee and any designated local ASGW members one of the following recommendations may be made to the Executive Board for appropriate action:

1. Advise that the charges be dropped.
2. Reprimand and admonishment against repetition of the charged conduct.
3. Notify the charged member(s) of his/her right to

a formal hearing before the ASGW Ethics Committee, and request a response be made to the Ethics Chairperson as to his/her decision on the matter. Such hearing would be conducted in accordance with the AACD Policy and Procedures for Processing Complaints of Ethical Violations, "Procedures for Hearings," and would be scheduled for a time coinciding with the annual AACD convention. Conditions for such hearing shall also be in accordance with the AACD Policy and Procedures document, "Options Available to the Ethics Committee, item 3."

4. Suspension of membership for a specified period from ASGW.

5. Dismissal from membership in ASGW.

Appendix G
ASGW Professional Standards for Group Counseling

PREAMBLE

Whereas counselors may be able to function effectively with individual clients, they are also required to possess specialized knowledge and skills that render them effective in group counseling. The Association for Specialists in Group Work supports the preparation of group practitioners as part of and in addition to counselor education. The *Professional Standards for Group Counseling* represent the minimum core of group leader (cognitive and applied) competencies that have been identified by the Association for Specialists in Group Work.

DEFINITION OF GROUP COUNSELING

Consists of the interpersonal processes and activities focused on conscious thoughts and behavior performed by individuals who have the professional credentials to work with and counsel groups of individuals regarding career, educational, personal, social and developmentally related concerns, issues, tasks or problems.

Approved by the ASGW Executive Board, March 20, 1983.

Source: Association for Specialists in Group Work, Alexandria, Va.: Author, 1983. Reproduced by permission of the AACD.

DESIGNATED GROUP COUNSELING AREAS

In order to work as a professional in group counseling, an individual must meet and demonstrate minimum competencies in the generic core of group counseling standards. These are applicable to all training programs regardless of level of work or specialty area. In addition to the generic core competencies, (and in order to practice in a specific area of expertise) the individual will be required to meet one or more specialty area standards (school counseling and guidance, student personnel services in high education, or community/mental health agency counseling).

GROUP COUNSELOR KNOWLEDGE COMPETENCIES

The qualified group leader has *demonstrated specialized knowledge* in the following aspects of group work:

1. Be able to state for at least three major theoretical approaches to group counseling the distinguishing characteristics of each and the commonalities shared by all.
2. Basic principles of group dynamics and the therapeutic ingredients of groups.
3. Personal characteristics of group leaders that have an impact on members; knowledge of personal strengths, weaknesses, biases, values and their impact on others.
4. Specific ethical problems and considerations unique to group counseling.
5. Body of research on group counseling in one's specialty area (school counseling, college students personnel, or community/mental health agency).
6. Major modes of group work, differentiation among the modes, and the appropriate instances in which each is used (such as group guidance, group counseling, group therapy, human relations training, etc.)
7. Process components involved in typical stages of a group's development (i.e., characteristics of group interaction and counselor roles).
8. Major facilitative and debilitative roles that group members may take.
9. Advantages and disadvantages of group counseling and the circumstances for which it is indicated or contraindicated.

GROUP COUNSELOR COMPETENCIES ⎯⎯⎯⎯⎯⎯⎯⎯

The qualified group leader has shown the following abilities:

1. To screen and assess readiness levels of prospective clients.
2. To deliver a clear, concise, and complete definition of group counseling.
3. To recognize self-defeating behaviors of group members.
4. To describe and conduct a personally selected group counseling model appropriate to the age and clientele of group leader's specialty area(s).
5. To identify accurately nonverbal behavior among group members.
6. To exhibit appropriate pacing skills involved in stages of a group's development.
7. To identify and intervene effectively at critical incidents in the group process.
8. To work appropriately with disruptive group members.
9. To make use of the major strategies, techniques, and procedures of group counseling.
10. To provide and use procedures to assist transfer and support of changes by group members in the natural environment.
11. To use adjunct group structures such as psychological homework (i.e., self monitoring, contracting).
12. To use basic group leader interventions such as process comments, empathic responses, self-disclosures, confrontations, etc.
13. To facilitate therapeutic conditions and forces in group counseling.
14. To work cooperatively and effectively with a co-leader.
15. To open and close sessions, and terminate the group process.
16. To provide follow up procedures to assist maintenance and support of group members.
17. To utilize assessment procedures in evaluating effects and contributions of group counseling.

Table G–1   Training in clinical practice

Type of Supervised Experience	Minimum Number of [clock] Hours Required: Master's or Entry Level Program
1. Critique of group tapes (by self or others)	5
2. Observing group counseling (live or media presentation	5
3. Participating as a member in a group	15
4. Leading a group with a partner and receiving critical feedback from a supervisor	15
5. Practicum: Leading a group alone, with critical self-analysis of performance; supervisor feedback on tape; and self-analysis	15
6. Fieldwork of Internship: Practice as a group leader with on-the-job supervision	25

Index